The Ukrainian-Polish Defensive Alliance, 1919–1921

The Ukrainian-Polish Defensive Alliance, 1919–1921

An Aspect of the Ukrainian Revolution

Michael Palij

 Canadian Institute of Ukrainian Studies Press
Edmonton   1995   Toronto

Canadian Institute of Ukrainian Studies Press
University of Alberta   University of Toronto
Edmonton, Alberta   Toronto, Ontario
T6G 2E8 Canada   M5S 1A1 Canada

Copyright © 1995 Canadian Institute of Ukrainian Studies
ISBN 0-895571-05-7

Canadian Cataloguing in Publication Data

Palij, Michael, 1914-
  The Ukrainian-Polish defensive alliance, 1919–1921:
an aspect of the Ukrainian revolution

Includes bibliographical references and index.
ISBN 1-895571-05-7

1. Ukraine - Foreign relations - Poland.
2. Poland - Foreign relations - Ukraine.
3. Ukraine - History - Revolution, 1917-1921.
4. Poland - History - Wars of 1918-1921. 5. Russo-
Polish War, 1919-1920. I. Title.

DK508.57.P7P3 1995   947'.71084'1   C95-930469-X

Map courtesy of *Encyclopedia of Ukraine*.

All rights reserved.

No part of this publication may be reproduced, stored in a retrieval system, or transmitted in any form or by any means, electronic, mechanical, photocopying, recording, or otherwise, without the prior permission of the copyright owner.

Printed in Canada

To the memory of my friends and relatives who believed in the freedom of Ukraine and died at Soviet hands because of that belief in July 1941 in Uman, Ukraine.

Contents

	Acknowledgements	viii
	Acronyms	viii
1.	The Prelude to the Ukrainian-Polish Alliance	1
2.	Symon Petliura—the Champion of Ukrainian National Liberation	12
3.	Józef Piłsudski—the Builder of the New Poland—and Political Developments in Poland	23
4.	The Organization of the Polish Army in France and Its Impact on the Ukrainian-Polish War	36
5.	The Ukrainian-Polish War in Galicia and Its Aftermath	48
6.	Piłsudski's Policy of Alliance versus Dmowski's Policy of Incorporation	59
7.	Ukrainian-Polish Diplomatic Relations and the Treaty of Warsaw	67
8.	The Genesis of the Polish-Soviet Russian War	80
9.	Ukrainian-Polish Socioeconomic Relations in Right-Bank Ukraine	92
10.	The Polish-Ukrainian Offensive, the Retreat from Ukraine, and the Reorganization of the Ukrainian Army	99
11.	The Soviet Offensive in Poland and the Battles of Warsaw and the Neman	124
12.	The Preliminary Peace Treaty and Armistice Agreement	137
13.	The Peace Treaty of Riga	161
14.	The Fate of the Ukrainian Army after the Treaties	171
15	The Second Winter Campaign	178
16.	Petliura's Exile and Assassination	184
17.	Conclusion	196
	Acronyms in the Notes and Bibliography	203
	Notes	208
	Bibliography: Primary Sources	249
	Bibliography: Secondary Sources	315
	Index	368

Acknowledgements

I am indebted to the University of Kansas General Research Fund for making it possible for me to undertake the travel necessary to complete my research. I am grateful to the staff members of various institutions for their assistance: the Reference Department of the Watson Library at the University of Kansas in Lawrence for obtaining source materials through interlibrary loan; the word-processing staff at the University of Kansas College of Liberal Arts and Sciences; the Bibliothèque Ukrainienne Simon Petlura in Paris; the Ukrainian National Home Archives in Toronto; the Ukrainian National Federation Library in Toronto; the Józef Piłsudski Institute of America in New York; the Société Historique et Litteraire Polonaise in Paris; the Library of Congress in Washington, DC; the New York Public Library; the Hoover Institution on War, Revolution, and Peace Library in Palo Alto, California; the University of Minnesota Library and Immigration Archives in Minneapolis; the University of Manitoba Library in Winnipeg; the University of Toronto Library; the University of Illinois Library in Urbana; and the St. Vladimir Ukrainian Institute Library in Toronto.

I am deeply indebted to Ola Faucher for her careful reading and initial editing of this book. I also thank Roger Anderson, Nan Hill, Ellen Brow, and Rachel Miller for reading some of the chapters. I am also indebted to my wife, Lubomyra, for helping me in my work.

Acronyms

The following acronyms are used in the text:

CP(B)U	Communist Party (Bolshevik) of Ukraine
POW	Polish Military Organization (Polska Organizacja Wojskowa)
PPS	Polish Socialist party (Polska Partja Socjalistyczna)
RUP	Revolutionary Ukrainian party (Revoliutsiina ukraïns'ka partiia)
TUP	Society of Ukrainian Progressives (Tovarystvo ukraïns'kykh postupovtsiv)
UHA	Ukrainian Galician Army (Ukraïns'ka Halyts'ka Armiia)
UNR	Ukrainian People's Republic (Ukraïns'ka Narodnia Respublika)
UNS	Ukrainian National Union (Ukraïns'kyi natsional'nyi soiuz)
USDRP	Ukrainian Social Democratic Workers' party (Ukraïns'ka sotsiial-demokratychna robitnycha partiia)
VA	Russian Volunteer Army (Dobrovol'cheskaia Armiia)
ZUNR	Western Ukrainian People's Republic (Zakhidn'o-Ukraïns'ka Narodnia Respublika)

CHAPTER 1

The Prelude to the Ukrainian-Polish Alliance

The political map of East Central Europe that had existed since the end of the eighteenth century was radically changed by World War I. The Central Powers' defeat and, above all, the Russian Revolution created new opportunities for the former subject peoples of the vanquished empires, and self-determination became the objective of many nations long forced to endure alien rule. The former subjects of Germany and Austria–Hungary, partly because of these states' defeat and partly because of their constitutional system and political traditions, found more favorable conditions for establishing political independence than the former subjects of the Russian Empire. In spite of military humiliation, revolution, and internal disintegration, Russia's power was rapidly reconsolidated by the Bolsheviks after November 1917, and reappeared as a challenge to the aspirations to independence of the seceding nations. The renascence of Russian power threatened both Ukraine and Poland; hence, the more farsighted leaders of those nations realized that only by combining forces could they resist occupation by Soviet Russia. Ukrainian-Polish political collaboration culminated in the Ukrainian–Polish alliance of 1920.

The revolutionary upheavals of 1917–20 occurred at an especially unfavorable time for Ukrainian national and political aspirations. When the March Revolution broke out in 1917, national development was not yet complete. The national revival that took place in Russian-ruled Ukraine before the Revolution of 1905 had been limited primarily to the cultural sphere because political parties were illegal and because administration of the country was mainly in the hands of non-Ukrainians. Given these conditions, little practical administrative and political experience was available to the Ukrainians. Consequently, their stunted political, cultural, and socioeconomic condition had a profound impact on the course of the 1917–20 revolution and the formation of Ukrainian statehood.

After the collapse of the Russian monarchy in 1917, the leaders of Ukraine declared the nation's right to self-determination. On 20 March 1917,[1] at the initiative of the Society of Ukrainian Progressives (TUP), the Ukrainian Central Rada (Council) was formed from the municipal and cultural organizations of Kyiv (Kiev) and representatives of political parties and professional organizations. Originally it served not as a parliament, but as a center of instruction and mutual information. Subsequently local councils, committees, or other organizations spontaneously recognized the authority of the Central Rada.[2]

To gain wider support and popular approval for its actions, the Rada convened the All-Ukrainian National Congress (Kyiv, 19–21 April 1917). Attended by some nine hundred representatives of soldiers, peasants, workers, cultural and professional organizations, and political parties, the congress sanctioned a larger Rada of similar composition under the presidency of Mykhailo Hrushevs'kyi, and inaugurated a new period of the revolution—a political struggle steering the nation away from reliance on the Russian Provisional Government toward political independence.

Cultural and political life flourished. Periodicals and publishing houses were revived or created to meet the demand for printed works, particularly school textbooks; organizations for the retraining of teachers were set up; and the number of Prosvita enlightenment societies, libraries, and bookstores grew. There was especially impressive activity in the Russian Army, where four million soldiers affirmed their Ukrainian nationality and a desire to form their own units. Ukrainian military councils, clubs, and other organizations began to emerge, demanding that the units quartered in Ukraine be composed only of Ukrainians.

The initiative for creating separate Ukrainian units came from the Ukrainian Military Club, which was founded on 29 March 1917 in Kyiv by officers such as Mykola Mikhnovs'kyi and the brothers Oleksander and Pavlo Makarenko, and from the Ukrainian Military Organizational Committee headed by Col. Pavlo Hlyns'kyi. Despite resistance by the Russian authorities, on 1 April the First Ukrainian Regiment was organized from soldiers temporarily stationed in Kyiv. After the regiment was approved by the commander of the Russian Southwestern Front, Gen. Aleksei Brusilov, it was reduced from 3,574 to 500 soldiers, and the regiment's first commander, Col. Demian Putnyk-Hrebeniuk, was arrested by the Russian military authorities. He subsequently disappeared and was perhaps executed, and a new commander, Col. Iurii Kapkan, was appointed.

Although the regiment was to be transferred to the front, the Russian press mounted a great campaign against it. In response Ukrainian soldiers began spreading the idea of Ukrainianizing all units in the Russian army and navy consisting of Ukrainians so as to defend Ukraine more effectively against the German and Austro-Hungarian armies and to speed up the orderly evacuation of millions of non-Ukrainian demobilized military personnel passing through Ukrainian territory.

At the initiative of the Ukrainian Military Club, the First All-Ukrainian Military Congress was held in Kyiv from 18 to 25 May 1917. The over seven hundred delegates at the congress, who represented nearly 1.5 million soldiers and sailors, adopted a resolution on the organization of separate military units drawn from Ukrainians in the Russian army. The congress created the Ukrainian Military General Committee to keep constant contact with the organizations of Ukrainian soldiers at the fronts, giving them orders and directives, to liaise between the Rada and the soldiers, and to influence the Rada to follow the soldiers' demands with respect to military and national questions. Both the Russian civil and military authorities opposed the Ukrainian military movement, calling its leaders chauvinists and Austro-German agents. The Russian regime, however, was afraid to take strong action against the committee, fearing that the Ukrainian soldiers at the fronts would revolt and thus bring about a Russian military collapse.

The vicissitudes of the revolution and the active participation of Ukrainian soldiers in national life impelled military leaders to expand the Ukrainianization of military units and to organize a national army. The Second All-Ukrainian Military Congress (Kyiv, 18–23 June 1917), which, despite a ban by the then Russian minister of war, Aleksandr Kerensky, was attended by 2,500 delegates representing 1,736,000 soldiers, elected an All-Ukrainian Council of Military Deputies, which entered the Rada as the representative of the Ukrainian soldiers. At the congress the Central Rada proclaimed its First Universal on 23 June 1917, and five days later the General Secretariat, the executive branch of the Ukrainian government, was established.³ Thereafter the First All-Ukrainian Peasants' Congress (Kyiv, 10–16 June 1917) and First All-Ukrainian Workers' Congress (Kyiv, 24–6 July 1917) sought to unify and direct the military, peasant, and labor movements and to give support to the Central Rada.

In the meantime, the Russian Provisional Government dispatched a delegation, under Kerensky, to Kyiv for negotiations with the Central Rada. On 16 July it recognized the autonomy of Ukraine and the Ukrainianization of fifteen divisions. That same day the Rada proclaimed its Second Universal allowing the national minorities in Ukraine to send representatives to the Rada, which was designated a territorial parliament. The Provisional Government, however, had no intention of honoring the agreement. To strengthen Ukraine's position vis-à-vis Russia, the Rada convened a congress of other nations of the former Russian monarchy (Kyiv, 21–8 September 1917). The Don Cossack, Estonian, Georgian, Latvian, Moldavian, Polish, Tatar, Turkestanian, Ukrainian, and Belarusian delegates in attendance discussed the transformation of the centralized Russian state into a federation of free states.

In response to Kerensky's tactics delaying the Ukrainianization of military formations, the Third All-Ukrainian Military Congress was called in Kyiv (2–12 November 1917). The Congress empowered the Military General Committee to demand from the Russian authorities the separation of Ukrainian soldiers and sailors into ethnically homogeneous units. After the Bolshevik coup d'état in Petrograd on 7 November 1917, the congress called upon the Central Rada and General Secretariat to assume full civil and military authority in Ukraine. On 20 November 1917 the Rada issued its Third Universal declaring de facto national independence and the creation of the Ukrainian People's Republic (UNR). Although relations with Russia were not broken off, the Rada did not recognize the Bolshevik regime.[4]

Although the collapse of Kerensky's government favored the course of Ukrainian independence, the establishment of a strong and stable Ukrainian government proved very difficult because of social and economic chaos and the administrative inexperience of the leaders. The greatest obstacle to establishing effective authority, however, was the concentration of Russian forces in Ukraine. In Kyiv, for example, there were some forty thousand Russian officers in 1917, while in the main Ukrainian cities there were close to one hundred thousand Russian officers early in 1918. Moreover, the movement through Ukraine of active and demobilized soldiers, and especially deserters, made it difficult to maintain order. Even prior to the revolution there were over 195,000 deserters, and on 1 August 1917 there were 365,000; together with those hiding to avoid conscription, the "greens," they totaled some two million by 1 October 1917.[5]

The Bolshevik seizure of power in Russia radically changed the course of the Ukrainian revolution. Prior to and during 1917 the Bolsheviks had opposed any Russian suppression of non-Russian nationalist movements within the empire. Under the Provisional Government they were willing to support the Central Rada's demand for a separate Ukrainian Constituent Assembly. Recognition of the nationalities was, however, primarily a political tactic aimed at weakening the monarchy and the Provisional Government and gaining the support of their enemies. Lenin saw nationalism as an ephemeral phenomenon that would yield to the internationalism of the proletariat and the new communist state. When this vision did not materialize, the Bolsheviks revised their policy of self-determination. This change was bound to be felt first and most strongly in Ukraine: that nation, because of its size, population, location, and natural resources, was considered more important to Russian interests than any other.

At first the Bolsheviks tried to prevent stabilization of the Ukrainian government by fomenting class hatred and sending Bolshevik bands into Ukraine. Subsequently the Russian Second Guard Corps led by the Bolshevik

Evgeniia Bosh, which was moving from the front to aid the Bolshevik uprising in Kyiv, was disarmed by the First Ukrainian Corps under Gen. Pavlo Skoropads'kyi and deported to Russia. Tensions between Ukraine and Soviet Russia mounted when the General Secretariat ordered troops in Ukraine not to obey the orders of the Bolshevik government. On 17 December the Bolsheviks sent the Central Rada an ultimatum that "recognized the complete independence of the Ukrainian Republic," but simultaneously accused the Rada of disarming Bolshevik forces in Ukraine and supporting Gen. Aleksei Kaledin's counterrevolutionary rebellion in the Don region. These practices were to be abandoned within forty-eight hours or the Bolshevik government would consider the Rada "in a state of open warfare against the Soviet Government in Russia and in Ukraine."[6] On 18 December 1917 the Secretariat rejected the Bolshevik ultimatum.

By early December the Bolsheviks had concentrated their forces near the Ukrainian border under the command of Vladimir Antonov. The Bolshevik invasion of Ukraine began on 7 January 1918. It was greatly facilitated by insurrections of mostly non-Ukrainian groups in the cities. The outnumbered and inadequately equipped Ukrainian troops gradually retreated while the Bolshevik forces occupied city after city. When some units of the Kyiv garrison left for the front, the local Bolshevik elements, consisting of Russian soldiers and workers under Bosh, staged an armed uprising, aiming to facilitate the imminent invasion of Kyiv by Bolshevik forces under Mikhail Muravev. After four days of heavy fighting the rebels were defeated. Subsequently, however, on 8 February 1918, after eleven days of heavy bombardment and street fighting, Bolshevik forces captured Kyiv. Consequently the Ukrainian troops retreated westward and the Rada was forced to evacuate to Zhytomyr.[7]

The only recourse left to the Central Rada was a separate peace with the Central Powers to obtain their support in defending the country. On 22 January 1918, in its Fourth Universal, the Rada announced: "On this day the Ukrainian People's Republic becomes an independent, subject to no one, free, sovereign state of the Ukrainian people."[8] The Rada feared that the peace negotiations between the Bolsheviks and the Central Powers begun at the end of December at Brest-Litovsk might result in Germany's ceding Ukraine to Soviet Russia. Although the Soviet delegation tried to prove that the Central Rada no longer existed, the Central Powers concluded a peace treaty with Ukraine on 9 February 1918 in order to secure Ukrainian supplies and put pressure on the Bolsheviks. In the treaty Ukraine, including the Kholm region, was recognized as an independent republic, and Austria promised to unite Bukovyna with Eastern Galicia and to set up a new Ukrainian crownland with political and cultural rights within the monarchy. In return Ukraine agreed to provide the Central Powers with surplus foodstuffs. Subsequently the Rada sought Austrian and German aid in expelling the Bolshevik forces, believing that an adequate force could be mounted from the existing Ukrainian units in the Austrian army and the Ukrainian prisoners of war from the Russian army held by the Germans. The Rada asked that those troops, estimated at thirty thousand, be deployed in Ukraine. The Central Powers refused, insisting that the time required to bring the troops from other areas was too great, though they undoubtedly were also anxious to assure their own control of Ukraine. Subsequently, by the end of April Austro-German forces, including some Ukrainian troops, had forced the Bolsheviks from Ukraine.[9]

After returning to Kyiv, the Central Rada faced overwhelming obstacles to the reestablishment of internal order. The retreating Bolshevik forces had pillaged and burned, looted banks, flooded mines, driven off cattle, and damaged factories and railroads. The country swarmed with foreign and reactionary military bands that opposed the republic. The Rada was also criticized for inviting the Austro-German troops into Ukraine. Although the latter had helped to expel the Bolshevik forces and the Rada publicly declared that Ukrainian sovereignty would not be limited, Ukraine became in effect an occupied country. Ukraine was partitioned into spheres of interest and authority was vested primarily in the German commander of Heeresgruppe Kiew, Field Marshal Hermann von Eichhorn, while Gen. Wilhelm Groener, the German chief of staff in Ukraine, was charged with securing supplies. The German and Austro-Hungarian diplomatic representatives played secondary roles.

At the beginning Austro-German policy vis-à-vis Ukraine was based on cooperation with the Central Rada. Soon, however, the Austro-German military authorities had abused their power, provoking strong public criticism. The Rada was caught between two opposing policies. Its policy was to weaken Bolshevik propaganda by announcing economic reforms in the Third and Fourth Universals, such as nationalization of agriculture, industry, and banks. Given their own economic state, the Central Powers were against these reforms. They were concerned mainly with having a Ukrainian government that could guarantee the delivery of supplies, and conditions in Ukraine were unfavorable to their interest. Although the peasants had appropriated the lands from the landlords, they hesitated to cultivate them because, faced with the landowners' intense reaction, they were uncertain about the future disposal of the harvest. With the approach of spring the German and Austrian authorities worried about future supplies. In light of scarce supplies and economic disorder, the German and Austrian authorities were more receptive to the wealthy classes, who were largely non-Ukrainian and hostile to the republic and who tried to discredit the Rada and hoped to depose it. On 6 April, as a result of this situation, von Eichhorn, without prior consultation with the Rada, issued an order stipulating that (1) cultivators of the soil would keep the crop and get current prices; (2) anyone holding more land than he could cultivate would be punished; (3) where peasants were unable to cultivate all the land and where landowners did exist, the peasants must do the planting, without prejudicing the rights of the land committees to divide the land; peasants were not to interfere with the cultivation, and land committees were to provide the landowners with horses, machinery, and seed; and (4) all robberies and despoilment of seeded land would be punished severely.[10]

Von Eichhorn's order came under severe criticism from the members of the Rada, who maintained that German troops had been invited into Ukraine for the purpose of maintaining order within limits designated by the government of the UNR. Arbitrary intrusion by German and Austrian military authorities in the social, political, and economic life of Ukraine could not be tolerated. The Rada members insisted that such interference would only further disorganize economic life in Ukraine and complicate social and political relations. Von Eichhorn contended that his order was not in conflict with the policy of the Ukrainian government and that he was merely reinforcing earlier instructions issued by the Ukrainian Ministry of Agriculture. Consequent increased German interference in Ukrainian internal affairs further strained German-Ukrainian relations. To strengthen its position, the Rada sought popular support by rescheduling the opening of a Ukrainian Constituent Assembly, which had earlier been postponed by the Bolshevik invasion, to 12 June. On 28 April, however, the German military authorities dissolved the Central Rada, and the next day a congress called by the Union of Landowners in Ukraine proclaimed Gen. Pavlo Skoropads'kyi the hetman of Ukraine.

With the fall of the socialist Central Rada and the establishment of the hetman government and so-called Ukrainian State, the second period of the national revolution began. The new government, with the assistance of the Austro-German military authorities and the largely non-Ukrainian landowners, attempted to restore the old order. Although the proclamation of 29 April was widely resented, it brought no open resistance because of the presence of German and Austro-Hungarian troops. The more conservative citizens accepted the new government, hoping it would protect Ukraine against another Bolshevik invasion and German interference in Ukrainian internal affairs. After the Rada's overthrow, the hetman issued a manifesto ordering the dissolution of the Rada and all land committees, and dismissed all ministers and their aides. All other civil servants, however, were to remain at their posts. The right of private ownership was restored, and all acts promulgated by the Rada or the Russian Provisional Government regarding property rights were abrogated. Skoropads'kyi promised to transfer land from the large estates to the landless peasants at face value, to safeguard the rights of the working class, and to provide for the election of a parliament. From the outset he wanted a government composed of moderate liberals, but his overtures to the Ukrainian Socialist-Federalist party to form it were refused. Gradually the gubernial and municipal administrations were largely staffed by conservatives recruited from among the national minorities and Russian refugees, partly because many Ukrainians refused to participate and partly because there was a huge shortage of qualified Ukrainian personnel. Consequently the hetman government became dependent largely on two forces inimical to the Ukrainian cause—the German and Austrian military authorities and the reactionary non-Ukrainian upper class.

In that situation normal national development was difficult; the hetman, however, made sincere efforts to promote national culture, to pursue an independent foreign policy, and to unite Ukrainian territories that were still separated from Ukraine. He converted the new Ukrainian National University in Kyiv into a state institution and established a new Ukrainian state university in Kamianets-Podilskyi, a historical and philological college in Poltava, an academy of sciences in Kyiv, chairs of Ukrainian history, language, literature, and law at the various universities, new secondary schools, a national gallery, a national museum, state archives, a central library, a Ukrainian state theater, and a theater school. The hetman sought to end the guardianship of the Central Powers, and received a pledge of their assistance in joining to Ukraine borderlands such as the Kholm region, Bessarabia, the Crimea, and the Kuban. He also tried to gain recognition from neutral states and possibly from the Entente, and to negotiate peace settlements with Soviet Russia and the Russian Volunteer Army (VA).

The most difficult problem facing the government was the organization of the Ukrainian army. Most of the military units had been demobilized by the Germans, and most of the remaining units' Ukrainian officers had been replaced mainly by Russians. Although an earlier Rada plan to organize a regular volunteer army was ordered by the hetman and general conscription was decreed, the army remained embryonic to the end of the hetman's rule. The German authorities and the Russian military commanders appointed by the hetman opposed the creation of a strong Ukrainian army as a threat to their positions.

Domestic and foreign conditions were unfavorable to Skoropads'kyi's political plans. His power had a weak foundation, and he was buffeted by the currents within the Austro-German military authorities and the non-Ukrainian, reactionary members of his government on the one hand, and within the Ukrainian nation on the other. The policy of his government was marked by many conservative decrees that turned the population against it. The appointment of non-Ukrainian landowners as heads of the provincial and county administrations brought about disastrous results. The government ordered that all property previously expropriated be restored to the landowners, and the landowners were authorized to use military force to regain their property and to collect compensation for damages. Consequently, many landowners undertook punitive expeditions using former Russian officers, adventurers, and criminals. Protected by German and Austrian troops, these expeditions looted, destroyed peasants' property, and meted out severe punishments, including executions, in the name of the hetman government, thereby discrediting it.[11]

The repressions elicited passive resistance and sabotage and then local and regional uprisings. Gradually both the punitive expeditions and defensive partisan uprisings spread and intensified, and neither the state police nor the German punitive detachments were able to control them. Although the partisans were initially successful in seizing territory, they could not stand for long against regular troops for they were disorganized and inadequately armed. Moreover, the German authorities arrested over ten thousand people and sent them to camps in Germany.

The leaders of the Central Rada called a number of illegal congresses to strengthen their position against the hetman government, such as the Second All-Ukrainian Peasants' Congress (8–10 May), which was attended by about twelve thousand delegates near Kyiv, and the Second All-Ukrainian Workers' Congress (13–14 May). Both congresses adopted resolutions calling for the restoration of the UNR, the transfer of land to the peasants without compensation to owners, the guarantee of all liberties proclaimed previously, and the formation of local armed groups for a popular uprising.

Simultaneously the leaders of the parties in opposition to the hetman government organized the Ukrainian National State Union, which in August was transformed into the Ukrainian National Union (UNS), to broaden their base of membership. Their aims were the establishment of a strong and independent Ukrainian state; a legal government responsible to a parliament; democratic, direct, general, equal, secret, and proportional suffrage; and the defense of the rights of the Ukrainian people and their state in the international sphere.

As long as German power was unbroken on the Western Front, the Central Powers were able to maintain their hold on Ukraine. After Germany was defeated, however, and signed an armistice with the Allies on 11 November that prescribed the immediate evacuation of German troops from Ukraine, the Skoropads'kyi government lost its support and Ukraine faced the possibility of a new Bolshevik invasion. Although the hetman tried to come to an understanding with the Entente, they did not favor Ukrainian independence, demanding instead Ukraine's federation with a non-Bolshevik Russia. Consequently, on 14 November the hetman decided upon federation, hoping this would convince the Entente of his good faith and loyalty.

Meanwhile, the leaders of the UNS made contact with the Union of Railroad Workers, peasant and partisan leaders, and a number of military units, especially the Sich Riflemen. On 13 November 1918 they met secretly in Kyiv and elected the Directory of the planned popular insurrection: Volodymyr Vynnychenko (president), Symon Petliura (commander in chief), Fedir Shvets', Panas Andriievs'kyi, and Andrii Makarenko. Bila Tserkva, where the Sich Riflemen were stationed, was chosen as the center of the insurrection and the headquarters of the Directory. Skoropads'kyi's declaration of federation with Russia only accelerated the beginning of the insurrection against his government.

On 16 November the Sich Riflemen began to move on Kyiv. On the way they were joined by other Ukrainian units and partisans. After several armed clashes with German troops, an agreement was concluded between the Germans and the Directory. The latter promised not to attack the Germans if they did not intervene in the internal Ukrainian struggle. Subsequently, after the Directory's troops defeated the hetman forces near Vasylkiv, partisan uprisings against the hetman government spread throughout Ukraine. Although German troops remained neutral in the countryside, after the Directory's troops besieged Kyiv the Germans retracted their earlier agreement and decided to hold the city. Soon, however, the Germans recognized the futility of their position and signed a new agreement with the Directory guaranteeing them safe passage home in return for their neutrality. On 14 December Directory troops entered Kyiv, and the next day the hetman abdicated. On 19 December the Directory moved to Kyiv and reestablished the UNR.[12]

The political vicissitudes in Ukraine were a result of the Central Rada inviting the Austro-German troops into Ukraine. Consequently its leaders, including Hrushevs'kyi and Vynnychenko, lost a degree of confidence among the people. Petliura, however, remained popular and was trusted by the population and the more disciplined military units. As a member of the Directory and commander in chief of the troops, he renewed the formation of a national army. Political conditions in Ukraine, however, were unfavorable for the Directory. Since the end of 1918 Ukraine had been surrounded by hostile neighbors. In the west the Poles had invaded Eastern Galicia and Western Volynia with the support of the Entente; in the south the Romanians occupied Bessarabia and Bukovyna; in the southeast the VA had begun preparatory operations for a major invasion with the support of the Entente; in the south French forces, including Greek, Russian, and Polish units, had intervened in the Odessa region; while in the northeast Bolshevik forces had renewed their invasion under the guise of a nominally Ukrainian Soviet government. In such circumstances Ukraine obviously needed a strong army to defend itself. Although a national army had not yet been organized, Petliura renewed the armed struggle against the Bolsheviks with new but weak troops. At the same time some members of the Directory, especially Vynnychenko, tried to negotiate with the Bolsheviks. Soon, however, they discovered that negotiations with the Bolsheviks meant only one thing—capitulation. When the Directory failed to find a modus vivendi with the Bolsheviks, on 16 January 1919 it declared that a state of war existed between Soviet Russia and Ukraine. But the Directory could offer no effective resistance to the advancing Red Army. As the latter approached Kyiv, on 2 February 1919 the Directory evacuated to Vinnytsia, and three days later loyal Ukrainian troops retreated from Kyiv to the west.

The critical military situation in Ukraine, especially the intervention of French forces in the south, brought about an internal political crisis and two opposing points of view within the Directory and the political parties. One group, headed by Vynnychenko, advocated seeking an understanding with the Bolsheviks, while the other, led by Petliura, urged joining the Entente against the Bolsheviks. Finally Petliura's viewpoint prevailed. In the meantime Vynnychenko's efforts at finding an agreement with the Bolsheviks brought about a cabinet crisis. During the Bolshevik invasion Petliura's supporters increasingly tried to win Entente support for their resistance. To facilitate the Directory's negotiations with the French representatives in Odessa, the Ukrainian Social Democratic and Socialist Revolutionary members of the government resigned, Petliura resigned from the Social Democratic party, and Vynnychenko handed over his authority as president of the Directory to Petliura on 11 February 1919.[13]

For a better understanding of political developments in Ukraine and its relations with Poland, it is necessary to examine Petliura's life and activities before he became president of the Directory and commander in chief of the Ukrainian army.

CHAPTER 2

Symon Petliura—the Champion of Ukrainian National Liberation

Symon Petliura was born on 10 May 1879 in Poltava into a family whose ancestors were Cossacks. Petliura's parents, Vasyl' and Ol'ha (née Marchenko), had four sons and five daughters. Three other children died in infancy. The family owned a small horse-and-carriage rental business. The oldest son, Ivan, was born in the early 1870s and died in 1900 during his last year at the Poltava Theological Seminary. The second-oldest son, Fedir, was born in 1876 and graduated in 1898 from that seminary. After teaching for two years, he attended the agricultural and forestry institute at Puławy, (Novo-Aleksandriia), Poland. After graduation he became the county agronomist in Kobeliaky county in Poltava gubernia and was active in revolutionary organizations there. In the early morning of 5 April 1907 he was found dead outside the door of his home. The youngest son, Oleksander, was born on 12 September 1888. He also attended the seminary in Poltava and then graduated from an officers' training school and served as an officer in the Russian army and a colonel in the Ukrainian army. One of the daughters, Mariianna, married Ivan Skrypnyk; their oldest son, Stepan, became Metropolitan Mstyslav of the Ukrainian Orthodox Church in the USA and died in 1993 as patriarch of the Ukrainian Autocephalous Orthodox church. Petliura's two youngest sisters, Maryna and Teodosiia, were arrested during the Ezhov terror of 1937 and disappeared. His father died in 1909, and his mother was arrested by the Bolsheviks in March 1919 and died three days after her release from prison.[1]

Petliura received his elementary education at the church school in Pavlenky, a suburb of Poltava, and in 1889 he began his secondary education at the ecclesiastical school (*dukhovnoe uchilishche*) in Poltava. From 1895 he studied at the theological seminary in Poltava, where he was one of the best students, sang in the student choir, and organized plays, concerts, and parties. His main extracurricular interest, however, lay in organizing meetings of secret self-education groups. Among the participants were students of the seminary, other secondary schools, and the universities of Kharkiv and Kyiv, as well as soldiers, who gathered in private houses and discussed Ukrainian history and various social, political, and national issues.

Thus Petliura's interest in politics developed very early. While at the seminary he began contributing to illegal publications and joined the clandestine Revolutionary Ukrainian party (RUP). At the beginning of 1901, only two weeks before his graduation, he was expelled from the seminary and was banned from enrolling at any other school. Although officially he was expelled because he had invited the Ukrainian composer Mykola Lysenko to give a concert at the seminary and to attend a meeting of the secret student group (*hromada*), the real reason was his expression of nationalistic and revolutionary convictions. After his expulsion Petliura tutored children of wealthy families in Poltava. In the spring of 1902 violent peasant uprisings occurred in Poltava and Kharkiv gubernias in which he and other students from the seminary played an important role as organizers. Fearing arrest, in the fall of 1902 he left for the Kuban.[2]

In the Kuban the tsarist authorities forbade Petliura to teach. At that time the otaman of the Kuban Cossacks, Gen. Ia. D. Malam, decided to publish a history of the Kuban Cossacks based on the archives of the Zaporozhian, Black Sea, and Kuban Cossacks in his office.[3] The otaman commissioned Fedir Shcherbyna to write the history.[4] Petliura's search for work brought him to Katerynodar, the capital of the Kuban. There his friends recommended him to Shcherbyna, who hired him as an assistant. Thus Petliura learned a great deal about the history of the Cossacks, their present life, and their traditions, and his archival work had a great influence upon the formation of his national conscience. While in the Kuban Petliura remained active in revolutionary politics and contributed to illegal Ukrainian publications. Consequently he was arrested in December 1903. After three months of imprisonment, his father bailed him out by selling his plot of woodland, and Petliura moved to Kyiv. In the fall of 1904 he illegally crossed the Russo-Austrian border near Kremianets, Volynia, and settled in Lviv, the center of Ukrainian national and political life at the time, under an assumed name, Sviatoslav Tagon. Petliura's intention was to study Ukrainian literature and literary criticism at Lviv University.[5]

While in Lviv Petliura was also active politically, and within the large group of young Ukrainians from Russian-ruled Ukraine there he soon became a leading RUP representative. He attended meetings, conventions, and lectures of various organizations; for a while was editor in chief of RUP organs such as the irregular *Pratsia* and monthly *Selianyn*; contributed to other Ukrainian periodicals; and helped smuggle illegal literature into the Russian Empire. In May 1905 he secretly attended the RUP congress in Kyiv. The 1905 Revolution enabled him to move back to Kyiv at the end of December.[6]

Lviv played an important part in the formation of Petliura's national consciousness and political outlook. There he developed a close association with Ukrainian students and prominent Ukrainians such as Mykola Hankevych, Volodymyr Levyns'kyi, Vasyl' Paneiko, Volodymyr Hnatiuk, and Ivan Franko. As a result of his relationship with Franko and Hnatiuk, the editors of *Literaturno-naukovyi vistnyk* and *Zapysky Naukovoho tovarystva im. Shevchenka*, Petliura contributed to these publications several articles on the history of the Ukrainian Cossacks in the eighteenth century based on the Katerynodar archives. He also learned a great deal from the Ukrainian-Polish national and political struggle in Galicia. In Lviv Petliura became acquainted with Russian revolutionary literature and thus gained an insight into the psychology and political aims of the Russian revolutionaries. Unlike some of his contemporaries, he was more concerned with the national than the social aims of the Ukrainian revolutionary movement. Previously he had advocated Ukrainian autonomy within the Russian monarchy; now he affirmed the goal of Ukrainian political independence.[7]

New political freedoms in the Russian Empire after the Revolution of 1905 encouraged Ukrainian leaders to intensify their political activities. The First Russian State Duma, which included forty-four Ukrainian members, gave them great hope. Consequently a Ukrainian center was established in St. Petersburg to provide information and assistance to them. The Ukrainian Social Democratic Worker's party (USDRP), the successor to RUP, began publishing a monthly party organ, *Vil'na Ukraïna*, in the fall of 1905, and established a publishing house, Borot'ba, in St. Petersburg. In mid-February 1906 the USDRP invited Petliura to take over editorship of its publications. Under his editorship *Vil'na Ukraïna* became more intellectual and more radical and more influential among Ukrainians. In addition to his editorial work, Petliura remained an activist, especially among students. He resumed organizing meetings, lectures, and concerts and was instrumental in the creation of the Ukrainian Club, the center of Ukrainian activities in St. Petersburg. In July 1906, however, *Vil'na Ukraïna* ceased to appear because of financial difficulties. Petliura returned to Kyiv, where he became secretary of the daily newspaper *Rada*.[8]

In July 1906 the First Duma was dissolved, and some two hundred of its members who had signed the Vyborg appeal were arrested.[9] Count Sergei Witte was dismissed from his position as the first constitutional prime minister of Russia, censorship of books and newspapers was tightened, and many Ukrainian scholars and politicians, especially members of parties and organizations, were forced to emigrate, went into exile, or settled in relatively freer centers such as St. Petersburg and Moscow, where some activity on behalf of the Ukrainian cause was still possible.

In May 1907 the USDRP began publishing the weekly organ *Slovo* to popularize the party's program and ideas among workers and peasants. Petliura was one of the paper's editors, who found it necessary to organize secret groups to assist in collecting information and organizing financial support and distribution. Petliura's contributions to *Slovo* were on various topics, primarily on Ukrainian literature and theater. He also wrote for the scholarly journal *Ukraïna* (1907), the successor to *Kievskaia starina* (1882–1906), and continued contributing to *Literaturno-naukovyi vistnyk* in Lviv while devoting some of his time to the USDRP. During the election campaign for the Second Duma he was a party candidate in Kyiv gubernia.[10]

At the beginning of 1909 political conditions in Ukraine and financial difficulties compelled Petliura to leave Kyiv for St. Petersburg. There he found employment as an accountant for a transportation firm and devoted his free time to cultural and political work among Ukrainians, especially students. Gradually Petliura was recognized as an authority among the city's Ukrainians and was often invited to appear as a speaker. His first main speech was delivered in the spring of 1911 at a concert commemorating the fiftieth anniversary of Taras Shevchenko's death.

In June 1910 Petliura married Olha Bil's'ka. The daughter of a teacher, she was born on 23 December 1885 in Mala Divytsia, Pryluky county, Poltava gubernia. She studied at the gymnasium in Pryluky and, after graduation, became a teacher in the same school and later at a gymnasium in Kyiv. Petliura and his wife lived in St. Petersburg until the fall of 1911, when they moved to Moscow. St. Petersburg was spiritually alien to Petliura, who complained that "it is suffocating for him in this swamp without sun, light, or warmth."[11] On 25 October 1911 his daughter Larysa was born. For a while Petliura worked as an inspector for the insurance society Rossiia in Moscow.

On 3 January 1912 Petliura and Oleksander Salikovs'kyi, an experienced journalist and editor, founded the monthly Russian-language journal *Ukrainskaia zhizn'* as the organ of a secret political organization, the Society of Ukrainian Progressives (TUP), founded in 1908. Because all Ukrainian political parties had been dissolved, TUP functioned as an umbrella organization of the Ukrainian national movement, and the journal was created to enlighten Russian society and Russified Ukrainians about Ukraine and its problems. Under Petliura and Salikovs'kyi, *Ukrainskaia zhizn'* maintained a high intellectual level. Many prominent Ukrainian scholars and politicians from both Russian- and Austrian-ruled Ukraine, as well as several prominent Russians, contributed to the journal.

As coeditor of the journal, Petliura gradually assumed a leading position among Ukrainians in Moscow, and the journal, which appeared until the beginning of the Revolution of 1917, became the focal point of the national and political life of Moscow's Ukrainian intelligentsia. In Moscow Petliura established close relationships with intellectuals from the countries subjugated by the Russian monarchy, and friendships with a number of leading Russian journalists, scholars, and politicians who defended the Ukrainian cause against both the regime and the Russian reactionary press. His closest friendship was with the Russian academician Fedor Korsh.[12]

Korsh told Oleksander Lotots'kyi that "Petliura's countrymen do not appreciate, do not understand the spiritual power concealed in him."[13] Korsh also prophesied Petliura's future role in Ukrainian national life:

> The Ukrainians do not know whom they have among themselves. They think that Petliura is a prominent editor, patriot, social leader, etc. All this is true, but it is not the whole truth.... He is from a breed of leaders; people from this dough once, in ancient times, established dynasties, and in our democratic time are becoming national heroes. He lives in unfavorable conditions, [and he] cannot reveal himself. Who knows whether everything will change around us? And when [it] changes he will be a leader of the Ukrainian people. Such is his destiny.[14]

With the outbreak of World War I the Russian regime suppressed all Ukrainian-language publications. *Ukrainskaia zhizn'* continued to appear because it was in Russian and was published in Moscow, and it was the only source of reliable information for Ukrainians, Russians, and foreigners about Ukrainian problems in the Russian Empire. Consequently, as editor Petliura unofficially performed some of the functions of a Ukrainian ambassador to Russia, and with the outbreak of the war he felt that he had to take a stand in the name of Ukrainian society. On 12 September 1914 he published in *Ukrainskaia zhizn'* a declaration entitled "Voina i ukraintsy" (The War and the Ukrainians). According to the declaration, the Ukrainians, as citizens of the Russian Empire, would fulfill their duties. They hoped, however, that the Russian regime and society would understand that they should receive certain rights that would secure their national aspirations. Petliura hoped that the declaration of loyalty to Russia would avert imminent repressions of Ukrainians and preserve their achievements. But his hope was not realized. After the outbreak of the war the tsarist regime closed down all Ukrainian presses and centers of Ukrainian cultural life, and the Ukrainians became convinced that the regime would not change its attitude toward Ukraine.

In addition to his journalistic work, Petliura edited two important books in Russian: *Ukrainskii vopros* and *Galichina, Bukovina, Ugorskaia Rus'*. The latter was used as a handbook by tsarist officials in the Western Ukrainian territories of the Austro-Hungarian monarchy while they were occupied by Russian forces during the war.

At the beginning of 1916 Petliura volunteered to work for the All-Russian Union of Zemstvos and Cities, a civilian auxiliary organization of the Russian military. By the summer of 1915 incompetence, corruption, and venality was widespread within the Russian bureaucracy, especially in the Ministry of War. Because of this and Russia's military failures, the union was authorized to supply the army with materiel and medical and sanitary services. Petliura served on Russia's Western Front at Minsk as a military official and later as an inspector. He proved to be a good organizer, administrator, and manager, and through his service he had opportunities to contact many Ukrainians in the army and to acquaint himself with military life and organizations.[15]

The outbreak of the March Revolution in 1917 and the collapse of the Russian monarchy brought about upheaval in Ukraine and accelerated the struggle for Ukrainian statehood. With the revolution a new period in Petliura's life began. Ukrainian soldiers in the Russian army delegated him to the First All-Ukrainian Military Congress. In contrast to other Ukrainian leaders, including Hrushevs'kyi and Vynnychenko, Petliura was less known. Because of his talent as a speaker and his knowledge, however, he became an influential figure at the congress and was elected to its presidium.[16] The organizers of the congress believed the only way to establish a Ukrainian state was through the organization of a Ukrainian regular army. The national leaders were divided over military policy, however. The idea of a professional army was not popular among some of them because they believed that such an army would be a threat to the revolution. The organizers, however, hoped that the congress would provide its support to their plan. Unfortunately they were only partly successful, because some of the delegates were influenced by the promises of the Russian revolutionaries and Russian "democracts." At that time many Ukrainians believed that Russia would not oppose Ukrainian independence so obstinately that it would be necessary to fight for it. A contemporary recalls that

> From the beginning of the Revolution of 1917 the Ukrainians were sure that revolutionary democratic Russia would not follow in the footsteps of the old autocratic satrapy in its attitude to the *"inorodtsi"* [aliens], including us Ukrainians. Moreover, most [Ukrainians] thought that the Russian democracy would come out sincerely and openly to meet the completely natural desires of all the nationalities of the former empire and would start to reconstruct the "prison of peoples" into a federative democratic republic.[17]

Petliura had a middle-of-the-road attitude toward the formation of a regular army. Although he shared the organizers' plan to "pull Ukrainian soldiers out of the hands of the Russian command and assemble them on one front," he cautioned them that, in his judgement, attitudes and circumstances did not favor the immediate organization of a Ukrainian army. The congress adopted general resolutions on the organization of separate military formations of Ukrainian soldiers from the Russian army. To carry them out, it created a seventeen-member Ukrainian Military General Committee headed by Petliura. The committee maintained constant contact with the organizations of Ukrainian soldiers at the fronts by letter, telegraph, and its bulletin, *Vistnyk*; dispatched delegates to or received delegations from those organizations; and gave them orders and directives. Thanks to Petliura's devotion to the committee's work, the Ukrainian soldiers became an organized and unified force.

Revolutionary events prompted the more patriotic Ukrainians to further the Ukrainianization of military units, and the Second All-Ukrainain Military Congress was held in Kyiv on 18–23 June 1917. The 2,500 delegates who attended represented 1,347 organizations, at the Russian fronts and 661 in the rear. They stressed mainly one goal: a free national life in a free democratic Ukraine. The congress elected an All-Ukrainian Council of Military Deputies consisting of 132 men (mostly officers), headed by Petliura. Subsequently the council entered the Central Rada as the representative of the Ukrainian military.

With the support of the congress, on 24 June 1917 the Central Rada proclaimed its First Universal: "Let the Ukrainian people on their own territory have the right to manage their own life.... No one knows better than we what we need and which laws are best for us."[18] Subsequently the Rada's General Secretariat, a Ukrainian government, was established. It was headed by Vynnychenko, while Petliura became the general secretary of military affairs. On 23 September 1917 the Council of Military Deputies dispatched a delegation headed by Petliura to the Headquarters of the Supreme Command of the Russian Army at Mahileu, where the delegation met Kerensky. Petliura conducted most of the prolonged negotiations with Kerensky, after which Kerensky agreed to the Ukrainianization of fifteen divisions. When Gen. Nikolai Dukhonin met the delegation, however, he informed it that he had not received enough information to carry out the agreement. Kerensky, it seems, was using delaying tactics, or he had no intention of honoring the agreement. The Russian Provisional Government only reluctantly agreed to a partial Ukrainianization of the troops. It needed the disciplined Ukrainian units to defend Russia because the Russian soldiers were demoralized by Bolshevik propaganda and did not wish to fight.[19] Kerensky expressed his view openly to Col. Viktor Pavlenko, the committee's liaison officer at the Russian headquarters: "You Ukrainians want to assemble all your forces at home to fight later against us. Try... dare! We would find enough forces at home to deal with you!"[20]

In response to Kerensky's hostility toward the Ukrainianization of the troops, the Ukrainian military leaders convened the Third All-Ukrainian Military Congress in Kyiv on 2–12 November 1917. It reflected the conflict between the Rada and the Provisional Government and the tension created by the subsequent Bolshevik coup in Petrograd on 7 November 1917. The congress reelected the Military General Committee headed by Petliura. As the head, Petliura distinguished himself by his initiative and activities; he did not, however, consistently carry out the committee's plans. He often compromised and remained loyal to the Russian Military Command. When the committee tried to assemble the Ukrainian soldiers on the Russian Southwestern and Romanian fronts, Petliura appealed to them to stay where they were. In spite of Petliura's loyalty, however, the Russian command and civil authorities distrusted and even hated him because he was the head of the committee. For them his loyalty was only a facade. Such an attitude undermined Petliura's popularity among the Ukrainian soldiers. The majority of the Ukrainian general secretaries also disliked Petliura because they were afraid he might use the troops in a dictatorial way.

In contrast to some of the general secretaries who called for "Ukraine without troops," Petliura was convinced that Russia would never abandon its desire to control Ukraine, that Ukrainian freedom and independence could only be maintained through hard, persistent, and bloody struggle, and that it was necessary to organize an army not through Ukrainianization of Russian units, but through the recruitment of volunteers for an independent Ukrainian army. His differences over political and especially military matters with Vynnychenko brought about Petliura's resignation as general secretary of military affairs on 6 January 1918. Subsequently he moved with a small staff of experts to Poltava gubernia, where he appealed to patriotic Ukrainian soldiers to join the new army. Soon after he succeeded in organizing a 250-man unit, the Kish Slobids'koï Ukrainy, consisting mainly of officers. Soon after another unit, consisting of 150 cadets of the Second Military School, joined Petliura. Subsequently the first unit was called the Red Haidamakas, while the second became the Black Haidamakas. Soon after a company of the two hundred Sich Riflemen commanded by Capt. Roman Sushko temporarily joined Petliura. These three units fought alongside other Ukrainian troops against the Bolshevik invasion that began on 7 January 1918.

During the invasion about ten thousand Bolsheviks in Kyiv staged an uprising on the night of 28 January 1918 and captured the Arsenal plant in the center of the city. The aim of the uprising was to help the Soviet Russian forces advancing from Left-Bank Ukraine toward Kyiv. If it succeeded, it would undermine the Ukrainian government and would discredit the Ukrainian delegation at Brest-Litovsk, thereby preventing it from carrying on negotiations with the Central Powers. Petliura transferred his units from the front to Kyiv to help suppress the uprising, and after four days of heavy fighting (1–4 February) the well-armed Bolsheviks were defeated. Although the Arsenal rebels had killed their wounded prisoners, Petliura prevented the execution of the 1,500 captured Bolsheviks, and they were later released.

The defeat of the Bolshevik invasion and uprising in Kyiv dramatically ended the period of Ukrainianization of Russian units and ushered in the new period of the organization of a national volunteer army. Petliura provided leadership and moral authority for this effort and the struggle against subsequent Soviet Russian invasions. The Arsenal rebellion was his Rubicon.[21]

Celebration of the victory in Kyiv was short-lived, however, because Soviet Russian forces under Mikhail Muravev regained the city after eleven days of bombardment and street fighting, on 8 February 1918. Consequently the Ukrainian government, which had evacuated to Zhytomyr while Ukrainian troops retreated westward, was forced to make a separate peace with the Central Powers to obtain their support in expelling the Bolshevik forces, believing that an adequate force could be composed of the existing Ukrainian units in the Austrian Army and the Ukrainian soldiers from the Russian Army captured and interned by the Germans. The Austrian and German authorities refused, arguing that the time needed to bring the troops from other areas was too great. Petliura opposed both the peace treaty with the Central Powers and bringing German and Austrian troops into Ukraine. He complained that the dominant Ukrainian political parties failed to recognize the principal problem:

> Whether Ukraine, as an independent state, ought in its foreign policy to rely on Europe or on Moscow-Asia.... [on this question the] SR [Ukrainian Party of Socialist Revolutionaries] and part of the SD [Ukrainian Social Democratic Worker's party] gave preference to Moscow and not to Europe. It is necessary [, however,] to depend on Europe, which ... did not know or understand us, and simultaneously to organize our own force.... From the time America became involved in World War I, I became convinced that the war would be won not by Germany, but by the Entente. I wanted to create a front—let it be militarily defeated temporarily; all the same we would win later politically.... I think that the orientation of some of our circles on Germany is a great mistake that will still cost us dearly. Germany needs the whole of Russia and not Ukraine alone.[22]

Petliura could not, however, influence ensuing developments. A day prior to the Germans' arrival in Korosten, where Petliura's headquarters were located, he called the officers of his units together to inform them that he had decided to resign from his post. An eyewitness wrote that Petliura stated: "What happened to Ukraine was not what I wished. Tomorrow the German echelons will march on the capital of Ukraine. My dear soldiers: I am leaving you because I cannot command the Kish Slobids'koï Ukraïny... [doing so] now would mean helping the [Germans'] occupation of Ukraine." His friends insisted that he remain with the units until they liberated Kyiv, however, and Petliura agreed.[23]

After the liberation of Kyiv on 2 March 1918, Petliura withdrew from military and political life, believing that the German presence was only temporary and that the Entente would win the war. Although he planned to devote himself to social concerns, he remained preoccupied with the military problem: "He spoke with enthusiasm about the necessity to have a dependable and trained national army because we would still have to fight Moscow for a long time, even in the absence of monarchism and faced with the most liberal regime."[24]

Petliura planned to establish a national daily newspaper. His friends, however, persuaded him to devote his time to the zemstvos, organizations of municipal self-government responsible for education, public health, public works, and transportation. Petliura was elected chairman of the Kyiv Gubernial Zemstvo. Subsequently, under his leadership the All-Ukrainian Union of Zemstvos was organized, and he was elected its head. Both posts allowed Petliura to utilize his organizational and administrative talents, and he was able to find a modus vivendi with the zemstvos' largely Russified personnel while firmly but tactfully directing their de-Russification. As a result, Petliura earned the respect of the zemstvo personnel and the population in general.

The national importance of the zemstvo union increased after the German military authorities dissolved the Central Rada on 28 April 1918 and a congress called by the right-wing Union of Landowners proclaimed Gen. Pavlo Skoropads'kyi the hetman of Ukraine. The union became a center of opposition to the Skoropads'kyi government. The congress of the union met in mid-June and sent a protest to the hetman objecting to the widespread arrests, including of national leaders; the denial of civil liberties; the punitive expeditions; and the suppression of the zemstvos and Prosvita societies. When this protest failed to change the hetman's policy, Petliura sent a memorandum to the German ambassador, Philip Mumm, with copies to the ambassadors of Austria-Hungary and Bulgaria, informing him of the arrests by both the government and the German military authorities. Petliura pointed out that such actions would not promote Ukrainian-German friendship. Petliura's activities and popularity worried both the hetman government and the German authorities, and on July 12 he himself was arrested. Although there were vocal protests against his arrest and petitions for his release, he was kept in jail until 11 November 1918.

Soon after Petliura's release, the leaders of the Ukrainian National Union elected him a member of the Directory, its five-member executive body, and commander in chief of the anti-hetman forces. After reaching an accord with the German forces being evacuated from Ukraine, on 14 December Petliura and his troops entered Kyiv, thereby forcing the hetman's abdication. On 19 December 1918 the Directory reestablished the UNR.

As a result of Petliura's activities during the Austro-German occupation and the hetman government's oppressive policies, his popularity and trust among the population and the troops increased substantially. Petliura was the only member of the Directory trusted by the disciplined military units, and they were held together by him. On 11 February 1919 Petliura succeeded Vynnychenko as president of the Directory. The task of governing Ukraine became for him a very difficult responsibility. Most of the leaders of the Central Rada had either left the country or withdrawn from political life. To cope with the critical political and military situation and to defend Ukrainian statehood, he chose to enter into a political and military alliance with Poland and simultaneously, through Poland, with the Allied Powers.[25]

CHAPTER 3

Józef Piłsudski—the Builder of the New Poland—and Political Developments in Poland

Józef Klemens Piłsudski was born on 5 December 1867 at Zulavas in Vilnius (Vilna) gubernia, Lithuania, into a family of Lithuanian-Polish landed gentry.[1] In the fall of 1877 he began his high-school education at a Russian gymnasium in Vilnius. The former capital of Lithuania was a cosmopolitan center where Lithuanians, Poles, Belarusians, and Jews had lived together for centuries, and there Piłsudski developed an understanding of the nationality problem and a sense of history. Tsarist policy had a different effect upon him. After the defeat of the 1863–4 Polish Insurrection against the Russian regime, oppression and Russification were the order of the day. The Russian teachers in Piłsudski's school distorted the histories of Lithuania and Poland, which were taught as the histories of the "northwestern Russian province" and the "Vistula land," and speaking Polish and Lithuanian in the schools, courts, and other public places was forbidden. As a result Piłsudski's patriotic feelings and his resentment toward the Russian regime deepened.[2] In later years he commented bitterly about his experiences:

> A whole ox's skin would not contain a description of the unceasing humiliating provocations from our teachers and the degradation of all that I had been accustomed to respect and love. I always count the years spent in the gymnasium amongst the most unpleasant of my life.[3]

Tragedy in Piłsudski's own family increased this resentment. His great uncle died in Russian exile; a cousin of his father was killed during the insurrection; another cousin's estate was confiscated by the Russians; and his blind grandmother was imprisoned for some time. In 1885 Piłsudski entered the medical school at Kharkiv University. Life in Kharkiv was quite different from that in Vilnius. Piłsudski was not impressed by the other Polish students there: they were "apathetic, almost without social ideas. Those who had them were almost entirely Russified. They tried to draw me into the student organization 'Narodna Wola' [Narodnaia Volia], but I steadily resisted."[4] For participating in the large demonstration at the university celebrating the twenty-fifth anniversary of the peasant emancipation, Piłsudski was jailed for six days. The following year the university authorities refused to reinstate him, and he returned to Vilnius.[5]

In Lithuania and Poland after 1863–4, Russian persecution made the people indifferent to national, social, and political problems. Those who had participated in the uprising were either dead, in prison, or abroad. Most young people were apathetic, while those who were radical joined the Russian revolutionaries. Piłsudski tried to awake the young from their lethargy. His previous acquaintance with the activities of the Russian revolutionaries gave him the idea of organizing people in Vilnius along the same lines, but adapted to Polish needs. He organized study circles whose participants made contact with workers in Vilnius but had no relations with socialist groups, although they read illegal socialist literature. They also discussed the struggles and political developments in the Russian cities. In 1887 Piłsudski's older brother, Bronisław, was implicated in the plot to assassinate Alexander III by procuring some chemicals needed by the conspirators, and Piłsudski himself came under suspicion because his brother had given his address to one of the conspirators. Consequently both brothers were arrested, Bronisław on 14 March in St. Petersburg and Józef on 22 March in Vilnius. On 1 May Bronisław was sentenced to fifteen years of hard labor on Sakhalin Island and Józef to five years' exile in eastern Siberia.[6] Piłsudski's exile greatly influenced the development of his national consciousness and political outlook. In later years he admitted that only in Siberian exile, "I became what I am."[7] While in transit, he participated in a mutiny in the prison in Irkutsk and was badly beaten. On 13 December he was sent to Kirensk, which some called hell on earth. The 6,000-kilometer journey took over eight months and was the worst part of his sentence. At the same time, however, Piłsudski had the opportunity to see and study the tsarist empire—its multinational composition, its brutal administrative system, and the mentality of its people—from inside. His experiences deepened his resentment toward Russia.

Piłsudski spent nearly two years at Kirensk. After he became very ill, he was transferred, on 18 August 1889, to Tunka in southern Siberia. More liberal conditions at Tunka gave him the opportunity to read a great deal of political literature by Marx, Engels, Herbert Spencer, and the Russian populists Nikolai Mikhailovskii, Dmitrii Pisarev, Mikhail Bakunin, Nikolai Chernyshevskii, Petr Lavrov, and Nikolai Dobroliubov, as well as novels by Dostoevskii, Tolstoi, and Turgenev. With other political prisoners he was able to discuss a wide range of national, social, and political problems. Among them were a Ukrainian, Dr. Afanasii Mykhalevych, and Bronisław Szwarce, a member of the Central National Committee in Warsaw responsible for the 1863–4 insurrection, who had been sentenced to twenty-eight years in Siberia. Szwarce greatly influenced Piłsudski, conveying to him the lessons of his experiences and convincing him that a successful uprising requires a well-prepared program of action.⁸

During his exile, Piłsudski became familiar with the Russian revolutionaries and their psychology and developed strong opinions about them. He was heard to say that

> They [the Russians] are all imperialists, more or less camouflaged, including the revolutionaries. An elemental centralism is characteristic of their minds, which eternally tends toward the absolute. They cannot support differences and do not know how to reconcile contradictions. They wear out their will and imagination to such an extent that ... they even reject completely the need for conscious social organizations, if only not to have to think of them. Let events follow their own elemental course; that solution is, in their view, the wisest because it is the simplest and the easiest. That is why there are so many anarchists among them. It is remarkable, nonetheless, that I met no republicans among the Russians."⁹

Piłsudski returned to Vilnius on 1 July 1892. Although he was only twenty-five years old, exile had tempered his will and his personality. It was, in a sense, part of his political education, and it gave him not merely the experience, but also the prestige that was essential for leadership. Piłsudski was a romantic idealist, but also a realist. In his opinion, if Poland wished to attain freedom, it could not rely on a future Russian revolution or internationalist movements, but only on its own strength. Exile had taught him that only force could prevail against brute force. He believed in the virtue of arms, but he realized that isolated revolutionary acts were a waste of time and too costly in terms of human suffering. When he returned home, he was ready for action and looked for the best way to rouse his people to begin an unconditional struggle against Russia and the tsarist system.¹⁰ His instinct and experiences had led him to think that the cause of political independence and the freedom of the working classes of Poland were complementary. A few years later he remarked: "The socialist in Poland must aim at the independence of his country, and independence is the obvious condition for the victory of socialism in Poland."¹¹ Piłsudski's later attitude toward socialism is reflected in his response to being addressed "Comrade Piłsudski" by a socialist delegation:

> Gentlemen, I am no longer your comrade. In the beginning we followed the same direction and together took a tramway painted red. But I left it at the station marked "Poland's Independence," while you are continuing the journey as far as the station "Socialism." My good wishes accompany you, but be so good as to call me "sir."¹²

Piłsudski's return from exile coincided with the growth in popularity of socialist ideas among the Poles. On 23 November 1892 four Polish socialist groups held a convention in Paris and united into one Polish Socialist party (PPS). Simultaneously a Group of Polish Socialists Abroad, composed of émigrés from Russian-ruled Poland, was organized. Subsequently, at the beginning of March 1893, the PPS was formed clandestinely in Warsaw; the Polish socialists from Vilnius joined it as a "Lithuanian Section." Piłsudski joined the party because he saw it as a strong revolutionary force that could be used to recruit and prepare the younger generation of Poles for a revolution against Russia.

Piłsudski began a period of intensive activity. He contributed many writings on sociopolitical problems to *Przedświt*, a Polish socialist newspaper published in London, where he formulated the principles of the new Polish revolutionary movement. He organized meetings of his close friends to discuss socialist literature and political problems and met with prominent Polish leaders visiting Vilnius. He also associated with radical workers in Vilnius to convey to them the idea of the restoration of an independent Poland. At the end of June 1893 the first congress of the PPS, representing the organizations of Warsaw, St. Petersburg and Vilnius, was held near Vilnius. One of its decisions was to publish a party organ, *Robotnik*, and its editorship was assigned to Piłsudski. The paper first appeared on 12 July 1894 in a small town near Vilnius, and at the beginning of June 1895 it was transferred to Vilnius. Piłsudski was assisted by Stanisław Wojciechowski, a future president of Poland. In addition to editing and writing, Piłsudski was responsible for procuring funds for the party and the publication of the newspapers at home and in London. To carry out his work, he travelled to other parts of Poland, to Russia, and to Ukraine. At the close of 1894 Piłsudski attended the second PPS congress in London, and at the third congress, held in Vilnius on 29 June 1895, he was elected to the party's Central Committee.[13]

The safety of Piłsudski and the clandestine PPS press became uncertain, and in the middle of October 1899 he and his wife of three months moved to Łódź, the industrial center of Poland, taking the press with them and installing it in their new apartment. On 21–2 February 1900, however, the tsarist police learned by accident of the press's whereabouts, and Piłsudski and his wife were arrested and jailed in the Warsaw Citadel, a tightly guarded prison. In prison Piłsudski feigned "psychosis hallucinatoria," and on 15 December 1900 he was transferred to a mental hospital in St. Petersburg. On 14 May 1901, with the help of two PPS members, Bronisław Mazurkiewicz and Aleksander Sułkiewicz, he escaped. Ten days later he was reunited with his wife, who had been freed on 21 January, and during the second half of June they crossed the Russo-Austrian border and lived for five weeks in Lviv. In the middle of November they travelled from Cracow to London to discuss PPS political and organizational work.[14]

After four months in London, Piłsudski returned home. For two months he remained mostly in Vilnius, but made trips to a number of cities, including Kyiv, where the newspaper *Robotnik* was now being secretly printed. His primary preoccupation was to make the party's work more effective by dividing Poland into organizational regions. In the middle of June 1902 the sixth PPS congress was held in Lublin. It resolved to publish the newspaper *Walka* as the organ of the PPS in Lithuania. Piłsudski was appointed its editor and elected to the Central Committee and Executive Committee of the PPS. After the congress Piłsudski returned to Cracow, where he started publishing *Walka*.

The relative freedom in the Austro-Hungarian Empire provided the party with a base for clandestine political activity in Russian-ruled Poland. From Cracow, an important Polish intellectual, cultural, and political center, it was easier to smuggle illegal material into Russian-ruled Poland. Therefore Piłsudski began transferring the party's agencies and publications from London to Cracow, and for the next twelve years, until World War I, he lived mostly in Cracow. During the years 1902–1905, Piłsudski played a leading role in the PPS. His influence steadily increased, and he became the acknowledged leader of the Polish revolutionary movement.[15] After the outbreak of the Russo-Japanese War in 1904, Piłsudski contacted the Japanese envoy in London and presented him with a memorandum proposing the formation of Polish legions in Japan to fight against Russia. In response, he received an invitation from the Japanese General Staff to come to Tokyo for further discussions. He arrived in Tokyo on 11 July 1904. In his memorandum to the Japanese Foreign Ministry in Tokyo, Piłsudski stated that in his judgment, among the oppressed nationalities in the Russian Empire, the Poles were the most politically conscious and most prepared to oppose the Russian regime. He pointed out that:

> This driving force the Poles possess, and the importance of the Poles among the component parts of the empire make us bold enough to set the political aim of splitting Russia into its component parts and securing in this way the independence of the countries attached to it by force. We consider it [this aim] not only as the fulfillment of our cultural aspirations for an independent existence, but also as its guarantee, because Russia, deprived of its conquests, would be weakened and no longer a formidable and dangerous neighbor.[16]

Piłsudski sought Japanese financial support, arms, and ammunition for his party's revolutionary work, and Japanese help in organizing a legion composed of Polish prisoners of war from the Russian army captured by the Japanese. He hoped that such support would lead to an uprising in Poland against Russia. In exchange, the PPS would supply intelligence to the Japanese about the Russian army.

Piłsudski encountered opposition in Japan from his principal political rival, Roman Dmowski, the leader of the Polish National Democratic party, who sought to promote Polish interests through an understanding with Russia. Dmowski had come to the conclusion that Russia would lose the war against Japan and would thus be weakened. Consequently its internal policy would change in favor of Poland.[17]

Dmowski, who had arrived in Tokyo almost two months before Piłsudski, presented petitions in English to prominent Japanese politicians concerning political conditions in the Russian Empire, the importance of the Polish problem, and the attitude of the Poles toward the Russian and Austrian occupational powers. He eventually convinced them that Piłsudski's plan was unrealizable. Piłsudski did manage, however, to achieve some minor successes in Japan, and during the war the Japanese authorities gave some arms and ammunition to the PPS and financed its diversionary actions against Russia. Moreover, the Japanese agreed to hold the Poles who had deserted from the Russian forces on the party's instructions in a special camp separate from other Russian prisoners and to give them special treatment. Eventually those prisoners would not be returned to Russia, but would be transported to the United States with the assistance of Polish organizations. Impressed by Japan's military strength, Piłsudski became very interested in military matters and began studying military science and history, particularly the Napoleonic campaigns and the Russo-Japanese and Balkan wars.[18]

After returning to Poland, Piłsudski devoted himself to the organization of combat units within the PPS, and armed demonstrations in Russian-ruled Poland. His concern was to prevent, or at least to retard, mobilization of Poles for the Japanese front, reasoning that it was better to resist Russia at home than to die for the oppressor in Manchuria. With this idea in mind, he visited the various PPS branches to sound out their views and ask for their help. To his disappointment, the party agreed only to organize a public demonstration against the mobilization. When the general mobilization was proclaimed, Piłsudski, through his friend Józef Kwiatka, the PPS leader in Warsaw, organized an armed demonstration in Warsaw on 13 November 1904. It was broken up by the police and army, but not before eleven people (including police) were killed and forty wounded. Similar demonstrations followed in other cities, including Łódź and Sosnowiec. Alarmed by the first public demonstrations in Poland since 1864, the tsarist regime responded by greatly reducing the mobilization in Poland.[19]

During the Russian Revolution of 1905, the PPS organized a Militant Organization (Organizacja Bojowa) and put Piłsudski in charge of it. In October 1905 it established a secret school in Cracow that trained small groups to engage in subversive activities in Russian-ruled Poland. Using arms and explosives supplied by the Japanese via London, these groups rescued Polish prisoners, attacked the police and their convoys, destroyed Russian monuments, and robbed banks, post offices, and mail trains to provide funds for the organization. Their most important action was the holdup of a mail train at a little railway station near Vilnius on 26 September 1908, in which Piłsudski took part. During the four years he was in charge of the organization, he resided in Cracow, but spent much of his time in Russian-ruled Poland and abroad.

As the organization's activities against the Russian regime increased, ideological differences within the PPS deepened concerning the involvement of all classes in revolutionary activities and the question of federation with Russia versus independence. At the PPS Congress held in Vienna (19–22 November 1906), these differences brought about a split in the party. Piłsudski and his supporters left the party and created the PPS—Revolutionary Faction, while the remainder became the PPS—Left Wing, which gradually moved ideologically toward the Social Democratic Party of the Kingdom of Poland and Lithuania.[20]

The Militant Organization and its activities were, in Piłsudski's mind, only the first stage in challenging the Russian regime in Poland. He also wanted to revive a militant spirit among the people at large. The nineteenth-century Polish uprisings, in his judgement, had failed because of inadequate preparation, and he maintained that the party must be strong enough in both arms and men to take advantage of any potential international crisis. The situation in Poland, however, was unfavorable for the realization of Piłsudski's ideas. Disillusionment had become widespread after the hopes of the Russian Revolution of 1905 had faded, and a modus vivendi with Russia had been generally accepted by most Poles. Although there were no tangible political gains from this understanding, there were certain economic ones. Russian-ruled Poland was becoming industrialized, and the imperial market was important to it. Moreover, the idea of a new constitutional Russia that would reunite Austrian-, German-, and Russian-ruled Poland was popular among the Poles, and the National Democrats called for a united front with Russia against Germany as Poland's main enemy.

The international political situation, however, favored Piłsudski's ideas. The Russo-Japanese War and the Revolution of 1905 had manifested the weakness of the tsarist regime but also the unreadiness of the liberal and revolutionary parties to take its place. An international crisis was imminent after Austria-Hungary annexed Bosnia and Herzegovina and thereby antagonized Serbia. In Piłsudski's judgement, a European war was merely a question of time. In light of this situation, he decided to abolish the Militant Organization, because it would not be able to defeat a regular army, and to create a nonpolitical military formation instead. In his judgement, "It must be all the people, not merely one group. No class, let it be the most powerful, can carry through against the oppressor a victorious insurrection. It can be accomplished only by the entire nation."[21]

In other words, an army had to precede the Polish state. At the end of June 1908, at Piłsudski's initiative, the leader of the Lviv branch of the Militant Organization, Kazimierz Sosnkowski, called a meeting of all branch leaders. At this meeting they agreed to create the nucleus of such an army, the Union of Active Struggle. The Militant Organization and the PPS were unwilling to approve this formation, but Piłsudski's threat of resignation from the party and the ensuing Bosnian crisis changed their minds. A similar organization, the Strzelec Society, was created in Cracow. Gradually branches of these organizations were formed in other places in both Austrian-ruled Galicia and Russian-ruled Poland. Their existence, however, was illegal, and Piłsudski realized that as long as these paramilitary groups acted secretly, they could not embrace all Polish youth. In 1910 he took advantage of a new Austrian law, which encouraged the creation of patriotic societies, to gain legal status for the Union of Active Struggle as the so-called Riflemen's Union. The Austrian authorities supplied its members with obsolete rifles for training and authorized them to wear uniforms. The union provided more advanced military training.[22]

As the union became stronger, Piłsudski's popularity among the Poles increased. In 1911 a rival, more conservative party formed its own paramilitary formation, the Drużyny Strzeleckie (Riflemen's Units). The older Sokół gymnastic society also became a paramilitary organization. Piłsudski's moral authority dominated in all of these organizations, and their leaders assured him that if war broke out, they would place themselves under his command. Each international crisis provided Piłsudski and the Poles with an impetus to new actions. After the outbreak of the Balkan Wars on 18 October 1912, the Poles' political activities increased, and on 10 November 1912 the Polish political parties called a convention in Vienna where the PPS initiated the creation of a Provisional Commission of Confederated Independence Parties responsible for military affairs. The commission appointed Piłsudski military commander of the Riflemen, gave them financial support, and defended them in the Galician Sejm and Austrian Parliament.

With the outbreak of World War I, the Riflemen's Union and the Drużyny were amalgamated, and Piłsudski formed a 144-man company of infantry from the two organizations. On 6–7 August 1914 this detachment crossed the Austro-Russian frontier into Russian-ruled Poland, which had been evacuated by Russian troops. On 12 August Piłsudski and an enlarged detachment of about 400 men entered the city of Kielce prior to the German and Austrian troops. For a while Kielce was Piłsudski's headquarters. In the meantime, representatives of the Polish parties in Austrian-ruled Poland formed a Chief National Committee in Cracow to oversee the formation of a Polish Legion. Piłsudski and his men joined the legion, and he became the commander of the its First Brigade. In order to have an organization that was independent of the Central Powers, he also created a secret Polish Military Organization (POW) under the command of Tadeusz Zieliński. The legion's three brigades and the POW would be, in Piłsudski's strategy, the nucleus of the future Polish army.[23]

Piłsudski entered the war on the side of the Central Powers because he saw Russia as the principal enemy of Poland. He recognized the Chief National Committee, an Austrophile organization, as the link between the legion and the Austrian authorities. Although Piłsudski had pledged loyalty to Austria-Hungary, he carried on an independent Polish policy. The legion was not a purely military formation; its origin, as well as its spirit, had been politically motivated. The legion became a problem for the Austrian military authorities because it disturbed the unity of the Austrian army. The enthusiasm of the legion, however, caused the Austrian authorities to believe that it might rouse the people in Russian-ruled Poland against the Russians. From the beginning of the war the legion's brigades operated against the Russians on different fronts. Piłsudski's brigade initially fought in a number of battles against the advancing Russians southeast of Cracow and then near Tarnów. Later it participated in the decisive Austro-German offensive following the victory at Gorlice in the spring of 1915. In November 1915 all of the legion's regiments were united as a single force under Gen. Stanisław Puchalski on the Volynian front, along the rivers Stokhid and Styr. At the beginning of 1916 the total strength of the legion was about 12,000 men (8,000 infantry, 1,000 cavalry, and 3,000 artillery with 36 guns). It played an important part in holding up the Brusilov offensive of June 1916 at the town of Kostiukivka. The fact that this was the first real war of the Poles with Russia since the Insurrection of 1863–4 proved an inspiration to Piłsudski and his brigade, even though the latter suffered serious losses. During this period, Piłsudski carried on energetic recruitment activity in Russian-ruled Poland. For his distinguished service at the front, he was promoted to brigadier by the Austrian Supreme Command on 15 November 1914.[24]

The war also brought Piłsudski disappointments. He had expected that as his troops entered Russian-ruled Poland, the population would rise up against the Russians. The majority of Poles showed no disposition for supporting Piłsudski, however. Both major Polish parties in Russian-ruled Poland, the National Democrats and Social Democrats, were pro-Russian. Their attitude was greatly strengthened by the 14 August 1914 manifesto of Grand Duke Nicholas, the commander in chief of the Russian army, proclaiming self-government for the Poles within the framework of the Russian Empire: "May the frontiers disappear that divide the Polish people, thus making of them a unity under the sceptre of the Emperor of Russia! Under that sceptre Poland will be born again, free in religion, in language, and in self-government (autonomy)."[25]

Piłsudski continued fighting on the side of the Central Powers on behalf of Poland's liberty until the summer of 1915. By that time the Russian troops were in full retreat from Poland, and Piłsudski believed Russia had already been defeated. For him the Germans were now the main opponent of Polish independence. Two-thirds of Russian-ruled Poland were occupied by the Germans and one-third by the Austrians. In light of these conditions, Piłsudski sought some guarantee that Poland would eventually become independent, but it soon became evident that the Central Powers had no intention of establishing an independent Poland. In view of this situation, Piłsudski perceived that inaction might be more successful than action. On 25 July 1916 he offered his resignation as brigade commander to the Austro-Hungarian General Headquarters, hoping to compel the Central Powers to make a concession on the Polish question. His resignation was accepted on 27 September. Many of the Brigade's officers followed his example, but the weakened Brigade continued fighting on the side of the Central Powers.

Military developments on the Eastern Front forced the Central Powers to modify their Polish policy. Although the Russians had been driven out from Poland by the summer of 1915, the war against Russia was not yet over. In the fall of 1915 the German advance on the Eastern Front was halted along the line Riga-Dvinsk-Pinsk-Dubno-Ternopil. The German military authorities planned to raise a Polish army in Poland, where only half of the man power had been mobilized by the Russian authorities, but the Polish leaders felt that only a Polish government could recruit Poles. The Central Powers soon came to the conclusion that in order to secure Polish recruits, it would be necessary first to solve the Polish question.

On 5 November 1916 the German and Austrian emperors issued a joint manifesto proclaiming an autonomous state on the territory of Russian-ruled Poland. This act had been prepared without Polish assistance, and the state's frontiers were not clearly defined. Subsequently, on 11 January 1917, the Central Powers called up a Polish Provisional Council of State. Piłsudski became the counselor of its Military Commission. The council was weak, however, for it did not represent the whole population and had only advisory functions. Real authority remained in the hands of the Central Powers. Subsequently the Germans proposed to form a Polish volunteer army using the legionnaires as cadres. Piłsudski wanted to use the POW instead, but this proposition was unacceptable to the Germans, who wanted to keep full control of this army. Piłsudski's objection to a German-controlled Polish army increased when the Russian Provisional Government recognized the principle of Polish independence on 29 March 1917. On 10 April the Austrian authorities handed over the Polish Legion to the German governor-general of Poland, Hans Hartwig von Beseler, and not to the Provisional Council of State. On 2 July Piłsudski resigned from the council in protest, and he advised his men not to take the oath of allegiance to the German emperor. On 9 July, 5,200 of the 6,000 men from Russian-ruled Poland who had followed Piłsudski's advice were sent to an internment camp; 3,000 of the 8,000 men from Austrian-ruled Poland were sent into reserve; while the remaining 5,000 were transferred to the Austrian eastern front. On 22 July the German authorities arrested Piłsudski and Col. Kazimierz Sosnkowski. By imprisoning Piłsudski, however, they vindicated his previous collaboration with them and improved his standing with the Poles and, especially, with the Allies.[26]

After Piłsudski's arrest the Provisional Council of State resigned, and on 12 September 1917 the Central Powers set up a Regency Council consisting of Archbishop Aleksander Kakowski of Warsaw, Prince Zdzisław Lubomirski, and Józef Ostrowski. Subsequently this body formed a Polish cabinet headed by Jan Kucharzewski. Germany's political and military situation in the fall of 1918 compelled the authorities to turn their attention to Piłsudski once again. At the end of October Count Harry Kessler visited Piłsudski to find out about his attitude toward Germany in case Poland should become independent, and to obtain a promise that he would refrain from any future aggressive policy. Piłsudski pointed out that he had never been hostile toward Germany, and that as a prisoner he could make no such promise. It is not clear whether he made any commitment regarding Poland's future western borders. But Piłsudski anticipated that the question of the borders would be decided neither in Warsaw nor in Berlin, but in Paris by the Entente. He alluded to this possibility by remarking to Kessler that "Poland will certainly accept all the gifts."[27] The outbreak of the revolution in Germany prompted the release of Piłsudski and Sosnkowski on 8 November 1918. Two days later they arrived in Warsaw.

At the beginning of the First World War, the Polish question was barely an international concern. During the latter phase of the war, both the Central Powers and Russia treated the Polish problem with restraint and conceded the possibility of limited geographical and political independence. The Poles accepted the concessions and thus strengthened their political position. By the end of 1917 their leaders had come to the conclusion that Polish independence was possible only in the case of an Allied victory. Following the collapse of the Russian and then of the Austrian and German empires, Polish aspirations became a reality. Militarily Poland contributed very little to achieving independence. On the eve of the armistice the question of Polish independence was, generally speaking, solved, and when Piłsudski arrived in Warsaw he was able to assume leadership of the Polish troops and the Polish state.

The fall of the three empires created chaos in Poland. The Regency Council set up by the Central Powers in 1917 was not able to exercise control and failed to form a government because of the lack of popular support. Simultaneously, in Lublin, Ignacy Daszyński proclaimed a socialist republic. The difficult political conditions compelled the Regency Council to turn over to Piłsudski the command of the troops that were at its disposal, and then, on 14 November, to dissolve itself and hand over its authority to Piłsudski until the formation of a national government. The German military acknowledged Piłsudski's authority. His first task was to get the German troops out of Poland. On 11 November he initiated a meeting with the German Soldiers' Council. Calling upon the German troops to preserve the peace and not to interfere in Poland's internal affairs, he promised to arrange for their immediate repatriation and to assure their personal safety as long as they laid down their arms and materiel before crossing the frontier. The Soldiers' Council accepted his proposal, and one week later the last of the 80,00 German troops had left Poland. Next Piłsudski dissolved Daszyński's government in Lublin through negotiation, and on 16 November he sent a message to all the governments of Europe and America announcing the formation of an independent Polish state. Two days later a socialist government was formed, headed by Jędrzej Moraczewski. On 22 November 1918 Piłsudski issued a decree declaring himself chief of state.

Piłsudski was confronted with new political and military problems. On 27 December 1918 an uprising against the Germans began in Poznań. Instigated by Ignacy Paderewski after his arrival from Paris, it resulted in the expulsion of the Germans from Prussian Poland, which legally, however, remained under German authority until the Peace Treaty of Versailles was signed on 28 June 1919. Poland also laid claim to Upper Silesia, which had not been a part of Poland since 1335. The Peace Conference solved this issue by a plebiscite held on 20 March 1921, and on 20 October the province was divided between Poland and Germany according to the principle of self-determination. In January 1919 a conflict between Poland and Czechoslovakia had also broken out over Teschen Silesia. It was resolved by the Conference of Ambassadors, which, on 28 July 1920, divided the province between the two countries.[28]

Internal conflict also plagued Poland. In Warsaw, on the night of 4–5 January 1919, a small rightist opposition, inspired by the National Committee in Paris, staged a coup d'état. The attempt was not well organized, and it failed the same day. Nevertheless, Moraczewski and his cabinet had to be dismissed, and the next day Piłsudski invited Paderewski to form a new cabinet. By appointing Paderewski, Piłsudski achieved a compromise with the right, many of whom were landowners, and the National Committee in Paris. Thus, his cabinet presented a facade of national unity at the Paris Peace Conference.[29] On 26 January 1919 Paderewski called an election, the result of which was a Sejm dominated by the National Democrats. With the help of the Entente, Piłsudski was free to turn his attention to the establishment of Poland's eastern borders with Ukraine, Belarus, Lithuania, and Soviet Russia.

CHAPTER 4

The Organization of the Polish Army in France and Its Impact on the Ukrainian-Polish War

Before 1917 Polish leaders organized military formations allied with the Central Powers to fight against Russia. The outbreak of the Russian Revolution in 1917 and the prospect of the defeat of the Central Powers encouraged Poles abroad to organize new military formations on the side of the Entente. The émigré leaders wanted all of these formations to be concentrated in one country and placed under one political authority in order to strengthen their position at the future peace conference.

At the beginning of World War I, Poles in France spontaneously set up a Committee of Polish Volunteers for Service in the French Army. On 20–22 August 1914 a military unit of about 200 volunteers was assigned to the First Regiment of the Foreign Legion and sent to Bayonne for training. It never became an independent Polish formation. An effort to organize similar detachments was prevented by the protest of the Russian ambassador in Paris, Aleksandr Izvol'skii. The Polish Legion fighting on the side of the Central Powers supplied him with the trump card that convinced France, as Russia's ally, to continue regarding the Polish question as an internal Russian problem. This situation prevailed until the outbreak of the March Revolution. On 29 March 1917 the Russian Provisional Government recognized, in principle, the independence of Poland in the territory where Poles constituted a majority of the population. At that time, however, the whole of Poland was under German and Austro-Hungarian occupation.[1]

When France's war effort became strained, its government asked Ambassador Izvol'skii to form military units from among Russian citizens living in France. Knowing that those citizens were unreliable, Izvol'skii advised the French government to turn for volunteers to the Polish immigrants in France and Poles in the German army interned there. In fact, the first petition concerning the creation of Polish units in France was written in the Russian embassy. Izvol'skii had reversed his previous attitude because he hoped to be able to control France's Polish troops and wanted to divert the Poles' attention away from the east and concentrate their energies on the Western Front. The French government accepted Izvol'skii's advice, and on 4 June 1917 the organization of an autonomous Polish army was decreed by President

Raymond Poincaré. According to the decree, (1) the army was under the authority of the French High Command but would fight under the Polish flag; (2) its raising and maintenance were guaranteed by the French government; (3) the regulations in force in the French Army would apply to it; (4) and it would be constituted from Poles already serving in the French forces and from other Poles in France who had enlisted voluntarily.[2] The position of the Polish Army was more clearly defined by another presidential decree issued on 31 May 1918.

After the initial decree, a Franco-Polish Military Mission, headed by a Gen. Louis Archinard, was created to carry out the formation of Polish troops in France. On 27 June 1917 an assembly camp near Sillé-le-Guillaume, Sarthe, was assigned for the recruits, and subsequently a number of recruitment offices were established, including ones in Lille, Boulogne-sur-Mer, Mans, Bordeaux, Lyon, and Nice. The recruits consisted of Poles serving in the French army, Polish settlers in France, Poles from the Russian brigades stationed in France, Polish refugees from Germany in Holland, and Poles in the German army interned in France. Many of the volunteers, including officers, were not the best candidates in terms of their physical condition or ideological orientation. Their main motive for joining was to get away from the trenches at the front or from prisoner of war camps to the safer training barracks in the rear. But conditions in the barracks were also bad, and the officers and noncommissioned officers, who came from the French, German, or Russian armies, did not speak Polish and treated the men badly. Moreover, as the number of recruits increased, the situation in the army worsened because of the shortage of officers and barracks, which the French army could not afford to supply because of its own needs. Consequently a number of new training camps, including ones in Laval, Mayenne, Potigny-Ussy, Leslay and Quintin, Côtes-du-Nord, were assigned for the recruits. The latter one became the main camp for training recruits as well as officers and noncommissioned officers.[3]

Alongside the organization of troops, Polish émigré leaders, mostly members of the National Democratic party and some conservatives, set up a Polish National Committee at Lausanne on 15 August 1917. Headed by Roman Dmowski, this committee established its headquarters in Paris, appointed representatives in London and Rome, recognized Ignacy Paderewski as its agent in the United States, and carried out a propaganda campaign in the Entente countries and the United States. As the Russian Provisional Government weakened and its armies disintegrated, the French authorities recognized the committee as the "official Polish organization" on 20 September 1917. Subsequently the other Allied governments also recognized the committee: Great Britain on 15 October, Italy on 30 October, and the

United States on 10 November. In order to strengthen its position, the committee claimed political control of the still forming Polish Army. On 20 March 1918 its request to this effect was granted by the French minister of foreign affairs, and on 28 September the French authorities signed an agreement with the committee. It consisted of eleven articles:

1. The Polish armed forces, wherever they may be raised to fight on the side of the Allies against the Central Powers, will constitute a unified autonomous allied army fighting under a unified Polish command;
2. This army will be placed under the supreme political authority of the Polish National Committee, whose headquarters is in Paris;
3. The commander in chief of the Polish Army will be appointed by the Polish National Committee and confirmed by the French government (eventually also by the other Allied governments);
4. The commander in chief of the Polish Army will be supported by a General Staff of the Polish Army, which will be headed by a French chief of staff selected by the commander in chief from a list supplied by the French minister of war;
5. All appointments in the Polish Army will be made by the commander in chief. Appointments made in France will be made in accordance with need and with the lists of qualifications that have been drawn up and published; in combat zones they will be made by the commander in chief; and in the interior by the inspector of training mentioned below. Appointments above the rank of regimental commander will be submitted for confirmation by the National Committee;
6. In France the Polish forces in the combat zone will depend for training on the commanding general under whose orders they fight. In the interior the Military Training Office will report to the commander in chief of the Polish Army; the commander in chief will be assisted in this matter by an inspector general of training for the zone of the interior, who will be chosen by the minister of war with the agreement of the commander in chief of the Polish Army;
7. For military operations the units of the Polish Army in the various theaters of war will be placed under the orders of the commanders of the armies to which they are attached. Communications between the Polish units of the combat zone and the commanding general of the Polish Army will be through the commanding general of the armies under whose orders these units function and in accordance with the chain of command;
8. The Franco-Polish Military Mission is the body accredited by the Government of France to the Polish National Committee and to the commander in chief of the Polish Army in all matters concerning this army. It is

charged with the implementation of all suitable measures to ensure the establishment and maintenance of the Polish Army in the manner described in the Decree of 4 June 1917. In all matters concerning the Polish Army, it is to be the intermediary between the Poles and the various French authorities. A National Committee member confirmed by the Government of France will be charged with ensuring a close liaison between the committee and the Military Mission;

9. Recruitment of the Polish Army will be carried out by the Polish National Committee. In France this will be done through the Franco-Polish Military Mission; outside of France it will be done by missions constituted by the Polish commander in chief with the agreement of the Franco-Polish Military Mission. The duties of the missions will be carried out in cooperation with the representatives of the Government of France in foreign countries;

10. The Polish National Committee may make agreements with the Allied governments for the possible posting to the Polish Army of officers or tactical units belonging to these nations. It will, however, reach agreement beforehand with the Government of France on these matters;

11. Minor questions arising from the implementation of the present agreement, and the modifications to bring this agreement into conformity with the decrees and memoranda presently governing the status of the Polish Army, will be the subjects of separate agreements.[4]

In light of the agreement, the Franco-Polish Military Mission now became concerned only with the maintenance of the Polish Army.

Prior to the organization of the Polish National Committee in Paris, the Polish organizations in America set up a Polish Central Committee of Safety from 25 September to 2 October 1914. On 21 January 1915 the latter resolved to cooperate with the Committee General in Switzerland headed by Henryk Sienkiewicz and Paderewski, and on 12 September 1916 it created a National Division to carry out political activities. A bureau for diplomatic work was opened in Washington under the supervision of Paderewski. Under his influence, on 22 January 1917 President Woodrow Wilson proclaimed a "unified and independent autonomous Poland" before the Congress of the United States. The Polish-American organizations decided to organize recruitment camps, but as long as the United States remained neutral, they could not do so on American soil. Consequently they turned to the Canadian authorities for permission to train Polish volunteers in Canadian schools, and in January 1917 the first group, consisting of twenty-three men, entered the officer school at the University of Toronto. Subsequently two other groups of volunteers, one consisting of forty-six men and the other of 110, entered the school. As the number of volunteers substantially increased, the new recruits were transferred in the summer of 1917 to another school at Camp Borden, Ontario. Later the training camp was transferred to Niagara-on-the-Lake, Ontario. In the meantime, on 19 March 1917, the Poles succeeded in opening an officer school with 250 volunteers at Cambridge Springs, Pennsylvania. After seven months it was transferred to Canada.[5] On 6 October 1917, six months after the United States had declared war on Germany, American authorities permitted the Polish-American leaders to conduct an enlistment campaign. Those who were eligible for service in the American army or responsible for their families, however, could not enlist.

The Polish-American recruitment caught the attention of the French authorities. Consequently, at the beginning of September 1917 the latter dispatched to America their own delegation to inform the Poles that a Polish Army was being organized in France. The recruitment of volunteers to that army brought about a conflict among the Poles in America. Those who were pro-Entente favored the recruitment; those who were pro-Central Powers were against it; while some were for enlistment in the United States Army only. Nonetheless, twelve and later forty-three recruitment centers were established in the United States. The volunteers were assembled in two camps, one at Niagara Fort, New York, the other at Niagara-on-the-Lake. After a short period of orientation in the camps, the volunteers were transferred to France for military training. Such recruitment continued until 7 February 1919. The first transport, consisting of 1,200 volunteers, left New York for France on 16 December 1917. During a period of sixteen months, 40,000 men enlisted, 30,000 were trained, and 24,260 went to France.[6]

Military activities in France also influenced Polish immigrants in Brazil. Although their number there was very small, they were also divided along pro-Entente or pro-Central Powers lines. A group of Polish volunteers tried to join to the Polish Legion commanded by Piłsudski, but Brazilian authorities did not let it leave for Poland. The position of the pro-Entente Poles was strengthened when Brazil declared war on Germany and when Poincaré issued his decree on the organization of Polish troops in France.

In the fall of 1917 the Franco-Polish Military Mission sent a representative to Brazil to encourage the recruitment of Polish volunteers. Consequently, at the end of December a meeting of some 500 delegates was held in Curitiba. A National Council was elected, and it subsequently elected a Central Committee with headquarters in Rio de Janeiro. The Brazilian recruitment effort faced transportation and communications difficulties and a lack of educated people among the Polish immigrants. The Central Committee organized one main camp at Cachoeira, where volunteers received preliminary training before going to France. The first transport of volunteers left Brazil for

France in January 1918. Altogether 300 volunteers were recruited in Brazil for the Polish Army in France.[7]

The recruitment of volunteers in Italy was much more promising. In the summer of 1917 Polish leaders there set up a Polish National Committee in Rome headed by Konstanty Skirmut to organize military units composed of Poles serving in the Austrian army who had been interned in Italy. The Italian government gave permission for the enlistment of such volunteers, provided that they would be transferred to France for training. At the end of 1917 the committee organized the first recruitment camp at Santa Maria, initially with 2,000 volunteers. Later two other camps were organized at Casa Giare and Capua Vettere in southern Italy. At the end of September 1918 the Franco-Polish Military Mission dispatched representatives headed by Maj. Leon Radziwiłł to Italy to help form military units. The mission organized three infantry regiments, and in December 1918 they were transferred to France. In the meantime, another camp with 15,000 volunteers at La Mandria di Chivasso in northern Italy was organized by Capt. Dienstl-Dąbrowa. From January through March 1919 the mission organized six more regiments of infantry, artillery, and sappers and one machine-gun unit. In April 1919 another regiment of infantry was organized. From November 1918 through April 1919 the mission recruited 38,000 men, including some 1,000 officers, who were transferred to France.[8]

While the organization of the Polish Army in France was taking place, the Polish National Committee began looking for a Polish commander. Political developments in the winter of 1918 presented the committee with the man it was looking for. On 9 February 1918 Ukraine, including the Kholm region, was recognized as an independent republic in the peace treaty between the Central Powers and Ukraine. In the treaty Austria promised to unite Bukovyna with Eastern Galicia and to set up a new Ukrainian crownland with political and cultural rights within the monarchy. Most Poles protested this agreement. A striking reaction came from the Second Polish Brigade commanded by Col. Józef Haller, then deployed as part of the Austrian army in the Bukovyna theater of operations. Haller and his brigade of 5,000 men left their positions on the night of 15–16 February 1918. Only the two infantry regiments, however, managed to cross over the front line to the eastern side at Rarancha. The brigade's command, artillery, technical units, and supply trains were surrounded by Austrian troops and were interned in camps in Khust, Dulove, Steblivka, and Sokyrnytsia in Transcarpathia. Subsequently, on 4 March 1918, 1,500 of Haller's men joined forces with the Polish Second Corps—the former soldiers of the Russian Ninth Army on the Romanian Front—commanded by Gen. Jan Stankiewicz, at Iaruha near Mohyliv-Podilskyi. The unified force of 6,000 infantry and 600 cavalry came under the command of Haller, who assumed the rank of general. On 13 May 1918 he and his troops were surrounded near Kaniv by the German army of Field Marshal Hermann von Eichhorn and forced to capitulate. Haller and a group of soldiers broke out of the encirclement, however, and made their way via Kyiv to Moscow. There, on 15 May, Haller met with the Polish Executive Committee of the Interparty Council, which had been organized on 8 September 1917 as a branch of the Polish National Committee in Paris. It recognized Haller's rank and agreed to establish a Polish Military Board that would recruit and organize Polish military detachments in Ukraine and Russia. On 4 July 1918 Haller and six of his officers left Murmansk on the British vessel *City of Marseille* bound for Le Havre. Thirty-six other Polish officers followed them to France.[9] On 14 July Haller arrived in Paris, where he was greeted enthusiastically by Dmowski. On 4 October the Polish National Committee appointed Haller commander in chief of the Polish Army in France.

The recruits of the Polish Army in France received preliminary training at Sillé-le-Guillaume. They were then assigned to camps in different parts of France, where they were armed and trained by French officers. The First Regiment of Polish Riflemen was formed on 10 January 1918; after five months of intensive training it was sent to the German front. Two other regiments were also organized, and together with the First they constituted the Polish First Division under the command of the French general Joseph Ecochard. Gradually other regiments and divisions were organized. As the First World War was coming to an end and the French troops were being demobilized, their arms, ammunition, and equipment were transferred to the Polish units. At the end of the war there were six well-armed Polish divisions (100,000 men) under the command of French generals. Only a few units participated in the fighting at the German front.

Because Poland was at war with the Ukrainians of Galicia, the Polish delegation in Paris tried desperately to obtain permission from the Supreme Council of the Peace Conference to transfer Haller's army from France to Poland. To achieve this goal, it disseminated propaganda associating the Ukrainian cause with Bolshevism and German intrigues in Eastern Europe. The British prime minister, David Lloyd George, recognized the Poles' intention. At a meeting of the heads of the Principal Allied and Associated Powers on 21 May 1919 in Paris, "he remarked that it seemed to him that Poles were using Bolshevism as a cloak for their imperialistic aims."[10] While the Ukrainians had been defending their own territory against the Bolshevik invasion, the Poles had not recognized Bolshevism as a peril. Only when the Bolsheviks began threatening Poland did the Poles begin bewailing the peril. At a meeting of the Polish National Committee in Paris on 30 January 1919, the representative of the Polish government, Kazimierz Dłuski, emphasized that "the Allies do not understand the magnitude of the danger of Bolshevism as a plague of the universe. [He stressed that] [T]his fact must be very strongly emphasized and exploited."[11]

Under the influence of Polish propaganda and French diplomatic support for the Poles, the Commission on Polish Affairs chose to advise the Supreme Council to send Haller's army to Poland:

> The loss of Lemberg [Lviv] [to the ZUNR] would have a tremendous effect throughout Poland and would be interpreted as a defeat to the Entente. This would immediately strengthen the position of the Bolsheviks; at the same time encouraging all agents employed by Germany in organizing plots against the Entente in Eastern Europe. In these circumstances the Commission for Polish Affairs considered it its duty once more to call the attention of the Supreme Council of the Conference to the necessity of arriving at the immediate decision as to the despatch of General Haller's troops to Poland.[12]

Before the Supreme Council reached its decision in this matter, however, Prime Minister Paderewski assured the prime ministers of the Entente and President Woodrow Wilson that Haller's army would be used exclusively against the Bolsheviks if it was allowed to go to Poland. Consequently the Supreme Council gave its consent, and at the beginning of December 1918 it authorized Marshal Ferdinand Foch to arrange with the German government the passage of the Polish Army to Poland by sea. The German government refused, however, on the ground that

> According to Art. XVI of the Armistice Treaty, the German Government was obliged to permit the Allies to have free access through Danzig and the Vistula in order to maintain quiet in the regions of old Russia. In concluding this Treaty we certainly envisaged the passage of Allied troops and not Polish troops. The German Government was not obliged to grant to the Polish army free access by Danzig and West Prussia.[13]

Apart from the legal aspects, the German authorities were concerned that the Poles would violate their hospitality. They pointed out that when Paderewski had been received on German soil, he had grossly violated Germany's hospitality by giving the signal for insurrection at Posen [Poznań]: "[Moreover] at the time of his stay at Danzig in December, 1918, he said: 'Let only the Polish divisions of France and Italy be at Danzig one day, then Danzig and all West Prussia will become Polish. In all Polish publications Haller's Army is designated as a Polish Army'."[14]

Subsequently, however, Foch met with the German representative, Minister Matthias Erzberger, at Spa, and on 4 April 1919 they signed an agreement to transport the Polish troops across Germany to Łódź by train. On 16 April the First Division left France, and on 23 April Haller departed for Poland via Mainz, Erfurt, and Leipzig. He arrived in Warsaw on 28 April. Huge transports of military equipment, arms, munitions, technical materials, medical supplies, and food accompanied the troops.

Contrary to the assurances Paderewski gave the prime ministers of the Entente and President Wilson, Haller's army was immediately deployed at the Ukrainian front in the regions of Zamość and Kovel. Lloyd George observed that "Haller's Army, which was ready for war when it arrived, was immediately marched into Galicia, ostensibly to drive off the Bolsheviks, but in reality to conquer the country and annex it to Poland."[15] Thanks to the divisions that had come from France and their huge stock of military supplies, Piłsudski was able to create a formidable force against the Ukrainian Galician Army (UHA).[16] On 14 May 1919 the Poles began a general offensive against the UHA and the UNR Army, and thus helped the Bolsheviks and Whites to make gains in Ukraine.

In addition to the Polish Army in France, Polish military formations were also organized in the Kuban under the auspices of the Russian Volunteer Army (VA). In August 1918 a few Polish officers delegated by Gen. Haller, while en route to Murmansk, were permitted by Gen. Mikhail Alekseev, the organizer of the VA, to form independent Polish military detachments. In the course of one month, one unit each of infantry, cavalry, and artillery had been formed, mainly from Haller's former troops that had capitulated to the Germans on 13 May 1918 near Kaniv in central Ukraine. Those detachments (700 men) were commanded by Col. (later Gen.) Zygmunt Zieliński and then by Gen. Jan Stankiewicz. Subsequently they formed the Fourth Division and were put under the political authority of the Polish Military Board, which jointly with Gen. Haller promoted Col. Lucjan Żeligowski to the rank of general and appointed him commander of the division. At the beginning of October 1918 Żeligowski arrived in the Kuban from the Crimea. Subsequently the Polish Military Board made an agreement with the VA commanded by Gen. Anton Denikin, the successor of Gens. Alekseev and Lavr Kornilov.[17] The agreement stipulated that

  a. The detachment of the Polish military forces on the territory of the VA is part of the independent Polish Army fighting on the French front and having the rights of an independent Allied army.
  b. The Polish political Supreme Committee, consisting of authorized representatives of political groups, is the political leader and representative of

the detachment of the Polish military forces on the territory of the VA.

c. The Polish military forces have been organized to fight against the Central Powers for the independence and complete unification of the Polish territories, including its own coastline.

d. The Polish military force organized and located on the territory of the VA reports in all operational matters to the command of the VA.

e. All matters pertaining to the internal life and size of the military force, uniforms, and service regulations are decided by the Polish High Command nominated by Gen. Haller in Paris, and relayed to the command of the VA. The internal life should be based on rigid discipline, without committees or the right to vote.

f. Officers and soldiers are paid from the Polish Army's own treasury. Because it is absolutely impossible to provide all materiel with its own monies, the detachment uses available supplies following the general guidelines of the VA, but a separate account will be kept for later billing.

g. When Polish interests require that the detachment leave the territory of the VA, the High Command of the VA will not oppose that decision, except in the case of strategic needs involving the VA and detachment of the Polish military forces.[18]

At the end of November 1918 the Fourth Division (1,500 men) was transferred, with the approval of the VA command, together with VA troops from Novorossiisk across the Black Sea on the steamer *Saratov* to Odessa. At that time authority over most of Odessa was in the hands of the UNR Directory. The arrival of those troops coincided with the imminent intervention of Franco-Greek expeditionary forces in southern Ukraine. On 17 December 1918, when the French 156th Division (1,800 men) under the command of Gen. Albert Borius reached Odessa from Salonika, the VA and Polish troops attacked the UNR forces under the cover of the guns of Allied warships. After hours of prolonged fighting the UNR troops withdrew from the city, and on the next day the French troops disembarked. The UNR troops (about 4,000 men) hesitated to employ their full firepower because the Directory was not in a position to enter into a war with France; rather, it was seeking understanding and technical aid from France against the Bolsheviks. Fighting continued, however, as the Entente forces expanded their occupation along the Black Sea coast.

With the assistance of the VA, the command of the Polish Division renewed their recruitment campaign, and by February 1919 the division had increased to 4,000 men, including 717 officers and 472 noncommissioned officers. Subsequently Gen. Żeligowski reorganized the division, forming detachments of infantry, cavalry, and artillery, a squadron of sixteen airplanes, and a unit of armored cars. A divisional hospital also was set up. For a while operations and provisions of the division were under the command of the VA Third Corps and the military governor of Odessa, Gen. Aleksei Grishin-Almazov, while politically it was subordinated to the French military command. Although later the division became part of the Entente forces, it subordinated itself to Piłsudski. The Polish division in the Odessa region had more political than military importance: it enhanced Poland's position at the Paris Peace Conference. It did not fight the real enemy—the Germans or the Bolsheviks—but the Ukrainians, who were struggling against a common foe.

As the Ukrainian-Polish war in Galicia intensified, Piłsudski and Haller demanded through Gen. Gustaw Ostapowicz, the head of the Polish Military Mission in Ukraine, that Gen. Henri Berthelot, the commander in chief of the Allied forces in South Russia and Romania, transfer the Fourth Division to the Galician front. According to their plans, this transfer would enable Polish troops to occupy Podillia and thus prevent the UNR Directory from giving military assistance to the UHA. It would also enable the Poles to secure the Lviv–Chernivtsi–Jassy–Bucharest railroad. On 12 March 1919 Prime Minister Paderewski sent an urgent dispatch to the Secretariat-General of the Peace Conference through the Inter-Allied Commission in Poland, insisting on transportation of the Fourth Division via Romania and Hungary to Galicia. These demands were realized a few weeks later.

While the French intervention in southern Ukraine continued, Soviet Russian forces again invaded Ukraine, in January 1919; the VA was moving into Ukraine from the Don; the Romanians occupied Bessarabia and Bukovyna; and the Poles were fighting the UHA in the west. In such circumstances, the UNR Directory could hardly offer effective resistance to the enemy forces. Consequently, at the beginning of February the Ukrainian troops retreated to the northwest. Meanwhile, one of the Directory's military commanders, Nykyfor Hryhor'iv, revolted against the policy of the Directory because it had forbidden him to move against the Entente forces.[19] Consequently Hryhor'iv and his force of 23,000 men joined the Bolsheviks, although they did not share their political goals. Because Bolshevik reserves were exhausted, responsibility for the offensive against the French fell upon Hryhor'iv. In March 1919 he advanced toward Odessa by railroad, taking station after station. After a fierce battle in Kherson, he drove the French troops from that city and demoralized those in Mykolaiv and Odessa. As Hryhor'iv approached, the French evacuated Mykolaiv, leaving the Germans to defend it. By negotiations and threats, Hryhor'iv forced the Germans to surrender. His victories improved the spirit of his troops and provided them with materiel while demoralizing the French troops to the point of mutiny.

They showed no interest in a foreign war that they neither wanted nor understood. Consequently, on 3 April several thousand Greek and Russian troops and thirty thousand Russian civilians departed from Odessa overland for Romania. The next day the Polish troops followed while conducting rearguard fighting, and on 10 April they crossed the Dniester River into Romania. On 5 April the last French ship left Odessa.

At the end of May the French command allowed Gen. Żeligowski to transport his division to Chernivtsi in Bukovyna. Subsequently Żeligowski offered assistance to Gen. Julian Stachiewicz, the commander of the Polish troops in Galicia, and on 17 June the Fourth Division was transported across the Romanian-Ukrainian border to Otynia in Galicia, where it immediately joined the fight against the UHA.[20]

CHAPTER 5

The Ukrainian-Polish War in Galicia and Its Aftermath

The collapse of the Habsburg monarchy in October 1918 created the opportunity for former Austro-Hungarian subjects to establish their own independent states. The monarchy's Ukrainians organized a National Rada (Council) in Lviv, which proclaimed an independent state—the Western Ukrainian People's Republic (ZUNR)—on 1 November 1918. The Rada announced autonomy for the republic's national minorities, with the right of representation in the government, and on 18 November it decided to include state secretaries for Polish, Jewish, and German affairs in the cabinet. Although Western Ukraine had been devastated by four years of war, was isolated from the outside world, and was without foreign help, the ZUNR government organized a fairly strong army (the UHA), installed an efficient administration, and established order and legality on its territory. The population manifested a high level of patriotism and sacrifice. To strengthen its position, the Rada decided to seek immediate unification with the UNR.

As early as 1 December 1918, ZUNR representatives L'onhyn Tsehel's'kyi and Dmytro Levyts'kyi signed a preliminary agreement of unification with the UNR Directory at Fastiv. Both sides agreed that because of its cultural, social, and legal particularities, the ZUNR was to enjoy autonomy. On 3 January 1919 the National Rada unanimously ratified the Fastiv Agreement, and on 22 January the act of union was approved by the Directory. According to the agreement, sovereignty was to reside in the Directory. The National Rada, however, was to exercise authority in Western Ukraine until the convocation of a UNR Constituent Assembly. Although the union of the two republics was a significant historic act, it was more symbolic than actual, because they were soon at war with different enemies: while the Western Province (Oblast) of the UNR, as the ZUNR was named after the act of union, fought against the Polish invasion, the UNR combated the second Soviet Russian invasion.[1]

The problems of union, consolidation, and defense were to be dealt with by the Congress of Toilers, a parliamentary assembly consisting of 528 indirectly elected delegates from the UNR and 65 from the ZUNR, which was convened in Kyiv on 22 January 1919. The congress, which was interrupted on 28 January by the Bolshevik advance on Kyiv, sanctioned the principle of general democratic elections to a Ukrainian parliament and to organs of local government. It adopted a resolution expressing "full confidence in and gratitude to the Directory for its great work in liberating the Ukrainian people from the landlord-hetman government." The most important achievements of the congress, however, were the formal proclamation of the union of the two Ukrainian republics and the legal confirmation of the Directory, which it invested with supreme authority, including the right to enact laws and to direct the defense of the state, until the next session of the congress.

While the Directory was struggling against the Bolsheviks and Whites and thus provided protection also for Poland, the ZUNR was defending its territory from a Polish invasion. Thus, as the Bolsheviks and Whites attacked the Ukrainians from the east, the Poles attacked them from the west. The creation of the ZUNR represented the triumph of the right of self-determination of the Ukrainian people in Eastern Galicia. But the Poles, who had also proclaimed their self-determination, did not acknowledge that right for Galicia's Ukrainians. They dreamed about restoring a Poland extending from the Baltic to the Black Sea. The ZUNR government believed that the Entente, which declared that the Treaty of Versailles was based on the principle of national self-determination, would compel the Poles to stop their invasion of the ZUNR. The Entente, however, limited its recognition of that principle to a few especially favored nations. Moreover, France was committed to the idea of a "strong Poland" that would serve a dual anti-German function: in coalition with France, Poland would be a military counterbalance while simultaneously constituting a barrier to the renewal of German economic and political influence in Russia. Hence France was the principal advocate of Poland's expansion. It championed Polish claims to German, Lithuanian, Belarusian, and, particularly, Ukrainian territories, and it looked with disfavor on Ukrainian independence.

Great Britain was the only power that opposed Polish expansion. Its leaders were convinced that if Poland was to be strong, both internally and externally, it was necessary that self-determination be the guiding principle in settling Poland's borders; if Poland absorbed alien minorities, its political effectiveness would decrease with its increase in size, and it would then become, like the former Austrian Empire, a conglomerate of nationalities. Italy's prime minister, Francesco Nitti, agreed:

> Poland was not created as the noble manifestation of the rights of nationality; ethnical Poland was not created, but a great state which, as she is, cannot live long, because there are not great foreign minorities, but a whole mass of populations which cannot co-exist. Poland, which has already the experience of a too numerous Israelitic population, has not the capacity to assimilate the

Germans, the Russians [i.e., Belarusians], and the Ukrainians which the Treaty of Versailles has unjustly given to her against the very declarations of Wilson.[2]

Consequently Poland would be surrounded by a ring of external enemies that would promote irredentism, foster division within its borders, and wait for an opportunity for military aggression. At the same time, Great Britain gave full support to the Russian anti-Bolshevik movement while seeking an agreement with the Bolsheviks. Neither of these policies was favorable to Ukrainian national aspirations. The United States, on the other hand, was little interested in Eastern Europe; its attitude was that nothing should be done to prejudice the future claims of the Russia that might emerge after the anti-Bolshevik victory. The uncertain political situation in Russia caused the Principal Allied and Associated Powers to postpone a definitive solution to the problem of Galicia because it would ostensibly serve as an important factor in any dealings with the future anti-Bolshevik Russian regime. Thus Ukraine was isolated from the Western powers.[3]

The Allies' vacillation on the Ukrainian question encouraged the Poles to seek a solution by force. When the ZUNR defensive campaign intensified, however, and threatened the Polish forces in Lviv with isolation and possible defeat, at the beginning of February 1919 the Supreme Council decided to send an Inter-Allied Mission to Poland to mediate in the Ukrainian-Polish War. It consisted of former French ambassadors to Petrograd—Joseph Noulens (chairman) and Gen. Henri Albert Niessel—and of Sir Esme Howard and Gen. Adrian Carton De Wiart of Great Britain, Gen. Francis J. Kernan and Prof. Robert Howard Lord of the United States, and Giulio-Cesare Montagna and Gen. Romei Longhena of Italy. This mission was accompanied by some fifty officials and generals. Its assignment was to report to the Commission on Polish Affairs, which was constituted on 12 February 1919 and consisted of Jules-Martin Cambon (chairman, France), Sir William George Tyrrell (Great Britain), Isaiah Bowman (United States), Pietro Thomasi Torreta (Italy), and K. M. Otchiai (Japan). The commission examined the mission's reports and submitted its findings to the Supreme Council.

To acquaint the commission better with conditions at the Ukrainian front, an Italian officer, Capt. Accame, who had spent a few weeks on the Ukrainian side of the front, reported that the soldiers of the UHA were fighting with the courage of the doomed, while "the Polish soldiers do not know why they are fighting, and it seems that their patriotism is stirred up only as a means of combating Bolshevism."[4] Earlier, on 19 January 1919, a similar confidential report had been made to Prime Minister Paderewski by Roman Knoll, a legation counselor and a Polish expert on Ukrainian questions in the Polish

Ministry of Foreign Affairs. In his report, which was based on his discussion with Col. A. Nieniewski, a deputy of Gen. Stanisław Szeptycki, Knoll characterized the disposition of the Polish soldiers: "According to his words, not only are our forces half as strong numerically as the enemy and lacking ammunition, but also the spirit of our troops is indifferent. Soldiers from Congress Poland, in the units of the Bug group, are saying that 'they want to go back to Poland because they do not see any reason to fight against Ruthenians concerning Ruthenian lands.'"[5]

The successful defense of Eastern Galicia by the UHA alarmed the Polish government and their Allied protectors. Consequently the Poles launched an intensive anti-Ukrainian propaganda campaign at home and abroad. They misinformed the world about the Ukrainians, presenting them as being anarchical by nature, illiterate, lacking their own intelligentsia, and unable to administer their own state or to form their own disciplined army. In Paris the Polish diplomats created an atmosphere of distrust toward the Ukrainian movement. Depending on tactical necessities, they persistently presented the ZUNR government as being avowedly "Germanophile," "Bolshevik," or both. For example:

> The Poles have not only the Bolshevists against them, but also the Tcheques and the Ukrainians, two peoples very ripe for Bolshevism, because they are very much under German influence. The Germans help not only the Bolshevists, but also the Ukrainians, and the Ukrainian people is led by a gang very similar to the Bolshevists. The true Ukrainians are not enemies of the Poles, as they have been voluntarily united with Poland for centuries, and have never been able to form a State of their own. The State which now bears the name Ukraine, is an artificial German creation, and serves the aims of the Germans. The real advantage of Poles and Ukrainians requires their close union, while war between these two peoples benefits only the Germans, who have succeeded in provoking it, because the Allies have not insisted on German demobilization, and on the return of all German officers from Poland and Ukraine to Germany.[6]

The Poles avoided mentioning, however, that in 1914 Austria and Germany created Polish military units commanded by Piłsudski and that these units fought on the Central Powers' side almost to the end of the war. They also failed to mention that the UNR Army fought both the Bolshevik and anti-Bolshevik Russian forces, thus defending Ukraine and Poland simultaneously. Moreover, the Poles ignored the thirteenth of President Wilson's Fourteen Points, which stated: "An independent Polish State should be erected which should include the territories inhabited by indisputably Polish populations, which should be assured a free and secure access to the sea, and whose political and economic independence and territorial integrity should be guaranteed by international covenant."[7] In reality, a Polish state with an indisputably non-Polish population had been erected, and this state had a markedly military and expansionist character.

With regard to the Polish claims to Eastern Galicia, an American reporter observed:

> When one talked with the Poles at Paris about their claims to different portions of German territory, they used to say: "Do not judge by a few cities, but go out in the country, and you will see that it is Polish. It is preposterous for Germany to claim these regions simply because some cities are German, largely so because of functionaries and their families." You granted the reasonableness of the argument, and then shifted the discussion to Eastern Galicia. You informed your Polish friends that you had done precisely this thing in Eastern Galicia and that your impression of the country, confirmed by reference to the statistics of the Poles themselves, had been that, outside of Lemberg [Lviv] and one or two other towns, there were no Poles at all except the great landowners, the very class the Poles railed against in Poznania and East Prussia. Enthusiasm for the principle of self-determination suddenly died.... A frown came over the face which had been almost tearful during the exposition of the wrongs of Polish peasants in Prussia.[8]

To help end the war, on 24 January 1919 the Commission on Polish Affairs sent a sub-commission to Galicia headed by the French general Joseph Berthélemy. The Berthélemy sub-commission demanded suspension of hostilities as a condition for peace negotiations, and the ZUNR government acceded to this demand. On 28 February the sub-commission presented a plan whereby the ZUNR would surrender to the Poles a third of its territory, including Lviv and the Drohobych-Boryslav oil fields. This proposal was unacceptable to the Ukrainians, and hostilities resumed.[9] On 18 April the Supreme Council created an Inter-Allied Commission, headed by Gen. Louis Botha of South Africa, to deal with the Ukrainian-Polish conflict. After several weeks of hearings, on 12 May the Botha Commission proposed a conditional armistice, leaving to the Ukrainians the Drohobych-Boryslav oil fields and limiting Polish and Ukrainian forces in Eastern Galicia to twenty thousand men each. Although the ZUNR representatives accepted these terms, the Polish military authorities not only rejected them, but continued to use force to maintain their claims. Consequently, on 27 May the president of the Peace Conference complained to Piłsudski that

The Polish authorities were in effect, if not in purpose, denying and rejecting the authority of the Conference of Peace. The Council feel it their duty, therefore, in the most friendly spirit but with the most solemn earnestness, to say to the Polish authorities that, if they are not willing to accept the guidance and decisions of the Conference of Peace in such matters, the Governments represented in the Council of the Principal Allied and Associated Governments will not be justified in furnishing Poland any longer with supplies or assistance.[10]

While the Botha Commission was working to settle the Ukrainian-Polish War, the Polish military authorities were concentrating large forces on the Ukrainian front. Although hostilities were to cease on 15 May, on 14 May the Polish forces renewed their general offensive against the UHA. This time they were greatly reinforced by Haller's six divisions (100,000 men) and by the Polish Fourth Division (4,000 men).[11] When the ZUNR government learned about the arrival of Haller's army and its subsequent offensive, it protested to the president of the Peace Conference, asking for a halt to the Polish offensive:

We lay before the Supreme Council of the Peace Conference at Paris a protest against the action of the Polish Government, which, notwithstanding the intention of the Entente Powers, throws Haller's Army, which was intended to fight the Bolshevists, against the Ukrainian Republic, which for the last four months has without help fought the Bolshevists and cannot succeed on account of the renewed attacks of the Poles, which oblige them to consecrate the best of their troops on the occidental front. The Government of the democratic republic of Western Ukrainia insists once more that the Governments of the Entente intervene to hasten the conclusion of an armistice on the Polish-Ukrainian front, so as to make it possible to concentrate all the Ukrainian forces against the Bolshevists.[12]

But the protest was ultimately ignored. Lloyd George observed that

The Supreme Council sent a message to General Haller ordering his withdrawal. Of this command he did not take the slightest notice. Subsequently he pretended that he had never received the telegram in time to act upon the instructions it conveyed. Whether it was intercepted and held up by Piłsudski's order, whether it had never been dispatched from France, or whether they were all in a conspiracy to ignore it, we never discovered. President Wilson was not overanxious to offend his Polish friends by pressing the inquiry too insistently.[13]

Esme W. Lord Howard, a member of the Inter-Allied Commission in Poland, also urged the Polish government not to send Haller's army against the Ukrainians:

> Colonel Kish of the Military Section, and a member of the Polish Ukrainian Armistice Committee, came to me in great agitation, saying that a telegram had come in from General Carton de Wiart (a member of the Inter-Allied Commission in Poland) to the effect that Haller's (Polish) army was on the point of attacking the Ukrainians. At his request I sent telegrams to M. Paderewski and General Piłsudski urging them to suspend attack and accept Armistice conditions.[14]

As the Polish troops advanced eastward, on 23 May the Romanian command of the Bukovyna-Khotyn front demanded that the UHA evacuate the southern part of Eastern Galicia. The resulting withdrawal was a serious setback to the UHA; it not only lost territory, but also its only supply of ammunition, and consequently became further isolated from the outside world. On 26 May the ZUNR authorities abandoned Stanyslaviv (now Ivano-Frankivske), the temporary capital, and retreated to Chortkiv. During this critical period, on 7 June, the UHA managed to launch the Chortkiv Offensive. After driving the Polish forces back to the west about eighty miles, after three weeks of successful fighting the Ukrainian advance halted, having expended all available ammunition and supplies. In the meantime the Poles concentrated a large force and launched a new offensive, and by the end of June the UHA began a general withdrawal, conducting only rearguard actions to assure an orderly retreat. A Polish participant in the war asserted that both the "The Poles and Ukrainians, because of a lack of their own military industries, were forced to seek foreign help. Toward the end of the armed activities, however, the Poles already had a constant supply of all kinds of war materiel, which remained in enormous quantity from the world war. The Ukrainians, however, remained, at the end, without help from the outside, and undoubtedly this helped the Poles to break the resistance of the enemy [Ukrainians]."[15]

Under these circumstances the UHA had no recourse but to abandon its territory and retreat across the river Zbruch, to where UNR troops held a narrow but gradually expanding strip of territory. Despite great efforts and sacrifices by the Ukrainian people, Eastern Galicia was finally occupied by Poland. It took nine months, however, for Poland, despite its greater military strength (including Haller's army and substantial French military, technical, and diplomatic support), to overcome the UHA. The ZUNR government was faced with two choices: to join the Directory against the Bolsheviks, or to accept the Bolsheviks' offer of an alliance and arms and ammunition against Poland. The government opted for the first choice, and on 16 July the UHA (about 100,000 men) and most ZUNR government officials began crossing the Zbruch.[16]

The Ukrainian ethnic territory occupied by Poland constituted 137,535 square kilometers, 55,700 of them in Eastern Galicia and 81,835 in northwestern Ukraine. This territory, which represented 35.3 percent of interwar Poland, was inhabited by over six million Ukrainians.[17] Lloyd George remarked that "The Poles in Galicia did not number more than one-fourth of the inhabitants. The rest were Ukrainian and hostile to the idea of Polish rule as the Poles themselves were to Russian rule."[18]

As the UHA was retreating, on 25 June the Council of Four decided the political fate of Eastern Galicia:

> To protect the persons and property of the peaceful population of Eastern Galicia from the dangers that the Bolshevik bands threaten them with, the Supreme Council of the Allied and Associated Powers has decided to authorize the forces of the Polish Republic to conduct their operations as far as the river Zbruch. This authorization does not in any way affect the decisions the Supreme Council will later take to regulate the political status of Galicia.[19]

On 2 July the Ukrainian delegation in Paris protested this act, declaring that "The decision of the Supreme Council does not mean the triumph of Justice and Right."[20] This protest was also ignored, and the Ukrainians considered that they had been betrayed by the Supreme Council. They had believed in the Entente's promises and had agreed to the armistices, while the Poles had strengthened their forces on the Ukrainian front.

On 10 September Austria ceded Galicia to the Principal Allied and Associated Powers in the Treaty of Saint-Germain, further complicating the status of Eastern Galicia. On 20 November the Supreme Council gave Poland the mandate in Eastern Galicia for twenty-five years, after which time a plebiscite should be held. The Poles objected to this arrangement. Stanisław Patek, the Polish delegate, argued that the existence of the Polish state depended on the incorporation of Eastern Galicia into Poland, pointing out that

> The Diet at Warsaw had unanimously voted that there could be no Poland without Eastern Galicia.... The Allied and Associated Powers must understand that the unanimous opinion of the Polish people had to be considered.... If the solution of a mandate were imposed upon Poland, Paderewski's cabinet would have to resign; the Polish Army, ill fed, ill clothed, engaged in a severe struggle

against the Bolshevists would be threatened with demoralization.... In the interior a famine threatened. The Polish army was strong and Poland counted on it as an element of order. If the Army became demoralized, Poland's situation would become most serious and it would be threatened with extinction.[21]

In spite of the critical attitude of some Entente leaders (Lloyd George, Nitti)[22] about the Poles' behavior, as a result of French pressure the Supreme Council abandoned the mandate on 22 December, and Eastern Galicia remained legally the possession of the Principal Allied and Associated Powers. After three years, on 15 March 1923, the Conference of Ambassadors, in the name of France, Great Britain, Italy, and Japan, recognized Poland's occupation of Eastern Galicia and approved the Treaty of Riga (18 March 1921) between Poland and Soviet Russia and Soviet Ukraine, which gave Poland the northwestern part of Ukraine (the Kholm region, western Polissia, and western Volynia).[23]

The arrival of the UHA east of the Zbruch strengthened the UNR militarily and politically. Almost immediately after the UHA crossed the Zbruch, it and the UNR Army began a joint offensive. After considering other alternatives, Petliura decided to push toward Kyiv, with precautionary thrusts to the north, toward Shepetivka, and to the south, toward Odessa. In spite of strong Bolshevik resistance, the Ukrainian troops advanced rapidly, aided by the uprisings of Ukrainian partisans in the Bolsheviks' rear and in part by the advance of Denikin from the southeast.[24] Although the Ukrainian command secured its rear in the west through the mediation of the Entente and by signing an armistice with the Poles on 1 September, it neglected to coordinate its advance with Denikin's simultaneous offensive in Left-Bank Ukraine or to issue a timely and precise order governing the actions of its troops in case they encountered VA troops.[25] Petliura hoped that the preemption of Kyiv might force Denikin to recognize their common interest—defeating the Bolsheviks—and to advance north rather than open another front.

In spite of the Bolsheviks' staunch defense in the Kyiv region, after several days of fighting the Ukrainian troops entered the capital on 30 August. On the next day, however, Denikin's superior force also approached Kyiv from the southeast and, instead of joining the Ukrainian troops against the Bolsheviks, forced its way into the city. Consequently the Ukrainian troops withdrew from the capital to avoid opening a third front. Denikin's attack against the Ukrainian troops saved, for a while, the Bolshevik position in Ukraine. To Denikin Ukrainian statehood was more menacing than Bolshevism in Russia. Although the Directory had tried to avert conflict with Denikin, both through negotiations with him and appeals to the Allies, it failed, and on 24 September it declared war and turned its main forces against his forces.[26]

The retreat from Kyiv was a great psychological and strategic blow to both the UNR Army and the UHA. Exhausted by constant fighting and lacking ammunition and equipment, they could not withstand for long the attacks of Denikin's well-nourished and well-armed troops. Moreover, a cold and rainy autumn and an early, severe winter, coupled with the lack of clothing and medical supplies, brought about a disastrous typhus epidemic. In the area of operations, all residences and public buildings were filled with sick soldiers; hospitals intended for a hundred patients were filled with more than a thousand. Thousands of soldiers died from the disease, while others, nearly barefoot and badly clothed, froze in the open fields. Peasants were also decimated by the disease after aiding the soldiers.[27] Meanwhile, an Entente blockade prevented the UNR government from obtaining medical supplies. Ultimately typhus reduced the fighting strength of the Ukrainian armies by seventy percent. This tragic situation was described by an American correspondent:

> It is not too much to say that about every third person in Kamenets [Kamianets-Podilskyi] has typhus. In other cities the situation is the same. In the army it is even worse. At Vapniarka I was with Petliura at a review of a frontier garrison where out of a thousand troops at least two hundred had had typhus. Against this epidemic Petliura's government is quite powerless to make headway. The Ukrainians are condemned to death by the fact that the Entente is backing Denikin. In an interview I had with Petliura he begged that, if only for humanity's sake, the Red Cross would send over a mission to fight typhus. Let me add here that right across the river in Romania are all the medical supplies necessary.... We do not ask for any gratuitous help from the allies. We only want our frontiers opened so that we can trade our products for manufactured articles and equipment. Let them open Odessa. We do not ask them to pour in supplies free of charge to us, as they do to Denikin."[28]

The UHA suffered the most. As Gen. Iurii Tiutiunnyk observed, its situation "was indeed desperate; there was no ammunition, medicine, food, clothing, no reinforcement of men and horses.... [Moreover,] there was no hope that the situation could soon change in our favor."[29] Gradually the Ukrainian troops retreated northwest, where they found themselves surrounded by hostile forces: the Poles to the west, the Bolsheviks to the northeast, and Denikin to the south and southeast.

In light of this situation, the UHA commander in chief, Gen. Myron Tarnavs'kyi, decided to negotiate with Denikin to save the rest of his troops. Although the president of the ZUNR, Evhen Petrushevych, opposed such a venture, an UHA delegation and representatives of the VA signed a preliminary treaty on 6 November 1919. Consequently Tarnavs'kyi and his chief of staff, Col. Alfred Shamanek, were relieved of their commands by the ZUNR government and court-martialed, but the final treaty was nevertheless signed in Odessa on 17 November and ratified two days later. Although the agreement was only a tactical expediency "to save the army," the Directory considered it an act of betrayal.[30]

Although Petliura was faced with a highly critical military situation, he never lost courage. Because he could no longer continue a regular war, he decided to pursue the fight against the Bolshevik and anti-Bolshevik Russian forces in the form of guerilla warfare and thus preserve the nucleus of his army. Part of it, some 14,000 men, was reorganized, and on 7 December 1919, under the command of Gen. Mykhailo Omelianovych-Pavlenko and Gen. Tiutiunnyk as his second, it moved far to the rear of both Russian forces to fight them and to support the Ukrainian partisans. Petliura realized, however, that Ukraine could not defend itself successfully without assistance from the West. Consequently he was compelled to seek Entente support through an alliance with Poland. This move, in his judgment, corresponded to the French plan for building a strong Poland as a barrier against Germany.[31]

CHAPTER 6

Piłsudski's Policy of Alliance versus Dmowski's Policy of Incorporation

Two conceptions had been developed in Poland concerning future relations with those countries that, like Poland, had liberated themselves from Russian occupation. One was promoted by the rather reactionary National Democratic party led by Roman Dmowski; the other, by the more progressive Polish Socialist party under Józef Piłsudski. The first party represented the large landowners, industrialists, the middle class, and expansionists who were not associated with any particular class. The strength of the second party was in the towns, among the lower middle class, and villages.

Originally Dmowski's political program discussed the future Poland as a purely ethnic state that united all the Polish territories occupied by the three imperial powers, but was dependent on Russia. After the outbreak of the Russian Revolution in 1917, however, Dmowski linked the cause of Poland with the Entente Powers. He argued that a small, ethnic Poland could not survive because of its geopolitical location: there was no place for a small Polish state between the inimical powers of Germany and Russia. Dmowski reasoned that "It has been necessary for a long time to understand that any Polish state established by anyone only on Polish ethnic territory cannot form an independent state. Its independence would always be a fiction and ephemeral."[1] Therefore, in his judgment, the Polish state had to be larger and stronger than ethnic Poland. Hence it had to expand at the expense of its eastern neighbors, absorbing Ukrainian lands, namely, all of Eastern Galicia, Kamianets-Podilskyi and Proskuriv counties in Podillia gubernia, and Volynia gubernia west of the rivers Horyn and Sluch; part of Belarus, i.e., two-thirds of Minsk gubernia, including Minsk and Pinsk; and part of Lithuania, i.e., almost all of Vilnius gubernia. Thus, Dmowski did not recognize the rights of self-determination for Ukraine, Belarus, and Lithuania.[2] The incorporated foreign lands would have to be colonized by Poles brought in from ethnic Poland, who would gradually assimilate the non-Polish population.

According to Dmowski Poland, could not be strong without being a centralized state with a population whose majority was Polish. For that reason he was against any federation with Lithuania, Belarus, and Ukraine, because Poland would ultimately be submerged by them. In this respect he echoed the earlier Polish politician and philosopher Hugo Kołłątaj (1750–1812), who had propagated Poland's union with its eastern neighbors rather than federation with them: "In the Poland of the future no one will be a Lithuanian or a Ruthenian, but all will be Poles."³ He would, however, make an exception for the Lithuanians; they would receive cultural autonomy because of Allied sympathies for Lithuania.⁴ Federation, in his judgment, implied weakness and paralysis; in addition, he believed no other peoples in that region were mature enough politically to federate with Poland.

The real reason Dmowski opposed federation, however, was that it would prevent the Polish state from colonizing the occupied territories and assimilating their population. Thus he stood for integral nationalism and was dedicated to the idea of making reborn Poland essentially a nation-state, even though it had incorporated large, non-Polish territories and a considerable non-Polish population. Dmowski realized, however, that a return to the frontiers of 1772 was impossible, because Poland was too weak and could not afford to secure the occupied peoples' allegiance nor to alienate Russia. Therefore he and his supporters, the National Democrats, advocated a rather limited territorial conquest whose population could be, in his opinion, easily colonized and assimilated. They thought in terms of the Treaty of Andrusovo of 1667, which implied a modus vivendi with Russia after its recovery from domestic war,⁵ and advocated a solution of the Russo-Polish territorial conflict by dividing Ukraine, Belarus, and Lithuania between Russia and Poland.

Dmowski believed that the main dangers to Poland's survival lay in the potential problems resulting from the incorporation of foreign peoples and in the threat posed by the German Empire. Therefore he opposed Piłsudski's idea of pushing Russia back to its ethnographic territories, believing that it exceeded Poland's ability and was contrary to Poland's interests. According to Dłuski, an understanding with a non-Bolshevik Russia was something Dmowski viewed as essential for the future of Poland.⁶

Dmowski considered Russia a potential ally against Germany, whose revival was his main worry. Ultimately he linked the overall security of Poland to gaining the support of France and to the interests of the Franco-Russian alliance. In light of his program, Dmowski and the National Democratic party had nothing to offer to the Ukrainians and Belarusians but colonization and assimilation. Even though their policy contradicted Poland's national interests, after the settlement of Poland's eastern border by the Treaty of Riga on 18 March 1921, Dmowski's close collaborator, Stanisław Grabski, gave an optimistic explanation:

> As long as there are territories in Poland with a majority of Orthodox or even Greek Catholic people, Russia will not cease dreaming about their recovery;

that is certain. But it is also certain that when the Polish-Russian borderland becomes Polish territory with a clear majority of Roman Catholic and Polish-speaking people, Russia will relinquish its aspirations for these territories. [Russia] will accept as a fait accompli that beyond the Sluch [River] is Poland.... Before Russia regains its aggressive power ... several decades will pass. A state can not recover quickly from ruin such as that into which Russia was plunged by the Bolshevik revolution. And during those several decades [of recovery] we can and should ensure that our state border will simultaneously be Poland's national [ethnic] border. At that time the age-old conflict between Poland and Russia over the Ruthenian [i.e., Ukrainian] lands would finally be decided and the object of conflict would cease to exist.[7]

Later Grabski pointed out that "At present, one of the most urgent priorities of the Polish national interest is to determine a prudent plan of colonization of the eastern gubernias associated with carrying out a thorough agricultural reform.... a proper plan must be developed for the movement of the agrarian population to the east from overpopulated western villages."[8] In his opinion, the resettlement of Poles in Ukrainian and Belarusian territories "should not be in conflict with the policy of assimilation of the Ukrainian and Belarusian population, but assist it."[9]

Dmowski's program of incorporation had considerable appeal to the followers of other Polish parties of the right and center and to many young Poles. It brought about a sharp split among the Poles from Ukraine, Belarus, and Lithuania, particularly the large landowners, whose class interests and nationalist zeal were interwoven. The latter formed a powerful pressure group and exercised a great deal of influence on the right-wing parties and the Polish government. Dmowski and his supporters condemned Piłsudski's policy of seeking relations with Poland's eastern neighbors as being dangerous to the cohesiveness of the Polish state.

Piłsudski's political conception was broader, more farsighted, and more audacious than Dmowski's program. According to Wasilewski, however, Piłsudski agreed with Dmowski concerning Poland's eastern boundaries.[10] Piłsudski planned to extend Polish political influence farther to the east. In a discussion with Michał Sokolnicki on the eve of the Treaty of Riga, he asserted that "Poland should not stretch to Minsk; it should, instead, embrace the regions of mixed Belarusian-Lithuanian-Polish population only, without being superior in number or culture to the other [non-Polish] population; finally, [it should incorporate] Volynia only in so far as it was necessary for [the mixed regions'] connection with eastern Little Poland [i.e., Eastern Galicia].... Piłsudski stated ...'I do not want to create contestable frontier problems in the future between Poland and Russia.'"[11]

According to Wasilewski, "The commander's plans in the east were linked with his conception of 'Great Poland,' which required a liberal treatment of the question of the lands of the former Grand Duchy of Lithuania and of Ukraine. This 'Great Poland' he [Piłsudski] contrasted with the National Democrats' conception of a 'Small Poland' that was nationalistic and alienating from itself its eastern neighbors, who should have clung to 'Great Poland' and rallied around it as a natural protector vis-à-vis the Russian threat."[12] In Piłsudski's judgment, an ethnic Polish state would be too weak to withstand revolutionary Russia alone. He also believed that a fragmented Eastern Europe, including Poland, would be independent for a brief period only, because it would soon fall prey to Russia, which, while controlling a vast colonial empire, coveted more territory. Dmowski's quasi-national state, with a population that was one-third non-Polish, would also be too weak and would explode in a crisis. Poland's Ukrainians, Belarusians, and Lithuanians would naturally gravitate toward their national centers, Kyiv, Minsk, and Kaunas, while politically they would be used against Poland by Moscow, or even by Berlin.

In contrast to Dmowski, Piłsudski was deeply distrustful of Russia, whether tsarist or Bolshevik. He was convinced that as long as Russia controlled a multinational empire, it would remain a threat to Polish independence. Piłsudski expressed his opinion in an interview with an English correspondent: "I think that the methods which have made Russian Socialism a policy of terrorism and of the total destruction of social life would be unthinkable in civilized countries.... Ask the Socialists of Great Britain whether they would like to have Lenin and Zinoviev reorganize their Government for them on the lines of Bolshevism. I think they would say 'No'. Do you wonder that I am afraid of the Bolsheviks coming here uninvited to organize the Polish Government?"[13] Piłsudski's objective was to weaken the Russian Empire by preventing it from reoccupying the newly established states. Consequently he wished to establish some form of political association between the new states and Poland. Some writers have called this association federal; more correctly it should be defined as an alliance. It was, however, never clearly defined. In his lecture of 24 August 1923 on the "Question of Vilnius," Piłsudski referred to the question of federation. In response to Paderewski, who wished to form a United States of Eastern Europe with the support of the United States, he stated: "I maintained that to go on this road, it seemed to me, was impossible. The principle of federation could not be applied in these lands. Moreover, we were coming with arms, which was contrary to the principles of federation. Besides, I did not see here those who wanted to join this federation.... As a federalist, I did not want to federate Poland with a party that would turn from us."[14]

Piłsudski's idea of association stemmed not from a doctrine, but from

Polish geopolitics and tradition. He was convinced that Poland's independence could not be secured in the long run without other independent countries between Poland and Soviet Russia. Therefore he sought cooperation with Poland's eastern neighbors. His spokesman, Dłuski, elaborated Piłsudski's view:

> Only Poland's close relations with those nations between the Baltic and the Black Sea, namely, Finland, Estonia, Latvia, Lithuania Belarus, and Ukraine, can be an effective dam against the pressure, simultaneously, from the East and from the West.... If those nations that were part of former Russia wish to live an independent life, giving them the possibility of developing their human and national characteristics in all aspects, and if they do not wish to be again [bound] in the chains of Muscovite tyranny, they should unite into one strong political federation having Poland as its nucleus.[15]

Piłsudski's objective was to establish a close political alliance with Finland, Estonia, and Latvia, a union with historic Lithuania and Belarus, and a political and military alliance with the UNR. His ambitious policy of alliance with Finland, Estonia, and Latvia rested on a weak foundation, because it would have practically no value unless Lithuania also joined. The Lithuanian leaders' attitude toward a union with Poland, however, was negative; they made it clear that they wished to be absolutely independent.

Piłsudski's "federal" policy, if it is possible at all to speak of one, was applied only to historic Lithuania.[16] He envisioned Lithuania connected in some imprecise way with Poland, either in a neo-Jagiellonian dynastic union or in a federation. According to Piłsudski, "the destinies of Poland and Lithuania had been linked together for centuries."[17] Earlier, during World War I, Piłsudski already believed that an independent Lithuanian state would be reborn, and he hoped that, as in the past, it would be in a close union with the future Poland.[18] In his conception, historic Lithuania, which included also Belarus, would consist of three gubernias: Western Lithuania with Kaunas; Belarus with Minsk; and Central Lithuania with Vilnius, which would be the capital of all three gubernias. In an interview on 2 May 1919, a French correspondent suggested to Piłsudski that "the ideal solution for Poland would be a union with all of historic Lithuania." Piłsudski replied: "Certainly, that is precisely what we need to aspire to, but this task is not devoid of difficulty. In my judgment the Belarusians and Poles could easily come to terms; with the Lithuanians, however, it will be more difficult."[19]

The Poles were harking back to the Polish-Lithuanian Commonwealth, which they wished to revive, while the Lithuanians wanted to avoid any such experiment. Piłsudski's effort to achieve some form of close association with

Lithuania, be it a union or federation, went through three phases. During their meeting in Vilnius on 30 December 1918, Polish and Lithuanian representatives tried to establish a political understanding. The Lithuanians agreed to negotiate if the Poles would recognize the independence of Lithuania, with Vilnius as its capital. The Bolshevik invasion and occupation of Vilnius and its region ended the first phase of Polish-Lithuanian negotiations.

A second attempt to unite was made prior to the April 1919 Polish expedition to Vilnius against the Bolsheviks. Piłsudski dispatched a confidential mission headed by Michał Romer to the Lithuanian government in Kaunas to propose a joint military operation and occupation of Vilnius commanded by Piłsudski. This act of solidarity would have historic significance for both countries. Lithuania would be united with the Vilnius region and gain Vilnius as its capital, while Poland, after the reconstruction of the historic Polish-Lithuanian Commonwealth, would become the dominant power in the Baltic region. The Lithuanians, however, turned down the Polish proposition because they had different goals. Referring to this problem on another occasion, Piłsudski's spokesman Antoni Sujkowski explained that if the Lithuanians had the opportunity to establish their own institutions in Vilnius, they would be satisfied; that would correspond with their concept of federation. Poland, however, would agree to this only under the condition that the Lithuanians would accept federation. Having Lithuanian central institutions in Vilnius, he argued, would not deprive the city of its Polish identity, but rather would promote the expansion of Polish influence throughout Lithuania.

The third serious attempt at finding some form of association with Lithuania was made by Piłsudski after his army had captured Vilnius. On 22 April 1919 Piłsudski issued a proclamation to the population of the former Grand Duchy of Lithuania in which he suggested union with Poland. The Lithuanians, however, declined his proposition; they viewed it as Polish imperialism, while the government in Kaunas demanded that Vilnius become part of the Lithuanian state. Even though the Lithuanians finally rejected union with Poland, Piłsudski did not abandon his goal.

In Piłsudski's conception, Lithuania assumed first place because of its key geopolitical position in a northern alliance that would also include Finland, Estonia, and Latvia. In case of failure, he feared that Lithuania would not only cut off the other Baltic states from Poland, but also would become a bridge for Poland's enemies, Russia and Germany. Therefore he attempted to realize his idea of a Baltic alliance at the Helsinki Conference held on 20–23 January 1920. Attended by representatives of Finland, Estonia, Latvia, Lithuania, and Poland, the conference dealt mainly with the question of relations between the Baltic states and Soviet Russia, the means of strengthening economic relations among those states, and the Polish-Lithuanian conflict over the Vilnius region.

The conference produced no positive results because of the Polish-Lithuanian conflict.

After the conference Piłsudski's attempt at a Baltic alliance collapsed. Consequently, on 8 October 1920, he ordered the so-called Lithuanian-Belarusian Division, composed of Poles from the Vilnius region, a regiment of cavalry, and a detachment of volunteers commanded by Gen. Lucjan Żeligowski, to occupy Vilnius and its region so as to force Lithuania to agree to a union with Poland. After the occupation Żeligowski established a Polish-ruled "Government of Central Lithuania," thereby violating the Suwałki Armistice concluded between Poland and Lithuania under the auspices of the League of Nations on 7 October 1920. Polish aggression displeased some Entente statesmen, especially the British, and representatives of foreign states assigned to the Lithuanian government protested Żeligowski's aggression. He not only ignored their protest, but ordered them to leave Vilnius.

To settle this conflict, the League of Nations invited both parties to a conference held in Brussels on 20 May 1921. Chaired by the Belgian minister Paul Hymans, the conference proposed a union between Poland and Lithuania in which Lithuania would be divided into two parts centered on Kaunas and Vilnius, each with its own parliament. The proposal was accepted in principle by the Poles, but rejected by the Lithuanians. The second Hymans plan of 3 September 1921 recommended that the Vilnius region be incorporated into Lithuania as an autonomous region. This proposal was rejected by the Poles. Piłsudski wanted to grant "Central Lithuania," which constituted about 37,000 square km. and had over 600,000 inhabitants, an autonomous status, hoping that in time the Lithuanians would agree to a union with Poland. Under the pressure of the Poles in Poland and in Vilnius, however, on 8 January 1922 an election was held in the Vilnius region under the auspices of Żeligowski. The assembly elected voted for incorporation of the Vilnius region into Poland, and on 24 March the Polish Sejm accepted its decision. In protest, the Lithuanian government severed relations with Poland. On 15 March 1923 the Conference of Ambassadors in Paris formally endorsed Piłsudski's fait accompli. But he not only failed to achieve some form of political association with Lithuania; he also created an abyss between Poland and Lithuania.

Piłsudski's plan of association between Belarus and Poland was much more fluid. Originally he had contemplated dealing with Belarus as part of historic Lithuania, and he maneuvered Belarus to induce Lithuania into a union with Poland. When Piłsudski's policy of union with Lithuania failed, Belarus's role diminished. In his opinion Belarus was not ready for political independence because its people and politics were less developed than Lithuania's. In the meantime, it was necessary to develop the Belarusian Piedmont in Poland. Piłsudski's closest collaborator, Leon Wasilewski, took a more pessimistic view. He viewed the Belarusians as "raw ethnografic material" who would not have, in the near future, prospects for developing their own national independence. Piłsudski believed, however, in the natural development of a national consciousness and culture in a people that had been awakened, and that national emancipation was inevitable.

When his plan for Poland's union with Lithuania and Belarus failed, Piłsudski continued searching for a workable political solution in Eastern Europe because he did not believe in the peaceful intentions of Soviet Russia. When, at the end of 1919, the Bolsheviks defeated the Denikin forces, he realized that the Bolshevik threat would soon extend also to Poland. In his judgment, Soviet Russia was playing for time to strengthen itself militarily and to make Poland subservient. It became clear to Piłsudski that Poland would need allies against the Bolsheviks.

Developments in Ukraine worked in Piłsudski's favor. The UNR Directory under Petliura was desperately struggling against both the Bolshevik and anti-Bolshevik Russian forces to maintain the independence of the UNR, and Petliura was thereby compelled to seek an alliance with Poland and thus an indirect alliance with the Entente. This gave Piłsudski an opportunity to conclude an alliance with Petliura—the Treaty of Warsaw—with the aim of defeating the Bolsheviks and thus maintaining the independence of Right-Bank Ukraine as a buffer between Poland and Soviet Russia.[20]

CHAPTER 7

Ukrainian-Polish Diplomatic Relations and The Treaty of Warsaw

Ukrainian-Polish diplomatic relations in 1917 and 1918 were inconsistent and weak, partly because of differing political situations in the two countries. Ukraine's independence had been achieved by means of a revolutionary struggle without outside assistance. Poland, on the other hand, became independent thanks not only to Polish efforts: Russia, Austria-Hungary, Germany, and, finally, the Entente Powers played a part for political and strategic reasons. The main factor that prevented the UNR and Poland from achieving friendly relations was, however, the war between Poland and the ZUNR that erupted in November 1918.

The UNR Directory's first attempt at contacting the Polish government was made on 31 December 1918, when Petliura sent a mission to Warsaw headed by V'iacheslav Prokopovych, the former UNR minister of education, to discuss the current policy and explore a basis for peace negotiations. The ensuing discussion, however, did not go beyond general problems, and the mission failed to achieve a positive result.[1] In the meantime, a Polish unofficial representative in Ukraine, Marian Szumlakowski, advised the UNR minister of foreign affairs, Kost' Matsiievych, to dispatch a mission to Poland, and on 4 April 1919 Matsiievych sent Borys Kurdynovs'kyi to exchange information with the Polish government. Kurdynovs'kyi overstepped his authority, however, and made a disadvantageous agreement with Prime Minister Paderewski that promised substantial territorial concessions to Poland. In exchange Poland pledged to recognize the independence of the UNR and to provide military assistance against the Bolsheviks. One Polish author later remarked: "As we see, Kurdynovs'kyi was not stingy in [his] promises. The agreement gave Poland all that one could only dream for." By the agreement Ukraine would have become Poland's protectorate, and the Directory did not ratify it. Paderewski, however, used it on Piłsudski's advice against the ZUNR delegation at the Peace Conference in Paris to argue that the Poles and the Directory were willing to solve the Polish-Ukrainian conflict peacefully.[2]

As the military situation in Ukraine worsened because of the war with the Bolsheviks, both UNR and ZUNR leaders came to the conclusion that a new basis for continuing the struggle was needed. At the end of April 1919 Petliura dispatched a small delegation, headed by Col. Dmytro Antonchuk, to determine whether there was a basis for peace on the Ukrainian-Polish front in Galicia. Later a larger delegation—Gen. Serhii Del'vig (chairman) and Col. Kamins'kyi and Antonchuk representing the UNR and Col. Kostiantyn Sliusarchuk, Capt. Kostiantyn Chekhovych, and a third member representing the ZUNR—was dispatched to the Polish command on 1 May 1919. The Polish delegation was chaired by Gen. Tadeusz Rozwadowski, the commander in Galicia. The negotiations took place in Lviv and dealt with military problems only. After three weeks, on 20 May 1919, the delegations signed a provisional peace agreement delineating the demarcation line between the Polish Army and the UHA of Zaliztsi–Ternopil–Kozova–Zastavtsi–Zolota Lypa River–Nyzhniv–Nezvyska. The Polish government and the Directory subsequently ratified the agreement without the participation of the ZUNR government, but a new Polish offensive annulled it.[3]

In the meantime, not wishing to break relations with the Directory, Piłsudski made contact with Petliura at the end of May 1919 at Chornyi Ostriv through a secret agent, Jan Zagłoba-Mazurkiewicz, who crossed the front line posing as a Ukrainian prisoner of war. After Zagłoba-Mazurkiewicz's return to Warsaw, contacts and exchanges of ideas between Piłsudski and Petliura continued.[4] In response to Piłsudski's mission, on 12 August 1919 Petliura sent a special mission to Poland headed by Pylyp Pylypchuk, a former UNR minister of communications, and including Volodymyr Tuliup, head of the Political Department in the Ministry of Foreign Affairs, and Cols. Klym Pavliuk and Iuliian Lypnyts'kyi. The Polish delegation consisted of August Zaleski (chairman), Maj. Ignacy Matuszewski, Col. Roman Knoll, and Marian Szumlakowski. During its two weeks in Warsaw the UNR delegation met Paderewski and Piłsudski. It was concerned mainly with the acquisition of materiel, the delineation of the Polish-Ukrainian frontier, guarantees of national and cultural rights for Ukrainians under Polish rule and non-Ukrainians in Ukraine, and the return of members of the Ukrainian Graycoats Corps (organized in Volodymyr-Volynskyi in 1918 from among Ukrainian prisoners of war interned in Austria as Russian army personnel) captured by the Poles. The Polish delegation pursued territorial concessions in the occupied territories, especially Eastern Galicia, and demanded that the UNR sever relations with the ZUNR president, Evhen Petrushevych, and guarantee that there would be no military formations on Ukrainian territory inimical to Poland. It also demanded that the UNR compensate the numerous Polish landowners in Right-Bank Ukraine for the loss of their properties.[5]

The Pylypchuk mission, just as earlier UNR missions, failed to achieve positive results because the Poles did not take the negotiations seriously. The

Polish deputy minister of foreign affairs, Władysław Skrzyński, wrote in a letter to the Polish envoy in London that "Poland's northeastern [i.e., Lithuanian and Belarusian] policy has certain lines of direction; our policy in Ukraine, however, has not. With Petliura, who would not renounce Eastern Galicia, we cannot negotiate, and a Petliura who would renounce it would lose the confidence of three-fourths of his troops."[6] On 16 August 1919 the Polish envoy in Paris, Maurycy Zamoyski, and the Polish delegation to the Peace Conference received from the Polish government instructions for discussion:

> If we obtain complete disinterest concerning Galicia and northern Volynia and a guarantee of good treatment of the Polish population [in Ukraine], and if we avoid recognition of Ukraine, we could eventually use them [Ukrainians] as an anti-Bolshevik force for faster termination of the war, which demands huge material and financial investment by our military forces. Also important is the very good harvest in Ukraine this year. [Therefore] Please direct the attention of the Entente to the fact that the winter campaign is approaching and that on the long anti-Bolshevik front, by which we are protecting Europe, the soldier needs warm clothes and a treasure of financial help is needed for provision of an army of a few hundred thousand.[7]

On 23 August Zamoyski was instructed, should there be a question concerning the negotiations with the Pylypchuk mission, to declare that "(1) negotiations were conducted with the aim of facilitating actions against the Bolsheviks; (2) Poland never recognized the Ukrainian state; (3) we [Poland] gained renunciation of Eastern Galicia by Ukraine, but because of the Allies we made no agreements concerning borders; and (4) the agreement is in the form of a one-sided declaration by Ukraine."[8]

Such attitudes by the Polish government were continued until the Polish army attained the desired frontiers. In late November 1919, however, the Denikin forces met serious setbacks and began a general retreat, and the Bolshevik threat to Poland consequently became real not only in the northeast, but also in the southeast. The Poles quickly realized that war with Soviet Russia was unavoidable and that they needed allies in that struggle. Because Petliura had already turned to Poland for assistance, Piłsudski saw an opportunity to seek reconciliation with the UNR in order to fight a common enemy. In his opinion, close ties with Ukraine were the key to finding a political settlement of the crisis in the region between the Baltic and the Black Seas, for an independent Ukraine would bring about the liberation of the Don and Kuban Cossacks as well as the Caucasian nations.[9] The advisability of such a policy became particularly apparent when Great Britain reversed its policy toward Soviet Russia and lifted its blockade, and when the Baltic states, where British influence predominated, initiated peace negotiations with Moscow. Estonia signed a peace treaty with Soviet Russia on 2 February 1920; Lithuania, on 12 July; Latvia, on 11 August; and Finland, on 14 October.[10]

After the experience of its previous diplomatic missions to Poland, the UNR government became convinced that it was necessary to send a plenipotentiary mission to Warsaw that had the support of all major political parties and enjoyed broad popular confidence. Such a mission left on 3 October 1919. It was headed by the UNR minister of foreign affairs, Andrii Livyts'kyi, and included the UNR representatives Leonid Mykhailiv, Prokip Poniatenko, Borys Rzhepets'kyi, and Petro Mshanets'kyi and the ZUNR representatives Stepan Vytvyts'kyi, Antin Horbachevs'kyi, and Mykhailo Novakivs'kyi. Two months later, on 7 December, Petliura joined the mission. Before major negotiations could begin, however, the mission was forced to issue a declaration on 2 December accepting the Zbruch River in Eastern Galicia and the Styr River in Western Volynia as the Polish-Ukrainian frontier, but not before its ZUNR members withdrew in protest.

Negotiations did not reach a decisive stage until the first half of March 1920. The Polish cabinet discussed the Ukrainian question on 13 April and submitted a draft treaty with Ukraine to the Foreign Affairs Committee for approval. The final text of the treaty consisted of a political agreement and a military convention.[11] According to the agreement, the Polish and UNR governments were "profoundly convinced that each nation possesses the natural right to self-determination and to define its relations with neighboring peoples ... and are equally animated by the desire of establishing the bases for concordant and friendly coexistence for the welfare and development of both peoples." The agreement consisted of the following articles:

1. Recognizing the right of Ukraine to independent political existence within its northern, eastern, and southern frontiers as they shall be determined by means of separate agreements concluded by the Ukrainian People's Republic with the respective border states, the Polish Republic recognizes the Directory of the independent Ukrainian People's Republic, headed by the Supreme Military Commander Symon Petliura, as the supreme authority of the Ukrainian People's Republic.

2. The frontiers between the Polish Republic and the Ukrainian People's Republic are established as follows: northward from the Dniester River along the Zbruch River and the former frontier between Austria-Hungary and Russia to Vyshhorodok; from Vyshhorodok northward through the Kremianets Hills; then in a northerly direction from Zdolbuniv and along

the eastern administrative boundary of Rivne county; continuing northward along the administrative boundary of former Minsk gubernia to its juncture with the Prypiat River; and then along the Prypiat River to its termination. The counties of Rivne, Dubno, and, in part, Kremianets, which presently are ceded to the Polish Republic, shall be subject to a more concise agreement to be concluded later. The final delimitation of the frontier shall be accomplished by a special Ukrainian-Polish commission composed of appropriate specialists.

3. The Polish Government recognizes as Ukrainian the territory east of the frontier as defined in Article 2 of this agreement, and extending to the 1772 frontiers of Poland (prior to the partition) that Poland now occupies or shall acquire in the future from Russia by military or diplomatic means.

4. The Polish Government is obligated not to conclude any international agreements directed against Ukraine; the government of the Ukrainian People's Republic is obligated similarly with respect to the Polish Republic.

5. The same national-cultural rights that the Government of the Ukrainian People's Republic ensures citizens of Polish nationality on its territory shall be ensured to citizens of Ukrainian nationality within the borders of the Polish Republic.

6. Special economic and commercial agreements are to be concluded between the Ukrainian People's Republic and the Polish Republic.

The agrarian question in Ukraine should be resolved by the Constituent Assembly. In the period preceding its convocation the legal status of landowners of Polish nationality in Ukraine shall be defined by a special agreement between the Ukrainian People's Republic and the Polish Republic.

7. A military convention is to be concluded and is to be regarded as an integral part of this agreement.

8. This agreement shall remain secret. It shall not be revealed to a third party nor published in whole or in part except with the mutual consent of both of the high contracting parties. An exception to this is Article 1, which shall be made public after the signing of this agreement.

9. This agreement shall enter into force immediately upon being signed by the high contracting parties.

Signed in Warsaw on this twenty-first day of April 1920 in two copies, one of which is in the Ukrainian language and one is in the Polish language. In case of doubt, only the Polish text is to be regarded as authentic.[12]

Three days after the political agreement was signed, a military convention was concluded:

1. This military convention comprises an integral part of the political treaty of 21 April 1920 and takes effect simultaneously and remains in force until the conclusion of a permanent military convention between the Polish Government and the Ukrainian.
2. The Polish and Ukrainian armies undertake operations jointly as allied armies.
3. In the event of a joint Polish-Ukrainian military action against the Bolshevik troops on the territory of Right-Bank Ukraine east of the existing Polish-Bolshevik front, the military operations take place after a mutual understanding has been reached by the Supreme Command of the Polish armies and the Supreme Command of the Ukrainian armies under the general direction of the Supreme Command of the Polish armies.
4. The Supreme Command of the Polish armies shall assign its own officers to the operational staff of the Ukrainian armies, and the Supreme Command of the Ukrainian armies, with the understanding of the Supreme Command of the Polish armies, shall assign to Polish commands, units, institutions, and so on its own liaison officers.
5. The troops assigned by the Supreme Command of the Ukrainian armies to the disposition of the Supreme Command of the Polish armies shall be deployed on Ukrainian territory by this command in accordance with operational needs defined by it, without, if possible, dividing them [the troops] into small tactical units. As actions advance, insofar as operational conditions allow, at the request of the Supreme Command of the Ukrainian armies the Supreme Command of the Polish armies shall gather the Ukrainian units together as soon as possible and shall assign them their own region of action and their own special strategic task, with the aim of returning them to the direct disposition of the Supreme Command of the Ukrainian armies.
6. From the start of a joint action against the Bolsheviks, the Ukrainian Government pledges to deliver to the Polish army that operates in this territory the necessary food supplies, in amounts according to the operational plan—the main commodities being meat, leaf fat, grains, groats, fruits, sugar, oats, hay, straw, etc.—on the basis of food-ration norms obligatory in the Polish army, as well as the necessary means for their conveyance.
   a. With this aim, civil commissioners or Ukrainian provision officers shall be assigned to the commands of the Polish divisions and armies; their duty shall be to supply a division (army) with the necessary

amount of food products and means for their conveyance.

b. In case of the non-delivery of the necessary products by the Ukrainian Government, the Ukrainian civil commissioner, with the understanding of the quartermaster's office of a division (army), shall carry out requisitions of the necessary products from the local population, paying by requisition receipts payable and guaranteed by the Ukrainian Government and issued in two languages—Polish and Ukrainian. The receipts shall indicate the kind and weight of the products, and as far as conveyances and horses are concerned, their number and time of employment. As much as possible, immediate payment of the full sum shall be made for the delivered conveyances at a price set by the Ukrainian Government. The receipt shall indicate that during the requisition the amount due was only partly paid and that the remainder shall be paid later by the Ukrainian Government.

The Ukrainian Government pledges to supply the Polish army with adequate cash to pay citizens part of the money owed them for commodities they have delivered according to maximum prices stipulated by the Ukrainian Government. The Polish army shall award a premium of requisition receipts and certificates payable in cash for salt, petroleum, or other commodities of primary necessity according to norms and instructions that shall be issued separately. Polish provision officers shall be assigned to the Ukrainian units with the aim of observing and executing the granting of uniform premiums.

c. Food commodities not supplied by the Ukrainian Government, and therefore delivered by the Polish Government, shall be calculated according to the Polish stipulated norms and charged to the Ukrainian Government in Polish currency in accordance with the prices regulated for the army troops in Poland.

d. Until the conclusion of a financial convention, the rate for exchanging Ukrainian currency into Polish currency that is obligatory in the army shall be stipulated by the Supreme Command of the Polish armies in agreement with the Supreme Command of the Ukrainian armies.

7. In case of occupation of the above-indicated territory by Polish-Ukrainian or only Polish armies, the Supreme Command of the Polish armies reserves the right to direct all railroad lines during a given military action; Ukrainian railroad personnel shall, however, remain at their posts. The Ukrainian authorities shall be notified concerning cases of and reasons for dismissal. Ukrainian liaison officers shall be assigned to the Polish military-railroad authorities in accordance with Paragraph 4. The Ukrainian Government shall begin organizing an entire railroad apparatus immediately with the aim of taking control of the railroads. The pro-

cedures and timetable for taking over shall be determined by a separate agreement. The Polish command shall assist the Ukrainian railroads by providing rolling stock, fuel, lubricants, and other materials necessary for the operation of the railroads and for ensuring their usability. Control of all transports and the movement of all railroad material shall be carried out according to regulations set by the appropriate orders of the Supreme Command of the Polish armies with the understanding of the Supreme Command of the Ukrainian armies.

8. From the moment of commencing a joint offensive and occupying new territory in Right-Bank Ukraine situated east of the existing line of the Polish-Bolshevik front, the Ukrainian Government shall organize there its own authority and administration, [both] civil and military. The rears of the Polish armies shall be guarded by the Polish field gendarmerie and the Polish rear army; their replacement by Ukrainian authorities shall proceed on the basis of a separate agreement reached after the formation of a Ukrainian gendarmerie and rear armies. Polish liaison officers shall be assigned to the Ukrainian administrative authorities for the duration of service by the Polish gendarmerie and rear armies.

   Authority in the presently occupied territories, which, in accordance with the political agreement, have been recognized as part of the Ukrainian People's Republic, shall remain for the time being in the hands of the Polish [authorities] while the Ukrainian Government is organizing its own administrative apparatus. Once it [the apparatus] has been organized, authority in these territories, with the agreement of the Polish Government, shall be transferred to the Ukrainian Government.

   From the moment of the signing of the present convention, the Ukrainian central state institutions in Kamianets-Podilskyi shall resume their functions.

9. After the fulfillment of a general plan of joint action, the evacuation of Polish armies from the territory of Ukraine should begin on the recommendation of one of the two contracting governments, while the technical execution of evacuation shall take place on the basis of a mutual understanding between the Supreme Command of the Polish armies and the Supreme Command of the Ukrainian armies.

10. The Ukrainian Government shall assume the costs of equipping, supplying, and maintaining organized Ukrainian units formed on the territory of Poland for which the Supreme Command of the Polish armies or the Polish Ministry of Military Affairs gave or shall give help in [the form of] food commodities, equipment, arms, ammunition, and all kinds of military materiel.

11. The organization of Ukrainian units shall continue on the territory of

Poland, as it took place heretofore in Brest, until such time when such organization shall be possible on its own [Ukrainian] territory.

12. The Supreme Command of the Polish armies pledges to supply the Ukrainian armies with arms, ammunition, equipment, and uniforms in quantities necessary for three divisions, in accordance with the budgets fixed for a Polish division with all its sanitary and other rear institutions, and to place these provisions at the disposition of the Ukrainian Ministry of Military Affairs. Things ordered or bought by the Ukrainian Government abroad, or exported or imported to the Ukrainian Army's place of sojourn thanks to the efforts of the Polish Government, shall be included in the amount of the above provisions.

13. The entire railroad spoil, except armored trains taken in battle, and other military booty, except movables taken in battle, constitute the property of the Ukrainian state. Details shall be stipulated in a separate agreement.

14. A detailed financial-economic agreement and a railroad convention related to the present convention shall be concluded additionally.

15. Both contracting parties have the right to propose the conclusion of a permanent military convention at a time considered suitable by each party. Until the conclusion of a new agreement the present convention is binding.

16. Both contracting parties pledge to keep this convention secret.

17. This convention is written in both the Polish and Ukrainian languages. Both texts are binding. In case of doubt, the Polish text is definitive.

The convention was signed in Warsaw on 24 April 1920. The Polish signatories were Maj. Walery Sławek and Capt. Wacław Jędrzejewicz; the Ukrainian, Gen. Volodymyr Sinkler and Col. Maksym Didkovs'kyi.[13]

The UNR agreement with Poland stemmed from the critical situation in Ukraine in the autumn of 1919. The Polish authorities took advantage of this situation to dictate their demands to the Ukrainian government. Petliura had been at the mercy of the Poles since December, when he sought refuge with them, and the treaty merely formalized that relationship, in which he was an instrument to be utilized and then discarded. During negotiations, the Poles did not hesitate to remind the Ukrainians that they were not equals because the latter possessed neither territory nor enough stability to govern. This attitude was reflected in the agreement itself, which had many weaknesses and shortcomings. In it Ukraine appeared as a junior partner. This was made clear in the first article, which did not provide for mutual recognition between the two contracting parties. Poland recognized Ukraine's right to independent political existence; it apparently did not require Ukrainian recognition of Polish independence. Moreover, the article provided for recognition of the

Directory as the government of Ukraine by Poland, but with the qualification that it be headed by Petliura. Such a provision was an error, because it ignored the fact that Petliura was mortal. If he resigned or was forced to resign could have been regarded legally as a violation of conditions implicit in the recognition. The second article provided for the cession of Eastern Galicia and Western Volynia to Poland. The third article placed Ukraine in a subservient position, for it recognized Poland's prior claim to its 1772 frontier and made the Ukrainians appear to be the objects of Polish beneficence. Furthermore, the fate of Left-Bank Ukraine was not included in the agreement, and Polish participation in the joint military operation was to end at the Dnieper. Thus the Poles were not bound to help the Ukrainians east of the Dnieper. In the fourth article the Polish government agreed not to make any international agreements against Ukraine, and the UNR similarly agreed not to be a party to any such agreements with respect to the Polish Republic. The fifth article was deceptive and unfair, because Poland agreed to grant to Ukrainians living within its frontiers the same rights Ukraine was to accord to Poles residing in Ukraine. Eastern Galicia and Western Volynia were Ukrainian ethnic territories where the Ukrainian population constituted a large majority, while there were fewer than one million Poles in Right-Bank Ukraine. In the sixth article the Polish government openly appeared as the protector of the interests of the great Polish landowners in Ukraine. To secure their position, two Poles were appointed to key UNR government positions—Stanisław Stempowski as minister of agriculture and Henryk Józewski as deputy minister of internal affairs—thereby facilitating Polish intervention in Ukrainian internal affairs. The eighth article, which provided for secrecy regarding everything but the fact of the treaty's existence, was necessitated by the sweeping concessions accepted by Petliura, which were not accompanied by any corresponding recompense on the part of the Poles.[14]

The Treaty of Warsaw was an expression of the mutual understanding between two national leaders, Petliura and Piłsudski. Both headed the struggle of their people, and both saw this agreement not as the beginning of a new era in relations between their two nations, but rather as a necessity dictated by the contemporary situation. Petliura viewed it as a tactical move aimed at establishing contact with Europe and gaining a respite before continuing the struggle. Piłsudski was in a very favorable position to carry out his plans and ideas. Petliura, however, was in an impossible position, and the treaty with Poland was simply an act of desperation. Poland, as the enemy only of Western Ukraine, was a lesser evil than Russia, which was the enemy of all of Ukraine. A victorious struggle against Russia was, in Petliura's opinion, a sine qua non for the continuing existence of the Ukrainian state. He understood that Russia would never freely allow an independent Ukraine to exist, either in full or in part. Although Petliura's aim was an independent, unified Ukraine, this goal, in his opinion, could be attained only if Ukraine strove for what was possible under given external and internal circumstances. In this respect Petliura was following the examples of the struggle for independence and unification of Italy, Romania, and Yugoslavia, and his policy, in his opinion, was one of realism. To the end of his life he remained convinced that the basis for the development of Ukrainian statehood must be former Russian-ruled Ukraine, and he regarded its defense against Soviet Russia as his primary aim, even if it had to be at the expense of Western Ukraine.[15]

A Polish author remarked on this situation and Petliura's critical position:

> The "Freedom" slogans of Piłsudski's federal plans were ... in practical life more "prosaic" and easily explainable in realistic language as expansion. Petliura, however, was compelled to reconcile his nationalism with the betrayal of Ukrainian national interests and to accept political, military, and economic domination by those who had strangled Western Ukraine's aspirations for freedom and, at the beginning of 1919, grabbed in military battles, even from Petliura himself, a sizable part of what was undoubtedly Ukrainian territory.[16]

Although the Poles were the main beneficiaries of the Warsaw Treaty, many of them opposed it because they feared a Ukrainian state, even one reduced in size, more than Soviet Russia. The main opponents were the National Democrats headed by Dmowski. They not only denied the Ukrainians the right to their own state: they did not even wish to recognize the existence of a Ukrainian nation, and their policy paralyzed Polish-Ukrainian negotiations and the subsequent agreement. Their representative in the government, Stanisław Grabski, manifested his opposition by resigning as chairman of the Foreign Affairs Committee.[17] According to his interview in *Gazeta Warszawska* on 27 April 1920, "The aim of the war [against Soviet Russia] should be the establishment of the Polish-Russian border, and we should not be concerned about Ukraine, which is not prepared for an independent life because in Ukraine there is lack of feeling for statehood." It was not, however, the lack of feeling that bothered Grabski, but his fear of fighting alongside Ukrainians for a common cause. He felt that

> Just as Poland needs Warsaw, so Ukraine needs Kyiv. But to have Kyiv in permanent possession, it would be necessary to go far beyond the Dnieper, and such a march would threaten [Poland] with a defeat like Napoleon's in 1812.... It is better to be a neighbor with Russia than a newly created Ukraine, because

we, as Poles, have more rights to the pre-partition lands lying east of the Zbruch than the Russians. Thanks to [these rights] we would have an easier situation than if we had next to us Ukraine, which, on the basis of the self-determination of nations, would demand rights to Eastern Little Poland [Eastern Galicia].[18]

Piłsudski had a different position. Although he was aware of the risk in supporting Ukraine, he understood that without Ukraine as an ally he could not defeat Soviet Russia and thus safeguard peace for Poland. There were, however, internal and external obstacles to his Ukrainian policy. The National Democrats' opposition to the treaty was strengthened by refugee Polish landowners from Right-Bank Ukraine, who sought the restitution of the tsarist regime and the establishment of friendly relations between the new Poland and Russia. The National Democrats' main concerns were the destruction of the ZUNR and the restitution of property to the Polish landowners in Right-Bank Ukraine; both, in their judgment, could be achieved by the victory of the Russian Volunteer Army. The increase in the importance of the Ukrainian question prompted Dmowski to go from Paris to Warsaw, where he warned other National Democratic leaders about the possible continuing existence of a Ukrainian state. If an independent Ukraine should be preserved, he asserted that it would be in the Polish interest for it to be as small as possible.[19]

Piłsudski asked Dmowski why the Polish delegation in Paris did not support the independence of Ukraine. At first Dmowski avoided a straight answer and argued that such support was impossible for two reasons. First, from the very beginning, namely, from the summer of 1917, the National Committee and the Polish delegation had presented to the Entente a definite plan for Poland's eastern borders that did not take into account the possibility of the eventual establishment of an independent Ukraine, and this plan had been accepted. Second, it was not known whether the Ukrainian state would be a viable one, or how it would behave toward Poland. Besides, the Entente were still hoping that the Bolshevik revolution would fail and a constitutional Russia would arise from the civil war. When his arguments failed to convince Piłsudski, Dmowski became more explicit: "On what ground could we demand for ourselves the annexation of eastern territories, including all of Eastern Galicia, if we would simultaneously support the claims of Ukrainians to these lands and to a great, independent Ukraine? Upon hearing this question Piłsudski grew impatient and became deeply upset."[20]

A major problem that Piłsudski could not ignore was the VA. In his judgment, even if Denikin submitted to the Entente and agreed to an independent Poland, he would not accept an independent Ukraine, Belarus, or Lithuania. According to B. Kutyłowski, a Polish envoy to the Ukrainian government,

The Russians are an unscrupulous opponent even to Ukrainian autonomy, [and] unwilling to consider favorably in the least measure a separate [Ukrainian] identity. As a result of [Russian] pressure, the local authorities [in occupied Ukraine] removed the Ukrainian language from the teaching program in the middle of the school year. [Russian] Newspapers denigrated Ukraine in various ways ... and [noted] the zeal of the [Ukrainian] people's efforts to unite with Russia. They proclaimed such slogans as "One and Indivisible Russia," which included the Kholm [region], Podlachia, and Eastern Galicia.[21]

Piłsudski had his own plans for Ukraine, Belarus, and Lithuania. These plans were dependent on Denikin's defeat. But because the Entente supported the VA because they viewed a non-Bolshevik Russia as a future ally against Germany, Piłsudski planned to act in Ukraine only after Denikin's defeat, when the Entente would have no reason to protest. Thus Piłsudski was compelled to deceive the Entente by acting against Denikin.

CHAPTER 8

The Genesis of the Polish-Soviet Russian War

Although the western and southern boundaries of Poland had been settled by the Peace Treaty of Versailles (conditional upon plebiscites for some territories) and the Conference of Ambassadors respectively, Poland's eastern border had not been resolved for two reasons. First, after the settlement of its western border by the Entente Powers and with their continued support, Poland was free to wage aggressive wars against its eastern neighbors, mainly Ukraine. Second, Article 87 of the Peace Treaty of Versailles had reserved for the Principal Allied and Associated Powers the right to delineate Poland's eastern frontiers, but they were not willing to make this decision without Russia. The Entente hoped that Bolshevism would be a passing phase and that an acceptable Russian regime would be established and invited to participate in international negotiations.

Piłsudski better understood both Bolshevik and anti-Bolshevik Russia and the political conditions in Eastern Europe than the Entente leaders. He expressed his understanding in a discussion with the British envoy to Poland, Sir Horace George Rumbold, on 15 December 1919. Rumbold wrote:

> Mr. Mackinder, General Keyes, and myself were received together by General Pilsudsky yesterday.... We asked General Pilsudsky whether, in his opinion, Bolshevism was merely a facade behind which a moderate party was developing. He replied emphatically that whilst a short time ago the moderate element seemed to be progressing, the extreme elements were now in command. He said that whilst the Bolsheviks would probably be prepared to make peace, they would never stick to any agreement they made, and he certainly would not enter into negotiations with them. At the beginning of the interview he expressed himself pessimistically about General Denikin's organization, but admitted that the Polish troops had only come into contact with loosely organized bands of Denikin's troops who were operating in the Ukraine. He spoke in the same manner about General Denikin to us.[1]

Piłsudski was convinced that Poland's eastern boundaries could only be established by military means. During 1919 and 1920, Polish-Soviet relations were essentially a competition for influence in Lithuania, Belarus, and Ukraine. In 1918 and 1919, while the Ukrainians were defending their land against the Bolshevik, White, and Polish invasions, the territories of Lithuania and Belarus were blocked off to both Soviet Russia and Poland by half a million troops of the German Oberkommando-Ostfront. The territory they controlled was nearly 1,500 miles long; it included Ukraine, Belarus, Lithuania, Latvia, and Estonia and stretched along Russia's western and southern borders from the Baltic Sea to the Don River. After the collapse of the Central Powers the Bolsheviks began advancing into these areas. Consequently the Entente included two clauses in the Armistice Convention of 11 November 1918 requiring Germany to maintain its forces in the east temporarily to prevent the Bolsheviks from occupying those territories. The Entente wished to establish some political order there prior to the German withdrawal, but gradually, by means of various agreements with local authorities, the German troops succeeded in withdrawing sooner than expected into East Prussia. By February 1919 the German Army had left most of Ukraine, Belarus, and Lithuania; some troops remained in Latvia until the beginning of July. As the Germans retreated, Bolshevik and Polish forces advanced into the evacuated territories from opposite directions.

Although Lithuania and Belarus had proclaimed national independence on 11 December 1917 and 25 March 1918 respectively, the Bolsheviks launched their offensive against both countries on 17 November 1918. On 10 December 1918 Minsk, the capital of Belarus, was occupied, and on 1 January 1919 the Belarusian Socialist Soviet Republic was proclaimed. Soon after, on 5 January, the Bolsheviks occupied eastern Lithuania, including Vilnius, and the Lithuanian government was forced to evacuate to Kaunas. In Vilnius the Soviet Republic of Lithuania was proclaimed on 16 January, and on 27 February both of the new Soviet republics were merged into the Socialist Soviet Republic of Lithuania and Belarus.

The Bolshevik occupation of these countries, and especially Vilnius, challenged Poland and Piłsudski, who had his own design on them. Piłsudski understood that Soviet Russia, just as tsarist Russia, was essentially imperialistic. The tsars had called their actions "the gathering up of Russian lands," whereas Soviet Russia disguised its aims behind the slogan of workers' solidarity. A Polish writer pointed out that "Piłsudski was aware that he was combating not this or other social system, but a Russia that had changed its colors in revolutionary fashion. Therefore he did not agree to wait for the verdict of international authorities, who considered Bolshevism a transitory phenomenon and did not wish to weaken the Russia of Denikin and Wrangel, but decided [instead] to solve the eternal conflict between Poland and Russia through direct combat."[2] Piłsudski hoped to be able to drive the Bolsheviks back to Russian's ethnic frontiers and to support, under Poland's hegemony, a bloc of independent states from the Baltic to the Black Sea.[3] The Poles and Bolsheviks first clashed in mid-February 1919 at Bereza Kartuzka, some sixty miles northeast of Brest-Litovsk. The conflict was confined for some time to small border skirmishes while each side sought to strengthen its forces and positions. Gradually Piłsudski became alarmed by the Entente's support for the White forces and by the activities of the Russian émigrés in Paris, who were trying to win Entente support for Russian claims to Western Ukraine. On 9 April 1919 those émigrés organized a Russian Political Conference in Paris, and on 10 May the conference submitted a memorandum to the president of the Peace Conference. While the UHA was fighting against the Polish invasion, Russian émigrés were claiming that the population of Eastern Galicia belonged to the "Russian family": "In Eastern Galicia, the Russians have a powerful majority in almost all regions, with very few exceptions. Moreover, Lemkovtchina [the Lemko region], which is part of Western Galicia, has in certain cantons a purely Russian character."[4] Thus this territory, they claimed, should belong to the future non-Bolshevik Russia, and they proposed that the Buh (Bug) River be the eastern border of Poland. This proposed border came to be known as the Curzon Line, after Lord George Curzon's note to Soviet Russia of 11 July 1920.

To counteract the Russians, Piłsudski decided to present the Supreme Council with a fait accompli by preparing for a mid-April offensive in the northeast against the Bolsheviks. Prime Minister Paderewski advised against such a move, expecting strong opposition from the Entente, who were still morally committed to their former Russian ally. "He believed that if he could win the support of America through President Wilson, who then exercised a considerable influence on European thinking, the whole affair could take a different turn, and one could obtain agreement for the setting up of the United States of Eastern Europe."[5] Piłsudski, however, believed that the only solution was a military one. Prior to the Polish offensive against the Bolsheviks, he dispatched a confidential mission to the Lithuanian government in Kaunas to solicit a joint military operation and occupation of Vilnius, but the Lithuanian government rejected his proposition. Simultaneously Piłsudski made preparations for a civil administration of the eastern territories that were to be occupied. This administration was to be composed of Polish refugees from the Vilnius region living in Warsaw. While the Ukrainian-Polish War in Galicia was still raging, Piłsudski concentrated troops in the Vilnius region. Under the command of Gens. Stanisław Szeptycki and Zygmunt Lasocki they secretly infiltrated the Bolshevik lines and, on 19 April 1919, attacked the enemy in Vilnius. After three days of fighting, on 21 April, they occupied the city and the surrounding area. Later they repulsed the Bolshevik counteroffensive to recapture Vilnius. On 22 April Piłsudski proclaimed to the Lithuanian population: "I wish to give you the opportunity to solve your internal, national, and religious problems according to your own desires, without any kind of violence or pressure from Poland."[6] The civil authorities would facilitate the manifestation of those desires through representatives chosen by an equal, secret, universal, and direct vote.

Although Piłsudski's proclamation created a favorable impression on Entente statesmen, the Lithuanians denounced the Poles as invaders, and their government in Kaunas demanded that Vilnius, the capital of the former Grand Duchy of Lithuania, should belong to the new Lithuanian state. An article published in a Vilnius newspaper stated that

> We know that imperialism has a firm, solid ground in Poland, that it is an expression of the vital needs of certain social groups.... How can we be certain that these tendencies would disappear at the touch of a magic wand? If such tendencies could be removed by means of proclamations issued by commanders in chief and heads of state, then we could agree. Unfortunately we know that *"nec Hercules contra plures."* What are lofty words worth when measured against the tangible, material facts of everyday life?[7]

When the Lithuanians rejected union with Poland and Polish-Lithuanian direct negotiations failed, the Supreme Council, on 18 June 1919, proposed a demarcation line between "Kaunas" and "Vilnius" Lithuania along the main railway route linking Hrodna, Vilnius, and Daugavpils. This line, however, was ignored in practice by the Poles. According to Georges Clemenceau, "The Poles had made an advance in Lithuania in defiance of the orders of the Conference. He thought that Marshal Foch should be requested, on behalf of the Council, to order the Poles to withdraw."[8] Consequently, on 26 July 1919, the council adopted a new line recommended by Foch's staff (the Foch Line).

The Polish victory in Vilnius encouraged Piłsudski to plan a new anti-Bolshevik campaign. But first he had to concentrate most of his forces against the UHA in Galicia and Volynia to end the Ukrainian-Polish War. In mid-July 1919, after heavy fighting, the Polish forces, strengthened by Haller's Army that had arrived from France, forced the UHA to retreat into the territory of the UNR. This victory over the UHA, the arrival of Haller's Army, and the signing of the Peace Treaty of Versailles by Germany, which removed the threat of conflict on Poland's western border, strengthened Piłsudski and freed him to renew the anti-Bolshevik campaign in the northeast.

Piłsudski decided to present Soviet Russia with a fait accompli by driving the Red Army out of Lithuania and Belarus. In July he launched his offensive. The main attack, under Gen. Szeptycki, was in the direction of Maladzechna,

Minsk, and Polatsk in Belarus, along the railroad lines. After heavy fighting, Bolshevik resistance was broken, and the Polish troops occupied Maladzechna and then Slutsk on 6 August and Minsk on 8 August. Occupation of those strategic places gave the Poles control of important railways and thus denied the Bolsheviks the means of bringing in reinforcements. Polish troops then advanced toward the Biarezina River, and by the end of August they occupied the city of Barysau and the fortress of Babruisk. Meeting weak Bolshevik resistance, they advanced northward toward Polatsk and Daugavpils.

The Polish successes in the north affected the front to the south, and the Volynian-Galician front under Gen. Wacław Iwaszkiewicz was divided in August 1919 into the Volynian front, commanded by Gen. Antoni Listowski, and the Eastern Galician front, which remained under Iwaszkiewicz. During the Bolshevik offensive in Right-Bank Ukraine, Red Army units there clashed with the Polish troops in Polissia and Volynia until the UNR troops drove the Bolsheviks out of the Right Bank. To concentrate on its war against the Bolshevik and anti-Bolshevik Russian forces, the command of the UNR Army signed an armistice with the Poles on 1 September 1919, thus formally ending the Ukrainian-Polish military conflict. As a result of successful military operations, the Polish front line was stabilized in mid-October and a strategic line was established in the north along the Dvina River near Daugavpils to Polatsk, then south along the Biarezina River to Babruisk, and along the rivers Ptsich, Ubort, Sluch, and Zbruch to the Dniester.[9]

The Polish penetration into Belarus and eastern Lithuania in the summer and autumn of 1919 was relatively easy because of weak Soviet resistance. During the second half of 1919 the Bolsheviks were in a critical situation: they were confronted by the anti-Bolshevik forces of Gen. Nikolai Iudenich in the northwest, Adm. Aleksandr Kolchak in the east, and Gen. Denikin in the southeast (Left-Bank Ukraine), as well as the united Ukrainian Galician and UNR armies in the southwest (Right-Bank Ukraine). The advance of those various forces was aided by the uprisings of various Ukrainian partisans, especially Nestor Makhno, in the Bolshevik rear. In light of these developments, the Bolshevik leaders concentrated the bulk of their forces against their main enemies, and Soviet Russia assumed a defensive policy toward Poland and the Baltic states. Consequently Poland became a sort of arbitrator in the struggle among Soviet Russia, the anti-Bolshevik Russian forces, and the UNR.

While fighting the Red Army in the northeast, Piłsudski could not ignore the VA. Denikin's successes against the Bolsheviks and the Ukrainians and his advance toward Moscow constituted a serious threat also to Poland. Piłsudski worried that if Denikin won the war, he would deny de jure recognition of Polish independence. According to Sir Horace Rumbold,

Piłsudski was "uncertain whether General Denikin, when once he has established himself at Moscow and overthrown the Bolshevists, will develop reactionary tendencies. Such tendencies could not fail unfavorably to affect this country."[10] Bohdan Kutyłowski, a Polish envoy to the UNR government, expressed the same concern about Denikin's policy toward Poland: "They [Russians] dream about the inclusion of Poland in the Russian state, and reluctantly agree with [Poland's] political independence. They are moved while drinking to comment about how Warsaw threw flowers at the Russian soldiers, how the Polish people hospitably carried them on their shoulders. They would like to return to this Warsaw and the Vistula Land, as they still call Poland."[11]

To acquaint himself better with Denikin's intentions toward Poland, on 26 September 1919 Piłsudski dispatched a military mission headed by Gen. Aleksander Karnicki, a former Russian officer, to Denikin's headquarters in Tahanrih. Soon after an economic mission under Jerzy Iwanowski joined Karnicki's Mission. It was imperative for Poland to maintain contact with Denikin because he enjoyed Entente Support. Piłsudski also wanted to obtain Denikin's guarantee of Poland's independence and to find out the actual strength and future potential of Denikin's army. Although Karnicki's mission received a cordial and ceremonial welcome, its achievements were minimal. During his meetings with Denikin to discuss the future of Polish-Russian relations, Denikin recognized the existence of the Polish state in principle, but left the settlement of its borders to the decision of the future Russian Constituent Assembly. Kolchak manifested the same attitude:

> Considering the creation of a unified Polish State to be one of the chief of the normal and just consequences of the world war, the government thinks itself justified in confirming the independence of Poland, proclaimed by the Provisional Russian Government of 1917, all the pledges and decrees of which we have accepted. The final solution of the question of delimiting the frontiers between Russia and Poland must, however, in conformity with the principles set for the above, be postponed till the meeting of the Constituent Assembly.[12]

Denikin viewed the future of the Baltic nations, Belarus, and Ukraine as Russian domestic problems, from the perspective of "One and Indivisible Russia." Karnicki reported that despite Denikin's successes, which resulted mainly from his army's technical superiority and supply of military equipment by the Entente, the VA had no great value. The soldiers were undisciplined and demoralized and would fight only if allowed to plunder the civilian population. Their behavior was unequivocally justified by one of their commanders, Gen. Vladimir Mai-Maevskii, in a conversation with Gen. Peter Wrangel:

"You see, in wartime you must leave no stone unturned and neglect no means by which you may achieve your ends. If you insist on the officers and men living like ascetics, they will not fight much longer." I was highly indignant. "Well, then, General," he said, "what is the whole difference between the Bolsheviks and ourselves?" He answered his own question without pausing, and he thought his answer irrefutable. "Is not the whole difference simply that the Bolsheviks have not scrupled about their means, and therefore have gained the upper hand?"[13]

Denikin attached great value to Polish armed assistance against the Bolsheviks because it would make his advance on Moscow considerably easier. But he was not willing to make any territorial concession to Poland or other nationalities and wanted to see the Polish state confined to the borders of former Congress Poland. Karnicki saw no possibility of obtaining a positive answer from Denikin concerning Poland and did not insist on one, because he became convinced that Denikin would not succeed in winning the war. As a result of Karnicki's mission, Piłsudski saw no reason for meeting any of Denikin's wishes. He was convinced that a White victory and subsequent reestablishment of a reactionary Russia would be more dangerous to Poland than the Bolsheviks. Consequently Poland's relations with Denikin lost their importance.[14]

Unlike Denikin, the Soviet Council of People's Commissars, on 29 August 1918, issued a decree stating that "All agreements and acts ... referring to the partitions of Poland are irrevocably annulled ... since they are contrary to the principle of self-determination of peoples."[15] Although this declaration was not sincere, it was effective propaganda, and it influenced Piłsudski to choose to assist the Bolsheviks to defeat Denikin not by military action, but by inaction. To weaken Denikin, he ordered Polish troops to cease their operations against the Red Army. A Bolshevik general, Nikolai Kakurin, later wrote that "A Polish attack at the time of Denikin's greatest success might have given him Moscow. But the reestablishment of a reactionary Russia constituted a danger to Poland. For even if Denikin had submitted to the will of the Allies to maintain a separate Poland, he would never have parted with Ukraine, or Lithuania, or Belarus, on all of which Piłsudski had designs."[16] The Polish minister of foreign affairs, Aleksander Skrzyński, confirmed this hypothesis: "Undoubtedly Denikin would have received with great gratitude the help of the Poles, but only on the understanding, scarcely concealed, that such help was forthcoming from the Poles as faithful subjects of Russia."[17]

Piłsudski did not wish for a quick defeat of Denikin, but rather for a prolonged war between the Whites and the Reds that would weaken both of them and give Poland time to strengthen its own forces for any future war.

According to Gen. Tadeusz Kutrzeba, it was clear to Piłsudski that the lesser of the two Russian evils was Denikin's defeat. A Polish war against the Bolsheviks with Denikin as their ally would be a war about Russia; while a war against the Bolsheviks without Denikin would be a war about Poland. In Piłsudski's judgment, even if Denikin submitted to the Entente and agreed to an independent Poland, he would not accept extending the Polish border beyond the Buh.[18] A Soviet historian described the deceptive Polish "Russian" strategy thus:

> In the fall of 1919, when the condition of Soviet Russia was particularly difficult, the White Poles, although they did not move all of their forces against us and did not join the alliance with Denikin, at the same time did not cease the war and [thus] achieved the highest military successes. At that time the RSFSR proposed peace on very advantageous conditions for them. But on the order of the Entente, Moscow's proposition was left unanswered.[19]

Piłsudski began negotiating with the Bolsheviks and dispatched a Polish Red Cross Mission headed by Michał Stanisław Kossakowski to meet with a Russian Red Cross Mission headed by Julian Marchlewski. On 11 October 1919 the missions met near Lutsk in Volynia to discuss an exchange of Polish and Soviet Russian prisoners of war and hostages. Their prolonged talks were clouded by distrust. Kossakowski suspected that the Bolsheviks' declared peaceful intentions toward Poland were not sincere because they were motivated by temporary domestic difficulties and civil war, while Marchlewski believed that Piłsudski had an agreement with Denikin and was carrying out the wishes of the Entente. Marchlewski felt that exchanging hostages was a small matter that could be solved in a few days, and he had been given diplomatic responsibilities by Lenin that went beyond the exchange of prisoners. Kossakowski, however, had no authority to conduct political negotiations.

More serious talks began on 16 October. On 5 November Piłsudski's confidant and spokesman, Capt. Ignacy Boerner, conveyed through Marchlewski Piłsudski's proposals to Lenin: Polish troops would refrain from advancing against the Red Army if a neutral zone ten kilometers wide was established, if Soviet Russia returned Daugavpils to Latvia and stopped the disseminating of Communist propaganda within the Polish Army, and if the Red Army stopped attacking the UNR. As soon as Lenin agreed to the proposals, Piłsudski would send a delegation to Moscow. On 23 November Marchlewski returned from Moscow with the reply that Lenin had accepted, with certain changes, some of Piłsudski's demands. He agreed to stop the Red Army advance against the Poles, to establish a neutral zone, and to refrain from disseminating propaganda among the Polish troops. Regarding Daugavpils, he pointed out that negotiations with Latvia were under way. As for the Ukrainian question, he explained that representatives of the Soviet Russian and UNR governments were negotiating, but insisted that Ukraine should not be an object of concern in the negotiations between Soviet Russia and Poland.

Piłsudski concluded that Lenin would not accept his conditions and that his political plans in Eastern Europe would have to be carried out by military means. Still the negotiations, which ended in November with no result other than the exchange of a few hundred prisoners and hostages, did postpone the war between Poland and Soviet Russia and thus gave the Bolsheviks enough time to defeat Denikin.[20]

Toward the end of 1919 Piłsudski abandoned all negotiations with the Bolsheviks and began preparing for military action. The Bolshevik leaders anticipated this new Polish offensive. According to Lenin, "Now we must make peace.... we shall play for time and use it to strengthen our army."[21] Consequently, on 22 December Georgii Chicherin, the commissar for foreign affairs, proposed peace by negotiations and declared the "firm wish of the Soviet Government to end all its conflicts with Poland" and that the "Soviet Government is convinced that all differences between them can be removed by a friendly agreement."[22] The Poles left this vague proposal unanswered, but in January 1920 two Polish divisions, commanded by Gen. Edward Rydz-Śmigły, and Latvian troops undertook a joint campaign against the Bolsheviks, and they captured Daugavpils on 3 January. Fearing that the Poles would continue their advance, the Bolsheviks sought to outmaneuver Poland politically by sending diplomatic notes proposing peace negotiations and disseminating revolutionary appeals to both the Polish government and the people. On 28 January the Soviet Russian government dispatched a peace proposal signed by Lenin, Chicherin, and Trotsky. It assured Poland that Soviet Russia "unconditionally recognizes the independence and sovereignty of the Polish Republic; that it entertained no aggressive intentions; that the Red Army would not advance beyond the then existing line; and that the Soviet State had not concluded agreements with Germany or any other Power aimed directly or obliquely against Poland."[23]

The Soviet government asserted that basic problems, including territorial and economic ones, could be settled peacefully. In response Stanisław Patek, the Polish minister of foreign affairs, informed Chicherin that the proposal was being considered. Meantime, Polish authorities sounded out the Entente governments' opinions and their willingness to cooperate with Poland by communicating to them the preliminary Polish conditions for peace:

a. Annulment of the crime of the partitions of Poland in which Russia participated;
b. Recognition of the States established after the fall of the former Russian empire which have governments de facto;
c. Restitution of state property comprised within the Polish frontiers of 1772;
d. Participation of Poland in the distribution of the gold reserves of the Russian State Bank, based on the balance of the 5th of August, 1914, and restitution of archives and libraries;
e. Ratification of the treaty by Russia;
f. Poland will decide the status of the territories situated to the west of the 1772 frontier, in accordance with the wishes of the population, to be expressed through a plebiscite.[24]

The Entente's reaction was rather unfavorable and contradictory. Although the French basically agreed with the Polish view, they suspected that Poland was pursuing a policy of expansion. The British advised the Poles to make peace with the Bolsheviks, but left it up to the Poles to come to an arrangement with Soviet Russia. Sir Horace Rumbold reported to his minister of foreign affairs, Lord Curzon, on 19 January that "Whilst it is right that the Poles should keep the Allied Governments informed, through the Allied representatives here, of their decision with regard to the Bolshevists' peace offer, it seems to me that the Poles wish to throw too much responsibility on the Allies in this matter, which, I think, ought to be determined principally by Poland's own interests."[25] The United States was reluctant to advise the Poles one way or the other.

Apparently Piłsudski was willing to make peace with Soviet Russia on the condition that the Entente Powers would participate. Otherwise he favored an armed conflict and taking advantage of the temporary Bolshevik weakness. Piłsudski believed that lasting peace could be achieved only after a military victory. In view of the contradictory advice coming from the Entente Powers, however, he tried to negotiate peace with the Bolsheviks. On 27 March Patek informed Chicherin that the Polish government would agree to begin negotiations on 10 April at Barysau in Belarus, near the front line, and offered a ceasefire in the area of Barysau for the duration. On 28 March Chicherin proposed Petrograd, Moscow, Warsaw, or towns in Estonia for the meeting, but Patek insisted on Barysau. In response Chicherin asked for an immediate suspension of hostilities along the entire front, which was about a thousand kilometers long. Patek, in turn, rejected Chicherin's counterproposal, insisting instead on his own previous proposal. On 8 April Chicherin tried to put

Poland in the wrong by sending a message to the Entente about the Soviet proposal in the hope that they would put pressure on Poland to make peace. From then on correspondence between Patek and Chicherin deteriorated into a meaningless dispute over whether Barysau was or was not a suitable place for negotiations. Each side blamed the other for the failure of the proposed negotiations. The Bolsheviks were opposed to Barysau for the same reasons that the Poles insisted upon it. The town was a railway junction on the main line from Moscow to Smolensk and Orsha, by which the Bolsheviks transported troops to the front. For the Poles negotiations there would prevent the movement of Bolshevik reinforcements.

Piłsudski was now convinced more than ever that the Bolshevik proposal was not sincere. Polish intelligence had disclosed that already by the end of 1919 the Bolsheviks were concentrating forces in Belarus and Ukraine. From the beginning of January to the end of April 1920, Bolshevik forces on the Soviet western front increased from four divisions and one infantry brigade to twenty and five respectively.[26] This increase was justified by Lenin because of continuing tensions. On 27 February he warned the War Council that "All the indications are that Poland will present us with absolutely impossible, even insolent conditions. It is essential that all our attention be turned to strengthening the Western Front. I consider it imperative that exceptional measures be taken to effect a lightning transfer of whatever [forces] we can from Siberia and the Urals to the west.... It is necessary to issue the slogan, 'prepare for war against Poland.'"[27]

Piłsudski was sure that the Bolsheviks were preparing a war against Poland, but that first they needed to consolidate their power in Ukraine and to defeat the Whites. In an interview given on 16 March to *Le petit parisien*, he stated: "I am convinced that Soviet Russia will attempt to attack Poland. Regardless of what government it will have, Russia is a sworn imperialist. It [imperialism] is in fact the principal feature of its political character. Its attack on Poland depends first of all on the Ukrainian question. If the problem of Ukraine would be settled to its advantage, then it would advance on Poland."[28] By the end of 1919 Piłsudski was confident of Poland's military power. On 13 November, in a discussion with the deputy commissioner-general of the Eastern Territory, Michał Stanisław Kossowski, he stated: "We can say simultaneously to both the Bolsheviks and Denikin: 'we are a power, and you are corpses.'... I am not afraid of Russia. If I wish, I can go even to Moscow now, and nobody would be able to oppose me; however, it is necessary to know clearly what we want and what we are striving for."[29] Piłsudski's confidence in Poland's power and political possibilities encouraged him to pursue a more active East European policy. Poland could either fight alone against a numerically superior enemy or seek allies among its newly independent neighbors. In Piłsudski's opinion Poland needed an ally, and Ukraine was the logical choice. The outcome of his plans for Eastern Europe was largely dependent on the success or failure of a Polish-Ukrainian alliance.

CHAPTER 9

Ukrainian-Polish Relations in Right-Bank Ukraine

The Polish-Ukrainian campaign against the Bolsheviks in 1920 can best be understood by exploring the complex socioeconomic relations between the Poles and Ukrainians in Right-Bank Ukraine, that is, the former gubernias of Kyiv, Podillia, and Volynia. The size of this area was 144,736 square versts.* According to the Russian census of 1897, it had a population of 9,577,010; by 1909 the population had increased to 11,191,496. The biggest social problem there was the question of land ownership. The economy of Right-Bank Ukraine was largely agrarian and was dominated by large estates, a sizable percentage of which were owned by magnates of Polish or Polonized Ukrainian descent. Before the 1917 Revolution those landowners possessed great power and privilege and were hence, by and large, loyal to the tsarist regime. Some Poles were also engaged in industry, especially in agricultural-based commercial and household milling, sugar refining, distilling, brewing, paper making, glassworks, and tobacco processing. Some also served as administrators in industry and government.

Although the number of Poles in Right-Bank Ukraine was small, their importance in economic and political life was disproportionately high. Their number and social structure is difficult to ascertain. Estimates are based on the 1897 census and on Polish private and church records. Polish sources treat all Roman Catholics in Right-Bank Ukraine as Poles, though there is evidence that a segment of them were Ukrainians. In 1897 the number of Poles in Right-Bank Ukraine was about 875,344, or between six and seven percent of the population; according to Russian official statistics in 1909, the number of Poles had fallen to 424,552, or 3.8 percent. The 1897 census indicates that 46.8 percent of the region's Roman Catholics were landowners; 16.2 percent were industrialists; 15.2 percent were professionals; 7.9 percent were workers; 3.9 percent were officials; 2.2 percent were tradesmen; and 7.3 percent were in other occupations.

After the outbreak of the revolution in 1917, the number of Poles in

---

* A verst is 1,067 metres.

Ukraine substantially increased as a result of the release of Polish prisoners of war by the Central Powers, the desertions of Poles from the Russian army, the return of Polish exiles from Siberia, and the release of inmates of Russian prisons. As early as the mid-summer of 1917, Piłsudski gave instructions to Polish agents to go to Russia and Ukraine to pull out as many Poles as possible from the Russian army and to gather them close to the Polish border. According to one eyewitness, "Hundreds of thousands of Poles found themselves in the territory of Russia.... They were officers and soldiers recruited to the tsarist army during the first year of the war, [or] condemned men and deportees liberated from prisons or from distant areas of Siberia after the fall of the tsarist regime."[1] Most of these Poles stayed in Ukraine until German troops left occupied Poland in 1919.[2]

Although antagonism between the landlords and peasants had existed before the revolution, mainly because of landlord opposition to the land reforms, after the outbreak of the revolution the conflict between them greatly increased when demoralized, retreating Russian troops passing through the villages plundered the estates and stirred up the peasants. One observer remarked that she "knew only that the defeated and insurgent Russian army, which had been scattered already for several months, plundered and burned estates and murdered landlords. Although the peasants joined those gangs of robbers, the leaders were the agitators and politicized soldiers."[3]

The magnitude of the destruction committed by the retreating Russian troops can be seen in official reports. Before the revolution such activity was promoted by a peculiar interpretation of the Regulation on Field Management of Troops:

> Mass arrests and deportations of aliens and criminal devastations of places by retreating troops aroused not only hatred, but also contempt within the western borderlands. The Minister of Justice, A. A. Khvostov, at a meeting on 2 September 1915, declared that the Council of Ministers had pointed several times to the terrible consequences of the system of devastation of places left behind by our troops. "People are driven out with whips, so it is hard to speak about spontaneity." To this Minister Aleksandr V. Krivoshein added: "General Nikolai N. Ianushkevich, in conversation with me concerning the refugees, told me straight-out that the war is conducted by fire and sword, and consequently let suffer those who are caught on the way."[4]

During the revolution the situation deteriorated. The destruction by troops was revealed at a convention of gubernial and county commissioners from the gubernias of Kyiv, Chernihiv, Poltava, Volynia, and Podillia held on 16–17 October 1917. The worst conditions existed in the gubernias adjacent to the front, Volynia and Podillia. According to Andrii Viazlov, the commissioner of Volynia, "On 10 October the soldiers carried out a 'pogrom' in the city of Ostrih; they also destroyed the town of Polonne. Throughout the gubernia, mass law-breaking has occurred on agrarian and forest soil." Karnachev, the commissioner of Liatychiv county in Podillia gubernia, reported that "the passing of the troops through the gubernia is equal to the Tatar invasion. In these counties everything was destroyed ... newly sown crops, domestic animals and poultry, ponds were drained, and settlements destroyed. The soldiers raped women."[5]

Later, in 1918, during the Bolsheviks' invasion and their subsequent retreat, the conflict between the landlords and the peasants intensified.[6] In places where the landlords had been honest and friendly to the peasants before the revolution, however, the peasants defended them against the demoralized Russian troops and later against Bolshevik agitators. According to a Polish witness from the village of Vinnykivtsi in Lityn county, Podillia gubernia, peasants defended his manor against Russian troops. He testified that "The peasants stood at close-range around the manor, [thereby] preventing the soldiers from entering the interior, and begged them not to destroy the property that he [the landlord] had left for them."[7] A similar event took place in the village of Mokra in Balta county. The daughter of a landlord recalls that "At the beginning we judged that, thanks to good relations of the manor with the village, there was no reason for fear. On one rainy evening, however, the coachman, Maksym, came running with a warning: a Bolshevik agitator was inciting peasants to [conduct] a 'pogrom.' The peasants resisted, [saying] the master is good, why kill him? The master's father was also good, and good is the master's wife. 'But there is a [six-year-old] son' insisted the agitator, 'who knows how he will be? It is necessary to kill the son.'"[8] Bolshevik agitation failed, however, to persuade the peasants.

Instability in Ukraine, peasant-landlord conflicts during the revolutionary period, and the friendly attitude of the Ukrainian government created favorable conditions for the organization of foreign military formations in Ukraine for the purpose of establishing national independence in their respective countries. At the end of 1917 the Central Rada permitted the Czechs and Slovaks to organize military units and gave them financial and material support. Later the government also gave similar support to the Poles, Armenians, Georgians, Siberians, Tatars, and Belarusians in Ukraine. The strongest military formations organized were the Polish. They remained in Ukraine while Poland was occupied by Austro-German troops almost to the end of 1918. The largest formations created in Ukraine were the Polish Second and Third Corps. The Second Corps was commanded by Gen. Jan Stankiewicz and consisted of former soldiers of the Russian Ninth Army who had served at the Romanian front. After it was reinforced by the Second Brigade commanded by Col. Józef Haller, which had crossed over from the Austrian front in Bukovyna to Right-Bank Ukraine in mid-February 1918, this corps had about 8,000 men and 6,500 horses. The Third Corps was commanded by Gen. Eugeniusz Michaelis de Henning and had 2,200 men, some of them in units stationed in other cities than the main command.[9] Another strong Polish unit that operated for a while in Ukraine was the Fourth Division. Consisting of 4,000 men commanded by Gen. Lucjan Żeligowski, it was organized in the Kuban under the auspices of the VA. In March 1919 it was transferred to southern Ukraine, where it joined the French and VA forces fighting against the UNR Army and, later, the Ukrainian partisans of Otaman Nykyfor Hryhor'ïv. A number of smaller Polish military detachments were also organized and operated in Ukraine.

The vicissitudes of the revolution and socioeconomic conditions in Right-Bank Ukraine facilitated conflict. Some of the Polish units violated Ukrainian hospitality by interfering in Ukrainian internal affairs and by fighting, especially against the peasants. The situation became more serious when the landlords began seeking support from the Polish detachments located in their areas against the peasants. Although the process of liquidating large estates in the former Russian Empire was taking place, in some areas in Right-Bank Ukraine the previous status of holdings was artificially maintained with the assistance of Polish armed detachments. In reference to this situation, a Polish writer remarked: "I felt pity and distaste for those soldiers who made a parody of the idea of the great Polish army [by] resurrecting the sad tradition of the private armies of the frontier 'kinglets.'"[10] The situation deteriorated further when some Polish magnates began organizing their own armed detachments consisting of their own sons and officials, or strengthened other existing military units. In their midst certain Poles spoke out against the organization of Polish military formations in Ukraine as being wrongheaded: "The Polish democratic group in Vinnytsia, headed by Stanislaw Stempowski, was ill-disposed to the idea of forming a Polish army in Ukraine [for it] assumed the role of Polish units de facto would lead to the guarding of estates and a struggle against the peasants. [Consequently] it would contribute only to deepening the animosity of the Ukrainian people toward the Polish people."[11]

The Polish units not only defended the estates of the magnates; to support their own existence, they also requisitioned food and horses from the Ukrainian population. When the latter began defending themselves against the requisitions, the Polish detachments undertook punitive expeditions into the countryside. Their destruction of peasant property and severe punishments, including executions, led to further conflict not only with the population, but also with the Ukrainian authorities, who had not sanctioned the requisitions.[12] On 16 March 1918 Col. von Rummel, the commander of a battery of the Third Corps stationed at Stara Syniava in Lityn county, dispatched an armed detachment to three villages to requisition seventy horses. In the evening, on its way back, the unit was fired upon from all sides by a group of peasants, who wanted to frighten the horses and scatter them in the hope that they would return to their homes. In the crossfire three soldiers were killed and three were wounded. In response von Rummel dispatched three punitive detachments, which killed or wounded forty to fifty people and burned one village and part of another.[13] At a dinner a Polish writer observed a group of officers who had taken part in the expedition:

> A topic of conversation was a story told by several officers who had just returned from a punitive expedition to a neighboring village [whose inhabitants] that had made an incursion onto one of the estates belonging to [Count] Potocki. With cheerful laughter, they recited how they captured the village, murdered peasants, and burned houses. Soon I realized that this company consisted predominantly of officers from among the circles of neighboring squires, who waged war with delight against the peasants to avenge the ruin and burning of their estates.[14]

This was not an isolated occurrence. Similar incidents in other places manifested the widespread abuse of Ukrainian hospitality by Polish troops. One Polish detachment, the Irregular Light-Cavalry Squadron, was commanded by Feliks Jaworski, a landowner from Tsyhanivka, Kamianets-Podilskyi county, who loved war for its own sake. The majority of his officers were squires from the same county who were adventurers like their commander. The squadron was organized in July 1917 and was initially stationed in Proskuriv (now Khmelnytskyi) and loosely connected with the Russian Fifth Army. Later it moved to Antoniny in Zaslav county and encamped at the estate of the Polish magnate József Potocki. There the detachment became independent of any higher authority. Jaworski fought fiercely against Ukrainian peasants to defend Potocki's countless estates. He terrorized the population to the end of February 1918. On 24 January 1918 one of his soldiers was shot in Rosolivtsi, a large village in Starokostiantyniv county outside his jurisdiction. In response Jaworski dispatched a punitive expedition to the village headed by an officer called Naruszewicz.[15] According to an eyewitness account, Naruszewicz ordered his irregulars to "'Let the Catholics alone, and do what you like to the others.' The gathering darkness was soon lit up by the fire of burning thatch. Rosolovtse flamed like a great torch, amidst the savage howls of fighting peasants and soldiers, the din of shots, the moaning of cattle and the lamentations of women. When the tardy January dawn stole upon the world, where cottages had been were burning ruins, over which towered skeletons of chimneys shooting up acrid smoke."[16]

Because of many such tragedies, on 30 March 1918 the UNR minister of defense issued an order prohibiting arbitrary requisitions:

> Already many times, information has been received concerning great damage to the people of the UNR caused by Polish troops. Therefore, for the future I order gubernial and county commanders and also county military heads to apply strictly the following ...
> 1. The Polish army has no right to interfere in the internal affairs of the Republic and cannot issue any decrees in this regard;
> 2. All arbitrary requisitions carried out by this army—of forage, grain, and all other products—must be immediately stopped, because this can be carried out only with the agreement and permission of the Ukrainian government;
> 3. There can be no sharing by Polish and Ukrainian detachments of arms or any other military property confiscated from inhabitants of the Ukrainian People's Republic.[17]

Because the government did not have adequate administrative power in the distant gubernias, however, the population there was largely responsible for their own defense. In light of their experiences with the Poles, the Ukrainians had little reason to believe that Polish attitudes toward Ukraine would improve in the future.

Because of pressure by the VA, a disastrous typhus epidemic, and a lack of ammunition and equipment, the UNR forces could no longer fight a regular war. They therefore decided to continue the struggle temporarily in the form of guerilla warfare. Faced with the VA's imminent occupation of Kamianets-Podilskyi—the temporary seat of the UNR government—and Podillia, Petliura turned to Piłsudski "with the request to order the occupation by Polish troops of those places being evacuated by the Ukrainian troops."[18] On 16–17 November 1919 the Polish Seventh Division occupied Kamianets-Podilskyi. From the first day there Polish troops behaved as an occupational force. They immediately began requisitioning state and private properties from warehouses, trains, grocery shops, hospitals, mills, factories, schools, state institutions, and other places. Many goods, including grain, sugar, leather, cloth, telephone apparatus, and medical supplies, were transported to Poland without permission from the Ukrainian authorities, and no receipts were given. The troops also destroyed libraries, bookstores, and even the portraits of prominent Ukrainians in schools and homes. Simultaneously the Poles took the entire administration of the area into their own hands. In Kamianets-

Podilskyi all Ukrainian signs were ordered to be repainted in Polish, and the Ukrainian flag was replaced by the Polish flag.

The Poles also launched searches and arrests of prominent Ukrainians, especially those from Galicia. The Polish commissioner-general, Antoni Minkiewicz, ordered the house arrest of the UNR ministers still in Kamianets-Podilskyi—Iosyf Bezpal'ko, Andrii Livyts'kyi, Ivan Ohiienko, and Prime Minister Isaak Mazepa.[19] Furthermore, on 9 January 1920 a Polish troop commander, Capt. Ocetkiewicz, issued a proclamation stating that the city, "the ancient frontier fortress, after many years of captivity, oppression, and humiliation, has returned to its former motherland [Poland]."[20] Although this proclamation was rescinded after the Ukrainian authorities issued a strong protest, it seriously disturbed the population of Podillia. According to Prime Minister Mazepa, "On my way to Kamianets I had the opportunity to observe that the Poles behaved as an occupying force on our territory. After arriving in Kamianets my conviction was only strengthened. Ohiienko informed me about the situation in Kamianets county. [He] stated categorically that the Polish authorities treated our people no better than the Bolsheviks."[21]

The Ukrainian authorities' appeal to the government in Warsaw regarding Polish military behavior was in vain, and the Polish troops evoked even greater indignation among the Ukrainian population. It also brought about dissatisfaction with the UNR government, which was seeking an alliance with the Poles.[22]

CHAPTER 10

The Polish-Ukrainian Offensive, the Retreat from Ukraine, and the Reorganization of the Ukrainian Army

The Polish offensive in Ukraine was not a separate campaign, but part of a larger defensive war against Soviet Russia. Piłsudski planned three stages of action to achieve victory over the Bolsheviks. First he facilitated the Bolshevik defeat of the VA, which was, in his opinion, more dangerous to Poland than the Bolsheviks. He then rejected the Bolsheviks' February 1920 peace proposal, because he believed they were playing for time to build up their military force and thus be able to negotiate from a position of strength, imposing political and military conditions that would make Poland subservient to Russia. Piłsudski's third action was the April 20 offensive in Right-Bank Ukraine aimed at defeating the Bolshevik forces concentrated there before they became strong enough to threaten Poland. These three actions led to the Bolshevik offensive in Poland and the subsequent Polish victory on the Wisła and Neman.

For Piłsudski the offensive in Right-Bank Ukraine had both strategic and political importance. The disintegration of the UNR regular front deprived Poland of an eastern buffer against both the Bolshevik and anti-Bolshevik Russian forces, and the subsequent Bolshevik victory over the VA resulted in the release of a large number of Bolshevik troops in the Don and Kuban regions; the Red Army command planned to transfer them to its western front with the intention of launching an offensive against Ukraine and Poland. Anticipating this, Piłsudski planned to strike first and defeat the Red Army before it was ready for a decisive battle. Although he considered the possibility of a Bolshevik counteraction in the north, Piłsudski chose Right-Bank Ukraine as the theater of his campaign. Kyiv was to be the campaign's focal point, because he expected to encounter a large concentration of Bolshevik forces there. By defeating the Bolsheviks Piłsudski expected to obtain suitable eastern borders for Poland and to secure its complete independence. He "reckoned that Poland must conquer its boundaries by the sword and not accept them as a present from Russia's hands."[1] Furthermore, Piłsudski wanted to cut off Soviet Russia from Ukraine's grain and mineral resources and to assist the UNR government under Petliura to reestablish its power. His policy toward Ukraine, however, was not based on what was good for Ukraine, nor was it derived from humanitarian or sentimental views. Piłsudski was convinced that any Russia, "white" or "red," was imperialistic. Therefore he wanted to have a Ukrainian buffer state that was dependent on and allied with Poland and would serve as a barrier against any invasion from Russia.

On the eve of the campaign Poland had twenty-one infantry divisions and seven cavalry brigades totaling over 600,000 men. The Polish forces advancing into Right-Bank Ukraine south from the Prypiat River were divided into three armies: the Third Army, commanded by Gen. Edward Rydz-Śmigły; the Second Army, commanded by Gen. Antoni Listowski; and the Sixth Army, commanded by Gen. Wacław Iwaszkiewicz. Two other groups also participated in the offensive. One consisted of two cavalry brigades (including six regiments) totaling about 2,000 men, under Gen. Jan Romer. The other was Col. Rybak's group consisting of one mountain brigade, one cavalry brigade, and one infantry regiment; on 26 May it merged with the Third Army. The three armies totalled nine infantry and two cavalry divisions, or 65,300 men, with 1,994 machine guns and 437 artillery guns. Two of the armies were joined by UNR divisions: the Third by the Sixth Sich Riflemen Division, and the Sixth by the Third Riflemen Division. Another UNR formation that joined the Polish troops was the Fifth Kherson Division. In addition, Gen. Mykhailo Omelianovych-Pavlenko's UNR army, which had returned from the anti-Bolshevik Winter Campaign at the beginning of May 1920, joined the offensive. The total manpower of the Ukrainian formations which had joined the Polish armies was over 14,000 men.

The Polish and Ukrainian troops faced two Bolshevik armies. The Soviet Twelfth Army (15,000 men) was commanded until 10 June by a former tsarist officer, Gen. Sergei Mezheninov, and then Gaspar Voskanov; it was composed of three divisions and three brigades deployed in Volynia (headquarters in Kyiv). The Soviet Fourteenth Army (7,000 men) was commanded by Gen. E. Uborevich, also a former tsarist officer, and was composed of four divisions and two brigades deployed in Podillia (headquarters in Zhmerynka). On the eve of the Polish-Ukrainian offensive, the total Bolshevik force consisted of over 22,000 men, 1,232 machine guns, and 236 artillery guns. The Twelfth Army was assigned the defense of the front line running along the Teteriv River and linking the towns of Lemakhiv, Radomyshl, Berdychiv, and Koziatyn. This 150-mile front was the gateway to Kyiv. The Fourteenth Army guarded the Dniester and Boh rivers.

On 25 April 1920, after the Treaty of Warsaw, the Polish Third and Second armies and the Ukrainian Sixth Sich Riflemen Division, jointly launched an offensive from Volynia, while the Polish Sixth Army and the Ukrainian Second Riflemen Division advanced from Podillia. Both groups advanced in

The Polish-Ukrainian Offensive 101

the direction of Kyiv. The stronger Third Army was instructed to deliver the main strike against the Soviet Twelfth Army, while the Sixth Army was to attack the Soviet Fourteenth Army along the Dniester and Boh in the direction of Odessa. A surprise initial tactical strike was delivered by the cavalry group of Gen. Romer at the railway junction of Koziatyn in the far rear of the Bolshevik forces.[2]

As the offensive proceeded, separate proclamations explaining its aims were issued by Piłsudski and Petliura to the population of Ukraine. On 26 April Piłsudski's proclamation stated:

> On my order the troops of the Republic of Poland advanced forward, penetrating deeply into the land of Ukraine. I want the population of this country to know that the Polish troops will remove from the territory inhabited by the Ukrainian people foreign invaders, against whom the Ukrainian people rose up in arms and defended their homes against violence, robbery, and pillage. The Polish troops will remain in Ukraine only as long as necessary to transfer authority for the country to the legitimate Ukrainian government. When the national government of the Ukrainian Republic has established state authority; when the troops of the Ukrainian nation have taken hold of its borders to protect their country against new invasion; when the free nation itself is in a position to decide its destiny, then the Polish soldiers will withdraw into the Republic of Poland.... I am convinced that the Ukrainian nation will use all its military efforts, with the aid of the Polish Republic, to achieve its freedom and to secure for the fertile soil of its homeland the happiness and prosperity that will result from work and tranquility once peace is reestablished. The troops of the Polish Republic guarantee to all people of Ukraine defense and protection, regardless of class, origin, or religion. I appeal to the Ukrainian people and all inhabitants of this land to bear patiently the hardships the difficult time of war imposes, [and] to support, within their power, the troops of the Polish Republic in their bloody struggle for their own life and freedom.[3]

The next day Petliura issued his proclamation:

> For three years, O Ukrainian people, you were struggling alone, forgotten by all peoples of the world.... The Polish people, in the person of its leader Józef Piłsudski and in the person of its government, honored the independence of your state.... The Polish Republic came forward offering real assistance to the Ukrainian People's Republic in its struggle against Russian Bolshevism, and provided the means to organize, within its borders, detachments of the Ukrainian army. This army is going to fight against the enemies

of Ukraine. Today, however, this army is not struggling alone, but together with the Polish army against the red imperialistic Bolsheviks, who are also threatening the freedom of the Polish people. The governments of Ukraine and Poland came to an agreement, and on its basis the Polish troops will enter together with Ukrainians into the territory of Ukraine as an ally against a common enemy. After a successful struggle the Polish troops will return to their own fatherland. Through the common struggle of the fraternal Ukrainian and Polish armies we will correct mistakes of the past, and by blood spilt jointly against the eternal historic enemy, Moscow, we will illuminate a new period of friendship between the Ukrainian and Polish peoples."[4]

As the Polish-Ukrainian troops combated the Bolsheviks in the west, Omelianovych-Pavlenko's army, which had been fighting the Bolsheviks in their rear, was recalled by the Ukrainian command and ordered to join forces with the other Ukrainian and Polish armies. During the six months of its successful campaign, Omelianovych-Pavlenko's army had inspired the population to resist the Bolshevik occupation. In his letter to the Central Committee, Trotsky conceded that "Petliura's troops have a proper, strong and purely military organization in their [the Bolsheviks'] rear, stronger than that of the Soviet authorities."[5] While retreating, Omelianovych-Pavlenko inflicted a serious blow to the Soviet Fourteenth Army near Rybnytsia in Bessarabia and Rudnytsia in Podillia, and a simultaneous wave of partisan uprisings paralyzed the Bolsheviks' operations and demoralized their troops. Winston Churchill confirmed that "the Ukrainians, under Petlura, have driven the Bolsheviks out of a large part of their territory, and are making an effort to establish an independent Ukraine free from Bolsheviks. Simultaneously with the Polish-Ukrainian advance, great popular risings occurred in the Ukraine against the Bolsheviks, and the liberating forces were shown every sign of welcome."[6] Trotsky admitted that the Ukrainian partisans "facilitated and accelerated the advance of the Polish troops."[7] The civilian population also welcomed the Polish troops and helped to fight the Bolsheviks. A Polish officer witnessed friendly receptions in the large village of Lytvynivka and in nearby Kyiv,[8] and another Polish officer attested that Ukrainian civilians helped the Polish troops to fight the Bolsheviks and to transport ammunition to the front.[9]

The success of the Polish-Ukrainian offensive was also, to a great extent, facilitated by UHA troops, which, because of difficult and complicated political conditions and for strategic reasons, had fought for a few months as part of the Soviet Twelfth and Fourteenth armies and were known as the Red UHA. On the eve of the offensive, the Red UHA consisted of three brigades totaling about twenty thousand men. Because of their mistreatment by the

Soviet command, the Second and Third brigades, which were part of the Fourteenth Army, turned against the Bolsheviks. The First Brigade, which was part of the Twelfth Army, later also switched sides. The breakaway of the UHA units opened up and disorganized part of the Bolshevik front and created panic among the Red Army troops. Soviet military historians admitted that

> The mutiny of the two Galician brigades totally broke the alignment of the Fourteenth Army.... Thus the mutiny of the two Galician brigades practically coincided with the beginning of the decisive advance of the Poles on the Southwestern Front; it not only reduced the already weakened forces of its Polish section, but proved totally disadvantageous for us and advantageous for the alignment of our opponent; it diverted the army and divisional reserves of the Fourteenth Army and part of the Twelfth toward carrying out tasks that had nothing in common with their primary destination.[10]

Gen. Kutrzeba wrote that "Because of these mutinies by the Ukrainian brigades, the Polish Sixth Army advanced during the offensive without great difficulties."[11]

As a result of the Polish-Ukrainian efforts, the Bolsheviks' resistance was broken and their front collapsed. A large amount of Red Army materiel was captured, including 40 artillery guns, 276 machine guns, 120 locomotives, and 3,000 freight cars; and over 11,000 prisoners of war were taken. Nonetheless, even though the Bolsheviks suffered heavy losses and were driven back, they retreated in an orderly manner toward Kyiv.[12] Now the aim of the Polish-Ukrainian offensive turned to reaching the Dnieper, taking Kyiv, and defeating the retreating Bolshevik forces.

According to Polish intelligence, the Soviet Twelfth Army had been ordered to defend resolutely the approach to Kyiv and the city itself. Even though there was no further information, especially whether the army was receiving new reserves to strengthen its defense, the Polish command decided to make "solid" preparations for attacking that army and delayed its advance on Kyiv. As a result of this voluntary delay from 27 April to 7 May, the Soviet Twelfth Army had time to retreat safely east from Kyiv. Consequently, when the commander of the Polish First Legionary Infantry Brigade dispatched a company of infantry toward Kyiv to locate the enemy, the company entered Kyiv on the afternoon of 7 May without resistance. There the company met the Polish First Light Cavalry Regiment, which had entered Kyiv that morning and also encountered no Bolshevik resistance. On 8 May the Polish Third Army and the Ukrainian Sixth Sich Riflemen Division entered Kyiv "without [firing] a shot." The bridges across the Dnieper had to be captured by force to prevent their destruction, however, and a ten-mile-deep bridgehead on the left bank of the Dnieper was established. Both actions were successfully accomplished on 9 May.

The liberation of Kyiv marked the end of the Polish-Ukrainian offensive. After that the Poles lost the initiative, and Polish and Ukrainian troops took up defensive positions from the Prypiat southward along the Dnieper, including bridgeheads on the left bank of the Dnieper east of Kyiv and Kaniv. From there the defense line swung southwest to Bila Tserkva, Skvyra, Lypovets, Kryzhopil, and Miaskivka to the Dniester at Iampil. Throughout May control of the Dnieper, mainly the eighty miles between Chornobyl and Trypillia, was hotly contested. The Soviet Twelfth Army had retreated undefeated to the Nizhyn region in Left-Bank Ukraine, but was reduced to 2,511 men. Subsequently it was reinforced by fresh units, including the Twenty-fifth Division from the Urals and the Bashkir Cavalry Brigade under M. Murtazin. As Piłsudski later asserted, however, "the powerlessness of the Soviet Twelfth Army, which was unable to recover from the defeat it had experienced in Ukraine,"[13] resulted in its playing only a minor role during Budennyi's counteroffensive. The Soviet Fourteenth Army, which had retreated into Left-Bank Ukraine east of Cherkasy, was strengthened by Hryhorii Kotovs'kyi's Cavalry Brigade.[14]

On 8 May the Polish High Command assured the Ukrainian population that Polish troops would leave Ukraine as soon as regular Ukrainian forces were organized and were able to defend the country:

> It is in the Polish interest to withdraw our troops from the occupied territories as quickly as possible and to establish good neighborly relations with the newly created Ukrainian state, as in this way a significant part of our eastern border will be secured from the direct danger of the Bolshevik forces. The Polish occupation of Ukraine must be calculated not in years, but in months. The sooner regular Ukrainian forces are formed, the sooner they will go to the front in order to liberate further the land of Ukraine from under the Bolshevik yoke, and the better the situation will be for the Polish State. The fewer the frictions and clashes with the Ukrainian authorities during [the period of] co-operation, the easier will Poland attain its ultimate aim.[15]

In the same vein, on 17 May in Vinnytsia, at a dinner arranged by the Ukrainian cabinet in his honor, Piłsudski made a speech in which he emphasized that

> Liberated Poland cannot really be free as long as all around persistently reigns the call of the captive subjection of national freedom to the domination of

terror. Poland, having attained the greatest treasure on earth, that is, freedom, decided to repel as far away as possible from its borders everything that would threaten this freedom. And [Piłsudski tried to assure the members of the cabinet] in the flash of our bayonets and our sabers you should not see a new imposition of foreign will. I wish that you would see in them the reflection of your own freedom.[16]

After the successful offensive in Right-Bank Ukraine, Polish public opinion, especially that of supporters of the National Democratic party, which had largely opposed Piłsudski's Ukrainian policy as adventurous, gradually shifted in Piłsudski's favor. When Piłsudski returned to Warsaw on 18 May 1920, he was met by jubilant crowds. That evening there was a formal session of the Sejm. Its speaker, Wojciech Trampczyński, a leading National Democrat, greeted Piłsudski, saying, "Since the time of Bolesław the Brave [the Polish king who captured Kyiv in 1018] ... the Polish nation has not experienced such military triumph.... By your military action you not only have attested to the bravery of the Polish armed forces, but have plucked from the breast of the nation its best longing, its knighthood in the service of nations. The whole of Poland is one in its desire that the people freed by our armies should determine their own fate."[17]

Already prior to the Polish-Ukrainian offensive UNR authorities had been working on strengthening their forces in order to liberate Ukraine from the Bolsheviks and to defend it. Gen. Kutrzeba felt that after Ukraine's liberation six Ukrainian divisions would be needed to defend the country. The organization of such a force was, in his judgment, achievable with respect to both manpower and materiel. The existing UNR Army, the Ukrainian reservists demobilized from the tsarist army, deserters from the VA and Bolshevik armies, and new recruits would all form part of the renewed Ukrainian force, which could be organized in six to twelve weeks.[18] The Polish authorities pledged and were able to assist in arming and equipping this army, because Poland had received a large amount of arms and equipment from abroad, particularly from France and America. As Kutrzeba pointed out, "in the military sphere, the aid given to us by France in [our] struggle with the Soviets was abundant. This aid was demonstrated mainly through the delivery of arms and military materiel."[19] Also war booty could be used to supply the army with arms and equipment. Instead of six divisions, however, the Polish authorities limited the number of Ukrainian troops under Petliura's command to only three divisions. In accordance with the military convention of the Treaty of Warsaw signed on 24 April 1920, "The Polish Supreme Command pledged to supply the Ukrainian forces with arms, ammunition, equipment, and uniforms in amounts necessary for three divisions, according to the estimate fixed for a Polish division and all of its sanitary and other rear establishments, and to place this supply materiel at the disposition of the Ukrainian Ministry of Military Affairs."[20] Unfortunately, however, during the offensive in Ukraine only two incomplete and poorly armed divisions participated.

The UNR government expended great efforts to strengthen its armed forces. During the winter of 1919–20 the Ministry of Military Affairs prepared a program to reorganize the UNR Army and to organize new units from the troops scattered throughout Ukraine and abroad, including those interned in Poland, into a unified formation. To realize this plan, Petliura negotiated with the Poles to allow him to organize Ukrainian units in Polish-controlled territory. One of his main aims was the long-delayed return from Italy of about 40,000 Ukrainian prisoners of war who had served in the Austrian army. Petliura sent Col. Evhen Konovalets' to Italy to negotiate their return, and in the middle of December 1919 the Ukrainian command in Vinnytsia dispatched sixteen officers and several noncommissioned officers to Mykolaiv in southern Ukraine to organize the returnees into regular units.

Besides the interned soldiers in Italy, there was an UHA Brigade of a few thousand well-trained men in Czechoslovakia. The Czechoslovak authorities were prepared to allow the brigade to leave the country if the Polish authorities consented, and Petliura authorized Gen. Viktor Zelins'kyi to negotiate with the Polish Ministry of Military Affairs. Petliura believed that a coalition between a strengthened UNR Army and the Polish army would establish a strong anti-Bolshevik front, and he expected that the Entente and Poland would supply his government and army with arms, equipment, and medicine. Unfortunately, in spite of his efforts, neither the Entente nor Poland supported Petliura's plan.[21]

In addition to the plan of bringing back Ukrainian soldiers from abroad, the UNR military authorities also prepared for the organization of Ukrainian military formations in Poland and for mobilization on liberated Ukrainian territory. One of the first such units in Poland was formed in Łańcut at the beginning of February 1920 from Ukrainian soldiers interned there by the Poles. In early March the formation was transferred to Berestia (Brest-Litovsk), where its organization continued under Col. Marko Bezruchko. New soldiers and officers arrived from other internment camps, including those in Starokostiantyniv, Rivne, and Lutsk. When the formation was formally organized, it was named the Sixth Sich Riflemen Division. The UNR military authorities intended that the division would become the core of a regular army. As of 25 April 1920 it was composed of two infantry brigades, an artillery regiment, a sapper company, a cavalry squadron, and auxiliary units. In all it consisted of 2,125 men, 239 of them officers. Although the division lacked arms, equipment, and even horses for the commanders, on 26–7 April it was transferred to Berdychiv, where it was subordinated in operative matters to the Polish Second Army commanded by Gen. Listowski. On 5 May, when the offensive on Kyiv was assigned to the newly reorganized Polish Third Army under Gen. Rydz-Śmigły, the division was subordinated to that army.[22] A Polish officer who fought alongside the Ukrainian troops under Col. Bezruchko testified that "His division matched in everything our best detachments. Its relations with us were the best, and [the division's] spirit was indeed admirable."[23]

In early February 1920, in Odessa, Col. Udovychenko, while still recovering from illness, organized a detachment of 48 men. To save his unit from Bolshevik encirclement, he moved westward toward Kamianets-Podilskyi through occupied territory to join the other Ukrainian formations. During the retreat his detachment was attacked, and he reached the city of Mohyliv-Podilskyi on 5 February with only five men. There he was appointed commander of a 125-man garrison, and on 23 February Prime Minister Mazepa commissioned him to organize a Separate Infantry Brigade in the region. In a short time Udovychenko integrated into his brigade some partisan units and UHA soldiers who had recovered from typhus. The brigade was substantially strengthened after the defeated Russian Volunteer troops of Gen. Nikolai Bredov appeared in the vicinity of Mohyliv-Podilskyi. Many of his troops were Ukrainian, and many of them joined Udovychenko's brigade, as did a cavalry regiment of Don Cossacks under Col. Mykhailo Frolov and a cavalry company of Kuban Cossacks under Capt. O. Iushkevych.

While a larger Bolshevik force approached Mohyliv-Podilskyi, on 3 March Udovychenko and his brigade retreated westward to join the Polish troops near Kamianets-Podilskyi. On 8 March the brigade was subordinated in operational matters to the Polish Eighteenth Division of Gen. Franciszek Krajowski. On 20 March it was united with the Ukrainian Fourth Riflemen Brigade of Col. Oleksander Shapoval, which had been organized in February 1920 in Kamianets-Podilskyi and consisted of three battalions, an artillery detachment, and a cavalry company. The united brigades became the Second Riflemen Division, and Udovychenko was appointed its commander. Although the new division was still in the process of formation and lacked manpower and, still worse, arms and equipment, it engaged in constant fighting against the Bolsheviks while defending the Polish-Ukrainian front in Podillia. The command of the Polish Eighteenth Division allowed Udovychenko to proclaim mobilization to strengthen his division and organize new formations. Other Polish authorities, however, delayed granting permission for mobilization, and even after permission was granted, Polish commanders obstructed the process and dispersed those already mobilized under various pretexts. Krajowski promised to supply badly needed arms and equipment to the UNR troops but delivered only limited quantities, even though the Polish army was well supplied by the Entente and thus was in a position to fulfill its obligations. Piłsudski issued appropriate orders, but strangely, they never reached Krajowski's headquarters. According to Gen. Volodymyr Sal's'kyi, the Ukrainian minister of military affairs, mobilization in Right-Bank Ukraine, which was controlled by the Polish administration, had been prepared; but the Polish civil authorities delayed granting permission until the Polish and UNR troops began retreating from the Right Bank, and failed to supply the UNR troops with arms, equipment, and uniforms. As a result, the UNR force grew very slowly. On 25 April 1920 the Second Riflemen Division was composed of two infantry brigades, an artillery brigade, a cavalry regiment, a sapper company, and auxiliary units totaling 1,779 men (317 officers) and 7 artillery guns, 29 machine guns, and 407 horses. On 29 May it was renamed the Third Iron Riflemen Division and Udovychenko was promoted to the rank of general.[24]

The UNR Fifth Kherson Division, which also participated in the Polish-Ukrainian offensive, was organized at the beginning of May 1920 under the command of Col. Andrii Dolud. About ninety percent of the division was composed of UHA soldiers who had escaped from Bolshevik or Polish captivity. Its nucleus was Col. Edmund Sheparovych's cavalry regiment of 716 men (90 officers). Gradually the division was strengthened by other soldiers who had recovered from typhus, and by 12 June it had 2,672 men (105 officers), a reserve brigade of about 80 officers, and an unknown number of men under the command of Maj. R. Knittel.[25]

Gen. Omelianovych-Pavlenko's army, after six months of fighting in the rear of the Bolshevik forces, was recalled on 6 May and united with the other UNR and Polish formations. Some troops continued fighting in the Bolshevik rear, however. The army had 6,347 men (397 officers), 14 artillery guns, and 144 machine guns. After it joined the offensive, the UNR Army consisted of seven divisions: the First Zaporozhian Division commanded by Gen. Andrii Hulyi-Hulenko; the Second Volynian Division commanded by Gen. Oleksander Zahrods'kyi; the Third Iron Riflemen Division commanded by Gen. Udovychenko; the Fourth Kyiv Division commanded by Gen. Iurii Tiutiunnyk; the Fifth Kherson Division commanded by Col. Dolud; the Sixth Sich Riflemen Division commanded by Gen. Bezruchko; and the Separate Cavalry Division commanded by Gen. Ivan Omelianovych-Pavlenko. Each of the infantry divisions consisted of three brigades, but also had one cavalry regiment, one artillery brigade, and one technical battalion. On 12 June the seven divisions totaled about 20,000 men (3,574 officers). Gen. Mykhailo Omelianovych-Pavlenko was appointed commander in chief of the reorganized

UNR Army. Although the military convention of the Treaty of Warsaw had stipulated that all UNR Army units would revert to the Ukrainian command, the army continued to be subordinated in operational matters to the Sixth and Third Polish armies.[26]

During the offensive UHA remnants also operated in Right-Bank Ukraine. In spite of the Polish occupation of Western Ukraine, they were willing to continue fighting against the Bolsheviks. During the last months of 1919 and the beginning of 1920, the state of the UHA had been critical. Its continuous and difficult campaign during a cold and rainy autumn and early severe winter, coupled with the lack of clothing and supplies, brought about a disastrous typhus epidemic. Of over 85,000 men in the UHA in July 1919, only 22,000 healthy men remained in January 1920. To protect its troops, especially the thousands of ill soldiers, from encirclement by the Bolsheviks, the UHA command sent them southward in the hope of crossing the border into Romania. But the Romanians, who had concluded an agreement with the Poles, refused to allow the UHA to cross the Dniester. Consequently, to avoid a rout by the Red Army, an UHA Revolutionary Committee was formed in Vinnytsia, and on 12 January 1920 it reached an agreement with the command of the Soviet Twelfth Army by which the so-called Red UHA became part of the Bolshevik forces.

Gradually, after some of the ill soldiers recovered, they again joined their former units, and in the middle of March 1920 the Red UHA was reorganized into three brigades, each with three infantry regiments, one cavalry regiment, and one artillery regiment. Subsequently they were moved to the front. The First Brigade, commanded by Col. Alfred Bisanz, was located in the Chudniv area; the Second, under Capt. Iuliian Holovins'kyi, in the Lityn area; and the Third, under Capt. Osyp Stanimir, in the Bar area. The opportunistic nature of the agreement with the Bolsheviks soon brought about serious negative consequences. Bolshevik commissars had organized Communist groups in the units to conduct intensive propaganda among the soldiers with the aim of undermining morale, eradicating nationalist feeling, and implanting Russian Communist ideology. The commissars also tried to destroy the officer corps by abolishing ranks and implanting disobedience and animosity among the soldiers toward their officers. When the attempt at Bolshevization failed, the Cheka arrested some officers. The UHA commander, Gen. Osyp Mykytka, and his chief of staff, Gen. Gustav Tsirits, were imprisoned in Moscow and executed there.

The reaction of the UHA troops was manifested during the Polish-Ukrainian offensive. Prior to the offensive, they had already begun to revolt against the Bolsheviks. On 6 April 1920 an insurrection broke out in the Third Brigade in Tyraspil, and its cavalry regiment (614 men) under Col. Sheparovych and a technical company (300 men) went over to the UNR army of Gen. Omelianovych-Pavlenko that was operating in the Bolshevik rear. UHA commanding officers formed a Military Committee in Birzulia to act as an anti-Bolshevik center in preparation for future action. The committee established contact with the commanders of the three brigades, with Gens. Omelianovych-Pavlenko and Udovychenko, and with local partisan groups. As soon as the UHA units encountered the advancing UNR troops, they sought to join them. On 23 and 24 April respectively, the Second Brigade (6,748 men) and the Third Brigade (3,813 men) mutinied against the Bolsheviks and joined the UNR and Polish troops. At the end of April the First Brigade (7,658 men), without knowing what had occurred in the other two brigades, also mutinied with the intention of joining the Polish-Ukrainian offensive. The brigades' switchover to the Polish-Ukrainian side, however, brought about tragedies for other UHA groups that remained behind the Bolshevik lines, as well as for the brigades themselves.

During the winter of 1919–20 a number of UHA soldiers were concentrated in the Odessa area; many of them were sick or recovering from illness. To assist them three centers, two hospitals, a few convalescence shelters, and an assembly station for the healthy were established in Odessa. When the Bolsheviks occupied that city, the UHA officers and soldiers there became the Cheka's main targets. On 23 April the soldiers at the assembly station were ordered to gather at the railroad freight station for transportation to Kyiv for "military reeducation." Two hundred and fifty soldiers and officers and a few women responded to the call. During the night the Cheka surrounded their transport and opened fire with machine guns, massacring them. The number killed is unknown because the Cheka buried the victims that same night, but railwaymen confirmed that at least sixty people were killed. The next morning the wounded were taken to hospitals. Those who survived were deported and drowned by the Cheka in the White Sea en route to concentration camps in the Solovets Islands.[27] (This practice was also later common under the Soviet regime.[28])

Before the UHA troops deserted the Bolsheviks, the command of the Second Brigade under Iuliian Holovins'kyi dispatched delegations to inform the operational division of the Polish forces and Petliura's headquarters of their intention to join the Polish-Ukrainian side. The brigade's command was strongly convinced that Polish military and political circles would be favorably disposed to their action. The reason for their action was later made clear by the officers of the brigades:

> Considering it our sacred duty to take an active part in establishing the Ukrainian state, we came over to this side in order to enter, with arms in hand,

The Polish-Ukrainian Offensive   111

the ranks of the Ukrainian Army. We stated that clearly to the Polish authorities, who, in spite of our action against the Bolsheviks, disarmed us and then interned us in a prisoner-of-war camp. We also stated our readiness to enter the Ukrainian Army through a separate delegation to Petliura, the commander in chief.[29]

The command's expectations were not realized. Even though the UHA spent several days successfully fighting against Bolshevik forces, the Poles did not show appreciation; instead they surrounded and disarmed the Second and Third brigades and later also the First Brigade (a total of 18,219 men) and seized their property, including forty-four heavy guns. All of the officers and some noncommissioned officers were deported to Poland and interned in camps at Tuchola, while the rank and file were demobilized. Afterwards the Polish press described the brigades as Bolshevik units that Polish troops had defeated and interned. From the very beginning of the Polish-Ukrainian War in Galicia in 1918, the Poles had described the UHA to the Entente statesmen as Bolsheviks. According to an author who had experienced this injustice and the sufferings experienced by the Ukrainian troops fighting against the Bolsheviks, "Tens of thousands of people died and the army perished while the civilized world calmly watched.... But who knows how the map of Europe would have looked if these 'Bolsheviks' had not, in the critical moment, barred the [Soviet] East from the West by their corpses and thus become spontaneous shields against the eastern storm."[30]

Besides the three UHA brigades, Sich Riflemen also operated against the Bolsheviks. Although they were composed largely of Galician Ukrainians, they were an integral part of the UNR Army. In July 1919 there were about 4,500 Sich Riflemen. Between 4 and 6 December their commanding officers, led by Col. Konovalets', decided at a meeting in Nova Chortoryia not to continue fighting as an UNR formation, because, in contrast to UNR authorities, they wanted to wage a regular war against the Bolsheviks and not engage in guerilla warfare. The soldiers were free either to join Omelianovych-Pavlenko's army or to demobilize. Some joined Omelianovych-Pavlenko, but the others were captured by the Polish troops, who unexpectedly seized the town and interned them in Lutsk and Rivne. A few months later some of the interned escaped abroad, while others eventually joined the Sixth Sich Riflemen Division.[31]

Ukrainian partisan groups, including that of Nestor Makhno, played an important role in the Bolshevik rear during the Polish-Ukrainian offensive.[32] According to Gen. Tiutiunnyk, during the winter of 1919–20 partisan activities continued, but "The advance of the Poles in Ukraine in the spring of 1920 to some extent demoralized the partisan movement. The more eager partisans did not restrain themselves and rose up, and thus gave the Poles the opportunity to advance to Kyiv without resistance. The majority [of the partisans], however, not knowing the attitude of the Poles toward Ukraine, behaved passively."[33] Although the Poles greatly profited from the fighting between the Ukrainian partisans and the Bolsheviks, the Polish military command soon began acting against the partisans. Toward the end of the offensive, on 6 May 1920, the command of the Polish Sixth Army issued operational order no. 728, which revealed the Polish aims and policy toward the strengthening of the Ukrainian army:

> Occupied places should be immediately pacified, [and we should] be confiscating arms and arresting those suspected of belonging to the Bolshevik army, not excluding Galicians previously belonging to the Bolshevik army. [This order was subsequently supplemented.] ... Ukrainian detachments fighting on the Bolshevik side that show readiness to join our side should be disarmed, and their soldiers should be treated on par with prisoners of war.... Detachments of the character of undisciplined bands, even if they are fighting against the Bolsheviks, should be disarmed and directed to [Twelfth Polish] divisional headquarters....[34]

One Polish officer gave some explanation for the negative Polish policy toward the Ukrainian partisans and the population at large. In the area of the Ros and Roska rivers south of Bila Tserkva, many villages were in the hands of about fifteen thousand local partisans under the command of Kurovs'kyi. Their disposition toward the Bolsheviks was openly hostile, while their and the civilian population's attitude toward the Polish troops was cordial. Because the Polish troops were maintained at the expense of the population through forced, excessive requisitions, however, the population eventually became demoralized.[35] Fearing that the population would sooner or later defend its rights, the Poles began disarming and interning the partisans.[36]

The UNR authorities favored the shift of the UHA to the Polish-Ukrainian side not only because it strengthened the anti-Bolshevik forces, but also because it seemingly renewed the Ukrainian unity that had been broken in the fall of 1919. Consequently an anti-Bolshevik united front was established. Although a stronger UNR Army was a necessity in fighting the Bolsheviks, the Polish authorities, contrary to the military convention of the Treaty of Warsaw, were not genuinely interested in strengthening the Ukrainian forces. Even though the existing units badly needed arms and equipment, the Polish command delivered them very slowly and in limited quantities. Moreover, the Poles not only disarmed the UHA brigades, which they seemed to consider more dangerous to Poland than the Bolsheviks, but also did not pass on their arms and equipment to the UNR Army. If the more than 23,000 well-trained and disciplined UHA soldiers and the numerous Ukrainian partisan groups had been allowed to remain part of the Polish-UNR troops, they would have played an important role in the campaign against the Bolsheviks.

Clearly the Polish government did not plan to assist the UNR government in building up a strong Ukrainian army. The Polish command simply needed the presence of some Ukrainian troops during its offensive in Ukraine so as to appease the population, which was antagonistic to all foreign forces, and thus make the campaign easier for the Polish troops.[37] As one Polish officer remarked, "When we started our offensive, only a small [sic] Ukrainian unit [the Third Iron Riflemen Division] stood with us. That unit had political and moral rather than strategic significance."[38] Yet, in spite of the negative Ukrainian policy of the Polish government, Polish historians have blamed the Ukrainians for making an inadequate contribution to the struggle against the Bolsheviks. In their opinion, "There was no spontaneous rise of the Ukrainians.... The reactions of the Ukrainian masses in 1920 proved that they were not yet mature enough for independence.... The Polish troops, which were engaged in a difficult struggle against the Bolsheviks, received inadequate support from their Ukrainian ally, whose forces did not exceed rather symbolic numbers."[39] Why the Ukrainian forces did not exceed "symbolic numbers" the author of this statement did not care to elaborate. In the same vein, another Polish historian wrote that "Piłsudski gambled on an upsurge of Ukrainian patriotism, which never materialized, although Petliura's small force fought bravely throughout the campaign."[40] Certainly a larger Ukrainian force would have also "fought bravely" had the Polish authorities not blocked its creation by disarming and interning the existing Ukrainian forces and preventing mobilization and the formation of new units.

During the offensive in Right-Bank Ukraine, the Polish military authorities did not act according to the Polish-Ukrainian agreement or respond to conditions as required. Although they needed both a strong ally and the cooperation of the Ukrainian civilian population to defend such a large territory against the Bolsheviks, the Poles not only prevented the strengthening of the UNR Army, but also acted as an occupying force, thus alienating the population. Polish troops interfered in Ukrainian internal affairs and established their own civil authorities, removing Ukrainian administrative personnel and replacing them with Poles. This interference particularly affected the railways, which, contrary to the agreement, the Poles took into their own hands. Moreover, the Polish troops requisitioned anything of value, be it state- or privately owned, especially postal and railroad properties. Even the train Petliura used was taken. Contrary to the Polish-Ukrainian agreement, those goods were transported to Poland.[41]

Polish policy in Ukraine eventually undermined Poland's defensive strength. More immediately it undermined the Polish military situation at the Bolshevik front. Although the possibility of a strengthened Bolshevik attack was imminent, little attention was paid to the lines of supply, and the Polish troops were poorly equipped. Liaison between the various units was also inadequate. Consequently the initially swift and triumphant Polish-Ukrainian offensive was short-lived. During the first days of May the Polish-Ukrainian forces captured Kyiv, but by mid-June they were in full retreat. Although the offensive took place in Ukraine, it nonetheless aroused Russian nationalists, who called for the defense of Russia. The 29 April 1920 appeal of the Bolshevik Central Committee was addressed not just to the working class, but to all citizens of Russia:

> Honorable citizens! Do not allow the will of the Russian people to be determined by the bayonets of Polish nobles, who have particularly shamelessly and repeatedly declared that it makes no difference to them who rules Russia, but only that Russia shall be helpless and weak.... The war against us by the Polish bourgeoisie is plunder, usurpation, bloody adventure. Our war against White Guard Poland is a revolutionary self-defense, the sacred protection of the working people's independence, [and ensures] a happy future for our children and grandchildren. And after the rout of Piłsudski's bands, the independence of Poland will remain for us inviolable. With the Polish proletariat and Polish peasantry, who will become full masters of their country, we will easily establish a brotherly union. Only our common gentry-bourgeois enemy divides us."[42]

The appeal called for a united Russian front, while in their propaganda about the war with Poland the Bolsheviks sought to divide the Poles in order to weaken them. For example, Lenin decreed in April 1920 that "All articles about Poland and the Polish war are to be passed by reliable editors who shall be personally responsible. Do not overdo it; that is, do not fall into chauvinism, and always distinguish the lords and capitalists of Poland from the workers and peasants."[43] The propaganda aroused the sympathies of Russians who previously had refused to serve the Bolshevik regime. Even many former tsarist officers, including some of the highest rank, joined the Bolshevik forces. Most prominent among them was Gen. Aleksei Brusilov, the commander in chief under the former Provisional Government. He appealed in *Pravda* to his former subordinates to "Forget the wrongs you have suffered. It is now your duty to defend our beloved Russia with all your strength and to give your lives to save it from irretrievable subjugation."[44] As a result,

"Separate groups of officers and soldiers on the eve of the war against the 'White Poles' switched over to the Red Cavalry Army from Denikin or were taken prisoner and enrolled in the Red Cavalry Army."[45] Although the Bolshevik leaders were glad to exploit this upsurge of Russian nationalism, for it resulted in an increase in the number of Red Army officers and strengthened the soldiers' morale, they made every effort in their propaganda to give the war a class, not a national, character. The Bolshevik slogan was always "Against the Polish Pans [Lords]," never "Down with Poland."[46]

The peace on the Ukrainian front was only temporary. On 14 May, to secure the Bolshevik strategic positions in Ukraine, the Soviet Fifteenth Army, consisting of six infantry divisions and one cavalry division under the former tsarist officer Avgust Kork, and units of the Northern Group under the former tsarist officer Evgenii Sergeev launched an offensive on the Belarusian Front. The Fifteenth Army was joined on 19 May by the Soviet Sixteenth Army under Nikolai Sologub, which advanced toward Minsk. The Bolshevik forces deployed for their offensive on the Northwestern Front totaled 92,400 men, under the supreme command of the former tsarist officer Gen. Mikhail Tukhachevskii. The Polish First Army that they attacked consisted of six infantry divisions and one cavalry brigade. Initially the Red Army compelled the Poles to retreat westward some 100 kilometers toward Maladzechna. After the First Army was strengthened by the Polish Fourth Army (four divisions) under Gen. Stanisław Szeptycki, who was appointed commander of both armies, and the Polesie Group (two infantry divisions) under Gen. Sikorski, Polish resistance stiffened. The Polish command reinforced the existing troops by forming an additional reserve army of three infantry divisions, two infantry brigades and a cavalry group under Gen. Kazimierz Sosnkowski, and on 2 June the Poles launched a counteroffensive. They repulsed the Bolshevik forces, inflicting heavy losses and forcing them to retreat nearly to their initial position along the Dvina, Auta, and Biarezina rivers.

Although the Bolsheviks did not achieve an important strategic success on the Belarusian Front, they compelled the Polish command to transfer some Polish units from the Ukrainian Front. Consequently, the Polish troops remaining in Ukraine were re-formed to face the threatening situation. On 28 May 1920 the Polish Second Army was dissolved, and its command was transformed into the command of the Ukrainian Front. The Third and Sixth armies and Gen. Jan Romer's Cavalry Group were subordinated to Gen. Antoni Listowski, who became the commander of the Ukrainian Front. The May campaign on the Belarusian Front facilitated the June Soviet offensive by the First Cavalry Army of Semen Budennyi, a former tsarist sergeant-major, which had been transferred from Northern Caucasia to the Ukrainian Front. Budennyi's army consisted of four cavalry divisions totaling 16,500 men, and was well armed with 304 machine guns, 48 mounted artillery guns, 5 armored trains, 8 armed cars, and 12 airplanes. Budennyi had captured those arms from Denikin's defeated VA, which had been abundantly supplied by Great Britain and France. His army was composed of Don and Kuban Cossacks, partisans, and adventurers who had been won over to the Bolshevik side in the course of the Russian Civil War. Those men had little in common with Bolshevik politics or ideology. According to Gen. Weygand, "It is as if he [Budennyi] is a new incarnation of a commander of the ancient Tatar hordes. During military operations, he gives evidence indeed of cruelty, spreading terror, burning hospitals, slaughtering the wounded, and not allowing for long the holding of prisoners of war."[47] A similar opinion about the Russian army was expressed by Tukhachevskii to Pierre Fervacque, a fellow prisoner of war in Germany: "The Russian Army is not like yours—the French. It is a horde, and its strength is in its being a horde."[48] Although he made this statement during the First World War, it is applicable to the campaign of 1920 as well.

The main characteristic of the First Cavalry Army was its great mobility and maneuverability. On 26 May 1920 Aleksandr Egorov, the commander of the Soviet Southwestern Front, ordered a general offensive from the mouth of the Prypiat to Koziatyn. After reaching Uman, Budennyi was ordered to strike in the direction of Koziatyn. His initial assault on the Polish Thirteenth Infantry Division at the Ros River south of Kyiv was repulsed after a week of heavy fighting.[49] In the forefront the Polish division had Ukrainian partisans under Kurovs'kyi and strongly anti-Bolshevik armed peasants from almost all the villages along the Roska River. Thus Ukrainian partisans and peasants constituted the first defensive line fighting Budennyi's advancing forces. After initial failure, Budennyi concentrated his attack on the Polish Third and Sixth armies' weakest point—where their flanks met. On 5 June he renewed his attack at Samhorodok southwest of Bila Tserkva, broke through the Poles' front line, and disrupted the Polish defenses for an area ten kilometers wide and fifteen kilometers deep. The battle at Samhorodok was the turning point in the Polish-Ukrainian offensive. At the same time the reinforced Soviet Twelfth Army and Aleksandr Golikov's Strike Group joined Budennyi's force advancing into the area of Kyiv. They tried to outflank the Polish Third Army from the north, while the Fastiv Army Group under Iona Iakir advanced via Bila Tserkva and Khvastiv to outflank it from the south. They succeeded in making deep raids in the direction of Koziatyn, Berdychiv, and Zhytomyr into the rear of the Polish troops, disorganizing them and creating panic. This critical situation prompted Piłsudski to order Rydz-Śmigły, the commander of the Third Army, to retreat toward Zhytomyr and challenge Budennyi, but his order failed to reach Rydz-Śmigły. Fearing that the Third Army might be cut off from the main Polish and Ukrainian troops, Piłsudski again ordered it to withdraw from the area of Kyiv, and on 11 June the Polish-Ukrainian troops began retreating along the entire front from the Prypiat to the Dniester.

During their retreat northwestward along the railroad line Kyiv-Malyn-Korosten, the Polish Third Army and the Ukrainian Sixth Sich Riflemen Division encountered Budennyi's army, which tried to outflank and destroy them. But in two battles, at Borodianka northwest of Kyiv from 11 to 13 June and at Horbuliv west of Radomyshl on 15 June, the Polish troops broke out of the encirclement. The next day, after crossing the Teteriv River, the Third Army established tactical contact with the main Polish force in the Malyn-Korosten area. Budennyi's plan to surround and destroy the Third Army and seize the military supplies concentrated in the areas of Koziatyn and Berdychiv failed. Moreover, at Borodianka between Kyiv and Malyn, Polish and Ukrainian troops repulsed the Soviet Twelfth Army, forcing it northward and preventing it from uniting with the striking group of Budennyi's army. Thus, the Bolshevik thrust was weakened.

During the Polish withdrawal from Ukraine, according to Gen. Kutrzeba,

> The Ukrainian population behaved exceptionally indeed.... The command of the Ukrainian division, in the persons of colonels Bezruchko and Zmiienko, behaved in an exemplary and soldierly manner, completely understanding the operational and tactical situation. It took upon itself to influence the population in regard to the maintenance of peace, safety, and eventual self-defense. At that time there appeared at the command [headquarters] of the Third Army a delegate from the [Ukrainian] anti-Bolshevik partisans in the Oster-Kozelets region (east of the Dnieper and Desna) with a proposal of cooperation with our army. It was accepted because the partisan actions in the Soviet rear during the [Bolshevik] attack on the Dnieper front could provide valuable help for us."[50]

Because the Polish retreat was hasty and not well planned, the Bolshevik forces were able to act more effectively and brutally. For example, after capturing Zhytomyr the Bolsheviks burned down its hospitals, killing the 600 wounded soldiers and medical personnel therein. News of Bolshevik cruelties spread throughout the region and created panic and fear among the soldiers and the civilian population.[51]

In light of the reversals in Ukraine, the Polish right began a campaign against Piłsudski, accusing him of adventurism and incompetence in military matters. Consequently, on 9 June the Cabinet of Prime Minister Leopold Skulski resigned, precipitating a lengthy cabinet crisis caused by an inter-party struggle over the appointment of an acting minister of foreign affairs. Finally, on 24 June a new cabinet was formed by Władysław Grabski, a National Democrat, with Prince Eustachy Sapieha as his minister of foreign affairs. In view of the critical military situation, on 1 July the Sejm approved the creation of a State Defense Council that would formally unite members of the government with nominees of the Sejm, Chief of State Piłsudski, and the high command of the army. The council consisted of eighteen members: the chief of state as its chairman; the marshal of the Sejm; three ministers; three generals; and ten representatives of the main political parties. Its prerogative was to decide on all matters of war and peace. During the next three months, until being disbanded on 1 October, the council de facto replaced the Sejm in these matters. On 3 July Piłsudski issued two proclamations in the name of the council. The first concerned the Soviet Russian invasion of Poland and called upon men to enlist to defend Poland. The second appealed to soldiers to make the greatest sacrifices and to be brave while defending their fatherland against the invaders. The council decided to reinforce the army by calling for volunteers, and Piłsudski decided to integrate the volunteer battalions with the regular army regiments.

Eventually the council decided that Poland's only salvation was peace with Soviet Russia, and on 5 July it resolved to appeal for assistance to the Allied Supreme Council, which at that time was conferring in Spa, Belgium, on the regulation of the international economic situation in Europe and inducing Germany to carry out the provisions of the Versailles Treaty. In his 6 July address to the Supreme Council, Prime Minister Grabski stated that

> Should the Polish Army, outnumbered by the enemy, be overwhelmed, the whole of Europe will be in danger; consequently, it is Poland's duty to warn the Supreme Council of this danger in order that it may make its decisions promptly. Should events force Poland to carry on the war, the material and moral assistance of the Allies will be needed. The Polish Government asks for assistance most insistently, assistance which must be immediate and efficient, and whichever may be the measures taken by the Supreme Council, the Polish Government will be ready to accept them."[52]

On 10 July Grabski signed an agreement with the Entente in which Poland agreed to a cease-fire with the prospect of negotiating peace with Soviet Russia. Poland was to withdraw to a line that had been designated by the Supreme Council on 8 December 1919, while the Bolshevik forces would stand twenty kilometers to the east. A conference to be held in London with invited representatives of Poland, Lithuania, Finland, Latvia, and the ZUNR would conclude a lasting peace between those countries and Soviet Russia.

Prior to this action, however, in case Soviet Russia agreed to an armistice, it would be necessary to have the assurance that Poland agreed to withdraw to the line assigned by the Supreme Council (which corresponded to the eastern frontier of the former Congress Kingdom), to attend the London conference, and to accept the decision of the Supreme Council regarding the border with Lithuania, the future of Eastern Galicia, the question of Teschen, and the Danzig treaty. If Poland accepted the above terms, the British government would immediately send a similar proposal to Soviet Russia. Should Russia refuse an armistice and cross the line, the Entente was obligated to give Poland aid, particularly war materiel, but contingent on the availability of supplies and on the heavy obligations undertaken elsewhere. This support would enable Poland to defend its independence.[53]

Following the Spa agreement, on 13 July, Grabski reported to the State Defense Council. He had accepted the agreement because, in his judgment, the Polish Army was not able to defend the country. Although there was some dissent, the majority of the council voted to accept British mediation in the Polish-Soviet negotiations. Continuing reversals at the front necessitated another council meeting on 19 July, at which the army and Piłsudski were blamed for all the military and political failures. Consequently Piłsudski offered to resign, but warned the Council that

> Victory depends three-fourths on the morale of the army and the people. Instead of faith and confidence, you show only quarrels, discussions and divisions. You stand near the abyss—perhaps tomorrow you will begin killing each other. I don't know what word I should use to inspire you with a spirit of unity and harmony. If my death would be necessary for that, I would be ready even to blow out my brains. How can I make you understand that this is the last moment for salvation; that you must unite and show your unity by forming a strong Cabinet? I am under a fire of accusations. I get disgusted with a state whose representative is treated in such a way. Don't make such a farce by giving me guardians and controllers. I put myself at your disposal. Select some one less irritating to you than I am, but give him full confidence and energetic support."[54]

After he left the room, the council voted unanimously for a resolution expressing full confidence in Piłsudski.

Because of the continuing crisis, Grabski's cabinet had a short existence; clearly a more representative cabinet was needed. Piłsudski felt that a cabinet should be selected from among the left, because the broad masses of the population should be the foundation of the state. On 24 July a coalition cabinet was formed, consisting of Wincenty Witos, the leader of the Piast party, as prime minister; Ignacy Daszyński, the leader of the Socialist party, as deputy prime minister; Eustachy Sapieha as minister of foreign affairs; and Gen. Kazimierz Sosnkowski as minister of war. After the Spa Conference, on 25 July, a special diplomatic-military mission sent by the British and French governments arrived in Warsaw. The British representatives were Lord Edgar Vincent D'Abernon, ambassador to Berlin; Gen. Sir Percy Radcliffe, director of military operations of the War Office; and Sir Maurice Hankey, secretary to the British cabinet. The French representatives were Jules Jusserand, ambassador to Washington; Gen. Maxime Weygand, chief of staff to Marshal Foch; and M. Vignon, counselor of the French embassy. The mission's members were to advise their governments on the measures to be taken to conclude an armistice between Poland and Soviet Russia and to assist the Polish government in defending its country.

The mission's members expected to be consulted and deferred to in all matters of Polish policy. Moreover, they (especially D'Abernon) urged the Polish leaders to "take advantage of Gen. Weygand's ... unrivalled experience and of his capacity for military organization." To their surprise, Piłsudski stated that "The greatest service the Mission could render Poland was to keep the communications through Danzig open. Poland was in urgent need of supplies.... He attached more importance to supplies than to military assistance in the form either of advice or foreign officers."[55] The mission's expectations that Weygand would be a military advisor to the Polish High Command were not realized because Piłsudski did not wish it so. On 29 July Weygand was appointed adviser to Gen. Tadeusz Rozwadowski, chief of the Polish General Staff, in matters of preparing and directing operations. Relations between the two generals proved to be very strained. Although they worked in the same building, they exchanged letters and notes instead of meeting to discuss problems. Nonetheless, until he left Warsaw on 25 August, Weygand and many other French officers contributed much to the Polish victory during this critical time.[56]

In mid-June Polish troops established a temporary front line along the Uzh River. There some success was achieved in the area of Zviahel by Romer's cavalry group. At the same time, however, the thrust of the Soviet Twelfth Army on the Polish northern flank in the Ovruch area broke the advance against Budennyi's cavalry and forced the Poles to retreat. Toward the end of June, after a series of skirmishes, the Polish and UNR troops retreated to a new line running from the Prypiat south along the rivers Ubort, Sluch, and Horyn and from there to the Dniester. The Polesie Group, the Polish Third Army, and the Ukrainian Sixth Sich Riflemen Division operated on the northern flank against the Soviet Twelfth Army. The Polish Sixth Army and UNR Sixth Division operated on the southern flank up to the Dniester against the Soviet Fourteenth Army. The newly reconstructed Polish Second Army under Gen. Kazimierz Raszewski, consisting of two infantry divisions, two infantry brigades, and one cavalry division, operated in the middle, which deeply curved westward, against Budennyi's cavalry army. The initiative along the entire front remained in the hands of the Bolshevik forces. Budennyi's swift maneuvers and attacks from the rear soon forced the Polish and Ukrainian troops to retreat westward. Although Rydz-Śmigły attempted to check Budennyi's advance by a concentric attack from the north, west, and south by all three Polish armies, he failed to stop Budennyi mainly because there was no co-ordination among the Polish units. At the beginning of July Budennyi crossed the Horyn River. After heavy fighting the stronghold of Rivne, an important railway and road junction in Volynia, fell on 10 July to Budennyi. Budennyi's success worsened the Polish strategic position, because the Polish Second Army was cut off from the southern Polish and UNR groups and was forced northward toward Sarny into wooded marshland. By mid-July the Polish and UNR troops established a temporary new front line along the rivers Zbruch and Styr, but under strong Bolshevik pressure they were forced to retreat westward. Meanwhile, from 12 to 26 July, Budennyi advanced along a hundred-kilometer stretch of highway connecting Rivne, Dubno, and Brody while fighting the Polish Eighth Infantry Division and part of the Second Army. On 12 August, after seizing Dubno, Budennyi received an order from Egorov, the commander of the Soviet Southwestern Front, to advance toward Lviv. After fighting his way to the environs of Lviv, Budennyi attempted to seize the city in one fell swoop, but because the Bolshevik command did not provide him with infantry, reserves, and adequate supplies, long and stubborn fighting tied him down instead. This situation was repeated in later fighting.[57]

From 6 May through 12 June 1920, the UNR troops on the southern flank were engaged in constant combat with the Bolsheviks while defending the line between Miaskivka near Chudniv and Iampil on the Dniester. When the Bolsheviks forced the Polish Sixth Army to withdraw to the northwest, the UNR troops in the south were left unprotected. Eventually the UNR troops also began retreating westward, but gradually, stopping and fighting at each natural defensive position and thus delaying the Bolshevik advance. By 14 July the UNR troops had established new positions along the Zbruch River from Husiatyn south to the Dniester, which they defended for nearly two weeks. Meanwhile Budennyi forced the Poles to retreat, and on 10 July he occupied Rivne. From there he advanced toward Lviv. As the situation on the Polish front north of the UNR positions worsened, the UNR troops withdrew westward on 27 July and established a new front along the Seret River from Chortkiv to the Dniester, and then, on 6 August, along the Strypa River from

Buchach to the Dniester. While Budennyi's cavalry approached Lviv, the Polish Sixth Army retreated westward, thus leaving the Ukrainian northern flank exposed. After heavy fighting, the UNR troops withdrew southward and established new positions along the right bank of the Dniester from Halych to the Romanian border near Zalishchyky. They also secured a bridgehead on the left bank of the Dniester and continued fighting against the Bolsheviks, thus securing the southern flank of the Polish Sixth Army.

At that time the largely Galician Ukrainian soldiers of the Fifth Kherson Division began to suspect that the Poles were tolerating the division only for the time being. Rumors began spreading among the officers and men about possible internment, especially when the Polish military police began making inquiries about the division and arresting some officers during their sick leave. Consequently the division's officers decided to separate from the Polish Army to avoid internment. On 31 August Gen. Antin Kraus and more than half of the division crossed the Carpathian Mountains into Czechoslovakia, where it was disarmed and interned in the camp at Liberec in the Sudetenland. Later the soldiers were transferred to the camp at Josefov.[58]

As the Polish Third Army withdrew from Kyiv, the Ukrainian Sixth Sich Riflemen Division retreated with it toward the Zhytomyr-Radomyshl-Malyn-Korosten line and then through the forests and marches of southern Polissia toward the Bilska Volia-Kholm-Krasnystaw-Hrubeshiv line. The division was almost constantly the rear guard covering the Polish retreat and protecting the transport and supply convoys while battling overwhelming Bolshevik forces. During the fighting, it lost more than half of its over two thousand soldiers, and by mid-August it had been reduced to just over eight hundred men. When the Polish Third Army broke through the tightening Bolshevik circle at Borodianka northwest of Kyiv, Gen. Rydz-Śmigły issued an order on 22 June 1920 in which he acknowledged that "The Sixth Ukrainian Division has preserved its moral strength as a faithful good friend, defending and guarding our northern flank despite its having had to abandon and surrender its fatherland as prey to the enemy."[59]

The division prepared to transfer south to the Dniester to strengthen the Polish-Ukrainian southern front. But the Polish command, in order to secure operations on the Warsaw front, decided to organize the two fortified cities between Warsaw and Lviv—Zamość and Krasnystaw—to prevent the advance of Budennyi's army toward Warsaw to assist Tukhachevskii. On 22 August the command of the Polish Third Army under Gen. Zygmunt Zieliński assigned several of the division's units—the staff company, a cavalry company, a battery of field artillery, and a technical battalion (two compaines of field engineers and one railroad company)—to defend Zamość. Because the main part of the division—two infantry brigades, one artillery group, one cavalry regiment, and one machine-gun detachment—was operating in the Krasnystaw-Hrubeshiv sector, the Polish command also strengthened Zamość with Polish units—two infantry battalions of young recruits, one artillery battery, one incomplete infantry regiment, and two armored trains. The Ukrainian and Polish units in Zamość (a total of about three thousand men) were put under the command of Col. Bezruchko and his staff. Bezruchko's first task was to construct an eighteen-kilometer defensive line around the city. This fortification, including two or three lines of barbed wire, was completed between 25 and 28 August by Ukrainian field engineers with the assistance of three thousand to five thousand inhabitants of Zamość and neighboring villages.

On the evening of 28 August Budennyi began intensive assaults using his force of over sixteen thousand cavalrymen. He had been ordered to take Zamość at any cost. The city was not prepared to withstand a siege, and its situation gradually became desperate because of the constant fighting and lack of food, medical supplies, sanitary services, and ammunition. Thatch had to be used to feed the horses. By isolating the city from the rest of the country, Budennyi hoped to force it to capitulate. But heavy artillery and machine-gun fire held his cavalry back until 31 August, when the Polish Army Group of Gen. Stanisław Haller, the Second Legionary Infantry Division, and two Ukrainian brigades relieved its defenders. Several days later the Ukrainian Sixth Sich Riflemen Division was transferred to the Dniester, where it joined the UNR army under Gen. Omelianovych-Pavlenko.[60]

The outcome of the Polish-Ukrainian offensive in Right-Bank Ukraine was reflected in the later Wisła campaign that led to the Polish victory over the Bolsheviks. In his 1937 book about the offensive, Gen. Kutrzeba concluded that "A general balance of gains and losses of our Kyivan campaign is favorable for us ... because it contributed in a positive way to making possible the Polish victory at the Vistula and ... the Neman."[61] In spite of substantial Ukrainian contributions and sacrifices in this joint campaign, however, Poland abandoned its ally, and the UNR was forced to fight the enemy alone. The struggle ended with the tragedy at Bazar and the subsequent occupation of Ukraine by the Bolsheviks.

CHAPTER 11

The Soviet Offensive in Poland and the Battles of Warsaw and the Neman

As the Polish and Ukrainian troops were retreating from Right-Bank Ukraine under pressure from the Soviet First Cavalry Army and Twelfth and Fourteenth armies, a large Bolshevik force at the Belarusian Front, under Tukhachevskii, was assembled in the regions of Vitsebsk and Polatsk. After its reorganization it consisted of four armies and one strike force. In the north, along the Dvina, the Fourth Army (four infantry divisions and two cavalry brigades) constituted the right flank of the front. Attached to it was the strike force of the Third Cavalry Corps (two cavalry divisions) under the command of Ghaia Ghai. In the south the Fifteenth Army (five infantry divisions and two cavalry brigades) was deployed along the Polatsk-Maladzechna railway line. The Third Army (four infantry divisions and one cavalry brigade) was deployed along the upper Biarezina. Along the lower Biarezina, from Barysau to Babruisk, was the Sixteenth Army (five infantry divisions), while along the Ipa River and in the area of Mazyr the Mozyr Group (two incomplete divisions, about 8,000 infantry and cavalry) formed the left flank of the front and served as the liaison between the Belarusian and Ukrainian fronts. The two fronts were separated by the well-nigh impassable swamps of Polissia. Tukhachevskii's 160,000 troops faced three Polish armies. On the northern flank was the First Army under Gen. Zygadłowicz (three infantry divisions and three infantry brigades) in the area between the Dvina and the upper Biarezina. To the south, along the Biarezina, was the Fourth Army under Gen. Stanisław Szeptycki (four incomplete infantry divisions). Farther south, along the Ptych and Prypiat Rivers, was the Polesie Group under Gen. Władysław Sikorski (three infantry divisions and one cavalry brigade). In addition, the Second Division was in the rear of the Belarusian Front and performed observational functions. The Polish troops—about 120,000 men—were under the general command of Szeptycki.

On 4 July Tukhachevskii launched his second Belarusian offensive south of the Dvina. His forces advanced in several columns. One main column moved along the axis of the Smolensk–Brest-Litovsk railway line. Another main column moved along the East Prussian border. Consisting of the Third Cavalry Corps and the Fourth Army, it made deep flanking movements in an attempt to move to the lower Wisła region and then to penetrate into the Polish rear. Tukhachevskii's plan was to outflank the Poles from the north in order to cut off rail and water communications with Danzig, the port through which the Entente's supplies reached Poland, and to drive the Polish troops into the Polissian swamps. During three days of battle at the rivers Auta and Biarezina, Szeptycki fought only from behind natural or previously constructed defense lines that would protect his rear and flanks from the enemy. But Tukhachevskii advanced much too fast, and as each new Polish line of defense was established, it could not be held and had to be abandoned. Constantly outflanked by the Third Cavalry Corps and the Fourth Army to the north, the Poles were forced to retreat to the Buh River.

The subsequent attempt to hold the Bolsheviks at the Buh failed, and on 1 August the fortress of Brest-Litovsk was occupied by Soviet forces. Although Polish resistance had not been broken, desertion and a great deal of confusion occurred among the men and officers because of the retreat, exhaustion, and lack of discipline. Tukhachevskii failed, however, to drive the Polish troops into the Polissian swamps, and Piłsudski ordered his army commanders to undertake a concerted counteroffensive across the entire front. He soon realized, however, that the regrouping and equipping of the units in necessary areas demanded more time than was available. In three and a half weeks the Poles retreated over 450 kilometers from the Biarezina to Białystok. On 13 July they abandoned Minsk; on 15 July, Vilnius, which afterward was taken over by Lithuanian troops; on 20 July, Hrodna; and on 26 July, Białystok. Thus, by late July they had retreated into Polish ethnographic territory.[1]

In view of the continuing Bolshevik advance westward, on 6 August Piłsudski decided to transfer the campaign to the middle Wisła. But first the Polish troops had to disengage from Tukhachevskii's armies to prepare for the defense at the Wisła. With the help of conscript labor, Piłsudski constructed fortified positions with a double line of trenches along the front near Warsaw and Modlin, and equipped them with artillery. New troops organized through mobilization were placed in the fortified areas as garrisons. Prior to his counteroffensive, Piłsudski remedied some of the Polish Army's weaknesses. He replaced Stanisław Haller with Tadeusz Rozwadowski as chief of the General Staff, and Szeptycki with Józef Haller as commander of the Northern Front. To check the Bolsheviks' threatening flanking movements in the north, Piłsudski organized the new Fifth Army under the command of Gen. Sikorski, and placed it on the left flank of the Polish front north of the Narew and Wisła. In the south, between Dęblin and Modlin, Piłsudski assembled newly mobilized units under his command to hold up the enemy's advance. Meanwhile Tukhachevskii's left-flank forces, the Fifteenth, Third, and Sixteenth armies, succeeded in establishing a long semicircular front extending from north of Modlin to Góra Kalwaria. Farther south, the Mozyr Group advanced westward and occupied territory east of the Wisła from Góra Kalwaria to Dęblin; there it faced the Polish Second Army and extended Tukhachevskii's left flank to the Wieprz. The Bolshevik Western Front, which stretched from East Prussia to Dęblin, was the main focus of the campaign, and the outcome of the war depended upon the campaign's results. The middle front, from Dęblin to Brody, linked the Northern and Southern fronts. Its swampy, wooded, river-cut terrain created a natural defense line and helped the Poles to hold the Bolsheviks in check. At the Southwestern Front, in Galicia from Brody to the Romanian border, the Soviet Twelfth, Fourteenth, and First Cavalry armies under Egorov (his political commissar was Joseph Stalin) were engaged in long fighting with stubborn Polish and UNR troops.

As Tukhachevskii's armies advanced deeper into Poland, their greatly extended supply lines required more troops to be withdrawn from the front for their defense. Overextension also brought about the disorganization of the lines themselves and that of the entire rear. Consequently it became difficult to bring up reinforcements to the front when they were badly needed. Meanwhile the Polish retreat had shortened the Polish supply lines, and therefore more battle-ready Polish troops could be brought to the front. The condition within the Bolshevik armies was revealed by Dmytro Manuïl's'kyi:

> Our defeat at the front was, first of all, a strategic defeat. Our army was advancing forward with such terrific speed that hundreds of versts remained between it and the reserves and material supplies. The line of our front was stretched out and became increasingly thinner. At that time the Polish army, clenching a striking fist, gained advantage through an unexpected counterattack and [had] a chance to break our front. Our army was scattered across a vast space, and consequently, as the result of [our] irrepressible advance, the link among individual units was lost.[2]

As a result of the changes that occurred on both sides, on the eve of the Battle of Warsaw the strength of the Polish-Ukrainian and Bolshevik troops was balanced. From north to south, the Polish Fifth Army (34,000 men) was deployed north of the Wisła around Modlin; the First (38,000 men), and Second (12,000 men) armies were west of Warsaw and held the Warsaw bridgehead; the Fourth Army (23,500 men) was around Dęblin; the joint Third Army and Ukrainian Sixth Sich Riflemen Division (25,000 men) were around Lublin; the Sixth Army (22,000 men), was near Lviv; and the UNR Army under Gen. Omelianovych-Pavlenko (24,000 men) was on the right bank of the Dniester from Halych to the Romanian border. Confronting them was the

Soviet Army of the West under Tukhachevskii: the Fourth Army (28,000 men) and the Third Cavalry Corps of Ghaia Ghai (4,700 men) north of Warsaw around Działdowo and Mława; the Fifteenth Army (26,000 men) north of Warsaw between the rivers Wkra and Narew; the Third Army (20,000 men) northeast of Warsaw around Ostrów Mazowiecki; and the Sixteenth Army (20,700 men) east of Warsaw around Węgrów and Sokołów Podlaski. To the south was the Mozyr Group (8,000 men) and the Army of the Southwestern Front under Egorov: the Twelfth Army (22,500 men) around Włodawa and Chełm (Kholm); the First Cavalry Army under Budennyi (30,000 men) around Lviv; and the Fourteenth Army (18,000 men) between Lviv and the Dniester. In all, 178,500 Polish and Ukrainian soldiers faced 177,900 Bolshevik troops.[3]

As Tukhachevskii's armies advanced into Poland, the Bolshevik leaders and troops were high-spirited and optimistic. They believed that Poland was seething with revolutionary ferment, and they expected the Polish workers and peasants to rise up against the bourgeoisie and landowners upon encountering the Red forces. They also felt that a rapid advance and quick victory would neutralize the Polish population. During their advance the Bolsheviks unfolded a vigorous propaganda campaign, and the Communist International issued appeals to the Polish workers to revolt:

> Workers of Poland! ... you will organize demonstrations and strikes on behalf of peace with Soviet Russia. The International is convinced that you will now exert your utmost efforts to strike White Poland in the rear, so that together with the workers of Russia you will win victory over the Polish landlords and capitalists. You know that Soviet Russia brings Poland not oppression, but national freedom, freedom from the chains of Allied capital, help in the fight against your own capitalists. The victory of workers' and peasants' Russia will be the victory of the Polish proletariat, brothers and allies of the Russian workers and peasants. To the attack, Polish workers![4]

The Bolsheviks and the Polish Communists also disseminated propaganda leaflets and proclamations exhorting Polish soldiers to desert and commit sabotage. In his speech at the Ninth All-Russian Conference of the Bolshevik party on 22 September 1920, a representative of the Polish Communist party, W. Ulman, assured the delegates at the conference that in spite of the Polish regime's terror in Poland, "A resistance against the war is growing, and a revolutionary explosion is imminent. They [the regime] would not shoot all of them [the resisters], and with the help of Soviet Russia we will make a revolution in Poland."[5] In order to make the Bolshevik propaganda more effective,

Moscow disposed of a host of spies, propagandists, secret emissaries and secret friends, who penetrated into Polish territory and undermined the resistance of certain element of the Polish population. In the astounding advance during July 1920 when the Russian Army drove the Poles back over 400 miles in forty days, the services rendered by the unarmed were not less effective than those brought about by military pressure. The system adopted was to avoid frontal attack whenever possible, and to turn positions by flank marches, infiltration and propaganda.[6]

The Bolshevik leaders were convinced that more pressure was needed to bring about class war and revolutionary upheavals within Poland before a Polish Soviet republic could emerge. In anticipation of victory, a Provisional Revolutionary Committee of Poland was formed on 23 July in Moscow from among leading Polish Communists such as Julian Marchlewski (chairman), Feliks Kon, Edward Próchniak, and Józef Unszlicht. Its de facto head was Feliks Dzierżyński (Dzerzhinskii), the head of the dreaded Soviet secret police, the Cheka. The committee issued a lengthy appeal to all Polish toilers. Its main points were:

> We must tear the factories and the coal mines out of the hands of the capitalists and robber-speculators. They shall pass into the possession of the people and under the administration of workers' committees. Estates and forests will also pass into the possession and under the administration of the people. Landowners are to be driven away; the management of the estates is to be entrusted to committees of farm laborers. [But] The land of working peasants is not to be touched. Power in the towns is [to be] transferred to workers' deputies; communal Soviets are [to be] created in the villages.[7]

On 30 July, as Tukhachevskii's forces moved closer to Warsaw, the Provisional Revolutionary Committee arrived in Białystok and waited aboard a train for Warsaw to fall. The train was equipped with its own press, office facilities, security services, and direct telephone line to Moscow. On 14 August the train moved to Wyszków, a town about thirty miles from Warsaw. The committee planned to enter Warsaw on 17 August, the day the city was expected to fall. There it would proclaim itself the Polish government and would convert Poland into a Soviet state.

Because of the situation at the front, many Polish politicians were, in contrast to the Bolsheviks' optimism, depressed and conciliatory and ready to make peace with Russia on almost any terms. In light of this situation, on 14 August the State Defense Council decided to dispatch a nine-man delegation to Minsk to begin peace negotiations with the Bolsheviks. The Bolshevik attitude to the delegation and its accompanying correspondents was highly hostile, and they were insulted and accused of being spies. For a few days the Poles received no lodging, and for most of the time they were not allowed to have telegraph or radio contacts with Warsaw and the outside world. Their correspondence was also strictly censored, and each Pole was followed around by Bolshevik secret police.[8] Eventually the Bolshevik authorities began negotiating with the Polish delegation under the pretext that they were prepared to make peace with Poland. The negotiations, however, "were designed with a view both to gain time for a military advance, and to give an opportunity for subversive propaganda in Poland to bear fruit. Among the erroneous ideas entertained by the Western Powers none was more dangerous than their belief that peace was possible with the Soviet. The Russian authorities were confident of their power to destroy the Polish Army and capture Warsaw."[9]

In view of the Bolsheviks' confidence in their victory, their terms for peace were exceedingly harsh, almost requiring Polish capitulation. They agreed that the Polish-Soviet border would follow more or less the ethnographic Polish boundary, but demanded that the future Polish army be limited to 50,000 men. They also called for the creation of a civilian militia of about 200,000 industrial workers controlled by the labor organizations of Soviet Russia and Poland; all arms not needed by the Polish army to be turned over to the Red Army; the prohibition of the importation of military materiel; the dismatling of the Polish armaments industry; Bolshevik control of important railroads in Poland; the departure of the Entente military mission from Poland; and free grants of farmland to war victims or their families in Poland. Some of the peace terms were solely propagandistic, because the Bolsheviks did not want peace at that time. They purposely prolonged the negotiations, hoping to impose conditions on Poland after the establishment of a Soviet regime there. By accepting the peace terms, Poland would have been at Moscow's mercy. Instead, while the Polish delegation negotiated at Minsk, Piłsudski organized a counterattack.[10]

As Tukhachevskii's armies moved closer to Warsaw, a Polish plan of defense became imperative. The Polish General Staff and Weygand advised Piłsudski to build a defensive line along the Wisła, behind which a counteroffensive would be prepared to begin from Modlin. They recommended striking at Tukhachevskii's right flank to cut it off from the Warsaw-Białystok railway and drive it south of the Buh. Earlier the Polish and UNR troops had been divided between two fronts, the Ukrainian and Belarusian, which were separated by the Prypiat. Now Piłsudski decided to open up a third front, and withdrew from the Southern Front the two most reliable infantry divisions—the Legion's First and Third—and one cavalry brigade.

Piłsudski had the Fourth Army south of Dęblin protecting the left flank. South of Lublin the Third Army guarded the right flank and the rear against the Soviet Twelfth Army. Piłsudski deployed his troops in a wide triangle formed by the Wisła and Wieprz and the line joining Dęblin and Lubartów. He planned to use this formidable strike force to attack the weak and overextended Mozyr Group northeast of the Wieprz, thereby forcing a wedge between Tukhachevskii's Western Front, which was centered on Warsaw, and Egorov's Southwestern Front, which was directed toward Lviv. Piłsudski exploited the Bolshevik High Command's faulty strategy of not coordinating the two Bolshevik fronts. He was convinced that the Mozyr Group would not offer serious resistance, and that by attacking it the Poles would simultaneously be able to penetrate the rear of the Soviet Sixteenth Army and to create panic and confusion there that would spread to the rears of the Third, Fifteenth, and Fourteenth Soviet armies deployed around Warsaw. They would also paralyze the Bolshevik supply system and lines of retreat. On 6 August Piłsudski presented his plan to the General Staff. Although they criticized it, Piłsudski held firm and immediately ordered the troops to assemble at specified locations. Preparations for the counterattack lasted until 16 August. On 12 August Piłsudski left Warsaw for Puławy, a city seventy miles to the southeast, where he planned to launch his counterattack.

Piłsudski planned to use the First and the Fifth armies around Warsaw and nearby Modlin in a primarily defensive role, to repulse Tukhachevskii's attacks. In his judgment, the more engaged the Bolshevik forces were in that region, the better chance of success he would have in striking Tukhachevskii's left flank and rear. Subsequently the First and Fifth armies would be able to divide and defeat Tukhachevskii's forces. Piłsudski expected Tukhachevskii to attack Warsaw from the east, and he hoped the city would hold up. But Tukhachevskii directed his armies first to the west and then turned to the south to attack the Polish troops by a wide outflanking maneuver north of Warsaw, acting on the hypothesis that the retreating Polish armies on his front were broken and therefore incapable of resistance until they withdrew across the Wisła. Accordingly, he advanced with great speed toward the Wisła to cut the Polish troops off from the Poznań region and to prevent the organized defense of the Warsaw area and the regrouping of the Polish armies west of the Wisła. In the meantime, on 13 August, half of the Soviet Third and Fifteenth armies attacked Warsaw from northeast of Modlin. The defenders held out, except in Radzymin fifteen miles northeast of Warsaw. After capturing the town, the Bolsheviks pushed west to Warsaw's second defensive line, thus creating panic among the Poles.

The Polish General Staff, with Weygand's help, gained control of the situation by strengthening the troops under Gen. Żeligowski. The next day the

Polish Fifth Army under Gen. Sikorski, which was deployed along the lower Wkra, launched a counterattack from Modlin against the Fifteenth and Third armies. Heavy fighting, particularly around Radzymin by the Tenth Division under Żeligowski, continued for three days. Radzymin changed hands twice before the Bolsheviks were forced from the town on 15 August. Finally the Poles succeeded in defeating the enemy in the area of Modlin and Nasielsk to the north, and the remnants of the defeated Soviet units retreated eastward. At that time the Soviet Sixteenth Army and the other half of the Third had attacked the bridgehead of Warsaw from the east. After initial successes during the first two days, they were repulsed with the help of French tanks and French officers, who not merely advised but participated in the fighting. As a result of Tukhachevskii's operation in the north, Piłsudski was prompted to start his counterattack one day sooner than planned.

On the early morning of 16 August, the Poles counterattacked from the Wieprz northward against Tukhachevskii's left flank. The Polish Fourth Army under Gen. Leonard Skierski advanced northward toward Siedlce to cut off the lines of retreat from Warsaw to Brest-Litovsk. While the Third Army under Gen. Zygmunt Zieliński advanced northeast from the Lublin-Kholm line toward Biała Podlaska and Brest-Litovsk. Supported by artillery, tanks, armored trains, and airplanes, Piłsudski's long forced march northward encountered no serious resistance; only some skirmishes with small Bolshevik detachments occurred. After the first two days of fighting it became clear that Piłsudski's counterattack had taken the Bolshevik High Command by surprise. His strike force rapidly penetrated into the rear of Tukhachevskii's left flank and defeated the Mozyr Group. The Soviet Sixteenth Army, which was regrouping after being routed near Warsaw, was caught between the strike force and the Polish First Army. In the ensuing fighting it was again defeated, and some 10,000 of its soldiers were taken prisoner. The disorganized survivors retreated northeast toward Białystok in panic, fearing being cut off. The Soviet Third and Fifteenth armies were also routed. They retreated northward toward Łomża and then eastward along the border of East Prussia toward Grajewo and Hrodna in panic, losing many prisoners and a great amount of military equipment along the way. In the meantime the Soviet Fourth Army and Third Cavalry Corps, not knowing about the situation on the left flank because they had lost contact with their command, advanced westward as previously ordered. On 19 August they captured Płock northwest of Warsaw, and tried to cross the Wisła and attack Warsaw from the west. They were repulsed, however, and on 21 August began retreating northeast toward Mława and Kolno. Polish troops pursued them, trying to cut off their lines of retreat. Although the Bolshevik units were outnumbered, had lost their artillery, and had many of their men taken prisoner by the Poles, they continued to resist. On 25 August, however, after several days of fighting, the Third Cavalry Corps and Fourth Army—about 30,000 men—were driven into East Prussia, where they were disarmed and interned.

To save Tukhachevskii's front, the Bolshevik High Command ordered Budennyi to advance in the direction of Warsaw. But Budennyi did not follow the order, because he had a goal of his own—capturing Lviv. Trotsky had ordered him to quit the siege of Lviv and move toward Warsaw, but not before capturing Zamość. Although Budennyi made great efforts to occupy that city, he failed because of the courage of its defenders. On 31 August the Polish and UNR troops appeared in Budennyi's rear and forced his army to retreat hurriedly eastward across the Buh in complete disorder and with heavy losses. Thus the ring of Tukhachevskii's forces was finally broken. Thereafter the Bolshevik frontal attacks lost their momentum, and the Poles turned from waging a defensive war to an offensive one. The Bolshevik leaders' expectation that victory was within their grasp was shattered.[11]

For the Bolshevik High Command the reverses in Poland were rapid, unexpected, and not immediately understandable. But the reasons were simple. Because of Tukhachevskii's speedy advance it had been extremely difficult to provide his forces with adequate supplies and reinforcements. As the front shifted farther west the forces weakened, and the faster they advanced, the faster they crumbled. The situation became critical because their supply lines became disorganized and inefficient as a result of overextension, while their rear hardly existed as an organized entity. When the vanguards were approaching the Wisła, their supply base was still in Minsk. Consequently Tukhachevskii's armies depended largely on booty and requisitions from the local population. Tukhachevskii admitted that "it was a heavy burden for the local population," and Marchlewski stated that "No doubt the peasants suffered very much from the Bolshevik requisitions and forced transportation services.... Hungry soldiers stripped orchards and gardens, devastated storerooms and often plundered. It is clear that this Red Army could not win the respect of the peasants."[12]

Thus it is no wonder that the Polish population detested them. At the same time Russia was exhausted by War Communism and military expansion, and the Bolshevik High Command had great difficulty bringing reinforcements and supplies to the front precisely when and where they were most needed. As well, health problems had reached a critical stage in the Red Army. Shortages of medical supplies, equipment, and services had resulted in widespread illness among the soldiers; many of them died from dysentery and typhus. Nevertheless, the Bolshevik High Command pressed the forces to advance westward. Tukhachevskii's problems were further compounded by the lack of military coordination between the Soviet Western and Southwestern fronts.

During their chaotic retreat from Poland, Tukhachevskii's forces lost contact not only with his headquarters but also with the unit commands. Because of panic and confusion in the rear, they were unable to fight back or retreat in order. They were hampered by the endless train of supply wagons and herds of cattle and horses requisitioned during the advance through Belarus and Poland. Tukhachevskii's armies were followed by 33,000 peasant carts, thousands of which were later captured by the Poles.[13] By the end of their campaign, the Bolshevik forces had suffered great losses. Some 25,000 men were killed or wounded; 66,000 were taken prisoner; and 231 guns, 1,023 machine guns, and 10,000 rounds of ammunition fell into Polish hands.

The inefficiency of the Bolshevik forces resulted primarily from their composition. They included many Russian peasant irregulars and captured soldiers of the VA and German, Austrian, Hungarian, and other armies who had been forced to serve in the Red Army. The forces were held together largely by Chinese and Latvian formations attached to each larger unit and by Communist political commissars assigned to each commander. The cadres trained in the tsarist army and the new Bolshevik military schools were poorly organized and undisciplined. During the rapid advance they got out of control and, therefore, were not able to fight effectively. Because of the great differences in their backgrounds, many Red Army soldiers were not devoted to the Bolshevik cause. According to Lord D'Abernon,

> Some Bolshevik prisoners ... were mild, downtrodden peasants without enthusiasm, fanaticism or conviction.... The soldiers do not talk of their Army as 'we' but of 'the Bolshevik Army,' as if they had nothing in common with it but forced service.... They said the Bolshevik Army was bad and short of ammunition—but the Denikin Army had been worse, the officers doing nothing but drinking and playing cards. The general impression they gave was that of good natured serfs, who were just driven forward by the Commissars and Chinese—their only desire was to get home. This applies to nine-tenths of the prisoners I have seen—the other tenth appear fanatical devils."[14]

When the Bolsheviks approached Warsaw, they were discouraged to find the Polish workers coming out not with red flags to greet them, but with rifles to fight them. They had grossly underestimated the strength of nationalism in the new Polish state, and a crucial factor in their defeat in Poland was their failure to arouse revolutionary support. The vast majority of Polish workers and peasants shared the bourgeoisie's and landlords' anti-Russian attitude, and it quickly became clear that a Soviet Poland could be established only through Bolshevik military conquest.[15]

On 25 August the fragments of Tukhachevskii's forces reached the Neman line and began regrouping. Meanwhile the Bolshevik High Command called up all available reserves from Russia, and soon new units arrived to strengthen Tukhachevskii. At this critical time, however, the High Command had to send some reserves to fight the VA under Gen. Wrangel, which was moving from the Crimea into southern Ukraine and the Kuban, as well as Ukrainian partisans. After the reinforcement of his forces and improvement of their morale, in early September Tukhachevskii established a new front along the rivers Neman and Shchara in Belarus. Its northern flank bordered on Lithuania; its southern flank, on the Polissian swamps. Four armies were deployed. In the north the Third Army was around Hrodna and received the strongest reinforcement. In the south the Fifteenth Army was around Vaukavysk, the Sixteenth Army was in the area of Belovezha, and the Fourth Army was along the Buh near Brest-Litovsk. Tukhachevskii hoped to regain his position in Poland. But the Polish Command anticipated his action.

Despite the Polish victory at the Wisła, Piłsudski realized the struggle for Poland was not over and that to achieve a real victory he had to defeat the Bolshevik forces that had retreated. Now Piłsudski had superiority in numbers, equipment, and troop morale, initiative, and momentum. Unlike Tukhachevskii, who, had remained at Minsk during the offensive and lost contact not only with his enemy, but also with his own forces, Piłsudski had moved from one part of the front to another to encourage his soldiers, get information, and evaluate the situation. On 25 August he halted his advance in order to reshape the front and regroup his troops. During the counterattack the Polish Northern Front had moved from south to north. Now Piłsudski had to turn it eastward to face the new Bolshevik front. This required changes on the Southern Front as well, and during the first half of September Piłsudski regrouped his troops accordingly. To strengthen them, he dissolved the First and Fifth armies and merged them with the remaining four armies. Of the latter, the Second Army was reorganized under Gen. Rydz-Śmigły into a strike force deployed around Hrodna, and the Fourth Army under Gen. Skierski was reinforced and deployed south of the Neman. The offensive against Tukhachevskii was carried on by these two armies.

Prior to further military operations, however, Piłsudski had to resolve an international political problem. On 10 July 1920 the Polish government had agreed at the Spa Conference that Polish troops would not cross the Curzon Line. Now it declared that the Spa agreement was null and void because it had been signed by Prime Minister Grabski under the condition that the Entente would protect Poland from a Bolshevik invasion, and the Entente had failed to give the promised protection. Consequently Piłsudski had decided to renew military operations, and the Entente were presented with a fait accompli.

After regrouping his troops, on 20 September Piłsudski resumed the campaign against Tukhachevskii. The Second Army carried out a frontal attack in the area of Hrodna, while the Fourth Army attacked in the direction of Vaukavysk. They met strong Bolshevik resistance, but this situation changed when Piłsudski applied Tukhachevskii's previous tactic on the Northern Front. By using a strike group formed from two infantry divisions and two cavalry brigades detached from the Second Army, Piłsudski outflanked the Soviet Third Army from the north and attacked its rear, thereby paralyzing the delivery of supplies, creating panic among the Bolshevik troops, and forcing them to retreat. On 25 September the Poles captured Hrodna and then advanced toward Lida, a rail and road junction. After three days of fighting the Third Army was defeated, and only part of it escaped under cover of night. Simultaneously the Polish Fourth Army attacked the Soviet Fifteenth and Sixteenth armies, and on 29 September it defeated and drove them toward Minsk. This battle became known as the Battle of the Neman. Piłsudski then pursued the retreating Bolsheviks to the river Shchara, where a new battle took place. After a few days the Bolsheviks were defeated and driven back toward Minsk. Piłsudski continued pursuing them and occupied Minsk on 5 October, after Tukhachevskii abandoned his headquarters. At the battles of the Neman and Shchara the Poles captured some 50,000 prisoners, 160 artillery guns, and other war materiel.[16]

The renewed campaign at the Belarusian Front gradually expanded to the south, from the Prypiat to the Dniester, and intensified. The aim of the Polish and UNR troops there was to defeat the Soviet Twelfth and Fourteenth armies. Concentric attacks were undertaken by the Polish Third Army in Volynia, while the Sixth Army and the UNR Army in Galicia strove to drive the Red Army from Western Ukrainian territory. On 12 September the Third Army under Gen. Sikorski and Gen. Krajowski's group (two infantry divisions) advanced along the Kholm-Kovel railroad line. Farther north a strike group with tanks, armored cars, and motorized infantry advanced eastward from Volodava to Ratne to outflank the Soviet Twelfth Army from the north and break its resistance. Farther south, from around Hrubeshiv, Gen. Stanislaw Haller's group (two infantry and two cavalry divisions) advanced eastward to capture Lutsk. Meanwhile Gen. Żeligowski's group (one infantry division and one Cossack cavalry brigade) captured Sokal and moved eastward. The Poles' unexpected attack resulted in the defeat of the Bolshevik forces in the area of Kovel and the capture of the city. Meanwhile, on 16 September, Haller's group captured Lutsk. During the fighting the Soviet Twelfth Army suffered heavy losses and was forced to retreat eastward. Budennyi's cavalry army failed to check the Polish advance at the Styr River, and the Poles pursued the retreating Bolsheviks eastward, capturing Rivne on 18 September and Ternopil on 20 September.

To the south, the UNR Army under Gen. Omelianovych-Pavlenko crossed the Dniester near Horodenka, Nyzhniv, and Iezupil on the night of 14–15 September, and under heavy Bolshevik fire attacked the Soviet Fourteenth Army. The Bolsheviks defending the crossings were all taken prisoner, while the forces in the rear retreated northeast. The UNR troops then moved northward in three directions: toward Chortkiv, toward Buchach, and between Pidhaitsi and Buchach. After four days of fighting they defeated the Bolsheviks and pursued them for over 100 kilometers into the triangular area between the Dniester and the Zbruch. On 18 September they established a new front line along the Zbruch. During the fighting in the triangle, they captured 1,217 prisoners, 68 machine guns, 915 wagons, and a considerable amount of other military equipment. After receiving new reserves, the Bolshevik forces tried to dislodge the UNR troops from their new positions, but failed. Although the latter were exhausted and lacked arms and ammunition, they fought the Bolsheviks with great courage.

The UNR Army needed to secure more territory to be able to mobilize new recruits, obtain more supplies, and establish contact with the Ukrainian partisans to the east and gain their cooperation. On 21 September it crossed the Zbruch and pushed the Bolshevik forces farther east to Nova Ushytsia. From there the Bolsheviks retreated to the Bar-Mohyliv railroad line near the Dniester, where they planned to establish a new defensive line with the help of armored trains. The UNR troops attacked again, however, and forced them to retreat still farther east to Vapniarka. The UNR troops then moved northwest to the Liatychiv-Bar line and the Zhmerynka-Mohyliv railroad. In the process the Soviet Fourteenth Army was routed.

In mid-October the Ukrainian-Bolshevik conflict greatly intensified as each side tried to take more territory before an expected cease-fire took place. On 18 October UNR troops attained the line running northwest from Iaruha on the Dniester to Ialtushkiv and then northeast to Lityn. Their command hoped that in a few days they would reach the strategically important railway junctions of Zhmerynka and Vapniarka. While the Ukrainian troops fought the Bolsheviks, a preliminary peace treaty and armistice agreement between Poland and Soviet Russia were signed on 12 October (they took effect on 18 October). Consequently a demarcation line was established and hostilities ceased on all fronts. To assure adherence to the cease-fire, the command of the Polish Army dispatched units to the line held by the Ukrainian troops to indicate that this was a Polish front.[17]

CHAPTER 12

The Preliminary Peace Treaty and Armistice Agreement

In light of the successful Polish counteroffensive, Polish-Soviet negotiations changed direction. During the negotiations in Minsk from 14 August through 2 September, the Bolsheviks had expected victory and the imminent collapse of Poland. The terms they presented amounted to Poland's disarmament, which, if accepted, would have turned Poland into a Soviet republic. When the Polish delegation, which was deprived of communication with Warsaw and the outside world, found out about the Polish successes at the front, however, it made demands of its own. One was the transfer of armistice negotiations to a neutral location. After hard bargaining, Riga, Latvia was the site both parties agreed upon.

The Polish delegation that returned from Minsk to Warsaw was reorganized and enlarged. One group was delegated by the Sejm, which consisted of six major political parties, and was represented by Stanisław Grabski, Władysław Kiernik, Norbert Barlicki, Adam Mieczkowski, Ludwik Waszkiewicz, and Michał Wichliński. The other group was delegated by the government and was represented by Witold Kamieniecki, Leon Wasilewski, and Gen. Mieczysław Kuliński. Jan Dąbski, the deputy foreign minister, was appointed the chairman. The new delegation, accompanied by several experts and a secretariat under Aleksander Ładoś, departed for Riga on 11 September. The joint Soviet Russian-Soviet Ukrainian delegation sent to Riga was represented by Leonid Obolenskii, Sergei Kirov, Dmytro Manuïl's'kyi, and Adol'f Ioffe, the chairman; the secretary was J. Lorenz. Ioffe, who was in constant touch with Lenin, conducted the negotiations, while the influence of the other members was slight. Unlike Dąbski, Ioffe was an experienced professional diplomat. Furthermore, as an American reporter remarked, "these Russians understand propaganda! That is where they are strong. The Poles do not refuse us the official text of their remarks, promising it early the next morning, but by that time the Russian side of the case and Ioffe's speech will already be in print across the Atlantic."[1]

When the Polish government accepted the Soviet proposal to negotiate an armistice and preliminary peace, it did not consult the UNR government. It thus violated the Treaty of Warsaw, in which the Polish government had agreed "not to conclude any international agreements directed against Ukraine." Moreover, when the Ukrainian government asked the Polish government for the right to participate in the negotiations, the Polish foreign minister, Prince Eustachy Sapieha, as revealed in his secret instructions to Polish diplomats abroad, referred the request to the Soviet Russian government:

> In our negotiations with the Bolsheviks the problem of Petliura shall not be taken into consideration at all; nevertheless, today I sent a message to [Soviet Deputy Commissar of Foreign Affairs Georgii] Chicherin informing him that Petliura's government wishes to negotiate with the Russian delegation at Riga. This proposal, however, should in no way create difficulties for the departure of our delegation, even if Chicherin rejects negotiations with Petliura, which I think is certain.[2]

In response to Sapieha's telegram of 15 September concerning the departure of the UNR representative Andrii Livyts'kyi for Riga, Chicherin replied that "a democratic Ukraine exists nowhere, and the Soviet Government considers Andrii Livyts'kyi a traitor and a rebel who may come to Riga only to raise, through Ioffe, intercession for amnesty."[3] When a correspondent later asked Grabski why the Polish delegation ignored the Treaty of Warsaw, Grabski replied that "it was merely a private agreement between Piłsudski and Petliura, [who were] personal friends; it was not ratified by the Polish Sejm, and therefore was not obligatory for the peace delegation."[4] This action not only violated the Ukrainian-Polish agreement, but also showed disregard for the loyalty of the Ukrainian side. Even Sapieha admitted that the army of "General Pavlenko for most of the time, even in the worst periods, fought most loyally on our side and continues to defend the important front line along the Dniester in Eastern Galicia."[5] A contemporary Polish writer warned the Polish leaders about the future consequences of Polish disloyalty toward the Ukrainians:

> A faithful ally, the Ukrainians, who with their army contributed to strengthening the southern front and the defense of Lviv against the Bolshevik invasion, shall, by our attitude in a decisive time for them, be won or lost for a long time.... We must remember that the conditions we shall present in Riga shall determine our position for the future not only toward Russia, but also toward Ukraine, Lithuania, and Belarus.... With Ukraine we concluded an agreement recognizing its independence and defending our border from its side. In its most difficult time Ukraine did not break this agreement and continued to stand by it with unprecedented loyalty. At present we must not abnegate it, the more so that [now] we have more opportunities to pursue an active policy in the east.[6]

Official armistice negotiations resumed in Riga on 17 September. During their first phase there was strong dissension among the Polish delegates for two principal reasons. First, because they had only general instructions from the Polish government, the final formulation of the armistice terms was left up to them, and they could not reach a concensus. Second, the delegation consisted of two distinct groups representing the divergent political conceptions of Dmowski or Piłsudski concerning the solution of the Ukrainian, Belarusian, and Lithuanian problems. Moreover one group, under Dąbski, viewed the border settlement with Soviet Russia as a permanent one, while the other, under Grabski, viewed it as temporary and hoped that the Bolshevik regime would eventually be overthrown by the tsarists. Sapieha shared Grabski's view: "We do not believe in the stability of the Bolshevik system in Russia. Therefore we shall maintain relations with all of the Russian organizations that might come to power by eventual changes or upheavals. Although we had the opportunity to take Minsk, Zhytomyr, and Kamianets[Podilskyi], for the sake of a future Russia we did not do it."[7]

Ładoś remarked that "Nearly as much energy was spent by the delegation on internal conflict as on actual negotiations with the adversary."[8] A major struggle occurred over the question of Poland's future eastern border, and the dissension weakened the Polish position vis-à-vis the Bolshevik delegation. The border question played into Grabski's hands. Gradually his view came to dominate, and consequently he was able to create an almost unanimous front within the "Sejm group," which abandoned Piłsudski's postulate of buffer states in Eastern Europe.

The first plenary session in Riga opened on 21 September. The two delegations, members of the diplomatic corps in Riga, representatives of the Latvian government, and correspondents assembled in the State Hall of the Schwarzhäupterhaus, where they were greeted by the Latvian foreign minister, Zigfrids Meierovics. Dąbski and Ioffe both thanked Latvia for its hospitality and then spoke of the need for a just and lasting peace. Both delegations faced a difficult task, for they had to not only negotiate an end to the war, but also solve the economic, financial, and cultural problems stemming from the foreign occupation of Poland for a century and a half.

At the session, one of the most important issues resolved was that of credentials. All participants, especially the UNR delegates or representatives, were uneasy about whether or not the Polish delegation would recognize the representatives of the Ukrainian Soviet Republic and negotiate with them as equals. Whether the Polish government betrayed or remained loyal to its official ally, the UNR under President Petliura, would determine the course of the Polish-Soviet negotiations. While UNR troops continued fighting the Bolsheviks alongside its Polish allies, the Polish delegation, following government instructions received prior to departure for Riga, recognized the Soviet Ukrainian representatives after only twenty minutes.[9] Recognition was given even though, as Dąbski admitted, "Soviet Ukraine and [Soviet] Belarus are fictions created by the Bolsheviks to disguise their all-Bolshevik imperialism."[10] In reality the Poles recognized the right of the Soviet Russian delegation to speak on behalf of Soviet Ukraine. Ironically the act of recognition was signed by Dąbski, the same man who, one year earlier, had signed the Treaty of Warsaw.

According to one eyewitness, "I watched carefully for signs of stress from the Soviet delegation. I remember well what emotion was apparent among the ranks of the Soviet delegation and how, immediately after [they left the cabinet room], Ioffe took out his cigarette case with a nervous motion and began frequently inhaling cigarette smoke. No wonder: in the course of some twenty minutes a huge rock onto which the boat of Polish-Soviet peace could have run [aground] was happily removed from the path."[11]

How important the recognition of the Soviet Ukrainian representatives was for the Soviet Russian regime can be seen from Chicherin's statement released from Moscow on 17 September: "Soviet Russia would willingly make any concessions if Poland agreed to recognize the government of Soviet Ukraine." According to the above eyewitness, "Chicherin knew what he was talking about. He knew that Soviet Ukraine is a fiction, that there is another Ukraine, a democratic one, which was twice recognized, on 10 January 1918 at Brest-Litovsk and on 30 June 1918 in Kyiv, by the Bolsheviks and with which Poland concluded a formal treaty."[12]

By this act of recognition the Polish delegation entirely reversed Poland's policy toward Ukraine. According to Wasilewski, Piłsudski had already stated his position on 30 March:

> As for Ukraine, we shall counterpose [Khristian] Rakovskii's [Soviet] Ukraine to Petliura's Ukraine, but we shall not discuss which one is the more authentic one, because we could do that endlessly. Let the Ukrainians decide for themselves. For this purpose we shall request the neutralization of Kyiv to convene there a constituent assembly from all of Ukraine within the borders recognized by us on the Right Bank and by them on the Left Bank of the Dnieper. That constituent assembly shall settle the Ukrainian question.[13]

Later, in the fall of 1923, Piłsudski explained to his friends why he betrayed Poland's ally, the UNR under Petliura, and accepted the Peace Treaty of Riga:

> The unsuccessful war of 1920 had so deeply shaken and horrified [Polish] society that [it] suddenly felt tired and unsure of itself. I could not ignore this

The Preliminary Peace Treaty 141

fact. [Moreover], At that time I and my policy were objects of a bitter and unscrupulous attack. The government and parliament were internally divided by this attack.[14]

During the second session, on 24 September, Ioffe stressed that Soviet Russia had recognized the independence and sovereignty of Poland, Ukraine, and Belarus as early as 1917, and that it had made peace with Lithuania in 1920. He stated that the Soviet Russian government considered that the basis of the Polish-Soviet peace settlement should be the confirmation by both sides of the independence of the Ukrainian and Belarusian Soviet republics and Lithuania, as well as the recognition of the independence of Eastern Galicia. It was prepared to agree to a universal, secret, direct, and equal plebiscite in Eastern Galicia, and believed that the future of the above-mentioned countries ought to be determined by their existing parliaments or soviets. During the negotiations, the Soviet Russian delegation exploited the issue of Eastern Galicia. The ZUNR government had been in exile in Vienna since mid-November 1919, and its president, Petrushevych, was actively lobbying international bodies on behalf of Eastern Galicia. Unsettled Polish-Soviet relations and the opening of negotiations in Riga gave Petrushevych additional opportunity to raise the question of Eastern Galicia and some hope that its lost statehood would be regained.

Petrushevych dispatched a delegation to Riga on 11 September. Its four members, Kost' Levyts'kyi (chairman), Osyp Nazaruk, Luka Myshuha, and Ernest Breiter, were to act as observers and report on the course of negotiations that affected Eastern Galicia. Because of travel difficulties, on 21 September the delegation dispatched a telegram from Stettin to the presidium of the peace conference, but the Poles intercepted and concealed it. The delegation finally arrived in Riga on 26 September, and the next day it submitted a second note to the Presidium expressing reservations about the legality of any decision on the political status of Eastern Galicia by the Polish and Soviet delegations without the consent of the ZUNR National Rada (parliament). It stressed that such a decision would violate the national self-determination of the people of that territory.[15]

Once the note was reported in Riga newspapers, the Polish delegation began spreading propaganda against the ZUNR delegation and their cause. On 30 September the Polish Press Bureau issued a release stating that

> In connection with the news in the local press about the arrival of the Ukrainian delegation, headed by K. Levyts'kyi and the Communist Breiter, the Polish agency informs the press that the above-mentioned persons represent nobody. The elements that, in 1918, established the Ukrainian Rada that was

headed by Petliura and was at war with Poland concluded a peace with Poland on the basis of the recognition of autonomy for Eastern Galicia and the formation of an independent Ukraine east of the Zbruch river.

Now there are two Ukrainian states, the first [being] Ukraine, [which] under Petliura and Pavlenko is fighting against the Bolsheviks and has seized Kamianets-Podilskyi, Proskuriv, and Novokostiantyniv, and the second [being] Soviet Ukraine under Rakovskii. Which of these parties wins shall be determined in the near future.

The third Ukraine, of the Germanophile Petrushevych who disassociated himself from Petliura and dispatched the delegate Levyts'kyi to Riga, is a figment; not one Ukrainian soldier would defend it.[16]

Next day the ZUNR delegation issued a response:

The Polish Press Bureau branded E. T. Breiter, the member of the Eastern Galician delegation, a "Communist." The intention is clear: to discredit the delegation before the Entente Powers. Breiter, a Pole [descended from a Polonized Swedish family], was for many years, from 1900, a member of the Austrian Parliament from the city of Lviv. He always stood on the principle of equality of rights for all nationalities in Galicia and, as an independent socialist, always unyieldingly struggled against abuses by the Galician bureaucracy.

The allegation that Petliura was the head of the Ukrainian Rada established in 1918 and that he concluded a peace treaty with Poland on the basis of recognition of autonomy for Eastern Galicia contradicts the facts. Since 1918 Petliura has been only a member of the Directory of Kyivan Ukraine [i.e., the UNR], and he was never a member of the Ukrainian National Rada of Eastern Galicia.

The truth is that now there are two Ukrainian states: Kyivan Ukraine, which previously was occupied by Russia and is now represented by the Soviet Ukrainian authorities at the peace conference, and East Galician Ukraine, which previously was occupied by Austria and whose National Rada dispatched the East Galician delegation here. As for Petliura, at present he is fighting jointly with the Poles near Proskuriv against the Bolshevik forces; and he has no relations with the East Galician National Rada.

The Polish allegation reproaches Dr. Petrushevych, the president of the East Galician National Rada, for being a "Germanophile." In the years 1914–17, when the Poles strove with great effort to gain favor from Germany, they accused the same Dr. Petrushevych of being an "Ententophile." Consequently this reproach led to the imprisonment of thousands of Galician Ukrainians in Austrian prisons.

Whether the East Galician question is imaginary, [and] without the support of a single Ukrainian soldier, other facts speak for themselves: the many years of bloody struggle and constant insurrection by the East Galician population against Polish annexation; stubborn Polish opposition against the plebiscite in Eastern Galicia; and the position of the Entente Powers, which consider Eastern Galicia a separate state.[17]

A few days later, on 5 October, Dąbski and Ioffe reached an agreement on all principal questions. The next day Nazaruk paid a visit to Manuïl's'kyi and asked him "what was happening to Galicia." Manuïl's'kyi replied: "We are signing a peace treaty, a harmful one for Galicia, Belarus, and Ukraine," and stated with sorrow that "The Poles also gave away my fatherland."[18] While the Polish and Soviet commissions completed the final draft of the preliminary peace treaty, the ZUNR delegation drew up a lengthy protest to the Riga conference, which was submitted on 7 October:

The Plenipotentiary Delegation of the National Rada of Eastern Galicia and its Government that came to Riga to protect the legitimate state rights of Eastern Galicia did not petition for participation in the Peace Conference's negotiations, for it considered the forum of interested belligerent parties, Poland and Soviet Russia and Soviet Ukraine, unqualified to discuss the matter of Eastern Galicia's statehood. Although, in the course of the Conference negotiations, the Delegation of Soviet Russia and Soviet Ukraine recognized the state independence of Eastern Galicia, it [subsequently] yielded to pressure from the Polish Delegation and agreed to accept in the preliminary peace treaty such a demarcation border that Galicia fell west of it. Consequently we consider it our duty, as representatives of the legal authority in Eastern Galicia, to register here a most resolute protest against all and any, even temporary, disposition of the territory of Eastern Galicia by Poland or by Soviet Russia and Ukraine, for any decision ... without the consent of the representatives of the National Rada of Eastern Galicia would be a violation of the rights of national self-determination of the population of that territory. Therefore such a decision can not have any significance, and its [Galicia's] people will never recognize it as valid. Arbitrary determination of the state territory of Eastern Galicia in the peace treaty between Poland and [Soviet] Russia and Ukraine directly violates the will of the people of Eastern Galicia that was recognized in the resolution of the Supreme Council of the Entente states adopted on 11 July 1919 and was also accepted by Poland, which guaranteed that the matter of Eastern Galicia's statehood would, on the basis of the right of national self-determination, be decided in the last instance by its population. Therefore we protest against the treatment of the matter of Eastern Galicia's statehood as an internal affair of Poland, because the

Ukrainian people of this territory, which never wanted and does want to belong to Poland, by accomplishing its right of statehood [in fighting] against Poland's annexational drives, attained during the last two years in [the arena of] international relations the recognition of Eastern Galicia as a separate state entity, [as] a separate subject of international law. Finally, by protesting against any and all importance, weight, and legal force of the peace treaty between Poland and Soviet Russia and Ukraine as pertaining to East Galician territory, we declare that the matter of the state independence of Eastern Galicia should be decided once and for all as soon as possible by a *world conference* according to the will of the population of this territory, because one cannot allow, after the dissolution of Austria, all of its [formerly subject] peoples to receive, on the basis of the right of self-determination, their own state territories, yet [allow] only the Ukrainian people on its own native Galician territory to be placed under the merciless rule of their age-old Polish enemy, which is even now destroying it in an unheard-of inhuman manner although Eastern Galicia has not been recognized as being part of Poland.[19]

Because the Soviet delegation recognized Eastern Galicia as part of the Polish state, the Polish delegation, as Manuïl's'kyi stated, "also gave away my fatherland," that is, the rest of Ukraine, to Soviet Russia. The recognition of "independent" Ukrainian and Belarusian Soviet republics meant recognition by Poland of the status quo in Ukraine and Belarus, that is, their Bolshevik control. Ioffe declared that to achieve a basic understanding, his government would withdraw its original terms presented to the Polish delegation at Minsk, such as reduction of the Polish Army, demobilization of the Polish war industries, the surrender of arms, and the return of the railway linking Vaukavysk and Grajewo to Soviet Russia. His government was also willing to offer Poland more favorable boundaries than the Entente had been able to offer. The Soviet-Polish border would run considerably to the east of the Curzon Line, and Eastern Galicia would remain within Poland, pending the result of a plebiscite. At the same time Ioffe presented the Soviet terms of armistice together with an ultimatum that Soviet Russia would resume a winter campaign: "If preliminary peace terms are not be signed within ten days, that is, by 5 October 1920, the Soviet government shall reserve the right to change the proposed terms."[20]

Although both sides needed the peace agreement, the Bolsheviks were in particular need of security in the west. Therefore their insistence on an accelerated armistice agreement was understandable. In a speech in Moscow to leather workers on 2 October, Lenin pointed out that "Because of the continuing [enemy] advancement on the Western and Wrangel's fronts, our position again is very bad... and now our main and principal task is victory over Wrangel.... It is necessary to end the war by all means and speed up the advance against Wrangel."[21] Lenin's fear was a real one, because in mid-September Wrangel was advancing from the Crimea in two directions: across the Dnieper so as to secure both banks of the Dnieper before a northern offensive, and into central Ukraine to establish contact with the Polish and UNR armies. In addition, the Bolsheviks were engaged in fighting against Ukrainian partisans. Therefore the Bolshevik command was compelled to transfer some units from the Polish front to southern Ukraine to prepare an offensive against Wrangel.

"I believed that from a political point of view it was wiser to make concessions to the enemy," Lenin admitted. "The temporary sacrifices of a bad peace seemed to me cheaper than the prolongation of war.... We are using the peace with Poland in order to descend upon Wrangel with all our strength and give him such a crushing blow that he shall leave us alone forever."[22] While speaking to the delegates of gubernial, country, and village executive committees of Moscow gubernia on 15 October 1920, Lenin declared: "We were compelled to hasten with peace because we wished to avoid a winter campaign, conscious that it is better to have an unwanted border, that is, to receive less territory in Belarus and to have an opportunity to liberate a smaller number of Belarusian peasants from under the yoke of the bourgeoisie, than to be exposed to the burden of a new winter campaign for the Russian peasants."[23] Taking into consideration the critical military situation, between 20 and 23 September Lenin sent Ioffe the following telegram:

> For us the whole essence is: first, to have an armistice soon, and second and most important, to have a real guarantee of effective peace within ten days. Your task is to safeguard this and verify the viability of the guarantees for effective implementation. If you can secure this, then make maximum [territorial] concessions up to the line running along the river Shchara, Ogiński Canal, rivers Iaselda and Styr, and then the state border between Russia [sic] and Eastern Galicia. If, in spite of all our efforts and concessions, this proves impossible to secure, then your sole task must be to unmask the Poles' procrastination and to convince them of the inevitability of a winter campaign."[24]

After a brief intermission, Dąbski presented Poland's preliminary terms, stressing its desire for a just peace, understanding, and reconciling the national interests of both sides. Subsequently he introduced eleven provisions:

1. Both contracting parties guarantee to respect each other's state sovereignty and to refrain from any interference in each other's internal affairs.

2. Delimitation of the state boundaries of both parties on territories detached from Poland by the Russian Empire should rest on mutual compliance with regard to:
   a. ending the campaign between Poland and Soviet Russia concerning disputed territories, and the creation of the basis for friendly coexistence. State boundaries shall be determined not on the basis of avenging historical wrongs, but on the basis of just conciliation of the vital interests of both parties;
   b. a just solution of disputed national problems on the said territories in the spirit of democratic principles;
   c. securing the lasting safety of each of the said states from eventual assault by the other side. Because Poland wishes peace and does not wish to impose by force its own peace terms, it therefore proposes to the other to decide on a mutually acceptable boundary line on the basis of the above principles.
3. Both parties assume the obligation to place in the peace treaty regulations regarding the free choice (option) of Polish, or Russian [or Ukrainian] citizenship, with the understanding that all persons should have freedom of choice without exception.
4. Both parties are obligated by the peace treaty regulations to guarantee persons of Polish nationality in Russia [or Ukraine] and persons of Russian [or Ukrainian] nationality in Poland rights safeguarding their free cultural and linguistic development and religious practices.
5. Both parties reciprocally renounce compensation, in any form, for costs incurred during the Polish-Soviet War and for damages caused by the war.
6. Both parties agree to place in the peace treaty regulations governing the exchange of prisoners of war and the repayment of expenses for their maintenance.
7. Upon signing the peace preliminaries, joint [Polish-Soviet] commissions are to be convoked to supervise the immediate exchange of civilian prisoners and interned persons and the return of hostages and prisoners of war.
8. Both parties agree to place in the peace treaty regulations governing amnesty for Polish citizens and persons of Polish origin in Russia and Ukraine, and for Russian [and Ukrainian] citizens and persons of Russian [and Ukrainian] origin in Poland.
9. Both parties agree to begin immediate negotiations regarding the conclusion of a peace treaty.
10. Both parties agree immediately after signing the Peace Treaty to begin negotiations regarding commercial and economic, sanitary, transportation, and postal and telegraph conventions.

11. Both parties declare that the resolution of accounts and liquidation questions in the peace treaty shall rest upon the following principles:
   a. Poland shall bear no obligations or burdens because part of the territories of the Polish Republic formerly belonged to the Russian Empire;
   b. both parties renounce all claims to state properties contained on the territory of the other party;
   c. both parties agree reciprocally to return in kind or in a corresponding equivalent the evacuated movable property of the state and of self-governing bodies, institutions, physical and legal persons, etc., with the exception of war booty;
   d. Russia shall return to Poland all archives, libraries, works of art, historical works, war trophies, relics, and similar articles of cultural achievement exported from Poland to Russia since the time of the partition of the Polish Commonwealth;
   e. both parties agree to a reciprocal settlement of the legal claims of physical and legal persons against the government and other institutions;
   f. both parties agree to the restitution or indemnity to the state and to legal and physical persons of possessions looted during the confiscation of the residences of Polish representatives in Russia by Soviet authorities;
   g. Russia accepts the clause that Poland and its citizens have the greatest privileges with regard to the restitution of property and compensation for losses incurred during the revolutionary period and the civil war in Russia.

Both contracting parties agree that the above points do not cover all matters regarding the settling and liquidation of accounts.[25]

At the next session of the peace conference, on 27 September, both sides issued responses to previous declarations. Ioffe analyzed the Polish terms of peace point by point, and ended by saying that the Polish delegation had not replied to the declaration of the Soviet Supreme Central Executive Committee. To avoid a prolonged discussion of this theoretical question and to expedite the negotiations, Dąbski proposed forming commissions that would work out the details of the treaty. Ioffe agreed, and four commissions with representatives and experts from both sides were set up: a General Commission comprised of all the Polish, Soviet Russian, and Soviet Ukrainian delegates, and commissions on territorial, legal, and economic and commercial questions. It was decided that their meetings would not be open to the public. At the 28 September session of the General Commission, Ioffe presented a draft of the preliminary peace agreement consisting of seventeen articles. It was an amalgamation of Ioffe's and Dąbski's articles:

1. Proceeding from the principle of self-determination, both contracting parties recognize without reservation ... the independence and sovereignty of the newly established ... Belarusian, Lithuanian, and Ukrainian republics.
2. Because national self-determination in Eastern Galicia has not yet assumed completed state forms, both contracting parties, recognizing in principle the independence of Eastern Galicia, agree that the final decision on its future should be determined through a referendum of the entire population, based on a universal, direct, equal, and secret vote.
3. Both contracting parties pledge to recognize the existing legal order in these republics and the state government that shall be established in Eastern Galicia by the will of its native peoples, and not to interfere in the internal affairs of these independent and sovereign republics.
4. Solemnly reaffirming its repeated declarations, Russia unreservedly recognizes the independence and sovereignty of the Polish republic ... [and] freely and forever renounces Russia's sovereign rights over the Polish people and its territories.
5. The contracting parties agree that the border between Belarus and Ukraine on the one hand and Poland on the other should, in its general features, run from the state border between Lithuania and Belarus to where the Svislach flows into the Neman, through the inhabited places of Svislach, Rudnia, Belovezha, Kamianets-Litovsk, Brest-Litovsk, Pishcha, Liuboml, Volodymyr-Volynskyi, and Hrybovytsia ... and then along the former border between Russia and Austria-Hungary to the Dniester River at the border with Romania....

    Within forty-eight hours of the signing of the preliminary agreement, military hostilities should cease, after which Polish troops should be withdrawn twenty-five versts to the west of the above border.... Russian armies also have the right to be not less than twenty-five versts east of the above border. The twenty-five-verst belts on both sides of the border shall be considered a neutral military zone.... Administration [there] ... shall be entrusted to the relevant governing bodies of Poland, Belarus, and Ukraine.
6. Both contracting parties pledge:
    a. Not to allow on their territories the formation and sojourn of governments, organizations, or groups whose goal is armed struggle against the other contracting party; and to take measures aimed at the immediate liquidation of such governments, organizations, and groups already created on the territories of both sides....
    b. To prohibit those powers that are actually in a state of war with one of the contracting parties, as well as organizations and groups that have

as their goal armed struggle against one of the parties, from importing into their ports and transporting across their territories anything that might be used against the other contracting party, such as armed forces, military property, military-technical means, and artillery, food, engineering, and flying materiel.
7. Both contracting parties pledge to include in the peace treaty provisions regarding the freedom of choice (option) of Russian, Ukrainian, or Polish citizenship, with the understanding that the rights that shall, on the basis of the peace treaty, be enjoyed by the citizens of both sides shall also be enjoyed equally by persons choosing their citizenship.
8. Both parties pledge to accept articles in the peace treaty guaranteeing the rights of national minorities and safeguarding the freedom of cultural, linguistic, and religious development.
9. Both contracting parties reciprocally renounce compensation for their wartime expenditures ... and indemnities for their wartime losses ... including [indemnities for] all types of requisitions....
10. Both contracting parties pledge to include in the peace treaty clauses on the exchange of prisoners of war and the repayment of the real expenses for their maintenance.
11. Both contracting parties pledge to establish, immediately after signing the preliminary peace treaty, joint commissions for the immediate exchange of state prisoners, interned persons, hostages, and, to the extent it is possible, prisoners of war.
12. Each contracting party pledges to include in the peace treaty a clause granting the broadest possible amnesty to citizens of the other side and to its own citizens for actions committed during the war in favor of the other side.
13. Immediately after [concluding] the current preliminary agreement, both contracting parties pledge to begin negotiations regarding a final peace treaty, whose basis should be the articles and terms of the current preliminary agreement.
14. Both contracting parties pledge to include in the peace treaty a clause regarding their mutual accounts and the liquidation of former relations resulting from the former inclusion of Poland in the Russian Empire. As their basis, both parties agree to accept the following principles:
    a. Any obligations for either side shall result from the former inclusion of Poland in Russia;
    b. Both parties renounce all charges resulting from the former inclusion of Poland in the Russian Empire, and mutually renounce all rights to state property associated with the territory of the other side;
    c. Both parties mutually pledge to restore in kind or in a corresponding

equivalent the evacuated movable property of the organs of self-government and of physical and legal persons if this property was removed to their own territory from the territory of the other side during the Russian-Ukrainian-Polish war;

d. Russia pledges to restore to Poland archives, libraries, art objects, military-historical trophies, monuments of antiquity, and similar objects of cultural value removed from Poland to Russia since the time of the partition of the Polish Commonwealth, provided that such objects have essential significance for Poland and provided that their transfer would not constitute a fundamental loss for the Russian archives, galleries, museums, and libraries in which they are preserved;

e. Both parties mutually pledge to regulate the private-legal and public-legal relations between citizens of the contracting parties and between the governments and citizens of the other party;

f. Both parties mutually pledge to grant the contracting parties and their citizens the rights of a most favored nation.

15. Both parties pledge to begin, immediately after signing the peace treaty, negotiations concerning consular, commercial, transit, sanitary, transportation, and postal-telegraphic conventions.

16. The present treaty shall be drawn up in Russian, Ukrainian, and Polish. For interpretation purposes, all three texts are to be considered authentic.

17. The present treaty is subject to ratification and enters into force upon ratification, provided that there is no other proviso in the treaty. All articles and terms of the present treaty should constitute the basis for the final peace treaty.[26]

Dąbski called Ioffe's draft a "new proposal," but Ioffe objected that it was not, because it had already been announced in Soviet and Polish declarations. Nonetheless Dąbski requested a few days' recess so that the Polish delegation could have time to study it.

During the recess Ioffe realized that the commissions' work was progressing too slowly. As a remedy he proposed to Dąbski to negotiate the main and controversial problems during private meetings between them at which the two secretaries, Ładoś and Lorenz, would be present; their decisions would then be submitted to the appropriate commissions for detailed elaboration. The first such confidential meeting took place on 1 October. Thenceforth confidential meetings occurred to the end of the conference, and they helped to expedite the negotiations. To facilitate negotiations by all delegates, it was decided to introduce the use of German. At the session of the General Commission on 4 October, Dąbski reproached Ioffe for the Soviet Russian "new proposal," especially for the inclusion of the question of Eastern Galicia.

Ioffe explained that the independence of Eastern Galicia was not a wish of the Red Army but the will of the population of Eastern Galicia, including political parties there whose Weltanschauung was considerably closer to Poland's than to Soviet Russia and Ukraine's. Dąbski declared that Eastern Galicia had to be excluded altogether not only from the treaty, but also from the discussion, and insisted that Eastern Galicia was an internal Polish problem. Ioffe then asked Dąbski: "'Then what is to be done in this case with Levyts'kyi? It is necessary to solve this question at least theoretically.' Dąbski replied that 'Levyts'kyi's arrival means nothing to us. When he finds out the direction in which problems are moving, Levyts'kyi will leave of his own accord,'"[27] and he declared emphatically: "I never will sit opposite Kost' Levyts'kyi."[28]

In subsequent discussions Dąbski threatened that "If the Soviet Russian delegation disagrees with such a declaration, then peace negotiations would be immediately broken off and the Polish delegation would return to Warsaw."[29] Ioffe pointed out that "Poland likewise desired to create buffer states. Russia had already created such states, but only in this form is their existence acceptable to Russia," and he insisted that "Ukraine is an independent state, although its government was composed of people sympathizing with Russia. Furthermore, they [Ukraine and Russia] are two states, but with only one [common] army; actually there are three [such] states, because there is also Belarus." Ioffe explained that such a policy was necessary because "the English workers are very concerned about Ukrainian and Belarusian self-determination, and therefore the Soviet Russian government must advance this problem. [Thus] Poland has to border on Ukraine and Belarus."[30]

Dąbski declined to enter into a theoretical discussion of the Soviet Russian concept of national self-determination in Ukraine and Belarus. According to him, in Soviet practice this problem was reduced to local self-government and to the dictatorship of the Party installed by force with the help of the Red Army. Dąbski pointed out that the Soviet draft contradicted the original declaration of the All-Russian Executive Committee, according to which Poland was to border on Soviet Russia and not on the Ukrainian and Belarusian Soviet republics. Ioffe explained that because the latter two republics had been recognized by Poland and Soviet Russia, Poland's boundary in the treaty should refer only to Ukraine and Belarus or to Poland's eastern boundary without mentioning what entities shared it.[31] Later, during one of their private sessions, Ioffe told Dąbski that the negotiations should be speeded up because the All-Russian Executive Committee was deliberating the question of peace with Poland. Ioffe wanted to provide the committee with proof that steps toward peace with Poland had been made, otherwise the pro-war faction in Moscow might gain the upper hand. Most probably this argument was only a tactical move.

The most important issue for both the Polish and Soviet Russian delegation was the delimitation of Poland's boundaries with Soviet Belarus and Ukraine. Before Dąbski could present Poland's territorial claims, however, he had to have a consensus within the Polish delegation. The question of Poland's eastern border was a complicated one, and it had created serious friction within the delegation. Two closely linked problems requiring separate solutions had arisen from two controversial political concepts regarding Poland's future relations with Ukraine, Belarus, and Lithuania. The concepts were articulated mainly by the National Democratic party under Dmowski and the Polish Socialist party under Piłsudski. According to Dmowski the Polish state had to be larger than ethnic Poland; hence it had to incorporate some Ukrainian, Belarusian, and Lithuanian territories. The rest of Ukraine and Belarus, however, had to be ceded to Soviet Russia so as to have a modus vivendi with it. Dmowski advocated conquest of a relatively limited territory that could be easily colonized and whose people could be eventually assimilated. Piłsudski's concept was broader. Although he agreed with Dmowski on Poland's eastern boundaries, he planned to extend Poland's political influence farther to the east by supporting dependent, democratic buffer states between Poland and Russia.

The struggle between the delegation's "Sejm group" and "governmental group" mirrored the political struggle between Dmowski and Piłsudski. Gradually Dąbski was overshadowed by Grabski, who championed the concept of the National Democratic party, "the party of the landlords and imperialists."[32] Grabski knew what he wanted to achieve in Riga. As chairman of the committee that drew up the proposals on Poland's eastern border, he had prepared a border plan in advance and swayed the delegates of the "Sejm group" to accept Dmowski's concept. Most of the delegates opposed the idea of allied buffer states, and Grabski skillfully utilized them to develop a consensus within the delegation. He believed "The only realistic Polish territorial policy in the east is the most profitable division of Ukrainian and Belarusian lands, which have been contested for centuries, between Poland and Russia."[33] Eventually even Dąbski no longer actively supported Piłsudski's concept, and Wasilewski, Piłsudski's closest collaborator, began supporting Grabski's view and subsequently subordinated himself to the delegation and became chairman of the Polish eastern-border commission.

Although the delegation was in contact with Warsaw, its relationship with it was not close. Sapieha, the foreign minister, did not seem to guide the negotiations. Piłsudski's influence, meanwhile, was indirect, and the position of his supporters in the delegation was weakened by the lack of decisive support by those circles who were its advocates. Even Gen. Kuliński, a representative of the army, was openly neutral. Consequently the political struggle within the delegation was minimal, because the majority already supported Dmowski's concept and Grabski's decisive action ensured that it had no serious opponents. Piłsudski had little influence on the further course of the negotiations in Riga. This was a great setback for his political plans.

Judging from the actions of its delegation in Riga, the Polish government had no intention of honoring the Treaty of Warsaw, not because Poland was too weak to carry out its obligations toward its ally, but because the government was against supporting the Ukrainian cause and because a large part of Polish society had annexationist ambitions. Most Poles dreamed of the restoration of the Polish state that had existed before its partitions from 1772 through 1795. This dream obsessed particularly those Poles who had owned large estates in Ukraine, Belarus, and Lithuania. Polish policy was manifested already at the beginning of the armistice negotiations in Riga, when the Polish delegation was authorized to recognize the full authority of the representatives of the Ukrainian SSR. By this recognition Poland abandoned Piłsudski's concept. During the second session, on 24 September, Ioffe brought up the question of Eastern Galicia in order to have a counterargument in case the Polish delegation insisted on reestablishing the UNR under Petliura. When Dąbski declared that Poland did not intend to champion Petliura's cause, Ioffe promised not to raise the question of Eastern Galicia again.[34]

Polish policy was also revealed by the Polish delegation's decision on Belarus. As the delegation began discussing Poland's claims in the north, Wasilewski and Kamieniecki proposed the creation of a democratic Belarus dependent on Poland. Their proposal was realistic because of the successful Polish military advance into Belarus and because the Soviet Russian delegation in Riga was consequently ready to make concessions. The resolution of Belarus's status depended almost entirely on the will of the Polish delegation. This possibility, however, was never exploited by the Polish delegation, because its majority opposed any concept of buffer states. According to Ładoś, there were two alternatives: either to establish a democratic Belarus closely linked with Poland, or to extend Poland's eastern border.

To test the Soviet attitude, Ładoś, with Dąbski's consent, raised the question of a democratic Belarus at a private meeting. Ioffe did not reject the proposal out of hand, for he was willing to make serious territorial concessions, including Minsk. Ioffe's only arguments were that the Soviet Russian government had social and political obligations toward the Belarusian peasants; it had promised to deliver them from the Polish landlords. Moreover, the workers of England were interested in seeing the federative development of the Soviet republics. Ładoś's proposal created real conflict among the majority of the Polish delegation, and only because of Dąbski's and Wasilewski's support was he not sent back to Warsaw for bringing up the

Belarusian question. When the idea of a Belarusian democratic state was rejected, Grabski persuaded the delegation to accept the principle that only that part of Belarus where the majority of population was Catholic should be incorporated by Poland.

Subsequently a new problem arose and caused heated debates. Wasilewski insisted that Minsk, the historic capital of Belarus, should also be incorporated by Poland. Grabski, however, objected to the incorporation of Minsk for fear that the city would become the center of a Belarusian national movement within Poland that would create trouble in the future and impair national consolidation. He believed that it would be better to cede the source of potential trouble to Soviet Russia. Wasilewski, on the other hand, wanted the Belarusian and Ukrainian national movements to be based and grow within Poland and to receive its support. He worried that if their centers were established on the other side of the Polish border, they would attract the Belarusians and Ukrainians living under Polish occupation and thereby create an irredentist problem within Poland. In the end, on 5 October, the delegation's majority voted against the incorporation of Minsk.[35]

While the Polish delegation debated Poland's eastern boundary, Ioffe drew Dąbski's attention to the fact that some Russians believed the Poles were prolonging negotiations because they were not genuinely interested in a peace agreement. The Bolsheviks were anxious for a quick settlement because they wished to free their forces for the struggle against Wrangel. Ioffe stated that Moscow would therefore agree to any border as long as the Lida-Baranavichy-Luninets-Sarny-Rivne-Brody railway line remained on the Soviet side. Dąbski, however, pointed out that Poland needed the railway line and could not abandon it. On 1 October Ioffe informed Dąbski that Moscow did not agree to a frontier east of the above railway line. On 2 October Dąbski, Kiernik, and Barlicki presented a counterproposal: the border was to run from the Dvina southward from where the Russian and Latvian borders met as far as Lida; from there along the above railway line, which would remain Polish; and from Brody to the Zbruch and down that river to the Dniester. The border would be protected by a "security strip" sixty to seventy kilometers wide east of it.

The next day Ioffe met with Dąbski, Grabski, Barlicki, and Kiernik to discuss the Polish proposal. After lengthy discussion he suggested that Moscow might consent to Poland's territorial claims, except in the north. He was apprehensive about the Polish demand for a corridor to Latvia. In his opinion Poland wanted it so as to deprive Soviet Russia of transit through Lithuania, thus cutting it off from a convenient land route to Germany and the rest of Europe, and to keep Lithuania under Polish control. He stated that if Lithuania agreed to cede the Vilnius area to Poland, the question of the corridor would be solved. On 5 October Ioffe informed Dąbski, Grabski,

Barlicki, and Kiernik that the Council of People's Commissars had authorized him to accept the entire Polish proposal as long as the Polish delegation agreed to reduce their claim to the gold in the former Imperial Bank of Russia.[36] The reason for the quick Soviet acceptance was explained by Lenin on 9 October. He stated that the Poles would derive little benefit from territorial acquisitions because "In those localities we give them in accordance with the peace agreement, Poland will maintain itself only by force." Meantime, he concluded, the Bolsheviks "will gain time ... and we shall be able to use it to strengthen our army."[37]

The critical military and political situation made both Soviet Russia and Poland more conciliatory. Both sides desired peace and were ready to make concessions, unfortunately at the expense of Ukraine, Belarus, and Lithuania. Although mistrust, hostility, and territorial claims persisted, the spirit of conciliation that prevailed led to a preliminary peace treaty. Because agreement was reached by 5 October on all principal questions, the work of all of the commissions in Riga was speeded up. Although it was difficult for the delegates to complete the final draft of the treaty in three languages within three days, it could have been signed on 8 October, as agreed. The Polish High Command, however, asked the Polish delegation to delay signing the treaty until Polish troops captured Minsk. Although the treaty was not binding until it was ratified and the war was to last for six more days, Ioffe considered the moment of its signing a victory for peace.

The preliminary treaty consisted of seventeen articles

1. Both delegations recognized the "independence" of Soviet Ukraine and Soviet Belarus and drew a border between them and Poland. The border was the most disputed question of all the seventeen articles. In case of differences between the treaty and any map, the terms of the treaty would be authoritative. Soviet Russia, Soviet Ukraine, and Poland renounced all rights and claims to territories located beyond their borders, while the territorial dispute between Poland and Lithuania was to be settled mutually by those two countries.

2. Both parties guaranteed to respect each other's national sovereignty and to refrain from intervening in each other's internal affairs. They agreed not to form nor support organizations whose aim was armed struggle against and abolition of the political and social order of the other. Each party also agreed neither to violate the territorial integrity of nor to allow the existence of organizations that would assume the role of the government of the opposite party. Upon ratification of the agreement, both parties obligated themselves not to support foreign military actions against the other party.

3. Both parties sanctioned the right of Poles to choose Russian or Ukrainian citizenship and the right of Russians or Ukrainians to choose Polish citizenship if they so wished. Such persons would enjoy all rights recognized by the treaty as belonging to the citizens of both parties.
4. Both parties guaranteed Polish citizens in Russia and Ukraine and Russian and Ukrainian citizens in Poland the same free development of their national civilizations, their languages, and their religions as enjoyed in their countries of origin.
5. Both parties renounced all claims to reparations for state costs incurred because of the war and for war losses sustained by both states or its citizens because of military operations and measures.
6. Both parties obligated themselves to exchange prisoners of war and repay the costs of their maintenance.
7. Joint commissions were to be created to oversee the immediate exchange, release, protection, and assistance of hostages, civilian prisoners, interned persons, prisoners of war, exiles, refugees, and emigrants.
8. Both parties obligated themselves to issue orders suspending legal, administrative, disciplinary, or any other persecution and legal punishments started against civilian prisoners, interned persons, hostages, exiles, emigrants, and prisoners of war. The suspension of punishment would not cause the release of such persons; instead they and their case files were to be handed over to the authorities of their country of origin. If such persons declared their unwillingness to return to their country of origin or if the authorities of that country did not allow them to return, they were liable to be deprived again of their liberty.
9. Both parties obligated themselves to introduce regulations regarding amnesty granted by Poland to Russian and Ukrainian citizens in Poland and by Russia and Ukraine to Polish citizens in Russia and Ukraine.
10. Both parties obligated themselves to include stipulations regarding the mutual settlement and liquidation of accounts; such stipulations were to be based on the following principles:
    a. Poland bears no obligations or burdens arising from the fact that part of the territories of the Polish Republic formerly belonged to the Russian Empire.
    b. Both parties renounce all claims to the state properties situated on the territory of the other party.
    c. In the calculation and settling of accounts, the active participation of the population of the Polish Republic in the economic life of the former Russian Empire is to be taken into consideration.
    d. Both parties obligate themselves mutually, at the request of the owners, to restore and deliver in kind or in a corresponding equivalent

the movable property of the state connected with the economic and cultural life of the country, and the movable property of self-governing bodies, institutions, and physical or juridical persons taken or evacuated by force or voluntarily since 1 August 1914, with the exception of war booty.

    e.   Measures are to be undertaken to restore to Poland the archives, libraries, works of art, historic war trophies, relics, and similar articles of cultural achievement exported from Poland to Russia since the partitions of Poland.

    f.   Both parties shall provide for the settlement of legally established claims by individuals or legal persons of both parties, such claims taking into account the time prior to the signing of the treaty and directed against the governments or institutions of the other party.

    g.   Russia and Ukraine undertake to restore to Poland and its citizens their property and to indemnify them for the losses of the revolutionary period and the civil war in Russia and Ukraine.

Both parties agreed that the above points did not cover all details requiring settlement.

11. Both parties agreed to enter into negotiations regarding an agreement on commerce and navigation, sanitation, communications, the mails and telegraphs, and the exchange of goods by way of compensation.

12. Both parties agreed to insert in the treaty provisions giving the right of transit to Poland through the territories of Russia and Ukraine and to Russia and Ukraine through the territories of Poland.

13. Both parties simultaneously concluded a special armistice of equal validity to the present treaty.

14. Russia and Ukraine declared that all their obligations toward Poland, and the rights accorded them by the treaty, would apply to all the territories east of the frontier as determined by article 1 of the treaty; these territories formed part of the former Russian Empire and were now represented by Russia and Ukraine.

15. Both parties obligated themselves, immediately upon signing the treaty, to start negotiations pertaining to the conclusion of a peace treaty.

16. Two copies of the treaty were prepared in Polish, Russian, and Ukrainian. For the purposes of interpreting the agreement the texts in all three languages were to be considered authoritative.

17. The agreement was subject to ratification and became valid with the exchange of ratification documents as long as the treaty and its appendices did not contain a different provision. The exchange of the ratification agreement and the preparation of a corresponding protocol was to take place in Liepāja, Latvia, within fifteen days, while the exchange of

ratification documents and the preparation of the protocol was to take place within six days after the expiration of the term provided for ratification.

An armistice agreement was signed at the same time as the preliminary peace treaty. It consisted of thirteen articles.

1. Both parties are obligated to suspend all military operations on land, on water, and in the air by midnight of 18 October 1920.
2. The armies of both parties shall remain in the positions occupied by them at the time of suspension of military operations, with the exception, however, that the Russo-Ukrainian armies must be situated at least fifteen kilometers away from the Polish front line.
3. The zone thus created, of fifteen kilometers in width, shall be a neutral zone administered by civil authorities.
4. In the sector from the Niasvizh region to the Dvina the Polish armies shall occupy the line of the state boundary fixed in Article 1 of the peace preliminaries, the Russo-Ukrainian armies taking positions fifteen kilometers to the east of that line.
5. Movements of the armies resulting from Articles 2 and 4 must take place at a rate of not less than twenty kilometers a day and shall begin not later than twenty-four hours after the suspension of military operations.
6. After the ratification of the peace preliminaries, the armies of both parties shall be withdrawn to their state territory at a rate of not less than twenty kilometers a day, and shall take up positions fifteen kilometers to each side of the boundary. The zone thus created, of thirty kilometers in width, shall constitute a neutral zone administered by civil authorities.
7. Within the neutral zone no military units should be maintained, except for Polish troops needed for the occupation of the territory as provided in Article 4. The other side must be informed about their strength and location.
8. Detailed regulations concerning the execution of this agreement are issued by the commands of both sides wherever necessary and after mutual agreement. A joint military commission shall be established to supervise the execution of the agreement.
9. In vacating the occupied territories the armies must leave untouched all governmental, public, and private properties found in the area, including buildings, railroads, rolling stock, bridges and station appurtenances, telegraphs, telephones, and other means of communication, grain stores in fields and in granaries, livestock, and industrial and agricultural

inventories. While withdrawing the armies must take no hostages nor evacuate the civilian population; they are not permitted to engage in repression of the population nor to expropriate, requisition, or forcibly redeem its property.

10. During the armistice period all communication by land, water, and air between both parties is suspended; exceptions shall be determined by joint military arbitration.
11. Military units and persons violating the regulations shall be considered prisoners of war.
12. The armistice is concluded for twenty-one days; each side can recall it upon a forty-eight-hour notice. If before the expiration of the armistice term neither side should cancel it, the armistice is automatically extended up to the time of the ratification of the final peace treaty, and each side has the right to recall by giving fourteen days' notice, without regard to the above regulations and in accordance with Article 17.
13. The present armistice constitutes an integral part of the peace preliminaries.[38]

In addition, a secret protocol dealing with the gold question was signed. it had four clauses.

1. In regard to paragraph three in article ten of the preliminary peace conditions, both parties agreed that the active participation of Poland in the economic life of the former Russian Empire includes accounts on the basis of Poland's participation informing gold reserves in the former Imperial Bank.
2. The means of settlement by Russia of an active balance in favor of Poland appeared as a result of mutual accounts, and shall be determined in the peace treaty. On account of debts due to Poland, Russia and Ukraine pledged to make advance payments in gold, raw materials, and concessions in state forests located near the border of Poland. These concessions are to be conveniently located for communication by railroad and water. The rate of the advance and conditions of separate payments and concessions are to be subject to the decision by a joint commission, which shall be formed during one month from the day of ratification of the armistice agreement and preliminary peace conditions.
3. Russia and Ukraine are obligated to repay Poland for the loss of state property and likewise physical and juridical persons detained or expropriated during the occupation of lodgings of Polish representatives in Russia or Ukraine by Russian or Ukrainian authorities, or to compensate them for incurred damages.

4. In regard to article twelve of the preliminary peace conditions, both parties resolved that transportation of goods from Russia and Ukraine and into Russia and Ukraine through Poland, likewise from and to Poland through Russia and Ukraine, would not be aggravated by any transit customs and any special transit collections. Poland, however, would retain freedom to regulate the conditions of transit for goods of German and Austrian origin imported from Germany and Austria through Poland into Russia and Ukraine. Although both parties agreed that the document would remain unpublished, it had the same force as the Preliminary Peace Treaty and the Armistice Agreement.[39]

On 12 October the two delegations met in a plenary session and signed the preliminary peace treaty, the armistice agreement, and the gold protocol, which were to go into effect on 18 October. Then Ioffe read their Russian text, Dąbski the Polish, and Manuïl's'kyi the Ukrainian. The documents were ratified unanimously by the Soviet government on 20 October, by the Soviet Ukrainian authorities on 21 October, and by the Polish Sejm on 22 October. The ratified documents were duly exchanged on 2 November at Liepāja, and both parties agreed to proceed to negotiations on a final peace settlement.

The preliminary peace treaty seemingly represented a compromise, mainly vis-à-vis territory, which was achieved at the expense of Ukraine and Belarus. If one considers the war aims of the contenders, however, it was not a compromise, because both of them failed to achieve that to which they strived. Soviet Russia had to postpone spreading the Bolshevik revolution into Western Europe, and Piłsudski's concept of buffer states allied with Poland was abandoned. Instead the buffer states remained under Soviet Russian domination.

CHAPTER 13

The Peace Treaty of Riga

After the preliminary peace treaty and armistice agreement had been signed, the Polish delegation returned to Warsaw. Shortly after it was reorganized. The new delegation that went to Riga was smaller and composed solely of government officials. This time the "Sejm group" was not included, and thus double representation was avoided and a source of dissension was eliminated. The new delegation consisted of Dąbski (the chairman), Stanisław Kauzik, Henryk Strasburger, Edward Lechowicz, Wasilewski, and a large staff of experts and a secretariat. The Polish High Command was represented by Col. Ignacy Matuszewski. The new Soviet Russian delegation consisted of Ioffe (the chairman), Jakub Fürstenberg-Hanecki, Emmanuel Kviring, and Leonid Obolenskii; a Ukrainian, Iurii Kotsiubyns'kyi, joined the delegation later.

Negotiations resumed at Riga on 17 November after a month's interval. By that time the methods adopted by the delegations were different from those used in earlier negotiations. At the first session joint commissions similar to those of the previous conference were set up to negotiate territorial, legal-political, and economic-financial questions and the exchange of prisoners of war and hostages. Subcommissions were created to elaborate details. The vital questions continued to be debated and decided by the chairmen during their frequent secret meetings, while editorial staff formulated the final texts. Experts were consulted more than they had been during the previous conference. Therefore there were only three plenary sessions: on 17 November 1920, 24 February 1921, and 18 March 1921. In contrast to the October 1920 conference, when the border question was the most difficult to settle, now the thorny issues were financial and economic ones. Because the vital questions had been already discussed during the preliminary peace agreements, however, negotiations of the final peace settlement seemed an easier task. They were limited primarily to developing and defining principles previously determined. Still, some questions had been hastily and insufficiently formulated in the hasty preliminary peace agreements, and the imprecise imterpretations created difficulties and conflicts. According to Ładoś, who was still the secretary of the Polish delegation, "one had to fight with extreme endurance for every word of the future treaty."[1]

During the conference the political situation was different from what it had been in October. Then the Polish military successes had compelled the Bolsheviks to be conciliatory, because they needed a speedy armistice and peace. Now the Bolsheviks had both, and neither side believed that war might be renewed. This new situation complicated and thus prolonged negotiations. Furthermore, the Bolsheviks' international relations had improved. After the Soviet defeat of Wrangel's forces in the middle of November 1920, the Allied Powers began competing with each other for concessions in Soviet Russia. At the same time Poland was experiencing tensions with Germany over Upper Silesia. A plebiscite was to take place there on 20 March 1921, and the Poles wanted to conclude peace with Soviet Russia before that date. Dąbski worried about the possibility of a Bolshevik-German agreement. He confessed that "The date of the Upper Silesian plebiscite hangs over me like a nightmare. I realize that if we lose the plebiscite or insufficiently win it, there will be people who would cast blame that the peace was not carried into effect soon enough."[2]

At the beginning of the negotiations tensions developed between the Polish and Soviet delegations. UNR troop activities on the Soviet southern front worried Moscow, and to prevent Polish troops from assisting the Ukrainians, Ioffe demanded that the Polish troops be withdrawn to Poland's state borders. He warned that otherwise he would suspend negotiations. The response of members of the Polish delegation varied. Dąbski wanted to dispel the Bolsheviks' fears of Polish military activity, while Matuszewski considered that the threat of a renewed war might make the Bolsheviks more conciliatory. There was progress on the negotiation of the repatriation of prisoners of war, civilian prisoners, hostages, and refugees, of amnesty for political offenders, and of the return of equipment taken from Polish factories during the Bolshevik invasion; but economic questions, especially the gold payments, were more difficult to solve. How much of Russia's gold reserves in the former Imperial Bank should be handed over to compensate Poland, especially for war damages, still had to be resolved. The Polish demand was based on (1) the amalgamation of the Polish State Bank with the Russian Imperial State Bank in the 1890s and the transfer of the Polish Bank's gold reserves from Warsaw to St. Petersburg; (2) the deposits in the Polish branches of the Russian Imperial Bank following the amalgamation; and (3) the damages caused by the Bolshevik invasion of Poland.[3] According to Polish estimates, Soviet Russia held 300 million to 400 million gold rubles belonging to Poland. The Bolsheviks, however, wanted to give Poland as little as possible from the gold reserves, because they were their only means of payment for military purchases abroad. Instead of gold, the Bolsheviks were willing to pay Poland the equivalent value in brilliants and raw material. They also offered

certain concessions of timber, coal, and other natural resources.
Dąbski became frustrated with the slowness and difficulty of the negotiations. He described the situation angrily:

> We are dealing with an adversary who laughs many times about his own "arguments"; who admits that he changes his position; who sometimes recalls the next day what he said the day before; who excuses himself by the difference in his social order; [and] who has an entirely different morality than the rest of the world. Therefore many [of their] promises and commitments have no value because they could be withdrawn at any moment. It is necessary to have the patience of a saint to listen to several hours of speeches by delegates who repeat the same thing ten times in order to tire and exhaust their adversary and force him to yield; who constantly threaten and beg and finally state that they have nothing to lose and nothing to give "because present-day Russia is naked and barefoot and you can get nothing from it, even if you would conquer Moscow by armed force."[4]

In light of this situation, the Polish government became nervous and sought to speed up the negotiations through direct intervention. Although Dąbski was against rushing matters, Sapieha dispatched telegrams to Chicherin and Rakovskii, the commissars of foreign affairs of Soviet Russia and Soviet Ukraine, complaining that the Bolshevik delegation was delaying concluding the peace agreement. Changes occurred when Dąbski and Ioffe began their own secret meetings.[5]

Dąbski proposed that Ioffe deal with the problem of rolling stock. The Polish Railway Subcommission claimed that Poland should receive from Soviet Russia 2,000 locomotives and an appropriate number of passenger and freight cars. Ioffe proposed only 350 locomotives and an appropriate number of cars. The next day, after a tense discussion, the Polish side lowered its demand to 509 locomotives and an appropriate number of cars, whereupon Ioffe raised the Soviet offer to 400 locomotives but then, on the advice of the Bolshevik experts, withdrew it. Eventually, after strenuous discussion, it was agreed that Poland would receive 300 locomotives, or the equivalent, in addition to the 255 locomotives already on Polish-held territory belonging to the Ukrainian railway system.[6]

Negotiations concerning basic economic problems greatly changed after the Polish minister of finance, Jan Steczkowski, and the Soviet Russian commissar of finance, Leonid Krasin, arrived in Riga. During their meetings they clarified important questions and instructed their respective delegations how to move the conference forward. In the middle of February 1921, at a secret meeting, Ioffe presented an offer to pay Poland ten percent of the estimated gold reserves held by Soviet Russia, that is, thirty million rubles' worth. Dąbski was prepared to accept the offer providing that this amount would be paid exclusively in gold, but Ioffe admitted that only part of the payment could be in gold, while the rest would be paid in platinum, valuable papers, gems from the treasury of the Russian tsars, and other valuables. Ioffe again offered concessions of timber, coal, and other natural resources, all of them in Ukraine, but on the advice of the Polish experts, these concessions and the tsars' treasure were not accepted because of their political implications and technical difficulties. If the concessions had been accepted, Poland would appear as an exploiter of a foreign country. After a few days of tense discussions, payment solely in gold was accepted.[7] Kauzik remarked, however, that "The rights were settled, but it is not known what will happen with the payment.... It is always so with the Bolsheviks: on the 'theory' and arguments they agree, but when it comes to payment they propose such ridiculous sums that in reality, if converted to gold rubles, the payment does not constitute great value."[8]

After the resolution of basic questions (the gold payment in particular) and the clarification of other matters by Steczkowski and Krasin, the negotiations accelerated. Finally, on 24 February 1921, three months after the opening of the conference, both delegations assembled in a plenary session to sign the (1) repatriation agreement, (2) additional protocol to the agreement on repatriation, (3) protocol extending the notification period prior to the renunciation of the armistice of 12 October 1920, and (4) additional protocol regarding the creation and competence of a joint border commission. The repatriation agreement consisted of thirty-eight articles. Three were essential. Article 1 obligated both parties "To proceed with the speedy repatriation of all hostages, civilian prisoners, interned persons, prisoners of war, exiles, refugees, and emigrants presently within the boundaries of their respective territories." In Article 28, both parties agreed that "The number of prisoners of war sent home shall not be less than 1,500 per week, and the total figure of persons of all categories repatriated shall not be less than 4,000 per week." Article 36 stated that "The present agreement has been concluded in execution of Article 7 of the Preliminaries of Peace ratified on 12 October 1920; it is not subject to ratification and is binding as soon as signed."[9] Consequently, by virtue of the repatriation agreement, during the three years from the middle of 1921 to the middle of 1924, nearly one million people returned from Soviet Russia to Poland.[10]

The negotiations were impeded by differences over the restitution of state property, commercial treaties, and diplomatic relations. The most contentious issue was that of the artistic treasures, libraries, and archives taken from Poland since 1915. The Bolshevik delegation insisted that they had to remain in Russia because their restitution to Poland would deplete Russian museums, libraries, and archives. From 8 March this issue was taken over by the chairmen, neither of whom was willing to compromise. Instead both Dąbski and Ioffe declared their willingness to go to war over that question.[11] The issue was finally resolved under the impact of the Kronstadt sailors' and workers' uprising against the Bolshevik regime, which forced the Soviet delegation to agree to restore all cultural valuables to Poland and hasten to settle all other problems.[12]

Another difficult problem was that of territory. The territorial commissions—the Polish under Wasilewski and the Bolshevik under Kviring—devoted their attention to the correction and more precise description of state borders than the one found in the preliminary treaty. The Polish delegation demanded that Poland's northeastern frontier run along the boundary of former Vilnius gubernia, and other corrections in Polesie (Polissia) voivodeship. The Bolshevik delegation acceeded. This territorial gain was strategically important for Poland. Toward the end of the negotiations, however, the boundary question was brought up again, this time by the Soviet delegation. At the suggestion of his secretary Shemiakin, Ioffe proposed adding to the text of the treaty that, in addition to the Belarusian and Ukrainian Soviet republics, Poland bordered, in the north, also on Soviet Russia. Dąbski dismissed the request. A few days later Kviring repeated Ioffe's request in a letter to Wasilewski, but his letter was not answered. Finally, however, the Polish delegation was forced to accept a revised Article 2, which stated that Poland bordered "on Russia, Ukraine, and Belarus."[13]

After both delegations completed their work, they wrote up the text of the peace treaty in Polish, Russian, and Ukrainian. In contrast with the Preliminary Peace Treaty, Belarus was now represented. The treaty consisted of the twenty-six articles agreed upon in the Preliminary Peace Treaty, but were presented in a more detailed and precise form and with a minor rectification of borders and terms that had been reserved for solution in the final treaty.

1. Both parties declare that the state of war between them shall come to an end.
2. The boundary between Poland, Soviet Russia, Belarus, and Ukraine is settled, with minor rectification in favor of Poland, as agreed in the Preliminary Peace Treaty.
3. Both Soviet Russia and Soviet Ukraine abandon all rights and claims to the territories situated west of the agreed border. Similarly, Poland abandons, in favor of Soviet Ukraine and Soviet Belarus, all rights and claims to the territory situated east of the border, while the districts that are the subject of dispute between Poland and Lithuania should be settled

by them.

4. In view of the fact that part of Poland formerly belonged to Russia, Poland shall not be held to have incurred any debt or obligation toward Soviet Russia, except as provided in the treaty. Similarly, no debt or obligation shall be regarded as incurred by Poland toward Belarus or Ukraine and vice versa, except as provided in the treaty.

5. Both parties pledge to respect each other's political sovereignty, to abstain from interference in each other's internal affairs, and not to support or create armed detachments with the objective of encouraging armed conflict against the other party so as to undermine its territorial integrity or subvert its political or social institutions.

6. All persons over the age of eighteen who are within the territory of Poland and, on 1 August 1914, were nationals of Russia shall have the right of opting for Russian or Ukrainian nationality. Similarly, all persons over the age of eighteen who are within the territory of Russia and of Ukraine, including the descendants of persons who took part in the Polish struggle between 1830 and 1865, shall be considered as citizens of Poland if they express such a desire. The choice made by the husband shall apply also to his wife and children under the age eighteen, if the husband and wife have not agreed to the contrary.

7. Russia and Ukraine pledge that persons of Polish nationality in Russia, Ukraine, and Belarus shall enjoy free intellectual development, the use of their national language, and the exercise of their religion. Similarly, Poland recognizes the same rights for persons of Russian, Ukrainian, and Belarusian nationality in Poland.

8. Both parties abandon all claims to repayment of expenses incurred by the state during the war and to indemnities for damages caused to their nationals by the war or military measures taken during the Polish-Soviet Russian-Ukrainian War.

9. The agreement concerning repatriation concluded between Poland, on the one side, and Russia and Ukraine, on the other, shall remain in force as agreed in the Preliminary Peace Treaty.

10. Each party guarantees to the subjects of the other party full amnesty for all acts directed against the government and the security of the state; as well, acts committed in the interest of the other party shall be regarded as political crimes and offenses within the meaning of this article.

11. Russia and Ukraine shall restore to Poland all war trophies, libraries, archives, works of art, and other objects of historical, ethnographic, artistic, scholarly, and archeological value that have been removed from the territory of Poland by Russia since 1772. Similarly, any collections or objects of historical value that have been removed from Russia and

Ukraine by Poland during the same period shall be restored to Russia and Ukraine.

12. Both parties agree that state property of whatever nature, including properties of all state institutions and possessions belonging to appanages and the Imperial Cabinet and Palaces that is within the geographic territory of both parties, or is to be restored to the parties by virtue of the treaty, shall be their property. Both parties, mutually renounce the right to any form of compensation that might involve the partition of state property, subject to any contrary provisions contained in the present treaty.

13. Russia and Ukraine agree to pay to Poland within one year after ratification of the present treaty the sum of thirty million gold rubles in specie and in bars, based on the active participation of the territory of Poland in the economic life of the former Russian state.

14. Both Russia and Ukraine shall hand over to Poland 300 locomotives, 260 passenger carriages, and 8,100 freight cars in addition to rolling stock for broad-gauge lines, that is, 259 locomotives, 435 passenger carriages, and 8,859 freight cars. The total value of the rolling stock to be restored to Poland shall be fixed at the sum of 13,149,000 gold rubles. The total value of any railway material other than rolling stock shall be fixed at the sum of 5,096,000 gold rubles.

15. Upon the request of the Polish government, supported by the declarations of the owners, Russia and Ukraine agree that restitution shall be made to Poland for the purpose of restoring property belonging to self-governing and municipal administrations, institutions, and legal and physical persons that was taken from Poland to Russia and Ukraine from 1 August 1914 through 1 October 1915. A restitution commission, composed of five representatives of each party and necessary experts, shall be created for the purpose of implementing the provisions of this article and shall reside in Moscow.

16. Russia and Ukraine agree to settle with Poland accounts relating to funds or capital bequeathed to physical and legal persons of Polish nationality or to Polish public or private scientific, religious, or charitable institutions or societies, which, by virtue of the regulations in force, were deposited on account in the state banks or credit institutions of the former Russian state. The fourteenth of January 1916 is accepted as the fixed date for the settlement of accounts. This action shall be effected by a joint commission for the settlement of accounts.

17. Russia and Ukraine undertake to settle accounts in respect to the deposits and securities of Polish physical and legal persons in Russian and Ukrainian state banks that have been nationalized and in state institutions

and savings banks. Russia and Ukraine shall respect the rights of Polish physical and legal persons as they have been recognized. A joint commission on the liquidation of accounts shall be entrusted with the settlement of questions.

18. A joint commission composed of five representatives of each party and the requisite number of experts, with its seat in Warsaw, shall be established to settle accounts provided for in articles 14, 15, 16, and 17 of the present treaty, and to draw up rules governing these settlements and fix the amount, method, and dates of payments. The first of October 1915 shall be the fixed date from which all accounts shall be settled.

19. Russia and Ukraine discharge Poland from all responsibility regarding debts and obligations incurred by the former Russian state, in particular obligations arising out of the issue of paper money, treasury bonds, debentures, and certificates of the Russian treasury.

20. Russia and Ukraine recognize ipso facto and without a special convention the claims of Poland and Polish nationals and legal persons to all rights, privileges, and similar benefits with regard to the restitution of property and compensation for damages incurred during the revolution and civil war in Russia and Ukraine.

21. Both parties agree to enter within six weeks from the date of ratification of the treaty into negotiations concerning a commercial convention and a convention regarding the exchange of goods by barter. They also agree to commence negotiations with a view to concluding consular, postal, telegraphic, railway, health, and veterinary conventions and a convention for the improvement of the conditions of navigation on the waterways of the Dnieper-Wisła and Dnieper-Dvina [basins].

22. Both parties agree to permit the forwarding of goods in transit subject to the following conditions:

    a. The principles laid down in this article shall serve as a basis for the future convention on transit.

    b. Both parties agree to the free transit of goods by railways and waterways.

    c. Both parties agree that goods transported to or from Russia and Ukraine through Poland and vice versa shall be exempt from customs or transit duties of any kind.

    d. The transportation of goods intended for armaments or for military equipment, and of all military stores, shall be prohibited.

    e. Goods from another state that are in transit through the territory of one of the parties shall not be subjected to a different or higher rate of duty than would be levied on similar goods if they were sent directly from their country of origin.

23. Russia and Ukraine declare that all undertakings entered into by them with regard to Poland, and all rights acquired by them by virtue of the treaty, shall apply to all territory situated east of the frontier of the state specified in article 11 of the treaty, which formed part of the former Russian state and was represented by Russia and Ukraine when this treaty was concluded. All above-mentioned rights shall [also] apply to Belarus and its citizens.
24. After ratification of the treaty, diplomatic relations between the contracting parties shall be resumed.
25. The treaty shall be drawn up in Polish, Russian, and Ukrainian in three original copies. All three texts shall be considered authoritative for purposes of interpreting the treaty.
26. The treaty shall be ratified and shall come into force from the time of the exchange of the protocols of ratification unless otherwise provided in the treaty or annexes.[14]

After the conclusion of the treaty on 18 March 1921 at 8:30 P.M. in a plenary session, both delegations, the Latvian government, the diplomatic corps, and the press assembled in the State Hall of the Schwarzhäupterhaus, where the terms of the treaty were read. The first ten articles were read by Dąbski in Polish; the next ten were read by Ioffe in Russian; and the remaining six articles were read by Kotsiubyns'kyi in Ukrainian. After the reading the members of both delegations signed the treaty. With its conclusion, negotiations came to an end. The Polish government ratified the treaty on 15 April, and the Soviet Russian government ratified it on 22 April. The documents were exchanged in Minsk on 30 April and thereby assumed legal force. Thus the war between Poland and Soviet Russia came to an end. The Entente Powers initially declined to recognize the treaty's validity because it had been negotiated without their participation. As a result of French pressure, however, it was finally recognized on 15 March 1923 in Paris by the Conference of Ambassadors in the name of France, Great Britain, Italy, and Japan. On 5 April 1923 the United States also recognized the treaty.[15]

By concluding of the Peace Treaty of Riga, Poland abrogated the Treaty of Warsaw it had concluded with the UNR. The Polish government had no intention of fulfilling the Treaty of Warsaw, not because Poland was too weak to carry out its obligations toward its ally, but because by that time it was against supporting Ukraine's independence. In spite of the UNR government's loyalty to Poland and its help in winning the war, the Polish government abandoned it. The reasons were plainly stated by Grabski: "The only realistic Polish territorial policy in the east is the most profitable division between Poland and Russia of the Ukrainian and Belarusian lands, which have been contested for centuries."[16]

The treaty had different meanings for Poland and Soviet Russia, because they were unequal contenders. By the treaty the Poles secured an independent Poland that included not only "the territories inhabited by indisputably Polish population," but also large non-Polish territories. The Poles welcomed the treaty because it promised peace and stability. In reality, however, it was a defeat for Poland, because it failed to safeguard its security. To quote Lenin, "The districts that we surrender to them by the peace agreement Poland will hold only by force."[17] Or, as Manuïl's'kyi put it, "Poland became a sort of new Austria with an utterly mixed foreign population. By its own policy, it created on its entire eastern border a permanent resistance movement."[18]

The treaty was only a temporary setback for Soviet Russia's political plans of expansion into Europe. At the same time it gave Soviet Russia the respite from war that it needed to be able to consolidate "socialism in one country." The Soviet "liberation and unification" of Ukrainian and Belarusian territories occupied by Poland was left for a more opportune time. Meanwhile, Poland did not secure a permanent peace with Soviet Russia by abandoning Ukraine and Belarus. The Peace Treaty of Riga left Poland in a defensive position vis-à-vis Soviet Russia, and it prevented the establishment of strong buffer states between Soviet Russia and Germany.

CHAPTER 14

The Fate of the Ukrainian Army after the Treaties

As a result of the new situation created by the Preliminary Peace Treaty and Armistice Agreement and of increased Bolshevik strength following the defeat of Wrangel's forces, the Ukrainian liberation struggle entered into a new stage of political and military crisis. On 9 November 1920, when the armistice agreement expired, all small Polish units withdrew from the Ukrainian front, leaving the UNR troops to fight the Bolsheviks alone. Moreover, the main Polish troops retreated westward, thus exposing the northern flank of the UNR army to Bolshevik attack. In the meantime the Bolshevik forces regrouped and were reinforced on the Ukrainian front by Russian, Kalmyk, Mordovian, Tatar and Turkmen units. The Bolshevik forces were superior to the UNR troops in manpower and materiel. They consisted of over 30,000 men, including 5,000 cavalry, 120 field guns, and 5 armored trains. The UNR troops were divided into three operational groups and a reserve group. Their right flank consisted of the Third Riflemen Iron Division and the First Machine-Gun Division commanded by Gen. Udovychenko. The central flank consisted of the Sixth Sich Riflemen Division and Fifth Kherson Division commanded by Gen. Bezruchko. The left flank consisted of the First Zaporozhian Division and Third Russian Cavalry Army under Gen. I. Peremykin; they were commanded by Gen. Havrylo Bazyl's'kyi. The reserve group consisted of the Fourth Kyiv Division, the Second Volynian Division, and the Separate Cavalry Division commanded by Col. Ivan Omelianovych-Pavlenko. The UNR forces had a total of 13,973 infantry and cavalry (2,100 officers), 675 machine guns, 74 field guns, 2 armored trains, and 3 airplanes. Although several thousand men, including ex-soldiers of the tsarist army, had been mobilized, most of them subsequently either were dismissed or had to remain in the rear because they lacked arms, clothing, and shoes; they did not participate in the defensive campaign. The Ukrainian command expected that the Poles would supply arms and ammunition to the UNR troops, but the Poles did not honor their commitment. Consequently the UNR had to rely on arms and ammunition captured from the enemy.

The UNR troops were supported by the Third Russian Cavalry Army, which had over 3,000 infantry and cavalry, 52 machine guns, and 12 field guns, and by a Cossack Cavalry Brigade under Capt. Iakovlev, which had over 2,000 men (190 officers), 38 machine guns, and 4 field guns. Both formations had been organized in Poland under the auspices of the Russian Political Liberation Committee headed by Boris Savinkov, whcih recognized the independence of the UNR. Both formations, however, were only in the initial stages of organization, and therefore only part of their troops participated in the struggle against the Bolsheviks.

In view of the Bolshevik strength, the situation of the Ukrainian army was very critical. Although the Armistice Agreement had designated a fifteen-kilometer-wide neutral zone east and west of the front line to be administered by civil authorities, four days later the Bolshevik command violated the agreement by imposing requisitions in this zone. The Bolsheviks not only took sugar from refineries, but also removed their machinery. Moreover, they brought in ammunition and fresh troops to strengthen their position. Thus, the armistice on the Ukrainian front was basically ignored. The UNR troops, in spite of their morale and courage, were physically exhausted and lacked clothing, shoes, arms, and ammunition. They had only 10 to 40 bullets per rifle, 2,000 to 3,000 bullets per machine gun, and 50 to 100 cartridges per field gun. Meanwhile the Bolshevik soldiers, according to those who had been captured, received as many bullets as they could carry, and they were well dressed and well fed. In light of such conditions, the UNR campaign against the Bolshevik forces had few prospects for success.

Early on 10 November 1920 the Bolshevik command launched a major attack along all fifty-four kilometers of the right flank with the aim of penetrating the gap between the right and central flanks in the area of Sharhorod. The Bolshevik force included the Cavalry Division under Hryhorii Kotovs'kyi (over eight hundred men) and the Eighth Cavalry Division under Vitalii Primakov, also known as the Red Cossack Cavalry Corps (about three thousand men). They were supported by the Forty-First Infantry Division. Their strategic aim was to strike against the strongest Ukrainian group, advance into its rear in the direction of Iaryshiv on the Dniester, and then surround and destroy it. Although they failed to surround the Ukrainian troops, they made a deep breakthrough and inflicted heavy casualties. One cavalry brigade tried to contain the Bolshevik advance, but it suffered heavy losses and was forced to cross the Dniester near Mohyliv into Romania, where it was disarmed and interned. Stubborn fighting continued, and some towns changed hands several times. Gradually the Ukrainian troops retreated westward while being constantly pursued by Bolshevik forces.

Meanwhile the UNR command expected that a decisive struggle would take place on its left flank. There the Bolsheviks, including the Bashkir Cavalry Brigade and part of the Eight Cavalry Division, were concentrated in the area of Lityn, Zhmerynka, and Kopaihorod. The Bolshevik command took advantage of the Polish retreat, which had left the left flank open from the north, to attack the Ukrainian troops. Initially the latter, with some help from the troops of Peremykin and Iakovlev, defended their positions. But they could not hold their ground for long without reserves, ammunition, medicine, and food.

In the course of nearly two weeks of heavy and unequal fighting, the Ukrainian troops suffered devastating human and material losses. For example, the Ninth Brigade of the Third Riflemen Iron Division, which was deployed in Sharhorod, on the eve of the fighting consisted of about a thousand men, but by the end of the campaign only seventy men remained. In some cases men reserved their last bullet for themselves to avoid Bolshevik capture and torture. In the end the Ukrainian troops and the Russian units of Peremykin and Iakovlev were forced to retreat westward across the Zbruch to avoid encirclement and destruction. On 21 November the UNR troops, government, and all government personnel began to evacuate to the town of Volochyska and from there to Polish-held Eastern Galicia. Because of their casualties and defeat, they lacked better prospects for the future.[1]

After crossing the border into Eastern Galicia, the UNR troops were compelled to surrender their arms, equipment, and horses, which they had also used to defend Poland, to their former ally. The Poles accepted the troops very reluctantly and with hostility. They carried out arbitrary requisitions under the pretext of searching for arms; many private items, including watches and rings, were confiscated and disappeared. After a few days the Ukrainian troops and government personnel—some thirty thousand people, including about two thousand women and children—were transported in unheated, dirty freight cars, with thirty to forty people per car, to internment camps in several towns in western Poland, including Dąbie, Kalisz, Strzałkowo, Szczepiórno, and Wadowice. The camps had been built by the Germans to hold prisoners of war during World War I. According to one internee, upon entering the camp at Wadowice, "In front of our eyes stood twenty-five or thirty black, deplorable [wooden] barracks, like coffins, on a space of about five and a half acres. This space was enclosed by a barbed-wire fence with sentry boxes [above it]."[2] The camps were guarded by Polish troops. Inside them, however, the Ukrainian units retained their administrative and organizational integrity, and the Polish authorities maintained direct contact only with the Ukrainian officer staff. From the outset, the situation in the camps was bad, and it grew worse. The barracks were overcrowded, and the food supplied by the Poles was scarce and of poor quality, amounting to about fourteen hundred to fifteen hundred calories per person per day; for some time horse meat was provided. The internees also lacked water for bathing, fuel for heating, and adequate clothing, and they suffered from body parasites. To improve physical conditions and morale in the camps, UNR diplomatic representatives appealed for aid to the Polish authorities and to international welfare organizations, including the YMCA and British Relief Mission. As a result, the Polish authorities gradually increased the quantity and quality of food supplies and assigned some money for medical supplies, while the YMCA supplied some clothing, bedding, canned food, medicine, and dried milk for the children. Moreover, some groups of internees were allowed to work in distant sawmills, sugar refineries, and latifundia, and some Polish officials showed sympathy for the internees as a whole. For example, the chief of the Polish General Staff, Gen. Stanisław Sikorski, wrote on 3 March 1922 to Polish military commanders that "The Ukrainians interned in the camps are [living] in difficult material and sanitary conditions. Their material misfortune is increased by their forced exile outside their own homeland. Appreciating the merit of their defense of the borders of the Polish Republic in 1920 and understanding their psychological condition, we should [in response], within the scope of our possibilities, correct their material misfortune."[3] To improve the material conditions of the internees and remedy their idleness, the camp administrations established various trade schools and workshops, including ones in carpentry, tailoring, and shoemaking, while the YMCA organized an embroidery enterprise that provided women with modest incomes. Artists' studios were also organized. Simultaneously, to overcome the widespread depression and morale problems caused by the hardships of the war and internment, the internees built churches in each camp and paid for them from their own funds. Gradually they also organized elementary and secondary schools, military schools, cultural-educational courses, literary groups, theaters, and choirs, and began publishing their own newspapers, journals, and books.[4]

The Bolsheviks sought to exploit the difficult conditions in the internment camps for their own political aims. Pursuant to article seven of the Preliminary Peace Treaty, the Soviet Russian mission in Warsaw had the right to appeal to the internees directly, and it stated that "As soon as the Treaty is signed, mixed commissions shall be set up which shall cause immediate steps to be taken to ensure the release of hostages and the prompt exchange of civil prisoners, interned persons and, as far as possible, prisoners of war; they will also organize the repatriation of exiles, refugees and emigrants. The above mentioned mixed commissions are entitled to protect and assist prisoners of war, civil prisoners, interned persons and hostages, and also exiles, refugees and emigrants."[5] In 1922 representatives of the mission visited the camps several times to urge the internees to request voluntary repatriation. They had little success, however. Only a few soldiers and civilian officials agreed to repatriation, and those who did never returned home. After its appeals to the assembled internees failed, the mission resorted to tempting internees individually. This approach proved to be no more successful.

The internees' feelings of betrayal by the Poles was alleviated on 15 May 1922 by Piłsudski's visit to the camp at Szczepiórno. There he expressed his feelings concerning the final result of the Polish-Ukrainian alliance of 1920. The camp's commandant, Gen. Bezruchko, was deeply touched by the visit, and the internees gave Piłsudski a friendly welcome. According to Piłsudski's aide, Juliusz Ulrych, "such seas of enthusiasm, such limitless feelings, such common affection I have seen nowhere and never experienced." When Piłsudski addressed the internees, no one raised "any requests, any problems." In his speech Piłsudski apologized for the Peace Treaty of Riga while expressing his regret regarding the historic dilemma of the two nations and the abandonment of his own policy.[6] After the visit the internees hoped that conditions would improve, but their hopes were dashed by Piłsudski's retirement from political life in May 1923.

While schools were being organized in the Polish camps, Ukrainian émigré institutions of higher learning were opened in Czechoslovakia. Since 1919 the UNR government had had a diplomatic mission there. At its request the Czechoslovak authorities had allowed many Ukrainian scholars to settle in the country, and now they allowed them to establish the Ukrainian Free University and Ukrainian Higher Pedagogical Institute in Prague, the Ukrainian Husbandry Academy in Poděbrady, and several gymnasiums. After news of the educational opportunities in Czechoslovakia reached the Polish internment camps, many younger internees escaped and made their way through the Carpathian Mountains to Czechoslovakia. Most entered schools; others found work. Consequently overcrowding in the Polish camps diminished, and life became more tolerable for those who remained.

A turning point for the internees occurred after Piłsudski returned to power in 1926. Toward the end of that year the UNR government-in-exile requested that Piłsudski grant certain relief reforms, including the formation of an official Ukrainian civic committee to care for all internees in Poland, health care for all disabled men and aged officers, and placing the administration of the camp at Kalisz in Ukrainian hands and turning it into a home for sick and infirm soldiers. Gradually all the requests were approved. First a Ukrainian Central Committee, with branches in all places where internees were concentrated, was established. The Kalisz camp was renamed the Ukrainian Station and was granted an independent administration, while other camps were abolished. All internees received legal status and the right to use Nansen passports. Those who were unable to work were transferred to the Ukrainian Station and, if they qualified, were granted modest pensions. Subsequently the

Polish authorities allowed the creation of a gymnasium and chauffeur courses for the residents.[7]

Most of the internees expected that they would be released soon and would return to Ukraine to continue the liberation struggle. They had information from the UNR government-in-exile that dissatisfaction with the Bolshevik regime was growing and that guerrilla warfare was being conducted by numerous partisan groups that, depending on the situation, could grow to encompass tens of thousands of people. The partisans had destroyed important bridges, railroad lines, and ammunition and food warehouses. They had also attacked smaller Bolshevik detachments carrying out requisitions, and administrative and police posts. Consequently the Bolshevik command had assigned large forces to combat them. The entire Soviet Sixth Army had been dispatched to fight against the partisan forces of Nestor Makhno, and almost the entire Soviet Seventh Division had been sent against the partisan leader Mordalevych. The partisan threat can be judged from Trotsky's secret instruction of 20 February 1920: "Liquidation of professional Ukrainian partisans represents a question of life and death [for Bolshevik rule] in Ukraine. Military detachments operating on Ukrainian territory are strictly prohibited to take into their ranks either partisan detachments or separate 'volunteers.' All partisan detachments should be immediately disarmed and disbanded, while those resisting should be destroyed."[8]

The Bolsheviks did not fight the UNR army and partisans in order simply to occupy Ukraine. The Red Army and Russian population had to be fed, and this was accomplished by forcibly expropriating foodstuffs through the so-called *prodnalog* (tax in agricultural products) imposed on the Ukrainian population. Almost three-fourths of all Bolshevik forces were sent into Right-Bank Ukraine: thirteen infantry divisions, one cavalry corps, the cavalry division of Hryhorii Kotovs'kyi, two border divisions, and several artillery brigades. In addition, "labor battalions" were stationed in each county center to carry out ruthlessly requisitions of food, livestock, and poultry. Thousands of people were shot, and entire villages were destroyed by artillery or burned to the ground for refusing to give up their goods. As a result of the requisitions and a bad harvest in 1921, a famine ensued. Oleksander Shul'hyn, the UNR foreign minister, later testified that "In 1921 Ukraine experienced a terrible famine even though our country was not short of grain—for it is the richest in Europe. But our granaries were pillaged, and while our grain was transported to the north [Russia], our people in Ukraine died of starvation."[9] Because of these desperate circumstances, a partisan delegation paid a visit to the UNR government-in-exile to beseech it to send officers and soldiers from the Polish internment camps to help fight the Bolshevik regime.

The policy of the UNR government-in-exile was oriented toward the Entente. Petliura trusted that the Allies and Poland would support the Ukrainian cause, and his trust induced the government-in-exile to try once again to overthrow the Bolshevik regime. Throughout Ukraine there were over two hundred partisan groups of varying strengths. In order to be more effective, they were guided by one center, the National Cossack Council in Kyiv. Messengers sent from Ukraine to the government-in-exile brought encouraging information about the partisans' activities. They also reported that the people were waiting for the government-in-exile and its interned troops to return to help the partisans and to coordinate their activities. This information and the desire of the interned soldiers to continue the struggle convinced the government-in-exile to organize fighting groups in Poland and send them into Ukraine.[10] Those groups' raids became known as the Second Winter Campaign.

CHAPTER 15

The Second Winter Campaign

The UNR government-in-exile underestimated the Bolsheviks' strength and ability to fight the partisans during the summer and fall of 1921. The Bolsheviks discovered and destroyed the National Cossack Council and executed its members and some partisan leaders. At the same time the government-in-exile chose not to acknowledge that Poland's civil administration, which was controlled by the National Democratic party, opposed Ukraine's independence and was trying to prevent the government-in-exile's activities. In spite of the real state of affairs, the government-in-exile decided to organize a Ukrainian Partisan Army to carry out raids into Soviet Ukraine and become both the nucleus and coordinating force of the partisan movement in the Bolshevik rear. Its direction was entrusted to Gen. Tiutiunnyk and Col. Iurii Otmarshtain (head of the operational staff). In preparation, Tiutiunnyk formed a Main Partisan Staff and Civil Administration and issued a call for volunteers. Although his action was secret, Polish military circles knew about it. Several thousand internees volunteered to join the UPA, but because of the obstacles put up by Polish authorities, only some two thousand volunteers were accepted. Most of the volunteers were soldiers of the Fourth Kyiv Division interned at Aleksandrów Kujawski. They were organized into two combat groups. The Volynian or Northern Group, commanded by Gen. Mykola Ianchenko, consisted of 650 volunteers and a brigade of the Ukrainian Sixth Division headed by Col. Roman Sushko. To this group the Main Partisan Staff and Civil Administration (some two hundred persons) was attached. The entire group was under the supreme command of Tiutiunnyk and Otmarshtain. The Podillian Group consisted of 620 volunteers, mainly cavalrymen, commanded by Col. Mykhailo Palii-Sydorians'kyi; Col. Serhii Chornyi was his deputy.

Although the raids were to take place in the early autumn of 1921, Polish authorities delayed authorizing transportation of the groups to the border until the end of October, by which time weather conditions were unsuitable for such an operation. The organizers faced a dilemma: should they begin the raids in late autumn, or should they postpone them until spring? Otmarshtain insisted on delaying until spring, but Tiutiunnyk decided to proceed with the raids in late autumn. A major problem for the groups was the lack of arms, clothing, and shoes. The Polish military was obliged to supply them with arms and equipment consisting mainly of the arsenal surrendered by the UNR troops in 1920, and Polish authorities promised to deliver them. At the same time they were divided on the question of the raids. Some wanted them and an uprising in Ukraine to take place for Poland's benefit, to frighten the Bolsheviks at the expense of the Ukrainians. Others opposed the raids and tried to prevent them. The delay of the raids and the failure to supply arms and clothing to the troops was the result of this vacillating Polish policy.

Finally, both groups were transported to border areas by freight trains in the guise of woodsmen. Their first destination was Lviv, where Tiutiunnyk was headquartered. In transit they were treated as prisoners and given only beggarly clothing and torn shoes; some were even barefoot and had no coats, only blankets. The Polish command promised to arm and cloth them at the next destination. From Lviv the Volynian Group was transferred to the Rivne area. There the men were quartered in villages and worked for food before being moved to the Kostopil area. Although there were a thousand of them, they received only a few hundred old rifles, six machine guns without bullets, and old spears and sabers, but no clothing or shoes.

As the group was transported closer to the Polish-Soviet border, it began maneuvering to hide from the Polish troops. The Soviet Russian mission in Warsaw, which had many agents in different places, was well informed about the planned raid, and it asked the Polish authorities to prevent it. In response the Polish command in Warsaw ordered two cavalry regiments stationed in Kovel and Rivne to overtake and disarm the group and return it to the camps. But Polish liaison officers attached to the Volynian Group and loyal to Piłsudski gave the cavalry regiments wrong directions and thus prevented them from locating the Ukrainian group. With difficulty, the Volynian Group reached the border near the village of Netreba, where it expected to receive the promised additional arms and clothing. Instead, however, the group learned that a detachment of forty-five Polish border cavalry police had received orders to prevent it from crossing the border. Consequently it was compelled to take the police by surprise and disarm them. The group faced new and even more difficult hardships after crossing the border.

The Podillian Group was sent to a border area in the south, near Husiatyn on the Zbruch. There the Polish command gave the 620 soldiers about a hundred old Russian rifles, a small amount of ammunition, three machine guns, a little dynamite, and some medicine, but no clothing, shoes, nor horses. To divert the Bolsheviks' away from the two groups, the Ukrainian command arranged an incursion from inside Romania by the small Bessarabian Strike Group organized and led by Gen. Andrii Hulyi-Hulenko. This group launched a raid on 3 November into the area of Tyraspil and Rozdilna, where the Soviet Fifty-First and Sixth divisions were deployed. After some skirmishes, it was defeated.

The Podillian Group crossed into Soviet Ukraine during the night of 25–6 October. Although it was poorly armed, it fought successfully against the Bolshevik border guards, police stations, and other administrative posts through surprise attacks, and captured badly needed arms, clothing, and horses. As the group moved deeper into Ukraine, it encountered Kotovs'kyi's cavalry division near Derazhnia. By surprise attacks, the Podillian Group, with the assistance of partisan groups, including ones headed by Shpak and Chorna Khmara, defeated two of Kotovs'kyi's regiments after heavy fighting, and captured more arms, ammunition, and horses. Col. Palii-Sydorians'kyi was wounded, but he and seventeen other soldiers made their way back to the border and crossed it near Korets. Subsequently Col. Chornyi took over command of the Podillian Group. Because Kotovs'kyi persistently pursued the group, Chornyi was forced to change the direction of his advance away from the area of Proskuriv, Liatychiv, and Liubar; instead he headed northeast into the forest. The group was constantly in desperate conditions: the men were hungry and cold, while their opponents were well armed, well dressed, and well fed. They sought food and shelter for themselves and their horses in villages, but the Bolshevik cavalry persistently hunted them down and forced them to hide in the forest. Consequently the group waged a losing battle not only against the Bolshevik cavalry, but also against the forces of nature. In spite of its hardships, however, it continued to fight in the area bounded by Novohrad-Volynskyi, Korosten, and Zhytomyr. From there it moved toward Malyn, crossing the Korosten-Kyiv railroad line; it then turned toward the Dnieper, crossed the Teteriv River, and entered the area near the village of Leonivka, where it expected to unite with the Volynian Group. Although both groups nearly rendezvoused, persistent attacks by the Bolshevik cavalry prevented them from doing so. The Podillian Group was forced to retreat westward through the Liubar and Iziaslav areas toward the border. To make its retreat safer, the group wore Bolshevik caps and posed as a "special detachment combatting banditry and counterrevolution." In this guise, the group's remaining 120 cavalrymen retreated day and night without rest. They crossed the Polish border on 6 December near the village of Moshchanytsia in Ostrih county. During its raid the group lost 500 men. The officers and soldiers who returned were disarmed by the Poles and again interned.

While the Podillian Group had moved from the southwest toward Kyiv, the Volynian Group advanced toward that city from the northwest. The plan had been to fight the Bolshevik forces from both directions simultaneously and then unite near Kyiv for a common action. To camouflage the raid by the main part of the group, Gen. Tiutiunnyk first dispatched a small unit under Gen. Nel'hovs'kyi into the Emelchyn area. The rest of the Volynian Group crossed the border during the night of 3–4 November between Korets and Olesko in Volynia. Tiutiunnyk's first concern was to capture arms, ammunition, and clothing from the Bolsheviks for his badly armed and poorly clothed soldiers, and he staged a surprise attack on a border-guard unit. Although the Bolshevik command knew about the raid, the group nonetheless succeeded in surprising and disarming the border guards and capturing some arms and horses. After this minor success, the group moved toward Korosten. The city and its vicinity were strategically important, and the terrain, covered by forests, marshes, and rivers, was suitable for partisan warfare. The group's main goal was to capture the depots of arms, ammunition, and clothing in the city and to use the city as its base for further operations. While moving through the area, the group encountered and fought a number of Bolshevik detachments, particularly those requisitioning food and other goods from Ukrainian peasants for transportation to Soviet Russia. After defeating a Bolshevik detachment, the Ukrainian troops redistributed captured requisitioned goods among the local peasantry.

In Korosten Tiutiunnyk surprised the Bolshevik garrison guarding the railroad station, and after heavy fighting his group captured the depots and took 300 prisoners. Leaving a detachment to hold the station, Tiutiunnyk attacked the town's garrison from two sides. During the attack, many Bolshevik prisoners were released, but the garrison proved to be much stronger than expected. Moreover, a few hours after the attack began, two Bolshevik armored trains arrived and began firing on the Ukrainian positions. With this support, the garrison launched a counterattack, and soon it became clear that the opposing forces were not equal. The Volynian Group was numerically weaker, badly armed, and poorly clothed. It had neither time nor opportunity to improve conditions, and Tiutiunnyk was unable to hold Korosten long enough to obtain arms and equipment from the arsenals. Even though the local people gave his soldiers food, clothing, and shoes whenever they could, this did not change the situation, because the Bolshevik forces were far superior in number and arms. After suffering serious losses, the Volynian Group retreated from Korosten. The only salvation was a quick retreat, first north to the forests of Polissia, and from there to the border. Otmarshtain and other officers urged Tiutiunnyk to do so, but the general decided instead to move northeast toward Kyiv in the expectation of uniting with the Podillian Group at Leonivka, some forty kilometers from Kyiv.

As the group advanced toward Kyiv, some partisan groups joined it, but Tiutiunnyk was unable to instigate widespread partisan uprisings because the Bolshevik command had concentrated superior forces, including Kotovs'kyi's cavalry, against the Volynian Group. Each time the Ukrainian soldiers entered a village to warm up and eat, the Bolshevik cavalry attacked them, and they had to retreat into the forest, where cold and hunger ruled. The winter weather had become a serious impediment; frostbite, wounds, and unavailable medical care gradually overtaxed the group's movement and diminished its effectiveness. In spite of these hardships and constant Bolshevik attacks, however, the group continued fighting with varying success. When the group finally approached Leonivka, it encountered strong Bolshevik forces instead of the Podillian Group. Not knowing the whereabouts of the Podillian Group, Tiutiunnyk retreated northward toward the Teteriv River to seek refuge in the forest. His soldiers were exhausted by uninterrupted fighting, frost, deep snow, hunger, and lack of sleep or rest. Lieut. Majewski, a Polish liaison officer attached to the Volynian Group, wrote, "I am simply amazed by the endurance and heroism of those people. I have been riding on my own horse from Poland, and now [even] I am reduced to a dead body. [But] Those soldiers have been marching on foot over 300 kilometers [; they are] barefoot, naked, [and have had only] three hours of rest in [every] twenty-four hours. In addition, there has been fighting each day."[1]

After crossing the Teteriv, the group retreated north over 175 kilometers while constantly fighting pursuing Bolshevik forces. On 17 November the group stopped to rest in the village of Mali Minky. There Bolshevik forces, including Kotovs'kyi's division, attacked it from two sides. The Ukrainian group fought courageously, but after all its bullets and grenades had been depleted, the Bolshevik cavalry broke through its ranks and killed over 100 of the wounded officers and soldiers resting on wagons and sleds. Some of the latter committed suicide with the help of their last bullet or grenade. During its raid the Volynian Group suffered about 500 casualties, and 359 of its men were captured by the Bolsheviks. The remaining fewer than 100 men, including Tiutiunnyk and his staff, managed to escape the Bolshevik encirclement because a Ukrainian commanding officer of a Bolshevik cavalry brigade did not carry out the order to occupy a ferry on the Uzh River. (This officer was later executed by the Bolsheviks.) Tiutiunnyk and his group used the ferry to cross into Polish-held territory. There the survivors of the Volynian Group, like those of the Podillian Group, were again interned.

The 359 officers and soldiers of the Volynian Group captured by the Bolsheviks were locked up in an unheated church in Mali Minky, where they were subjected to cold, hunger, and interrogations. When local people tried to bring food and water to the prisoners, the Bolshevik guards shot at them. Kotovs'kyi personally interrogated almost all of the prisoners. At the end of the interrogations, he offered pardons to those who agreed to join the punitive detachments fighting the Ukrainian partisans. When the prisoners categorically refused his offer, Kotovs'kyi declared, "Then we will execute you." In response a soldier named Shcherbak spoke out for the entire group: "We know what will happen to us, and we are not afraid to die, but we will not enter into your service. If you execute us, be aware that the entire Ukrainian people will avenge us, and when the Ukrainian soldiers learn about your disgraceful work, for [shedding] our blood they will destroy everything that has any connection with you, the persecutors." The whole group then shouted "hurrah" in support of Shcherbak's statement and sang the Ukrainian national anthem.[2]

The case of the captured Ukrainian group was taken over by an extraordinary commission consisting of Illia Harkavyi (chairman), Livshits, Ivanov, Kotovs'kyi, and Frinovskii; Litvinov was its secretary. Tried for attempting to overthrow the Bolshevik regime and for banditry, all 359 prisoners were sentenced to death by firing squad. The verdict was signed by Iona Iakir, the commander in chief of the Crimean and Kyiv military districts, I. Pauka, the chief of staff, and Volodymyr Zatons'kyi, a member of the Revolutionary Committee of the region. The prisoners were transferred to the town of Bazar, about fifty kilometers northeast of Korosten, where they were again held in an unheated church. Later they were forced to dig a long trench in a ravine near the cemetery, while the Bolsheviks gathered people from the surrounding villages to witness how they punished those who resisted Soviet rule. The mass execution was carried out publicly on 21 November by machine gunners commanded by Primakov. Just before they were shot the prisoners sang the Ukrainian national anthem. Those only wounded were dumped into the trench and buried alive along with the dead. One of the wounded victims regained consciousness and managed to climb out of the grave at night and crawl to a nearby house, where the owner hid and nursed him in a barn for about one month. After the survivor regained some strength, the owner transported him to the Polish border. From there he made his way to a hospital in Brest-Litovsk, where he died of tuberculosis in 1924 or 1925.[3] As an epilogue to the massacre at Bazar, the Bolsheviks held a general parade of the Red Cossack Cavalry Division to celebrate their victory over the Ukrainian liberation struggle.[4]

CHAPTER 16

Petliura's Exile and Assassination

When the UNR troops had crossed into Poland and were interned, the UNR government, including Petliura, V'iacheslav Prokopovych, Pylyp Pylypchuk, and Andrii Livyts'kyi, sought refuge there. Petliura and other members of the government-in-exile settled in Tarnów with the consent of their Polish hosts. From there they organized and directed actions aimed at overthrowing the Bolsheviks and liberating Ukraine. Encouraged by the popular resistance in Ukraine to the Bolshevik occupation, Petliura organized the Second Winter Campaign in the hope that with the help of the Entente and Poland, the Bolshevik regime would be overthrown.

After the tragic failure of the Second Winter Campaign, Petliura turned his attention to international diplomatic activities in an attempt to increase support for Ukrainian independence in the European community. Under an assumed name he moved to Warsaw, where he intervened on behalf of the Ukrainian troops interned by the Polish administration. After a while Petliura faced a lack of cooperation from the Polish authorities, who prevented him from engaging in important political activities. Meantime the Soviet regime repeatedly demanded that the Polish government extradite Petliura on the grounds that he was a "rebel" and not entitled to asylum. Gradually life in Warsaw became psychologically unbearable for Petliura, while for the Polish government his presence handicapped the maintenance of good relations with its Soviet neighbor. Petliura's situation in Warsaw worsened after Piłsudski retired from political life in May 1923, and he decided to leave Poland after the discovery that a Bolshevik agent was trailing him. On 31 December 1923 Petliura left Warsaw under the assumed name of Stepan Mohyla. He was accompanied by Prokopovych, the former prime minister, who was also travelling under an assumed name. Their first destination was Budapest by way of Vienna, where they stayed for a day. In Budapest Petliura expected to have some freedom to engage in diplomatic activities, for there a UNR diplomatic mission was still active and the Hungarian government, after the experience of Béla Kun's Communist regime, was sympathetic to the Ukrainian cause. After a while Petliura realized that he could not successfully carry out important political activities from Budapest, because Hungary was not an important player in European politics. Moreover, the Ukrainian émigré community there was much too small to give Petliura the moral and financial support he needed for his political activities. Consequently, at the beginning of June 1924 Petliura, again under his assumed name and accompanied by Prokopovych, moved to Zürich.

In Zürich Petliura's living expenses were paid by Baron Mykola Vasyl'ko, the UNR ambassador to Switzerland since 1920. There Petliura contacted foreign diplomats and informed them about the Ukrainian cause and its struggle against the Bolsheviks. In his work he was aided by Vasyl'ko's connections and invaluable experience as a politician and diplomat. Unfortunately, Vasyl'ko died unexpectedly on 2 August 1924, and Petliura left Zürich for Geneva on 8 August.

In Geneva Petliura lobbied members of the League of Nations and sought their support for the Ukrainian cause. He also informed other international organizations about the Ukrainian struggle for freedom, among them the International Federation of League of Nations Societies, the International League of Invalids, the International League of Women for Peace and Freedom, and scholarly conferences. Petliura also initiated tours of the Ukrainian Republican Choir conducted by Oleksander Koshyts' throughout Western Europe, the United States, and Canada to acquaint the Western public with Ukraine and its culture. The more active Petliura became, the greater moral and financial support he needed not only from Ukrainian émigrés, but also from émigré groups of other nations occupied by Soviet Russia. Because the centers of most of these groups were mainly in France, Petliura decided to move to Paris. On 16 October he left Geneva.

In Paris Petliura rented a two-room apartment at 27 rue Belgrand. In March 1925 he moved to a small hotel at 7 rue Thenard in the Latin Quarter. Because of financial difficulties, it was several months before his wife Ol'ha and daughter Lesia joined him in Paris. The family shared two rooms, which did not befit Petliura's status as a former head of state. They had no kitchen and had to eat in restaurants almost every day. Petliura maintained relations with various French and foreign political circles through extensive correspondence, and continued to worry about the UNR soldiers interned in Poland. Owing to his efforts, a few thousand internees were allowed to come to France to work, and higher military education in foreign armies for younger and more qualified Ukrainian officers was attained by his government-in-exile in 1928. By 1936 over fifty young officers were serving in various foreign armies, including the Polish, French, Finnish, and Turkish. To document and promote the ongoing liberation struggle, Petliura established the weekly *Tryzub* (1925–40). Edited by Prokopovych, it was the unofficial organ of the

UNR government-in-exile. Petliura also initiated the creation of the journal *Tabor* (1923–4, 1927–39, Kalisz and Warsaw). Edited by Gen. Viktor Kushch, it published pioneer studies of Ukrainian military history. Petliura contributed many political articles to émigré Ukrainian journals and newspapers and wrote a booklet on the Ukrainian émigré community and its duty in which he promoted the struggle to free Ukraine.

The various governments-in-exile and national committees jointly concluded that liberation from Soviet Russia depended above all on a common front of all the subjugated nations. Consequently an international Promethean League was established in 1925 in Warsaw and then moved to Paris, largely on the initiative of Petliura and other members of the UNR government-in-exile. The establishment of the league followed the example of the Congress of Nations Formerly Ruled by Tsarist Russia held in Kyiv between 21 and 28 September 1917. Prof. Roman Smal'-Stoc'ky, an émigré Ukrainian, was the league's president until 1939. The league claimed to represent Azerbaijani, Crimean Tatar, Don and Kuban Cossack, Georgian, Idel-Ural Tatar, Ukrainian, and Turkestanian (Turkmen, Tajik, Kazakh, and Kyrgyz) aspirations and about 80 million captive non-Russians. The Armenians did not formally join the league, because their national aspirations were directed mainly against Turkey. Later, less important branches of the league were established, including ones in Berlin, Bucharest, Harbin, Helsinki, Istanbul, Prague, and Tehran. The league's efforts were directed by a council and its ideological, educational, women's, youth, and press sections. The various Promethean clubs held meetings and lectures and published books and brochures, and its members contributed articles to the foreign press and émigré periodicals. Alongside the clubs, a Committee of Friendship of Caucasia, Turkestan, and Ukraine was established in Paris. There, in 1926, émigré Georgians began publishing a monthly review in French, *Prométhée*, edited by Georgi Gvazava. It was replaced by the bimonthly *La Revue de Prométhée* (1938–40), edited by Oleksander Shul'hyn. Both publications informed the Western public about the fate of the captive nations and their struggle against Soviet rule.

The Promethean League maintained links with underground organizations in the captive homelands. It also lobbied the League of Nations and Western governments and sent them memoranda and memorials. In Poland the Promethean movement was supported financially by governmental and semigovernmental institutions and especially by military circles. There the main Promethean center was the Oriental Institute in Warsaw, which, in cooperation with the Oriental Youth Circle, published the quarterly *Wschód* (1930–9), the weekly *Biuletyn Polsko-Ukraiński* (1922–39), and the biweekly *Myśl Polska* (1936–9). All three periodicals were edited by Włodzimierz Bączkowski.[1]

The activities of the UNR government-in-exile and the Promethean League were quite successful. The Bolshevik regime was aware of Petliura's leadership role therein and that he was the symbol of Ukrainian political aspirations and the most popular figure in Ukraine. Singling him out as the most dangerous opponent to its rule in Ukraine, the regime speculated that if Petliura were dead, many Ukrainian émigré groups would completely break down and the spirit of resistance in Ukraine would be undermined. The Soviet regime persistently pursued Petliura's destruction. During the first Bolshevik invasion of Ukraine in January 1918, when UNR troops retreated from Kyiv, Bolshevik agents shot some forty innocent men there because they resembled Petliura. The Bolshevik plot to assassinate Petliura accelerated when Piłsudski returned to power after the parliamentary regime in Poland was ousted on 12 May 1926. The Bolsheviks feared that Piłsudski and Petliura would revive the Polish-Ukrainian united front against Soviet Russia and would try to liberate Ukraine once again.

In spite of warnings by members of the UNR government-in-exile and senior Ukrainian military officers that his life was in danger, Petliura did not take their advice to go into hiding. For a while aides guarded Petliura when he went out. Later, however, he went out unguarded with his wife and daughter and alone. On 25 May 1926, because his wife was ill, Petliura went by himself to the restaurant Boullion Chartier on rue Racine. While returning home from the restaurant, he stopped to peruse the window display of the bookstore at the corner of boulevard Saint-Michel. There Petliura was approached by an unknown man who called out his name, and when Petliura turned around the man pointed a pistol at him and fired. The assassin was Samuel (Shalom) Schwartzbard, a Jewish watchmaker. Struck by three bullets, Petliura fell to the sidewalk, after which seven more shots were fired at him point blank; a final shot was not discharged because the pistol's firing mechanism jammed.[2] The assassination was described by Schwartzbard himself:

Here's my chance, I thought. 'Are you Petlura?' I asked him. He did not answer, simply lifting his heavy cane. I knew it was he! I shot once, twice, three, four, five times! He fell, the crowd rushed in on me. My only worry was whether it was really Petlura.... When a policeman told me it was Petlura I threw my arms about his neck in joy!"[3]

Still breathing feebly, Petliura was taken to the Hôpital de la Charité on rue Jacob. There, one and a half hours later, he died at the age of 47. On 30 May his body was transferred to a Romanian church on rue Jean de Beauvais, which Petliura attended each Sunday. After the funeral service there he was buried in the Montparnasse cemetery.[4]

Schwartzbard was arrested and taken to a police station, where he told Magistrate Peyere at the preliminary examination that he had killed Petliura to avenge the pogroms to which his people had been subjected in Ukraine on Petliura's orders.[5] In fact, however, as president of the UNR, Petliura had condemned the pogroms and had issued a special order on 26 August 1919 exhorting the population not to commit wrongs against the Jews and declaring that perpetrators of such crimes would be severely punished.[6] Petliura also made an important contribution to the freedom of the Jews in Ukraine. On 20 November 1917, in its Third Universal, the Ukrainian Central Rada had proclaimed that "The Ukrainians, having gained freedom for themselves, will firmly defend the freedom of national development of all nationalities living in Ukraine. Therefore we declare that we recognize the right of the Russian, Jewish, Polish, and other nationalities to national-personal autonomy to secure for themselves the right and freedom of self-rule in questions of national life."[7] Ukrainian Jews, with few exceptions, welcomed the manifesto as a fulfillment of their hopes and political aspirations. Subsequently, on 22 January 1918, the UNR government, in which Petliura was secretary of military affairs, unanimously adopted the Law on National-Personal Autonomy. Solomon Goldelman, a Jewish-Ukrainian economist and UNR deputy minister of trade and industry and of labor, wrote that "the great extent of national autonomy granted the Jewish minority in Ukraine stands alone in the entire history of the Jewish people in the diaspora."[8] Similarly, the representative of the Jewish Social Democratic Bund in the Rada, Moisei Rafes, welcomed the law as "an act of the greatest value, which is not to be found in any other country of Europe."[9] Thus, it is clear that the wrongs of which Schwartzbard accused Petliura were not committed by Petliura or under his orders, but by renegade troops, partisans, Red Army soldiers, and the VA during its invasion of Ukraine in 1919.

In response to the report on pogroms of the Committee of Assistance to Pogrom Victims of the Russian Red Cross in Kyiv, Arnold Margolin, a Jewish-Ukrainian lawyer, politician, and UNR deputy foreign minister, wrote that

> In this report it is pointed out that under the Ukrainian Central Rada, under the Hetman Skoropadski [sic], and during the first two months of the Directory, there were no pogroms. Pogroms began after the defeats of the armies of the Ukrainian Directory by the Bolsheviki.... An entirely different picture is presented when one compares this series of pogroms with the pogroms instituted by the army of Denikin. Here it is no longer a question of a retreat and consequent chaos. On the contrary, the more successful the offensive, the better organized was the propaganda from above and the more violent and

deliberate became the pogroms. If in the regular Ukrainian army the decay started at the tail, here the poison of decomposition was lodged in the head. The officers of Denikin openly declared that they were not fighting the Bolsheviki but the Jews. "Beat the Jews and save Mother Russia![10]

According to evidence obtained from Schwartzbard and witnesses during his preliminary examination and trial, he was born in Smolensk in 1886 but grew up in Balta, Podillia gubernia, where his parents had moved. (Balta was a commercial town whose population in 1880 was eighty percent Jewish.) In 1905 Schwartzbard survived a pogrom in Balta instigated by the Russian police. That year he illegally crossed into Romania. On 18 August 1908 he and others were arrested in Vienna while trying to rob a restaurant. Schwartzbard was sentenced to four months of hard labor. After serving his sentence he moved to Budapest, where he was arrested for a similar crime and deported from Hungary. Schwartzbard justified his criminal activities on the basis of his anarchist convictions. It is not clear how he came to Paris in 1910. There he found a job in a watch factory and married a Jewish woman in 1914. Following the outbreak of the First World War, Schwartzbard joined the Foreign Legion. Later he was transferred to the French 363d Infantry Regiment and was sent to the front. In 1916 he was wounded; after recovering he left the army. In September 1917, with the assistance of the Russian Military Mission, Schwartzbard traveled by ship to Russia in the company of his wife and a few Russians with whom he had served in the army. The purpose of his trip was never clearly established. During his trip he carried pro-Bolshevik propaganda, however, and was arrested and handed over to the Russian authorities in Archangel. After the Bolshevik coup he joined the Red Army and fought in it, mainly in Ukraine. In 1920 he returned to Paris and received an official discharge from the French army. There he opened a watch and jewelry store on boulevard Menilmontent and was active in an anarchocommunist organization. In 1925 Schwartzbard became a French citizen.

According to witnesses, the plan to assassinate Petliura was worked out by the GPU (secret police) in Moscow and was brought out by Mikhail Volodin. Volodin worked abroad as an agent from 1920, first in Poland and then in Czechoslovakia, from which he was expelled. In 1922 he appeared in Berlin posing as an anarchist. In early August 1925 Volodin came to Paris, where he mingled among the Slavic émigrés as a political agitator. Volodin met Schwartzbard through Elia Dobkowski, the former deputy commissioner general of the Central Jewish Commission in France, with whom he had become acquainted in Berlin. Volodin recruited Schwartzbard and helped him to work out his strategy for assassinating Petliura. In Schwartzbard's house police found a registered letter he had written to his wife to explain his actions. The letter had been registered at the post office at the City Hall at 2:35 P.M., thirty-five minutes after the assassination, when Schwartzbard was already under arrest. Volodin was suspected of posting the letter. At Schwartzbard's trial Dobkowski testified that Volodin played a key role in the plot to assassinate Petliura. On the eve of the trial, Dobkowski wrote a pamphlet that discussed Volodin's involvement in the crime. "In the last days of March, he [Volodin] returned very upset because he had learned that he would certainly be called by the judge. He feared being confronted by Petliura's wife and daughter because he dined on the eve of the crime with Schwartzbard in a restaurant where Petliura usually dined."[11] Volodin told Dobkowski that he had to leave Paris for Russia. When the police found out about his involvement and came to his residence, he had already disappeared.[12]

Seventeen months of investigation took place before Schwartzbard's trial began on 18 October 1927 at the Criminal Court of the Seine. Judge Flory presided. The plaintiffs were the widow, Mrs. Ol'ha Petliura, and Col. Oleksander Petliura, the victim's younger brother. They were represented by César Campinchi and Albert Willm. The public prosecutor was Atty. Gen. Pierre Reynaudel. The chief defense counsel was Henri Torrès. Some two hundred witnesses were summoned—forty by the prosecutor, sixty by the plaintiffs, and about one hundred by the defense. They included poets, writers, senators, professors, and other people well known in France. The defense summoned many character witnesses who did not contribute evidence pertaining directly to the assassination. Most of the witnesses, particularly those called by the defense, never lived in Ukraine, and therefore knew very little about developments there, let alone the assassination or Schwartzbard. During the trial Schwartzbard was supported by a Jewish public committee, which helped him and Torrès and portrayed Schwartzbard as a Jewish national hero.

Although the courtroom was the largest in Paris, it was too small to hold everyone who sought to attend the trial. The trial drew a large number of journalists and correspondents from around the world. Virtually every Jewish newspaper in the world was represented. From the outset the trial was a spectacle. According to one American reporter, "Emotion dominated the scene from start to finish. Such cold abstractions as law and reason found no place in the crowded court-room. Theatrical display and the appeal to sheer feeling were everywhere present in the trial of Samuel Schwartzbard."[13]

The defense built its case on the assumption that Schwartzbard acted alone as a "righteous avenger." During the trial, however, a number of witnesses testified that Schwartzbard had accomplices. Gen. Mykola Shapoval, a prominent Ukrainian émigré in Paris, testified that Volodin knew Schwartzbard; Volodin had often met with Shapoval and had asked for Petliura's address a number of times. Dobkowski wrote in a long letter to the prosecutor that "In order to arrive at the truth of Petliura's assassination, I consider it indispensable to call your attention to the advisability of arresting Volodin at once, or at least making certain of his presence. I already exerted all efforts to have him summoned before the examiner and arrested as an accomplice of Schwartzbard, since he himself admitted his part in the crime."[14] That Schwartzbard had accomplices is evident also from the fact that when Petliura went alone to the restaurant on rue Racine, Schwartzbard immediately left his shop, and that the assassin's letter to his wife was posted when he was already under arrest. In spite of the evidence pointing to Volodin's involvement, he was not brought to trial.

The trial was influenced by international politics, history, and prejudice. Moscow, in particular, used the trial not only to undermine the reputation of Petliura and of the Ukrainian liberation movement, but also to instigate mutual Jewish-Ukrainian animosity. Defense counsel Torrès, a highly successful criminal lawyer, dominated the proceedings and skillfully diverted the court's attention away from the defendant by dwelling on the pogroms. The defense called many Jewish witnesses to testify about pogroms, starting with the reign of Emperor Titus Flavius Vespasianus (79–81). This tactic complicated the case and confused the court. For two days Torrès sought to prove Petliura's personal responsibility for pogroms. Some witnesses, however, testified to the contrary. Dobkowski was questioned by Magistrate Peyere, and his testimony was damaging to his friend Schwartzbard. Dobkowski cited Vladimir Jabotinsky, a Zionist leader born in Odessa: "The fact is that neither Petliura, nor Vynnychenko, nor any other prominent members of the Ukrainian government were pogromists. I grew up with them. I fought with them against anti-Semitism. You will never convince a Zionist such as myself that people of this type could be called anti-Semitic."[15]

In his testimony, another witness, Prince Jean de Tokhary, stated:

"Gentlemen, I have come to tell you what I know about the deceased, with whom I was closely associated in my work. I was under his direction and he always confided in me. Therefore, I can tell you about his opinions and about the directives I received from him. His sympathies never changed with regard to France and her allies. I see in the newspapers that the assassin, in attempting to justify his deed, is blackening the memory of his victim by accusing him of having ordered or tolerated the pogroms. As an official of government, I know and can affirm the opposite to be true—he protected all national minorities in Ukraine, as long as he was head of the state. Returning to Paris after him, I can testify that this incorruptible man lived a simple daily life in poverty, despite his modest means. His integrity, his patriotism, his moral courage were above reproach: There could not have been a better Chief-of-State of Ukraine."[16]

When Torrès failed to prove his point, he changed his line of argument to claim that Petliura, as the UNR head of state and commander in chief of the UNR Army, was ultimately responsible for the acts of his soldiers and everything that occurred in the territory under his control. He insisted that Petliura neither suppressed disorders nor punished the guilty. Campinchi insisted that Petliura was not responsible for the pogroms, but that the Jewish population suffered from both Denikin's army and the Bolsheviks, who had occupied most of Ukraine. He pointed to a book containing 300 pages of Petliura's proclamations and orders in defense of the Jews. Gen. Shapoval declared that UNR regular troops had never participated in pogroms and that Petliura condemned such tactics. He stressed that "Petliura was not anti-Semitic. He was a humanitarian—a friend of the Jews. 'He lies! He lies!' chorused a score of voices in a score of different tongues.... Torrès interrupted [Shapoval] to brand Petliura a dictator and necessarily responsible in person for the acts of his subordinates."[17] In response, Willm stated:

"Gentlemen of the Jury, it is necessary to realize that Petlura, as a symbol of Ukraine's national independence, is an enemy of the Tsarist Empire as well as of those who joined the Moscow regime after the Bolshevik revolution. It so happened that on the devastated soil of Ukraine there wasn't a moment of peace or security. Otaman Petlura had to fight against Denikin's White Russians and Trotsky's Red Army. Additionally, he had to battle against the piratical bands of demobilized Russian elements ... and, furthermore, to lead and maintain a country plunged into complete anarchy."[18]

To blacken Petliura further, Torrès began accusing him of Germanophilism and hostility to France and its allies. Contrary to that accusation, however, in mid-November 1918 Petliura led the insurrection against Hetman Skoropads'kyi's regime, which was supported by the German occupational forces, and he later made efforts to gain French support for the UNR and, in 1920, the Ukrainian-Polish alliance. Petliura's pro-French policy was corroborated by Gen. Georges Tabouis, a member of the former French military mission in Kyiv, and by his successor, Col. Henri Freydenberg. Tabouis testified by letter that

"I have not forgotten the good relations between Otaman Petlura and myself ... nor the patriotic ardor.... I understand your desire to defend the memory of this man from the taint with which his enemies wish to stain it for only political and nonreligious reasons. To say that Petliura was anti-Semitic! What a sinister trick."[19]

Petliura's Exile and Assassination 193

And in his letter Freydenberg wrote:

I remember that there were at least two Jews as ministers in the Directorate [Directory]. I have spoken with many of your ministers and they always insisted on Petlura's efforts to prevent the pogroms, which was to be expected considering the altruistic sentiments of Symon Petlura. I am certain, moreover, that Petliura always acted as a friend of France and spared no efforts to collaborate in the friendliest manner with the French occupation forces.[20]

Torrès prolonged his interrogation to prevent his opponents from refuting his accusations and witnesses from speaking on Petliura's behalf. He never missed an opportunity to interrupt a witness who provided important testimony unfavorable to Schwartzbard. When he could not distract a witness, he abusively tried to discredit him or to cast suspicion on his moral qualities, objectivity, and honesty. Torrès referred to witnesses who were veterans of the UNR army as bandits. In spite of such behavior, the presiding judge did not reprimand him, even when the counsel for the prosecution and witnesses appealed to him for intervention. While questioning witnesses, Torrès always inserted facts or questions that were completely unconnected with the case, so as to obscure the content of the testimonies and to confuse the jury. Through this tactic he gradually transformed the victim into the accused and the assassin into the righteous avenger. This turn was accomplished skillfully, owing to Torrès's thorough acquaintance with the dossier and by his use of gaps in the evidence to his advantage. As a result, Petliura was put on trial. Willm tried to refute the portrayal of Schwartzbard as a righteous avenger:

"If Schwartzbard were really seeking, as he insists, to avenge the unfortunate brothers of his race, why did he not execute his revenge while in Russia, where courage would have been demanded of him to accept the consequences of his crime?... But this is not how he acted. He waited till his victim was in exile, till he found himself in impoverished circumstances, living in a quiet quarter of Paris, patiently awaiting the moment when he could again take up the struggle for his country's independence."[21]

Torrès sought Schwartzbard's acquittal. Such a decision, however, could occur only if there was formal proof of Petliura's responsibility for pogroms. Torrès could not supply such proof. As an experienced counsel, however, he understood that the jury's verdict would be based largely on emotional responses rather than on legal rules. Therefore he called many witnesses to testify to Schwartzbard's integrity prior to his act of assassination and to his service in the French army, or to accuse Petliura of responsibility for the pogroms. When more witnesses were to testify on Petliura's behalf, Torrès proposed ending the trial. Unfortunately Campinchi agreed, and at the close of the eighth session, the court concurred so as not to prolong the trial.

In his summation, Willm appealed:

"Gentlemen of the Jury, do not forget that for several years Petlura was in retirement, that he betook himself under the mantle of the generous laws of France, which have always been liberal and hospitable to those seeking asylum after military disaster or political persecution, and that it was when the former Otaman was alone and unprotected and peacefully leaving a restaurant that the accused stood waiting with his weapon cocked—as he himself has told you—and after calling 'It is you Pane [Mister] Petlura?' that he shot him the moment he turned. Then with incredible cruelty and cowardice, he kept firing at the fallen wounded man. No! He had no right shortly after being accepted by the French community to taint that community by so abominable a crime, because it is dangerous to everyone, and we could then be exposed to the malice of those who roam our streets armed and ready to kill, without being certain of the character of their victims. We surrender assassins to those who want them and who wish to transform them into national heroes."[22]

In his final appeal to the jury, Campinchi anticipated the outcome:

"And you, the French Jury, who value human life, will you let this man go free? Schwartzbard, you would leave in triumph. Outside this court I've seen over five hundred people who are ready to carry you out on their shoulders as a hero, while the widow of Petlura, alone, silent and worn out, would depart in solitude, clothed in mourning and become still more depressed. It is curious that Justice should exalt an assassin, and so brazenly reject the rights of the victim."[23]

In his concluding remarks, Atty. Gen. Reynaudel stated that

"Petlura was never an enemy of the Jews. He never advocated pogroms. On the contrary, he loved Jews. I reached this conviction, Gentlemen, first, after examining Petlura's deeds; second, after hearing the tributes paid him by his co-workers, compatriots and by Jews. Solemnly Petlura always condemned and forbade pogroms with the most severe sanctions. With Napoleonic inspiration, he spoke of the common suffering of both Jews and Ukrainians, and preached fraternity among these two peoples. 'Pogroms,' he said, 'are a crime against humanity.' Petlura repeatedly and admirably proposed the union of Jews and Ukrainians as the only means of working for his aim of an independent

Ukraine. To Schwartzbard I say: 'You have nothing with which to reproach Petliura. You had nothing to reproach him with in the past. And in the future you had nothing to fear from him.'"[24]

Torrès's tactics, however, were not intended to aid justice and to enlighten the jury about the reasons that led to the tragedy, but to appeal to their emotions and prejudices. His tactics proved successful. The jury "followed the dictates of its heart rather than of its head in rendering its verdict"[25] and found Schwartzbard not guilty.[26]

CHAPTER 17

Conclusion

The political map of East Central Europe, as it had existed for generations, was radically changed by World War I. The defeat of the Central Powers and the Revolution of 1917 created new political opportunities for the former subject peoples of the old empires. Ukraine was fertile ground for the growth of a national self-determination movement. To preserve the unity of the Russian Empire, the tsarist regime had systematically suppressed all manifestations of Ukrainian culture for generations and had placed the administration of Ukraine mainly in the hands of non-Ukrainians. Consequently, when the revolution broke out, the establishment and maintenance of Ukrainian statehood proved difficult because the number of qualified personnel needed to run the new Ukrainian state's infrastructure was inadequate. Moreover, efforts to establish Ukrainian independence were further weakened internally by the large non-Ukrainian communities in Ukraine, especially in the cities and industrial centers, among whom a neutral or even hostile attitude toward Ukrainian statehood was widespread. The concentration in Ukraine of the Russian armies fighting against the Austro-German armies, and the great number of deserters hiding in Ukraine, also hindered the Ukrainian government's attempts at establishing a strong authority and maintaining order.

Nevertheless, Ukrainian leaders, with the support of the All-Ukrainian Military and Peasants' and Workers' congresses, declared their nation's right to self-determination and formed a pre-parliament, the Central Rada, composed of representatives of municipal, cultural, and professional organizations and various political parties. The Rada inaugurated a new period in the national revolution—a struggle whose goal was consolidating the supreme political authority of the independent Ukrainian People's Republic. The Rada failed, however, to create a regular army that could ensure the defense of Ukraine. Because the Rada already faced huge internal obstacles, the success of its efforts to achieve and maintain independence depended heavily on the absence of external pressure, which only strong support by the Entente could have assured. But the Entente leaders remained faithful to their pro-Russian policy and irreconcilably opposed to Ukrainian statehood.

Conclusion

The relatively peaceful and constructive period that ensued in Ukraine immediately after the outbreak of the revolution was threatened by the political changes in Russia. In spite of Russia's military humiliations and internal disintegration, its power was rapidly reconsolidated by the Bolsheviks following their victorious coup in November 1917. The Bolsheviks immediately challenged the aspirations of the newly created nation-states on the territory of the former Russian Empire. Ukraine became the main object of their aggression because of its strategic location and natural resources.

After it became clear that the weak and inadequately equipped forces of the nascent Ukrainian state could not contain the Bolshevik assault, the Rada signed a separate peace treaty with the Central Powers at Brest-Litovsk on 9 February 1918 so as to obtain their aid in expelling the Bolsheviks. Although Ukraine's new allies were instrumental in driving the Bolshevik forces from Ukraine, they also abused their powers there. Their Ukrainian policy was short-sighted, for it was concerned mainly with ensuring the delivery of supplies from Ukraine. Consequently, when the Rada introduced economic reforms that were unacceptable to the Austro-German military authorities, they dissolved the Rada and replaced it with a conservative puppet regime headed by Gen. Pavlo Skoropads'kyi as hetman of Ukraine.

The hetman tried to gain national support for his regime by inviting representatives of various parties to join his government and help pursue an independent foreign policy. But he failed to gain their cooperation. Instead the party leaders organized a national union to oppose the hetman and elected a UNR Directory as its executive organ. As long as German power was unbroken on the Western Front, Austro-German troops were able to maintain control in Ukraine. After the defeat of the Central Powers, however, the hetman government lost the little support it had and was overthrown by the troops of the Directory. The new UNR government faced even more serious domestic and foreign problems than its predecessor. Many bureaucrats of the hetman regime went into hiding, and the Directory was left with even fewer trained personnel to run the state. Besides seemingly insurmountable domestic difficulties, the Directory was also threatened by new foreign invasions.

Following the breakup of the Habsburg monarchy, the Ukrainian population of Eastern Galicia, Bukovyna, and Transcarpthia had organized a Ukrainian National Rada in Lviv, which proclaimed an independent Western Ukrainian People's Republic on 1 November 1918. The Directory and the National Rada proclaimed the union of the two Ukrainian republics on 29 January 1919. Soon after newly united Ukraine faced a military threat from three sides—from the Poles in the west, the VA in the southeast, and the Bolsheviks in the northeast—while lacking adequate arms, military equipment, and medical supplies and while a typhus epidemic decimated its army.

In these circumstances some members of the UNR government, headed by Vynnychenko, favored negotiations with the Bolsheviks; others, led by Petliura, favored a united front with the French against the Bolsheviks, despite French support for a "united and indivisible Russia." Petliura's view prevailed, the Ukrainian Social Democrats and Socialist Revolutionaries withdrew from the government, and Vynnychenko, the president of the Directory, handed over his authority to Petliura.

Meanwhile, the superior invading forces of the Bolsheviks and the VA forced the battered UNR Army to retreat to the westernmost limits of Right-Bank Ukraine. Petliura realized that Ukraine would not survive its war with the Russians without Entente aid. In his opinion, Poland was the bridge to the Entente, and he made genuine attempts to come to terms with the Polish government in order to conclude a political and military alliance with Poland and thus win French support for the struggle against the Bolsheviks. For Petliura such an alliance corresponded to the French plan for a strong Poland as a barrier against Germany. Unlike Ukraine, Poland was protected by the victorious Entente, while the Ukrainians served as a buffer between Poland and Soviet Russia. But the renascence of Russian power ultimately threatened Poland, for the Bolshevik leaders' aim was the military and political triumph of Bolshevism throughout Europe.

Despite the Bolshevik threat, Poland's leaders did not have a unanimous policy toward Soviet Russia. Poland was dominated by two parties—the National Democrats headed by Dmowski and the Socialists under Piłsudski—with different defensive policies based on opposing attitudes toward Poland's eastern neighbors. Dmowski favored strengthening Poland through the partial territorial conquest of its eastern neighbors. To assure that conquest and gain security for Poland, he proposed offering Poland's agreement to Soviet Russia's occupation of a larger part of Poland's eastern neighbors. Dmowski also linked the overall security of Poland with the Franco-Russian alliance, and he feared a smaller but independent Ukraine even more than a strong and hostile Soviet Russia.

Piłsudski was more farsighted and more audacious. He was convinced that Poland's independence could not be secured without the independence of other states in Eastern Europe. Piłsudski understood that the Entente Powers protected Poland from Germany, but that there was no power to check Soviet Russia's aggressive policy. Consequently, Piłsudski's plan was to support and unite with those countries between Poland and Russia, which he viewed as Poland's natural allies against Russia. He wished to extend Polish influence farther to the east than Dmowski did, and envisioned a liberal "Great Poland" loosely associated with Lithuania, Belarus, and Ukraine. Piłsudski did not believe that Soviet Russia had peaceful intentions, and he felt it would be impossible to secure a lasting peace with Russia without first defeating it. Like Petliura, he realized that only as allies could Poland and Ukraine both resist absorption by Russia.

Diplomatic relations between Ukraine and Poland were practically nonexistent in 1917 and 1918, primarily because of the Polish-Ukrainian War in Galicia. A serious threat from both the Bolshevik and White forces compelled the UNR government to initiate peace negotiations with the Polish government in the summer of 1919. Although the struggle of the UNR Army against the Russians also protected Poland, the Poles ignored the Ukrainians' help and took advantage of their critical situation until they had conquered the Ukrainian territory they desired. It was only after the defeat of the VA that the Bolshevik threat to Poland became real. In the meantime, Petliura had turned to Poland for assistance, thereby offering Piłsudski an opportunity to seek an alliance with Ukraine against Soviet Russia.

In October 1919 the Ukrainian government dispatched a diplomatic mission to Warsaw headed by Minister of Foreign Affairs Andrii Livyts'kyi. Before the negotiations began, the Polish delegation, which consisted mainly of the supporters of the National Democratic party, took full advantage of Ukraine's critical military situation to force the mission to issue a declaration accepting a border that left Western Ukraine within Poland. In the end the Treaty of Warsaw, which consisted of a political agreement and a military convention, reflected the Ukrainian delegation's desperation. Although the Ukrainians viewed the independence and unity of Ukraine as its ultimate goal, they were compelled to recognize Poland's claim to Western Ukraine. Yet, the fate of Left-Bank Ukraine was not addressed in the treaty. For Petliura the treaty was a tactical move aimed at establishing contact with the Entente Powers. He failed, however, to gain French support, while the British showed no interest in supporting a Ukraine allied with a Poland that they considered a French creation.

The aims of the joint Polish-Ukrainian war of 1920 with Soviet Russia that followed the signing of the Treaty of Warsaw were independence and peace for both Poland and Ukraine after defeating the Bolsheviks. Piłsudski wanted to forestall an anticipated Bolshevik offensive in Ukraine, where most of the Red forces were concentrated. During the April offensive the Bolshevik forces were driven back toward Kyiv with the help of a wave of Ukrainian partisan uprisings. But the Bolsheviks were not completely defeated, and they were able to retreat from Kyiv safely. Instead of pursuing them, the Polish command began building a defensive line.

Prior to the offensive, the Ukrainian government tried to strengthen its armed forces by organizing new units from troops scattered throughout Ukraine and abroad and by mobilizing civilians. But only two poorly armed divisions were created, because the Poles put up obstacles and did not supply the Ukrainians with promised military materiel. Even though it was a real necessity, the Poles were not interested in strengthening the UNR Army, and they even disarmed and interned the Galician brigades of over 23,000 men that joined the Polish side. The Poles also disarmed and interned various Ukrainian partisan groups at the end of the offensive.

Following the Bolshevik retreat east across the Dnieper River, the Red Army Command began reorganizing and reinforcing its forces in preparation for a counteroffensive under Budennyi. But the Polish command paid little attention to strengthening its defenses. In mid-May the Bolsheviks attacked on the Belarusian Front. The Poles forced them to retreat, but not before transferring many troops from the Ukrainian Front and thus weakening their position there. The Bolsheviks launched two offensives in Ukraine. The first was repulsed, but the second disrupted the Polish front line and was a turning point in the war. In mid-June the Polish and Ukrainian troops began a forced retreat along the entire front from the Prypiat to the Dniester.

While the Poles retreated into Poland, the Ukrainian troops established positions along the right bank of the Dniester and fortified and defended the border city of Zamość. As Bolshevik forces advanced deeper into Poland, Piłsudski fortified his positions around Warsaw and organized new units to strengthen his forces. The French government supplied materiel and sent a military mission to help organize the Polish defense. Because of a Bolshevik strategic mistake—the lack of coordination of military actions on both fronts—the Poles were able to organize a surprise attack, and after three days of fighting they defeated the Bolsheviks and split their fronts. As the Bolshevik forces under Tukhachevskii retreated eastward, many of them were captured, and they lost much materiel. Although Budennyi was ordered to reinforce Tukhachevskii, he could not do so after failing to capture Zamość. There the successes of Budennyi's cavalry ended.

Thereafter the Poles went on the offensive. Tukhachevskii had retreated eastward to the Neman. There he assembled his forces and received reinforcements with which he hoped to regain lost positions. Piłsudski, however, decided to attack and defeat the Bolsheviks before they were ready for new battle. Owing to the Poles' superior manpower, he succeeded. The Bolshevik position was further undermined by the Ukrainian partisans and the advance of Gen. Wrangel's White troops from the Crimea. As UNR troops continued fighting the Bolsheviks, the Poles and the Soviet Command signed a preliminary peace treaty and armistice agreement in mid-October 1920.

In spite of substantial Ukrainian contributions and sacrifices in the joint war against Soviet Russia, Poland abandoned its ally, and the UNR was forced to fight the enemy alone. After the tragedy at Bazar, Bolshevik power in Ukraine was consolidated. Poland seemed to have lost nothing after the failure of Polish-Ukrainian cooperation. In the long run, however, both it and Ukraine lost much because of their failure to develop a solid and durable alliance. While Russia's power was diminished during the early stages of the revolution, it would have been in Poland's interest to aid Ukraine and thereby strengthen its own future security vis-à-vis both Germany and Russia. Poland was politically shortsighted to come to terms with the Bolsheviks at Ukraine's expense.

A preliminary peace treaty and armistice agreement between Poland and Soviet Russia and Soviet Ukraine were signed on 12 October 1920. The final Peace Treaty of Riga was signed on 18 March 1921. The contracting parties recognized the "independence" of Ukraine and agreed on the frontiers, which were substantially the same as those agreed to in the Treaty of Warsaw. The Polish delegation at Riga, consisting again mostly of Dmowski's supporters, treated the Soviet Ukrainian delegation as representatives of an independent Ukraine. According to the fourth article of the Treaty of Warsaw, the Polish government had agreed "not to conclude any international agreement directed against Ukraine." But it did not consult the UNR government before accepting the Soviet Russian proposal to negotiate an armistice and a preliminary peace. While Ukrainian troops continued fighting the Bolsheviks alongside Polish troops, the Polish delegation, after twenty minutes of negotiations, recognized the credentials of the representatives of the fictitious Soviet Ukrainian republic. By this one act the delegation reversed Polish policy toward Ukraine and ignored both the Treaty of Warsaw and Ukrainian loyalty to Poland. The Polish government had no intention of fulfilling that treaty, not because Poland was too weak to carry out its obligation toward Ukraine, but because the Poles had not intention of defending the cause of Ukrainian independence.

The Treaty of Riga signalled the defeat of Piłsudski's conception and the victory of Dmowski's program. At that time both Piłsudski and Petliura considered the treaty as an interlude in the anti-Bolshevik struggle. Future political developments would annul the treaty and the war would continue, they thought. In the meantime, Piłsudski retired from political life in May 1923, while Petliura left Warsaw at the end of 1923 and settled in Paris with his family. After three years Piłsudski reentered political life by ousting the parliamentary regime on 12 May 1926, and became the virtual dictator of Poland. Piłsudski's reappearance on the political stage alarmed Moscow. Two weeks later, on 25 May 1926, Petliura was assassinated in Paris by Moscow's agent Samuel Schwartzbard, a naturalized Frenchman from Smolensk.

Polish-Ukrainian political and military collaboration is an important part of the history of Eastern Europe in the years immediately following the Russian Revolution and World War I. Although the Treaty of Warsaw between

Ukraine and Poland became defunct after the conclusion of the Peace Treaty of Riga, the idea of an alliance between these two large Slavic nations remained alive. The Treaty of Warsaw is a symbol of an historical current in Polish-Ukrainian relations that may well assert itself again.

Acronyms in the Notes and Bibliography

A   Ameryka (Philadelphia)
AKP   Al'manakh-kalendar Soiuzu katolykiv Ameryky "Provydinnia" (Philadelphia)
AR   The American Review of Reviews
ARR   Arkhiv russkoi revoliutsii (Berlin)
AUNS   Al'manakh Ukraïns'koho narodnoho soiuzu (Jersey City)
B   Bellona (Warsaw, 1919–50; London, 1950–)
BM   Bunt Młodych (Warsaw)
BPU   Biuletyn Polsko-Ukraiński (Warsaw)
BSBUVK   Biuleten' Soiuzu buvshykh ukraïns'kykh voiakiv u Kanadi (Toronto)
BUNDS   Biuleten' Ukraïns'koho natsional'no-derzhavnoho soiuzu (New York)
Byl   Byloe (Paris)
CH   Current History (New York)
ChSh   Chervonyi shliakh (Kharkiv)
CM   The Century Magazine (New York)
D   Dilo (Lviv)
DL   Donskaia letopis' (Belgrade)
DN   Dzieje Najnowsze (Wrocław)
Dor   Dorohovkaz (Toronto)
DP   Dziennik Polski i Dziennik Żolnierza (London)
EEQ   East European Quarterly
F   Fashist (Putnam, Connecticut)
GM   Golos minuvshago (Paris)
GMChS   Golos minuvshago na chuzhoi storone (Paris)
Gos. izd-vo Gosudarstvennoe izdatel'stvo
GP   Gazeta Poranna (Lviv)
GW   Gazeta Wieczorna (Lviv)
H   Hurtuimosia (Prague)
HU   Homin Ukraïny (Toronto)
IKAChK   Istorychnyi kaliendar-al'manakh Chervonoï kalyny (Lviv)

IKC	Ilustrowany Kurjer Codzienny (Cracow)
IM	Istorik-marksist (Moscow)
IS	Istorik i sovremennik (Berlin)
JAH	Journal of American History
JCEA	Journal of Central European Affairs (Boulder)
JCH	Journal of Contemporary History
JGO	Jahrbücher für Geschichte Osteuropas (Vienna)
K	Kultura (Paris)
KA	Krasnyi arkhiv (Moscow)
KAD	Kaliendar-al'manakh "Dnipro" (Lviv)
KAV	Kalendar-al'manakh "Vidrodzhennia" (Buenos Aires)
KChK	Kaliendar "Chervonoï kalyny" (Lviv)
KH	Kwartalnik Historyczny (Warsaw)
KhU	Khliborobs'ka Ukraïna (Vienna)
KI	Kommunisticheskii internatsional (Moscow)
KL	Kurjer Lwowski (Lviv)
KP	Kalendar "Provydinnia" (Philadelphia)
KUI	Kaliendar "Ukraïns'koho invalida" (Lviv)
KUNS	Kaliendar Ukraïns'koho narodnoho soiuzu (Jersey City)
KW	Kurjer Warszawski (Warsaw)
LA	The Living Age (Boston)
LChK	Litopys "Chervonoï kalyny" (Lviv)
LD	The Literary Digest (New York)
LNV	Literaturno-naukovyi vistnyk (Lviv)
LR	Letopis' revoliutsii/Litopys revoliutsiï (Kharkiv)
LS	Leninskii sbornik (Moscow)
M	Meta (Munich)
MN	Myśl Narodowa (Warsaw)
MS	Le Monde Slave (Paris)
MU	Moloda Ukraïna (Paris)
N	Niepodległość (Warsaw, London)
NB	Nasha bat'kivshchyna (New York)
NCA	The Nineteenth Century and After (London)
NChS	Na chuzhoi storone (Berlin)
ND	Natsional'na dumka (Prague)
NDni	Novi dni (Toronto)
NDP	Najnowsze Dzieje Polski: Materiały i Studia z Okresu 1914-1939 (Warsaw)
NE	The New Europe (London)
NH	Nova hromada (Vienna)

NIKTP	*Narodnii iliustrovanyi kaliendar tovarystva "Prosvita"* (Lviv)
NiP	*Naród i Państwo* (Warsaw)
NK	*Nash klych* (Buenos Aires)
NKul	*Nasha kul'tura* (Warsaw)
NL	*Novyi litopys* (Winnipeg)
NP	*Nasha pratsia* (Minneapolis)
NS	*Na slidakh* (Ontario, Calif.)
NSl	*Nashe slovo* (Munich)
NU	*Nova Ukraïna* (Prague)
NYT	*The New York Times*
NZh	*Novyi zhurnal* (New York)
O	*Ovyd* (Buenos Aires, 1949–55; Chicago, 1957–76)
OB	*Orzeł Biały* (London, Brussels)
P	*Proboiem* (Prague)
PD	*Przegląd Dyplomatyczny* (Warsaw)
PEW	*Problemy Europy Wschodniej* (Warsaw)
PH	*Przegląd Historyczny* (Warsaw)
PIB	*Politychnyi informatsiinyi biuleten'* (Warsaw)
PK	*Pamiętnik Kijowski* (London)
PoR	*The Polish Review* (New York)
PR	*Proletarskaia revoliutsiia* (Moscow)
PW	*Przegląd Współczesny* (Cracow)
R	*Robotnik* (Warsaw)
RD	*Rozbudova derzhavy* (Montreal, Toronto)
RM	*Russkaia mysl'* (Paris)
RN	*Rozbudova natsiï* (Prague)
RP	*The Review of Politics*
RR	The Russian Review
RW	*Rząd i Wojsko* (Warsaw)
S	*Suchasnist'* (Munich)
SD	*Samostiina dumka* (Chernivtsi)
SDZSRR	*Studia z Dziejów ZSRR i Europy Środkowej* (Warsaw)
SEER	*Slavonic and East European Review* (London)
Sh	*Shturm* (Neu-Ulm)
SM	*Sprawy Międzynarodowe* (Warsaw)
SN	*Sprawy Narodowościowe* (Warsaw)
SNDP	*Studia z Najnowszych Dziejów Powszechnych* (Warsaw)
SoR	*Soviet Russia* (New York)
SR	*Slavic Review*
SS	*Soviet Studies* (Glasgow)

StD	Strilets'ka dumka (Starokostiantyniv)
StV	Studens'kyi visnyk (Prague)
SU	Samostiina Ukraïna (Chicago)
Sv	Svoboda (Jersey City)
SV	Sichovi visty (Lviv)
T	Tabor (Warsaw)
TM	Trybuna molodykh (Paris)
TN	The Nation (New York)
TP	Tydzień Polski (Warsaw)
Tr	Tryzub (Paris, 1925–40; New York, 1961–75)
TrU	Trybuna Ukraïny (Warsaw)
TU	Trudova Ukraïna (New York)
UIn	Ukraïns'kyi invalid (Kalisz, 1923–31; Lviv, 1937–9)
UIs	Ukraïns'kyi istoryk (New York)
UIZh	Ukraïns'kyi istorychnyi zhurnal (Kyiv)
UK	Ukraïns'ke kozatstvo (Chicago, Toronto)
UKom	Ukraïns'kyi kombatant (Munich)
UP	Ukraïns'kyi prapor (Vienna)
UPS	Ukraïns'ke pravoslavne slovo (South Bound Brook)
UQ	The Ukrainian Quarterly (New York)
UR	Ukrainian Review (Munich, London)
URob	Ukraïns'kyi robitnyk (Toronto)
US	Ukraïns'kyi skytalets' (Liberec, 1920–2; Josefov, 1922; Vienna, 1922–3)
UV	Ukraïns'ki visti (Neu-Ulm, 1945–78; Detroit, 1978–)
V	Vistnyk (Lviv)
VI	Voprosy istorii (Moscow)
VK	Visti kombatanta (Toronto)
Vo	Volia (Vienna)
Voz	Vozrozhdenie (Paris)
VR	Voina i revoliutsiia (Moscow)
VSh	Vyzvol'nyi shliakh (London)
VSVU	Vistnyk Soiuza vyzvolennia Ukraïny (Vienna)
VU	Vil'na Ukraïna (Detroit, 1954–60; New York, 1961–72)
VV	Voennyi vestnik (Moscow)
Vyz	Vyzvolennia (Vienna)
W	Wiadomości (London)
WAP	Wojskowa Akademia Polityczna: Zeszyty Naukowe, Seria Historyczna (Warsaw)
WN	Wiek Nowy (Lviv)

WP	*Wiadomości Polskie* (London, Paris)
Ws	*Wschód* (Warsaw)
WsP	*Wschód Polski* (Warsaw)
WW	*Wissen und Wehr* (Berlin)
ZD	*Za derzhavnist'* (Kalisz, 1929–35; Warsaw, 1935–8; Toronto, 1964–6)
ZDSPR	*Z Dziejów Stosunków Polsko-Radzieckich: Studia i Materiały* (Warsaw)
ZH	*Zeszyty Historyczne* (Paris)
ZPW	*Z Pola Walki* (Warsaw)

Notes

Notes to Chapter 1

1. Most dates are new style. In certain sources, however, it was impossible to determine which dating system was being used.
2. Pavlo Khrystiuk, *Zamitky i materiialy do istoriï ukraïns'koï revoliutsiï: 1917–1920 rr.*, reprint (New York: Vydavnytstvo Chartoryis'kykh, 1969), 1: 16.
3. N. N. Sukhanov, *The Russian Revolution 1917: A Personal Record* (London: Oxford University Press, 1955), 113 ff; George Vernadsky, *A History of Russia* (New York: New Home Library, 1944), 236–7; V. Kedrovs'kyi, "Ukraïnizovani chastyny i reguliarna armiia," *VK*, 1968, no. 2 (33), 37–9; M. Halahan, "Bohdanivs'kyi polk," *LChK*, 1937, no. 6, 3–5; Ia. Dziabenko, "Pershyi ukraïns'kyi viis'kovyï z'ïzd," *UK*, 1954, no. 2, 9–13; Stepan Lazurenko, "Bohdanivtsi na fronti 1917 roku," *Tr* (New York), 1965, no. 33, 13–15, no. 34, 15–18; Serhii Shemet, "Mykola Mikhnovs'kyi: Posmertna zhadka," *KhU* 5, (1924–5): 3–30; Pavlo Skoropads'kyi, "Uryvok zi 'Spomyniv'," *KhU* 5, (1924–5): 31–66; Ie[vhen] Chykalenko, *Uryvok z moïkh spomyniv za 1917 r.* (Prague: Vyd. Fondu im. Ie. Chykalenka pry Ukraïns'komu akademichnomu komiteti, 1932), 8–20; Bohdanivets', "Rozstril bohdanivtsiv na stantsiï Post Volyns'kyi," *KAV na 1957 rik* (Buenos Aires), 102–10; Iakiv Zozulia, "Vseukraïns'ki viis'kovi z'ïzdy v 1917 r.," *VK*, 1967, no. 4 (28), 29–34; B. Martos, "Pershi kroky Tsentral'noï Rady," *UIs*, 1973, no. 3–4, 99–112.
4. James Bunyan and H. H. Fisher, comps., *The Bolshevik Revolution, 1917–1918: Documents and Materials* (Stanford: Stanford University Press, 1934), 435; Khrystiuk, *Zamitky i materiialy*, 2: 39, 46, 194; Iakiv M. Zozulia, comp., *Velyka ukraïns'ka revoliutsiia: Materiialy do istoriï vidnovlennia ukraïns'koï derzhavnosty: Kalendar istorychnykh podii za liutyi 1917 r.–berezen' 1918 r.*, ed. B. Martos et al (New York, 1967), 26, 31; "Tretii vseukraïns'kyi viis'kovyi z'ïzd u Kyievi," *VSVU*, no. 179 (1917), 773–5.
5. David Plotkin [D.Kin], *Denikinshchina* (Leningrad: Priboi, 1927), 9; I. A. Poliakov, *Donskie kazaki v bor'be s bol'shevikami: Vospominaniia* (Munich, 1962), 26; Victor Chernov, *The Great Russian Revolution* (New Haven: Yale

University Press, 1936), 416.
6. Bunyan and Fisher, *The Bolshevik Revolution*, 440.
7. O. Udovychenko, "Bii za Arsenal," *BUNDS*, no. 28 (1958), 6–9; Stepan Lazurenko "Bohdanivtsi v boiakh za Kyïv," *Tr* (New York), 1961, no. 4 (10), 14–19; Iurii Lypa, "Zdobuttia Arsenalu: Spohad pro velykyi rik," *KAV na 1957 rik* (Buenos Aires), 107–9; A. Marushchenko-Bohdanivs'kyi, "Shturm Arsenalu," *T*, 1927, no. 5, 20–3; Vsevolod Petriv, *Spomyny z chasiv ukraïns'koï revoliutsiï, 1917–1921* (Lviv: Chervona kalyna, 1927), 1: 114–15, 120–6, 130; Andrii Iakovliv, "Petliura i borot'ba za Arsenal: Uryvok zi 'Spomyniv'," in *Symon Petliura—derzhavnyi muzh*, ed. Nataliia Livyts'ka-Kholodna et al (New York: Ukraïns'kyi natsional'no-derzhavnyi soiuz, 1957), 91–3; V. Fylonovych, "S. Petliura—postat' natsional'no-derzhavnoho chynu," *H*, 1936, nos. 1–2 (17–18), 10–17; K. Smovs'kyi, "Moia sluzhba Ukraïni pid komanduvanniam Hol. ot. Symona Petliury," *NP*, 1954, nos. 6–7.
8. V. Vynnychenko, *Vidrodzhennia natsiï*, vol. 2 (Vienna: Dzvin, 1920), 246–7.
9. Fritz Fischer, *Germany's Aims in the First World War* (London: Chatto and Windus, 1967), 497–8; John W. Wheeler-Bennett, *Brest-Litovsk: The Forgotten Peace* (New York: W. W. Norton, 1938), 220; Gustav Gratz and Richard Schulder, *The Economic Policy of Austria-Hungary during the War in Its External Relations* (New Haven: Yale University Press, 1928), 255; Khrystiuk, *Zamitky i materiialy*, 2: 138–9.
10. Dmytro Doroshenko, *History of Ukraine, 1917–1923* (Winnipeg: Hetman Movement Leadership, 1973), 34–5.
11. I. Mazepa, *Ukraïna v ohni i buri revoliutsiï, 1917–1921*, vol. 1 (Munich: Prometei, 1950), 53–5; Khrystiuk, *Zamitky i materiialy*, 3: 39–41; Doroshenko, *History of Ukraine*, 36–50, 259–65; Vasyl' Ivanys, *Symon Petliura—prezydent Ukraïny, 1879–1926* (Toronto: Ukrainian War Veterans' League of Canada, 1952), 65–77; Dmytro Dontsov, *Rik 1918* (Toronto: Homin Ukraïny, 1954), 32–5; Iwan Majstrenko, *Borot'bism: A Chapter in the History of Ukrainian Communism* (New York: Research Program on the U.S.S.R., 1954), 72–4; Mykola Kovalevs'kyi, *Pry dzherelakh borot'by: Spomyny, vrazhennia, refleksiï* (Innsbruck: Maria Kowalewsky, 1960), 477–97; Michael Palij, *The Anarchism of Nestor Makhno, 1918–1921: An Aspect of the Ukrainian Revolution* (Seattle: University of Washington Press, 1976), 33–40; John S. Reshetar Jr., *The Ukrainian Revolution, 1917–1920: A Study in Nationalism* (Princeton: Princeton University Press, 1952), 145–52.
12. Dmytro Doroshenko, *Istoriia Ukraïny 1917–1923. rr.*, reprint (New York: Bulava, 1954), 2: 386–408; Khrystiuk, *Zamitky i materiialy*, 3: 87–120; Vynnychenko, *Vidrodzhennia natsiï*, 3: 73, 163–8; Viktor Andriievs'kyi, *Z mynuloho* (Berlin: Ukraïns'ke slovo, 1921), 2, pt. 1, 210–11; Serhii Shemet, "Do istoriï Ukraïns'koï demokratychno-khliborobs'koï partiï," *KhU* 1 (1920): 63–79;

M. Bezruchko, "Sichovi striltsi v borot'bi za derzhavnist'," *ZD* 2 (1930): 47–72; Zenon Stefaniv, *Ukraïns'ki zbroini syly 1917–1921 rr.* (Munich: Soiuz ukraïns'kykh veteraniv, 1941), 1: 110–15; Osyp Dumin [A. Krezub, pseud.], "Povstannia proty het'mana Skoropads'koho i Sichovi stril'tsi: Kil'ka zavvah do ioho istoriï," *LNV*, 1928, no. 11, 219–25; V. Prokhoda, "Sirozhupannyky v povstanni proty uriadu het'mana Skoropads'koho," *T*, no. 9 (1928), 90–5; Osyp Nazaruk, *Rik na Velykii Ukraïni: Konspekt spomyniv z ukraïns'koï revoliutsiï* (Vienna: Ukraïns'kyi prapor, 1920), 75–80.

13. Arnold D. Margolin, *From a Political Diary: Russia, the Ukraine, and America, 1905–1945* (New York: Columbia University Press, 1946), 37–71; Nazaruk, *Rik na Velykii Ukraïni*, 123–33; V. Prokhoda "Symon Petliura, vozhd' ukraïns'koho viis'ka," *T*, nos. 28–9 (1936), 3–49; Mytyta Shapoval, *Velyka revoliutsiia i ukraïns'ka vyzvol'na programa* (Prague: Vil'na spilka, 1927), 132–5; A. I. Denikin, *Ocherki russkoi smuty*, vol. 4 (Paris: J. Povolozky, 1925), 71–5; I. Drabatyi, "Epizod z evakuatsiï Kyieva v 1919 r.," *Tr* (New York), no. 30 (1964), 3–6; L'onhyn Tsehel's'kyi, *Vid legend do pravdy: Spomyny pro podiï v Ukraïni zv'iazani z pershym lystopadom 1918 r.* (New York: Bulava, 1960), 289–310; A. A. Gol'denveizer, "Iz kievskikh vospominanii, 1917–1921 g.g.," *ARR* (Berlin) 6 (1922): 236–303; Dmytro Doroshenko, *A Survey of Ukrainian History*, edited, updated (1914–75), and with an introduction by Oleh W. Gerus (Winnipeg: Humeniuk Publication Foundation, 1975), 638–41.

Notes to Chapter 2

1. Stepan Skrypnyk (Metropolitan Mstyslav), "Do zhyttiepysu Symona Petliury," *UPS*, 1966, no. 5, 6–8; M. B., "Rodyna Petliuriv," *Sv*, 12–13 November 1976; Oleksander Stovba, "Materiialy do rodu Petliur," *UIs*, 1979, no. 1–4, 70, 75–7; "Polkovnyk Oleksander Petliura," *Dor*, 1965, no. 5–6, 7–8; V. Koroliv-Staryi, "Z moïkh spomyniv pro Symona Petliuru," *Zbirnyk pam'iaty Symona Petliury, 1879–1926*, ed. I. Mazepa et al (Prague: Mizhorhanizatsiinyi komitet dlia vshanuvannia pam'iati Symona Petliury, 1930), 177; Ivan Rudychiv, "Symon Petliura v molodosti: Spomyn," in *Symon Petliura v molodosti: Zbirka spomyniv,* ed. A. Zhuk (Lviv: Khortytsia, 1936), 5; *Symon Petliura: Statti, lysty, dokumenty*, vol. 1, ed. L. Drazhevs'ka et al (New York: Ukrainian Academy of Arts and Sciences in the U.S., 1956), 459–62; Maksym Slavins'kyi, "Symon Petliura, 1879–1926," in *Symon Petliura—derzhavnyi muzh*, ed. Nataliia Livyts'ka-Kholodna et al (New York: Ukraïns'kyi natsional'no-derzhavnyi soiuz, 1957), 16–21; Vasyl' Ivanys, *Symon Petliura—prezydent Ukraïny, 1879–1926* (Toronto: Ukrainian War Veterans' League of Canada, 1952), 11–24; Alain Desroches, *The Ukrainian Problem and Symon Petlura (The Fire and Ashes)* (Chicago: Ukrainian Research and Information Institute, 1970), 30–2; Leonid

Poltava, *Symon Petliura: Al'bom–biohrafiia* (Paris, 1949); John S. Reshetar Jr., *The Ukrainian Revolution, 1917–1920: A Study in Nationalism* (Princeton: Princeton University Press, 1952), 263–4; "Symon Petliura," *Sv*, 25 May 1951.

2. Rudychiv, "Symon Petliura v molodosti," 6–17; Koroliv-Staryi, "Z moïkh spomyniv pro Symona Petliuru," 177–9; V. Koroliv-Staryi, "Pys'mennyts'kyi shliakh S. V. Petliury: Detal' do biohrafii," *Tr* (Paris), 1927, no. 22–3, 22–7; Skrypnyk, "Do zhyttiepysu Symona Petliury," 6–8; O. Lotots'kyi, "Lystky z pam'iaty (na mohylu nezabutn'oho)," *Tr* (Paris), 1926, no. 45, 2–3; Andrii Zhuk, "Iz spomyniv pro S. Petliuru, 1901–1907," in *Symon Petliura v molodosti*, 22–6; Iurii Kollard, *Spohady iunats'kykh dniv, 1897–1906* (Toronto: Sribna surma, 1972), 43–54; Liubov Mykhailova, "Spohady," *Tr* (New York), no. 35 (1965), 4–5; V. Fylonovych, "S. Petliura—postat' natsional'no-derzhavnoho chynu," *H*, no. 17–18 (1936), 10–17; V. H., "Velykyi syn ukraïns'koho narodu," *UPS*, 1973, no. 5, 4–6.

3. There were 200,000 packages of documents, some with 200 documents each (F. Shcherbyna, "Symon Petliura na Kubani," in *Zbirnyk pam'iati Symona Petliury*, 190).

4. Shcherbyna's *Istoriia Kubanskago voiska* was published in Ekaterinodar. Vol. 1 (1910) had over 700 pages, and vol. 2 (1913) had 850 pages (Vasyl' Bidnov, "Pershi roky literaturnoï diial'nosty S. V. Petliury, 1902–1907 rr.," in *Symon Petliura—derzhavnyi muzh*, 129).

5. Shcherbyna, "Symon Petliura na Kubani," 189–94; V. I[vany]s. "Petliura na Kubani," *Sv*, 23 May 1951; Mykola Porsh, "Na spil'nomu shliakhu," in *Symon Petliura v molodosti*, 35–6; M. Slavins'kyi, "Symon Petliura, 1879–1926," in *Zbirnyk pam'iati Symona Petliury*, 10.

6. Lev Hankevych, "Sviatoslav Tagon u L'vovi: Do vzaiemyn naddnistrians'koï i halyts'koï revoliutsiinoi molodi," in *Symon Petliura v molodosti*, 68–77; Koroliv-Staryi, "Pys'mennyts'kyi shliakh S. Petliury," 22–7; Porsh, "Na spil'nomu shliakhu," 45–7; Ivanys, *Symon Petliura—prezydent Ukraïny*, 22–3; V. Sadovs'kyi, "S. Petliura v Kyievi v 1906–1907 rr.: Iz spomyniv," *Tr* (Paris), 1927, no. 22–3, 18–19; Volodymyr Levyns'kyi, "Naddniprians'ka politychna emigratsiia u L'vovi v rr. 1904–1905," in *Symon Petliura v molodosti*, 83–5.

7. Porsh, "Na spil'nomu shliakhu," 35–47; Levyns'kyi, "Naddniprians'ka politychna emigratsiia," 81–5; Hankevych, "Sviatoslav Tagon," 68–70; Bidnov, "Pershi roky literaturnoï diial'nosty S. V. Petliury," 132–3; Volodymyr Doroshenko, "Ukraïns'ka students'ka hromada u Moskvi, 1898–1905 rr." in *Z mynuloho: Zbirnyk*, vol. 2, ed. R. Smal'-Stots'kyi (Warsaw: Ukraïns'kyi naukovyi instytut, 1939), 159; Andrii Zhuk, "Do kharakterystyky S. Petliury," in *Symon Petliura v molodosti*, 92–4; Sadovs'kyi, "S. Petliura v Kyievi," 18–22.

8. Volodymyr Sikevych, "Symon Vasyl'ovych Petliura," *Iliustrovanyi kaliendar "Ukraïns'koho holosu na rik 1942* (Winnipeg, 1941), 49–53; Panas Fedenko,

"Symon Petliura i trahediia Ukraïny," *NDni*, no. 292 (1974), 5–11; Sadovs'kyi, "S. Petliura v Kyievi," 18–22; Sadovs'kyi, "S. Petliura v RUP i USDRP: Iz spomyniv," *Tr* (Paris), 1935, no. 21–2, 8–13; Porsh, "Na spil'nomu shliakhu," 54–8; I. Mazepa, *Ukraïna v ohni i buri revoliutsiï, 1917–1921*, vol. 3 (Munich: Prometei, 1951), 125–7.

9. After the dissolution of the Duma on 8 July 1906 some two hundred of its members journeyed to nearby Vyborg, Finland, where they issued an appeal to the population to engage in passive resistance by refusing to pay taxes or respond to conscription. The appeal elicited no popular response, but the signatories were sentenced to three months in prison and were disfranchised, thus forfeiting their parliamentary careers (Michael T. Florinsky, *Russia: A History and An Interpretation* [New York: MacMillan, 1953], 2: 1192; Alexander Kerensky, *Russia and History's Turning Point* [New York: Duell, Sloan and Pearce, 1965], 73).

10. Sadovs'kyi, "S. Petliura v Kyievi," 18–21; Lotots'kyi, "Lystky z pam'iati," 2–8; M. B., "Rodyna Petliuriv," *Sv*, 12 November 1976; Pavlo Zaitsev, "Ol'ha Petliura, 1885–1959," *M*, 1960, no. 1; Stovba, "Materiialy do rodu Petliur," 69–78.

11. Slavins'kyi, "Symon Petliura, 1879–1926," in *Zbirnyk pam'iati Symona Petliury*, 10–11.

12. H. Kozlovs'kyi, "Z zhyttia ukraïns'koï kol'oniï v Moskvi v 1900 rr.," in *Z mynuloho: Zbirnyk*, vol. 1, ed. R. Smal'-Stots'kyi (Warsaw: Ukraïns'kyi naukovyi instytut, 1938), 124; M. K., "Larysa Petliurivna," *Dor*, 1965, no. 5–6, 6–7; Fylonovych, "S. Petliura," 10–17; Fedenko, "Symon Petliura," 5–11; V. Prokhoda, "Symon Petliura: Vozhd' ukraïns'koho viis'ka," *T*, no. 28–9 (1936), 15–25; A. Vetlugin, *Geroi i voobrazhaemye portrety* (Berlin: "Russkoe tvorchestvo, 1922), 85–6; Zhuk, "Do kharakterystyky Symona Petliury," 96–7; Slavins'kyi, "Symon Petliura, 1879–1926," in *Symon Petliura—derzhavnyi muzh*, 16–24.

13. Lotots'kyi, "Lystky z pam'iati," 8.

14. Slavins'kyi, "Symon Petliura," 21.

15. Dmytro Doroshenko, *Moï spomyny pro nedavnïe mynule (1914–1920)*, 2d ed. (Munich: Ukraïns'ke vydavnytstvo, 1969), 19–21; Zhuk, "Do kharakterystyky S. Petliury," 98–9; Ol. Salikovs'kyi, "Pro odnu ne napysanu knyzhku: Uryvok iz spomyniv," *KAD na rik 1927*, 102–7; Vasyl' Koroliv-Staryi, *Simon Petlura: Héros national, ukrainien* (Prague: Čas, 1919), 14–25; St. Siropolko, "Z zhyttia ukraïns'koï kol'oniï v Moskvi: Storinka zi spohadiv," *KAD na rik 1927*, 35–40; T. Olesiiuk. "S. V. Petliura ta ukraïns'ke studenstvo," *StV*, 1926, no. 7–8, 9–15; D. Andriievs'kyi, "Symon Petliura," *KAD na rik 1927*, 7–13; *Symon Petliura: Statti, lysty, dokumenty*, vol 1, ed. L. Drazhevs'ka et al (New York: Ukrainian Academy of Arts and Sciences in the U.S., 1956), 184–7; "Symon Petliura," *Sv*, 25 May 1951.

16. V. H., "Velykyi syn," 5; M. K., "Larysa Petliurivna," 6; Prokhoda, "Symon Petliura," 7–49; Ivanys, *Symon Petliura*, 40–2; Ia. Dziabenko, "Pershyi ukraïns'kyi viiskovyi z'ïzd," *UKb*, 1954, no. 2, 9–12.
17. Volodymyr Kedrovs'kyi, *1917 rik: Spohady chlena Ukraïns'koho Viis'kovoho Heneral'noho Komitetu i tovarysha sekretaria viis'kovykh sprav u chasi Ukraïns'koï Tsentral'noï Rady* (Winnipeg: Trident Press, 1967), 122.
18. Robert Paul Browder and Alexander F. Kerensky, eds., *The Russian Provisional Government, 1917: Documents* (Stanford: Stanford University Press, 1961), 1: 383.
19. A soldier of the Czechoslovak Brigade in the Russia Army reported the following:

    Our Czechoslovak brigade was in a position next to Ukrainian units. A few days before our attack we exchanged gunfire with the Germans and even came to skirmishes. Our activity, however, was very disliked by a Russian reserve division composed half of Bolsheviks. Each day they demanded that we stop "provoking" the Germans. This was very damaging to our enthusiasm; we thought, however, that with the arrival of Kerensky's order to attack, our "peace-loving" comrades would follow us.... As we were leaving the trenches, treacherous "brotherly" bullets began whistling behind our backs. By one of them I was wounded in my right shoulder. All of us were seized by despair, for we found ourselves [caught] in the middle. From the front and from the rear death equally threatened. We stopped, not knowing which way to go: back or forward!? Suddenly Ukrainian units appeared, surrounded the mutinous division, and forced it to stop the fratricide. Immediately our brigade again rushed to attack and took the German trenches and about 1,800 prisoners.

    Such events happened in almost all sectors of the front. V. K., "Z Druhoho Vseukraïns'koho z'ïzdu," *LNV*, 1923, no. 10, 146–7.
20. V. K., "Z Druhoho vseukraïns'koho z'ïzdu," 145.
21. Iurii Lypa, "Zdobuttia Arsenalu: Spohad pro velykyi rik," *KAV na 1957 rik*, 107–9; O. Udovychenko, "Bii za Arsenal," BUNDS, no. 28 (1958), 6–9; Fylonovych. "S. Petliura," 10–17; V. Fylonovych, "Chomu dymisionuvav Symon Petliura?" *Dor*, 1966, no. 9, 15–16; Mykola Padalka, *Vystup polubotkivtsiv 4–6 lypnia 1917 roku v m. Kyievi na foni politychnoï sytuatsiï toho chasu* (Lviv: the author, 1921), 1–16; Arkhyp Kmeta, "Pam'iati nezabutn'oho," *T*, no. 5 (1927), 15–19; Agaton Dobrians'kyi, "Tsars'ka imperiia vpala, rik 1917: Uryvok iz spomyniv," *IKAChK na 1937 rik*, 13–20; Prokhoda, "Symon Petliura," 5–12; V. Prokhoda, "Iak Symon Petliura stav vozhdem ukraïns'koï armiï," *H*, no. 20–1 (1936), 20–4; Zozulia, "Vseukraïns'ki viis'kovi z'ïzdy," 28–34; Kedrovs'kyi, *1917 rik*, 56, 120–2, 151; V. K., "Povalenie bol'shevykamy Rosiis'koho Tymchasovoho Uriadu i perekhid vlady na Ukraïni do Tsentral'noï Rady: Skorochenyi uryvok zi spomyniv," *LNV*, 1925, no. 1, 29–45; V. Kedrovs'kyi, "S.

V. Petliura i orhanizatsiia ukraïns'koï armiï," *Ukraïns'kyi pravoslavnyi kalendar na 1967* (South Bound Brook), 98–104; Il'ko Havryliuk, "Druhyi viis'kovyi z'ïzd," in *Zbirnyk pam'iati Symona Petliury*, 203–9; V. K., "Vseukraïns'kyi viis'kovyi hen. komitet i Tymchasove Pravytel'stvo: Uryvok iz spomyniv," *LNV*, 1923, no. 5, 34–41; "Tretii vseukraïns'kyi viis'kovyi z'ïzd u Kyievi," *VSVU*, no. 179 (1917), 773–5; Khrystiuk, *Zamitky i materiialy*, 2: 39–46, 194; Ie. Chykalenko, *Uryvok z moïkh spomyniv za 1917 r.* (Prague: Fond im. Ie. Chykalenka pry Ukraïns'komu akademichnomu komiteti, 1932), 28–31; K. Smovs'kyi, "Moia sluzhba Ukraïni pid komanduvanniam Holovnoho otamana Symona Petliury," *NP*, 1954, nos. 6–7.
22. Fylonovych, "Chomu dymisionuvav Symon Petliura?" 15–16.
23. Smovs'kyi, "Moia sluzhba Ukraïni."
24. Koroliv-Staryi, "Z moïkh spomyniv," 183.
25. Khrystiuk, *Zamitky i materiialy*, 2: 138–9, 3: 87–90, 146–8, 4: 15–20, 40, 91; D. I. Doroshenko, "Voina i revoliutsiia na Ukraine," in *Revoliutsiia na Ukraine po memuaram belykh*, ed. S. A. Alekseev (Moscow: Gos. izd-vo., 1930), 64–97; O. Shul'hyn, "Symon Petliura ta ukraïns'ka zakordonna polityka," in *Zbirnyk pam'iati Symona Petliury*, 173–6; Iakiv Zozulia, "Obloha Kyieva, vidstup ukraïns'koï armiï na Volyn' ta orhanizatsiia sanitarnoï sluzhby," *ZD* 11 (1966): 42–6; Kost' Matsiievych, "Na zems'kii roboti," in *Symon Petliura—derzhavnyi muzh*, 60–7; Doroshenko, *Moï spomyny pro nedavnie-mynule*, 232–9; Pavlo Skoropads'kyi, "Uryvok zi 'Spomyniv'," *KhU* 5: 31–92; Stepan Lazurenko, "Bohdanivtsi v boiakh za Kyïv," *Tr* (New York), 1961, no. 4, 14–19; St. Siropolko, "Dva areshtuvannia S. Petliury za het'mana P. Skoropads'koho," *KAD na rik 1938*, 74–7; Fylonovych, "S. Petliura," 10–17; M. Bezruchko, "Sichovi striltsi v borot'bi za derzhavnist'," *ZD* 2 (1930): 47–72; Osyp Dumin [A. Krezub, pseud.] "Povstannia proty het'mana Skoropads'koho i Sichovi stril'tsi: Kil'ka zavvakh do ioho istoriï," *LNV*, 1928, no. 11, 219–25; Osyp Nazaruk, *Rik na Velykii Ukraïni: Konspekt spomyniv z ukraïns'koï revoliutsiï* (Vienna: Ukraïns'kyi prapor, 1920), 65–78; Prokhoda, "Symon Petliura," 28–31; I. Drabatyi, "Epizod z evakuatsiï Kyieva v 1919 r.," *Tr* (New York), 1965, no. 30, 306; A. A. Gol'denveizer, "Iz kievskikh vospominanii, 1917–1921 gg.," *ARR* 6 (1922): 236–303; Arnold D. Margolin, *From a Political Diary: Russia, the Ukraine, and America, 1905–1945* (New York: Columbia University Press, 1946), 37–71; Mykyta Shapoval, *Velyka revoliutsiia i ukraïns'ka vyzvol'na programa* (Prague: Vil'na spilka, 1927), 132–5; I. Mazepa, "Tvorena derzhava: Borot'ba 1919 roku," in *Zbirnyk pam'iati Symona Petliury*, 22–3; Panas Fedenko, "Holovnyi otaman," *Nsl*, no. 5 (1977), 22–61; Vasyl' Prokhoda, *Symon Petliura* (San Diego, 1968), 46–8.

Notes to Chapter 3

1. There are many biographies of Piłsudski. See, for example, Wacław Jędrzejewicz, *Kronika życia Józefa Piłsudskiego, 1867–1935* (London: Polska Fundacja Kulturalna, 1977); Stanisław Mackiewicz, *Klucz do Piłsudskiego* (London: the author, 1943) Wacław Lipiński, *Wielki Marszałek, 1867–1935* (Warsaw: Gebethner i Wolff, 1937); Wacław Sieroszewski, *Józef Piłsudski* (Lviv: Państwowe Wydawnictwo Książek Szkolnych, 1933); Robert Machray, *The Poland of Piłsudski* (London: Allan and Unwin, 1936); W. Pobóg-Malinowski, *Józef Piłsudski*, 2 vols. (Warsaw: Gebethner i Wolff, 1935); Grace Humphrey, *Piłsudski: Builder of Poland* (New York: Scott and More, 1936); and Ralph Butler, "Józef Piłsudski, Aristocrat–Revolutionary," *Atlantic Monthly*, August 1923, 269–70.
2. Jędrzejewicz, *Kronika*, 1: 19–20; Sieroszewski, *Józef Piłsudski*, 8–10, 16–17; Eric J. Patterson, *Piłsudski, Marshal of Poland* (London: Arrowsmith, 1935), 29; Humphrey, *Piłsudski*, 23–4; Andrzej Garlicki, *U źródeł obozu belwederskiego* (Warsaw: Państwowe Wydawnictwo Naukowe, 1978), 11; Leon Wasilewski. "Stosunki polsko-litewskie w dobie popowstaniowej," *N* (Warsaw), 1929, no. 3, 30, 42–5; Leonas Sabaliunas, "Social Democracy in Tsarist Lithuania, 1893–1904," *SR*, 1972, no. 2, 323.
3. Joseph Pilsudski, *The Memories of a Polish Revolutionary and Soldier*, trans. and ed. D. R. Gillie (London: Faber and Faber, 1931), 13.
4. Ibid., 15.
5. Jędrzejewicz, *Kronika*, 1: 32–7; Pilsudski, *Memories*, 15–16; Mackiewicz, *Klucz do Piłsudskiego*, 11–12.
6. Jędrzejewicz, *Kronika*, 1: 37–9; Pilsudski, *Memories*, 15; Humphrey, *Piłsudski*, 23–4; Garlicki, *U źródeł*, 11; Sieroszewski, *Józef Piłsudski*, 8–10, 16–18; Wacław Gąsiorowski, *Historja Armji Polskiej we Francji*, vol. 1 (Warsaw: Dom Książki Polskiej, 1931), 10–18; Butler, "Józef Piłsudski," 270–1.
7. Pilsudski, *Memories*, 16.
8. Pilsudski, *Memories*, 17–26; Jędrzejewicz, *Kronika*, 1: 40–50; Sieroszewski, *Józef Piłsudski*, 18–19; Lipiński, *Wielki Marszałek*, 20–1.
9. Wacław Sieroszewski, *Józef Piłsudski* (Chicago: Centralny Komitet Obrony Narodowej, 1915), 26; see also Pilsudski, *Memories*, 27–8.
10. Sieroszewski, *Józef Piłsudski* (1933), 20–2.
11. Pilsudski, *Memories*, 27; see also Jędrzejewicz, *Kronika*, 1: 163.
12. Humphrey, *Piłsudski*, 189.
13. Butler, "Józef Piłsudski," 271–2; Józef Piłsudski, "Jak stałem się socjalistą, 1903," in his *Pisma, mowy, rozkazy: Wydanie zbiorowe prac dotychczas drukiem ogłoszonych*, vol. 2, ed. Michał Sokolnicki and Juljan Stachiewicz (Warsaw: "Polska Zjednoczona," 1930), 3–12; Sieroszewski, *Józef Piłsudski* (1933), 23–5;

Jędrzejewicz, *Kronika*, 1: 55–69, 114, 188; Pilsudski, *Memories*, 30–3; Humphrey. *Piłsudski*, 53–5; Lipiński, *Wielki Marszałek*, 24–7; Patterson, *Piłsudski*, 40–2; Machray, *The Poland of Piłsudski*, 30–2.

14. Jędrzejewicz, *Kronika*, 1: 121–47; Machray, *The Poland of Piłsudski*, 31; Oleksander Lotots'kyi, *Storinky mynuloho*, repr. ed. (South Bound Brook: Ukrainian Orthodox Church in the U.S.A., 1966), 3: 243–4; G. Daniłowski, "Józef Piłsudski," *SL*, 1914, 20; Stanisław Szpotański, "Piłsudski o swoim pobycie w szpitalu sw. Mikolaja," *N* (Warsaw) 16 (1937), no. 3, 490–4; Patterson, *Piłsudski*, 40–7.

15. Jędrzejewicz, *Kronika*, 1: 148–56, 162–4; Humphrey, *Piłsudski*, 86–7; Machray, *The Poland of Piłsudski*, 31–2; Pilsudski, *Memories*, 34–5.

16. Józef Piłsudski, *Pisma wybrane* (London: M. I. Kolin, 1943), 38.

17. Władysław Pobóg-Malinowski, *Józef Piłsudski, 1867–1914* (London: Komitet Wydawniczy, 1965?), 260–1; Jędrzejewicz, *Kronika*, 1: 174–84; Machray, *The Poland of Piłsudski*, 36–9; Sieroszewski, *Józef Piłsudski* (1933), 25–6; Humphrey, *Piłsudski*, 88–9; Patterson, *Piłsudski*, 52–3; Rom Landau, *Piłsudski, Hero of Poland* (London: Jarrolds, 1930), 75–8; Józef Piłsudski, *Poprawki historyczne* (Warsaw: Instytut Badania Najnowszej Historji Polski, 1931), 24–6.

18. Andrzej Sujkowski, "Dmowski, Roman, 1864–1939," in *Polski Słownik Biograficzny*, vol. 5 (Cracow: Polska Akademia Umiejętnośći, 1939–46), 213–17; Pobóg-Malinowski, *Józef Piłsudski*, 257–61; Landau, *Piłsudski*, 75–7; Aleksandra Piłsudska (Alexandra Pilsudski), *Memoirs of Madame Pilsudski* (London: Hurst and Blackett, 1940), 101–4, 182–3; Pilsudski, *Memories*, 45–6, 181–3; Jędrzejewicz, *Kronika*, 1: 175–84, 220; Stanisław Skwarczyński, "Twórca Awangardy: działalność Józefa Piłsudskiego w latach 1893–1918," *N* (London) 7 (1962): 158–9; James Douglas, "W zaraniu dyplomacji polskiej—misja Ligi Narodowej i P.P.S. w Japonji, 1904–1905," *N* (Warsaw) 5, no. 2, 178–85; Roman Wapiński, *Narodowa Demokracja, 1893–1939: Ze studiów nad dziejami myśli nacjonalistycznej* (Wrocław: Zakład Narodowy im. Ossolińskich, 1980), 27–9.

19. Pilsudski, *Memories*, 155–9; Piłsudska, *Memoirs*, 102–6; Jędrzejewicz, *Kronika*, 1: 185–7; Humphrey, *Piłsudski*, 88–92; Sieroszewski, *Józef Piłsudski* (1933), 24–6; Landau, *Piłsudski*, 75–6; Skwarczyński, "Twórca Awangardy," 158–60.

20. Pilsudski, *Memories*, 160–2; Jędrzejewicz, *Kronika*, 1: 191–205; Piłsudska, *Memoirs*, 182–3; Landau, *Piłsudski*, 78–9.

21. Humphrey, *Piłsudski*, 96.

22. Pilsudski, *Memories*, 179–201; Piłsudska, *Memoirs*, 113, 197; Leon Wasilewski, *Józef Piłsudski Jakim Go znałem* (Warsaw: Rój, 1935), 102–5; Sieroszewski, *Józef Piłsudski* (1915), 64–73; V. M. Chernov, *Pered burei: Vospominaniia* (New York: Izdatel'stvo im. Chekhova, 1953), 296–7; Patterson, *Piłsudski*, 56–8; Jędrzejewicz, *Kronika*, 1: 213–5; Humphrey, *Piłsudski*, 116–20; Jan Molenda,

Piłsudczycy a Narodowi Demokraci (Warsaw: Książka i Wiedza, 1980), 26–9; Skwarczyński, "Twórca Awangardy," 160–72; Piłsudski, *Poprawki historyczne*, 27–9; Michał Sokolnicki, *Rok czternasty* (London: Gryf, 1961), 23–7; Daniłowski, "Józef Piłsudski," 20.
23. Zofja Zawiszanka, "Do historji Drużyn Strzeleckich," *N* (Warsaw) 2 (1930), no. 2, 267–84; Skwarczyński, "Twórca Awangardy," 167–8; Jędrzejewicz, *Kronika*, 1: 243–6, 276–84, 303; Pilsudski, *Memories*, 182–8; Piłsudska, *Memoirs*, 204–6, 213–18, 223–5; Wasilewski, *Józef Piłsudski*, 124–5, 131–3; Stefan Arski and Józef Chudek, comps., *Galicyjska działalność wojskowa Piłsudskiego, 1906–1914: Dokumenty* (Warsaw: Państwowe Wydawnictwo Naukowe, 1967), 658–60; Patterson, *Piłsudski*, 62–3; Humphrey, *Piłsudski*, 122; Sieroszewski, *Józef Piłsudski* (1915), 82–8; Landau, *Piłsudski*, 100–1; Sokolnicki, *Rok czternasty*, 207–14; Robert Machray, *Poland, 1914–1931* (London: Allen and Unwin, 1932), 64–5; *The Cambridge History of Poland: From Augustus II to Piłsudski, 1697–1935* (Cambridge: The University Press, 1951), 464–5.
24. "Niezwykła wyprawa Piłsudskiego," *SL*, 1914, 22–3.
25. Machray, *Poland, 1914–1931*, 51; see also Raymond Leslie Buell, *Poland: Key to Europe* (New York: Knopf, 1939), 65–6.
26. Pilsudski, *Memories*, 349–53; Piłsudska, *Memoirs*, 226–7; Jędrzejewicz, *Kronika*, 1: 291–2; Sławoj Felicjan Składkowski, *Moja służba w Brygadzie: Pamiętnik polowy*, vol. 1 (Warsaw: Instytut Badania Najnowszej Historji Polski, 1932); Humphrey, *Piłsudski*, 130; Patterson, *Piłsudski*, 69–73; Machray, *The Poland of Piłsudski*, 62–6; Landau, *Piłsudski*, 106–7; Michał Sokolnicki, "Na przełomie polityki legionowej: Epizody roku 1916," *N* (London) 5 (1955): 5–6; Wacław Lipiński, "Aresztowanie Józefa Piłsudskiego w lipcu 1917 r. w świetle nieznanych dokumentów niemieckich," *N* (Warsaw) 18 (1938), no. 1, 141–50; George Vernadsky, *A History of Russia* (New York: New Home Library, 1944), 223; Stanley Pliska, "The 'Polish-American Army,' 1917–1921," *PoR*, 1965, no. 3, 46–7; Piłsudski, *Poprawki historyczne*, 70–2; Stanisław Głąbiński, *Wspomnienia polityczne: Pod zaborem austriackim*, pt. 1 (Pelplin: Drukarnia i Księgarnia Spółki z Ograniczoną Odpowiedzialnością, 1939), 292–3.
27. Wacław Lipiński, "Zwolnienie Józefa Piłsudskiego z Magdeburga w świetle relacji niemieckiej," in his *Z dziejów dawnych i najnowszych: Szkice i studja historyczne* (Warsaw: Wojskowy Instytut Naukowo-Wydawniczy, 1934), 428.
28. Karol Matkowski and Stanisław Biegański, "Sprawa polska na konferencji międzynarodowej w Spa," *B* (Warsaw) 39 (1932), no. 1, 18–21; Machray, *Poland, 1914–1931*, 125; Buell, *Poland*, 71–3; H. H. Fisher, *America and the New Poland* (New York: Macmillan, 1928), 136–47; *Documents on British Foreign Policy, 1919–1939*, ser. 1, vol. 2, ed. E. L. Woodward and Rohan Butler (London: His Majesty's Stationary Office, 1948), 77–9; Marian Kukiel, *Dzieje Polski porozbiorowej, 1795–1921* (London: B. Świderski, 1961), 561–5; Leon

Wasilewski, *Granice Rzeczypospolitej Polskiej* (Warsaw: Dom Książki Polskiej, 1926), 10–11; Richard M. Watt, *Bitter Glory: Poland and Its Fate, 1918 to 1939* (New York: Simon and Schuster, 1979), 80–1; A. Przybylski, *Wojna Polska, 1918–1921* (Warsaw: Wojskowy Instytut Naukowo-Wydawniczy, 1930), 30–2; H. W. V. Temperley, ed., *A History of the Peace Conference of Paris*, vol. 6 (London: H. Frowde and Hodder and Stoughton, 1924), 248–66.
29. Józef Skrzypek, *Zamach stanu płk. Januszajtisa i ks. Sapiehy 4–5 stycznia, 1919 r.* (Warsaw: Spółdzielnia Wydawnicza, 1948), 18–36; Watt, *Bitter Glory*, 84–8; Wacław Jędrzejewicz, *Piłsudski: A Life for Poland* (New York: Hippocrene Books, 1982), 76–9.

Notes to Chapter 4

1. Wacław Gąsiorowski, *Historja Armji Polskiej we Francji* (Warsaw: Dom Książki Polskiej, 1931), 111–12, 132–3, 170–6, 194, 234; Wacław Lipiński, "Bajończycy i Armia Polska we Francji," *B* (Warsaw) 33 (1929), no. 11, 70–6; idem., "Dziennik bajończyka Marjana Himner," *N* (Warsaw) 1 (1930), no. 2, 303–27; Józef Sierociński, *Armja Polska we Francji: Dzieje wojsk Generała Hallera na obczyznie* (Warsaw: the author, 1929), 38–9, 112; Mieczysław Pruszyński, "Rozmowa historyczna ze St. Grabskim," *BM* (Warsaw), 20 November–5 December 1935.
2. A. Merlot, *L'armée Polonaise: Constitution en France et organisation, juin 1917–avril 1919* (Paris: Imprimerie Levé, 1919), 12; see also Lipiński, "Bajończycy," 80–1.
3. Edward Ligocki, *O Józefie Hallerze: Zycie i czyny na tle współczesności dziejowej* (Warsaw: Komitet Obywatelski Obrony Państwa, 1923), 279–84; Sierociński, *Armja Polska*, 111–17; Lipiński, "Bajończycy," 80–93, 101; Wincenty Skarzyński, *Armja Polska we Francji w świetle faktów* (Warsaw: n.p., 1929), 65, 74–5; Gąsiorowski, *Historja Armji*, 115, 267, 299–300; Jim Poker, *Błękitni rycerze* (Warsaw: Rój, 1931), 14–29, 56, 184–92.
4. Merlot, *L'armée Polonaise*, 60–2; see also Lipiński, "Bajończycy," 97–8.
5. Stanley R. Pliska, "The 'Polish-American Army', 1917–1921," *PoR*, 1965, no. 3, 49–51; Skarzyński, *Armja Polska*, 33–7, 45–8; Lipiński, "Bajończycy," 84–6; Marian Marek Drozdowski, *Ignacy Jan Paderewski: Zarys biografii politycznej* (Warsaw: Interpress, 1979), 81–96; Sierociński, *Armja Polska*, 38–9, 51–2, 79–80; Ligocki, *O Józefie Hallerze*, 299; Gąsiorowski, *Historja Armji*, 291.
6. Henryk Lokański, *Sześć lat wojny polskiej* (Chicago: n.p., 1920), 55; Pliska, "The 'Polish-American Army'," 56–7; Skarzyński, *Armja Polska*, 23–4, 48, 53–6; Lipiński, "Bajończycy," 84–5; Sierociński, *Armja Polska*, 91–2, 101, 106–8; Ligocki, *O Józefie Hallerze*, 300; Drozdowski, *Ignacy Jan Paderewski*, 102, 131; Maximilien Weygand, *Bitwa o Warszawę: Odczyt wygłoszony w*

Brukseli (Warsaw: Mazowiecka Spółka Wydawnicza, 1930), 30–1.
7. Sierociński, *Armja Polska*, 177–84; Lipiński, "Bajończycy," 84–5.
8. Sierociński, *Armja Polska*, 155–9, 168–9; Ligocki, *O Józefie Hallerze*, 292–4; Lipiński, "Bajończycy," 104–6; Joseph Pilsudski, *The Memories of a Polish Revolutionary and Soldier*, trans. and ed. D. R. Gillie (London: Faber and Faber, 1931), 352; *Polska Armja Błękitna* (Poznań: Drukarnia sw. Wojciecha, 1929), 26; Marjan Kukiel, *Dzieje Polski porozbiorowej, 1795–1921* (London: B. Świderski, 1961), 540–2.
9. Józef Haller, *Pamiętniki: Z wyborem dokumentów i zdjęć* (London: Veritas Foundation Press, 1964), 134, 171–2; Ligocki, *O Józefie Hallerze*, 192–6, 206, 243–4; Sierociński, *Armja Polska*, 135; Włodzimierz T. Kowalski, "At Brest and at Versailles," *Polish Perspectives* (Warsaw) 21, no. 11, 19–20; Lipiński, "Bajończycy," 94; Skarzyński, *Armja Polska*, 80; Pliska, "The 'Polish-American Army'," 55; Izydor Modelski, *Józef Haller w walce o Polske niepodległą i zjednoczoną* (Toruń: Drukarnia Robotnicza, 1936), 9–18, 72–5, 87; Zdzisław Oplustill, *Polskie formacje wschodnie, 1918–1919* (Warsaw: Perzyński, Niklewicz, 1922), 44–5, 103–4, 118–23; Józef Wielowiejski, "Ze wspomnień o s.p. Romanie Dmowskim," *Przegląd Współczesny*, 1939, no. 4 (204), 57; Stanisław Biegański, "Tajny układ między Austro-Węgrami a Ukrainą z 8 lutego 1918 r.," *N* (London) 12 (1979): 60–6; Wacław Lipiński, "Sprawy wojskowych formacyj polskich na Wschodzie: Według relacji ks. Kazimierza Lutosławskiego," *N* (Warsaw) 16 (1937): 633–45; Stanisław Głąbiński, *Wspomnienia polityczne* (Pelplin: Instytut Józefa Piłsudskiego, 1939), 324–5; Roman Górecki, "Z moich wspomnień, 15–21 lutego 1918," in *Wspomnienia legjonowe: Materiały z dziejów walk o niepodległość*, vol. 1, ed. Janusz Jędrzejewicz (Warsaw: Instytut Badań Najnowszej Historji Polskiej, 1924), 171–5; Roman Bataglia, *Prądy polityczne w Polsce i w Europie w ciągu XIX i XX wieku* (Warsaw: Dom Książki Polskiej, 1935), 34; Vasyl' Vyshyvanyi, "U.S.S-tsi z vesny 1918 roku do perevorotu v Avstriï," *Zaporozhets': Kalendar dlia naroda na rik 1921* (Vienna), 84–5; Titus Komarnicki, *Rebirth of the Polish Republic: A Study in the Diplomatic History of Europe, 1914–1920* (Melbourne: Heinemann, 1957), 173.
10. U.S. Department of State, *Papers Relating to the Foreign Relations of the United States, 1919: The Paris Peace Conference*, vol. 5 (Washington: U.S. Government Printing Office, 1946), 781.
11. Józef Kukułka, "Niektóre aspekty międzynarodowe polityki Piłsudskiego wobec ziem litewsko-białoruskich w pierwszej polowie 1919 roku," *SNDP* 2 (1962): 45; Wielowiejski, "Ze wspomnień o s. p. Romanie Dmowskim."
12. David Hunter Miller, *My Diary at the Conference of Paris with Documents*, vol. 17 (New York: Appeal Printing Co., 1926), 179–80.
13. Ibid., 357.

14. Ibid.
15. David Lloyd George, *Memoirs of the Peace Conference* (New Haven: Yale University Press, 1939), 1: 204.
16. Poker, *Błękitni rycerze*, 308–10; Haller, *Pamiętniki*, 196–8; Pilsudski, *Memories*, 352–3; Pliska, "The 'Polish-American Army'," 47–9; *Polska Armja Błękitna*, 12–13; Modelski, *Józef Haller*, 22–4; Sierociński, *Armja Polska*, 117–20, 125, 146–52; Ligocki, *O Józefie Hallerze*, 301–2, 317–20; Lipiński, "Bajończycy," 105–9; Wacław Lipiński, "Z historji Armji Polskiej we Francji," *N* (Warsaw) 6, no. 4 (1932), 468–9; Michał Budny, "Misja Generała Berthélemy w Polsce w relacji Romana Michałowskiego," *N* (London) 15 (1982): 193; "General Haller's Army," *The Morning Post* (London), 7 July 1919; Miller, *My Diary*, 420–1; Robert Machray, *The Poland of Piłsudski* (London: Allen and Unwin, 1936), 87–8; Hans Roos, *A History of Modern Poland* (New York: Knopf, 1966), 67–8.
17. Tadeusz Kawalec, *Historja IV-ej Dywizji Strzelców Generała Żeligowskiego w zarysie* (Vilnius: Harcerska Spółka Wydawnicza, 1921), 2–10; Lipiński, "Sprawy wojskowych formacyj," 633–45; Modelski, *Józef Haller*, 18; Józef Zając, *Dwie wojny: Mój udział w wojnie o niepodległość i w obronie powietrznej Polski* (London: Veritas Foundation Press, 1964), 71–3; A. Denikin, "Pol'sha i Dobrovol'cheskaia armia," *GM*, no. 4 (1926), 177–8.
18. Oplustill, *Polskie formacje*, 191–3.
19. Nykyfor O. Hryhor'iv (1885?–1919), was born in Dunaivtsi, Ushytsia county, Podillia gubernia. He joined the Russian Cossack cavalry in 1904 and fought in the Russo-Japanese War. After distinguished service, he joined the police force in Proskuriv. In 1914 he volunteered for the army and eventually rose to the rank of staff captain. He was wounded several times and decorated for distinguished service.

During the 1917 Revolution Hryhor'iv commanded a military train station at Berdychiv and was active in the Ukrainian military movement. When the Central Rada fell, he initially supported the hetman regime but became disillusioned. Petliura commissioned him in August 1918 to prepare an uprising against the hetman regime and the Austro-German troops in Kherson gubernia. Hryhor'iv became famous during the fighting against the Germans.

After the Red Army command ordered Hryhor'iv's units to invade Romania, Hryhor'iv organized an open revolt, against which the Red command mobilized all available forces in Ukraine. At the end of May Hryhor'iv's main forces were defeated, but he continued to wage a partisan war against the Bolsheviks.In the meantime Denikin's forces began a major advance into the Left Bank and forced Makhno and his troops to retreat westward into Hryhor'iv's area. There the two partisan leaders carried on negotiations about joining forces. Makhno, however, viewed Hryhor'iv as a rival, because both of them operated in and recruited

from the same region. On 27 July, after the two met at Lozova, Oleksandriia county, to discuss unification, Makhno and his associates had Hryhor'ïv assassinated.
20. Kawalec, *Historja IV-ej Dywizji*, 11–40; Oplustill, *Polskie formacje*, 171–6, 191–8; Lipiński, "Sprawy wojskowych formacyj," 642–4; Lucjan Żeligowski, "Notatki z roku 1920," *N* (London) 3 (1951): 164; Aleksy Deruga, *Polityka wschodnia Polski wobec ziem Litwy, Białorusi i Ukrainy, 1918–1919* (Warsaw: Książka i Wiedza, 1969), 209–22, 231; Sierociński, *Armja Polska*, 199–207; Vladimir Margulies, *Ognennye gody: Materialy i dokumenty istorii voiny na iuge Rossii* (Berlin: Manfred, 1923), 33–7; William Chamberlin, *The Russian Revolution, 1917–1921*, vol. 2 (New York: Macmillan, 1935), 165; Anton I. Denikin, *Ocherki russkoi smuty*, vol. 5 (Paris: J. Povolozky, 1926), 11; *Sprawy polskie na Konferencji Pokojowej w Paryżu w 1919 r.: Dokumenty i materiały*, vol. 2, ed. Remigiusz Bierzanek and Józef Kukułka (Warsaw: Państwowe Wydawnictwo Naukowe, 1967), 262; John S. Reshetar, Jr., *The Ukrainian Revolution, 1917–1920: A Study in Nationalism* (Princeton: Princeton University Press, 1952), 238–9; Michael Palij, *The Anarchism of Nestor Makhno, 1918–1921: An Aspect of the Ukrainian Revolution* (Seattle: University of Washington Press, 1976), 124–7; Matvii Stakhiv and Jaroslaw Sztendera, *Western Ukraine at the Turning Point of Europe's History, 1918–1923* (New York: Shevchenko Scientific Society, 1969), 2: 245 ff.; Pavlo Shandruk, *Arms of Valor* (New York: Robert Speller and Sons, 1959), 86–7; Stanisław Biegański. "Polska wobec Europy Południowo-Wschodniej na przełomie 1918–1919," *N* (London) 10 (1976): 54.

Notes to Chapter 5

1. S. Vytvytsky and S. Baran, "The Western Ukrainian National Republic (ZUNR-ZOUNR), 1918–23," in *Ukraine: A Concise Encyclopaedia*, ed. Volodymyr Kubijovyč, vol. 1 (Toronto: University of Toronto Press, 1963), 772–3; L'onhyn Tsehel's'kyi, *Vid legend do pravdy: Spomyny pro podiï v Ukraïni zv'iazani z pershym lystopadom 1918 r.* (New York: Bulava, 1960), 143–5, 258–60; Mykola Kovalevs'kyi, *Pry dzherelakh borot'by: Spomyny, vrazhennia, refleksiï* (Innsbruck: Maria Kowalewsky, 1960), 536; V. Vynnychenko, *Vidrodzhennia natsiï*, vol. 3 (Vienna: Dzvin, 1920), 242–3.
2. Francesco S. Nitti, *Peaceless Europe* (London: Cassell, 1922), 142–3.
3. I. Mazepa, *Ukraïna v ohni i buri revoliutsiï, 1917–1921*, vol. 1 (Munich: Prometei, 1950), 87–95; Pavlo Khrystiuk, *Zamitky i materiialy do istoriï ukraïns'koï revoliutsiï, 1917–1920 rr.*, vol. 4 repr. ed. (New York: Vydavnytstvo Chartoryis'kykh, 1969), 57–68; Tsehel's'kyi. *Vid legend*, 180–1; H. W. V. Temperley, ed., *A History of the Peace Conference of Paris*, vol. 6 (London: H.

Frowde and Hodder and Stoughton, 1924), 239–40; A. Denikin, "Pol'sha i Dobrovol'cheskaia armiia," *GMChS*, no. 4 (1926), 175–87; Moisei G. Rafes, *Dva goda revoliutsii na Ukraine: Evoliutsiia i raskol "Bunda"* (Moscow: Gos. izdvo, 1920), 143–52; John S. Reshetar, Jr., *The Ukrainian Revolution, 1917–1920: A Study in Nationalism* (Princeton: Princeton University Press, 1952), 231–2; Tadeusz Kutrzeba, *Wyprawa Kijowska 1920 roku* (Warsaw: Gebethner i Wolff, 1937), 314–20.
4. Aleksy Deruga, *Polityka wschodnia Polski wobec ziem Litwy, Białorusi i Ukrainy (1918–1919)* (Warsaw: Książka i Wiedza, 1969), 227.
5. Ibid., 225.
6. Wincenty Lutosławski, *Bolshevism and Poland* (Paris: M. Flinkowski, 1919), 32–3.
7. Robert Lansing, *The Peace Negotiations: A Personal Narrative* (Boston: Houghton Mifflin, 1921), 316.
8. Herbert Adams Gibbons, "The Ukraine and the Balance of Power," *CM*, July–October 1921, 470.
9. Esme Howard, *Theatre of Life: Life Seen from the Stalls, 1903–1936* (Boston: Little, Brown, 1936), 314–15; Michał Budny, "Misja Generała Berthélemy w Polsce w relacji Romana Michałowskiego," *N* (London) 15 (1982): 184–202; "Generał Berthélemy do Generała Franchet d'Esperey," *N* (London), 15 (1982): 199–200; Gigi Michelotti, "Why Poland Fails," *LA*, 11 September 1920, 630–4; Laurence J. Orzel, "A 'Hotly Disputed' Issue: Eastern Galicia at the Paris Peace Conference, 1919," *PoR*, 1980, no. 1, 52; Włodzimierz T. Kowalski, *Rok 1918* (Warsaw: Krajowa Agencja Wydawnicza, 1978), 203–4; Deruga, *Polityka wschodnia Polski*, 240–3; Mykhailo Lozyns'kyi, *Halychyna v rr. 1918–1920*, repr. ed. (New York: Chervona kalyna, 1970), 147ff; Reshetar, *The Ukrainian Revolution*, 273–4; "Misya francuzko-angielska przyjeżdża dziś do Lwowa," *WN*, 24 January 1919; "Czy pamiętacie gen. Berthélemy'ego, serdecznego przyjaciela Lwowa?," *GP*, 11 May 1923; "Przyjazd misyi koalicyj do Lwowa," *WN* 24 February 1919; Vytvytsky and Baran, "The Western Ukrainian National Republic," 774–5.
10. David Hunter Miller, *My Diary at the Conference of Paris with Documents*, vol. 18, (New York: Appeal Printing Co., 1926), 428.
11. Arnold D. Margolin, *From A Political Diary: Russia, the Ukraine, and America, 1905–1945* (New York: Columbia University Press, 1946), 42–4; Edward Ligocki, *O Józefie Hallerze: Życie i czyny na tle współczesności dziejowej* (Warsaw: Komitet Obywatelski Obrony Państwa, 1923), 317–20; Liubomyr Savoika, "Iak povstala armiia Halliera," *Visti* (New York), no. 122 (1966), 65–6; *Dokumenty i materiały do historii stosunków polsko-radzieckich*, vol. 2, ed. Natalia Gąsiorowska-Grabowska et al (Warsaw: Książka i Wiedza, 1964), 266–7; Hans Roos, *A History of Modern Poland* (New York: Knopf,

1966), 67–8; Marian Kukiel, *Dzieje Polski porozbiorowej, 1795–1921* (London: B. Świderski, 1961), 561–6; Tadeusz Piszczkowski, *Odbudowanie Polski, 1914–1921: Historia i polityka* (London: Orbis, 1969), 246–8; Izydor Modelski, *Józef Haller w walce o Polske niepodległą i zjednoczoną* (Toruń: Drukarnia Robotnicza, 1936), 23–4; *Polska Armja Błękitna* (Poznań: Drukarnia sw. Wojciecha, 1929), 12–14; Lozyns'kyi, *Halychyna*, 134ff.; R. Dashkevych, *Artyleriia Sichovykh stril'tsiv u borot'bi za Zoloti kyïvs'ki vorota* (New York: Chervona kalyna, 1965), 62–72.

12. Miller, *My Diary*, 489.
13. David Lloyd George, *Memoirs of the Peace Conference*, vol. 1 (New Haven: Yale University Press, 1939), 204.
14. Howard, *Theatre of Life*, 372.
15. Józef Sopotnicki, *Kampanja polsko-ukraińska: Doświadczenia operacyjne i bojowe* (Lviv: Odrodzenie, 1921), 31.
16. M. Kapustians'kyi, *Pokhid ukraïns'kykh armii na Kyïv–Odesu v 1919 rotsi: Korotkyi voienno-istorychnyi ohliad*, vol. 2 (Munich: Vydavnytstvo Khvyl'ovoho, 1946), 52–9; Osyp Nazaruk, *Rik na Velykii Ukraïni: Konspekt spomyniv z ukraïns'koï revoliutsiï* (Vienna: Ukraïns'kyi prapor, 1920), 183–7; Lozyns'kyi, *Halychyna*, 168–9; Osyp Levyts'kyi, *Halyts'ka armiia na Velykii Ukraïni: Spomyny z chasu vid lypnia do hrudnia 1919* (Vienna: n.p., 1921), 9–11; Luka Myshuha, *Pokhid ukraïns'kykh viis'k na Kyïv, serpen', 1919* (Vienna: Ukraïns'kyi prapor, 1920), 6–8.
17. Emil Revyuk, ed., *Polish Atrocities in Ukraine* (New York: United Ukrainian Organizations of the United States, 1931), 487–91; Volodymyr Kubiiovych and Zenon Kuzelia, eds., *Entsyklopediia ukraïnoznavstva*, vol. 1 (Munich: Molode zhyttia, 1949), 25; M. K., "Ukraïns'ka natsional'na terytoriia i kil'kist' ukraïntsiv v Polshchi," *NIKTP na rik 1926*, 57–60; *The Eastern Provinces of Poland* (London, 1944), 6–7; Nik. Berezhanskii, "Pol'sko-sovetskii mir v Rige: Iz zapisok byv. redaktora," *IS* 3 (1923): 128; Matthew Stachiw, *Ukraine and the European Turmoil, 1917–1919*, vol. 1 (New York: Shevchenko Scientific Society, 1973), 16–17.
18. Lloyd George, *Memoirs*, 1: 205.
19. Lozyns'kyi, *Halychyna*, 143.
20. Ibid., 143.
21. *Documents on British Foreign Policy, 1919–1939*, ser. 1, vol. 2, ed. E. L. Woodward and Rohan Butler (London: His Majesty's Stationary Office, 1948), 364–5. The Poles assumed the same annexationist attitude toward Lithuania. One deputy in the Polish Constituent Assembly proclaimed, to the accompaniment of laud cheers: "There is no Poland without Vilna!" (*Monitor Polski* [Warsaw], 24 November 1919; quoted in Alfred E. Senn, *The Emergence of Modern Lithuania* [New York: Columbia University Press, 1959], 191.)

22. Cf. Lloyd George, *Memoirs*, 1: 201; 2: 647; and Nitti, *Peaceless Europe*, 180. Lloyd George (1: 201), for example, recalls: "No one gave more trouble than the Poles.... There were few provinces in a vast area inhabited by a variety of races that Poland could not claim as being historically her inheritance of which she had been reft. Drunk with the new wine of liberty supplied to her by the Allies, she fancied herself once more resistless mistress of Central Europe. Self-determination did not suit her ambitions. She coveted Galicia, the Ukraine, Lithuania and parts of White Russia. A vote of the inhabitants would have emphatically repudiated her dominion. So the right of all peoples to select their nationhood was promptly thrown over by her leaders. They claimed that these various races belonged to the Poles through the conquering arm of their ancestors."

23. Temperley, *History of the Peace Conference*, 266–74, 300–1; *Documents on British Foreign Policy*, 219, 280–5, 363–6, 377–8, 383–4; Alexander Skrzyński, *Poland and Peace* (London: Allen and Unwin, 1923), 34–5; Orzel, "A 'Hotly Disputed' Issue,' 54–6; Pavlo Shandruk, *Arms of Valor* (New York: Robert Speller and Sons, 1959), 86–7; Volodymyr Galan, *Bateriia smerty* (New York: Chervona kalyna, 1968), 82–4; I. Rohatyns'kyi, "Chortkivs'ka ofenzyva," *IKAChK na 1931 rik*, 58–64; Liubomyr Makarushka, "Fragmenty z Chortkivs'koï ofenzyvy," *IKAChK na 1935 rik*, 68–80; Zenon Stefaniv, "Dva roky v ukraïns'kii armiï: Spomyny 17-litn'oho pidkhorunzhoho," *LChK*, 1932, no. 11, 13–16; Hnat Martynets', "Napad rumuniv na ZUNR 25 travnia 1919 r.," in *Ukraïns'ka Halyts'ka Armiia*, vol. 3, ed. Myron Dol'nyts'kyi (Winnipeg: D. Mykytiuk, 1966), 109–18.

24. Iaromyr Diakiv, "Strategichne polozhennia UHA po perekhodi cherez Zbruch litom 1919 r.," *US*, no. 28 (1923), 13–16; Myshuha, *Pokhid*, 6–8; Levyts'kyi, *Halyts'ka armiia*, 9–12; Mazepa, *Ukraïna v ohni*, 2: 17–23; Reshetar, *The Ukrainian Revolution*, 284–6; Oleksander Dotsenko, *Litopys ukraïns'koï revoliutsiï: Materiialy i dokumenty do istoriï ukraïns'koï revoliutsiï, 1917–1923*, vol. 2, pt. 4 (Lviv: the author, 1923), 14; Andrii Holub, "Zbroina vyzvol'na borot'ba na Khersonshchyni v zapilliu voroha, 1917–1919 roky," *ZD* 11: 183.

25. When the UNR troops approached Kyiv, their command issued a vague order: "It is absolutely essential not to enter into hostile action; ask the Denikin troops not to occupy those localities that are already in our hands or that we will soon take; ask them to withdraw from the region of our advance in order not to delay us; apply all efforts to find out details of the organization, condition of the troops, strength, intent, morale, armaments, uniforms, and ammunition of the Denikin Army.... find out the attitude of the Denikin troops toward the Ukrainian state and toward our troops." (Dotsenko, *Litopys*, 9–10).

26. Dotsenko, *Litopys*, 15–16. Shandruk, *Arms of Valor*, 104; Levyts'kyi, *Halyts'ka armiia*, 50–4; Oleksander Udovychenko, *Tretia Zalizna dyviziia: materiialy do*

istorii Viis'ka Ukraïns'koï Narodn'oï Respubliky, rik 1919, vol. 1 (New York: Chervona kalyna, 1971), 112–13, 115–16; Myshuha, *Pokhid ukraïns'kykh viis'k*, 12–18; Anton I. Denikin, *Ocherki russkoi smuty*, vol. 5 (Paris: J. Povolozky, 1926), 123.

27. Shandruk, *Arms of Valor*, 112; *Istoriia ukraïns'koho viis'ka* (Winnipeg: Kliub pryiateliv ukraïns'koï knyzhky, 1953), 564–5; M. Omelianovych-Pavlenko, *Zymovyi pokhid, 6. XII. 1919–6. V. 1920*, vol. 1 (Kalisz: Ukraïns'ke voienno-istorychne tovarystvo, 1920), 41.
28. Henry G. Alsberg, "The Situation in the Ukraine," *TN* 109 (1919): 569–70.
29. Iurii Tiutiunnyk, *Zymovyi pokhid 1919–20 rr.*, vol. 1 (New York: Vydavnytstvo Chartoryis'kykh, 1966), 9.
30. Lozyns'kyi, *Halychyna*, 193–4; Levyts'kyi, *Halyts'ka armiia*, 139–41. For the text of the treaty see Lozyns'kyi, *Halychyna*, 198–9; Tiutiunnyk, *Zymovyi pokhid*, 12–13; Dmytro Paliïv, "Zymovyi pokhid," *LChK*, 1935, no. 7–8, 8.
31. Oleksander Dotsenko, *Zymovyi pokhid (6.XII.1919–6.V.1920)* (Warsaw: Ukraïns'kyi naukovyi instytut, 1932), viiiff.; Margolin, *From a Political Diary*, 52; Shandruk, *Arms of Valor*, 116; I. Mazepa, *Ohneva proba: Ukraïns'ka polityka i strategiia v dobi Zymovoho pokhodu 1919–20* (Prague: Proboiem, 1941), 24, 29–31; Paliïv, "Zymovyi pokhid," *LChK*, 1935, no. 6, 8–9.

Notes to Chapter 6

1. Roman Dmowski, *Polityka polska i odbudowanie państwa*, vol. 1, 3d ed. (Hannover: Perzyński, Niklewicz, 1947), 95.
2. K. Długi, *Wspomnienia z Paryża od 4. I. do 10. VII. 1919 r.* (Warsaw, 1929), 35–6.
3. Szymon Askenazy, *Szkice i portrety* (Warsaw: Instytut Wydawniczy "Biblioteka Polska," 1937), 7.
4. Artur Leinwand, *Polska Partia Socjalistyczna wobec Wojny Polsko-Radzieckiej: 1919–1920* (Warsaw: Państwowe Wydawnictwo Naukowe, 1964), 16–17.
5. As a result of constant invasions by Asiatic hordes, including the Tatars, the strength of the Ukrainian state gradually weakened. The Poles took advantage of this situation and tried, through military force and political maneuvers, to dominate Ukraine. When Poland and Muscovy saw that neither of them could dominate all of Ukraine, in 1667 they concluded the Treaty of Andrusovo, according to which Ukraine was divided between them along the Dnieper River. Right-Bank Ukraine remained under Poland, while the Left Bank fell to Muscovy. Kyiv was initially granted to Muscovy for two years (it later became a permanent possession), and the Zaporozhian Cossack lands were placed under the joint protection of Poland and Muscovy. This settlement brought about an enormous hostile reaction in Ukraine and led to prolonged wars against both

occupational powers, especially Poland. Poland was thus gradually weakened and finally, in 1772, 1793, and 1795, partitioned among Russia, Prussia, and Austria.
6. Dłuski, *Wspomnienia*, 35; Józef Skrzypek, *Zamach stanu płk. Januszajtisa i ks. Sapiehy 4–5 stycznia 1919 r.* (Warsaw: Spółdzielnia Wydawnicza, 1948), 37–41.
7. Stanisław Grabski, *Uwagi o bieżącej historycznej chwili Polski* (Warsaw: Perzyński, Niklewicz, 1922), 149.
8. Stanisław Grabski, *Z zagadnień polityki narodowo-państwowej* (Warsaw: Perzyński, Niklewicz, 1925), 34.
9. Ibid., 32.
10. Leon Wasilewski, *Józef Piłsudski Jakim Go znałem* (Warsaw: Rój, 1935), 172.
11. Michał Sokolnicki, "Józef Piłsudski a zagadnienia Rosji," *N* (London) 2 (1950): 65.
12. Wasilewski, *Józef Piłsudski*, 172–3.
13. Aleksandra Piłsudska (Alexandra Pilsudski), *Memoirs of Madam Pilsudski* (London: Hurst and Blackett, 1940), 206.
14. Józef Piłsudski, *Pisma, mowy, rozkazy: Wydanie zbiorowe prac dotychczas drukiem ogłoszonych*, vol. 6 (Warsaw: Instytut Badań Najnowszej Historji Polski, 1931), 200–1.
15. Dłuski, *Wspomnienia*, 35.
16. Borys Rzhepets'kyi, a member of the UNR delegation that signed the Treaty of Warsaw, asserted that Piłsudski never spoke to the delegation of his design of federation for Eastern Europe. (H. V. S., "Dopovid' d-ra Dzievanovs'koho 'Pilsuds'kyi i Ukraïna v rokakh 1918–21'," New York, 2 June 1963, ms.)
17. Piłsudska, *Memoirs*, 293.
18. Alfred E. Senn, *The Emergence of Modern Lithuania* (New York: Columbia University Press, 1959), 61–3.
19. Piłsudski, *Pisma*, 5 (1933): 70.
20. *Dokumenty i materiały do historii stosunków polsko-radzieckich*, vol. 2, ed. Natalia Gąsiorowska-Grabowska et al (Warsaw: Książka i Wiedza, 1964), 139–65; Karol Grunberg, *Polskie koncepcje federalistyczne, 1864–1918* (Warsaw: Książka i Wiedza, 1971), 243–90; Konstantin Symmons-Symonolewicz, "Polish Political Thought and the Problem of the Eastern Borderlands of Poland, 1918–1938," *PoR*, 1959, no. 1–2, 65–7; Kazimierz Okulicz, "Ostatni akt dramatu Józefa Pilsudskiego, 1920–1922," *ZH* 9 (1966): 7–45; Henry G. Alsberg, "The Russo-Polish Peace," *TN*, 24 November 1920, 587–8; Edmund Charaszkiewicz, "Przebudowa wschodu Europy," *N* (Warsaw) 5: 149–50; Dłuski, *Wspomnienia*, 32–9, 42–3; Jan Rozwadowski, *My a Ruś* (Cracow: Księgarnia J. Czerneckiego, 1917), 2–3; H. W. V. Temperley, ed., *A History of the Peace Conference of Paris*, vol. 6 (London: H. Frowde and Holder and Stoughton, 1924), 309–10; Josef Korbel, *Poland between East and West: Soviet and German Diplomacy toward Poland, 1919–1933* (Princeton:

Princeton University Press, 1963), 11–12; H. H. Fisher, *America and the New Poland* (New York: Macmillan, 1928), 263–5; Tadeusz Katelbach, "Rola Piłsudskiego w sprawie polsko-litewskiej," *N* (London) 1 (1948): 101–16; Piotr Wandycz, *France and Her Eastern Allies, 1919–1925: French-Czechoslovak-Polish Relations from the Paris Peace Conference to Locarno* (Minneapolis: University of Minnesota Press, 1962), 180–5; Marian Kukiel, *Dzieje Polski porozbiorowej, 1795–1921* (London: B. Świderski, 1961), 590–3; Kazimierz Maciej Smogorzewski, *La Pologne restaurée* (Paris: Gebethner et Wolff, 1927), 155–7; M. K. Dziewanowski, *Joseph Piłsudski: A European Federalist, 1918–1922* (Stanford: Hoover Institution Press, 1969), 81–5; Tytus Komarnicki, "Piłsudski a polityka wielkich mocarstw zachodnich," *N* (London) 4 (1952): 44–5; Titus Komarnicki, *Rebirth of the Polish Republic: A Study in the Diplomatic History of Europe, 1914–1920* (Melbourne: Heinemann, 1957), 49–50, 484; Zygmunt Jundzill, "Niefortunna Wyprawa Kowieńska," *N* (London) 5 (1955): 206–11; Sokolnicki, "Józef Piłsudski," 51–70.

Notes to Chapter 7

1. Oleksander Dotsenko, *Litopys ukraïns'koï revoliutsiï: Materiialy i dokumenty do istoriï ukraïns'koï revoliutsiï, 1917–1923*, vol. 2, pt. 5 (Lviv: the author, 1924), 7–8; Paweł Szandruk, "Geneza umowy polsko-ukraińskiej z 21. IV. 1920 r.," *W*, 1935, no. 2, 39; Aleksy Deruga, *Polityka wschodnia Polski wobec ziem Litwy, Białorusi i Ukrainy (1918–1919)* (Warsaw: Książka i Wiedza, 1969), 233–4.
2. *Dokumenty i materiały do historii stosunków polsko-radzieckich*, vol. 2, ed. Natalia Gąsiorowska-Grabowska et al (Warsaw: Książka i Wiedza, 1961), 259–60; Józef Lewandowski, "U źródeł Wyprawy Kijowskiej," *WAP* 7 (1962): 95–7; J. Piłsudski, "List do I. Paderewskiego w Paryżu," *N* (London) 7 (1962): 38; D. Antonchuk, "Ukraïns'ko-pol's'ki perehovory pro zamyrennia u travni 1919: Vystup Kurdynovs'koho; uryvok zi spomynyv," *IKAChK na 1939 rik*, 176–7; Matvii Stakhiv, *Ukraïna v dobi Dyrektoriï UNR*, vol. 7 (Scranton: Ukrainian Workingmen's Association, 1966), 159; Dotsenko, *Litopys*, 4, pt. 4, 45, 62–71; idem, 2, pt. 5, 9; Piotr Wandycz, "Z zagadnień współpracy polsko-ukraińskiej w latach 1919–20," *ZH* 12 (1967): 9.
3. Antonchuk, "Ukraïns'ko-pol's'ki perehovory," 174–8; M. Omelianovych-Pavlenko, *Ukrains'ko-pol's'ka viina, 1918–1919* (Prague: Merkur-fil'm, 1929), 69; Lewandowski, "U źródeł," 98.
4. Tadeusz Kutrzeba, *Wyprawa Kijowska 1920 roku* (Warsaw: Gebethner i Wolff, 1937), 51.
5. Dotsenko, *Litopys*, 2, pt. 4, 43–61, 72–7; idem, pt. 5, 10–12; Lewandowski, "U źródeł," 98–9; V. Prokhoda, "Sirozhupannyky v povstanni proty uriadu het'mana

Skoropads'koho," *T*, no. 9 (1928), 90; idem, "Siri abo Sirozhupannyky," *VK*, 1967, no. 4 (28), 35.
6. Lewandowski, "U źródeł," 100.
7. *Dokumenty i materiały*, 230–1; see also Lewandowski, "U źródeł," 99–100.
8. *Dokumenty i materiały*, 331–2; Wandycz, "Z zagadnień," 10–12; Lewandowski, "U źródeł," 100.
9. Kutrzeba, *Wyprawa Kijowska*, 50–1, 228.
10. Louis Fischer, *The Soviets in World Affairs: A History of the Relations between the Soviet Union and the Rest of the World, 1917–1929*, vol. 1 (Princeton: Princeton University Press, 1951), 254–6.
11. Dotsenko, *Litopys*, 2, pt. 4, 81–2; idem, pt. 5, 13–14; Kutrzeba, *Wyprawa Kijowska*, 51; John S. Reshetar, Jr., *The Ukrainian Revolution, 1917–1920: A Study in Nationalism* (Princeton: Princeton University Press, 1952), 299; I. Mazepa, *Ukraïna v ohni i buri revoliutsiï, 1917–1921*, vol. 3 (Munich: Prometei, 1952), 13; Lewandowski, "U źródeł," 101; P. Fedenko, "The Period of the Directory," in *Ukraine: A Concise Encyclopaedia*, vol. 1, ed. Volodymyr Kubijovyč (Toronto: University of Toronto Press, 1963), 765–7.
12. "Tekst umowy politycznej polsko-ukraińskiej z 22, 4, 20," Warsaw, 21 April 1920, ms. at the Józef Piłsudski Institute of America, New York; "Politychna konventsiia mizh ta U.," Warsaw, 21 April 1920, ms. at the Bibliothèque Ukrainienne Symon Petlura, Paris; see also S. Shelukhyn, *Varshavs'kyi dohovir mizh poliakamy i S. Petliuroiu 21 kvitnia 1920 roku* (Prague: Nova Ukraïna, 1920), 13–14.
13. "Konwencja wojskowa między Polską a Ukrainą," Warsaw, 24 April 1920, ms. at the Józef Piłsudski Institute of America; "Viis'kova konventsiia pomizh Pol'shcheiu i Ukraïnoiu," Warsaw, 24 April 1920, ms. at the Bibliothèque Ukrainienne Symon Petlura.
14. Mazepa, *Ukraïna v ohni*, 5, 8–9, 14; S. Shelukhyn, *Varshavs'kyi dohovir* (Toronto: Ukraïns'kyi robitnyk, 1947), 13ff.; Reshetar, *The Ukrainian Revolution*, 301–5; Lewandowski, "U źródeł," 109.
15. Symon Petlura, "Lyst Holovnoho otamana Symona Petliury do odnoho z ioho heneraliv," *NS*, 1955, no. 1, 18; Petro Sahaidachnyi, *V ioho tini: Symon Petliura v istoriï ukraïns'koho narodu* (New York: Ukraïns'ke vydavnytstvo, 1951), 22.
16. Henryk Jabłoński, "Z dziejów genezy sojuszu Piłsudski-Petlura: Początki konfliktu zbrojnego XI. 1918–III. 1919," *WAP* 5 (1961): 58.
17. Titus Komarnicki, *Rebirth of the Polish Republic: A Study in the Diplomatic History of Europe, 1914–1920* (Melbourne: Heinemann, 1957), 573; Aleksy Deruga, "Początek rokowań o sojusz między Piłsudskim a Petlurą, styczeń–lipiec 1919," *ZDSPR* 6 (1970): 47.
18. Kutrzeba, *Wyprawa Kijowska*, 88.

19. Lewandowski, "U źródeł," 104.
20. Stanisław Głąbiński, *Wspomnienia polityczne* (Pelplin: Spółka z Ograniczoną Odpowiedzialnością, 1959), 429.
21. *Dokumenty i materiały*, 132.

Notes to Chapter 8

1. *Documents on British Foreign Policy, 1919–1939*, ser. 1, vol. 3, ed. E. L. Woodward and Rohan Butler (London: His Majesty's Stationary Office, 1949), 787.
2. Aleksander Kawałkowski, *Z dziejów odbudowy państwa: Szkice* (Warsaw: Wojskowy Instytut Naukowo-Wydawniczy, 1933), 16.
3. Adolf Juzwenko, "Misja Marchlewskiego w 1919 roku na tle stosunków polsko-radzieckich," in *Z badań nad wpływem i znaczeniem Rewolucji rosyjskiej 1917 roku dla ziem polskich*, ed. Henryk Zieliński (Wrocław: Towarzystwo Naukowe, 1968), 31–3; Juljusz Łukasiewicz, "Uwagi o polityce ukraińskiej Marszałka Piłsudskiego," *WP* (London), 1941, no. 50; Stefan Arski, "Wojna roku 1920," *Polityka* (Warsaw), 2 July 1960; Władysław Pobóg-Malinowski, *Najnowsza historia polityczna Polski, 1864–1945*, vol. 2 (London: B. Świderski, 1956), 198; Edgar Anderson, "The British Policy toward the Baltic States, 1918–1920," *JCEA* 19, no. 3, 277–83; Jerzy Ochmański, *Historia Litwy*, 2d ed. (Wrocław: Zakład Narodowy im. Ossolińskich, 1982), 295–6; Józef Skrzypek, *Zamach stanu płk. Januszajtisa i ks. Sapiehy 4–5 stycznia, 1919 r.* (Warsaw: Spółdzielnia Wydawnicza, 1948), 43.
4. David Hunter Miller, *My Diary at the Conference of Paris with Documents*, vol. 18 (New York: Appeal Printing Co., 1926), 274.
5. Piłsudski writing about Paderewski, cited in M. K. Dziewanowski, *Joseph Piłsudski: A European Federalist, 1918–1922* (Stanford: Hoover Institution Press, 1969), 133.
6. Józef Piłsudski, *Pisma, mowy, rozkazy: Wydanie zbiorowe prac dotychczas drukiem ogłoszonych*, vol. 5 (Warsaw: Instytut Badania Najnowszej Historii Polski, 1933), 129.
7. *Głos Litwy* (Vilnius), 29 May 1919, as quoted in Dziewanowski, *Joseph Piłsudski*, 136.
8. *Documents on British Foreign Policy, 1919–1939*, ser. 1, vol. 1 (1948), 59.
9. Adam Przybylski, *Wojna Polska, 1918–1921* (Warsaw: Wojskowy Instytut Naukowo-Wydawniczy, 1930), 56–61, 92–3, 102–8, 117–20; Piotr S. Wandycz, "Secret Soviet-Polish Peace Talks in 1919," *SR* 24, no. 3 (1965), 434–5; H. W. V. Temperley, ed., *A History of the Peace Conference of Paris*, vol. 6 (London: H. Browde and Hodder and Stoughton, 1924), 245–6; Piotr S. Wandycz, *France and Her Eastern Allies, 1919–1925: French-Czechoslovak-Polish Relations from*

the Paris Peace Conference to Locarno (Minneapolis: The University of Minnesota Press, 1962), 29–48; William Henry Chamberlin, *The Russian Revolution, 1917–1921*, vol. 2 (New York: The University Library, 1965), 122–3; Dziewanowski, *Joseph Piłsudski*, 73, 95–9; Anton I. Denikin, *The White Army* (Westport, Conn.: Hyperion Press, 1973), 185–6; Isaak Mazepa, *Ohneva proba: Ukraïns'ka polityka i strategiia v dobi Zymovoho pokhodu, 1919–20* (Prague: Proboiem, 1941), 50–1; Marian Kukiel, *Dzieje Polski porozbiorowej, 1795–1921* (London: B. Świderski, 1961), 567–9; Aleksy Deruga, *Polityka wschodnia Polski wobec ziem Litwy, Białorusi i Ukrainy (1918–1919)* (Warsaw: Książka i Wiedza, 1969), 115–20, 288–99; idem., "Przyczynki do genezy Litewskiej Republiki Radzieckiej i dziejów wojny domowej na przełomie lat 1918–1919," *ZDSPR* 9 (1973): 214–17; idem., "Przed i po Wyprawie Wileńskiej 1919 r.," *ZDSPR* 10 (1973): 56–60; Jerzy Iwanowski, "Gdyby Denikin zwyciężył, czerwony totalizm zostałby białym," *DP*, 19 September 1947; Józef Kukułka, "Niektóre aspekty międzynarodowe polityki Piłsudskiego wobec ziem litewsko-białoruskich w pierwszej połowie 1919 roku," *SNDP* 2 (1962): 35–6; *The Proclamation of Byelorussian Independence, 25th of March 1918* (London: Association of Byelorussians in Great Britain, 1968), 6–8; G. Paszkiewicz, "Wypad na Kliczew 12, XII, 1919," *B* (Warsaw) 13 (1924), no. 3, 253–9; Bolesław Zawadzki, *System obrony w 1920 roku* (Warsaw: Wojskowy Instytut Narodowo-Wydawniczy, 1926), 7–12; Artur Leinwand, *Polska Partia Socjalistyczna wobec Wojny Polsko-Radzieckiej, 1919–1920* (Warsaw: Państwowe Wydawnictwo Naukowe, 1964), 87–90; *Dokumenty i materiały do historii stosunków polsko-radzieckich*, vol. 2, ed. Natalia Gąsiorowska-Grabowska et al (Warsaw: Książka i Wiedza, 1964), 140–1.
10. *Documents on British Foreign Policy*, ser. 1, vol. 3, 611.
11. *Dokumenty i materiały*, 132. The pro-Russian attitude of the Poles was manifested at the beginning of the war. According to Tadeusz Hołówko, who witnessed this phenomenon in Warsaw, "A regiment of [Russian] Cossacks was marching with a band at its head ... [and] surrounded by a crowd of enthusiastic Polish public shouting 'long live our troops, long live our defenders.' Ladies in a feverish state, with radiant eyes, were quickly buying flowers and running between the rows of horses to hand them to the officers, [while] the gentlemen emptied their cigarette cases and thrust the cigarettes upon the Cossacks, who from high up with indulgent smiles accepted these signs of admiration." (Tadeusz Hołówko, "Ze wspomnień 'germanofila'," in *Wspomnienia legjonowe: Materiały z dziejów walk o niepodległość*, vol. 1, ed. Janusz Jędrzejewicz [Warsaw: Instytut Badań Najnowszej Historji Polskiej, 1924], 21.)
12. *Documents on British Foreign Policy*, ser. 1, vol. 3, 363.
13. Peter N. Wrangel, *The Memoirs of General Wrangel, the Last Commander-in-Chief of the Russian National Army*, transl. Sophie Gouston (London: Williams

and Norgate, 1929), 127.
14. Denikin, *The White Army*, 327–9; Pobóg-Malinowski, *Najnowsza historia*, 2: 204–6; Iwanowski, "Gdyby Denikin zwyciężył"; Mieczysław Pruszyński, "Rozmowa historyczna ze St. Grabskim," *BM*, 20 November–5 December 1935; Haller, "Instrukcja do Generała Karnickiego, Szefa Polskiej Misji Wojskowej przy gen. Denikinie," Warsaw, 8 August 1919, 1–4, ms. at the Józef Piłsudski Institute of America, New York.
15. Jane Degras, ed., *Soviet Documents on Foreign Policy* vol. 1 (London: Oxford University Press, 1951), 98.
16. N. E. Kakurin, *Kak srazhalas' revoliutsiia*, vol. 2 (Moscow: Gos. izd-vo, 1926), 321.
17. Alexander Skrzyński, *Poland and Peace* (London: Allen and Unwin, 1923), 39.
18. Tadeusz Kutrzeba, *Wyprawa Kijowska 1920 roku* (Warsaw: Gebethner i Wolff, 1937), 24–5; A. Denikin, "Pol'sha i Dobrovol'cheskaia armiia," *GMChS*, 1926, no. 4, 180–1; Weronika Gostyńska, "Stosunki polsko-radzieckie a państwa Bałtyckie, wrzesień–grudzień 1919 r.," *ZDSPR* 14 (1976): 31–2; W. A. Zbyszewski, "Denikin, zdolny generał i ograniczony polityk: Czy Polska mogła uratowac białą Rosję," *DP*, 12 August 1947.
19. P. V. Suslov, *Politicheskoe obespechenie sovetsko-pol'skoi kampanii 1920 goda* (Moscow: Gos. izd-vo, 1930), 18–19.
20. Józef Sieradzki, *Białowieża i Miklaszewicze: Mity i prawdy; Do genezy wojny pomiędzy Polską a RSFRR w 1920 r.* (Warsaw: Wydawnictwo Ministerstwa Obrony Narodowej, 1959), 15–28; Kutrzeba, *Wyprawa Kijowska*, 21–32; Kukiel, *Dzieje Polski porozbiorowej*, 572–4; Wandycz, "Secret Soviet-Polish Peace Talks in 1919," 425–49; Edward Hallet Carr, *The Bolshevik Revolution, 1917–1923*, vol. 3 (New York: Macmillan, 1953), 154–5; Piotr Wandycz, "Z zagadnień współpracy polsko-ukraińskiej w latach 1919–20," *ZH* 12 (1967): 11–13; Aleksy Deruga, "Początek rokowań o sojusz między Piłsudskim a Petlurą, styczeń-lipiec 1919," *ZDSPR* 6 (1970): 46–7; Józef Lewandowski, "U źródeł Wyprawy Kijowskiej," *WAP* 7 (1962): 90–1; E. G. Val', *Kak Piłsudskii pogubil Denikina* (Tallinn: the author, 1938), 1–4, 50–1; Mazepa, *Ohneva proba*, 62–3; Stanisław Haller, "Nasz stosunek do Denikina," *KW*, 13 June 1937; Adam Krzyżanowski, "Z historji stosunków polsko-rosyjskich nazajutrz po wojnie swiatowej," *PW* 58 (1936): 72–5; Przybylski, *Wojna Polska*, 102–8; Skrzyński, *Poland and Peace*, 40–1.
21. *LS* 36 (1959): 130.
22. Louis Fischer, *The Soviets in World Affairs: A History of the Relations between the Soviet Union and the Rest of the World, 1917–1929*, vol. 1 (Princeton: Princeton University Press, 1951), 242.
23. Ibid., 242.
24. Józef Korbel, *Poland between East and West: Soviet and German Diplomacy*

toward Poland, 1919–1933 (Princeton: Princeton University Press, 1963), 35; Robert Machray, *Poland, 1914–1931* (London: Allen and Unwin, 1932), 141–2; S. Konovalov, ed., *Russo-Polish Relations: An Historical Survey* (Princeton: Princeton University Press, 1945), 71–2; Titus Komarnicki, *Rebirth of the Polish Republic: A Study in the Diplomatic History of Europe, 1914–1920* (Melbourne: Heinemann, 1957), 565.

25. *Documents on British Foreign Policy*, ser. 1, vol. 3, 765.
26. Kutrzeba, *Wyprawa Kijowska*, 45; Wacław Jędrzejewicz, "Rokowania borysowskie w 1920 roku," *N* (London) 3 (1951): 47–59; Korbel, *Poland*, 33–7; Machray, *Poland*, 141–3; Konovalov, *Russo-Polish Relations*, 71–3; Komarnicki, *Rebirth*, 564–6; Val', *Kak Piłsudskii*, 34.
27. *Dokumenty i materiały*, 613.
28. Józef Kalinowski, "Stosunki polsko-rosyjskie w latach 1914–1945," 8, ms. copy in my possession.
29. Lewandowski, "U źródeł," 101–2.

Notes to Chapter 9

1. Bogusław Międziński, "Wojna i pokój," *K*, 1966, no. 5, 116–17.
2. Joachim Bartoszewicz, *Na Rusi polski stan posiadania: Kraj, ludność, ziemia* (Kyïv: L. Dzikowski, 1912), 3–20; Aleksander Weryha-Darowski, *Kresy Ruskie Rzeczypospolitej: Województwa Kijowskie, Wołynskie, Bracławskie i Podolskie* (Warsaw: Koło Polaków Ziem Ruskich w Warszawie, 1919), 9–11; Marjan Tokarzewski, *Straż przednia: Ze wspomnień i notatek* (Warsaw: Polski Instytut Wydawniczy, 1925), 17–18; "Ukraïntsi-katolyky na Pravoberezhnii Ukraïni," *VSVU*, no. 168 (1917), 600; Józef Lewandowski, *Federalizm: Litwa i Białoruś w polityce obozu belwederskiego, XI. 1918–IV. 1920* (Warsaw: Państwowe Wydawnictwo Naukowe, 1962), 18–23; *Demokrata Polski* (Warsaw), 18 June 1917, as quoted in Henryk Jabłoński, *Polska autonomia narodowa na Ukrainie, 1917–1918* (Warsaw: Towarzystwo Miłośników Historii, 1948), 17–18; Franciszek Rawita-Gawroński, "Wartość i straty majątku polskiego w Rosji," *PW*, 1925, no. 40, 255–66.
3. Wanda Wyhowska de Andreis, *Między Dnieprem a Tybrem* (London: Polska Fundacja Kulturalna, 1981), 36.
4. E. G. Val'. *Kak Piłsudskii pogubil Denikina* (Tallinn: the author, 1938), vi–viii.
5. Dmytro Doroshenko, *Istoriia Ukraïny, 1917–1923 rr.*, vol. 1, *Doba Tsentral'noï Rady*, 2d ed. (New York: Bulava, 1954), 150.
6. Witold Walewski, "Wspomnienia o Podolu," *PK* 3 (1966): 19–22, 35–7; Stanisław Stempowski, "Wspomnienia," *ZH*, no. 24 (1973), 70–6, 100–2; Wiktor Dzierżykraj-Stokalski, *Dzieje jednej partyzantki z lat 1917–1920* (Lviv: the author, 1927), 19, 34–5, 48.

7. Stempowski, "Wspomnienia," 73–4.
8. Wyhowska de Andreis, *Między Dnieprem a Tybrem*, 36–7.
9. Iv. Za-ych, "Chuzhozemni viiskovi formuvannia v Ukraïns'kii Derzhavi," *IKAChK na 1939 rik*, 88–101; Stempowski, "Wspomnienia," 98–131; Tadeusz Hołówko, *Przez dwa fronty: Ze wspomnień emisariusza politycznego z 1918 roku: Z Warszawy do Kijowa* (Warsaw: Dom Książki Polskiej, 1931), 90–5, 103, 227–9.
10. Hołówko, *Przez dwa fronty*, 118.
11. Ibid., 169–70.
12. Stokalski, *Dzieje jednej partyzantki*, 31–5; Józef Haller, *Pamiętniki z wyborem dokumentów i zdjęć* (London: Veritas Foundation Press, 1964), 139–47.
13. Stempowski, "Wspomnienia," 99–101.
14. Hołówko, *Przez dwa fronty*, 123.
15. Stokalski, *Dzieje jednej partyzantki*, 50–1; Sophia Kossak, *The Blaze: Reminiscences of Volhynia, 1917–1919* (London: Allen and Unwin, 1927), 94ff.; Hołówko, *Przez dwa fronty*, 128–31.
16. Kossak, *The Blaze*, 100.
17. Stempowski, "Wspomnienia," 103.
18. Oleksander Dotsenko, *Litopys ukraïns'koï revoliutsiï: Materiialy i dokumenty do istoriï ukraïns'koï revoliutsiï, 1917–1923*, vol. 2, pt. 5 (Lviv: the author, 1924), 135.
19. I. Mazepa, *Ukraïna v ohni i buri revoliutsiï, 1917–1921*, vol. 2 (Munich: Prometei, 1951), 188–99; idem., *Ohneva proba: Ukraïns'ka polityka i strategiia v dobi Zymovoho pokhodu, 1919–1920* (Prague: Proboiem, 1941), 52–3; Dotsenko, *Litopys*, 127–31, 293ff.; Xawery Orłowski, "Projekt tyczący sie akcji Sprzymierzonych na Ukrainie," Warsaw, 1 November 1919, ms.; Włodzimierz Wisłocki, "W Kamieńcu Podolskim—grudzien 1919," *PK* 3 (1966): 235–40; O. R., "Kamianets' pid pol's'koiu vladoiu," *Vo*, 1919, no. 5, 212–13; "Do Vsyokoho Uriadu Richi Pospolytoï Pol's'koï," *Vo*, 1919, no. 5, 215–16; Ivan Ohiienko, *Riatuvannia Ukraïny: Na tiazhkii sluzhbi svoiemu narodovi*, rev. ed. (Winnipeg: Society of Volyn, 1968), 23, 44–8.
20. Ohiienko, *Riatuvannia Ukraïny*, 57, 71.
21. Mazepa, *Ohneva proba*, 53.
22. M. K. Dziewanowski, *Joseph Piłsudski, A European Federalist, 1918–1922*. (Stanford: Hoover Institution Press, 1969), 66–7; Pavlo Shandruk. *Arms of Valor* (New York: Robert Speller and Sons, 1959), 118–19, 210.

Notes to Chapter 10

1. E. G. F. Val', *Kak Pilsudskii pogubil Denikina* (Tallinn: the author, 1938), 3.
2. Tadeusz Kutrzeba, *Wyprawa Kijowska 1920 roku* (Warsaw: Gebethner i Wolff,

1937), 82, 91–5; Marian Kukiel, *Zarys historji wojskowości w Polsce* (London: Orbis, 1949), 233–4; Zbigniew Lewiński, "Zagon na Koziatyn," *B* (Warsaw), April 1921, 306–16; *Ukraïns'ko-moskovs'ka viina 1920 roku v dokumentakh*, vol. 1, ed. Volodymyr Sal's'kyi, comp. Pavlo Shandruk (Warsaw: Ukraïns'kyi naukovyi instytut, 1933), 3–4; Oleksander Udovychenko, *Tretia Zalizna dyviziia*, vol. 2 (New York: Chervona kalyna, 1982), 41–7; Oleksander Udovychenko, *Ukraïna u viini za derzhavnist': Istoriia orhanizatsiï i boiovykh dii Ukraïns'kykh Zbroinykh Syl* (Winnipeg: D. Mykytiuk, 1954), 142–3; Volodymyr Bemko, "Likvidatsiina komisiia UHA," in *Ukraïns'ka Halyts'ka Armiia u 40-richchia ïï uchasty u vyzvol'nykh zmahanniakh (materiialy do istoriï)*, vol. 1 (Winnipeg: D. Mykytiuk, 1958), 560–1; Norman Davies, *White Eagle, Red Star: The Polish-Soviet War, 1919-1920* (London: Macdonald, 1972), 106–9; Lev Shankovs'kyi, *Ukraïns'ka Halyts'ka Armiia: Voienno-istorychna studiia* (Winnipeg: D. Mykytiuk, 1974), 262–3; A. Przybylski, *Wojna Polska, 1918–1921* (Warsaw: Wojskowy Instytut Naukowo-Wydawniczy, 1930), 138–9; W. Ordon, "Polska ofenzywa na Ukrainie," *RW*, 1920, no. 19, 7–8, and no. 20, 6–8; Adam Skwarczyński, "Niepodległa Ukraina," *RW*, 1920, no. 18, 1–2.
3. Józef Piłsudski, *Pisma, mowy, rozkazy: Wydanie zbiorowe prac dotychczas drukiem ogłoszonych*, vol. 5 (Warsaw: Instytut Badania Najnowszej Historji Polski, 1933), 168–9.
4. I. Mazepa, *Ukraïna v ohni i buri revoliutsiï, 1917–1921*, vol. 3 (Munich: Prometei, 1951), 6–7.
5. Jan M. Meijer, ed., *The Trotsky Papers, 1917–1922*, vol. 2 (The Hague: Mouton, 1971), 176.
6. Winston S. Churchill, *The Aftermath* (New York: Scribner, 1929), 277–8.
7. L. Trotsky, *Kak vooruzhalas' revoliutsiia: Na voennoi rabote*, vol. 2, pt. 2 (Moscow: Vysshii voennyi redaktsionnyi sovet, 1924), 138.
8. Adam Ludwik Korwin-Sokołowski, *Fragmenty wspomnień, 1910–1945* (Paris: Spotkania, 1985), 47–8.
9. N. N., "Pobratymcy broni: List rannego oficera," *RW*, 1920, no. 30, 10.
10. N. E. Kakurin and V. A. Melikov, *Voina s belopoliakami 1920 g.* (Moscow: Gosudarstvennoe voennoe izdatel'stvo, 1925), 93–5.
11. Kutrzeba, *Wyprawa Kijowska*, 99.
12. Lewiński, "Zagon," 306–16; Kutrzeba, *Wyprawa Kijowska*, 99, 251–3.
13. Edgar V. D'Abernon, *The Eighteenth Decisive Battle of the World: Warsaw, 1920* (London: Hodder and Stoughton, 1931), 130.
14. Kutrzeba, *Wyprawa Kijowska*, 104–8, 251–2; Tadeusz Machalski, *Ostatnia epopeja: Działania kawalerii w 1920 roku* (London: B. Świderski, 1969), 45–54; Przybylski, *Wojna Polska*, 136–42; Wacław Jędrzejewicz, *Piłsudski: A Life for Poland* (New York: Hippocrene Books, 1982), 104; Petro Samutyn, "VI Sichovo-strilets'ka dyviziia: Orhanizatsiia v Beresti i pokhid na Kyïv u 1920 r.,"

VK, 1971, no. 5 (55), 27–32; *Ukraïns'ko-moskovs'ka viina*, 1: 2; Udovychenko, *Ukraïna u viini*, 143–4; John Erickson, *The Soviet High Command: A Military-Political History, 1918–1941* (New York: St. Martin's Press, 1962), 86–7; Davies, *White Eagle*, 115–16.
15. Kutrzeba, *Wyprawa Kijowska*, 254.
16. Piłsudski, *Pisma, mowy, rozkazy*, 5: 171.
17. Jędrzejewicz, *Piłsudski*, 104.
18. Kutrzeba, *Wyprawa Kijowska*, 253–5.
19. Ibid., 314.
20. "Konwencja wojskowa między Polską a Ukraina," Warsaw, 24 April 1920, ms.
21. "Pytannia, iaki pidneseni heneralom Zelins'kym pidchas rozmovy ioho z heneralom Airys," Warsaw, 16 September 1920, ms.; Mazepa, *Ukraïna v ohni*, 3: 40–2; Volodymyr Bemko, "Halychany v Odesi," in *Ukraïns'ka Halyts'ka Armiia*, 1: 538–44; *Ukraïns'ko-moskovs'ka viina*, 1: 2; Mykhailo Kurakh, "Chy Sichovi stril'tsi braly uchast' u Zymovomu pokhodi?," VK, 1961, no. 1–2, 32–3; A. Shustykevych, "Spomyny z Odesy," *IKAChK na 1928 rik*, 102–3; Symon Petliura, *Statti, lysty, dokumenty*, vol. 1, ed. L. Drazhevs'ka et al (New York: Ukrainian Academy of Arts and Sciences in the U.S., 1956), 264.
22. Samutyn, "VI Sichovo-strilets'ka dyviziia," 27–32; *Ukraïns'ko-moskovs'ka viina*, 1: 2; Vsevolod Zmiienko, "Rolia nashoï VI-oï Sichovoï dyviziï v ukraïns'kii derzhavnii spravi," 1921, ms.; Mazepa, *Ukraïna v ohni*, 2: 214.
23. N. N., "Pobratymcy broni," 9.
24. Kutrzeba, *Wyprawa Kijowska*, 254–6; Pavlo Shandruk, *Arms of Valor* (New York: Robert Speller and Sons, 1959), 122–4; Udovychenko, *Tretia Zalizna*, 2: 37–41; *Ukraïns'ko-moskovs'ka viina*, 1: 1–3; Mazepa, *Ukraïna v ohni*, 2: 209–12; Piotr Wandycz, "Z zagadnień współpracy polsko-ukraińskiej w latach 1919–20," ZH 12 (1967): 20–2; V. Sal's'kyi, "Do statti 'Ukraïntsi v bytvi z Turkamy pid Vidnem 12 veresnia 1683 r.," *Nemezida* (Warsaw) 1 (1936): 33–5; Korwin-Sokołowski, *Fragmenty wspomnień*, 44–50, 185–91.
25. O. Dumin, "5-ta Khersons'ka strilets'ka dyviziia ta ïï perekhid na Zakarpattia v serpni 1920 r.," ZD 9 (1938): 76–91; Iurii Naumenko, "Moia sluzhba v 5 Khersons'kii strilets'kii dyviziï," ZD 7 (1935): 165–80; "Z armiieiu generala Pavlenka," *"Kaliendar "Kanadiis'koho ukraïntsia" na rik 1921*, 86–98; O. Z., "Hirs'ka brygada UHA ta ïï perekhid na chekhoslovats'ku terytoriiu," LChK, 1938, no. 7–8, 13–14; D. M., "Perekhid hrupy Kravsa do Chekho-Slovachchyny," in *Ukraïns'ka Halyts'ka Armiia*, 1: 590–3.
26. Udovychenko, *Ukraïna u viini*, 133–4, 142–3; *Ukraïns'ko-moskovs'ka viina*, 1: 6, 21, 36; Shandruk, *Arms of Valor*, 122–6; Osyp Stanimir, *Moia uchast' u vyzvol'nykh zmahanniakh, 1917–1920* (Toronto: the author, 1966), 172–3; Shankovs'kyi, *Ukraïns'ka Halyts'ka Armiia*, 258–65; I. Mazepa, *Ohneva proba: Ukraïns'ka polityka i stratehiia v dobi Zymovoho pokhodu, 1919–1920* (Prague:

Proboiem, 1941) 95–100; Oleksander Dotsenko, *Litopys ukraïns'koï revoliutsiï: Materiialy i dokumenty do istoriï ukraïns'koï revoliutsiï*, vol. 2, pt. 5 (Lviv: the author, 1925), 257–9.
27. Nykyfor Hirniak, "Ukraïns'ka Halyts'ka Armiia v soiuzi z chervonymy," in *Ukraïns'ka Halyts'ka Armiia*, 1: 527–9; T. Dats'kiv, "Masakra halychan v Odessi v r. 1920," *URob*, 14 September 1951; H. Havryliv, "Vid bil'shovykiv do Petliury: Zi spomyniv," *LChK*, 1936, no. 9, 17–20; Denys Onyshchuk, "Ostannii akt: Uryvok zi spomyniv," *LChK*, 1938, no. 9, 4–10; Osyp Nymylovych, "Spomyny pro ostanni dni 3-ho polku 1-oï brygady USS," *LChK*, 1936, no. 5, 20–1; Petro Holyns'kyi, "Ostanni dni UHA: Uryvky zi spomyniv," *IKAChK na 1931 rik*, 142–55; Ivan Baidok, "Nastup na Vynnytsiu v kvitni 1920 r.," *LChK*, 1936, no. 6, 11–14; Shustykevych, "Spomyny z Odesy," 102–14; Izydor Sokhots'kyi, "Iak my staly bol'shevykamy," in *Ukraïns'ka Halyts'ka Armiia*, vol. 5 (1976), 62–5; *Mizh molotom a kovadlom: Prychynky do istoriï ukraïns'koï armiï* (Lviv: Chernova kalyna, 1923), 61–79.
28. See Karlo Stajner, *Seven Thousand Days in Siberia* (New York: Farrar, Straus, and Giroux, 1988), 41.
29. *Mizh molotom*, 78.
30. A. Shustykevych, "Z ostannikh boïv: Osin' 1919 roku na Velykii Ukraïni," *IKAChK na 1929 rik*, 145.
31. Articles by Volodymyr Bemko, Volodymyr Klodnyts'kyi, V. K., and D. M. in *Ukraïns'ka Halyts'ka Armiia*, 1: 538–58, 590–3; Vasyl' Kuchabs'kyi, *Korpus Sichovykh stril'tsiv: Voienno-istorychnyi narys* (Chicago: Iuvileinyi komitet dlia vidznachennia 50-richchia stvorennia formatsiï Sichovykh stril'tsiv, 1969), 390–1, 442–6; R. Davnyi, *Pro Sichovykh stril'tsiv* (Vienna: Chornohory, 1921), 69–72; Kurakh, "Chy Sichovi stril'tsi," 24–36; Ivan Ivanets', "Pid Chudnovom: Kinets' Brygady USS," *IKAChK na 1935 rik*, 83–96. The Sich Riflemen were organized in November 1917 in Kyïv from Galician Ukrainians in the Austrian army held as prisoners of war in Russia. Some writers call the formation the Kyivan Sich Riflemen. As the formation grew from a battalion into a corps, many Ukrainians from central and eastern Ukraine joined it. The Sich Riflemen were the best and most reliable Ukrainian military formation during the Ukrainian revolution. See Dmytro Herchanivs'kyi, "Pochatky Sichovykh stril'tsiv," *VK*, 1967, no. 2, 29-36; idem., "Prykmetni rysy Sichovykh stril'tsiv," *VK*, 1968, no. 3, 16–22; Hryts' Hladkyi, "Sichovi stril'tsi," *LChK*, 1935, no. 6, 4–6; M. Bezruchko, "Sichovi stril'tsi v borot'bi za derzhavnist'," *ZD* 3 (1932): 104–8; *Dokumenty i materiały do historii stosunków polsko-radzieckich*, vol. 3, ed. Natalia Gąsiorowska-Grabowska et al (Warsaw: Książka i Wiedza, 1964), 20.
32. W. Ordon, "Polska ofenzywa na Ukrainie," *RW*, 1920, no. 20, 8.
33. Iurii Tiutiunnyk, *Zymovyi pokhid 1919–20 rr.* (Kolomyia, 1923; reprint, New York: Vydavnytstvo Chartoryis'kykh, 1966), 81.

34. Udovychenko, *Tretia Zalizna*, 2: 43–5.
35. T. Kurcjusz, "Pierwsze spotkanie 13-ej Dywizji Piechoty z Budiennym," *B* (Warsaw), 1921, no. 1, 475–87; no. 2, 577–89; no. 3, 696–704; no. 4, 781–92.
36. Ibid., no. 1, 477–9.
37. Shankovs'kyi, *Ukraïns'ka Halyts'ka Armiia*, 264–5; Mazepa, *Ukraïna v ohni*, 3: 22–3.
38. N. N., "Pobratymcy broni," 9.
39. Tadeusz Piszczkowski, *Odbudowanie Polski, 1914–1921: Historia i polityka* (London: Orbis, 1969), 294–5.
40. M. K. Dziewanowski, *Joseph Piłsudski: A European Federalist, 1918–1922* (Stanford: Hoover Institution Press, 1969), 296.
41. Mazepa, *Ukraïna v ohni*, 3: 19–23, 41–2; Wandycz, "Z zagadnień," 18–21; N. N., "Pobratymcy broni," 9; Kutrzeba, *Wyprawa Kijowska*, 82. Mykola Halahan, *Z moïkh spomyniv*, vol. 4 (Lviv: Chervona kalyna, 1930), 275–98.
42. *Dokumenty i materiały*, 18–19.
43. *LS* 34 (1942): 293.
44. *Pravda* (Moscow), 7 May 1920, as quoted in Davies, *White Eagle*, 135.
45. G. Gai, *Na Varshavu: Deistviia 3-go konnogo korpusa na Zapadnom fronte* (Moscow: Gos. izd-vo, 1928), 9, as quoted in P. V. Suslov, *Politicheskoe obespechenie sovetsko-pol'skoi kampanii 1920 goda* (Moscow: Gos. izd-vo, 1930), 35.
46. William Henry Chamberlin, *The Russian Revolution, 1917–1921*, vol. 2 (New York: The University Library, 1965), 302–3; I. Markhlevskii [J. Marchlewski], *Voina i mir mezhdu burzhuaznoi Polshei i proletarskoi Rossiei* (Moscow: Gos. izd-vo, 1921), 18–21.
47. Maximilien Weygand, *Bitwa o Warszawę: Odczyt wygłoszony w Brukseli* (Warsaw: Mazowiecka Spółka Wydawnicza, 1930), 11.
48. Pierre Fervacque, *Le Chef de L'Armée Rouge—Mikail Toukatchevski* (Paris: Bibliothèque Charpentier, 1928), 36.
49. On 28 May 1920, when the assault began, the Polish Thirteenth Infantry Division had about 8,000 men, including 201 officers, 443 machine guns, and 39 artillery guns (Kurcjusz, "Pierwsze spotkanie," 475–87)
50. Kutrzeba, *Wyprawa Kijowska*, 181–2.
51. Kurcjusz, "Pierwsze spotkanie," 475–87; Kutrzeba, *Wyprawa Kijowska*, 144–223; Machalski, *Ostatnia epopeja*, 61–3; Jędrzejewicz, *Piłsudski*, 104–7; Przybylski, *Wojna polska*, 143–53; Erickson, *The Soviet High Command*, 84–91; Davies, *White Eagle*, 124–6; Shandruk, *Arms of Valor*, 124–6.
52. Titus Komarnicki, *Rebirth of the Polish Republic: A Study in the Diplomatic History of Europe, 1914–1920* (Melbourne: Heinemann, 1957), 607.
53. *Dokumenty i materiały*, 156–62.

54. Grace Humphrey, *Piłsudski: Builder of Poland* (New York: Scott and More, 1936), 204–5.
55. D'Abernon, *Eighteenth Decisive Battle*, 32.
56. M. Kukiel, "Dramat Generała Weyganda," *B* (London), 1949, no. 2, 3.
57. Przybylski, *Wojna polska*, 152–5; Jędrzejewicz, *Piłsudski*, 107–8; Robert Machray, *Poland, 1914–1931* (London: Allen and Unwin, 1932), 147–9; Davies, *White Eagle*, 160–3; W. F. Reddaway, *Marshal Piłsudski* (London: G. Routledge, 1939), 131–5; Weygand, *Bitwa o Warszawie*, 17–18; D'Abernon, *An Ambassador of Peace: Pages from the Diary*, vol. 1 (London: Hodder and Stoughton, 1929), 69–71; Piotr S. Wandycz, "General Weygand and the Battle of Warsaw of 1920," *JCEA* 19, no. 4, 357–65; Weygand, "The Repulse of the Bolshevik Invasion of Poland," *The American Army and Navy Journal*, no. 48 (1922), 1174–5; Artur Leinwand, *Polska Partia Socjalistyczna wobec Wojny Polsko-Radzieckiej, 1919–1920* (Warsaw: Państwowe Wydawnictwo Naukowe, 1964), 168–81.
58. Dumin, "5-ta Khersons'ka," 76–91; Naumenko, "Moia sluzhba," 165–80; Ol. Udovychenko, "Forsuvannia Dnistra pid Horodnytseiu 14 veresnia 1920 roku," *ZD* 4 (1934): 190–6; Udovychenko, *Tretia Zalizna*, 2: 49–90; Udovychenko, *Ukraïna u viini*, 143–7; O. Demchuk, "Z zhyttia-buttia v tabori v Iozefovi, rik 1921," *US*, no. 11 (1922) 7; Mazepa, *Ukraïna v ohni*, 3: 48–9.
59. Lector, "Wspomnienia o Wyprawie Kijowskiej 1920 r.," *BPU*, 1937, no. 2, 18.
60. Wiktor Romanów-Głowacki, "Jeszcze o Zamościu w 1920 roku," *DP*, 22 August 1946; Mikołaj Bołtuc, "Budenny pod Zamościem," *B* (Warsaw), 22, no. 3 (1926), 203–29; Tadeusz Różycki, "Możliwość interwencji konnej armji Budiennego w Bitwie Warszawskiej," *B* (Warsaw) 19, no. 2 (1925), 288–93; Kutrzeba, *Wyprawa Kijowska*, 206–7; Zmiienko, "Rolia VI-oï Sichovoï dyviziï," 1–5; Domarats'kyi, "Oborona Zamostia," 1–3, ms.; *Oborona Zamostia VI. Sichovoiu strilets'koiu dyviziieiu Armiï UNR u 1920 r.* (Toronto: Hrupa voiakiv VI. Sichovoï strilets'koï dyviziï i prykhyl'nykiv, 1956), 3–31; M. Bytyns'kyi, "Oborona Zamostia: Spohad z nahody 35 rokovyn," *NDni*, no. 68 (1955), 22–3.
61. Kutrzeba, *Wyprawa Kijowska*, 344.

Notes to Chapter 11

1. Józef Piłsudski, *Year 1920 and Its Climax Battle of Warsaw during the Polish-Soviet War, 1919–1920* (London and New York: Piłsudski Institute of America/Piłsudski Institute of London, 1972), 119–22; A. Przybylski, *Wojna Polska, 1918–1921* (Warsaw: Wojskowy Instytut Naukowo-Wydawniczy, 1930), 155–71; Piotr S. Wandycz, *Soviet-Polish Relations, 1917–1921* (Cambridge: Harvard University Press, 1969), 200–25; John Erickson, *The Soviet High*

Command: a Military-Political History, 1918–1941 (New York: St. Martin's Press, 1962), 92–4; N. E. Kakurin and V. A. Melikov, *Voina s belopoliakami 1920 g.* (Moscow: Gosudarstvennoe voennoe izdatel'stvo, 1925); J. F. C. Fuller, *Decisive Battles: Their Influence upon History and Civilization* (New York: Charles Scribner and Sons, 1940), 946–50; Maximilien Weygand, *Bitwa o Warszawę: Odczyt wygłoszony w Brukseli* (Warsaw: Mazowiecka Spółka Wydawnicza, 1930), 11–13; Henryk Piątkowski, "Krytyczny rozbiór 'Bitwy Warszawskiej' 1920 roku," *B* (London), 1957, no. 1, 3–36; Lucjan Żeligowski, "Notatki z roku 1920," *N* (London) 3 (1951): 161–6; V. P. Savchenko, "Vtracheni mozhlyvosti dlia peremohy v lystopadi 1920 r.," *T*, no. 2 (1924), 99–151.
2. D. Manuil'skii, "O rizhskikh peregovorakh," *KI*, 1920, no. 15, 3.
3. Fuller, *Decisive Battles*, 954.
4. *The Communist International, 1919–1943: Documents*, vol. 1, ed. Jane Degras (London: Cass, 1971), 91–2.
5. *Pravda* (Moscow), 23 September 1920, as quoted in P. N. Ol'shanskii, *Rizhskii mir: Iz istorii bor'by Sovetskogo Pravitel'stva za ustanovlenie mirnykh otnoshenii s Pol'shei, konets 1918–mart 1921 g.* (Moscow: Nauka, 1969), 134–5.
6. Edgar V. D'Abernon, *The Eighteenth Decisive Battle of the World: Warsaw, 1920* (London: Hodder and Stoughton, 1931), 28.
7. Ivan I. Skvortsov-Stepanov, *S Krasnoi Armiei na panskuiu Pol'shu: Vpechatleniia i nabliudaniia* (Moscow: Gosizdat, 1920), 92–5, as quoted in William Henry Chamberlin, *The Russian Revolution, 1917–1921*, vol 2 (New York: The University Library, 1965), 309.
8. Nik. Berezhanskii, "Pol'sko-sovetskii mir v Rige: Iz zapisok byv. redaktora," *IS* 2 (1922): 112.
9. D'Abernon, *Eighteenth Decisive Battle*, 27.
10. Louis Fischer, *The Soviets in World Affairs: A History of the Relations between the Soviet Union and the Rest of the World, 1917–1929* (Princeton: Princeton University Press, 1951), 266–8; Chamberlin, *Russian Revolution*, 2: 306–8; Richard M. Watt, *Bitter Glory: Poland and Its Fate, 1918 to 1939* (New York: Simon and Schuster, 1979), 142–5; I. Markhlevskii, *Voina i mir mezhdu burzhuaznoi Pol'shei i proletarskoi Rossiei* (Moscow: Gos. izd-vo, 1921), 21–5; Berezhanskii, "Pol'sko-sovetskii mir," 110–15; Adam Wierny, *Na szlakach dziejowych Romana Dmowskiego* (Piotrków: the author, 1939), 113–15.
11. Maximilien Weygand, "The Repulse of the Bolshevik Invasion of Poland," *The American Army and Navy Journal*, 1922, no. 47, 1141–2; Weygand, *Bitwa o Warszawę*, 21–9; Wacław Jędrzejewicz, *Piłsudski: A Life for Poland* (New York: Hippocrene Books, 1982), 112–17; Piotr S. Wandycz, "General Weygand and the Battle of Warsaw of 1920," *JCEA*, 1960, no. 4, 357–65; M. Kukiel, "Dramat generała Weyganda," *B* (London), 1949, no. 2, 3–11; M. Kukiel, "Rozbior

Operacji Warszawskiej z punktu widzenia obrony," *B* (Warsaw) 22, no. 2 (1926), 98–9; Erickson, *The Soviet High Command*, 93–7; Fuller, *Decisive Battles*, 954–9, 965–7; Kakurin and Melikov, *Voina s belopoliakami*; Mikołaj Bołtuć, "Budienny pod Zamościem," *B* (Warsaw) 22, no. 3 (1926), 214–16; Żeligowski, "Notatki," 161–6; Przybylski, *Wojna Polska*, 194–6; Savchenko, "Vtracheni mozhlyvosti," 101–7.
12. Fuller, *Decisive Battles*, 949; Markhlevskii, *Voina i mir*, 22–6, 36.
13. Fuller, *Decisive Battles*, 949.
14. D'Abernon, *Eighteenth Decisive Battle*, 76–7.
15. Weygand, *Bitwa o Warszawę*, 24–30; Chamberlin, *Russian Revolution*, 2: 317; Josef Korbel, *Poland between East and West: Soviet and German Diplomacy toward Poland, 1919–1933* (Princeton: Princeton University Press, 1963), 63–5; Kukiel, "Rozbiór Operacji Warszawskiej," 102–23; Edward Hallett Carr, *The Bolshevik Revolution, 1917–1923*, vol. 3 (New York: Macmillan, 1953), 209–10; Grace Humphrey, *Piłsudski: Builder of Poland* (New York: Scott and More, 1936), 234–5; Fuller, *Decisive Battles*, 960–73.
16. *Dokumenty i materiały do historii stosunków polsko-radzieckich*, vol. 3, ed. Natalia Gąsiorowska-Grabowska et al. (Warsaw: Książka i Wiedza, 1964), 406; Piłsudski, *Year 1920*, 35–9; Weygand, "The Repulse," 1174–5; Fuller, *Decisive Battles*, 960–73; Jędrzejewicz, *Piłsudski*, 125–7; Przybylski, *Wojna Polska*, 191–7, 214–25; Tadeusz Kutrzeba, *Bitwa nad Niemnem, wrzesień-pazdziernik 1920* (Warsaw: Wojskowy Instytut Naukowo-Wydawniczy, 1926); Savchenko, "Vtracheni mozhlyvosti," 106–8.
17. Pavlo Shandruk, *Arms of Valor* (New York: Robert Speller and Sons, 1959), 128–30; Watt, *Bitter Glory*, 149–51; Norman Davies, *White Eagle, Red Star: The Polish-Soviet War, 1919–20* (London: Macdonald, 1972), 232–7; Przybylski, *Wojna Polska*, 208–11; Oleksander Udovychenko, *Ukraïna u viini za derzhavnist': Istoriia orhanizatsiï i boiovykh diï Ukraïns'kykh Zbroinykh Syl, 1917–1921* (Winnipeg: D. Mykytiuk, 1954), 150–3; Savchenko, "Vtracheni mozhlyvosti," 104–8; Berezhanskii, "Pol'sko-sovetskii mir," 129–30.

Notes to Chapter 12

1. Leonhard Horst, "At the Riga Peace Conference," *LA*, 20 November 1920, 459.
2. *Dokumenty i materiały do historii stosunków polsko-radzieckich*, vol. 3, ed. Natalia Gąsiorowska-Grabowska et al. (Warsaw: Książka i Wiedza, 1964), 409–10.
3. Nik. Berezhanskii, "Pol'sko-sovetskii mir v Rige (Iz zapisok byv. redaktora)," *IS*, 2 (1922): 123.
4. Ibid., 124.
5. *Dokumenty i materiały*, 409.

6. Adam Płomieńczyk, "Polskie warunki pokoju," *RW*, 5 September 1920, 36.
7. *Dokumenty i materiały*, 464.
8. Aleksander Ładoś, "Wasilewski w rokowaniach ryskich: Wspomnienia osobiste," *N* (Warsaw) 16 (1937): 234.
9. Jan Dąbski, *Pokój Ryski: Wspomnienia, pertraktacje, tajne układy z Joffem, listy* (Warsaw: n.p., 1931), 77–8; Iwan Kedryn, "Istota Traktatu Ryskiego," *BPU* 1933, no. 3, 10–14.
10. Dąbski, *Pokój Ryski*, 184.
11. Berezhanskii, "Pol'sko-sovetskii mir," 122.
12. Ibid., 123–4.
13. Leon Wasilewski, *Józef Piłsudski, Jakim Go znałem* (Warsaw: Rój, 1935), 219–20.
14. L. K., "Ekspozytura Ministerstwa Spraw Wojskowych do spraw ukraińskich w roku 1920," *N* (London) 7 (1962): 236–45.
15. *Ukraïns'ka deliegatsiia Skhid'noï Halychyny v Ryzi* (Vienna: Uriad presy i propagandy ZUNR, 1920), 4–16; Osyp Nazaruk, *Halyts'ka deliegatsiia v Ryzi 1920 r.: Spomyny uchasnyka* (Lviv: Ukraïns'ka khrystyians'ka organizatsiia, 1930), 3–49, 86.
16. Nazaruk, *Halyts'ka deliegatsiia*, 98–9.
17. Ibid., 99–101.
18. Ibid., 140, 142.
19. Ibid., 145–7.
20. Dąbski, *Pokój Ryski*, 82; Berezhanskii, "Pol'sko-sovetskii mir," 133–5.
21. V. I. Lenin, *Polnoe sobranie sochinenii*, 5th ed., vol. 4 (Moscow: Gos. izd-vo politicheskoi literatury, 1963), 331–2.
22. Louis Fischer, *The Soviets in World Affairs: A History of the Relations between the Soviet Union and the Rest of the World, 1917–1929* (Princeton: Princeton University Press, 1951), 272.
23. Lenin, *Polnoe sobranie sochinenii*, 41: 363.
24. *LS* 36 (1959): 123.
25. Dąbski, *Pokój Ryski*, 83–6; *SoR*, December 1920, 591–3; Władysław Pobóg-Malinowski, *Najnowsza historia polityczna Polski, 1864–1945*, vol. 2 (London: B. Świderski, 1956), 368–70; Ładoś, "Wasilewski," 232–7.
26. Dąbski, *Pokój Ryski*, 92–6; *Dokumenty i materiały*, 437–41 (Russian document); Berezhanskii, "Pol'sko-sovetskii mir," 139–41.
27. Dąbski, *Pokój Ryski*, 106–7.
28. Nazaruk, *Halyts'ka deliegatsiia*, 115.
29. Berezhanskii, "Pol'sko-sovetskii mir," 126.
30. Dąbski, *Pokój Ryski*, 105–6.
31. Ibid., 96–107; Stanisław Dąbrowski, "The Peace Treaty of Riga," *PoR*, 1960, no. 1, 6–10; Piotr S. Wandycz, *Soviet-Polish Relations, 1917–1921* (Cambridge: Harvard University Press, 1969), 264–5; Nazaruk, *Halyts'ka deliegatsiia*, 131–3.

32. Henry G. Alsberg, "The Russo-Polish Peace," *TN*, 24 November 1920, 587.
33. Stanisław Grabski, "Jeszcze o rokowaniach ryskich," *MN*, 1933, no. 8, 83.
34. Ładoś, "Wasilewski," 232–8; Dąbrowski, "The Peace Treaty of Riga," 9–13; I. Markhlevskii, "Mir s Pol'shei," *KI*, 1920, no. 14, 2751–4.
35. Stanisław Grabski, *The Polish-Soviet Frontier* (London: Keliher, Hudson and Kearns, 1943), 29–31; Ładoś, "Wasilewski," 235–8; Dąbski, *Pokój Ryski*, 107–10; Karol Poznański, "Jak to naprawdę było w Rydze z Mińskiem?," *TP*, 28 November 1964; Wandycz, *Soviet-Polish Relations, 1917–1921*, 266–7; Dąbrowski, "The Peace Treaty of Riga," 10–13.
36. Dąbski, *Pokój Ryski*, 107–16; Wincenty Witos, *Moje wspomnienia*, vol. 2 (Paris: Instytut Literacki, 1964), 364–72; Alsberg, "The Russo-Polish Peace," 587–8; Dąbrowski, "The Peace Treaty of Riga," 13–15; Titus Komarnicki, *Rebirth of the Polish Republic: A Study in the Diplomatic History of Europe, 1914–1920* (Melbourne: Heinemann, 1957), 732–7.
37. *LS* 36 (1959): 130.
38. *Soviet Treaty Series: A Collection of Bilateral Treaties, Agreements and Conventions, Etc., Concluded between the Soviet Union and Foreign Powers*, vol. 1, *1917–1928*, comp. and ed. Leonard Shapiro (Washington: The Georgetown University Press, 1950), 67–9; *Dokumenty i materiały*, 465–75; Berezhanskii, "Pol'sko-sovetskii mir," *IS* 3 (1922): 117–23.
39. *Dokumenty i materiały*, 476–7.

Notes to Chapter 13

1. Aleksander Ładoś, "Wasilewski w rokowaniach ryskich: Wspomnienia osobiste," *N* (Warsaw) 16 (1937): 240.
2. Jan Dąbski. *Pokój Ryski: Wspomnienia, pertraktacje, tajne układy z Joffem, listy* (Warsaw, 1931), 173.
3. "Poland on a Firmer Footing," *CH* 13 (1921): 520.
4. Dąbski, *Pokój Ryski*, 174.
5. Prochor N. Olszański, "Od preliminariów pokojowych do traktatu pokojowego," *ZDSPR* 3 (1968): 97–101; Dąbski, *Pokój Ryski*, 129–32; Ładoś, "Wasilewski," 240–3; Stanisław Dąbrowski, "The Peace Treaty of Riga," *PoR*, 1960, no. 1, 19–23; Piotr S. Wandycz, *Soviet-Polish Relations, 1917–1921* (Cambridge: Harvard University Press, 1969), 279–82; Karol Poznański, "Ryga, 1920–1921," *W*, 14 April 1957.
6. Dąbski, *Pokój Ryski*, 168–70.
7. Ładoś, "Wasilewski," 244–7; Dąbski, *Pokój Ryski*, 165–80; Nik. Berezhanskii, "Pol'sko-sovetskii mir v Rige: Iz zapisok byv. redaktora," *IS* 2 (1922): 143–7.
8. Dąbski, *Pokój Ryski*, 174.

9. *Soviet Treaty Series: A Collection of Bilateral Treaties, Agreements and Conventions, Etc., Concluded between the Soviet Union and Foreign Powers,* vol. 1, *1917–1928,* comp. and ed. Leonard Shapiro (Washington: The Georgetown University Press, 1950), 88–92; *Dokumenty i materiały do historii stosunków polsko-radzieckich,* vol. 3, ed. Natalia Gąsiorowska-Grabowska et al. (Warsaw: Książka i Wiedza, 1964), 551–65.
10. Poznański, "Ryga, 1920–1921."
11. Dąbski, *Pokój Ryski,* 182; Poznański, "Ryga, 1920–1921"; Berezhanskii, "Pol'sko-sovetskii mir," 145–9.
12. For accounts of the uprising, see David Footman, *The Russian Revolution* (New York: G. P. Putnam and Sons, 1964), 118–29; and Lancelot Lawton, *The Russian Revolution, 1917–1926* (London: Macmillan, 1927), 94–5.
13. Dąbski, *Pokój Ryski,* 183–5; Ładoś, "Wasilewski," 248.
14. *Soviet Treaty Series,* 1: 105–16; *Dokumenty i materiały,* 1: 572–609; Dąbski, *Pokój Ryski,* 206–24.
15. Dąbski, *Pokój Ryski,* 187–98; Ładoś, "Wasilewski," 248–50; Wandycz, *Soviet-Polish Relations,* 283–90; Olszański, "Od preliminariów pokojowych," 115–17.
16. Stanisław Grabski, "Jeszcze o rokowaniach ryskich," *MN,* 1933, no. 8, 83.
17. *LS* 36 (1959): 130.
18. Dmitrii Manuïl'skii, "O rizhskikh peregovorakh," *KI,* 1920, no. 15, 3078–9.

Notes to Chapter 14

1. V. Sal's'kyi, ed., *Ukraïns'ko-moskovs'ka viina 1920 roku v dokumentakh,* vol. 1 (Warsaw: Ukraïns'kyi naukovyi instytut, 1933), 297–8, 317, 329–30; V. P. Savchenko, "Vtracheni mozhlyvosti dlia peremohy v lystopadi 1920 r.," *T,* no. 2 (1924), 108–51; Oleksander Udovychenko, *Ukraïna u viini za derzhavnist': Istoriia orhanizatsiï i boiovykh diï Ukraïns'kykh Zbroinykh Syl, 1917–1921* (Winnipeg: D. Mykytiuk, 1954), 152–61; Oleksander Udovychenko, "Vid Dnistra do liniï peremyr'ia i vidvorot za Zbruch," *ZD* 6 (1936): 77–109, 7 (1936): 152–64; Pavlo Shandruk, *Arms of Valor* (New York: Robert Speller and Sons, 1959), 130–3; Erich Wollenberg, *The Red Army; A Study of the Growth of Soviet Imperialism* (London: Secker and Warburg, 1940), 58–61; Iurii Naumenko, "Moia sluzhba v 5-ii Khersons'kii strilets'kii dyziziï," *ZD* 7 (1936), 165–80; O. Dumin, "5-ta Khersons'ka strilets'ka dyviziia ta ïï perekhid na Zakarpattia v serpni 1920 r.," *ZD* 9 (1938): 76–91; V. Kushch, "Slid pamiataty," *T,* no. 7 (1928), 32–4.
2. A. Marushchenko-Bohdanivs'kyi, "Materiialy do istoriï 1-ho kinnoho Lubens'koho imeny zaporozhs'koho polkovnyka Maksyma Zalizniaka polku," *ZD* 9 (1938): 216.
3. Ibid., 219.

4. Shandruk, *Arms of valor*, 134–6; P. Shandruk, "Ukraïns'ka armiia v borot'bi z Moskovshchynoiu," *ZD* 4 (1934): 201–36; Udovychenko, *Ukraïna u viini*, 161–2; V. Tatars'kyi, *Pid chotyrma praporamy: Spohad* (Munich: the author, 1983), 77–85; Liubov Mykhailova, "Spohady pro Symona Petliuru," *Kyïv* (Philadelphia), 1964, no. 4 (85), 111–15; *Ukraïns'ko-moskovs'ka viina*, 297–360; *Istoriia ukraïns'koho viis'ka* (Winnipeg: I. Tyktor, 1953), 567–8.
5. *Soviet Treaty Series; A Collection of Bilateral Treaties, Agreements and Conventions, Etc., Concluded between the Soviet Union and Foreign Powers*, vol. 1, *1917–1928*, comp. and ed. Leonard Shapiro (Washington: The Georgetown University Press, 1950), 68.
6. K. L., "Ekspozytura Ministerstwa Spraw Wojskowych do spraw ukraińskich w roku 1920," *N* (London) 7 (1962): 242.
7. Shandruk, *Arms of Valor*, 134–42.
8. Iurii Tiutiunnyk, *Zymovyi pokhid 1919–20 rr.* (New York: Vydavnytstvo Chartoryis'kykh, 1966), 79.
9. Alain Desroches, *The Ukrainian Problem and Symon Petlura (The Fire and the Ashes)* (Chicago: Ukrainian Research and Information Institute, 1970), 88.
10. Marushchenko-Bohdanivs'kyi, "Materiialy," 206–25; Vl. Shmerling, "Grigorii Kotovskii," *VV*, 1940, no. 8, 9–13; L. Poltava, "Povstantsi na pivdni Ukraïny v 1920–21 rokakh," *VK*, 1967, no. 3, 32–5; Udovychenko, *Ukraïna u viini*, 161–4; N. P-pa, "Protybol'shevyts'ki povstannia v Ukraïni 1921 r.," *VK*, 1969, no. 6, 57–67; Kharytyna Pekarchuk, "Voiats'kym shliakhom," *Nashe zhyttia* (Philadelphia), 1969, no. 9, 31–2, no. 10, 31–3; Viktor Ianovs'kyi, "'Za Ukraïnu, za ïï doliu'," *ZD* 3 (1932): 172–91.

Notes to Chapter 15

1. Hryts' Rohoznyi, "Bazar," *SD*, 1934, no. 5–6, 428.
2. I. Dombrovs'kyi, "Druhyi zymovyi pokhid: Spohady uchasnyka," *Kalendar-al'manakh Ukraïns'koï narodnoï pomochi, 1914–1954* (Pittsburgh), 119.
3. Viktor Ianovs'kyi. "'Za Ukraïnu, za ïï doliu'," *ZD* 3 (1932): 190.
4. Dombrovs'kyi, "Druhyi zymovyi pokhid," 113–21; Mykola Staroviit, *U Lystopadovomu reidi: Spohady uchasnyka* (Los Angeles, 1968), 7–53; *Lystopadovyi reid* (Toronto: Ukraïns'kyi voienno-istorychnyi instytut, 1957), 7–14; Osyp Dobrotvors'kyi, "Lystopad 1921 roku na Velykii Ukraïni," *Pryiatel' ukraïns'koho zhovnira: Kalendar na 1923 rik* (Lviv), 146–54; Hr. Maslivets', "Podil's'ka hrupa: U 55-ti rokovyny 2-ho zymovoho pokhodu," *BUNDS*, no. 21 (1956), 1–5; Petrenko, "Lystopadovyi reid 1921 r. cherez pol's'ko-ukraïns'kyi kordon: Spomyny z II zymovoho pokhodu v lystopadi 1921," *LChK*, 1934, no. 6, 6–8; Hryts' Rohoznyi, "Bazar," *SD*, 1934, no. 2, 131–48, no. 3, 209–28, no. 5–6, 422–49; Pavlo Shandruk, *Arms of Valor* (New York: Robert Speller and Sons,

1959), 134–7; Vasyl' Padalka, "Reid rozvidchoho viddilu sotnyka V. Padalky: Materiialy do vyvchennia 2-ho zymovoho pokhodu," *Visti* (Munich) no. 114 (1964), 44–7, no. 115, 93–4, no. 116, 129–31, no. 117 (1965), 17–19, no. 118, 65–7, no. 119, 92–5; "Protybol'shevyts'ki povstannia v Ukraïni v 1921 r.," *VK*, 1969, no. 6 (43), 57–67; Hryhir Samchuk, "Chomu trahediia Bazaru?," *Tr* (Paris), 1938, no. 1–2, 29–32; M. Bytyns'kyi, "Navkola Bazaru," *VK*, 1971, no. 6 (56), 11–17; I. K. Koz'ma, "L'odovyi pokhid i hen. Iu. Tiutiunnyk," *VK*, 1972, no. 1 (57), 20–8; O. Udovychenko, "Reid henerala Huloho-Hulenka," *BSBUVK*, no. 9 (1961), 9–12; Mykhailo Palii-Sydorians'kyi, "'Na reidi': Zi spohadiv," *T*, no. 5 (1930), 9–13; L. Poltava, "Povstantsi na pivdni Ukraïny v 1920–21 rokakh," *VK*, 1967, no. 3 (28), 32–5; M. Kapustians'kyi, "Otamany-heneral-khorunzhi Vasyl' i Iurko Tiutiunnyky," *Rozbudova derzhavy* (Toronto), 1958, no. 1 (22), 1–6; A. Marushchenko-Bohdanivs'kyi, "Materiialy do istoriï 1-ho Kinnoho lubens'koho im. zaporozhs'koho polkovnyka Maksyma Zalizniaka polku," *ZD* 9 (1938): 206–25; Vas. Zaryts'kyi, "Vypad povstanchoho zahonu vid Husiatyna pid Kyïv 1921 r.," *IKAChK na 1932 rik*, 87–97; O. Shpilins'kyi, "Bazar," *ZD* 3 (1932): 109–34; Petro Vashchenko, "Do reidu 1921 roku," *ZD* 3 (1932): 135–9; M. Chyzhevs'kyi, "15 dib na okupovanii Moskvoiu Ukraïni: Z 4 po 19 lystopada 1921 roku," *ZD* 3 (1932): 140–54; Ivan Rembolovych, "Reid 1921 roku," *ZD* 3 (1932): 156–71; Ianovs'kyi, "'Za Ukraïnu, za ïï doliu'," *ZD* 3 (1932): 172–91; Serhii Chornyi, "Storinka z Druhoho zymovoho pokhodu," *ZD* 3 (1932): 192–205; Dmytro Zorenko, "Na partyzantsi," *ZD* 3 (1932): 206–25.

Notes to Chapter 16

1. Alain Desroches, *The Ukrainian Problem and Symon Petlura (The Fire and the Ashes)* (Chicago: Ukrainian Research and Information Institute, 1970), 66–76; Pavlo Shandruk, *Arms of Valor* (New York: Robert Speller and Sons, 1959), 143–51; Vasyl' Ivanys, *Symon Petliura—Prezydent Ukraïny, 1879–1926* (Toronto: Ukrainian War Veterans' League of Canada, 1952), 215–35; V. Ivanys, "Symon Petliura iak hromadianyn, polityk, derzhavnyi muzh," *NL*, no. 12 (1964), 51–63; Ivan Kedryn, "Kul't Symona Petliury," in *Symon Petliura: Zbirnyk Studiino-naukovoï konferentsiï v Paryzhi, traven' 1976*, ed. Volodymyr Kosyk (Munich: Ukraïns'kyi vilnyi universytet, 1980), 209–17; I. Kedryn, "Symon Petliura," *KChK na 1927 rik*, 143–51; V. Fylonovych, "S. Petliura—postat' natsional'no-derzhavnoho chynu," *H*, no. 17–18 (1936), 10–17; Liubov Mykhailova, "Spohady pro Symona Petliuru," *Kyïv* (Philadelphia), 1964, no. 4, 111–15; Jarosław Dryhynycz, "Symon Petlura," *W*, 1936, no. 1–2, 44–51; Panas Fedenko, "Symon Petliura i trahediia Ukraïny," *NDni*, no. 292 (1974), 5–11; Ievhen Bachyns'kyi, "'Iablunia tsvite: Deshcho z davnikh spomyniv pro Petliuru," *Tr* (Paris), 1938, no. 22, 15–23, no. 25, 3–9; V. Kedrovs'kyi, "Pam'iati

Holovnoho otamana S. Petliury," *Biuleten' Ob'iednannia prykhyl'nykiv Ukraïns'koï Narodn'oï Respubliky v SShA* (New York), 1965, no. 4, 2–6; Il'ko Havryliuk, *Veleten' dukha: Pam'iati Symona Petliury* (Chernivtsi: Iu. Hlyvko, 1928), 3–38; V. Prokopovych, "Ostannia podorozh," *Tr* (Paris), 25 May 1931, 26–33; "Memorjał 'Prometeusza'," *BPU*, 1937, no. 5, 56; W. B., "J. Piłsudski a idee prometejskie," *BPU*, 1938, no. 20, 209–11; Sergiusz Mikulicz, *Prometeizm w polityce II Rzeczypospolitej* (Warsaw: Książka i Wiedza, 1971), 106–230; Roman Smal-Stocky, "The Struggle of the Subjugated Nations in the Soviet Union for Freedom," *UQ*, 1947, no. 4, 324–35; Włodzimierz Bączkowski, *Prometeizm na tle epoki: Wybrane fragmenty z historii ruchu* (n. p.: the author, 1984), 1–27.
2. Desroches, *The Ukrainian Problem*, 72–6; Allen W. Dulles, "The Craft of Intelligence," *Encyclopaedia Britannica Book of the Year, 1963*, 20; *Symon Petliura—derzhavnyi muzh*, ed. Nataliia Livyts'ka-Kholodna, Zakhar Ivasyshyn, and Artem Zubenko (New York: Ukraïns'kyi natsional'no-derzhavnyi soiuz v SShA, 1957), 69–75, 119–27; Sydir Korbut, *Symon Petliura* (Lviv: Ukraïns'ke vydavnytstvo, 1941), 48–51.
3. "The Lurid Trial of Petlura's Slayer," *LD*, 1927, no. 8, p. 36.
4. Ian Tokarzhevs'kyi-Karashevych, "Symon Petliura v Paryzhi, 1924–1926," in *Symon Petliura—derzhavnyi muzh*. 119–27.
5. The word pogrom (from the Russian) means a purposeful devastation of property, usually accompanied by beatings, looting, rape, and even killing of innocent people. Pogroms were either approved or condoned by the tsarist police and officials. They took the form of mob attacks against non-Russian persons, especially Jews, and their property. The Russian police did nothing to stop the pogroms, nor did they punish those responsible for them. The first extensive pogroms followed the assassination of Tsar Alexander II in 1881, and the most severe anti-Jewish pogrom took place in Kishinev, Bessarabia, in 1903. In Russia proper there were practically no pogroms, because the number of Jews there had been limited and was less than one percent of the total population. There they lived mainly in the cities as doctors, lawyers, druggists, artisans, and merchants. Practically all the Jews in the Russian Empire, ninety-five percent or even more, were confined to Poland and especially to the "pale of settlement," that is Ukraine, Belarus, Lithuania, and Bessarabia. See Arnold D. Margolin, *The Jews of Eastern Europe* (New York: Seltzer, 1926), 16–17, 70–2; *The Universal Jewish Encyclopedia*, 8: 559–62.
6. The text of Petliura's anti-pogrom order to UNR troops reads:
    Daily Order by the Supreme Commander of the Troops of the Ukrainian People's Republic No. 131, Issued on August 26, 1919.
    This order will be read in the divisions, the brigades, the regiments, the battalions and the companies of the armies of the Dnieper and the Dniester

and in the detachments of the insurgents.

The sinister men of the "Black Hundreds" and the "Red Hundreds" are but one band. They are assiduously weaving the spider's web, provoking pogroms on the Jewish population, and on many occasions they have incited certain backward elements of our army to commit abominable acts. They thus succeeded in defiling our struggle for liberty in the eyes of the world and in compromising our nation's cause.

Officers and Cossacks! It is time to know that the Jews have, like the greater part of our Ukrainian population, suffered from the horrors of the Bolshevik–Communist invasion and follow the way to the truth. The best Jewish groups, such as the "Bund," the "Unified," the "Poale-Zion" and the "Volks-Party" have willingly placed themselves at the disposal of the sovereign and independent Ukraine and cooperated with us.

It is time to learn that the peaceful Jewish population, its women and children, have been oppressed in the same way as ours and deprived of national liberty. This population has lived with us for centuries and shared our pleasures and our sorrows.

The chivalrous troops who bring fraternity, equality and liberty to all the nationalities of Ukraine must not listen to the invaders and provocateurs who thirst for human blood. Neither can they remain indifferent in the face of the tragic fate of the Jews. He who becomes an accomplice to such crimes is a traitor and an enemy of our country, and he must be placed beyond the pale of human society.

Officers and Cossacks! The entire world is amazed at your heroism. Do not tarnish it, even accidentally by an infamous adventure, and do not dishonor our republic in the eyes of the world; our enemies have exploited the pogroms against us. They affirm that we are not worthy of an independent and sovereign existence and that we must be enslaved once again.

Officers and Cossacks! Insure the victory by directing your arms against the real enemy, and remember that our pure cause necessitates clean hands. I expressly order you to drive away with your arms all who incite you to pogroms and to bring them before the courts as enemies of the State. And the tribunals will judge them for their acts and the most severe penalties of the law will be inflicted upon all those found guilty.

The Government of the Ukrainian People's Republic has addressed an appeal to all inhabitants of the country to resist the activities of our enemies who provoked the pogroms of the Jewish population.

I order all troops to listen well and to retain this appeal and to spread it as much as possible among their comrades and among the people.

Petlura Commander in Chief
(*New York Times*, 20 June 1926, section 8)

7. V. Vynnychenko, *Vidrodzhennia natsii*. vol. 2 (Vienna: Dzvin, 1920), 78–9.
8. Solomon I. Goldelman, *Jewish National Autonomy in Ukraine, 1917–1920* (Chicago: Ukrainian Research and Information Institute, 1968), 14.
9. Ivanys, *Symon Petliura*, 148.
10. Margolin, *The Jews of Eastern Europe*, 126–8.
11. Elie Dobkowski, *Affaire Petlura-Schwartzbard* (Paris: L'Union Federative Socialiste, 1927), 54.
12. Ibid., 17–60; Desroches, *The Ukrainian Problem*, 66–82; "The Lurid Trial," 36, 41–2; Margolin, *The Jews of Eastern Europe*, 126–42; Margolin, *Ukraïna i politika Antanty: Zapiski evreia i grazhdanina* (Berlin: S. Efron, 1922), 270–5; A. Iakovliv, *Paryz'ka trahediia 25 travnia 1926 roku: Do protsesu Shvartsbarda* (Prague: Mizhorhanizatsiinyi komitet dlia vshanuvannia pam'iati Symona Petliury v Prazi, 1930), 228–58; Taras Hunczak, "A Reappraisal of Symon Petliura and Ukrainian-Jewish Relations, 1917–1921," *Jewish Social Studies*, 1969, no. 3, 163–83; Ievhen Onats'kyi, *Ukraïns'ka mala entsyklopediia*, vol. 14 (Buenos Aires: Administratura UAPTs v Argentini, 1967), 2075–6.
13. "The Lurid Trial," 36.
14. Desroches, *The Ukrainian Problem*, 94–5.
15. Dobkowski, *Affaire Petlura-Schwartzbard*, 9.
16. Desroches, *The Ukrainian Problem*, 87.
17. "The Lurid Trial," 41.
18. Desroches, *The Ukrainian Problem*, 98.
19. Ibid., 89–90.
20. Ibid., 90.
21. Ibid., 98–9.
22. Ibid., 99–100.
23. Ibid., 102.
24. Ibid., 103.
25. "The Lurid Trial," 36.
26. Lev Bykovsky, *Solomon I. Goldelman: A Portrait of a Politician and Educator, 1885–1974; A Chapter in Ukrainian-Jewish Relations* (New York: Ukrainian Historical Association, 1980), 83–9; Hunczak, "Reappraisal," 163–83; Arnold Margolin, *Ukraine and Policy of the Entente* (N.p.: A. Margolina, 1977), 194–256; Shandruk, *Arms of Valor*, 143–51; *Symon Petliura—derzhavnyi muzh*, 119–27; Desroches, *The Ukrainian Problem*, 66–108; Dobkowski, *Affaire Petlura-Schwartzbard*, 9–62; F. Pigido et al, eds., *Material Concerning Ukrainian-Jewish Relations during the Years of the Revolution (1917–1921): Collection of Documents and Testimonies by Prominent Jewish Political Workers* (Munich: Ukrainian Information Bureau, 1956), 22–102; Ivanys, *Symon Petliura*, 236–55; Iakovliv, *Paryz'ka trahediia*, 7–35; Iakovliv, "Paryz'ka trahediia," in *Zbirnyk pam'iati Symona Petliury*, 228-58; Tokarzhevs'kyi-Karashevych, "Symon Petliura v Paryzhi," 119–27.

Bibliography

Primary Sources (Documents and Memoirs)

Ademar. "Kurin' smerty: Spomyny z Podillia z 1920 r." *IKAChK na 1929 rik*, 151–2.

"Ad'iutant Holovnoho otamana." *Tr* (New York), no. 9 (1961), 12–15.

Agapev, V. P. "Korpus Generala Dovbor-Musnitskago." *BD* (Berlin), no. 4 (1928), 180–94.

Akty i dokumenty dotyczące sprawy granic Polski na Konferencji Pokojowej w Paryżu, 1918–1919. Paris: n.p., 1920.

Aleksashenko, Andrei P., comp. *Protiv Denikina: Sbornik vospominanii*. Moscow: Voennoe izdatel'stvo, 1919.

Alekseev, I. *Iz vospominanii levogo esera*. Moscow: Gosizdat, 1922.
Recollections by a Left Russian Socialist Revolutionary about the underground movement in Ukraine in 1917 and 1918.

Alekseev, S. A., comp. *Revoliutsiia i grazhdanskaia voina v opisaniiakh belogvardeitsev*. 5 vols. Moscow: Gos. izd-vo, 1926–30.
A compilation of memoirs by leading military and political figures, including VA generals such as Denikin, Wrangel, Lukomskii, and Krasnov, and materials on such anti-White movements as the Greens and Makhno and on events in Ukraine.

———. *Revoliutsiia na Ukraine po memuaram belykh*. Moscow: Gos. izd-vo, 1930.
Selections from memoirs by leading Russian and Ukrainian military and political figures dealing with the Ukrainian revolution.

Al'mendingen, G. "K pis'mu v redaktsiiu rotmistra Labinskago." *Pereklichka* (New York), no. 106 (1960), 13–15.

Alys'kevych, Mykola. "Piv roku pid bol'shevykamy." *LChK*, 1933, no. 9, 21–3; no. 10, 10–13; no. 11, 20–2; no. 12, 20–4.

———. "Vyshkil Komandy etapu U.H.A. na Ukraïni: Spomyn." *LChK*, 1932, no. 3, 14–17.

Andriievs'kyi, Viktor. *Z mynuloho*. 2 vols. Berlin: Ukraïns'ke slovo, 1923.
Recollections of events from May 1917 through the summer of 1919, primarily

in Poltava gubernia, where the author was a prominent politician.

Andrukh, Ivan. "Sichovi stril'tsi u Korpusi gen. Natiïva: Zi spomyniv b. p. Ivana Andrukha." *LChK*, 1930, no. 4, 5–8.

Andrusiak, Mykola. "Sered ostankiv U.H.A.: Spomyny." *IKAChK na 1932 rik*, 113–15.

Antonchuk, D. "Ukraïns'ko-pol's'ki perehovory pro zamyrennia v travni 1919, vystup Kurdynovs'koho: Uryvok zi spomyniv." *IKAChK na 1939 rik*, 174–8. An eyewitness's account of Polish-Ukrainian negotiations in May 1919.

Antonov-Ovsiienko, Volodymyr (Antonov-Ovseenko, Vladimir A.). "V borot'bi proty Denikina i soiuznyts'koï okupatsiï." *LR*, 1931, no. 1 (45), 111–54.

———. "V borot'bi proty Dyrektoriï," *LR*, 1929, no. 5–6 (38–9), 142–86; 1930, no. 1 (40), 103–32; no. 2 (41), 104–51; no. 3–4 (42–3), 78–107; no. 5 (44), 173–93. An account of the UNR Directory's social policy in 1919, the Bolshevik intervention of 1919, the struggle for power in Ukraine, the French intervention, and Makhno's campaigns against Denikin.

———. "V borot'bi za Radians'ku Ukraïnu." *LR*, 1931, no. 2 (46), 85–114; no. 3 (47); no. 4 (48), 78–107; 1932, no. 5 (49), 112–52.
A detailed account, based on the author's memoirs and documents, of Makhno's campaigns against Denikin in the spring of 1919, the conflict with the Bolsheviks, Makhno's alleged cooperation with Hryhoriïv, and Hryhoriïv's uprising against the Bolsheviks.

———. *V revoliutsii*. Moscow: Gos. izd-vo politicheskoi literatury, 1957.

———. *V semnadtsatom godu*. Moscow: Gos. izd-vo khudozhestvennoi literatury, 1933.

———. *Zapiski o grazhdanskoi voine*. 4 vols. Moscow: Vysshii voennyi redaktsionnyi sovet, 1924–33.
Fairly objective, well-documented memoirs by one of the commanders of the Red Army, which include orders, telegrams, letters, and recorded conversations and deal with the campaigns on the Volga and Ukrainian fronts and with the organization, tactics, and strategy of the Red Army.

Anulov, F. "Protiv Iuzhnoi gruppy voisk 12-oi armii na Ukraine: Vospominaniia." *VR*, 1926, no. 1–2, 60–74.

Arbatov, Zinovii Iu. "Ekaterinoslav, 1917–1922 gg." *ARR* 12 (1923): 83–148.
Valuable memoirs on the vicissitudes of the revolutionary period in Katerynoslav, stressing the terror of the Denikin and Bolshevik forces.

Arkas, Mykola M. "U hostiakh v otamana Bozhka." *KUNS*, 1965, 111–14.

Arski, Stefan, and Józef Chudek, comps. *Galicyjska działalność wojskowa Piłsudskiego, 1906–1914: Dokumenty*. Warsaw: Państwowe Wydawnictwo Naukowe, 1967.

Artiushenko, Iurii. "Do istoriï ukraïns'koï armiï ta ïï tradytsiï." *BSBUVK*, 1962, no. 12, 7–9.

———. *Heneral Borys Podzhio: Spohad.* Chicago: Ukraïns'kyi voienno-istorychnyi instytut, 1955.

———. "Mizh frontamy: Uryvok iz spohadiv iz kintsia 1919-ho i pochatku 1920-ho roku." *KUI na rik 1938*, 81–3.

———. "Symon Petliura." *SU*, 1964, no. 5, 1–4.

———. "Zmahannia ukraïns'koho narodu v 1917–21 rokakh." *Kalendar "Slovo" na 1978 rik* (Toronto), 52–60.

Astrov, N. "Iasskoe soveshchanie: Iz dokumentov." *GMChS* 16, no. 3 (1926), 39–76.

Aten, Marion, and Arthur Orrmont. *Last Train over Rostov Bridge.* New York: Messner, 1961.

Auerbakh, V. A. "Revoliutsionnoe obshchestvo po lichnym vospominaniiam." *ARR* 14 (1924): 5–38; 16 (1925): 49–99.

Memoirs of the revolution largely in Ukraine, including Katerynoslav gubernia.

Aussem, V. "K istorii povstanchestva na Ukraine: O dvukh partizanskikh diviziiakh." *LR*, 1926, no. 5, 7–21.

An authoritative article by a Bolshevik partisan leader describing the organization of Bolshevik partisans in the neutral zone in the second half of 1918; with an appendix of five documents.

Averdukh, K. K. (Averius). *Odesskaia "Chrezvychaika", bol'shevistskii zastenok: Fakty i nabliudaniia.* Kishinev: n.p., 1920.

B., D. "Z boïv za Sicheslav: Voiennyi spomyn." *Iliustrovanyi kaliendar "Kanadiis'koho ukraïntsia" na rik 1928* (Winnipeg), 203–7.

B., P., and B. O. "2. (kolomyis'ka) brygada v chervnevii protyofenzyvi 1919 r.: Uryvok iz dnevnyka." *US*, no. 13 (1922), 3–5; no. 14, 11–14; no. 15, 11–12.

B., N. "Polevyi lazaret IX Halyts'koï brygady." *LChK*, 1935, no. 12, 17–18.

Babiuk, Andrii. "Utecha USS z hlybyny Rossiï." *VSVU*, no. 108 (1916), 483–5.

Bachyns'kyi, Ievhen. "'Iablunia tsvite': De-shcho z davnikh spomyniv pro Petliuru i osobyste znaiomstvo z nym v Zhenevi." *Tr* (Paris), 1938, no. 22 (622), 15–23; no. 25 (625), 3–9.

Bachyns'kyi, Leonid. "General-polkovnyk Oleksa Halkin." *LChK*, 1938, no. 12, 6.

———. "Polkovnyk Borys Palii-Neïlo." *LChK*, 1936, no. 12, 18–19.

Bachyns'kyi, Vasyl'. "Povstanchyi viddil Bratslavs'koho povitu." *LChK*, 1930, no. 3, 5–6.

———. "Vesna 1920 roku." *LChK*, 1934, no. 4, 2–3.

Baidok, Ivan. "Nastup na Vynnytsiu v kvitni 1920 r." *LChK*, 1936, no. 6, 11–14.

Baiko, Mykola. "4 zhovtnia 1919 roku." *ZD* 2 (1930): 148–50.

Bandrowski, Juliusz K. *The Great Battle on the Vistula.* London: Low and Marston, 1921.

Bane, Suda Lorena, and Ralph Haswell Lutz, eds. *Organization of American Relief in Europe, 1918–1919: Including Negotiations Leading Up to the Establishment of the Office of Director General of Relief at Paris by the Allied and Associated Powers*. Stanford: Stanford University Press, 1943.

Baranowski, Władysław. "Rozmowy z Piłsudskim od 1916–1931 r." *N* (Warsaw) 18 (1938): 21–66.

Batsutsa, Iu. "Moï zustrichi z Holovnym otamanom." *Sv*, 1957, no. 100.

Bechhofer, C. E. *In Denikin's Russia and the Caucasus, 1919–1920: Being the Record of a Journey to South Russia, the Crimea, Armenia, Georgia, and Baku in 1919 and 1920*. London: Collins, 1921.

An account by a British war correspondent emphasizing conditions within the VA from October 1918 through March 1920.

Bekesevych, P. "Moï spomyny z ostannikh dniv okupatsiï Ukraïny avstro-nimets'kymy viis'kamy." *LChK*, 1931, no. 3, 4–6.

Beliaevskii, Vasilii A. *Kto vinovat: Vospominaniia o belom dvizhenii, 1918–1920*. Buenos Aires: Talleres Gráficos "Dorrego," 1960(?).

Beloe delo: Letopis' beloi bor'by. 7 vols. Edited by A. A. Lampe. Paris and Berlin: Mednyi vsadnik, 1926–33.

A collection of documents and memoirs about the White movement, including accounts of the civil war in the south by V. Shul'gin, A. Filimonov, P. Shatilov, and others. Vols. 5–6 contain Wrangel's memoirs.

Belyi arkhiv. Edited by Ia. M. Kisovoi. 3 vols. Paris, 1926–8.

Documents, memoirs, and articles on the history of the Bolshevik and anti-Bolshevik Russian movements, including transcripts of conferences, correspondence among its leaders, accounts by participants, and agents' reports from major cities.

Belyi, M. P., R. A. Kuznetsova, and K. F. Chumak, comps. *Vospominaniia o G. I. Kotovskom*. Kishinev: Kartiia moldoveniaske, 1961.

Ben', Vasyl'. "Vtecha S. Petliury z Kyieva: Spomyny." *KAD na rik 1934*, 99–100.

Berehul'ka, A. "Liutyi 1918 roku v Kyievi." *BSBUVK*, 1962, no. 10, 13–16.

Berezhanskii, Nik. "Pol'sko-sovetskii mir v Rige (Iz zapisok byv. redaktora)." *IS* 2 (1922): 110–47; 3 (1923): 109–50.

Berezhnyts'kyi, Mykhailo. "Ostannii rik na Velykii Ukraïni: Uryvok zi spomyniv." *IKAChK na 1934 rik*, 132–44.

Berkman, Alexander. *The Bolshevik Myth: Diary, 1920–1922*. New York: Boni and Liveright, 1925.

Critical observations of two years of political life in Soviet Russia and Ukraine by a Russian-American anarchist who met a number of revolutionary leaders.

Bezruchko, Marko. "Grupa S.S. v boiakh na pidstupakh do Kam'iantsia-Podil's'koho: Bii pid Smotrychem 22 lypnia 1919 roku." *IKAChK na 1927 rik*, 114–24.

———. "Sichovi stril'tsi v borot'bi za derzhavnist'." *ZD* 2 (1930): 47–72; 3 (1932): 55–108.

Bidnov, V. "Pershi dva akademichni roky Ukraïns'koho derzhavnoho universytetu v Kam'iantsi-Podil's'komu: Uryvok iz spohadiv." *LNV*, 1928, no. 11, 233–40; no. 12, 325–33.

Bielecki, Tadeusz. *W szkole Dmowskiego: Szkice i wspomnienia*. London: Polska Fundacja Kulturalna, 1968.

"Bii pid Krutamy." *Studens'kyi shliakh* (Lviv), 1933, no. 10–12, 262–87.

"Bii pid Krutamy 29 sichnia 1918," *NIKTP na 1938 rik*, 99–101.

Bilous, Iv. "Boï pid Korostenem v sichni 1919 roku." *VK*, 1969, no. 2 (38), 22–4.

Bizants. "Iahol'nytsia." *IKAChK na 1923 rik*, 52–9.

Bobriv, Vasyl'. "Do zustrichiv ta portretiv." *Sv*, 3 October 1927.

———. "Zustrichi ta portrety: Otaman Zelenyi." *Sv*, 27 July 1927.

"Boevye dokumenty N. A. Shchorsa." *Voenno-istoricheskii zhurnal* (Moscow), 1939, no. 1, 122–5.

Bohdanivets'. "Rozstril bohdanivtsiv na stantsiï Post Volyns'kyi." *KAV na 1957 rik* (Buenos Aires), 102–6.

Bohun, M. "Fragmenty zi spomyniv pro 'Narodnu oboronu Khersons'koi guberniï': Na peredodni kintsia Denikinshchyny na Khersonshchyni." *US*, no. 24 (1923), 32–7.

Boncza-Tomaszewski, Tadeusz. "Dembowa Wólka: Fragment wspomnień." *Pamiętnik Kijowski*, 3 (1966): 75–95.

Borkovs'kyi, Ivan. "Udar na Chortkiv." *LChK*, 1938, no. 7–8, 5–10.

Borman, Arkady. "My Meetings with White Russian Generals." *RR* 27, no. 2 (1968), 215–24.

Borodyievych, Ievhen. *V chotyrokutnyku smerty: Prychynky do tragediï U.H.A. na Velykii Ukraïni: Iz voiennoho zapysnyka 3-oï bryhady*. Lviv: Naukove tovarystvo im. Shevchenka, 1921. Reprint, New York: Hoverlia, 1975.

Bosh, Evgeniia B. *God bor'by: Bor'ba za vlast' na Ukraine s aprelia 1917 g. do nemetskoi okkupatsii*. Moscow: Gos. izd-vo, 1925.

———. *Natsional'noe pravitel'stvo i Sovetskaia vlast' na Ukraine*. Moscow: Kommunist, 1919.

An account by a prominent Russian Communist of the Bolshevik invasion and underground activities in Ukraine from 1917 through the first half of 1918.

Bozhyk, Stepan. "Deshcho pro ukraïns'kykh partyzan v 1918 rotsi: Uryvok z dennyka." *IKAChK na 1924 rik*, 140–4.

Brandt, Rolf. "With the Soviet Army." *LA*, 2 October 1920, 28–30.

Bredis, Ie. "Partiine pidpillia v Odesi za denikinshchyny: Narys." *LR*, 1930, no. 3–4 (42–3), 110–37.

Brzoz, Czesław, and Adam Rolin'ski, eds. *Bij bolszewika!: Rok 1920 w przekazie historycznym i literackim*. Cracow: Libertas, 1990.

Brusilov, A. A. *Moi vospominaniia*. Moscow: Gos. izd-vo khudozhestvennoi literatury, 1950.

Brylyns'kyi, Maksym. "Na marginesi knyzhky 'General Tarnavs'kyi'." *LChK*, 1936, no. 3, 11–14.

———. "Z denikintsiamy: Opovidannia-spomyn." *LChK*, 1929, no. 2, 8–10.

———. "Zatyshok Sekhina: Epizod z chasiv moskovs'koï okupatsiï v Halychyni." *KUI na rik 1938*, 49–51.

Budberg, Aleksei P. *Dnevnik belogvardeitsa (Kolchakovskaia epopeia)*. Leningrad: Priboi, 1929.

Budennyi, Semen M. "K stat'e Riubi 'Operatsii konnitsy Budennogo vo vremia pol'skogo otstupleniia s Ukrainy'." *VR*, 1926, no. 12, 3–9.

———. *Krasnaia konnitsa: Sbornik statei*. Moscow: Gos. izd-vo, 1930.

Budny, Michał. "Misja Generała Berthélemy w Polsce w relacji Romana Michałowskiego," *N* (London) 15 (1982): 184–202.

Budnyi, Vsevolod B. "Heneral Mykhailo Krat—komandyr 1-oï Ukraïns'koï dyviziï UNA." *Sv*, 16–18 October 1979.

Bunyan, James, and H. H. Fisher, comps. *The Bolshevik Revolution, 1917–1918: Documents and Materials*. Stanford: Stanford University Press, 1934.

———. *Intervention, Civil War, and Communism in Russia, April–December, 1918: Documents and Materials*. Baltimore: The Johns Hopkins Press, 1936. A compilation of documents and texts, mostly from Soviet Russian sources; a useful guide to further study of the subject.

Burachyns'kyi, Andrii. "Moia vidpovid'." *LChK*, 1930, no. 6, 7–10.

Burcew, Włodzimierz. "Moje spotkanie z Piłsudskim w więzieniu na Syberii i za granicą." *N* (Warsaw) 18, no. 3 (1938), 331–44.

Burnadz, M. "Na ukraïns'ko-rumuns'komu pohranychu: Spomyn." *IKAChK na 1931 rik*, 131–41.

Bykovs'kyi, Lev. *Na kavkaz'ko-turets'komu fronti: Spomyny z 1916–1918 rr.* Winnipeg: Instytut doslidiv Volyni, 1968.

———. "Spohady pro pochatky UVK v 1917." *UK*, 1972, no. 4 (22), 16–19.

Bytyns'kyi, M. "Do 15. richnytsi boiu pid Krutamy." *H*, 1933, no. 10, 12–19.

———. "Kruty." *BSBUVK*, 1962, no. 4, 10–12.

———. "Navkolo Bazaru." *VK*, 1971, no. 6 (56), 11–17.

———. "Oborona Zamostia: Spohad z nahody 35 rokovyn." *NDni*, no. 68 (1955), 22–3.

———. "Symon Petliura: Do 10. richnytsi smerty." *H*, 1936, no. 1–2, 7–8.

Carton de Wiart, Adrian. *Happy Odyssey: The Memoirs of Lieutenant-General Sir Adrian Carton de Wiart*. Foreword by Winston S. Churchill. London: Jonathan Cape, 1950.

Ch., M. "Desiat' dniv u Kyïvi v sichni 1919 r.: Spomyny z Trudovoho kongresu." *LChK*, 1931, no. 5, 5–8; no. 6, 3–6. Memoirs about the participation of the Galician delegation at the Labor Congress in Kyiv in January 1919, the unification of the UNR and ZUNR, and political conditions there.

Ch., V. "Spohad pro povstannia proty Het'mana v Poltavi." *T*, no. 9 (1928), 96–100.
Chabanivs'kyi, V. "Vstup ukraïns'kykh viis'k do Kyïva 31 serpnia 1919 roku." *ZD* 8 (1938): 152–5.
Chaika, Leonid. "Na krain'omu khutori: Zi spohadiv povstantsiv." *IKAChK na 1925 rik*, 119–23.
Chaikovs'kyi, Iosyf. "Spohady." *A*, 24 June, 1 July, 22 July 1983.
Cheriachukin, A. "Donskiia delegatsii na Ukrainu i v Berline v 1918–1919 g." *DL* 3 (1924): 163–231.
  Valuable memoirs of the Don Cossack envoy to the hetman government dealing with the negotiation of the Ukrainian-Don Cossack border, the political conditions in Ukraine, the anti-hetman activities of Denikin's followers, the uprising against the hetman, and the establishment of the UNR Directory.
Cherikover, I. "Antisemitizm i pogromy na Ukraine v period Tsentral'noi Rady i Getmana." In S. A. Alekseev, comp., *Revoliutsiia na Ukraine po memuaram belykh*, 239–76. Moscow: Gos. izd-vo, 1930.
Chciuk, Andrzej. "List do redakcji." *K*, 1960, no. 4, 150–1.
Chervontsi: Spohady veteraniv Chervonoho kozatstva (Kyiv: Molod', 1968).
Chmielewski, Jan. E. "Pierwsze lata korporacji studentów polaków w Kijowie r. 1884–1892: Garść wspomnień." *N* (Warsaw) 19 (1939), no. 1 (51), 107–35.
Chojnowski, A. *Piłsudczycy u władzy: Dzieje Bezpartyjnego Bloku Współpracy z Rządem*. Wrocław: Ossolineum, 1986.
Chornyi, Serhii. "Storinka z Druhoho zymovoho pokhodu," *ZD* 3 (1932): 192–205.
Chotyry, Od. "Iz zapysnyka harmatchyka." *IKAChK na 1922 rik*, 35–9.
Choulgine, A. [Shul'hyn, Oleksander]. *L'Ukraine contre Moscou, 1917*. Paris: F. Alcan, 1935.
  Memoirs by the minister of foreign affairs of the UNR government-in-exile dealing mainly with Ukraine's diplomatic relations with the Entente and Soviet Russia.
Chubatyi, Mykola. "Rizdviani sviata 1919 roku: Spomyny z-pered 32 rokiv." *Sv*, 6 January 1951.
Chubinskii, M. "'Na Donu': Iz vospominanii ober-prokurora." *DL* 1 (1923): 131–68; 3 (1924): 268–309.
Ch-yi, V. "Zymoiu 1919–20 r." *US*, no. 5 (1921), 28–32.
Chykalenko, Hanna. "Materiialy do biohrafiï Ievhena Chykalenka." *LNV*, 1930, no. 6, 510–23; no. 7–8, 631–42.
Chykalenko, Ievhen. *Shchodennyk, 1907–1917*. Lviv: Chervona kalyna, 1931.
———. *Uryvok z moïkh spomyniv za 1917 r.* Prague: Fond im. Ie. Chykalenka pry Ukraïns'komu akademichnomu komiteti, 1932.
———. "V Kyievi tomu 25 lit: Vyïmka iz shchodennyka." *KP*, 1933, 88–108.
Chykalenko, Levko. "Literatura desiatykh rokovyn." *PIB*, 1937, no. 5–6, 1–11.
———. *Nasha bat'kivshchyna: Spohady, 1918–1919*. N.p.: n.d.
———. "Pomylka Tsentral'noï Rady." *KAD na rik 1937*, 96–100.

An authoritative account of the Central Rada's agrarian policy, Bolshevik propaganda in Ukraine, and the feelings of the peasantry.

———. "Sionisty i 'Sionisty'." *Tr* (Paris), 1926, no. 49, 2–6.

———. *Uryvky zi spohadiv z rokiv 1919–1920.* New York: Nasha bat'kivshchyna, 1963.

Chyzhevs'kyi, M. "15 dib na okupovanii Moskvoiu Ukraïni: Z 4 po 19 lystopada 1921 roku." *ZD* 3 (1932): 140–55.

Czerniawski, Jerzy. "Z mojej służby w Belwederze." *ZH* 33 (1975): 148–87.

Czernin, Ottokar. *In the World War.* London: Cassel, 1919.

"D. Doroshenko pro P. Skoropads'koho 1919 r." *SD*, 1934, no. 11–12, 857–9.

D., N. "Z moïkh spohadiv pro M. Hrushevs'koho: Protses SVU; smert' i pokhoron M. Hrushevs'koho." *Ukraïna* (Paris) 9 (1953): 744–7.

Dąbski, Jan. *Pokój Ryski: Wspomnienia, pertraktacje, tajne układy z Joffem, listy.* Warsaw: n.p., 1931.

Danilov, I. "Vospominaniia o moei podnevol'noi sluzhbe u bol'shevikov." *ARR* 14 (1924): 39–131; 16 (1925): 162–230.

A valuable account by a Bolshevik officer who defected to the West, which describes the Bolshevik campaigns against Makhno from the end of 1920 to the spring of 1921.

Danylovych, Kost'. "Kil'ka zustrichiv z Holovnym otamanom na Velykii Ukraïni roku 1919." *Tr* (Paris), 1936, no. 21–2 (525–6), 16–23.

Dashkevych, Roman. "Marshal Pilsuds'kyi i pochatky ukraïns'kykh zbroinykh syl pered svitovoiu viinoiu: Spomyn." *D*, 24 May 1935.

———. "Zdobuttia Kyieva." *VK*, 1966, no. 1 (22), 18–21.

Daushkov, Serhii. "Ostannia stiika: Opovidannia z rumuns'koho frontu." *IKAChK na 1931 rik*, 101–5.

———. "Strashni khvylyny: Uryvky zi spomyniv." *IKAChK na 1932 rik*, 38–46.

Davatts, Vladimir Kh. *Gody: Ocherki piatiletnei bor'by.* Belgrade: Russkaia tipografiia, 1926.

———. *Na Moskvu.* Paris: I. Rirakhovskii, 1921.

Davnyi, R. *Pro sichovykh stril'tsiv.* Vienna: Chornohora, 1921.

Memoirs of an officer describing the organization of the Sich Riflemen and the campaign against the Bolsheviks and VA from the fall of 1917 to the end of 1919; it includes an article by Dmytro Doroshenko about the cadets massacred by the Bolsheviks at Kruty.

Degras, Jane, ed. *The Communist International, 1919–1943. Documents.* London: Cass, 1971.

———. *Soviet Documents on Foreign Policy.* Vol. 1, *1917–1924* London: Oxford University Press, 1951.

Degtiarev, L. "Politotdel v otstuplenii: Vospominaniia iz voiny s poliakami 1920 g." *PR*, 1924, no. 12 (35), 212–47.

"Deiatel'nost' Taganrogskago tsentra Dobrovol'cheskoi armii, 1918–1919 g.g." *BA* 2–3 (1928): 133–7.

Denikin, Anton I. "Bor'ba generala Kornilova." *F*, no. 37 (1937), 12–13.

An account of the formation of VA by Gen. Alekseev in the Don region at the end of 1917.

———. *La décomposition de l'armée et du pouvoir, février–septembre 1917*. Paris: J. Povolozky, 1922.

———. "Getmanstvo i Direktoriia na Ukraine." In S. A. Alekseev, comp., *Revoliutsiia na Ukraine po memuaram belykh*, 136–185. Moscow: Gos. izd-vo, 1930.

A selection from vols. 3–5 of the author's memoirs, *Ocherki russkoi smuty*, dealing with the hetman government, German, Bolshevik, and anti-Bolshevik Russian policies in Ukraine in 1918, the establishment of the UNR Directory government, and French intervention in southern Ukraine.

———. "Kubanskii pokhod." *F*, no. 41 (1938), 13–17; no. 42 (1938), 2–15.

An account of the war between the VA and Red Army in the Kuban during the winter and spring of 1918, the death of Gen. Kornilov, the formation of a VA unit in Jassy by Gen. Drozdovskii, and its march to the Don.

———. *Ocherki russkoi smuty*. 5 vols. Paris: J. Povolozky, 1921–6.

Valuable memoirs, which include numerous documents, of the period from the outbreak of World War I to April 1920 by the commander of the VA.

———. "Okrainnyi vopros." *Poslednyia novosti* (Paris), n.d.

———. "Po'sha i Dobrovol'cheskaia armiia." *GMChS* 17, no. 4 (1926), 175–87.

———. *The Russian Turmoil: Memoirs Military, Social and Political*. London: Hutchinson, 1922.

———. *Sprostowanie historji: Odpowiedź Polakom*. Paris: Dobrowolec, 1937.

———. *The White Army*. London: Jonathan Cape, 1930. Reprint, Westport, Conn.: Hyperion Press, 1973.

"Denikintsy o sostoianii svoego tyla: Soobshchenie Kandidova." *KA*, 1935, no. 5 (72), 191–9.

A report sent to Gen. Wrangel at the end of March 1920 by a member of a military court; it describes the causes of the evacuation of Odessa by the VA and its demoralization.

Dennyk Nachal'noï komandy Ukraïns'koï Halyts'koï Armiï. New York: Chervona Kalyna, 1974.

Derevenskii, Iv. "Bandity: Ocherki perioda grazhdanskoi voiny." *Byloe* (Leningrad) 24 (1924): 252–73.

An account by a Soviet agent in a Ukrainian village of the activities of Orlyk, Struk, and other partisan leaders in the Kyiv region and of the peasants' attitude from August 1920 to May 1922.

Derkach, Hryhorii. "29. kvitnia 1918 r. u svitli 'Spomyniv' Het'mana Pavla

Skoropads'koho." In *Za velych natsiï: U dvadtsiati rokovyny vidnovlennia Ukraïns'koï Hetmans'koï Derzhavy*, 25–31. Edited by Mykola Pasika, Mykhailo Karpyshyn, and Teofil' Kostruba. Lviv, 1938. Reprint, New York: Bulava, 1955.

Diachenko, Petro. "Chorni zaporozhtsi: Spomyny komandyra polku Chornykh zaporozhtsiv." In *U 50-richchia Zymovoho pokhodu Armiï UNR*, 166–95. Edited by M. Krat and F. Hrinchenko. New York: Ordens'ka rada Ordena Zaliznoho khresta Armiï UNR, 1973.

Diakiv, Iaromyr. "Strategichne polozhennia UHA po perekhodi cherez Zbruch litom 1919 r." *US*, no. 28 (1923), 13–16.

A valuable account of conditions in the UHA in the summer of 1919 and of its strategy for an offensive against the Bolsheviks in Odessa or Kyiv.

Die deutsche Okkupation der Ukraine: Geheimdokumente. Strasbourg: Prométhée, 1937.

A collection of secret official German documents published abroad by the German Communist party during the Nazi-Soviet propaganda war. The documents emphasize German military domination and interference in Ukrainian civilian life, the requisitioning of food and raw materials, and Germany's commercial rapacity; they castigate all Ukrainians who did not resist the Central Powers or who participated in non-Communist activity in support of Ukrainian independence.

Direktivy komandovaniia frontov Krasnoi Armii, 1917–1922 gg.: Sbornik dokumentov. 2 vols. Compiled by T. F. Kariaeva. Moscow: Voennoe izdatel'stvo, 1971.

Divnych, Antin. "V Zhytomiri: Nacherk iz pobutu U.H.A. v 1919 r." *IKAChK na 1923 rik*, 101–6.

Dłuski, Kazimierz. *Wspomnienia z Paryża od 4. I. do 10. VII. 1919 r.* Warsaw: n.p., 1929.

"Dnevnik i vospominaniia kievskoi studentki," *ARR* 15 (1924): 209–52.

A diary describing political events in Kyiv from February 1919 through March 1920 and stressing the Bolshevik and VA terror there.

Do Ministerjum Spraw Zagranicznych: O przedstawicielstwach i organizacyach ukraińskich zagranicą. Warsaw, 27 May 1920. Ms.

Do Naczelnego Dowództwa W. P. w Warszawie. London, 14 February 1920. Ms.

Dobkowski, Elie. *Affaire Petlura-Schwartzbard*. Paris: L'Union Federative Socialiste, 1926.

Dobranitskii, M. "Zelenye partizany, 1918–1920 gg." *PR*, 1924, no. 8–9, 72–98.

Dobrians'kyi, Agaton. "Tsars'ka imperiia vpala, rik 1917: Uryvok iz spomyniv." *IKAChK na 1937 rik*, 13–20.

Dobrynin, V. *Bor'ba s bol'shevizmom na iuge Rossii: Uchastie v bor'be donskogo kazachestva, fevral' 1917–mart 1920; Ocherk*. Prague: Slavianskoe izdatel'stvo, 1921.

A survey of Don Cossack campaigns against the Bolsheviks by the chief of intelligence and the operational department of the Don Cossack Army.
"Documents and Information." *Bulletin of Ukrainian Information* (Geneva), 2 May 1931, 7–12.
Documents on British Foreign Policy, 1919–1939. Edited by E. L. Woodward and Rohan Butler. London: His Majesty's Stationary Office, 1948.
"Doklad nachal'niku operatsionnago otdeleniia germanskago vostochnago fronta o polozhenii del na Ukraine v marte 1918 goda." *ARR* 1 (1921): 288–94.
A report by a German publicist, Collin Ross, sent from Kyiv to the Command of the German Eastern Front in March 1918 about conditions in Ukraine.
"Doklad o deiatel'nosti Kievskago tsentra Dobrovol'cheskoi armii." *BA*, 2–3 (1928): 119–32.
Dokument sudovoï pomylky: Protses Shvartsbarda. Paris: Natsionalistychne vydavnytstvo v Evropi, 1958.
"Dokumenty." *PD*, 1919, no. 14, 597–607.
"Dokumenty dyplomatyczne Rządów Sowieckich Republik Rosji, Ukrainy, Litwy, Białorusi i Łotwy, rok 1919." *PD*, 1919, no. 13, 554–8.
Dokumenty i materiały do historii stosunków polsko-radzieckich, vols. 2–3. Edited by Natalia Gąsiorowska, I. A. Chreniow, et al. Warsaw: Książka i Wiedza, 1964.
Dokumenty Naczelnego Komitetu Narodowego, 1914–1917. Cracow: Naczelny Komitet Narodowy, 1917.
Dokumenty o razgrome germanskikh okkupantov na Ukraine v 1918 godu. Edited by I. I. Mints and E. N. Gorodetskii. Moscow: Gospolitizdat, 1942.
"Dokumenty: O urzędzie 'Polskiego kraju'." *N* (Warsaw), 1932, no. 2, 291–307; no. 3, 435–52.
Dol'nyts'kyi, Myron. "Nad propastiu." *US*, no. 10 (1921), 8–9; no. 11, 6–7; no. 12, 9–11; no. 13, 5–7; no. 14, 5–7; no. 15 (1922), 6–8.
Dombrovs'kyi, I. "Druhyi zymovyi pokhid: Spohady uchasnyka." *Kalendar-al'manakh Ukraïns'koï narodnoï pomochi, 1914–1954* (Pittsburgh), 113–21.
Dombrovs'kyi, Oleksander. "Nad svizhoiu mohyloiu (Polkovnyk Oleksander Petliura)." *Sv*, 21 March 1951.
Dontsov, Dmytro. "Mazepyns'kyi myr, 1918–1928." *IKAChK na 1928 rik*, 37–43.
———. *Rik 1918, Kyiv: Zapysky.* Toronto: Homin Ukraïny, 1954.
A valuable diary of events in Kyiv from May 1918 through February 1919.
Dniprovyi, M. "Skoropads'kyi ta ioho 'Ukraïns'ka Derzhava'." *VU*, no. 3 (1954), 34–8.
Doroshenko, Dmytro. "Deshcho pro zakordonnu polityku Ukraïns'koï Derzhavy v 1918 r." *KhU* 2 (1920–1): 49–64.
———. "Iak ukraïntsi naddniprians'ki pomahaly svoïm naddnistrians'kym bratam u chasi halyts'koï ruïny 1914–1916 rokiv: Uryvok iz spomyniv." *KAD na rik 1924*, 23–39.

———. "Getmanstvo 1918 goda na Ukraine: Po lichnym vospominaniiam i dokumentam." *GMChS* 8, no. 5 (1927), 133–64.

———. *Moï spomyny pro davnie-mynule (1901–1914 roky)*. Winnipeg: Trident Press, 1949.

———. *Moï spomyny pro nedavnie mynule (1914–1920)*. 4 vols. Lviv: Chervona Kalyna, 1923–4. Reprint, Munich: Ukraïns'ke vydavnytstvo, 1969.

Valuable memoirs based on archival materials and the author's own recollections of conditions in Ukraine and the revolutionary years, emphasizing the persecution of Ukrainian national life in Russian-occupied Galicia during World War I.

———. "Pis'mo." *Voz*, September–October 1951, 152–7.

A letter written in response to S. Melgunov's article about Russo-Ukrainian relations. Doroshenko maintains that the Ukrainian people do not hate Russians, but are striving for the independence of both Ukraine and Russia.

———. "Voina i revoliutsiia na Ukraine: Iz vospominanii." *IS* 1 (1922): 207–45; 2 (1922): 180–205; 4 (1923): 178–209; 5 (1924): 73–125.

Memoirs of the Central Rada's conflict with the Provisional Government and Russian political groups, the first Bolshevik invasion, and the invitation to Austro-German troops to help repel the enemies.

Doroshenko, Volodymyr. "Mykhailo Hrushevs'kyi—hromads'kyi diiach, polityk i publitsyst." *O* (Chicago), 1957, no. 6, 15–19; no. 10, 23–6; no. 11, 18–19.

———. "Pershyi prezydent vidnovlenoï ukraïns'koï derzhavy: Mykhailo Hrushevs'kyi, ioho zhyttia i diial'nist'." *O*, 1957, no. 1, 25–6; no. 2–3, 27–32.

———. "Politychnyi rozvytok Naddniprians'koï Ukraïny." *KAD na rik 1935*, 50–66.

———. "U dvadtsiatlitniu richnytsiu." *KAD na rik 1937*, 32–8.

Doroshenko-Savchenko, Natalia. "Dni radosty i nadiï." *Literaturnyi i hromads'ko-politychnyi kaliendar-al'manakh Dnipro na rik 1937*, 86–96.

———. "Pochatky ukraïns'koï revoliutsiï v Proskurovi: Ukraïns'ka hromada v Proskurovi ta ïï pratsia." *KAD na rik 1932*, 44–58.

———. "Poltavs'ki spomyny, 1917–20: Fragmenty." *KAD na rik 1933*, 56–92.

Dorożyńska [Zaleska], Elżbieta. *Na ostatniej placówce: Dziennik z życia wsi podolskiej w latach 1917–1921*. Warsaw: Gebethner i Wolff, 1925.

A Polish landowner and physician's diary of vicissitudes in Podillia gubernia in 1917–21.

Dotsenko, Oleksander. "Istoriia Zvenyhorods'koho kosha Vil'noho kozatstva." *IKAChK na 1933 rik*, 85–103.

———. *Litopys ukraïns'koï revoliutsiï: Materiialy i dokumenty do istoriï ukraïns'koï revoliutsii, 1917–1923*. Vol. 2, pts. 4–5. Lviv: the author. 1923–4. Reprint, Philadelphia: Doslidchyi instytut modernoï ukraïns'koï istoriï, 1988.

An authoritative work by Petliura's aide on the revolutionary period, based on official documents, the author's archives, diaries, recollections, and interviews with political and military leaders, and on contemporary Ukrainian and foreign publications.

———. *Zymovyi pokhid (7.XII.1919–6.V.1920)*. Warsaw: Ukraïns'kyi naukovyi instytut, 1932.

Dowbór-Muśnicki, Józef. *Krótki szkic do historiji I Polskiego Korpusu*. 3 vols. Warsaw: Placówka, 1919.

———. *Moje wspomnienia*. 2 vols. Warsaw: n.p., 1935.

Drabatyi, I. "Epizod z evakuatsiï Kyieva v 1919 r." *Tr* (New York), no. 30 (1964), 3–6.

———. "Holovnyi otaman Symon Petliura i Pershyi Ukraïns'kyi viis'kovyi z'ïzd u Kyievi." *Tr* (New York), no. 44 (1967), 20–1; no. 45 (1967), 17–19.

Drozdovskii, Mikhail G. *Dnevnik*. New York: Vseslavianskoe izdatel'stvo, 1963. A VA officer's diary describing the advance of his unit from Jassy through southern Ukraine to the Don from February through April 1918, conditions in Ukraine, the attitude of the population toward the Reds, Whites, and Germans, and the conflict within the VA.

Drymmer, Wiktor T. "Wspomnienia." *ZH* 28 (1974): 172–94; 29 (1974): 173–218.

Dubiv, Volodymyr. "Ulamok z moho zhyttia: Spomyn." *VSh*, June 1966, 737–44; July 1966, 916–23. An account of Bolshevik persecution in a Kharkiv prison at the end of 1920.

Dubreuil, Charles. *Deux années en Ukraine, 1917–1919*. Paris: H. Paulin, 1919.

Dubynets', Ivan. *Horyt' Medvedyn: Istorychno-memuarnyi narys*. New York: DOBRUS, 1952. Memoirs of the anti-Bolsehvik uprising in Medvedyn, Kaniv county, and its suppression at the end of 1920.

Dudko, Fedir. "Vid Muraviova do Dyrektoriï: Spomyny z 1918 roku." *KAD na rik 1938*, 41–60.

———. "Z bil'shovyts'koho Kyieva do Kyieva ukraïns'koho: Spohad pro muraviovs'ki chasy." *IKAChK na 1938 rik*, 54–65.

Duduk, Pavlo. "Kozaky na Oleksandrivshchyni: Spohad." *UK* 1973, no. 3, 24–6.

Dumin, Osyp (Krezub, A., pseud.). "Avstriis'ka 'intryga' i Lystopadovyi perevorot." *LChK*, 1933, no. 7–8, 13–18.

———. "Deshcho do istoriï pryhotuvannia povstannia proty het'mana Skoropads'koho." *VK*, 1964, no. 1 (13), 108–17.

———. "Deshcho pro stan Armiï UNR na perelomi 1918–19 r.: Na marginesi zvitu gen. Hrekova." *LChK*, 1934, no. 3, 4–8.

———. "Deutsche in der ukrainischen Armee, 1917–1920: Ein Kapitel aus der deutsch-ukrainischen Zusammenarbeit." *Volksforschung* (Stuttgart) 5 (1941–2): 37–49.

———. "Do istoriï povstannia otamana Zelenoho proty Dyrektoriï." *Sv*, 1927, nos. 227–8.

———. "Hrupa polk. Rogul's'koho: Zamitky i materiialy do ïï istoriï." *IKAChK na 1929 rik*, 51–64.

———. "Halychane i ïkh viis'kovo-organizatsiina pratsia na Nadniprianshchyni v 1917–1919 rr." *Nedilia: Kaliendar-al'manakh na 1930 rik* (Lviv), 85–92.

———. "Het'man Pavlo Skoropads'kyi, iak komandant I. Ukraïns'koho korpusa i nakaznyi otaman Vil'noho kozatstva." In *Za velych natsiï: U dvadtsiati rokovyny vidnovlennia Ukraïns'koï Het'mans'koï Derzhavy*, 46–52. Edited by Mykola Pasika, Mykhailo Karpyshyn, and Teofil' Kostruba. Lviv, 1938. Reprint, New York: Bulava, 1955.

———. "Iak zhynuv otaman Zelenyi." *LNV*, 1927, no. 10, 109–13.

An authoritative account of the relations between the partisans led by Zelenyi and the UNR Army and of Zelenyi's assassination by Denikin's intelligence.

———. "Kozats'kym shiakhom: Zi spomyniv pro pobut v partyzans'komu viddili v Hoshchovi." *SV*, 1922, no. 5–6; 1923, no. 1–2.

———. "Mestnyky: Spomyny iz partyzanky na Velykii Ukraïni." *KChK na 1924 rik*, 158–66.

An account of Ukrainian partisan activities in Poltava guberniia in July 1921.

———. "Motovylivs'kyi bii: Krytychni zavvahy do ioho istoriï." *IKAChK na 1928 rik*, 70–5.

———. "Na vesni revoliutsiï: Uryvok zi spomyniv." *IKAChK na 1932 rik*, 9–15.

———. "Nimtsi v ukraïns'kii armiï 1917–1920 rr." *P*, 1942, no. 2, 89–99.

———. "Obloha Kyïva: Spohady z lystopada–hrudnia 1918 r." *LNV*, 1928, no. 1, 25–40; no. 3, 242–51; no. 4, 309–24.

———. "Ofenzyva Kerens'koho." *IKAChK na 1937 rik*, 40–6.

———. "Partyzans'kyi zahin imeny otamana Zelenoho." *KChK na 1925 rik*, 110–16.

———. *Partyzany: Spomyny*. 2 vols. Lviv: Chervona kalyna, 1930.

———. "Partyzany: Zbirka spomyniv iz partyzanky na Naddniprians'kii Ukraïni." *LNV*, 1925, no. 7–8, 246–61; no. 9, 10–24.

———. "Persha umova Dyrektoriï UNR z nimtsiamy z dnia 17. XI. 1918 r." *LNV*, 1928, no. 5, 458–64.

———. "5-ta Khersons'ka strilets'ka dyviziia ta ïï perekhid na Zakarpattia v serpni 1920 r." *ZD* 9 (1938), 76–91.

———. "Pochatok Halyts'koho kurinia S.S." *IKAChK na 1926 rik*, 55–60.

———. "Povstannia otamana Zelenoho proty Dyrektoriï v sichni 1919 r." *LNV*, 1927, no. 5, 26–41.

———. "Povstannia proty het'mana Skoropads'koho i Sichovi stril'tsi: Kil'ka zavvah do ioho istoriï." *LNV*, 1928, no. 11, 219–25; no. 12, 309–18.

———. "Pro dzherela ukraïns'koho viis'kovoho rukhu v 1917 r.," *V*, 1937, no. 7–8, 587–91.

———. "Tabor okremoho zahonu S.S. v Bilii Tserkvi," *LChK*, 1935, no. 3, 2–4.

———. "Tsily nimets'koï viis'kovoï polityky na Ukraïni 1918 r." *LChK*, 1929, no. 1, 14–17; no. 2, 4–8.

———. "Ukraïns'ka viis'kova i voienna literatura." *LChK*, 1938, no. 7–8, 15–18; no. 9, 19–21; no. 10, 18–21.

———. "'Ukraïns'ki Termopyli': V desiatu richnytsiu boiu pid Krutamy." *LNV*, 1927, no. 2, 105–9.

———. "Uryvky spomyniv z 1917–1920 r." *IKAChK na 1931 rik*, 52–5.

———. "U vyzvolenomu Kyïvi: Spohady z hrudnia 1918–sichnia 1919." *LNV*, 1932, no. 2, 138–47; no. 3, 218–26; no. 4, 334–7; no. 6, 525–30.

———. "Z Kyieva do Sarn i nazad: Spohad." *IKAChK na 1938 rik*, 45–54.

———. "Za khlibom." *Litopys* (Berlin), no. 19–20 (1924), 292–8.

Dunin-Kozicka, Marja. "Bolszewicy w Kijowie, rok 1919." *PW*, 1925, no. 34, 193–212; no. 35, 339–66.

———. *Burza od wschodu: Wspomnienia z Kijowszczyzny, 1918–1920.* Warsaw: Dom Książki, 1929.
A Polish landowner's description of vicissitudes in Kyiv gubernia during the Bolshevik and VA invasions.

Dydyk, Evhen. "Z povstantsiamy: Vesna 1920 r. na Velykii Ukraïni." *IKAChK na 1930 rik*, 80–8.

Dykans'kyi, Z. "Dva spohady." *Tr* (New York), no. 8 (1961), 19–21.

Dymowski, Tadeusz. *Moich 10 lat w Polsce odrodzonej.* Warsaw: n.p., 1928.

Dziabenko, Ia. "Pershyi ukraïns'kyi viis'kovyi z'ïzd, 19–22. V. 1917." *UK*, 1954, no. 2, 9–13; no. 3, 24–9.

Dzierżykraj-Stokalski, Wiktor. *Dzieje jednej partyzantki z lat 1917–1920.* Lviv: the author, 1927.

Egorov, A. I. *Razgrom Denikina 1919.* Moscow: Gosudarstvennoe voennoe izdatel'stvo, 1931.
A detailed study, based on personal experiences, archival materials, and secondary sources, by the Red commander at the Southwestern Front of the strategic plans and events of the Bolshevik campaign of 1919 against Denikin.

Ezavitav, K. *Belorussy i poliaki: Dokumenty i fakty iz istorii okkupatsii Belorussii poliakami v 1918–1919 godakh.* Kaunas: Izdatel'stvo im. F. Skoryny, 1919.

"Fakty i dokumenty." *RW*, 7 December 1919.

Fedenko, Panas. "Holovnyi otaman." *NSl*, no. 5 (1977), 22–61.

———. *Holovnyi otaman: Iz kul'turnoï ta politychnoï diial'nosty Symona Petliury.* Munich: Nashe slovo, 1976.

———. *Isaak Mazepa: Borets' za voliu Ukraïny.* London: Nashe slovo, 1954.

———. *Mynulo pivstolittia: Zymovyi pokhid Armiï Ukraïns'koï Narodn'oï Respubliky, 1919–1920 rr.* New York: Svoboda, 1972.
Memoirs of the Winter Campaign in the rear of the Bolshevik and VA forces from December 1919 to May 1920.

———. "Pam'iati heroïv Krut." *NB* (New York), 1 February 1966.
———. "P'iatdesiat rokiv tomu: Spomyny pro upadok tsars'koho rezhymu v liutomu 1917 r." *Sv*, 9–11 March 1967.
———. "Sorok-littia Zymovoho pokhodu Ukraïns'koï Respublikans'koï Armiï, 6 hrudnia 1919–5 travnia 1920." *VU*, no. 25 (1960), 42–9.
———. "Symon Petliura i trahediia Ukraïny." *NDni*, no. 292 (1974), 5–11.
———. "U storichchia Pilsuds'koho." *Sv*, 29 July 1967.
———. *Vlada Pavla Skoropads'koho: P'iatdesiati rokovyny perevorotu v Ukraïni*. London: Nashe slovo, 1968.
———. "Z ostannikh dniv I. P. Mazepy." *NSl*, no. 3 (1973), 119–27.
Fediv, Ihor. "Koniukhy: Uryvok z dnevnyka—15. V.–30. VI. 1917." *IKAChK na 1932 rik*, 149–57.
Fedorchuk, Iaroslav. *Memorandum on the Ukrainian Question in Its National Aspect*. Compiled on behalf of the Cercle des Ukrainiens, Paris, and the Ukraine Committee. London: F. Griffiths, 1914.
Fedorovych, Rudol'f. "Istorychnyi dokument: Zamist' kvitiv na nevidomu mohylu sv. p. muchenykovi polkovnykovi Petrovi Bolbochanovi." *UK*, 1973, no. 3, 22–4.
Fervacque, Pierre. *Le chef de l'Armée rouge, Mikail Toukatchevski*. Paris: Bibliothèque Charpentier, 1928.
Filippov, N. *Ukrainskaia kontr-revoliutsiia na sluzhbe u Anglii, Frantsii i Pol'shi*. Moscow: Moskovskii rabochii, 1927.
An account of the UNR Directory's foreign relations, supplemented by a number of documents, including the Ukrainian-Polish political and military conventions of 21 and 24 April 1920.
Filonenko, Ie. "Volyns'ki povstantsi v krivavykh dniakh 1920–1924 rokiv." *ZD* 8 (1938), 215–35.
———. *Zbroina borot'ba na Volyni: Spomyn uchasnyka*. Winnipeg: Volyns'kyi vydavnychyi fond, 1958.
Frish, Roman. "Iz dniv slavy artylieriï U.H.A.: Storinka do istoriï b. Harmatn'oho polku U.H.A." *IKAChK na 1928 rik*, 146–50.
Frunze, Mikhail V. *Izbrannye proizvedeniia*. Moscow: Voennoe izdatel'stvo, 1965.
A collection of articles and speeches on the organization of the Red Army, its struggle during the Civil War, its military and political education, and the role of its rear.
———. "Pamiati Perekopa i Chongara: Stranichka iz vospominanii." *VV*, 1928, no. 6, 40–8.
Fylonovych, V. "Boï za Zhytomyr." *H*, no. 9 (1932), 25–31.
———. "Chomu dymisionuvav Symon Petliura?" *Dor*, 1966, no. 9, 15–16.
———. "Fragmenty." *H*, no. 17–18 (1936), 27–8.
———. "S. Petliura—postat' natsional'no-derzhavnoho chynu." *H*, no. 17–18 (1936), 10–17.

———. "U 45-tylittia vidnovlennia ukraïns'kykh zbroinykh syl." *BSBUVK*, 1962, no. 12, 2–6.

———. "Zymovyi pokhid." *H*, no. 13 (1935), 6–12.

Galan, Volodymyr. *Bateriia smerty*. New York: Chervona Kalyna, 1968.

———. "Bohdanivs'kyi polk." *KAV na 1957 rik* (Buenos Aires), 98–101.

———. "Boï o Chortivs'ku Skalu pid L'vovom v 1919 r.: Spomyny z oblohy L'vova Ukr. Hal. Armiieiu, 1918 do 1919 roku." *US*, no. 45–6 (1923), 23–31.

———. "Na Kyïv," *IKAChK na 1931 rik*, 72–5.

———. "Perekhid za Zbruch." *VK*, 1969, no. 1 (38), 21–3.

Gaulle, Charles de. "Bitwa o Wisłę: Dziennik działań wojennych oficera francuskiego." *ZH* (Paris) 19 (1971): 3–18.

Gendler, M. "O revoliutsionnykh sobytiiakh v Volyn'skoi gub. (m. Berezna) 1917–1919 g." *LR*, 1922, no. 1, 202–5.

"General'nyi Sekretariiat proholoshuie ziedynennie Ukraïny po tim botsi frontu." *VSVU*, no. 179 (1918), 770–1.

Genkin, E. B., comp. *Razgrom nemetskikh zakhvatchikov v 1918 godu: Sbornik materialov i dokumentov*. Moscow: Gosudarstvennoe politicheskoe izdatel'stvo, 1943.

A collection of documents dealing with German policy in Eastern Europe (largely in Ukraine) and the struggle of the population against the Germans from February 1918 to February 1919.

Georgievskii, I. "Ot"ezd generala Denikina." *RM* (Paris), 5 December 1974.

Germany and the Revolution, 1915–1918: Documents from the Archives of the German Foreign Ministry. Edited by Z. A. B. Zeman. London: Oxford University Press, 1958.

Gippius, Z. "Pol'sha 20-go goda: Zapiski iz dnevnika." *Voz* (Paris), 1951, no. 12, 118–32; no. 13, 130–42.

Gizhovs'kyi, Volodymyr. "Iz kyïvs'kykh spomyniv 1917–1918 rr." *Kaliendar "Hromada" dlia robitnychoho narodu v misti i seli na rik 1924* (Lviv), 153–6.

Głąbiński, Stanisław. *Wspomnienia polityczne*. Pelplin: Spółka z Ograniczoną Odpowiedzialnością, 1959.

Gol'del'man, Solomon. *Lysty zhydivs'koho sotsiial-demokrata pro Ukraïnu: Materiialy do istoriï ukraïns'ko-zhydivs'kykh vidnosyn za chas revoliutsiï*. Vienna: Hamoin, 1921.

Gol'denveizer, A. A. "Begstvo: Iiul'–oktiabr' 1921 g." *ARR* 12 (1923): 167–86.

———. "Iz kievskikh vospominanii, 1917–1921 gg." *ARR* 6 (1922): 161–303.

Gołoczewski, W. *Walecznych tysiąc: Pamiętnik z wojny polsko-bolszewickiej*. Warsaw: n.p., 1934.

Gonta, Dmytro. "Na pantsyrnyku 'Khortytsia'." *IKAChK na 1932 rik*, 71–86.

Górecki, Roman. *Z moich wspomnień o Józefie Piłsudskim: W siódmą rocznicę zgonu*. London: M. I. Kolin, 1942.

Gostyńska, Weronika. "Materiały archiwalne o tajnych rokowaniach polsko-radzieckich w Baranowiczach i Białowieży." *ZDSPR* 4 (1969): 150–72.

Grazhdanskaia voina, 1918–1921. 3 vols. Edited by A. S. Bubnov, S. S. Kamenev, and R. P. Eideman. 3 vols. Moscow: Voennyi vestnik, 1928–30.
A valuable collection dealing with the Russian Civil War, the Bolshevik and German interventions in Ukraine, and the Polish-Soviet War in 1920. Vols. 1–2 consist of memoirs and articles; vol. 3 is a collective monograph.

Grazhdanskaia voina na Ekaterinoslavshchine, fevral' 1918–1920 gg.: Dokumenty i materialy. Edited by A. Ia. Pashchenko. Dnipropetrovsk: Promin, 1968.
A biased collection of documents dealing with partisan activities and the Bolshevik struggle for power in Katerynoslav gubernia. It contains 292 documents in chronological order, most of them published for the first time.

Grazhdanskaia voina na Ukraine, 1918–1920: Sbornik dokumentov i materialov. Edited by S. M. Korolivskii, N. K. Kolesnik, and I. K. Rybalka. Kyiv: Naukova dumka, 1967.

Grzybowski, Kazimierz. "The Jakhontov Papers: Russo-Polish Relations, 1914–1916." *JCEA* 18, no. 1 (April 1958), 3–24.

Grzybowski, Wacław. "Samotność Józefa Piłsudskiego: Kilka uwag i wspomnień." *N* (London) 8 (1972): 167–75.

———. "Spotkania i rozmowy z Józefem Piłsudskim." *N* (London) 1 (1948): 89–100.
An essay about the author's conversations with Piłsudski on various topics, including Ukrainian-Polish relations in 1920.

Gul', Roman. "Kievskaia epopeia, noiabr'-dekabr' 1918 g." *ARR* 2 (1922): 59–86.
An informative account about the Ukrainians' struggle, largely in Kyiv, against the German and Russian forces in November and December 1918.

———. *Ledianoi pokhod: S Kornilovym*. Berlin: S. Efron, 1921.
An account by a Russian officer of Kornilov's campaigns against the Bolsheviks in the Don and Kuban regions in the winter of 1917–18.

Gulevich, K., and Gassanova, R. "Iz istorii bor'by prodovolstvennykh otriadov rabochikh za khleb i ukreplenie sovetskoi vlasti, 1918–1920 gg." *KA*, 1938, no. 4–5 (89–90), 103–53.

Gurev, V. I. *Ekaterinoslavskii pokhod: Vospominaniia*. 1939. Ms.
Unpublished memoirs by a Russian officer describing the activities in late 1918 of the Eight Corps organized under the hetman regime and stationed in Katerynoslav.

Gurko, V. I. "Iz Petrograda cherez Moskvu, Parizh i London v Odessu, 1917–1918 g.g." *Arkhiv russkoi revoliutsii* 15 (1924): 5–84.
A first-hand account of the early formation of the anti-Bolshevik Russian organizations, the conflict between their pro-German and pro-Allied orientations, the records of their Jassy Conference that appealed for Allied aid, the activities

of their delegations in Paris and London, and the French intervention in southern Ukraine.

———. "Politicheskoe polozhenie na Ukraine pri getmane." In S. A. Alekseev, comp., *Revoliutsiia na Ukraine po memuaram belykh*, 212–21. Moscow: Gos. izd-vo, 1930.

Haidukevych, Ostap. *Bulo kolys': Iz zapysnyka polevoho dukhovnyka UHA*. Lviv: Chervona kalyna, 1935.

Halahan, Mykola. "Deliegatsiia na Kuban', hruden' 1917 r." *IKAChK na 1931 rik*, 36–46.

———. "Na Tret'omu viis'kovomu z'ïzdi: Fragment spohadiv." *NU*, 1925, no. 2–3, 71–7.

———. *Z moïkh spomyniv*. 4 vols. Lviv: Chervona kalyna, 1930.

Valuable memoirs by a Ukrainian Social Democrat and diplomat of underground activities in the Russian Empire prior to 1905, the disintegration of the tsarist regime, and the vicissitudes of World War I and the Ukrainian revolution. The author focuses on the activities of the political parties, the organization of Ukrainian military formations, the conflict with the Russian regime, and his diplomatic missions in the Kuban, Romania, and Hungary.

Hal'chevs'kyi-Voinarovs'kyi, Iakiv (Pravoberezhets', Ia., pseud.). "Nezabutni heroï vyzvol'noï borot'by: Spohady povstantsia," *TrU*, no. 2–3 (1923), 74–8.

———. *Proty chervonykh okupantiv*. 2 vols. Cracow: Ukraïns'ke vydavnytstvo, 1942.

Haller, Józef. *Generał Haller, Dowódca Armji, do Naczelnego Dowództwa Wojsk Polskich w Warszawie*. Ms.

———. *Pamiętniki: Z wyborem dokumentów i zdjęć*. London: Veritas Foundation Press, 1964.

———. *Naczelne Dowództwo W. P. Generał Rodziewicz*. Lviv. Ms.

———. *Instrukcja do Generała Karnickiego, Szefa Polskiej Misji Wojskowej przy Gen. Denikinie*. Warsaw, 8 August 1919. Ms.

———. *Intryga Skoropadskiego*. Warsaw, 9 June 1920. Ms.

Halushchyns'kyi, Mykhailo. *Z Ukraïns'kymy sichovymy stril'tsiamy: Spomyny z rr. 1914–1915*. Lviv: Dilo. 1934.

Halyn, M. "Sposterezhennia i vrazhinnia viis'kovoho likaria z chasiv velykoï viiny i revoliutsiï, 1914–1918." *ZD* 4 (1934): 237–66; 5 (1935): 227–42; 6 (1937): 181–212.

Harusewicz, Mieczysław. *Za carskich czasów i po wyzwoleniu; Jan Harusewicz: Wspomnienia-dokumenty*. London: Veritas Foundation Press, 1975.

Havans'kyi, Roman. "Pam'iatnoho 1919 roku: Spomyny z Velykoï Ukraïny." *IKAChK na 1929 rik*, 120–32.

Havryliuk, Il'ko. "Chetvertyi universal: Spohady." *LNV*, 1927, no. 1, 16–24.

———. "Druhyi viis'kovyi z'ïzd." *Sh* (Neu-Ulm), 1953, no. 3–4 (5–6), 19–21.

———. *Veleten' dukha: Pam'iati Symona Petliury*. Chernivtsi: Iu. Hlyvko, 1928. Sketchy reminiscences about Petliura.

———. "Z velychn'oho mynuloho." *ZD* 1 (1929): 124–34.

———. "Vid bol'shevykiv do Petliury: Zi spomyniv poruchnyka UHA." *LChK*, 1936, no. 9, 17–20.

Henning-Michaelis, Eugenjusz de. *Burza dziejowa: Pamiętnik z wojny światowej, 1914–1917*. 3 vols. Warsaw: Gebethner i Wolff, 1928–9.

Herchanivs'kyi, Dmytro. "Pochatok Sichovykh stril'tsiv." *VK*, 1967, no. 2 (27), 29–36.

———. "Prykmetni rysy Sichovykh stril'tsiv (SS)." *VK*, 1968, no. 3 (34), 16–22.

Hirniak, Nykyfor. "Avstriis'ki ta nimets'ki heneraly i dyplomaty proty Vasylia Vyshyvanoho: Dokumenty." *Visti* (Munich), June 1961, 51–3; September 1961, 79–84; December 1961, 124–6; March 1962, 18–21; June 1962, 64–6; September 1962, 89–90.

———. *Ostannii akt trahediï Ukraïns'koï Halyts'koï Armiï*. Perth Amboy: Ukraïns'kyi viis'kovo-istorychnyi instytut v SShA, 1960.

Hnoiovyi, Ivan. "Spomyn pro 19-i pishyi ukraïns'kyi polk r. 1917." *T*, no. 6 (1928), 49–62.

———. "Z ukraïns'koho rukhu Sicheslavs'koï zalohy v rotsi 1917." *ZD* 6 (1936): 110–18.

Hodgson, John E. *With Denikin's Armies: Being a Description of the Cossack Counter-revolution in South Russia, 1919–1920*. London: L. Williams, 1932. An account by a war correspondent of the *Daily Express*.

Hoffmann, Max. *Der Krieg der versäumten Gelegenheiten*. Munich: G. Pehl, 1924. Memoirs of the chief of staff of the German Eastern Front dealing with German policy in Eastern Europe, including the Treaty of Brest-Litovsk and the evacuation of the front after November 1918.

Holota, Iakiv. "Z zhyttia i buttia v tabori v Libertsi." *US*, no. 5 (1921), 33–5.

Holovnyi Otaman Symon Petliura. The Hague, 27 April 1920. Ms.

Hołówko, Tadeusz. *Ostatni rok*. Warsaw: Książnica Atlas T.N.S.W., 1932.

———. *Przez dwa fronty: Ze wspomnień emisarjusza politycznego z 1918 roku*. 2 vols. Warsaw: Dom Książki Polskiej, 1931.

———. *Przez kraj czerwonego caratu*. Warsaw: n.p. 1931.

———. "Ze wspomnień 'Germanofila'." In *Wspomnienia legjonowe: Materiały z dziejów walk o niepodległość*, vol. 1, 18–55. Edited by Janusz Jędrzejewicz. Warsaw: Instytut Badań Najnowszej Historji Polskiej, 1924.

Holub, Andrii. "Zbroina vyzvol'na borot'ba na Khersonshchyni v zapiliu voroha, 1917–1919 roky." *ZD* 11 (1966): 175–89.

Holyns'kyi, Hr. "Ukraïns'ki povstantsi." *US*, no. 12 (1922), 15–16.

———. "Ukraïns'ki seliany ta radians'ka vlada na Ukraïni." *US*, no. 13 (1922), 15–16.

Holyns'kyi, Petro. "Ostanni dni UHA: Uryvky zi spomyniv." *IKAChK na 1931 rik*, 142–55.

Holzer, Jerzy. "Rozmowa Piłsudskiego z hrabią Kesslerem." *KH* 68 (1961): 447–50.
Honcharenko, Averkii. "Bii pid Krutamy." *BSBUVK*, no. 10 (1962), 4–8.
Horbenko, Kh. "Spohady pro Denikinshchynu." *StD*, no. 48–9 (1919).
Horbovyi, M. "Vid'ïzd U.S.S na Velyku Ukraïnu 1918 r." *IKAChK na 1932 rik*, 66–70.
Hordiienko, Havrylo. "Khto vyzvolyv Oleksandrivs'k v 1918 rotsi." *UK*, 1974, no. 2 (28), 38–41.
———. *Pid shchytom Marsa: Spohady*. Philadelphia: the author, 1976.
Hornykiewicz, Theophil, ed. *Ereignisse in der Ukraine, 1914–1922: Deren Bedeutung und historische Hintergründe*. 4 vols. Philadelphia: W. K. Lypynsky East European Research Institute, 1966–9.
House, Edward Mandell, and Seymour, Charles, eds. *What Really Happened at Paris: The Story of the Peace Conference, 1918–1919, by American Delegates*. Westport, Conn.: Greenwood Press, 1976.
Howard, Esme. *Theatre of Life: Life Seen from the Stalls, 1903–1936*. 2 vols. Boston: Little, Brown, 1935–6.
Hrekiv, O. "Vesna 1918 roku v Ukraïni." *ZD* 10 (1964): 23–6.
Hrushets'kyi, Ivan. "Uryvky zi spohadiv: Moï zustrichi z Holovnym otamanom." *BSBUVK*, no. 19 (1964), 5–6.
Hryhoriïv, Nykyfor. *Natsional'ne pytannia na Skhodi Evropy: Materiialy i dokumenty*. Prague: Nova Ukraïna, 1925.
Hryhorijiv, Nikifor. *The War and Ukrainian democracy: A Compilation of Documents from the Past and Present*. Toronto: Industrial and Educational Publishing Co., 1945.
Hryhorovych, M. "Ukraïns'kyi viis'kovyi rukh na Prydniprianshchyni v 1917 r." *IKAChK na 1937 rik*, 17–20.
Hryniuk, Petro. *Politychnyi i viis'kovyi dohovir z Pol'shcheiu*. Ms.
———. *1920 rik*. Ms.
Hryshko, H. "1917 rik v Odesi: Spomyny z chasiv vyzvol'nykh zmahan'." *RN*, 1930, no. 5–6, 128–35; no. 7–8, 178–87; no. 9–10, 237–45; no. 11–12, 281–92.
Hrytsyk, Ustia. "Deshcho z toho, shcho perezhyla." *IKAChK na 1930 rik*, 89–97.
Hupka, Jan. *Z czasów wielkiej wojny: Pamiętnik nie kombatanta*. 2d ed. Lviv: Księgarnia Gubrynowicz i Syn wł. A. Krawczyński, 1937.
Hunczak, Taras, ed. *Ukraine and Poland in Documents, 1918–1922*. 2 vols. New York: Shevchenko Scientific Society, 1983.
———. *The Ukrainian Revolution: Documents, 1919–1921*. New York: Ukrainian Academy of Arts and Sciences in the United States, 1984.
Iakir, Iona E. *Vospominaniia o grazhdanskoi voine*. Moscow: Voennoe izdatel'stvo, 1957.
   An account by a Red Army commander of the campaign against the UNR Army and VA.

Iakovliv, Andrii. "Beresteis'kyi dohovir i sprava avtonomiï Skhidn'oï Halychyny: Uryvok spomyniv z r. 1918." *KAD na rik 1938*, 14–21.

———. "Petliura i borot'ba za Arsenal: Uryvok zi 'Spomyniv'." In *Symon Petliura—derzhavnyi muzh*, 91–3. Edited by Nataliia Livyts'ka-Kholodna, Zakhar Ivasyshyn, and Artem Zubenko. New York: Ukraïns'kyi natsional'no-derzhavnyi soiuz, 1957.

———, ed. *Documents sur les pogromes en Ukraine et l'assassinat de Simon Petlura à Paris, 1917–1921*. Paris: Librairie du Trident, 1927.

Ianchevs'kyi, Mykola. "Zi spomyniv." *ZD* 2 (1930): 137–47.

Ianovs'kyi, Viktor. "'Za Ukraïnu, za ïï doliu'." *ZD* 3 (1932): 172–90.

Ieremiïv, Mykhailo. "Za lashtunkamy Tsentral'noï Rady: Storinky zi spohadiv." *UIs*, 1968, no. 1–4 (17–20), 94–104.

An account by the secretary of the Central Rada about its work.

Ieroshevych, P. "Spohady z chasiv het'mana Pavla Skoropads'koho na Ukraïni i povstannia narodu ukraïns'koho proty vlady het'mana ta nimtsiv-okupantiv." *T*, no. 9 (1928), 57–80; no. 10 (1929), 75–83.

Ievtymovych, Vartolomei. "Do istoriï Kam'ianets'koï spil'noï iunats'koï shkoly." *LChK*, 1936, no. 4, 4–6.

———. "Pershe stavlennia v Het'mana." In *Za velych natsiï: U dvadtsiati rokovyny vidnovlennia Ukraïns'koï Het'mans' koï Derzhavy*, 143–59. Edited by Mykola Pasika, Mykhailo Karpyshyn, and Teofil' Kostruba. Lviv, 1938. Reprint, New York: Bulava, 1955.

———. "Pochatky ukraïns'koho viis'kovoho shkil'nytstva v 1917–1918 r." *LChK*, 1937, no. 12, 7–11.

———. "Polkovnyk Petro Bolbachan i ioho ostanni dni." *UK*, 1976, no. 1 (35), 11–19.

———. "Poruchnyk Mykola Mikhnovs'kyi: Tvorets' novitn'oho ukraïns'koho viis'ka." *IKAChK na 1937 rik*, 46–53.

———. *Viis'ko ide: Uryvok zi spohadiv pro berezen' 1917 r. v Kyïevi*. Lviv: I. Tyktor, 1937.

Igrenev, G. "Ekaterinoslavskiia vospominaniia (avgust 1918 g.–iiun' 1919 g.)." *ARR*, 3 (1922): 234–43.

An account of the struggle between UNR and Bolshevik forces for control of Katerynoslav from August 1918 through June 1919.

Ilashchuk, Mykola. "III. kurin' 8 brygady v nastupi na Kyïv." *US*, no. 16 (1922), 15–16; no. 17, 9–10; no. 18, 5–7.

Ilashchuk, Vasyl'. "Na ridnii zemli v nevoli: V chotyrolitni rokovyny zdobuttia Kyïva." *US*, no. 39–40 (1923), 40–55; no. 41–2, 35–48; no. 43–4, 43–55.

Il'nyts'kyi, A. "Rozhin nimtsiamy Tsentral'noï Rady: Spohad." *VU*, no. 52 (1966), 24–7.

"Instruktsiia Trots'koho ahitatoram-komunistam na Vkraïni." *Syn Ukraïny* (Warsaw), 7 August 1920.

"Interv'iu z het'manom Skoropads'kym." 15 October 1920. Manuscript of interview for *La Gazette de Lausanne*.

Istoriia Ukraïny v dokumentakh i materialakh. Vol. 3. Compiled by M. N. Petrovs'kyi and V. K. Putilov. Kyiv: Akademiia nauk URSR, 1941.

"Istorychnyi dokument (lyst Holovnoho otamana Symona Petliury do Marshala Iuzefa Pilsuds'koho)." *Tr* (New York), no. 35 (1965), 7–9.

Iunakiv, Mykola L. "Materiialy dlia moho zhyttiepysu." *Tr* (Paris), 1931, no. 30–2 (289–90), 3–12.

———. "Uryvok z avtobiohrafiï." In *Symon Petliura—derzhavnyi muzh*, 148–52. Edited by Nataliia Livyts'ka-Kholodna et al. New York: Ukraïns'kyi natsional'noderzhavnyi soiuz, 1957.

Iurtyk, H. "Druhyi vseukraïns'kyi viis'kovyi z'ïzd, Pershyi universal: Zi spomyniv." *LNV*, 1923, no. 3, 228–34; no. 4, 306–14.

———. "Pershyi Symferopol's'kyi polk im. Het'mana Petra Doroshenka: Zi spomyniv." *LNV*, 1923, no. 1, 31–42.

———. "Stykhiia: Zi spomyniv." *LNV*, 1922, no. 3, 223–38.

———. "Tvorymo: Zi spomyniv." *LNV*, 1923, no. 6, 147–59.

———. "Zvenyhorods'kyi kish Vil'noho kozatstva." *LNV*, 1922, no. 2, 125–33.

Ivanets', Ivan. "Pid Chudnovom: Kinets' Brygady USS." *IKAChK na 1935 rik*, 83–96.

Ivanyna, Nestor. *Zalizni roky: Spomyny, 1914–1922*. Lviv: I. Tyktor, 1937.

Ivanys, Vasyl'. "Petliura na Kubani." *Sv*, 23 May 1951.

———. *Stezhkamy zhyttia: Spohady*. 5 vols. Toronto: Peremoha, 1958–62.

Memoirs by the former head of the Kuban Cossack government, based on the author's reminiscences, documentary material, and interviews covering the period from the end of the nineteenth century to the 1950s.

"Iz istorii grazhdanskoi voiny na Ukraine v 1918 g." *KA* 95 (1939): 73–102.

Documents dealing with the uprisings against the Germans in Zvenyhorodka and Tarashcha counties, and the organization of Bolshevik partisans in the neutral zone from March 1918 through March 1919.

"Iz istorii organizatsii komitetov nezamozhnykh krestian Ukraïny." *Istorik-marksist* 58 (1936): 164–75.

A report about the organization and work of the Committees of Poor Peasants in Soviet Ukraine from 1 July to 10 September 1920.

"Iz istorii sovvlasti na Ukraine: O Pervom vseukrainskom s"ezde sovetov i Pervom Sovetskom Pravitel'stve Ukrainy." *LR*, 1924, no. 4 (9), 166–85.

Memoirs and documentary materials on the attempt to establish the first Soviet government in Ukraine.

"Iz istorii vneshnei politiki pravitel'stva Vrangelia: Ekonomicheskie otnosheniia s Frantsiei." *KA* 32 (1929): 125–57.

Reports from Paris by a commercial agent of Wrangel's government about the activities of his agency from May to July 1920. It includes documents about the foundation of a Russo-French society for trade, industry, and transportation.

"Iz materialov kievskoi chrezvychaiki." *BA* 2–3 (1928): 113–16.
A brief description of the people executed by the Cheka in Kyiv for alleged anti-Bolshevik activities.

Janowska, Halina, and Tadeusz Jędruszczak, eds. *Powstanie II Rzeczypospolitej: Wybór dokumentów, 1866–1925*. Warsaw: Ludowa Spółdzielnia Wydawnicza, 1984.

Jastrzębski, Wincenty. "Między Piotrogradem a Warszawą." *NDP* 12 (1967): 155–89.

Jędrzejewicz, Janusz, ed. *Wspomnienia legjonowe: Materiały z dziejów walk o niepodległość*. 2 vols. Warsaw: Instytut Badań Najnowszej Historji Polskiej, 1924–5.

Józefski, Henryk. "Zamiast pamiętnika." *ZH* 59 (1982): 3–163; 60 (1982): 65–157; 63 (1983): 3–86.

Jundzill, Zygmunt. "Niefortunna Wyprawa Kowieńska." *N* (London) 5 (1955): 206–11.
An account of Piłsudski's attempt to unite or federate Poland with Lithuania in 1918–19.

K. "Armeis'ka hrupa gen. Kravsa v nastupi na Kyïv." *US*, no. 8 (1921), 3–8; no. 9 (1921), 13–16.

K., K. "Ukr. parliamentar do rosyis'koï Dobrovol'choï armiï." *US*, no. 10 (1921), 3–4.

"K istorii frantsuzskoi interventsii na iuge Rossii, dekabr' 1918-aprel' 1919 g." *KA* 19 (1926), 3–38.
A collection of reports from an associate of the South Russian National Center and V. Shulgin to Adm. Kolchak about the French intervention and conditions in southern Ukraine, emphasizing the French attitude toward the VA and UNR government.

"K istorii grazhdanskoi bor'by na Ukraine: K voprosu ob organizatsii Vremennogo Raboche-Krest'ianskogo Pravitel'stva Ukraïny." *LR*, 1924, no. 4 (9), 151–65.
A valuable account of political conditions in Ukraine, which includes a number of documents.

Kakhovskaia, I. K. "Delo Eikhgorna i Denikina: Iz vospominanii." In *Puti revoliutsii: Stat'i, materialy, vospominaniia*, 191–260. Berlin: Skify, 1923.
Memoirs of a Russian Left Socialist Revolutionary dealing with the assassination of Field Marshal Eichhorn in Kyiv in late July 1918, the attempt on the life of Skoropads'kyi, and Denikin's occupation of Kyiv in August 1919.

———. "Terroristicheskii akt protiv Gen. Eikhorna." *LR*, 1923, no. 2, 172–84.

Kalichak, I. *Zapysky chetaria: Spomyny, 1918–1919*. Lviv: Chervona kalyna, 1931.

Kalinowski, Józef. *Stosunki polsko-rosyjskie w latach 1914–1945*. London, 1949. Ms.

Kalynovych, Ivan. "Kozats'ka pomsta: Spohad." *UK*, 1972, no. 2 (20), 17–19.
Kamenets'ka, Nataliia. "Spomyn pro Holovnoho otamana." *Sv*, 25 May 1976.
Kandiskaliv, P. Dolyna troiand i smerty; spohady: Materiialy dlia istoriï tak zvanoho "belogo dvizheniia." Ms., 1964.
Kaplystyi, Makar. "Moia uchast' v ukraïnizatsiï 133 rosiis'koï pishoï dyviziï." *VK*, 1971, no. 2 (52), 27–37.
Kapulovskii, I. "Organizatsiia vostaniia protiv getmana." *LR*, 1923, no. 4, 95–102.
Memoirs dealing with the organization of partisan groups and uprising against the hetman regime's police and German troops in Zvenyhorodka county in the spring and summer of 1918.
Karinskii, N. "Epizod iz evakuatsii Novorossiiska." *ARR* 12 (1923): 149–66, 194–6.
Karnicki. Do Szefa Sztabu Generalnego w Warszawie. Novorossiisk, 18 March 1920. Ms.
Kasprzycki, Tadeusz. *Kartki z dziennika oficera 1. Brygady*. Warsaw: Wojskowy Instytut Naukowo-Wydawniczy, 1934.
Kedrovs'kyi, Volodymyr. "Pam'iati Holovnoho otamana S. Petliury." *Biuleten' Ob'iednannia prykhyl'nykiv Ukraïns'koï Narodn'oï Respubliky v SShA* (New York), 1965, no. 4, 2–6.
———. "Pershe zasidannia Druhoho Vseukraïns'koho Viis'kovoho Heneral'noho Komitetu: Vyryvok zi spohadiv." *ZD* 1 (1929): 118–23.
———. "Pershi dni bol'shevyts'koho panuvannia: Spohady." *LNV*, 1926, no. 2, 120–30.
———. "Povalennie bol'shevykamy Rosiis'koho Tymchasovoho Uriadu i perekhid vlady na Ukraïni do Tsentralnoï Rady: Skorochenyi uryvok zi spomyniv." *LNV*, 1925, no. 1, 29–45.
———. "Povstannia proty Het'mana: Uryvok iz spohadiv." *LNV*, 1928, no. 5, 36–47; no. 6, 125–32.
———. "Pryïzd moskovs'kykh ministriv do Kyïva v kintsi chervnia 1917 roku i viis'kova sprava: Uryvok zi spomyniv." *LNV*, 1923, no. 12, 333–8.
———. *Ryzhs'ke Andrusovo: Spomyny pro rosiis'ko-pol's'ki myrovi perehovory v 1920 r.* Winnipeg: Ukraïns'ka vydavnycha spilka v Kanadi, 1936.
———. "S. V. Petliura i orhanizatsiia ukraïns'koi armiï." *Ukraïns'kyi pravoslavnyi kalendar na 1967 rik* (South Bound Brook), 98–104.
———. *1917 rik: Spohady chlena Ukraïns'koho Viis'kovoho Heneral'noho Komitetu i tovarysha sekretaria viis'kovykh sprav u chasi Ukraïns'koi Tsentral'noï Rady*. Winnipeg: Trident Press, 1967.
Authoritative memoirs by a high-ranking UNR officer and diplomat describing the vicissitudes of the Ukrainian revolution from March through October 1917 and the organization of Ukrainian military formations.
———. "Ukraïnizatsiia v Rosiis'kii armiï." *UIs*, 1967, no. 3–4 (15–16), 61–77.
An account of the formation of separate Ukrainian military units in the Russian army during the first half of 1917.

———. "Ukraïns'ki povstans'ki otamany." *Sv*, 2 October 1934.
A valuable characterization of a number of partisan leaders and their negative role.

———. "V borot'bi za derzhavnist'." *ZD* 10 (1964): 9–22.

———. "Vserosiis'ka demokratychna narada v Peterburzi 14–23 veresnia 1917 roku: Skorochenyi uryvok zi spomyniv." *LNV*, 1923, no. 7, 221–9.

———. "Vseukraïns'kyi Viis'kovyi Heneral'nyi Komitet i Tymchasove Pravytel'stvo: Uryvok iz spomyniv." *LNV*, 1923, no. 5, 34–41.

———. "Z chasiv rozvalu: Zi spohadiv." *LNV*. 1929, no. 7–8, 616–732.

———. "Z Druhoho Vseukraïns'koho viis'kovoho z'ïzdu." *LNV*, 1923, no. 10, 142–8.

Kedryn, Ivan. "Pam'iati Andriia M. Livyts'koho: Spohad." *Sv*, 6–8 August 1964.

———. *Paraleli v istoriï Ukraïny: Z nahody 50-richchia Ryz'koho myru*. New York: Chervona Kalyna, 1971.

Kharakternyk. "Moia podorozh do Kyïva cherez front u kvitni 1919 r.: Uryvok zi spohadiv." *IKAChK na 1928 rik*, 114–19.

———. "Zhadky z mynuloho." *LNV*, 1924, no. 7–9, 285–98; 1925, no. 2, 134–42; no. 6, 127–32; no. 10, 126–31; no. 11, 219–29; 1926, no. 1, 33–43; no. 3, 207–15; 1927, no. 11, 227–38; 1928, no. 6, 503–10.
An account of Russian activities in Ukraine during the second half of 1918 and the uprising against the hetman government.

Khlebnikov. "Perekop: Vospominaniia." *VR* 11 (1935): 22–8.

Khrystiuk, Pavlo. *Zamitky i materiialy do istoriï ukraïns'koï revoliutsiï, 1917–1920 rr.* 4 vols. Vienna, 1921–2. Reprint, New York: Vydavnytstvo Chartoryis'kykh, 1969.
An authoritative history of the Ukrainian revolution based on documents and the author's experiences as a senior UNR official. Numerous documents are integrated into the text.

Kirimer, Cafer Seydahmet. "Moje wspomnienie z rozmowy z Marszałkiem Józefem Piłsudskim." *N* (London) 2 (1950): 41–50.

Kiselev, Mikhail. *Agitpoezd: Vospominaniia o bor'be s kontrrevoliutsiei na Ukraine, 1918–1919 gg.* Moscow: Molodaia gvardiia, 1933.
An account by a Red Army officer of Bolshevik propaganda in Ukraine and the campaign against the UNR Army and VA, focussing on the Bolshevik retreat from Ukraine.

K-k, R. "Ulychni boï v Kyïvi," *US*, no. 6 (1921), 24–8; no. 7, 12–17; no. 8, 9–14; no. 9, 17–19; no. 10, 5–6.

K-kyi, Ivan. "Bii pid Krutamy: Spohady uchasnyka, khorunzhoho Vasylia Shcherbaka." *Sv*, 29 January 1951.

Klodnyts'kyi, Osyp. "Moia sluzhba v UHA." *VK*, 1969, no. 2 (38), 24–32.

Kmeta, Arkhyp. "Pam'iati nezabutn'oho." *T*, no. 5 (1927), 15–19.

Kochehar, Mykhailo. "Tretii viis'kovyi z'їzd u Kyїvi." *IKAChK na 1935 rik*, 128–9.
Kokh, H. *Dohovir z Denikinom vid 1. do 17. lystopada 1919 r.* Lviv: Chervona kalyna, 1930.
An account of the agreement between the UHA and VA.
Kollard, Iurii. *Spohady iunats'kykh dniv, 1897–1906: Ukraїns'ka students'ka hromada v Kharkovi i Revoliutsiina ukraїns'ka partiia (RUP).* Toronto: Sribna surma, 1972.
Koltuniuk, Roman. "Z klishchiv smerty." *US*, no. 20 (1922), 32–6; no. 21, 12–16; no. 22, 17–22; no. 23 (1923), 37–40; no. 24, 22–6; no. 25, 20–3; no. 27, 40–4; no. 28, 26–30; no. 31–2, 18–25; no. 33.
Komandarm Iakir: Vospominaniia druzei i soratnikov. Moscow: Voennoe izdatel'stvo, 1963.
Komandarm Uborevich: Vospominaniia druzei i soratnikov. Moscow: Voennoe izdatel'stvo, 1964.
Komitet uczczenia czynu zbrojnego Józefa Piłsudskiego 6-go sierpnia 1914: Sprawozdanie. London, 1964.
Komitety nezamozhnykh selian. Odessa: Informatsionno-instruktivnyi podotdel, Otdelenie upravleniia gubrevkoma, 1920.
"Komunikat Warszawskiego Sztabu Generalnego z dnia 27-go marca 1919 r." *WN* (Lviv), 30 March 1919.
Kononenko, Kharytia. "Dvi manifestatsiї: Spohady z pershykh dniv revoliutsiї 1917 r." *Literaturnyi i hromads'ko-politychnyi kaliendar-al'manakh Dnipro na rik 1937*, 80–5.
Konovalets', Evhen. "Prychynky do istoriї roli Sichovykh stril'tsiv v ukraїns'kii revoliutsiї." *RN*, 1928, no. 1, 18–23; no. 2, 60–4; no. 3, 104–10; no. 4, 153–8; no. 5, 199–204; no. 6, 241–4.
———. *Prychynky do istoriї ukraїns'koї revoliutsiї.* Prague: Provid ukraїns'kykh natsionalistiv, 1928.
Memoirs of the Ukrainian revolution by the Sich Riflemen's commander.
Konwencja Wojskowa między Polską a Ukrainą. Warsaw, 24 April 1920. Ms.
Korduba, Myron. "Perevorot na Bukovyni: Z osobystykh spomyniv." *LNV*, 1923, no. 10, 135–41; no. 11, 229–39; no. 12, 321–33.
———. "V posol'stvi do het'mana." *LChK*, 1926, no. 12, 12–14; 1927, no. 1, 5–10; no. 2, 11–15.
Korniїv, V. "Spohady pro ukraїnizatsiiu 36 pishoho orlovs'koho polku (X korpusu Rosiis'koї armiї) v rotsi 1917." *ZD* 1 (1929): 62–70.
Korol', Nestor. *Iak Pavlo Skoropads'kyi stav het'manom Ukraїny: Uryvok zi spohadiv.* New York: the author, 1967.
Koroliv-Staryi, Vasyl'. "Kinets' Het'manatu: Fragment spohadiv." *KAD na rik 1928*, 79–95.
A valuable account of the uprising against Skoropads'kyi, the negotiations that

led to his capitulation, and the arrival of the Directory in Kyiv.

———. "Nachal'nyi otaman Symon Vasyl'ovych Petliura: Biohrafichnyi ocherk." *UP*, 1919, no. 13.

———. "Pys'mennyts'kyi shliakh S. Petliury: Detal' do biohrafiï." *Tr* (Paris), 1927, no. 22–3, 22–7.

Korostovetz, Vladimir. *Seed and Harvest*. London: Faber and Faber, 1931.
Memoirs by an official of the Russian Foreign Ministry describing the life of his family and the course of the revolution mainly in Ukraine to the end of 1919.

Korsak, V. *U belykh*. Paris: Knizhnyi magazin Moskva, 1931.
An account by a VA officer about the attack of the VA forces under Gen. Bredov against the UNR troops in Kyiv and of the later fighting between the VA and the Bolsheviks, with emphasis on the suffering of Kyiv's population under Denikin's occupation from August to December 1919.

———. *U krasnykh*. Paris: Knizhnyi magazin Moskva, 1930.

———. *Velikii iskhod*. Paris: Knizhnyi magazin Moskva, 1931.

Korwin-Sokołowski, Adam L. *Fragmenty wspomnień, 1910–1945*. Paris: Spotkania, 1985.

Kossak, Sophia. *The Blaze: Reminiscences of Volhynia, 1917–1919*. London: Allen and Unwin, 1927.

Koval'-Medzvieds'ka, K. "Kyïvs'ki perezhyvannia v 1919 r." *ZD* 8 (1938): 142–51.

Koval'-Stepovyi, P. "Shliakhamy zrady: Spomyn pro Liubars'ku tragediiu 1919 roku." *KAD na rik 1933*, 45–9.
An account of political and military conditions in Right-Bank Ukraine in the autumn of 1919, with emphasis on Volokh's betrayal at Liubar in November.

Kovalevs'kyi, Mykola (Kowalewski, Mikołaj). *Polityka narodowościowa na Ukrainie Sowieckiej: Zarys ewolucji stosunków w latach 1917–1937*. Jerusalem: Wydział Opieki nad Żołnierzem DTWA Jednostek Wojska na Śr. Wschodzie, 1947.

———. *Pry dzherelakh borot'by: Spomyny, vrazhennia, refleksiï*. Innsbruck: Maria Kowalewsky, 1960.

———. *L'Ukraine et la Guerre Polono-Soviétique de 1920*. Ms.

Kovtiukh, E. *Ot Kubani do Volgi i obratno: Iz vospominanii o pokhodakh i boiakh krasnykh tamanskikh chastei*. Moscow: Gosudarstvennoe voennoe izdatel'stvo, 1926.

———. *Zheleznyi potok v voennom izlozhenii*. 2d ed. Moscow: Gosudarstvennoe voennoe izdatel'stvo, 1931.

Kovzhun, Pavlo. "Sproba organizatsiï ukraïns'koho legionu na botsi Antanty: Spohad." *IKAChK na 1937 rik*, 104–7.

Kozachenko, P. "Heroï Krut." *Sv*, 30 January 1951.

Kozar, L'ongin. "Symon Petliura u vadovyts'komu tabori." *Biuleten' Holovnoï upravy Soiuzu ukraïns'kykh veteraniv*, no. 2 (May 1949), 9–10.

Kozerovskii, V. *V plenu u interventov.* Moscow: Molodaia gvardiia, 1925.
An account of the Polish-Soviet War of 1920 by a former prisoner of war in Poland.

Koz'ma, I. K. "'L'odovyi pokhid' i hen. Iu. Tiutiunnyk." *VK*, 1972, no. 1 (57), 20–8.

Kozub, Ivan. "Povstannia proty het'manshchyny ta petliurovshchyny: Notatky z istoriï povstans'koho rukhu v Pereiaslavs'komu, Pyriatyns'komu ta Zolotonos'komu povitakh, kinets' 1918–pochatok 1919 r.r." *LR*, 1930, no. 5, 274–88.

Krakh germanskoi okkupatsii na Ukraine: Po dokumentam okkupantov. Edited by M. Gorkii, I. Mints, and R. Eideman. Moscow: Gos. izd-vo, 1936.
A collection of diplomatic papers, military reports, and other materials of the German Command and Austro-German envoys on German colonial policy, repressions, punitive expeditions, and military disintegration in Ukraine.

Krasnaia kniga: Sbornik diplomaticheskikh dokumentov o russko-pol'skikh otnosheniiakh v 1918–1920 gg. Moscow: Gos. izd-vo, 1920.

Krasnov, P. N. "Vsevelikoe voisko donskoe." *ARR* 5 (1922): 190–321.

———. "Iz vospominanii o 1917–1920 gg." *ARR* 8 (1923): 110–65; 11 (1923): 106–65.

Krat, Mykhailo. "Iak to bulo u Zymovomu pokhodi." *UK*, 1974, no. 4 (30), 26–9.

———. "Vapniarska operatsiia." *ZD* 8 (1938): 66–80.

Kravs, Antin. *Za ukraïns'ku spravu: Spomyny pro III. korpus U.H.A. pislia perekhodu za Zbruch.* Lviv: Chervona kalyna, 1937.

———. "Zav'iazok moieï hrupy: Uryvok zi spomyniv." *US*, no. 16 (1922), 4–7; no. 17, 4–6.

Kritskii, M. "Istoki dobrovol'chestva i ego sushchnost'." *Voz*, no. 193 (1968), 33–52; no. 194, 42–59; no. 195, 53–66; no. 196, 64–79; no. 197, 56–68; no. 200, 67–86; no. 201, 79–89; no. 202, 92–103; no. 203, 74–89; no. 204, 99–110; no. 206 (1969), 57–68.

———. "Krasnaia Armiia na Iuzhnom fronte v 1918–1920 gg. po dokumentam i sekretnym prikazam, zakhvachenym v boiakh 1-ym korpusom Dobrovol'cheskoi armii." *ARR* 18 (1926): 254–300.

Krylovets'kyi, Ilarion. "Moi spohady z chasiv zbroinoï vyzvol'noï borot'by: Uryvok spohadiv." *UK*, 1973, no. 4, 8–11.

"Krym u 1918–1919 gg.: Materialy osvedomitel'nykh organov Dobrovol'cheskoi armii i diplomaticheskogo predstavitelia Vsevelikogo voiska donskogo; soobshchenie A. Gukovskogo." *KA* 27 (1928): 142–81; 29 (1928): 55–85.
Telegrams from the VA chief of staff in Symferopil to the VA representative at the Entente Command in the Crimea about the intervention and conditions in southern Ukraine, Bolshevik propaganda activities among the French troops, and the Tatar movement in the Crimea.

Krushyns'kyi, Fedir. "Holovnyi otaman: Spohady ad'iutanta." *MU*, 1935, no. 1–2, 6–11.
Kryshevskii, N. "V Krymu, 1916–1918 gg." *ARR* 13 (1924): 71–124.
Kryzhanivs'kyi, P. "Dvi zustrichi z S. Petliuroiu: Uryvok iz spohadiv." *Uln*, no. 9–10 (1928), 6–12.
Krzemieński, Jakub. "Rozmowa Komendanta ze mną." *N* (London) 5 (1955): 212–16.
Kukiel, M. "Dokumenty do historji planu Operacji Warszawskiej." *B* (Warsaw) 20 (1925): 114–36.
Kułakowski, Mariusz. *Roman Dmowski w świetle listów i wspomnień*. London: Gryf, 1968.
Kulczycki, Jerzy. *Dziennik dowódcy kompanji: Iz walk w Małopolsce Wschodniej i nad Dźwiną w 1919 roku*. Warsaw: Wojskowy Instytut Naukowo-Wydawniczy, 1927.
Kumaniecki, Kazimierz Władysław, ed. *Odbudowa państwowości polskiej: Najważniejsze dokumenty, 1912–styczeń 1924*. Warsaw: Księgarnia J. Czerneckiego, 1924.
Kunstman, Zdzisław. "Wspomnienia o atamanie Petlurze: Rozmowa z majorem Leonem Kniaziołuckim." *BPU*, 26 July 1936, 306–7.
Kupchyns'kyi, Roman. "Zustrich na fronti." *Kalendar-al'manakh na 1967 rik* (Jersey City), 139–44.
Kurakh, Mykhailo. "Chy Sichovi stril'tsi braly uchast' u Zymovomu pokhodi?" *VK*, 1961, no. 1–2, 24–36.
A valuable eyewitness account of the Ukrainian Sich Riflemen and their fate at the end of 1919.
Kurka, I. "Vesna 1920 r. v. Odesi." *IKAChK na 1932 rik*, 117–24.
Kurovs'kyi, Volodymyr. "Na okupovanykh nimtsiamy zemliakh Kholmshchyny, Pidliashshia i Polissia: Iz spomyniv syn'ozhupannyka." *KAD na rik 1931*, 81–5.
Kuryliuk, Evhen V. Iak ia distav pliamystyi tyf v Ukraïni 1919 r. Chicago, May 1978. Ms.
———. "Moï dvi zustrichi iz 'Zubatoiu' v Ukraïni 1919 r.: Esei z perezhytoho." *UK*, 1978, no. 3–4, 37–40.
Kushch, V. "Slid pam'iaty." *T*, no. 7 (1926), 32–4.
An eyewitness account of the crossing of the Zbruch on 21 November 1920 by the UNR Army and the Russian units of Gen. Peremykin and Capt. Iakovlev.
Kushchyns'kyi Antin. "Dva braty kozats'ki heneraly." *UK*, 1975, no. 1, 11–18.
———. "Kil'ka dokumentiv pro 'ukraïns'ke pytannia' u Vrangelia." *Tr* (Paris), 1926, no. 26–7, 23–7.
———. "Ukraïns'ke Vil'ne kozatstvo v rokakh 1917–18." *UK*, 1971, no. 1, 22–4; no. 2, 16–23.
———. "Kozats'ki ideï henerala Mykhaila Omelianovych-Pavlenka: Spohady i arkhivni akty." *UK*, 1969, no. 3–4, 27–32.

Kustelian, M. "Denikinskoe podpol'e." *LR*, 1926, no. 2, 7–12.
Memoirs of Bolshevik underground agents' activities in the Kyiv region during the VA occupation of 1919.
Kuz', Kuz'ma, "Pid Malymy Min'kamy, 1921–1971." *VK*, 1971, no. 6 (56), 6–10.
Kuz'ma, Oleksa. "Chomu ukraïntsi stratyly L'viv? Iz spomyniv." *KP*, 1933, 108–17.
———. "Na rozputti: Prychynky do istoriï UHA." *Iuvileinyi al'manakh tovarystva Prosvita* (Lviv, 1928), 182–99.
Kuznetsov, V. *Voina s Pol'shei: Vospominaniia*. Moscow: GIZ, 1927.
L., L. "V Chotyrokutnyku smerty (Peredrizdviani spomyny z 1919 r.)." *LChK*, 1930, no. 2, 3–4.
L-ii, A. Politychna konventsiia mizh P. ta U. Paris. Ms.
L-oi, L. "Ocherki zhizni v Kieve v 1919–20 gg." *ARR* 3 (1921): 210–33.
Ładoś, Aleksander. "Wasilewski w rokowaniach ryskich: Wspomnienia osobiste." *N* (Warsaw) 16, no. 1 (1937), 230–50.
Lansing, Robert. *The Peace Negotiations: A Personal Narrative*. Boston: Houghton Mifflin, 1921.
Lazurenko, Stepan. "Bohdanivtsi na fronti 1917 roku." *Tr* (New York) no. 33 (1965), 13–15; no. 34, 15–18.
———. "Persha krov i pershi zhertvy vyzvol'nykh zmahan' 1917–1920 rokiv." *BSBUVK*, 1962, no. 12, 4–8.
———. "Povstannia proty het'mana i druha viina z bol'shevykamy, 1918–1919 rr." *Tr* (New York), no. 39 (1966), 17–18; no. 40, 3–5; no. 41, 6–9; no. 42 (1967), 13–15.
Lazurko, Omelian. "Deshcho iz sanitarnykh vidnosyn UHA (Spomyny)." *US*, 1923, no. 5 (27), 31–6; no. 6 (28), 19–23; no. 7 (29), 22–5; no. 9–10 (31–2), 26–9; no. 12 (34), 19–22; no. 13 (35), 21–7; no. 14 (36), 12–16.
League of Nations Treaty Series. Vol. 6, 51–169. Lausanne: Imprimeries Réunies, 1921.
Lector. "Wspomnienia o Wyprawie Kijowskiej 1920 r." *BPU*, 1937 no. 2, 17–18.
Leikhtenbergskii, G. N. "Kak nachalas' 'Iuzhnaia armiia'." *ARR* 8 (1923): 166–82.
An account of the VA in Ukraine from July through December 1918.
———. *Vospominaniia ob "Ukraine" 1917–1918 gg*. Berlin: Detinets, 1921.
A Russian noble's memoirs of his experiences and anti-Ukrainian activities from 1917 through the end of 1918.
"Leon Wasilewski do Józefa Piłsudskiego o przebiegu ryskich rokowań pokojowych, 1920–1921." *ZPW*, no. 60 (1972), 177–82.
Leontiev, L., and L. Kurylov. *Daiosh Kyïv: Z istoriï 44-ï Kyïvs'koï dyviziï*. Kharkiv: Derzhavne vydavnytstvo Ukraïny, 1929.
Leontovych, Volodymyr. "Spohady." *Tr* (Paris), 1929, no. 22–3, 9–15; no. 24, 9–14; no. 26, 7–12; no. 27, 7–12; no. 41, 5–11; no. 42, 7–10; no. 44, 15–18; no. 45, 7–9.

———. *Spomyny utikacha*. Berlin: Ukraïns'ke slovo, 1922.
———. "Uryvok spohadiv iz revoliutsiinykh chasiv." *KAD na rik 1936*, 67–76.
Levyts'kyi, Evhen. "Ukraïna pislia viiny." *Sv*, 19–20 and 22–5 September 1924.
Levyts'kyi, Kost'. "Pershyi Derzhavnyi Sekretariiat u L'vovi." *US*, no. 33 (1923), 15–18.
———. "Rozpad Avstriï i ukraïns'ka sprava: Politychni spomyny z r. 1918." *Vo* (Vienna), 1920, no. 2, 54–9.
———. *Velykyi zryv: Do istoriï ukraïns'koï derzhavnosty vid bereznia do lystopada 1918 r. na pidstavi spomyniv ta dokumentiv*. Lviv: Chervona kalyna, 1931. Reprint, New York: Vydavnytstvo Chartoryis'kykh, 1968.
Levyts'kyi, Modest. "Kozak i S. Petliura: Iz spohadiv." In *Symon Petliura—derzhavnyi muzh*, 95–8. Edited by Nataliia Livyts'ka-Kholodna et al. New York: Ukraïns'kyi natsional'no-derzhavnyi soiuz, 1957.
Levyts'kyi, Osyp. *Halyts'ka Armiia na Velykii Ukraïni: Spomyny z chasu vid lypnia do hrudnia 1919*. Vienna: n.p., 1921.
A valuable account by an UHA officer of the UHA campaign in Right-Bank Ukraine from July through December 1919.
Lipiński, Wacław. "Aresztowanie Józefa Piłsudskiego w lipcu 1917 r. w świetle nieznanych dokumentów niemieckich." *N* (Warsaw) 18, no. 1 (1938), 141–50.
———. "Dziennik bajończyka Marjana Himnera." *N* (Warsaw) 1, no. 2 (1930), 303–27; 2, no. 1 (1930), 133–56.
———. *Od Wilna po Dynaburg: Wspomnienia z ofensywy 5 P. P. Legjonów*. Warsaw: Główna Księgarnia Wojskowa, 1920.
———. "Rząd Jędrzeja Moraczewskiego i zamach 5. I. 1919 r.: Według relacyj z r. 1923 i dokumentów współczesnych." *N* (Warsaw) 15 (1937): 403–17.
———. "Uwolnienie Józefa Piłsudskiego z Magdeburga według relacji hr. Harry Kesslera." *N* (Warsaw) 18 (1938): 462–70.
———. "Wywiad u Marszałka Piłsudskiego w Sulejówku z dn. 10. II. 1924 r." *N* (Warsaw) 7, no. 1 (1933), 63–80.
Lisovskii, N. "Otkhod III-i armii ot Varshavy v 1920 g." *VR*, 1924, no. 8, 89–102; 1925, no. 1, 166–78.
Liutarevych, P. "Istoriia odnoho povstannia na Poltavshchyni ta ukraïns'ke pidpillia v rokakh 1920–1926." *Ukraïns'kyi zbirnyk* (Munich) 4 (1955): 131–55.
Liutyi-Liutenko, Ivan. *Vohon' z Kholodnoho Iaru: Spohady*. Detroit: the author, 1986.
Livyts'kyi, Andrii. *Vidnosyny Zakhid-Skhid i problemy ponevolenykh Moskvoiu natsii*. Munich: Ukraïns'ke informatsiine biuro, 1975.
Livyts'kyi, Mykola A. *DTs UNR v ekzyli mizh 1920 i 1940 rokamy*. Munich: Ukraïns'ke informatsiine biuro, 1984.
Lloyd George, David. *Memoirs of the Peace Conference*. 2 vols. New Haven: Yale University Press, 1939.

Lobanov-Rostovsky, A. *The Grinding Mill: Reminiscences of War and Revolution in Russia, 1913–1920.* New York: Macmillan, 1935.
A Russian prince's account, based on the diary he kept while serving in the Russian army.

Lotots'kyi, Oleksander. "Lystky z pam'iati: Na mohylu nezabutn'oho." *Tr* (Paris), 1926, no. 45. 2–8.

———. *Storinky mynuloho.* 4 vols. Reprint, South Bound Brook: Ukrainian Orthodox Church in the USA, 1966.

Lozyns'kyi, Mykhailo, ed. *Décisions du Conseil Suprême sur la Galicie Orientale: Les plus importants documents.* Paris: Bureau Ukrainien, 1919.

Luchanko, H. "Ternopil'tsi na oboronu Kyieva: Spomyny." *VK*, 1972, no. 2 (45), 25–33.

Lukasevych, Lev. *Rozdumy na skhylku zhyttia.* New York: Ukraïns'ke pravoslavne vydavnytstvo sv. Sofiï, 1982.

———. "Sen'ior ukraïns'koï dyplomatiï: Pam'iati grafa Mykhaila Tyshkevycha." *KAD na rik 1931*, 93–7.

Lukomskii, Aleksander S. *Memoirs of the Russian Revolution.* London: T. F. Unwin, 1922.

———. *Vospominaniia.* 2 vols. Berlin: O. Kirchner, 1922.
Memoirs by a Russian general, based on his experiences and on documents, dealing with the Russian Revolution, the Civil War, the organization of the VA, its operations and policies, and its relations with the British and French during the intervention in southern Ukraine.

Lulu, L. "Desiatylittia perekhodu Zbrucha, 1919, 16, VII.– 1929: Spomyn." *IKAChK na 1929 rik*, 76–81.
An account of the joint campaigns of the UHA and UNR Army against the Bolsheviks in the summer of 1919.

———. "Spohady pro podiï pid Krutamy." *LNV*, 1926, no. 4, 309–13.

Lutsiv, Luka. "1918 rik ochyma Ukraïns'koho sichovoho stril'tsia." *AUNS na rik 1968*, 129–37.

Luts'kyi, Ostap. "Na Velykim Luzi: Z pobutu USS-iv na Vel. Ukraïni." *NIKTP na rik 1926*, 108–12.

Lymanets', V. "Kruty: Vidrodzhennia ukraïns'koï strategiï." *T*, no. 33 (1937), 6–12.

Lypa, Iurii. "Dva roky." *Al'manakh "Novoho chasu": Kaliendar dlia vsikh na rik 1938*, 9–17.

———. "Zdobuttia Arsenalu: Spohad pro velykyi rik." *Kalendar-al'manakh na 1957 rik* (Buenos-Aires), 107–9.

Lytvyts'kyi, M. "Persha zustrich z S. Petliuroiu: Spohad." *StV*, 1926, no. 7–8, 30–2.

M., E. "Pam'iati Vasylia Tiutiunnyka." *KAD na rik 1931*, 97–112.

M., P. "Zhytomyr-Korosten'; Iz voiennykh zapyskiv." *US*, no. 16 (1922), 12–13; no. 17, 12–14; no. 18, 2–5.

Maevskii, Vladimir A. *Gvardeiskie sapery.* Novi Sad: S. F. Filonov, 1938.

An account by a VA officer of the Austro-German punitive expeditions in Ukraine in 1918 and Denikin's campaigns of 1919 in Left-Bank Ukraine.

———. *Povstantsy Ukraïny, 1918–1919 g.g.* Novi Sad, 192?

Memoirs by a VA officer of the Ukrainian partisan struggle against the Austro-German troops, Bolsheviks, and VA from the second half of 1918 through the beginning of 1920. The emphasis is on the partisan leader Kotsur, who operated in the Kremenchuk, Chyhyryn, Znamianka, and Oleksandriia regions.

Mahalevs'kyi, Iurii. "Oborona Kyieva v sichni 1918 r.: Spomyny." *KAD na rik 1934*, 59–76.

———. "Oleksandrivs'k-Kyïv: Spomyn, 1917–1918." *KAD na rik 1931*, 61–72.

An account of political conditions in Ukraine and the UNR forces in Kyiv and Oleksandrivsk that fought against the Bolshevik invasion at the end of 1917.

———. "Ostatnii akt tragediï." *LNV*, 1927, no. 9, 41–54; no. 10, 114–29; no. 11, 217–26; no. 12, 301–21.

———. "Uryvok iz spomyniv." *IKAChK na 1929 rik*, 155–61.

Reminiscences of political conditions in Ukraine and the suppression of the Bolshevik uprising in Kyiv during the winter of 1918.

Maiborodov, Vladimir. "S frantsuzami." *ARR* 16 (1925): 100–61.

A detailed account by a Russian monarchist of the French intervention in southern Ukraine and of relations between the representatives of the VA and the French command in Odessa.

Maiorov, M. *Z istoriï revoliutsiinoï borot'by na Ukraïni, 1914–1919.* Kharkiv: Derzhavne vydavnytstvo Ukraïny, 1928.

An account by a member of the Bolshevik underground of Bolshevik activities, mostly in Kyiv, during World War I and of the struggle for power in Ukraine in 1917–19. It includes a survey of the activities of the CP(B)U.

Makarushka, Liubomyr. "Fragmenty z Chortkivs'koï ofenzyvy." *IKAChK na 1935 rik*, 68–80.

A valuable account by an UHA officer of the Polish invasion of Western Ukraine and of the Chortkiv Offensive in June 1919.

Maksymchuk, Ivan. *Kozhukhiv: Spomyny.* Lviv: Chervona kalyna, 1930.

Makukh, Ivan. "Na perelomi: Uryvok zi spohadiv." *Zhyve slovo* (Lviv), 1939, no. 1, 25–30.

Maliarevskii, A. [Sumskoi, A.]. "Na pereekzamenovke: P. P Skoropadskii i ego vremia." *Arkhiv grazhdanskoi voiny* (Berlin) 2 (1922): 104–42.

A Russian journalist's critical account of the hetman government. The author maintains that Skoropads'kyi's mission was to reestablish the ancien régime in Russia, using Ukraine as a base for the struggle against the Bolsheviks.

Mandryka, M. I. "Deshcho za roky 1917 ta 1918: Z moïkh neopublikovanykh spomyniv." *UIs*, 1977, no. 1–2, 85–95; no. 3–4, 75–82.

Manilov, V., ed. *Iz istorii Oktiabr'skoi revoliutsii v Kieve: Vospominaniia uchastnikov.* Kyiv: Derzhavne vydavnytstvo Ukraïny, 1927.

———. *Pid hnitom nimets'koho imperiializmu (1918 r. na Kyïvshchyni): Statti, spohady, dokumenty, khronika.* Kyiv: Derzhavne vydavnytstvo Ukraïny, 1927.

Margolin, Arnold D. *From a Political Diary: Russia, the Ukraine, and America, 1905–1945.* New York: Columbia University Press, 1946.

———. *Ukraïna i politika Antanty: Zapiski evreia i grazhdanina.* Berlin: S. Efron, 1922.

A valuable source on UNR relations with the Entente in 1918–20 by a prominent Jewish-Ukrainian jurist, politician, member of the UNR mission in Paris, and UNR envoy to London. Published in English translation as *Ukraine and Policy of the Entente.* N.p.: A. Margolina, 1977.

Margulies, Manuil S. *God interventsii.* 3 vols. Berlin: Z. I. Grzhebin, 1923.

Memoirs by a left-wing Russian liberal critical of the Allies. Vol. 1 covers the period from September 1918 to April 1919; vol. 2, April to September 1919; and vol. 3, September 1919 to December 1920.

Margulies, Vladimir. *Ognennye gody: Materialy i dokumenty po istorii voiny na iuge Rossii.* Berlin: Manfred, 1923.

Valuable memoirs, which include documents and other materials, of the revolutionary period in southern Ukraine and the Hryhor'ïv and Makhno partisan movements from mid-March 1917 to mid-August 1919.

Maritchak, Teodor. "Na perelomi: Shchodennyk pidkhorunzhoho z 1918 roku." *LChK*, 1936, no. 1, 16–19; no. 2, 21–2; no. 3, 20 3; no. 4, 19–21; no. 5, 14–16; no. 6, 18–21.

———. "Otaman Voloshchuk pro Chortkivs'ku ofenzyvu." *LChK*, 1937, no. 3, 3–6; no. 4, 9–14.

Martos, Borys. *Vyzvol'nyi zdvyh Ukraïny.* New York: Naukove tovarysto im. Shevchenka, 1989.

———. "Z pryvodu statti Hen. shtabu hen. Oleksandra Vyshnivs'koho v 'Narodnii voli'." *VU*, no. 67 (1972), 6–16.

Marushchenko-Bohdanivs'kyi, A. "Materiialy do istoriï 1-ho kinnoho lubens'koho im. zaporozhs'koho polkovnyka Maksyma Zalizniaka polku." *ZD* 5 (1935): 209–26; 6 (1936): 193–228; 7 (1937): 213–25; 8 (1938): 177–214; 9 (1938): 206–25.

———. "Shturm Arsenalu: Shkitsy z perezhytykh refleksii." *T*, no. 5 (1927), 20–3. A valuable account by a UNR officer of the defeat of the Bolsheviks barricaded in the Arsenal in Kyiv from 1 to 4 February 1918.

———. "Ukraïnizatsiia chastyn v Rosiis'kii armiï." *IKAChK na 1935 rik*, 130–4.

———. "'Zanapastyly Bozhyi rai'." *T*, no. 9 (1928), 101–13.

Maslivets', Hryts'. "Podil's'ka hrupa: U 35-ti rokovyny 2-ho zymovoho pokhodu." *BUNDS*, no. 21 (1956), 1–5.

———. "Pravda pro Tiutiunnyka." *VK*, 1972, no. 4 (60), 36–40.
———. "Spohad." *BUNDS*, no. 9 (1955), 9–13.
  A valuable account of the raid of the Podillian Group into Right-Bank Ukraine.
Matchak, M. "Pochatky Sichovykh stril'tsiv." *IKAChK na 1937 rik*, 72–5.
Matushevs'kyi, F. "Iz shchodennyka ukraïns'koho posla." In *Z mynuloho*. Vol. 1, 138–57. Edited by R. Smal'-Stots'kyi. Warsaw: Ukraïns'kyi naukovyi instytut, 1938.
Mazlakh, Sergei. "Oktiabr'skaia revoliutsiia na Poltavshchine." *LR*, 1922, no. 1, 126–42.
  Memoirs of Bolshevik activities in Poltava gubernia in the fall of 1917 and its occupation by Red troops in the winter of 1918.
Meleshko, Fotii. "Pivdenno-skhidna hrupa Armiï UNR." *VK*, 1970, no. 3–4, 60–71; no. 5, 7–11; no. 6, 9–15; 1971, no. 1, 21–6.
———. "Rizdvo 1919 roku: Vytiah iz zahal'nykh spomyniv." In *U 50-richchia Zymovoho pokhodu Armiï UNR*, 149–55. Edited by M. Krat and F. Hrinchenko. New York: Ordens'ka rada Ordena Zaliznoho khresta Armiï Ukraïns'koï Narodn'oï Respubliky, 1973.
"Memorandum to the Government of the United States on the Recognition of the Ukrainian People's Republic." Washington, DC, 1920.
"Memorial and Petition for Liberty: Presented to the President of the United States and to the Peace Conference in Paris by the Delegates of the Ukrainian Convention of the State of Connecticut on the Day of the Third of August, 1919, in the Ukrainian Hall, New Britain, Connecticut."
Meyer, Henry Cord. "Germans in the Ukraine, 1918: Excerpts from Unpublished Letters." *American Slavic and East European Review* 9 (1950): 105–15.
  A record of German policy in Ukraine as witnessed from a high bureaucratic level; it indicates the ineffectivness of even moderate civilian opposition during the last days of the Second Reich.
Miakotin, V. "Iz nedalekogo proshlogo: Otryvki vospominanii." In *Revoliutsiia na Ukraine po memuaram belykh*, 222–38. Edited by N. N. Popov. Moscow: Gos. izd-vo, 1930.
  A valuable account of life in Kyiv and Odessa under the hetman government, with emphasis on the activities of refugees from Soviet Russia.
Michalski. Depesza z Konstantynopola. Warsaw, 5 May 1920. Ms.
———. Do Naczelnego Dowództwa W. P. w Warszawie. Sevastopil, 10 May 1920. Ms.
Międziński, Bogusław. "Moje wspomnienia," *ZH* 33 (1975): 3–27; 34: 134–86; 35 (1976): 85–117; 36: 97–187; 37: 61–222.
———. "Wspominając Sawinkowa." *ZH* 32 (1975): 39–49.
Miliukov, P. N. "Dnevnik." *NZh*, no. 66 (1961), 173–203; no. 67 (1962), 180–218.
  The diary of Miliukov's negotiations with the Germans in Kyiv, his activities against the hetman government, and his work in the VA.
Mirchuk, Ivan. "Spomyny pro nedavnie mynule." *URob*, 12 November 1948.

Mirna, Z. "Zhinky v Ukraïns'kii Tsentral'nii Radi." *Kaliendar "Ukraïns'koho holosu" na rik 1958* (Winnipeg), 109–17.

Mizh molotom a kovadlom: Prychynky do istoriï Ukraïns'koï armiï. Lviv: Chervona kalyna, 1923.

Moffat, Jay Pierrepont. *The Moffat Papers: Selections from the Diplomatic Journals, 1919–1943*. Cambridge: Harvard University Press, 1956.

Mogilianskii, N. M. "Tragediia Ukrainy: Iz perezhitogo v Kieve v 1918 godu." *ARR* 11 (1923): 74–105.

An account of events largely in Kyiv in 1918, with emphasis on the population's conflict with the Austro-German forces and the hetman administration.

Monkevych, Borys. *Chorni zaporozhtsi: Zymovyi pokhid i ostannia kampaniia Chornykh zaporozhtsiv*. Lviv: Dobra knyzhka, 1929.

———. "Pionery ukraïns'koho viis'ka: Pam'iati nevidomoho kozaka." *T*, no. 4 (1927), 9–18.

———. *Slidamy novitnikh zaporozhtsiv*. Lviv: Dobra knyzhka, 1928.

———. *Spomyny z 1918 r*. Lviv: Dobra knyzhka, 1928.

Moriaki v bor'be za vlast' sovetov na Ukraine, noiabr' 1917–1920 gg.: Sbornik dokumentov. Compiled by V. I. Aleksandrova and T. S. Fedorova. Kyiv: Akademiia nauk URSR, 1963.

A biased collection of 509 documents and other materials from various Russian and Ukrainian archives.

Moshyns'kyi, V. "Z dalekoho mynuloho: Spohad." *UK*, no. 64 (1982), 5–57.

Moszyński, Emilian, and R. Józef Moszyński. "Szkice i wspomnienia z Ziemi Owruckiej na Wołyniu." *PK* 2 (1963): 217–32.

Mstislavskii, S. D. "Medovyi mesiats: Iz vospominanii o Denikinshchine na Ukraine." *Byl*, no. 25 (1924), 221–46; no. 26, 159–76; no. 27–28, 301–33; no. 29 (1925), 180–98; no. 30, 176–94.

A detailed account of Denikin's rule in Kyiv in 1919, which includes documentary material, by a member of the Central Committee of the Russian Socialist party active in the underground in Kyiv gubernia.

Mudryi, Vasyl'. "Proskurivs'kyi pohrom: Uryvok zi spomyniv." *NIKTP na rik 1926*, 113–24.

M. V. Frunze na frontakh grazhdanskoi voiny: Sbornik dokumentov. Moscow: Voenizdat, 1941.

Documents (orders, telegrams, appeals, and other material) dealing with Frunze's activities on the Ukrainian and other fronts from January 1919 to December 1920.

Myhovych, P. "Pry I-ii brygadi ChUSS: Khronolohichnyi khid podii." *LChK*, 1938, no. 10, 11–15; no. 11, 16–19; no. 12, 11–14; 1939, no. 1, 17–19; no. 2, 17–19.

———. "Pry VII-ii brygadi UHA." *LChK*, 1937, no. 5, 5–9; no. 6, 6–10; no. 7–8, 3–7; no. 9, 4–6; no. 10, 17–19; no. 11, 4–6; 1938, no. 2, 5–8; no. 3, 13–16; no. 4, 5–8; no. 5, 14–17; no. 6, 5–8; no. 7–8, 25–9.

Mykhailyk, Mykhailo. "Ukraïns'ke selo v chasy natsional'noï revoliutsiï: Spomyn z chasiv borot'by za vyzvolennia odnoho sela." *LChK*, 1933, no. 1, 10–14; no. 2, 5–9.
   An account of the struggle of the population of Hlodosy, Kherson gubernia, against Russian Army deserters, the Bolsheviks, Austro-German troops, and the VA during the years 1917–1920.
——. "Ukraïns'kyi natsional'nyi rukh v Krymu v 1917 r." *LChK*, 1932, no. 6, 12–14; no. 7–8, 22–6.
   An account of the vicissitudes of the Revolution of 1917 in the Crimea and Ukrainian organizations there.
——. *Za strilets'ku slavu: Spomyny z rr. 1919–20.* Lviv: I. Tyktor, 1936.
Mykhailova, Liubov. "Spohady." *T* (New York), no. 35 (1965), 4–6.
——. "Spohady pro Symona Petliuru." *Kyïv* (Philadelphia), 1964, no. 4 (85), 111–15.
Myronov, Ie. "Z pidpillia za Tsentral'noï Rady i het'manshchyny: Spohady pro pidpil'nu robotu na Katerynoslavshchyni 1918 r." *LR*, 1930, no. 3–4, 138–47.
   Memoirs of Bolshevik underground activities in Katerynoslav gubernia in 1918.
Myshuha, Luka. *Pokhid ukraïns'kykh viis'k na Kyïv: serpen', 1919.* Vienna: Ukraïns'kyi prapor, 1920.
Mytsiuk, O. *Doba Dyrektoriï UNR: Spomyny i rozdumy.* Lviv: Hromads'kyi holos, 1939.
N., J. "Ś. p. generał W. Zmijenko: Wspomnienia pośmiertne." *BPU*, 1938, no. 43, 466–7.
N., N. "Pobratymcy broni: List rannego oficera." *RW*, 25 July 1920.
   An account by a Polish officer of Polish-Ukrainian military cooperation against the Bolsheviks during the spring offensive of 1920, the national consciousness of the Ukrainian population, and the assistance they gave to the Polish troops.
Na granicy epok: Wspomnienia o udziale Polaków w Rewolucji Październikowej i wojnie domowej w Rosji, 1917–1921. Edited by Zbigniew Iwańczuk et al. Warsaw: Książka i Więdza, 1967.
"Nachalo Vrangelevshchiny." *KA* 21 (1927): 174–81.
Naczelne Dowództwo W. P. Sztab Generalny. Instrukcja dla rokowań o zawieszenie broni z delegacją ukraińską w Dęblinie. Warsaw, 7 August 1919. Ms.
Nakaz Holovnoï komandy viis'k Ukraïns'koï Narodn'oï Respubliky, No. 131 (26 August 1919). Ms.
Naumenko, Iurii. "Kruty i Bazar." *BPU*, 1933, no. 1, 30–3.
——. "Moia sluzhba v 5-ii Khersons'kii strilets'kii dyviziï." *ZD* 7 (1937): 165–80.
   A detailed account by a UNR officer of the campaign against the Bolsheviks on both sides of the Zbruch from July to the end of November 1920.

———. "Na perelomi." *ZD* 5 (1935): 186–96.
Nazaruk, Osyp. *Halyts'ka deliegatsiia v Ryzi 1920 r.: Spomyny uchasnyka.* Lviv: Ukraïns'ka khrystyians'ka organizatsiia, 1930.
———. *Rik na Velykii Ukraïni: Konspekt spomyniv z ukraïns'koï revoliutsiï.* Vienna: Ukraïns'kyi prapor, 1920.
A jurist and editor's account of political events in Ukraine from November 1918 through November 1919, as seen from the decision-making centers.
———. "Spomyny pro te, iaki buly pershi kroky het'mans'koï ideï u hlybyni narodnikh mas pislia velykoï katastrofy nashoï derzhavnosty." In *Za velych natsiï: U dvadtsiasti rokovyny vidnovlennia Ukraïns'koï Het'mans'koï Derzhavy.* 39–49. Edited by Mykola Pasika, Mykhailo Karpyshyn, and Teofil' Kostruba. Lviv, 1938. Reprint, New York: Bulava, 1955.
———. "Ukraïns'ka armiia v chasi katastrofy." *UP*, 13 January 1920.
A valuable account of the UHA struggle against the Red Army and VA and its physical condition in the fall of 1919.
———. "V ukraïns'kii dypl'omatychnii sluzhbi v rokakh 1915–1923." *LChK*, 1938, no. 10, 16–17.
Nebutev, Ivan Alekseev. *Iz vospominanii levogo esera: Podpol'naia rabota na Ukraine.* Moscow: Gos. izd-vo, 1925.
Nemirovich-Danchenko, G. V. *V Krymu pri Vrangele: Fakty i itogi.* Berlin: P. Ol'denburg, 1922.
An account of Wrangel's campaign in 1920 stressing his socioeconomic policy in the Crimea and conditions there.
Neufeld, Dietrich. *A Russian Dance of Death: Revolution and Civil War in the Ukraine.* Winnipeg: Hyperion Press, 1977.
Nikulin, Ia. *Na fronte grazhdanskoi voiny, 1918–1921 g.g.: Ocherki i vospominaniia.* Petrograd: Priboi, 1923.
Nimchuk, Ivan, ed. *Choho pryishly nimtsi na Ukraïnu? Ofitsiial'ni povidomlennia, dumky, rozmovy.* Vienna: Vidrodzhennia, 1918.
Nimylovych, Osyp. "Spomyny pro ostanni dni 3-ho polku 1-oï brygady USS." *LChK*, 1936, no. 5, 20–1.
Nishchenko, Kornel'. "Spohady pro pochatok vyzvol'nykh zmahan'," *AUNS na rik 1968*, 105–20.
Notes présentées par la délégation de la République Ukrainienne à la Conférence de la Paix à Paris. 2 vols. Paris: Robinet-Houtain, 1919.
Official communications of the UNR delegation to the Paris Peace Conference from February to 15 July 1919.
Nyzhankivs'kyi, Stepan. "Z Ukraïns'koiu Halyts'koiu Armiieiu: Na spomyn velykoï doby." *ND* (Prague), 1927, no. 6, 22–7.
Oberuchev, Konstantin M. *V dni revoliutsii: Vospominaniia uchastnika Velikoi russkoi revoliutsii 1917-go goda.* New York: Narodopravstvo, 1919.

———. *Vospominaniia.* New York: Gruppa pochitatelei pamiati K.M. Oberucheva, 1930.

Memoirs by a Russian officer of his activities from the last quarter of the nineteenth century through November 1917, with emphasis on his service as military commissioner of Kyiv gubernia in 1917.

Obolenskii, V. "Krym v 1917–1920 g.g." *NChS,* no. 5–6 (1923), 5–40.

Memoirs by the former chairman of the Tavriia Gubernia Zemstvo of Wrangel's plan for land reform and his domestic policy in the Crimea.

———. "V period Krymskago pravitel'stva." *NChS,* no. 7 (1924), 81–110.

Oborona Zamostia, 1920–1955. Toronto: Ukraïns'kyi voienno-istorychnyi instytut, 1956.

Obrona Lwowa 1–22 listopada 1918: Relacje uczestników. Vols. 2–3. Edited by Eugeniusz Wawrzkowicz and Józef Klink. Lviv: Towarzystwo Badania Historji Obrony Lwowa i Województw Południowo-Wschodnich, 1936, 1939.

"Ocherk vzaimootnoshenii Vooruzhennykh sil iuga Rossii i predstavitelei frantsuzskago komandovaniia." *ARR* 16 (1925): 233–62.

Ohiienko, Ivan. "Urochystyi v'ïzd S. Petliury do Kam'iantsia-Podil's'koho 1-ho travnia 1920 r." *NKul,* 1936, no. 5 (14), 321–31.

Okunevs'kyi, Iaroslav. "Rozmova z arkhykniazem Vil'hel'mom dnia 4 serpnia 1918 roku." *D,* 8–10 May 1931.

Details of the conversation between the author, an admiral of the Austrian Navy, and Archduke Wilhelm von Habsburg on 4 August 1918 concerning the Ukrainian question and the latter's close ties with Ukrainian circles.

Omel'chenko, T. "Moï spohady pro synikh." *ZD* 7 (1937): 57–67.

Omelianovych-Pavlenko, Mykhailo. "Na choli zaporozhtsiv v 1919 r. u borot'bi z denikintsiamy." *KAD na rik 1930,* 46–60.

Valuable reminiscences by the commander of the Zaporozhian Corps of its campaigns against the VA in the fall of 1919.

———. *Na Ukraïni, 1917–1918.* Prague: Stilus, 1935.

An authoritative account of the revolution in Ukraine, with emphasis on Katerynoslav gubernia.

———. *Na Ukraïni, 1919: Perehovory i viina z rosiis'koiu Dobrovol'choiu armiieiu: Spomyny holovy delegatsiï ta komandyra Zaporiz'koï hrupy.* Prague: Stilus, 1940.

A valuable account of UNR negotiations with Denikin in mid-September 1919 for a joint operation against the Bolsheviks, set against the background of partisan fighting in the Bolshevik and VA rears.

———. "Pochatok 1919 roku." *RN,* 1929, no. 1–2, 38–47; no. 3–4, 109–17; no. 5, 166–76; no. 6–7, 210–17; no. 8–9, 276–81.

———. *Spomyny.* Lviv: Ukraïns'ka vydavnycha spilka, 1930.

Reminiscences by the commander of the UHA and later the UNR Army, of the campaigns against Poland, the Bolsheviks, and the VA.

———. *Ukraïns'ko-pol's'ka viina, 1918–1919.* Prague: Merkur-fil'm, 1929.

———. *Zymovyi pokhid, 6, XII, 1919 – 6, V, 1920.* Kalisz: Ukraïns'ke voienno-istorychne tovarystvo, 1929.

Memoirs of the guerrilla war in the VA and Bolshevik rears from December 1919 to May 1920, based on the author's diaries and experiences.

Onats'kyi, Ievhen. "Akademiia pam'iati Symona Petliury ta Evhena Konoval'tsia." *NK*, 1947, no. 20.

———. "Po pokhylii ploshchi: Zapysky zhurnalista i dyplomata." *S*, 1967, no. 5, 94–118; no. 7, 86–108; no. 8, 92–120; no. 9, 92–113; no. 10, 113–22; no. 11, 92–110; no. 12, 107–21; 1968, no. 1, 103–14; no. 4, 109–18; no. 6, 114–21; no. 7, 104–15; no. 8, 108–16; no. 9, 101–8.

———. "S. Petliura—chesnist' z ideieiu." *O* (Buenos Aires), May 1955, 1–2.

———. "Tvorennia dyplomatychnoï misiï pry Vatykani za Karmans'koho i Tyshkevycha." *Biuleten': Materiialy IV-oï naukovoï konferentsiï NTSh* (Toronto), no. 1 (4) (1953), 33–60.

———. "Ukraïns'ka dyplomatychna misiia v Italiï za pershykh shist' misiatsiv svoieï diial'nosty." *KAV na 1956 rik.*

Onyshchuk, Denys. "Ostannii akt: Uryvok zi spomyniv 2-hoho tiazhkoho dyvizionu 3 brygady Ch.U.H.A." *LChK*, 1938, no. 9, 4–10.

Opałek, Mieczysław. *W dworku na Litwie: Z lat dziecinnych Józefa Piłsudskiego.* Cracow: Drukarnia Ludowa, 1917.

"Organizatsiia vlasti na iuge Rossii v period grazhdanskoi voiny, 1918–1920 gg." *ARR* 4 (1922): 241–51.

Documents on the organization of VA authority on the territory under its control from September 1918 to November 1920.

Orłowski, Xawery. *Projekt tyczący sie akcji Sprzymierzonych na Ukrainie.* Warsaw, 1 November 1919. Ms.

Osipov, I. *Na prolome: Ocherki 1914–1920 g.g.* Peremyshl: Sovremennaia biblioteka, 1922.

Memoirs of a Ukrainian Russophile describing Russian wartime policy in Galicia and Denikin's attitude toward the Galician Ukrainian refugees in the Don region.

Oskilko, Volodymyr. *Do iasnovel'mozhnoho pana nachal'nyka Panstva Pol's'koï Respubliky.* Kielce, 5 June 1919. Ms.

Ostroverkha, Mykhailo. "Mobilizatsiia na Ukraïni: Spohad z 1919-ho roku." *KUI na rik 1937*, 79–80.

———. "Nashe prave krylo v ofenzyvi pislia chortkivs'koho prolomu." *KUI na rik 1938*, 117–19.

———. "Pid Chornym Ostrovom: Fragment iz chervnia 1920 r." *KAD na rik 1935*, 100–3.

———. "U moskovs'komu poloni, 1916–1918 rr." *LChK*, 1936, no. 4, 15–18.

———. "Zhmut spohadiv." *AUNS na 1967 rik*, 145–50.
Ostrovershenko, Ivan. "Z vyzvol'noï borot'by: Spohad." *Dor*, 1966, no. 9, 7–9; no. 10, 5–6.
"'Ot vlasti otkazyvaius' (Dokumenty o getmanshchine iz arkhiva Kharkovskogo gubernskogo starosty)." *LR* 1924, no. 2, 224–31.
Telegrams and dispatches of county captains and declarations by landowners indicating the growth of peasant dissatisfaction with and uprisings against the hetman regime.
Otechestvennaia voina protiv germanskikh okkupantov v 1918 godu. Moscow: Gospolitizdat, 1941.
Appeals, orders, letters, telegrams, and reports dealing with the struggle of the people against the German troops in Ukraine and Belarus from February 1918 to March 1919.
Otreshko-Ars'kyi, Mykola. "Proryv frontu." *Tr* (New York), no. 80 (1976), 13–22.
———. "Spil'na voienna shkola Armiï UNR." *Tr* (New York), no. 72 (1973) 10–17; no. 73, 12–19.
———. "Spohad pro Symona Petliuru." *Biuleten' Holovnoï upravy Soiuzu ukraïns'kykh veteraniv*, May 1949, 5–8.
Padalka, Vasyl'. "Reid rozvidchoho viddilu sotnyka V. Padalky: Materiialy do vyvchennia 2-ho Zymovoho pokhodu." *Visti* (Munich), no. 114 (1964), 44–7; no. 115, 93–4; no. 116, 129–31; no. 117 (1965), 17–19; no. 118, 65–7; no. 119, 92–5.
Paladiichuk, S. "Spohady pro 'Hrebenkivshchynu'." *Tr* (New York), no. 42 (1967), 11–13.
Palii-Sydorians'kyi, Mykhailo. "'Na reidi': Zi spohadiv." *T*, no. 5 (1930), 9–13.
Paliïv, Dmytro. "Na chystu vodu: Spomyn." *VK*, 1971, no. 1 (51), 11–20.
———. "Nashe viis'ko: Ukraïns'ka Halyts'ka Armiia." *NIKTP na rik 1922*, 145–9.
———. "P'iatdesiatrichchia USS, 1914–1964." *Kalendar "Ukraïns'kykh vistei"* (Edmonton), 1963, 58–67.
———. "Zhmut spomyniv: Za generalamy." *IKAChK na 1935 rik*, 40–6.
———. "Zymovyi pokhid." *LChK*. 1935, no. 6, 8–9; no. 7–8, 7–10.
Pan'kiv, I. *Na pantsyrnomu potiahu "Otaman Mel'nyk": Spohady z 1918–1919 rokiv*. Winnipeg: Novyi shliakh, 1954.
P-pa, N. "Protybol'shevyts'ki povstannia na Ukraïni v 1921 r. na osnovi ofitsiinykh bol'shevyts'kykh zvidomlen' i inshykh nepublikovanykh materiialiv." *LChK*, 1932, no. 6, 19–22; no. 9, 6–7.
Pasmanik, D. S. *Revoliutsionnye gody v Krymu; Prilozhenie: Pis'mo I.I. Petrunkevicha o russkoi intelligentsii*. Paris: Imprimerie de Navarre, 1926.
Reminiscences by a conservative observer about vicissitudes in the Crimea from February 1917 to April 1919.
Paszkiewicz, G. "Wypad na Kliczew 12, XII, 1919." *B* (Warsaw) 13 (1924): 253–9.

Patlakh. "Kiev v ianvare 1918 goda: Vospominaniia." *LR*, 1923, no. 5, 18–24.
Pekarchuk, Stepan. "Povstannia na Bratslavshchyni." *LChK*, 1930, no. 4, 9–10.
An account of the uprising against the Bolsheviks in Bratslav county in April 1919.
———. "Voiats'kym shliakhom." *Nashe zhyttia* (Philadelphia), 1969, no. 9, 31–2; no. 10, 31–3.
Perfets'kyi, A. "Smert' chety kinnykh chornomortsiv: Pam'iati poliahlykh." *IKAChK na 1925 rik*, 116–19.
Pelens'kyi, Damian. "Osin' 1918 roku: Uryvky zi spomyniv." *IKAChK na 1934 rik*, 75–83.
Pelens'kyi, Oleksander. *Svitova kontsertova podorozh Ukraïns'koï respublikans'koï kapeli: Spomyn uchasnyka*. Lviv: the author, 1933.
"Pershyi mizhnarodnii akt vidrodzhenoï ukraïns'koï derzhavy: U 20-littia Beresteis'koho myra," *"Ukraïns'kyi invalid": Zahal'nyi kaliendar ukraïns'koho narodu na rik 1938*, 53–6.
Pervaia konnaia v izobrazhenii ee boitsov i komandirov. Moscow: Gosizdat, 1930.
Peskarpoli, Antoniia. "Interv'iu z S. Petliuroiu: Iz zapysok ukraïns'koho zhurnalista." *NK*, 7 June 1956.
Petliura, Symon. "A Letter from Symon Petliura to Canada." *HU*, 29 July 1978.
———. "Lyst do henerala Mykoly Udovychenka." *BUNDS*, 1958, no. 28, 1–5.
———. "Lyst do Zhana Pelis'ie." *NK*, 7 June 1956.
———. "Lyst Holovnoho otamana Petliury do odnoho z ioho generaliv." *NS*, 1955, no. 1, 16–19.
———. *Statti, lysty, dokumenty*. 2 vols. New York: Ukrainian Academy of Arts and Sciences in the US, 1956, 1979.
———. "Suchasna ukraïns'ka emigratsiia ta ïï zavdannia." *NB*, 1 February 1966.
———. "Try lysty Holovnoho otamana sl. pam. S. V. Peliury." *RD*, 1952, no. 1, 19–22.
Petrenko. "Lystopadovyi reid 1921 r. cherez pol's'ko-ukraïns'kyi kordon: Spomyny z II Zymovoho pokhodu v lystopadi 1921." *LChK*, 1934, no. 6, 6–8.
Petriv, Tamara. "Vesna 1917 roku u Kyïevi." *BSBUVK*, 1962, no. 12, 10–12.
Petriv, Vsevolod. "Iz zustrichei z Symonom Vasyl'ovychem Petliuroiu." *H*, no. 17–18 (1936), 26.
———. *Spomyny z chasiv ukraïns'koï revoliutsiï, 1917–1921*. 4 vols. Lviv: Chervona kalyna, 1927–31.
Valuable memoirs by a high-ranking UNR officer, with special reference to the formation of the Ukrainian armed forces and descriptions of some of its leaders, including Petliura, Bolbachan, and Archduke Wilhelm von Habsburg.
———. "Uryvky zi spomyniv." *IKAChK na 1929 rik*, 29–39.
———. "Zhytomyrs'ka iunats'ka shkola: Formuvannia, nauka, boï, pershyi vypusk ukraïns'koï starshyny; storinky z nedrukovanoho shchodennyka." *LChK*, 1936,

no. 5, 18–19; no. 6, 7–10; no. 7–8, 15–18; no. 10, 11–15; no. 11, 14–17; 1937, no. 1, 19–21; no. 3, 14–17.

Piętkiewicz, Kazimierz. "Wspomnienia szkolne z Suwałszczyzny, 1876–1884." *N* (Warsaw) 1, no. 2 (1930), 357–66.

Pigido, F.; et al, eds. *Material Concerning Ukrainian-Jewish Relations during the Years of the Revolution (1917–1921): Collection of Documents and Testimonies by Prominent Jewish Political Workers*. Munich: Ukrainian Information Bureau, 1956.

Piłsudska, Aleksandra (Pilsudski, Alexandra). *Memoirs of Madame Pilsudski*. London: Hurst and Blackett, 1940.

———. *Pilsudski: A Biography by His Wife Alexandra Pilsudski*. New York: Dodd, Mead, 1941.

———. *Wspomnienia*. London: Gryf Publications, 1960.

Piłsudski, Józef. *Erinnerungen und Dokumente*. 4 vols. Essen: Essener Verlags-Anstalt, 1935–6.

———. *Korespondencja, 1914–17*. Edited by Stanisław Biegański and Andrzej Suchcitz. London: Instytut Józefa Piłsudskiego, 1984.

———. "Listy." *N* (Warsaw) 15 (1937): 117–36, 243–60, 418–33; 16: 374–9, 495–512; 18 (1938): 67–75, 205–41, 345–78; (London) 7 (1962): 4–126.

———. "Listy do Leona Wasilewskiego." *ZH* 19 (1971): 142–4.

———. "Listy Józefa Piłsudskiego z okresu PPS, 1898–1904." *N* (London) 11 (1978): 3–44; 12 (1979): 3–42; 13 (1980): 3–23.

———. *The Memories of a Polish Revolutionary and Soldier*. Translated and edited by D. R. Gillie. London: Faber and Faber, 1931. Reprint, New York: AMS Press, 1971.

———. *Moje pierwsze boje: Wspomnienia spisane w twierdze magdeburskiej*. Warsaw: Instytut Józefa Piłsudskiego, 1938.

———. *Pisma, mowy, rozkazy: Wydanie zbiorowe prac dotychczas drukiem ogłoszonych*. 8 vols. Warsaw: Instytut Badania Najnowszej Historji Polski, 1930–1.

———. *Pisma wybrane*. London: M. I. Kolin, 1943.

———. *Pisma zbiorowe: Wydanie prac dotychczas drukiem ogłoszonych*. 10 vols. Warsaw: Instytut Józefa Piłsudskiego, 1937–8.

———. *Poprawki historyczne*. Warsaw: Instytut Badania Najnowszej Historji Polski, 1931.

———. "Psychologia więźnia: Odczyt wygłoszony w Warszawie na zaproszene Komitetu b. Więźniów Politycznych w dn. 24 maja 1925 roku." *K*, 1986, no. 7–8, 3–15.

———. "Sześć listów Józefa Piłsudskiego do Stanisława Szeptyckiego z okresu Wojny Polsko-Radzieckiej." *DN*, 1971, no. 3, 157–73.

———. *W ćwierćwiecze zgonu: Szkic biograficzny—Józef Piłsudski mówi—Komendant i Marszałek w poezji i pieśni—za życia i po śmierci—głosy zagranicy—u wrót Wawelu*. London: Komitet Uczczenia Pamięci Józefa Piłsudskiego w 25-lecie Jego Zgonu, 1960.

———. *Wybór pism*. New York: Instytut Józefa Piłsudskiego, 1944.

———. "Wyjątki z listów." *N* (London) 1 (1948): 9–11.

———. *Year 1920 and Its Climax Battle of Warsaw during the Polish-Soviet War, 1919–1920: With the Addition of Soviet Marshal Tukhachevski's March beyond the Vistula*. London and New York: Piłsudski Institute of America/Piłsudski Institute of London, 1972.

Piontkovskii, Sergei A. *Grazhdanskaia voina v Rossii, 1918–1921: Khrestomatiia*. Moscow: Izdatel'stvo Kommunisticheskogo universiteta, 1925.

A collection of documents, correspondence, memoirs, and other materials dealing with the Russian Civil War and intervention in southern Ukraine.

"Pislia pidpysannia myru v Beresti pomizh oserednymy derzhavamy i Ukraïnoiu (Vytiahy z nakaziv avstriis'kykh i nimets'kykh komand): Podav I. K." *LChK*, 1937, no. 2, 2–3.

"Pis'mo gen. D. G. Shcherbacheva gen. A. I. Denikinu." *KA* 21 (1927): 220–3.

Pobóg-Malinowski, Władysław. *Narodowa demokracja, 1887–1918: Fakty i dokumenty*. Warsaw: Drukarnia "Polska Zjednoczona," 1933.

———. "Nieznane listy Piłsudskiego." *ZH* 2 (1962): 141–53.

"Poland's Eastern Policy: An interview with Prime Minister Skulski." *LA*, 24 July 1920, 213–15.

Poliakov, Ivan Alekseevich. *Donskie kazaki v bor'be s bol'shevikami: Vospominaniia*. Munich, 1962.

Politychna konventsiia mizh P. ta U. Warsaw, 21 April 1920. Ms.

Polovoi-Polianskii, K. "Vooruzhennaia bor'ba s denikintsami na Verkhnedneprovshchine i Kremenchugshchine: Iz vospominanii." *LR*, 1926, no. 6 (21), 86–97.

An account of partisan activities in the VA rear in Ukraine in 1919.

Pomarański, S., ed. *Pierwsza wojna polska, 1918–1920: Zbiór wojennych komunikatów prasowych Sztabu Generalnego za czas od 26, XI, 1918 r. do 20. X, 1920 r.* Warsaw: Główna Księgarnia Wojskowa, 1920.

Poniatyshyn, Petro. "Ukraïns'ka sprava v Amerytsi pid chas Pershoï svitovoï viiny." *AUNS na 1967 rik*, 185–96.

Popov, Nikolai N. "Ocherki revoliutsionnykh sobytii v Kharkove ot iiunia 1917 g. po dekabr' 1918 g." *LR*, 1922, no. 1, 16–34.

An account of the Bolshevik struggle in Kharkiv against the Central Rada and the hetman regime from June 1917 through December 1918.

Porokhivs'kyi, Ihnat. "Pam'iatna nich u povstanchomu shtabi: Spomyn." *LChK*, 1936, no. 1, 7–10; no. 2, 18–20.

———. "Persha ukraïns'ka dyviziia: Spomyn." *KAD na rik 1936*, 50–67.

———. "Shtab Pivdennoho frontu, 14-ho hrudnia 1918 r.–15-ho sichnia 1919 r.:

Spomyn." *LChK*, 1938, no. 7–8, 15–18; no. 9, 17–20.

———. "Spohady pro l-yi Ukraïns'kyi korpus." *KAD na rik 1934*, 26–54.

Poselstwo Rzeczypospolitcj Polskiej, Copenhagen. Wizyta przedstawiciela ukraińskiego Dr. D. Lewickiego w Poselstwie. 9 May 1920. Ms.

Poznański, Karol. "Jak to naprawdę było w Rydze z Mińskiem?" *TP*, 28 November 1964.

———. "Pokój Ryski." *W*, 27 April 1957.

———. "Ryga, 1920–1921." *W*, 14 April 1957.

An account by a member of the secretariat of the Polish delegation about the peace negotiations in Riga.

Pravoberezhets', Ia. "Nezabutni heroï vyzvol'noï borot'by: Spohady povstantsia." *TrU*, no. 2–4 (1923), 74–8.

Prokhoda, Vasyl'. "Iak Symon Petliura stav vozhdem Ukraïns'koï Armiï." *H*, no. 20–1 (1936), 20–4.

———. "Petliura ta zbroina borot'ba." *H*, no. 11 (1933), 10–13.

———. "Podiï u borot'bi za Ukraïnu." *Tr* (New York), no. 41 (1966), 4–6; no. 42 (1967), 8–11; no. 43, 17–19; no. 44, 11–14; no. 45, 12–14; no. 46, 16–18; no. 47 (1968), 14–18.

———. "Siri abo sirozhupannyky." *VK*, 1967, no. 4 (28), 35–42; 1968, no. 2 (33), 40–4; no. 3 (34), 37–41.

Memoirs of the campaigns of the Graycoats division during the Bolshevik invasion of Ukraine in 1919.

———. "Sirozhupannyky v povstani proty uriadu het'mana Skoropads'koho." *T*, no. 9 (1928), 90–5.

———. *Symon Petliura*. Neu-Ulm: "Ukraïns'ki visti," 1968.

———. "Symon Petliura, vozhd' ukraïns'koho viis'ka." *T*, no. 28–9 (1936), 3–49.

———. "Zapysky do istoriï sirykh (sirozhupannykiv)." *ZD* 1 (1929): 72–117.

———. *Zapysky nepokirlyvoho: Istoriia natsional'noho usvidomlennia, zhyttia i diial'nosty zvychainoho ukraïntsia*. Toronto: Proboiem, 1967.

Prokopovych, V'iacheslav. "Ne plachem, a mechem." *Ukraïns'ka trybuna* (Warsaw), 6 December 1921.

———. "Ostannia podorozh." *Tr* (Paris), 1931, no. 20–1, 26–33.

An account of Petliura in Poland in 1924 and his move to Paris via Budapest and Vienna.

Protest of the Ukrainian Republic to the United States against the Delivery of Eastern Galicia to Polish Domination. Washington, DC, 1919.

"Protokoły posiedzeń Komitetu Narodowego Polskiego w Paryżu z okresu 2 października 1918 do 23 stycznia 1919 r. (wybór)." *NDP* 2 (1959): 111–82.

Protsenko, Petro. "Oskilkivshchyna." *LChK*, 1934, no. 4, 16–18.

———. "Ukraïnizatsiia na Pivnichnomu fronti Rosiis'koi armiï." *ZD* 6 (1937): 229–37.

Pruszyński, Mieczysław. "Rozmowa historyczna ze St. Grabskim." *BM*, 20 November–5 December 1935.
Prykhod'ko V. "Ukraïna v potiahakh: Spomyn z 1917 roku." *IKAChK na 1937 rik*, 138–46.
Przebieg pertraktacji o zawieszeniu broni na Froncie Ukraińskim. Warsaw, 20 August 1919. Ms.
Ptashyns'kyi, P., ed. "Do istoriï nimets'ko-avstriis'koï interventsiï na Ukraïni." *Arkhiv Radians'koï Ukraïny*, 1932, no. 1–2, 64–106.
Twenty-two hitherto unpublished documents pertaining to Austro-German policy in Ukraine.
Pyl'kevych, Oleksander. Do Przewodniczącego Ukraińskiej Komisji Likwidacyjnej. Strzałkowo, 16 August 1921. Ms.
Pys'mennyi, Stepan. "Symon Petliura: Spohad suchasnyka." *UPS*, 1966, no. 5, 6–8.
Quaroni, Pietro. *Diplomatic Bags: An Ambassador's Memoirs*. Translated and edited by Anthony Rhodes. New York: D. White, 1966.
Radians'ke budivnytsvo na Ukraïni v roky hromadians'koï viiny, lystopad 1918–serpen' 1919: Zbirnyk dokumentiv i materialiv. Edited by M. A. Rubach. Kyiv: Akademiia nauk URSR, 1962.
Radziejowski, Janusz. "Ruch narodowy i rewolucyjny na Ukrainie w okresie działalności Centralnej Rady, marzec 1917–kwiecień 1918 r." *SDZSRR* 9 (1973): 53–84.
Rafes, Moisei G. *Dva goda revoliutsii na Ukraine: Evoliutsiia i raskol "Bunda."* Moscow:, Gos. izd-vo, 1920.
A biased but informative account of the Ukrainian revolution, mainly from 1917 through the beginning of 1919, and the attitude of the Social Democratic Jewish Bund toward the Ukrainian state by one of its leaders, who later became a Bolshevik. It includes a number of documents.
———. "Moi vospominaniia." *Byl*, no. 19 (1922), 177–97.
Raievs'kyi, S. "Moia sluzhba pid komanduvanniam sv. p. Symona Petliury." *UKom*, 1947, no. 1, 15–21.
Raievs'kyi, Vasyl'. "Z moïkh spomyniv." *IKAChK na 1932 rik*, 26–35.
Rakitin, N. *Zapiski konarmeitsa*. Moscow: Voennoe izdatel'stvo, 1929.
An account of the 1920 Soviet-Polish War by a Bolshevik officer.
Rakovskii, Khristian G. "Il'ich i Ukraina." *LR*, 1925, no. 2, 5–10.
A brief account of Lenin's Ukrainian policy from the second half of 1918 through the summer of 1919. Originally it appeared in *Kommunist* (21 January 1925).
"Raport Gen. sht. podpolkovnika N. predstaviteliu Dobrovol'cheskoi armii v g. Kieve." In *Belyi arkhiv*, vol. 2–3, 138–44. Edited by Ia. M. Kisovoi. Paris, 1928.
Raport konfidenta Berlińskiego o stosunkach ukraińsko-niemieckich. Warsaw, 31 May 1920. Ms.

"Raport sostoiashchago v shtabe predstavitelia Verkhovnago kommandovaniia Dobrarmii Gen. sht. podpolkovnika S-go predstaviteliu Verkhovnago kommandovaniia v Kieve." In *Belyi arkhiv*, vol. 2–3, 145–50. Edited by Ia. M. Kisovoi. Paris, 1928.

A report by a high-ranking VA officer about his secret activities in the Red Army in Ukraine during the summer of 1919.

"Raport Wojskowego Generalnego Gubernatorstwa w Lublinie z roku 1916." *N* (London), 9 (1974): 309–44.

Ravich-Cherkasskii, M. "Fevral'–dekabr' 1917 g. v Ekaterinoslave." *LR*, 1922, no. 1, 74–80.

An account of Bolshevik activities among the workers and soldiers in Katerynoslav in 1917.

Rekis, O. "Z bil'shovyts'koho pidpillia v Odesi, 1918–1919 rr." *LR*, 1931, no. 1–2, 169–86.

"Relacja żandarmerii rosyjskiej o aresztowaniu Józefa Piłsudskiego w 1900 r." *N* (Warsaw) 19, no. 2 (1939), 225–32.

Rembolovych, Ivan. "Reid 1921 roku." *ZD* 3 (1932): 156–71.

———. "1918 rik na Chernyhivshchyni." *ZD* 8 (1938): 86–98.

Rey, Mikołaj. "Memoriał Gen. Tadeusza Rozwadowskiego w sprawie wschodnich granic Polski." *PW*, no. 92 (1929), 414–28.

Riappo, Anfisa. "Revoliutsionnaia bor'ba v Nikolaeve: Vospominaniia." *LR*, 1924, no. 4, 5–43.

Memoirs by a Bolshevik agent of relations between the authorities in Mykolaiv and German and Entente troops during the first half of 1919, and of Hryhor'iv's and Makhno's uprisings against the Red troops.

———. "Vostanie nikolaevskogo proletariata protiv nemtsev." *LR*, 1922, no. 1, 107–23.

Memoirs of the uprising against the German troops in Mykolaiv at the end of March 1918.

Roberts, Carl Eric B. *In Denikin's Russia and the Caucasus, 1919–1920*. London: Collins, 1921.

An informative account by a British journalist of the Russian Civil War and the Allied intervention in southern Ukraine and northern Caucasia.

Rohoznyi, Hryts'. "Bazar." *SD*, 1934, no. 2, 131–48; no. 3, 209–28; no. 5–6, 422–49.

A valuable, critical account by a UNR Army officer of the raid into Right-Bank Ukraine in November 1921.

———. *14-tym rokovynam herois'koï smerty 359 lytsariv pid Bazarom*. Lviv: Desheva knyzhka, 1935.

Roja, Bolesław. *Legendy i fakty*. Warsaw: Księgarnia F. Hoesicka, 1931.

Romaniuk, Leonid. "Vid Bershadi do Chartoryï: Naperedodni Zymovoho pokhodu." *VK*, 1972, no. 2 (58), 23–31.

Romanov, A. A. "V Tavriiu za volei: Vospominaniia ochevidtsa." *Istoricheskii vestnik* (St. Petersburg) 84 (1901): 264–73.

Romer, Jan. *Pamiętniki.* Lviv: Książnica-Atlas, 1938.

Rozhin, Ivan. "Spohad pro slavnoho komandyra." *Tr* (New York), no. 2 (1960), 19–22.

Rozwadowski, Adam J. *Generał Rozwadowski.* Cracow: Księgarnia Krakowska, 1929.

Rubach, M. A. "Do istoriï ukraïns'koï revoliutsiï: Zamitky i dokumenty, hruden' 1917 – sichen' 1918 r." *LR*, 1926, no. 1, 41–84; no. 6, 7–56.

Rudychiv, Ivan. "Symon Petliura v molodosti: Spomyn." In *Symon Petliura v molodosti: Zbirka spomyniv*, 3–17. Edited by A. Zhuk. Lviv: Khortytsia, 1936.

Rutkowski. Raport z podróży jazdy służbowej do Lwowa. Warsaw, 29 May 1920. Ms.

Rybakov, M. "Deistviia letiuchego korpusa tov. Nestorovicha." In *Sbornik trudov Voenno-nauchnogo obshchestva pri Voennoi akademii* (Moscow) 4 (1923): 104–34. A detailed account by a Bolshevik officer of the campaigns against the partisans during the winter of 1921 in Poltava gubernia.

S., V. "Ekspeditsiia L. B. Kameneva dlia prodvizheniia prodgruzov k Moskve v 1919 godu." *PR*, 1925, no. 6, 116–54.

Sadovs'kyi, Mykhailo. Letter to Michael Palij. Toronto, 1 January 1961.

———. "Mykola Iunakiv: Heneral'noho shtabu heneral-polkovnyk Armiï UNR." *VK*, 1971, no. 3–4 (53–4), 38–44.

———. "S. Petliura v Kyievi v 1906–1907 rr.: Iz spomyniv." *Tr* (Paris), 1927, no. 22–3, 18–22.

———. "S. Petliura v RUP i USDRP: Iz spomyniv." *Tr* (Paris), 1935, no. 21–2, 8–13.

———. "Shliakhy ukraïns'koï revoliutsiï." *KAD na rik 1928*, 13–26.

———. "359 bezsmertnykh." *Sv*, 21 and 23 November 1956.

Sahaidachnyi, Petro. "Polkovnyk Evhen Konovalets'." *LChK*, 1938, no. 7–8, 2–4.

Sakhno, V. "Delegatom vid povstantsiv, lystopad–hruden' 1919 r." *T*, no. 7 (1928), 70–83.

Salikovs'kyi, Ol. "Pro odnu nenapysanu knyzhku: Uryvok iz spomyniv." *KAD na rik 1927*, 102–7.

Samiilenko, Stepan. *Dni slavy: Spohady polkovnyka ukraïns'koï armiï.* New York: Ukrainian Academy of Arts and Sciences in the US, 1958.

———. "Dole! De ty? Uryvok zi spohadiv 'Na zmushenii chuzhyni'." *AUNS na rik 1979*, 70–82.

———. "Kruty." *BSBUVK*, 1962, no. 10, 9–10.

Samushyns'kyi, Stepan. "Spomyny z italiis'koho polonu." *RN*, 1928, no. 9, 339–47.

Samutyn, Petro. "VI Sichovo-strilets'ka dyviziia: Orhanizatsiia v Beresti i pokhid na Kyïv u 1920 r." *VK*, 1971, no. 5 (55), 27–32. An authoritative survey about the formation of the Sixth Sich Riflemen Division and its participation, with Polish troops, in the Kyïv offensive against the Bolsheviks in the spring of 1920.

———. "Ukraïns'ki zbroini syly v rotsi 1920." *AUNS na iuvileinyi rik 1968*, 139–50.

Savchenko, Volodymyr. "Narys borot'by Viis'ka U.N.R. na Livoberezhzhi naprykintsi 1918 ta pochatku 1919 rr. na pidstavi dokumentiv ta opovidan' svidkiv." *ZD* 5 (1935): 158–85; 6 (1936): 119–54.

———. "Spomyny viis'kovyka z 1918 r." *KAD na rik 1938*, 60–74.

———. "Ukraïns'kyi rukh u rosiis'kykh chastynakh u 1917 ta 1918 r.r." *ZD* 4 (1934): 145–60.

Savinkov, Boris. "General Kornilov: Iz vospominanii." *Byl*, no. 31 (1925), 182–97.

Schräder, Friedrich. *Eine Fluchtlingsreise durch die Ukraine: Tagebuchblätter von meiner Flucht aus Konstantinople*. Tübingen: J. C. B. Mohr, 1919.

Sereda, Mykhailo. "Holovnyi otaman." *LNV*, 1931, no. 5, 482–9.

———. "Na vulytsiakh Kyieva z 30 sichnia do 8 liutoho 1918." *IKAChK na 1938 rik*, 23–32.

———. "Otamanshchyna." *LChK*, 1929, no. 3, 22–4; 1930, no. 1, 10–12; no. 2, 6–8; no. 3, 15–17; no. 4, 12–14; no. 5, 12–14; no. 6, 17–20; no. 7–8, 21–5; no. 11, 11–13; no. 12, 18–20.

Biographical sketches by a Ukrainian officer of a number of partisan leaders, which describe their campaigns against the Bolshevik and White forces.

———. "Pershi ukraïns'ki viis'kovi chastyny." *IKAChK na 1929 rik*, 45–51.

———. "Storinka z istoriï vyzvol'noï borot'by." *LChK*, 1931, no. 11, 15–17.

An account of the Ukrainianization of the 34th Russian Army Corps under Gen. Pavlo Skoropads'kyi in the summer of 1917 and the corps's campaign against the Bolshevik forces under Evgeniia Bosh.

———. "Viis'kova narada v kabineti general'noho sekretaria Porsha dnia 18 (5 st. st.) sichnia 1918 r." *LChK*, 1937, no. 5, 2–3.

Serge, Victor. *Memoirs of a Revolutionary, 1901–1941*. London: Oxford University Press, 1963.

Memoirs by a Belgian-born former Bolshevik of political conditions in Soviet Russia, which also provide some information about the partisan struggle in Ukraine.

Sergeev, A. *Denikinskaia armiia sama o sebe: Po dokumentam sobrannym na boevykh liniiakh voennym korrespondentom "Rosta"*. Moscow: Gos. izd-vo, 1920.

Seymour, Charles. *The Intimate Papers*. 2 vols. Boston: Houghton, Mifflin, 1926.

Shapoval, Mykyta Iu. "Het'manshchyna i Dyrektoriia: Uryvok zi spomyniv." *Ukraïns'ke hromads'ke slovo* (New York), 1954, no. 1, 8–10; no. 2, 28–32; no. 4, 81–6; no. 9, 208–12; no. 10, 233–8; no. 11, 257–62; no. 12, 277–9.

———. *Velyka revoliutsiia i ukraïns'ka vyzvol'na prohrama*. Prague: Vil'na spilka, 1927.

A valuable history of the Ukrainian revolution based mainly on the author's reminiscences.

———, and O. Slobodych. *Velykyi zryv: Narys istoriï ukraïns'koï revoliutsiï, 1917–1920.* Lviv: Samoosvita, 1930.

Shatilov. "Pamiatnaia zapiska o Krymskoi evakuatsii: Dokumenty iz arkhiva Russkoi Armii." In *Beloe delo: Letopis' beloi bor'by*, vol. 4, 93–107. Edited by A. A. Lampe. Berlin: Mednyi vsadnik, 1928.
Documents pertaining to the evacuation of the VA from the Crimea in the fall of 1920.

Shchegolev, Pavel E., ed. *Frantsuzy v Odesse: Iz belykh memuarov gen. I. A. Denikina, M. S. Marguliesa, M. V. Braikevicha.* Leningrad: Krasnaia gazeta, 1928.
A reprint of Russian military and political leaders' memoirs of the French intervention in Odessa.

Shchurovs'kyi, Volodymyr. "Spomyny z perebuvannia U.S.S. na Naddniproviu v 1918 r." *LNV*, 1925, no. 3, 218–28.

———. "Ukraïns'ki sichovi stril'tsi na Zaporizhzhu." *IKAChK na 1929 rik*, 40–4.

Shchekun, O., ed. *Perekop: Sbornik vospominanii.* Moscow: Gosudarstvennoe sotsial'no-ekonomicheskoe izdatel'stvo, 1941.

———. "Razgrom Vrangelia." *KA* 72 (1935): 3–44; 73: 9–73.
M. V. Frunze's orders and telegrams to and from the headquarters of the Soviet Fourth, Sixth, Thirteenth, First Cavalry, and Second Cavalry armies from September through November 1920.

Shaposhnikov, Boris M. *Na Visle: K istorii kampanii 1920 goda.* Moscow: Gosudarstvennoe voennoe izdatel'stvo, 1924.
An account of the Polish-Soviet War of 1920 by a prominent Soviet military writer, based on his own observations and documents.

Shekhtman, Iosif B. *Pogromy Dobrovol'cheskoi armii na Ukraine: K istorii antisemitizma na Ukraine v 1919–1920 g.g.* Berlin: Ostjudisches historisches Archiv, 1932.

Shelukhyn, Serhii. "Doba Tsentral'noï Rady." *VU*, no. 52 (1966), 29–49.

———. *Lyst do S. Petliury pro Ryzhs'kyi dohovir.* Paris: Postup, 1948.

Shemet, Serhii. "Do istoriï Ukraïns'koï demokratychno-khliborobs'koï partiï." *KhU* 1 (1920): 63–79.
An authoritative account of the Ukrainian Democratic Agrarian party's activities by one of its founders.

———. "Mykola Mikhnovs'kyi: Posmertna zhadka." *KhU* 5 (1924–5), 3–30.

Sheparovych, Olena Fedak. "Z povstantsiamy: Spomyn." *IKAChK na 1922 rik*, 99–108.

Shepel', Zynaïda. "Bat'ko povstantsia: Spohad." *LChK*, 1932, no. 2, 5.
An account of the partisan leader Iakiv Shepel and his father's execution by the Bolsheviks, written by their sister and daughter.

Shiller, A. E. "An Officer's Experience with Bolshevism." *CH*, September 1919, 514–16.

Shkil'nyk, Mykhailo. *Ukraïna u borot'bi za derzhavnist' v 1917–1921 rokakh: Spomyny i rozdumy.* Toronto: Basilian Press, 1971.

Shkuro, A. G. *Zapiski belogo partizana.* Buenos Aires: Seiatel', 1961.

Memoirs by one of Denikin's generals, written in 1920–1, about his campaigns during World War I and against the Bolsheviks and Ukrainian partisans.

Shlikhter, A. G., ed. *Chernaia kniga: Sbornik statei i materialov ob interventsii Antanty na Ukraine v 1918–1919 gg.* Kharkiv: Derzhavne vydavnytstvo Ukraïny, 1925.

A valuable collection of documents, including captured material, and of articles by Soviet Russian and Ukrainian eyewitnesses on the Allied intervention and its economic background in southern Ukraine.

Shpilins'kyi, O. "Bazar, 1921–1931 r." *ZD* 3 (1932): 109–34.

———. "Zamitky do istoriï 3-ho pish. polku im. het'mana Nalyvaika." *T*, no. 12 (1929), 54–69.

Shteifon, Boris A. "Bredovskii pokhod: Vospominaniia." In *Beloe delo: Letopis' beloi bor'by*, vol. 3, 91–139. Edited by A. A. Lampe. Paris: Mednyi vsadnik, 1927.

Shteinman, F. "Otstuplenie ot Odessy, ianvar' 1920 g." *ARR* 2 (1925): 87–97.

An account of the German colonists in the VA who fought against the Bolsheviks in southern Ukraine, their retreat to Romania, and their difficulties with the authorities there.

Shukhevych, Stepan. *Spomyny z Ukraïns'koï Halyts'koi Armii, 1918–1920.* 5 vols. Lviv: Chervona kalyna, 1928–9.

Memoirs by a high-ranking UHA officer describing the army's war with Poland, the Bolsheviks, and the VA, physical conditions and epidemics, and its conflict with the UNR Directory over the latter's agreements with Denikin and Poland.

———. *Vydysh brate mii: Visim misiatsiv sered USS-iv.* Lviv: Chervona kalyna, 1930.

———. "Za het'mans'kykh chasiv v Odessi." *IKAChK na 1931 rik*, 47–52.

An account of the formation of Ukrainian units from Galician soldiers in the Austrian army in Odessa at the end of 1918.

Shul'gin, V. V. "Kontrabandisty: Otryvok iz vpechatlenii." In *Beloe delo: Letopis' beloi bor'by*, vol. 1, 159–202. Edited by A. A. Lampe. Berlin: Mednyi vsadnik, 1926.

———. *1920 god: Ocherki.* Sofia: Rossiisko-bolgarskoe knigoizdatel'stvo, 1921.

A survey of the Russian Civil War.

Shul'hyn, Oleksander. "Mykhailo Serhiiovych Hrushevs'kyi, iak polityk i liudyna." In *Zbirnyk na poshanu Oleksandra Shul'hyna, 1889–1960*, 143–55. Edited by Volodymyr Ianiv. Paris: Naukove tovarystvo im. Shevchenko, 1969.

———. "Storinka mynuloho: Pam'iati A. D. Margolina." *O*, 1957, no. 9, 19–22.

Shumovs'kyi, Arsen. "Ukraïnizatsiia 10-ho korpusu Rosiis'koï tsars'koï armiï v 1917 rotsi." *BUNDS*, 1962, no. 12, 13–15.

Shustykevych, A. "Spomyn z Odesy." *IKAChK na 1928 rik*, 102–14.

———. "Z ostannykh boïv: Osin' 1919 roku na Velykii Ukraïni." *IKAChK na 1929 rik*, 114–48.

Sidorov, A. H. "Z istoriï borot'by proty Vrangelivshchyny i bandytyzmu na Mykolaïvshchyni 1920 r." *LR*, 1931, no. 1, 187–202. Useful memoirs of the struggle between Ukrainian partisans and Soviet troops in Mykolaiv gubernia in 1920.

Siedlecki, Adam G. *Cud Wisły: Wspomnienia korespondenta wojennego.* Warsaw: Perzyński, Niklewicz, 1921.

Siedlecki, Stanisław. "'Futorek' na Ukrainie pod Złotopolem: Dzieje placówki niepodległościowej." *N* (Warsaw) 15 (1937): 19–42.

Sikar, Stepan M. "Try spomyny: 1. Delegaty Sovnarkomu do Uriadu UNR v 1919 r. 2. Bat'ko Makhno. 3. Basarabs'ka dyviziia 1919 r." *NSI*, no. 3 (1973), 89–108.

Sikevych, V. *Storinky iz zapysnoï knyzhky*. 7 vols. Winnipeg: Ukraïns'ka strilets'ka hromada, 1941–51.

Simiantsev, Valentyn. *Roky kozakuvannia, 1917–1923: Spohady*. Philadelphia: the author, 1976.

Simovych, Vasyl'. "Iak zustrily revoliutsiiu 1917 r. poloneni ukraïntsi v taborakh." *IKAChK na 1937 rik*, 148–50.

Sinel, Allen A., "Ekaterinoslav in Revolution: Excerpts from the Diary of Princess Urusov." *RR*, 1970, no. 2, 192–208.

Siropolko, Stepan. "Dva areshtuvannia S. Petliury za het'mana P. Skoropads'koho." *KAD na rik 1938*, 74–7.

———. "F. Korsh i ioho molodyi druh—S. Petliura." *Tr* (Paris), 1936, no. 21–2, 14–16.

———. "Liternaturno-zhurnalistychna diial'nist' S. V. Petliury." *Tr* (Paris), 1936, no. 27–8, 8–14; no. 29–30, 2–5.

———. "Storinka z pryvatnoho zhyttia S. V. Petliury." *Tr* (Paris), 1931, no. 20–1, 24–5.

———. "Vyïzd S. V. Petliury z Kyïva do povstanchoho viis'ka v lystopadi 1918 r." *Tr* (Paris), 1934, no. 19–20, 6–7.

———. "Z zhyttia ukraïns'koï kol'oniï v Moskvi: Storinka zi spohadiv." *KAD na rik 1927*, 35–40.

———. "Zems'kyi diiach S. V. Petliura i het'man P. Skoropads'kyi: Z arkhivnykh materiialiv." *Tr* (Paris), 1927, no. 22–3, 27–31.

Skalski, Teofil. "Garstka wspomnień z mojego życia." *ZH* 45 (1978): 57–138; 46: 184–207.

Skarzyński, Wincenty. *Armja Polska we Francji w świetle faktów: Nakreślił ze swojego pamiętnika Wincenty Skarzyński*. Warsaw: Zakłady graficzne Straszewiczów, 1929.

Składkowski, Sławoj Felicjan. *Moja służba w Brygadzie: Pamiętnik polowy.* 2 vols. Warsaw: Instytut Najnowszej Historji Polski, 1932–3. Reprint, Warsaw: Bellona, 1990.

S-ko, V. "25 rokiv tomu: Spohady z Livoberezhzhia." *AUNS na iuvileinyi rik 1968,* 163–72.

Skobtsov, D. "Drama Kubani: Noiabr', 1919 g." *GMChS* 14, no. 1 (1926), 223–62.

Skoropads'kyi, Pavlo. "Ukraïns'ka kul'turna pratsia za het'manshchyny 1918-ho roku: Storinka spomyniv." *NKul,* 1936, no. 4, 241–6.

———. "Uryvok zi 'Spomyniv'." *KhU* 4 (1924): 3–40; 5 (1924–5): 31–92.

Skoropads'kyi's valuable and informative account of his military and political activities, including the Ukrainianization of the Russian Thirty-Fourth Corps from March 1917 to April 1918.

Skvortsov-Stepanov, Ivan I. *S Krasnoi Armiei na panskoiu Pol'shu: Vpechatleniia i nabliudeniia.* Moscow: Gosizdat, 1920.

An account by a Bolshevik officer of the Bolshevik offensive in Poland in July 1920 and the reasons for its failure.

Skwarczyński, Stanisław. "Kilka rozmów z Komendantem." *N* (London) 7 (1962): 219–24.

———. "Przemiany duchowe Józefa Piłsudskiego w latach 1905–1922." *N* (London) 10 (1976): 3–16.

———. "Twórca Awangardy: Działalność Józefa Piłsudskiego, 1893–1918." *N* (London) 7 (1962): 156–72.

Skydan, M. "Shliakh l-ho Halyts'koho korpusu v pokhodi na Kyïv." *LChK,* 1936, no. 2, 7–10; no. 3, 14–19; no. 4, 10–14; no. 5, 9–13.

Slashchev, Ia. *Krym v 1920 g.: Otryvki iz vospominanii.* Moscow: Gos. izd-vo, 1924.

———. "Materialy po istorii grazhdanskoi voiny v Rossii: Operatsii belykh, Petliury i Makhno v iuzhnoi Ukraine v poslednei chetverti 1919 goda." *VV,* 1922, no. 9–10, 38–43; no. 11; no. 12; no. 13, 49–51.

An authoritative account of the campaign of the VA Third Corps against UNR troops and partisans in Right-Bank Ukraine in the last quarter of 1919.

Śliwiński, Artur. "Marszałek Piłsudski o sobie." *N* (Warsaw) 16 (1937): 376–3; 18 (1938): 195–204.

———. "Rozmowa z Beselerem." *N* (Warsaw) 5, no. 1 (1931), 71–82.

Slobids'kyi, V. "V zapili voroha: Spomyny z nahody 15-littia Zymovoho pokhodu." *H,* no. 13 (1935), 16–21.

Smal'-Stots'kyi, Roman, ed. *L. Vasilievs'kyi, M. Halyn, S. Stempovs'kyi, A. Topchybashy, Tabuï: Spohady.* Warsaw: Ukraïns'kyi naukovyi instytut, 1932.

Smovs'kyi, Konstantyn. "Kyïvs'ki kureni U.V.K." *UK,* 1969, no. 3–4, 20–1.

———. "Moia sluzhba Ukraïni pid komanduvanniam Holovnoho otamana Symona Petliury." *NP,* 1954, no. 6, 6–8; no. 7, 4–6.

———. "Nashchadok Iaroslava Mudroho: Spohad u 28. richnytsiu smerty S. Petliury." *UKom*, no. 2 (1954), 7–8.

———. "35-ta richnytsia povstannia proty het'mana." *BUNDS*, no. 5 (1954), 13–17.

———. "U 28-mu richnytsiu smerty Symona Petliury." *UKom*, no. 2 (1954), 5–7.

Sokil, Ivan. "Vid Zbrucha do Kyieva: Slidamy III. kurenia 5-oï sokal's'koi brygady: Spomyn uchasnyka pokhodu." *LChK*, 1938, no. 5, 3–5.

Sokolnicki, Michał. *Polska w pamiętnikach Wielkiej Wojny, 1914–1918*. Warsaw: Biblioteka Polska, 1925.

Sokolov, K. N. *Pravlenie generala Denikina: Iz vospominanii*. Sofia: Rossiisko-bolgarskoe knigoizdatel'stvo, 1921.
Memoirs of the VA by a legal advisor to Denikin's Special Council, with emphasis on the VA administration in the occupied territories.

Solovei, Dmytro. *Rozhrom Poltavy: Spohady z chasiv vyzvol'nykh zmahan' ukraïns'koho narodu, 1914–1921*. Winnipeg: Trident Press, 1974.

Soltykevych, Iaroslav. *Pryvorittia: Zapysky likaria USS pro odyn fragment trahedi UHA v 1919–20 rr*. Toronto, Nasha slava, 1955.

———. *Shliakh U.S.S. do Makivky*. Toronto, 1952.

Sosnowski. Do Generalnej Adjutantury Naczelnego Wodza. Warsaw, 19 April 1920. Ms.

Soviet Treaty Series: A Collection of Bilateral Treaties, Agreements and Conventions, Etc., Concluded between the Soviet Union and Foreign Powers. Vol. 1. *1917–28*. Compiled and edited by Leon Shapiro. Washington: The Georgetown University Press, 1950.

Speller, John P. "The Savinkov-Piłsudski correspondence." *East Europe*, 1975, no. 4–5, 6–8.

"Spisek habsbursko-ukraiński przeciw Polakom: 2 listy ks. Wasyla Habsburga do metropolity Szeptyckiego." *GP* (Lviv), no. 4549 (February 1919).

"Spohad pro S. Petliuru." *Ukraïns'ke pravoslavne slovo*, 1986, no. 4–5, 11–12.

"Spomyny narodn'oho uchytelia z Volyni (Z dniv nastupu nimtsiv i avstriitsiv u chervni 1915 r.)." *US*, 1923, no. 3 (25), 32–5; no. 4 (26), 32–7.

"Sprava Halychyny na Myrovii konferentsiï v Paryzhi 1919 roku i dal'sha ïï dolia azh do rishennia Rady ambasadoriv." *Biuleten' Vydavnychoho komitetu Ukraïns'koï iednosty u Frantsiï* (Paris), no. 1 (1938), 1–2.

Sprawy polskie na konferencji pokojowej w Paryżu w 1919 r.: Dokumenty i materiały. 3 vols. Edited by Remigiusz Bierzanek and Józef Kukułka. Warsaw: Państwowe Wydawnictwo Naukowe, 1965–8.

Srokowski, Stanisław. *Z dzikich pól: Wspomnienia z zimy 1919/20 na południu Rosji*. Poznań: n.p., 1925.

Stanimir, Osyp. *Moia uchast' u vyzvol'nykh zmahanniakh, 1917–1920*. Toronto: the author, 1966.

———. "Z italiis'koho frontu na ukraïns'kyi v lystopadi 1918 r." *VK*, 1966, no. 2 (23), 26–33.
Staroviit, Mykola. *U Lystopadovomu reidi: Spohady uchasnyka*. Los Angeles, 1968.
Steblik, Władysław. "Epizod z walk 12 Pułku Piechoty w Wojnie 1920 roku." *B* 24, no. 2 (1926), 167–78.
Stechyshyn, Stepan. "Zi spomyniv polonenoho." *LChK*, 1932, no. 7–8, 17–21.
An account of the disintegration of the tsarist regime and the subsequent chaotic conditions created by Bolshevik propaganda.
Stefaniv, Zenon. "Dva roky v ukraïns'kii armiï: Spomyny 17-litn'oho pidkhorunzhoho." *LChK*, 1932, no. 9, 8–10; no. 10, 9–13; no. 11, 13–16; no. 12, 6–8.
An account by a young officer of the uprising against Skoropads'kyi and of the UNR campaigns against the Bolsheviks, Poles, and VA.
Stempowski, Stanisław. *Pamiętniki, 1870–1914*. Wrocław: Zakład im. Ossolińskich, Polska Akademia Nauk, 1953.
———. "Ukraina, 1919–1920." *ZH* 21 (1972): 64–88.
———. "Wspomnienia." *ZH* 23 (1973): 101–40; 24 (1973): 68–76.
Stovba, Oleksander. "Materiialy do rodu Petliur." *UIs*, no. 61–4 (1979), 69–78.
Struts', Volodymyr. "Shist' tyzhniv v denikinis'kim poloni: Spomyn." *LChK*, 1933, no. 7–8, 26–30.
———. "Try misiatsi u povstantsiv." *IKAChK na 1934 rik*, 102–12.
Sulkivs'kyi, B. "Z istoriï formuvannia 2-ho Sichovoho zaporizhs'koho korpusu na Pivdenno-zakhidn'omu fronti v rotsi 1917: Spomyny." *T*, no. 4 (1927), 71–86.
Sumskii, S. "Odinnadtsat' perevorotov: Grazhdanskaia voina v Kieve." In *Revoliutsiia na Ukraine po memuaram belykh*, 99–114. Edited by N. N. Popov. Moscow: Gos. izd-vo, 1930.
Memoirs by a Bolshevik journalist of conditions in Kyiv during the Bolshevik invasion of January 1918, and of German policies in Ukraine to April 1918.
Sushko, Roman. "Brat na brata: Materiialy do istoriï udarnoï hrupy S.S." *IKAChK na 1928 rik*, 53–8.
———. "Moï spomyny pro Pershu sotniu S.S." *ND*, 1927, no. 1, 28–34; no. 2, 23–37.
———. "Sichovi stril'tsi za Tsentral'noï Rady: Moï spomyny pro 1. sotniu S.S." *IKAChK na 1928 rik*, 9–37.
Suslyk, L. R. *Kryvavi storinky z nepysanykh litopysiv: Kozats'ko-khutorians'ka Poltavashchyna v borot'bi proty moskovs'koho komunizmu*. Derby: the author, 1956.
Memoirs of the partisan movement in Poltava gubernia and the author's experiences in Soviet concentration camps.
Sworakowski, Witold. "Nieznane listy rosyjskie Józefa Piłsudskiego." *ZH* 15 (1969): 13–220.

Sydorenko, Hryhorii. *Les problèmes nationaux de l'Ukraine a la Conférence de Paris: Interview de M. Sydorenko*. Paris: Robinet-Houtain, 1919.

Szeptycki, Stanisław. *Front Litewsko-Białoruski, 10 marca 1919–30 lipca 1920*. Cracow: Krakowska Spółka Wydawnicza, 1925.

A polemical work on the Polish-Soviet War by the commander of the Polish Northeastern Front.

Szpinger, Stefan. *Z Pierwszą Konną*. Łódź: Wydawnictwo Łódzkie, 1967.

Szpotański, Stanisław. "Piłsudski o swojim pobycie w szpitalu Św. Mikołaja." *N* (Warsaw) 16, no. 3 (1937), 491–4.

Piłsudski's reminiscences of his imprisonment and escape.

Talan, Pavlo. "Spohad u 35–ti rokovyny." *BUNDS*, no. 21 (1956), 6–9.

Tarczyński-Alf, Tadeusz. *Wspomnienia oficera Pierwszej Brygady*. London: Polska Fundacja Kulturalna, 1979.

Tarnogrodskii, N. "Vozniknovenie i pervye shagi bol'shevitskoi organizatsii na Podolii: Otryvok iz vospominanii." *LR*, 1923, no. 5. 212–18.

Tatars'kyi, V. *Pid chotyrma praporamy: Spohad*. Munich: the author, 1983.

Tekst umowy politycznej polsko-ukraińskiej z 22, 4, 20. Warsaw, 21 April 1920. Ms.

Temnyts'kyi, Volodymyr, and Iosyp Burachyns'kyi. *Les atrocités polonaises en Galicie Ukrainienne: Note telegramme adressé par Voldemar Temnytsky et Joseph Bouratchinski à M. Clemenceau*. Paris: Bureau Ukrainien, 1919.

Terlets'kyi, Omelian. "Z zhyttia polonenykh ukraïntsiv v Nimechchyni v 1916 rotsi." *LChK*, 1932, no. 7–8, 8–10.

"Testament polityczny Symona Petlury." *BPU*, 1937, no. 35, 396–7.

Tintrup, Hans. *Krieg in der Ukraine: Aufzeichnungen eines deutschen Offiziers*. Essen: Essener Verlagsanstalt, 1938.

Memoirs by a German infantry officer of his service in Ukraine from the beginning of 1917 to January 1919.

Tokarzewski, Marjan. *Straż przednia: Ze wspomnień i notatek*. Warsaw: Polski Instytut Wydawniczy, 1925.

Tol'ko fakty: Istoricheskie dokumenty ob okkupatsii nemtsami Ukrainy v 1918 g. Moscow: Partiino-politicheskaia rabota v VMF, 1941.

Topchybashi, A. M. "Zustrichi z Symonom Petliuroiu." *Tr* (Paris), 1932, no. 22, 2–8.

"Tretii Vseukraïns'kyi viis'kovyi z'ïzd u Kyïvi." *VSVU*, no. 179 (1917), 773–5.

Trotskii, Lev (Trotsky, Leon). *How the Revolution Armed*. 2 vols. Translated and annotated by Brian Pearce. New York: New Park Publications, 1979.

———. *Kak vooruzhalas' revoliutsiia: Na voennoi rabote*. 5 vols. Moscow: Vysshii voennyi redaktsionnyi sovet, 1923–5.

Articles, speeches, lectures, proclamations, orders, and other documentary materials concerning the formation of the Red Army.

———. *My Life: An Attempt at An Autobiography*. New York: Scribner, 1931.

———. The Trotsky Archives. Harvard College Library, Cambridge.
This massive archive contains about 800 letters and telegrams sent by Lenin to Trotsky and vice versa during 1918 and 1919.

———. *The Trotsky Papers, 1917–1922*. 2 vols. Edited and annotated by Jan Meijer. The Hague: Mouton, 1964.

Trubetskoi, E. N. "Iz putevykh zametok bezhentsa." *ARR* 18 (1928): 137–207.
Memoirs of the author's experiences, conditions in Ukraine and the Kuban, the French intervention, and Denikin's policy in Ukraine from September 1918 through June 1919.

Trutenko. *3-tia Zalizna dyviziia na pochatku Zymovoho pokhodu, 6-XII-1919–7-Iv, 1920*. n. p., n.d. [1920s].

"Try lysty Holovnoho otamana sl. p. S. Petliury." *RD*, 1952, no. 1, 19–22.

Tryl'ovs'kyi, Kyrylo. "Moja znajomość z Józefem Piłsudskim." *N* (Warsaw) 8, no. 3 (1933), 443–56.

———. "Shche pro Piłsuds'koho." *Sv*, 9 July 1935.

Trymailo, Ivan. "Herois'ka smert' Semena Hryzla, pershoho orhanizatora UVK: Spohad spivuchasnyka podii i ioho pobratyma." *UK*, 1971, no. 4, 18–19.

Tsapko, Ivan. "Ostannii bii Armiï UNR." *VK*, 1961, no. 3, 19–24.

———. "Partyzany na Skhidnii Ukraïni: Starobil's'kyi partyzans'kyi zahin." *Visti* (Munich), 1963, no. 109, 6–8; no. 111, 85–9.
A valuable account of the organization of partisan groups in Left-Bank Ukraine and their campaigns against the Bolsheviks in late 1918 and 1919.

———. "Persha ukraïns'ka viis'kova misiia v Krymu, traven' 1920 r." *VK*, 1963, no. 3 (11), 19–26.

———. "Ukraïns'ki viis'ka pered zavishenniam zbroï, zhovten' 1920." *VK*, 1964, no. 1 (13), 7–15.

Tsebrii, Osyp. "Vospominaniia partizana." *Delo truda—probuzhdenie* (Paris), 1949, no. 31, 17–19; no. 32, 13–14; no. 33, 41–2; no. 34 (1950), 20–2.
An account of a peasant partisan detachment that fought the Austro-German punitive expeditions in 1918 in Right-Bank Ukraine and of its efforts to coordinate its activities with Makhno's army.

Tsehel's'kyi, L'onhyn. *Vid legend do pravdy: Spomyny pro podiï v Ukraïni zv'iazani z pershym lystopadom 1918 r.* New York: Bulava, 1960.
Controversial memoirs by a former UNR deputy foreign minister of Ukrainian national aspirations from November 1918 to February 1919.

Ts'okan, Il. *Vid Denikina do bil'shevykiv: Fragment spomyniv z Radians'koï Ukraïny*. Vienna: Ukraïns'kyi prapor, 1921.
Memoirs by an UHA officer of the UHA's war with the VA and Bolsheviks at the turn of 1920.

Tukhachevskii, M. N. *Pokhod za Vislu*. Moscow: Gos. izd-vo, 1923.

Lectures on the Polish-Soviet War in Poland in 1920, originally delivered at the Moscow Military Academy.

Turbiak, S. "Walki III Dywizjonu Lotniczego z Konną Armją Budiennego pod Lwowem: Wspomnienia i uwagi." *B* (Warsaw), 1922, no. 2, 122–31.

Tymoshevs'kyi, Volodymyr. *Istoriia ukraïns'koï vlady, 1917–1919*. Vienna: Ukraïns'ka partiia samostiinykiv-sotsiialistiv (U.N.P.), 1920.

Tyshkevych, Mykhailo. "Uryvky z spohadiv." *LNV*, 1928, no. 3, 229–41; no. 5, 29–36; no. 7–8, 250–60; no. 9, 52–8; no. 10, 766–85.

———. "Z lystiv, 1915–1930." *V*, 1939, no. 9, 643–67.

———. "Z nedavn'oho mynuloho." *ZD* 7 (1937): 229–31.

———. "Zhmen'ka spohadiv z nedavn'oho mynuloho." *UIn*, no. 7–8 (1928), 8–9.

"1919 god v Ekaterinoslave i Aleksandrovske." *LR*, 1925, no. 4 (13), 74–103.

"U 60-richchia aktu zluky u spohadakh ioho tvortsiv i suchasnykiv." *AUNS na rik 1979*, 49–52.

U.R.L. Szef Sztabu Generalnego I-e Kwatermistrzowstwo do Szefa Sztabu Generalnego Wojsk Polskich. 24 July 1920. Ms.

Udovychenko, Oleksander. "Bii za Arsenal." *BUNDS*, no. 28 (1958), 5–9.

———. "Forsuvannia Dnistra pid Horodnytseiu, 14 veresnia 1920 roku." *ZD* 4 (1934): 190–200.

———. "Liudyna hlybokoï viry." *H*, no. 17–18 (1936), 21–3.

———. "Reid henerala Huloho-Hulenka," *BSBUVK*, no. 9 (1961), 9–12.

———. *Tretia Zalizna dyviziia: Materiialy do istoriï Viis'ka Ukraïns'koi Narodn'oï Respubliky, rik 1919*. 2 vols. New York: Chervona kalyna, 1971, 1982.

A valuable study, based on archival materials and the author's recollections, of the Third Iron Division and its campaign against the Bolsheviks and VA from April to December 1919.

———. "Vid Dnistra do liniï peremyr'ia i vidvorot za Zbruch: Boiovi chyny Pravoi hrupy Armiï UNR." *ZD* 5 (1935): 76–123; 6 (1936): 77–109; 7 (1937): 152–64.

Ukrainian Bulletins from the Ukrainian Press-Bureau (Copenhagen), no. 2 (28 April 1919), 1–11.

Ukraïns'ka deliegatsiia Skhidn'oï Halychyny v Ryzi. Vienna: Uriad presy i propagandy ZUNR, 1920.

Ukraïns'ka Halyts'ka Armiia: Materiialy do istoriï. 5 vols. Edited by Myron Dol'nyts'kyi et al. Winnipeg: D. Mykytiuk, 1958–76.

A major collection of documents, reports, and memoirs dealing with the UHA and its wars with the Poles, Bolsheviks, and VA from 1918 to 1923.

Ukraïns'ko-moskovska viina 1920 roku v dokumentakh. Edited by V. Sal's'kyi. Compiled by P. Shandruk. Warsaw: Ukraïns'kyi naukovyi instyt, 1933.

Ulrych, Juljusz. "Ze wspomnień 1919–21." In *Pamiętnik trzydziestolecia niepodległości Polski*, 25–7. New York: National Committee of Americans of Polish Descent, 1948.

U.S. Department of State. *Papers Relating to the Foreign Relations of the United States: The Lansing Papers, 1914–1920.* 2 vols. Washington: U.S. Government Printing Office, 1939.

———. *Papers Relating to the Foreign Relations of the United States: The Paris Peace Conference, 1919.* 5 vols. Washington: U.S. Government Printing Office, 1946.

———. *Papers Relating to the Foreign Relations of the United States, 1918–1919: Russia.* 3 vols. Washington: U.S. Government Printing Office, 1931–7.

Uwolnienie Piłsudskiego: Wspomnienia organizatorów ucieczki. Edited by M. Paszkowska et al. Warsaw: Ognis, 1924.

V., A. "Dnevnik obyvatelia." *ARR* 4 (1922): 252–88.

A diary of the revolution from July 1918 to April 1919, largely in the Crimea, by an escapee from Soviet Russia.

V., Dmytro. "Lystopad v 1918 r. na Ukraïni: Vyrvanyi lystok z voiennykh spomyniv." *US,* no. 9 (1921) 5–13; no. 10, 2–3; no. 11 (1922), 11–12; no. 12, 4–6; no. 13, 13–14.

"V tylu 'Vooruzhennykh sil iuga Rossii'." *KA* 34 (1929): 224–8.

Valentinov, A. A. "Krymskaia epopeia po dnevnikam uchastnikov i po dokumentam." *ARR* 5 (1922): 5–100.

An account of the VA in southern Ukraine, based on documents and the author's diary written while at Wrangel's headquarters from May to November 1920.

Varetskii, Dm. "Marshal V. K. Bliukher." *NZh,* no. 27 (1951), 250–65.

Memoirs by a Red Army officer describing conditions in Katerynoslav gubernia and the struggle of Marshal Bliukher's Red forces against the partisans there in the summer of 1921.

Vashchenko, Petro. "Do reidu 1921 roku." *ZD* 3 (1932): 135–9.

Vasyl'kivs'kyi, L. "Rozdumy na skhyli zhyttia: Spohady." *S,* 1969, no. 1, 92–106; no. 3, 107–20; no. 4, 112–21; no. 5, 103–14.

Velyhors'kyi, Ivan. "Z Horodenky pid Nyzhniv." *IKAChK na 1925 rik,* 85–7.

Velikaia Oktiabr'skaia sotsialisticheskaia revoliutsiia na Ukraine, fevral' 1917–aprel' 1918: Sbornik dokumentov i materialov. 3 vols. Edited by S. M. Korolivskii. Kyiv: Gos. izd-vo politicheskoi literatury USSR, 1957.

More than two thousand Soviet documents on the Ukrainian revolution issued from February 1917 to April 1918.

Venhrynovych, Stepan. "Vesna 1920 roku: Uryvky z dnevnyka." *IKAChK na 1931 rik,* 155–60.

Viis'kova umova finansovo-hospodarcha zavarta pomizh Ministerstvom sprav viis'kovykh Rechi Pospolytoï Pol's'koï i Uriadom Ukraïns'koï Narodn'oï Respubliky. Ms.

Vinaver, M. *Nashe pravitel'stvo: Krymskiia vospominaniia, 1918–1919 g.g.* Paris: Imprimerie d'art Voltaire, 1928.

Vinnyts'kyi, S. "Spomyn pro pryïzd Holovnoho otamana Viis'ka U.N.R. do mista Iampolia na Podilliu v travni 1920 r." *T*, no. 3 (1924), 18–22.

Vinogradov, M. Chemu ia byl svidetelem. 25 November 1954. Ms.

An account by a VA officer of the campaigns against Ukrainian partisans and Bolsheviks in Left-Bank Ukraine in 1919 and the beginning of 1920.

Vintoniak, Ivan. "Ukr. halyts'kyi kurin' u Poltavi 1918 r." *US*, no. 13 (1922), 1–3; no. 14, 9–11; no. 15, 9–11; no. 16, 2–4.

Vodianyi, Iakiv. "Na rozstril: Zi spomyniv." *LNV*, 1923, no. 6, 104–12.

———. "Ukraïns'ke Vil'ne kozatstvo ta ioho z'ïzd v Chyhyryni 3. X. 1917." *LChK*, 1930, no. 10, 4–7.

———. "Vystup Vil'noho kozatstva proty moskaliv na st. Vinnytsi: Uryvok iz spohadiv." *ZD* 5 (1935): 202–6.

Volkov, Vitalii. "Zdobuttia Kyieva: Epizod." *Slovo: Zbirnyk* (New York) 3 (1969): 444–8.

Volyts'kyi, Vasyl'. *Na L'viv i Kyïv: Voienni spohady, 1918–1920*. Toronto: Homin Ukraïny, 1963.

Memoirs by a former UNR soldier of his combat experiences from the end of 1918 through the spring of 1920.

Voronovich, N. "Mezhdu dvukh ognei: Zapiski zelenogo." *ARR* 7 (1923): 53–183.

"Vosstanovlenie sovvlasti na Ukraine: Materialy k piatiletiiu vziatiia Khar'kova 12 dekabria 1919 g." *LR* 10 (1925): 56–8.

An order issued by the Kharkiv Military-Revoliutionary Committee, appeals of the All-Ukrainian Revolutionary Committee to CP(B)U organizations, and other documents of December 1919.

"Vrangelevshchina: Iz materialov parizhskogo posol'stva Vremennogo Pravitel'stva." *KA* 39 (1930): 3–46; 40: 3–40.

Correspondence of the Russian Provisional Government's embassy in Paris with VA representatives abroad and Wrangel's government, which describes the political conditions in areas under Wrangel's control in Ukraine from June to November 1920.

Vygran, Vl. Vospominaniia o bor'be s makhnovtsami. San Francisco, 15 March 1954. Ms.

Memoirs by a VA officer of Denikin's military operations against Makhno in Left-Bank Ukraine from the fall of 1918 to the end of 1919.

Vynnychenko, Volodymyr. *Shchodennyk*. Vol. 1. *1911–1920*. Edited by Hryhory Kostiuk. Edmonton and New York: Canadian Institute of Ukrainian Studies and the Volodymyr Vynnychenko Commission of the Ukrainian Academy of Arts and Sciences in the U.S., 1980.

———. *Vidrodzhennia natsiï*. 3 vols. Vienna: Dzvin, 1920.

Memoirs of the years 1917–1921 by the former vice-president of the Central Rada, head of the UNR General Secretariat and Directory, and USDRP leader.

Vynnyk. Ivan. "Voienna Zhytomyrs'ka iunats'ka shkola: Boï Zhytomyrs'koï pishoï iunats'koï shkoly." *Tr* (New York), no. 74 (1974), 3–7.
Vynnyts'kyi, Roman. "Pokhid na Krym." *IKAChK na 1929 rik*, 21–9.
Vyshnivs'kyi, Oleksander. "Do istoriï synikh i zaliznykh: Zi spohadiv komandyra 7-ho Syn'oho polku." *ZD* 7 (1937): 68–191.
———. "Iuzef Pilsuds'kyi: Etapy zhyttia i diial'nosty." *PIB*, no. 5–6 (1937), 11–17.
———. "Otaman i otamaniia." *Sv*, 16–17 and 19 May 1951.
An account by a UNR general of the partisans' role in the struggle against Ukraine's enemies in 1917–21.
———. "Vapniarka: Zi spohadiv komandyra Syn'oho polku." *ZD* 4 (1934): 161–71.
———. "Zapovit Symona Petliury: Zamist' kvitiv na mohylu." *Tr* (New York), no. 34 (1965), 5–7.
Vyshyvanyi, Vasyl'. "U.S.S-tsi z vesny 1918 roku do perevorotu v Avstriï," *Zaporozhets': Kaliendar dlia narodu na rik 1921* (Vienna), 84–98.
Vyslots'kyi, Ivan. "16 misiatsiv u riadakh Kyïvs'kykh sichovykh stril'tsiv, 1918–1919." *LChK*, 1935, no. 7–8, 29–34; no. 9, 14–18; no. 10, 6–7; no. 11, 20–2; no. 13, 9–12.
Walewski, Witold. "Wspomnienia o Podolu." In *Pamiętnik o Podolu*, vol. 3, 9–74. London, 1966.
Washburn, Stanley. *Field Notes from the Russian Front*. London: Andrew Melrose, 1915.
Wasilewski, Leon. *Józef Piłsudski Jakim Go znałem*. Warsaw: Rój, 1935.
Memoirs of Piłsudski's life and activities from 1896 by a close friend and collaborator.
———. Letter to Piłsudski. Tallinn, 15 May 1920. Ms.
Wędziagolski, Karol. *Pamiętniki: Wojna i rewolucja, kontrrewolucja, bolszewicki przewrót, warszawski epilog*. London: Polska Fundacja Kulturalna, 1972.
Wertheimer, Fritz. *Durch Ukraine und Krim*. Stuttgart: Franckh, 1918.
An unfavorable account by a German traveler of the war in Ukraine and the Crimea and German interests there from March to May 1918.
Weygand, Jacques. "Weygand mój ojciec." *ZH* 19 (1971): 19–35.
Wielhorski, Władysław. "Moje pierwsze spotkanie z Józefem Piłsudskim." *N* (London) 8 (1972): 159–60.
Wielowieyski, Józef. "Ze wspomnień o ś. p. Romanie Dmowskim." *PW*, 1939, no. 4 (204), 53–60.
Wierzejski, Witold K. "Fragmenty z dziejów polskiej młodzieży akademickiej w Kijowie, 1864–1920." *N* (Warsaw) 19 (1939): 418–70.
Wisłocki, Włodzimierz. "Sojusz polsko-ukraiński w 1920 roku." *PK* 3 (1966): 173–83.
———. "W Kamieńcu Podolskim—grudzień 1919." *PK* 3 (1966): 235–40.
An account of the Polish occupation of Kamianets-Podilskyi in December 1919.

"With the retreating Bolsheviki." *LA*, 6 November 1920, 325–32.
Witos, Wincenty. *Moje wspomnienia*. Paris: Instytut Literacki, 1964.
Włoskowicz, Al. Do Adjutantury Generalnej. Warsaw, 21 May 1920. Ms.
———. Dowództwo 6. Armji, Oddział II: Meldunek specjalny. Ms.
———. Komunikat o Armji Pawlenki. Ms.
Wrangel, Peter N. (Vrangel', Petr). *Always with Honour*. Foreword by Herbert Hoover. New York: Robert Speller and Sons, 1947.
Memoirs of the years 1917–20 with a critical review of VA operations and valuable material on Allied policy and aid.
———. Letter to Denikin (translation into Polish). Sevastopol, 1919[?] Ms.
———. "Mart 1920 goda: Iz vospominanii." In *Beloe delo: Letopis' beloi bor'by*, vol. 1, 61–75. Edited by A. A. Lampe. Berlin: Mednyi vsadnik, 1926.
———. *Vospominaniia generala barona P. N. Vrangelia: Materialy sobrannye i razrabotannye P. N. Vrangelem, G. N. Leikhtenbergskim i A. P. Livenom*. Edited by A. A. von Lampe. Frankfurt am Main: Possev, 1969.
———. "The White Armies in Russia and Later." *The English Review* (London), October 1927, 375–94.
A sketchy account of British and French attitudes toward Wrangel, of his defeat, and of the escape of his forces from the Crimea in the autumn of 1920.
Wyhowska de Andreis, Wanda. *Między Dnieprem a Tybrem*. London: Polska Fundacja Kulturalna, 1981.
Xydias, Jean. *L'intervention française en Russie, 1918–1919: Souvenirs d'un témoin*. Paris: Les Editions de France, 1927.
Memoirs by a Greco-Russian financier in Odessa of the Allied intervention in southern Ukraine, with emphasis on the leading personalities in the anti-Bolshevik Russian ranks, French policy, and French relations with the VA and UNR government.
Z., O. [Zales'kyi, Osyp]. "Hirs'ka brygada UHA ta ïï perekhid na chekhoslovats'ku terytoriiu." *LChK*, 1938, no. 7–8, 13–14; no. 10, 8–9.
"Z armiieiu generala Pavlenka." *Kaliendar "Kanadiis'koho ukraïntsia" na rik 1921* (Winnipeg), 86–98.
"Z frontu: Z listu żołnierza 36 p.p." *RW*, 2 February 1919, 8–9.
Zadoianyi, Vasyl'. "Druhyi Vseukraïns'kyi viis'kovyi z'ïzd: Spohad uchasnyka." *Tr* (New York), no. 44 (1967), 15–20; no. 45, 2–6.
———. "Heneral Iurko Tiutiunnyk: U 50-tu richnytsiu Pershoho zymovoho pokhodu Armiï UNR v zapillia voroha." *Tr* (New York), no. 59 (1970), 13–18; no. 60, 10–16; no. 61, 11–19; no. 62 (1971), 6–16; no. 63, 10–20; no. 64, 9–16; no. 65, 11–17; no. 66 (1972), 9–15; no. 67, 15–21.
———. "Iak tvorylysia ukraïns'ki zbroini syly na pochatku revoliutsiï 1917 roku." *Tr* (New York), no. 42 (1967), 16–19; no. 43, 11–13; no. 68 (1972), 9–21; no. 69, 23–4.

———. "Khronika ukraïns'koï vyzvol'noï borot'by doby 1917–21 rokiv." *Tr* (New York), no. 33 (1965), 10–13; no. 34, 20–2; no. 35, 13–15.

———. "Naslidky Beresteis'koho dohovoru." *Tr* (New York), no. 78 (1975), 7–10.

———. "Povstannia u Zhmeryntsi: Spohad uchasnyka." *Tr* (New York), no. 38 (1966), 5–9; no. 39, 13–17; no. 40, 5–11.

———. "Povstans'ka stykhiia." *Tr* (New York), no. 46 (1967), 11–15; no. 47, 8–14; no. 48, 14–18; no. 49 (1968), 4–8.

Memoirs of the partisan uprisings against the landowners and German punitive expeditions in Tarashcha and Zvenyhorodka counties in the summer of 1918, their suppression, and the partisans' retreat to the neutral zone.

———. "Stanovyshche v Ukraïni do i pislia prykhodu avstro-nimets'kykh viis'k, berezen'–kviten' 1918 r." *Tr* (New York), no. 69 (1972), 14–21.

Zahora, Feliks. "Wyprawa kijowska w świetle 'Pism, mów, rozkazów'." *BPU*, 1937, no. 21 (212), 229–32.

Zaitsev, Pavlo. "Petliura: Fragmenty spohadiv." *KAV na 1951 rik*, 41–8.

Zakharovych, Iv. "Pershyi den' svobody, pryneseno na vistriakh bagnetiv: Spomyn z chasu pershoï navaly moskaliv na vil'nyi Kyïv." *IKAChK na 1938 rik*, 32–44.

Zaklyns'kyi, Myron. "Karni ekspedytsiï U.S.S.-iv u Khersonshchyni." *IKAChK na 1933 rik*, 67–77.

An account of the Sich Riflemen's activities and Austrian military policy in Kherson gubernia from June to October 1918.

———. "Lystopadovyi zryv." *VK*, 1969, no. 6 (43), 13–20.

———. "Nastup USS-iv na Oleksandrivs'k 1918 r." *IKAChK na 1932 rik*, 46–51.

———. "Sichovi stril'tsi na Khersonshchyni." *IKAChK na 1933 rik*, 54–67.

A detailed account of the hetman regime's and Austrian troops' policies and of the cooperation between the Sich Riflemen and the local population in Kherson gubernia in the summer of 1918.

———. "Tyf u Halyts'kii Armiï: Spohad." *V*, 1935, no. 12, 873–83.

Zales'kyi, Osyp. "Lystopadovyi spohad." *O*, 1958, no. 8 (97), 8–10.

Zalesskii, P. "Glavnyia prichiny neudach belago dvizheniia na iuge Rossii." In *Belyi arkhiv*, vol. 2–3, 151–69. Edited by Ia. M. Kosovoi. Paris, 1928.

An account of the causes of the defeat of the White movement in Ukraine by the governor of Kharkiv gubernia under the hetman regime.

———. *Vozmezdie: Prichiny russkoi katastrofy*. Paris: Muzei sovremennykh sobytii v Rossii, 1925.

Zaryts'kyi, Vasyl'. "Neskinchena sprava." *IKAChK na 1931 rik*, 106–21.

———. "Vypad povstanchoho zahonu vid Husiatyna pid Kyïv 1921 r." *IKAChK na 1932 rik*, 87–97.

———. "Z pid Kyïva do L'vova." *LNV*, 1928, no. 12, 334–42.

Zatonskii, V. "K voprosu ob organizatsii Vremennogo Raboche-Krestianskogo Pravitel'stva Ukraïny, noiabr' 1918 g." *LR*, 1925, no. 1 (10), 139–49.

Zavads'kyi, Viktor. "Natsional'na-personal'na avtonomiia." *LNV*, 1928, no. 2, 159–65.

———. "Znadibky do istoriï 1-ho ukraïns'koho polku im. het'mana Bohdana Khmel'nyts'koho." *KAD na rik 1928*, 113–16.

Zelenyi, Bohdan. "Ostanni dni Halyts'koï armiï: Vytiahy z dnevnyka." In *Ukraïns'ka strilets'ka hromada v Kanadi, 1928–1938*, 149–52. Saskatoon: Ukraïns'ka strilets'ka hromada v Kanadi, 1938.

Żeligowski, Lucjan. "Notatki z roku 1920: Z papierów pośmiertnych." *N* (London) 3 (1951): 161–6.

———. *Wojna w roku 1920: Wspomnienia i rozważania*. Warsaw: Instytut Badania Najnowszej Historji Polski, 1930.

Zelins'kyi, Viktor. Pytannia, iaki pidneseni heneralom Zelins'kym ... pidchas rozmovy ioho z heneralom Anris, nachal'nykom Frantsuz'koï viis'kovoi misiï v Polshchi, 16. 9. 20. r. Warsaw, 16 September 1920. Ms.

———. *Syn'ozhupannyky*. Berlin: Ukraïns'ke natsional'ne ob'iednannia, 1938. An account of the organization and activities of the two Ukrainian Bluecoats divisions in 1917–18 by their general.

———. Viis'kovomu ahentu v Paryzhu polkovnykovi Kolosovs'komu. Warsaw, 21 November 1920. Ms.

Zhuk, Andrii. "Iak diishlo do zasnuvannia 'Soiuzu vyzvolennia Ukraïny'." *KAD na rik 1935*, 103–17.

———. "Persha partiina konferentsiia R.U.P." *KAD na rik 1936*, 96–101.

———. "Ukraïntsi u rosiis'koho voiennoho gubernatora L'vova—Sheremetieva: Iz zapysok ochevydtsia." *Krivavoho roku videns'kyi iliustrovanyi al'manakh na 1917 rik* (Vienna), 122–9.

———. "Verbna nedilia u Kyievi 1918 roku:; Uryvok iz spomyniv." *KAD na rik 1938*, 22–40.

———, ed. *Symon Petliura v molodosti: Zbirka spomyniv*. Lviv: Khortytsia, 1936.

Zhurba, Halyna. "Rik 1917: Spomyny." *NIKTP na rik 1938*, 67–9.

Zieliński, Adam. "Korespondencja z Jerzym Stempowskim, 1941–1942: Myśli o problemach polsko-ukraińskich." *ZH* 45 (1978): 8–56.

Zieliński, Zygmunt. "Z pierwszych walk II. Brygady Legjonów: Listy do rodziny." *B* (Warsaw), 1926, no. 2, 113–22.

Zilyns'kyi, P. "Ostannimy z Kyieva: Iz spomyniv starshyny." *KAD na rik 1934*, 59–76.

Zinevych, Nykanor. "Persha zustrich z Holovnym otamanom." *LChK*, 1936, no. 5, 6–7.

Zmiienko, Vsevolod. Rolia nashoï, VI-ï Sichovoï, dyviziï v ukraïns'kii derzhavnii spravi. 1921. Ms.

———. Zamostia. 1920. Ms.

Zorenko, Dmytro. "Na partyzantsi." *ZD* 3 (1932): 206–25.

Zotov, S. A. "Ot Voronezha do Rostova: Vospominaniia k 15-letiiu l-i Konnoi armiï." *VR*, 1934, no. 11–12, 7–17.

Zozulia, Iakiv. *Kinets' rosiis'koï vlady v Ukraïni: Ohliad podiï ta osobysti spohady.* 2d. rev. ed. New York: the author, 1964.

———. "Naddniprians'ka pomich Halychyni v 1919 r." *VU*, no. 35–6 (1962), 91–101.

———. "Obloha Kyieva, vidstup ukraïns'koï armiï na Volyn' ta orhanizatsiia sanitarnoï sluzhby." *ZD* 11 (1966): 42–64.

———. "Symon Petliura." *VU*, no. 46 (1965), 4–8.

———. "Vidhuky pershoho lystopada na Velykii Ukraïni." *VU*, no. 63 (1970), 33–40.

———. "Vseukraïns'ki viis'kovi z'ïzdy v 1917 r." *VK*, 1967, no. 4 (28), 29–34.

———, comp. *Velyka ukraïns'ka revoliutsiia: Materiialy do istoriï vidnovlennia ukraïns'koï derzhavnosty; kalendar istorychnykh podiï za liut. 1917 r.–ber. 1918 r.* 2d ed. New York: Ukrainian Academy of Arts and Sciences in the U.S., 1967.

Zubov, Valentin. *Stradnye gody Rossii: Vospominaniia o revoliutsii, 1917–1925.* Munich: W. Fink, 1968.

Zubyk, Roman. "Okremyi zaliznyi zahin na zadakh bol'shevykiv: Na osnovi zapysok." *IKAChK na 1922 rik*, 70–5.

Związek Demokracji Polskiej na Rusi: Do Naczelnika Państwa i Wodza Naczelnego. Warsaw, 22 August 1919. Ms.

Secondary Sources

Adams, Arthur E. "Bolshevik Administration in the Ukraine, 1918." *RP* 20 (1958): 289–306.
———. "The Bolsheviks and the Ukrainian Front in 1918–1919." *SEER* 36 (1958): 396–417.
———. *Bolsheviks in the Ukraine: The Second Campaign, 1918–1919*. New Haven: Yale University Press, 1963.
   A well-documented study of the Bolshevik effort to occupy Ukraine after the fall of the hetman regime, with emphasis on the struggle with Otaman Hryhor'ïv.
Agureev, K. V. *Razgrom belogvardeiskikh voisk Denikina, oktiabr 1919–mart 1920*. Moscow: Voennoe izdatel'stvo, 1961.
Ajnenkiel, Andrzej. *Od rządów ludowych do przewrotu majowego: Zarys dziejów politycznych Polski, 1918–1926*. Warsaw: Wiedza Powszechna, 1968.
"Akademja ku czci Szymona Petlury w Instytucie Wschodnim w Warszawie." *BPU*, 1936, no. 23 (162), 240–1.
Aleksashenko, A. P. *Krakh denikinshchiny*. Moscow: Izdatel'stvo Moskovskogo universiteta, 1966.
Aleksandrowicz, St. "Bój 13 pułku ułanów pod Janowem 25. VII. 1920." *Przegląd Kawalerii i Broni Pancernej* (London) 8, no. 59 (1970), 207–18.
Alsberg, Henry G. "The Russo-Polish Armistice." *CH* 13 (1921): 233–8.
———. "The Russo-Polish Peace." *TN* 111 (1920): 587–8.
———. "The Situation in the Ukraine." *TN* 109 (1919): 569–70.
Ambrosius, Lloyd E. "Wilson, the Republicans, and French Security after World War I." *JAH* 59, no. 2 (1972), 341–52.
Anderson, Edgar. "The British Policy toward the Baltic States, 1918–1920." *JCEA* 19, no. 3 (1959), 276–89.
Andriievs'kyi, A. M. "Varshavs'kyi dohovir." *URob*, 12 November 1948.
Andriievs'kyi, Dmytro. "Soiuz z Pol'shcheiu." *RN*, 1931, no. 7–8, 162–6.
———. "Symon Petliura." *KAD na rik Bozhyi 1927*, 7–13.
———. "Ukraïns'ka sprava na mizhnarodnii shakhivnytsi." *RN*, 1931, no. 9–10, 213–18; no. 11–12, 257–65.
Andriievs'kyi, Viktor. *V desiatu richnytsiu, 22. I. 1918–22. I. 1928: Promova na urochystii akademiï v Ukraïns'kii stanytsi pry m. Kalish 22. I. 1928*. Kalisz: Tabor, 1928.
Andrusiak, Mykola. "Dumky Hrushevs'koho pro potrebu ukraïns'koï armiï." *LChK*, 1935, no. 3, 7–8.
Antonchuk, Demyd. "Svitlii pam'iati Holovnoho otamana." *H*, no. 24 (1938), 7–11.
———. "Vapniars'ka Respublika." *ZD* 9 (1938): 153–63.
Anusz, Antoni. *Naród, armja i wódz*. Warsaw: Biuro Propagandy Wewnętrznej, 1920.
———. *Pierwszy Marszałek Józef Piłsudski*. Warsaw: Wojskowy Instytut Naukowo-Wydawniczy, 1927.
Apolla, Arnaldo. "Fighting the Bolsheviki." *LA*, 7 June 1919, 325–31.
Arciszewski, Franciszek Adam. *Ostróg-Dubno-Brody: Walki 18 Dywizji Piechoty z Konną Armją Budiennego, 1 lipca–6 sierpnia 1920*. Warsaw: Wojskowy Instytut Naukowo-Wydawniczy, 1923.
Argus. "Frantsuz'ka interventsiia v Odesi." *Tr* (Paris), 1928, no. 38 (144), 12–14.

"Armiia Zelenoho i Sichovi stril'tsi." *StD*, no. 54 (October 1919).
Arski, Stefan. "Zmowa grabieżców: Sojusz Piłsudskiego z Denikinym przeciw rewolucji." *Nowa Kultura* (Warsaw), 1950, no. 6, 6; no. 7, 5–6.
"Artylerja konna w walkach naszej jazdy z kawalerją Budiennego." *B* (Warsaw), 1921, no. 2, 129–31.
Assassinés par Moscou: Petlura—Konovaletz—Bandera. Munich: Editions Ukrainiennes, 1962.
"At Zeligowsky's Headquarters." *LA*, 12 February 1921, 399–403.
"Ataman Petlura." *K*, 1958, no. 4, 78.
B., M. "Rodyna Petliuriv." *Sv*, 12 November 1976.
Babii, Ol. "Choho vchyt' nas 1. lystopad 1918 r." *RN*, 1929, no. 10–11, 311–17.
———. "Petliura i Halychyna." *StV*, 1926, no. 7–8, 21–8.
Bączkowski, Włodzimierz. "Abecadło problemu polsko-ukraińskiego." *BPU*, 1938, no. 26 (265), 277–8.
———. "Co zagraża polskości na południowym wschodzie Rzeczypospolitej?" *BPU*, 1936, no. 7 (146), 57–8.
———. "Europa wschodnia a obrona państwa." *PEW* 1, no. 2 (1939), 77–91.
———. *Grunwald czy Piławce*. Warsaw: Wydawnictwo Myśli Polskiej, 1938.
A work dealing with Poland's historical dilemma: should it ally with Ukraine, Belarus, and Lithuania to fight against the Germans, as it did in the Battle of Tannenberg in 1410, or should it struggle against them and thus suffer defeat and subsequent decline, as in the Cossack-Polish wars of the seventeenth century?
———. "J. Piłsudski a idee prometejskie." *BPU*, 1938, no. 20 (259), 209–11.
———. "Petlurowstwo i Piłsudskizm: Przeciwieństwa i analogie." *BPU*, 1937, no. 9 (200), 93–5; no. 10 (201), 109–12.
———. *Prometeizm na tle epoki: Wybrane fragmenty z historii ruchu*. N. p.; the author, 1984.
———. *Rosja wczoraj i dziś: Studium historyczno-polityczne*. Jerusalem: the author, 1946.
———. "Sprawa ukraińska." *K*, 1952, no. 7–8 (57–8), 64–84.
———. "Sprawa ukraińska w świetle obrony państwa." *BPU*, 1937, nos. 4–6 (195–7).
———. *U źródeł polskiej idei federacyjnej*. Jerusalem: the author, 1945.
———. *U źródeł upadku i wielkości: Zagadnienie kresów wschodnich na tle dziejów polsko-moskiewskich; polski "inferiority complex"; problemat ukraiński; kim jesteśmy?; pomniejszycielstwo Rzeczypospolitej; ignorancja polska; zarys podstaw rozwiązania problematu ukraińskiego*. Warsaw: Księgarnia F. Hoesicka, 1935.
———. "Wyprawa kijowska: W drugą rocznicę zgonu Wielkiego Marszałka." *BPU*, 1937, no. 20 (211), 217–20.
———. "Z dziedziny polskiej polityki wschodniej." *Ws* 4, no. 1–2 (1932–3), 1–6.
Bagiński, Henryk. "Jarosław Dąbrowski o sprawie ruskiej." *N* (Warsaw), 1934, no. 3, 455–69.
———. *Wojsko Polskie na wschodzie, 1914–1920*. Warsaw: Główna Księgarnia Wojskowa, 1921.
———. "Zdzisław Oplustill: 'Polskie formacje wschodnie, 1918–1919'." *B* (Warsaw), 1922, no. 3, 219–24.

Baibak, P. T. "Symon Petliura—symvol derzhavnosty ta reformator doby." *Sv*, 4–6 and 10–11 October 1979.
Baier, Mykola. *Prychyny agrarnoï revoliutsiï na Ukraïni i shliakhy do rozv'iazky agrarnoï spravy*. Kyiv: Vydavnytstvo UNP Svoboda i pravo, 1920.
Balck. "Der russisch-polnische Krieg 1920." *WW*, 1930, no. 7, 425–40.
Balkun, F. "Interventsiia v Odesse, 1918–1919 gg." *PR*, 1923, no. 6–7 (18–19), 196–221.
Bandrowski, Julius K. *The Great Battle on the Vistula*. Translated by Harriet E. Kennedy. London: Low and Marston, 1921.
Baranowski, Władysław. "Zagraniczna akcja niepodległościowa w czasie Wielkiej Wojny we Włoszech, 1914–1915." *N* (Warsaw), 1938, no. 3 (47), 403–20.
Barr, James, and Rhys J. Davies. *Report on the Polish-Ukrainian Conflict in Eastern Galicia*. London: House of Commons, 1931.
Bartel, Paul. *Le maréchal Piłsudski*. Paris: Plon, 1935.
Bartlitz, Stanisław. "Działania w obszarze Ihumenia w maju 1920 r." *B* (Warsaw), 1933, no. 3–4, 193–233; no. 5–6, 393–434.
Bartoszewicz, Joachim. *Na Rusi: Polski stan posiadania, kraj, ludność, ziemia*. Kyiv: L. Idzikowski, 1912.
———. *Znaczenie polityczne kresów wschodnich dla Polski*. Warsaw: A. Michalski, 1924.
Bartoszewicz, Kazimierz. *Dzieje Galicyi, jej stan przed wojną i "wyodrębnienie."* Warsaw and New York: Gebethner i Wolff and Polish Book Import Co., 1917.
Batorskii, M. "Iz proshlogo XVI armii." *VR*, 1927, no. 8, 181–9.
Batowski, Henryk. "Linia Curzona a była Galicja Wschodnia." *ZDSPR* 3 (1968): 170–7.
Baudouin de Courtenay-Jędrzejewiczowa, C. "Patriotyzm Piłsudskiego." *N* (London) 6 (1958): 23–60.
Baumgart, Winfried. "Ludendorff und das Auswärtige Amt zum Besetzung der Krim 1918." *JGO* 15, no. 4 (December 1966), 529–38.
Beh. "Nieznana inicjatywa Piłsudskiego." *K*, 1956, no. 5, 124–7.
Benedykt, Stefan. "Kijowskie 'poprawki historyczne'." *ZH* 31 (1975): 201–8.
Berbenets', Panas. "Symon Petliura: Do p'iatoï richnytsi ioho trahichnoï smerty." *T*, no. 16 (1931), 4–28.
Biegański, Stanisław. "Gen. Weygand o Bitwie Warszawskiej." *B* (London), 1957, no. 1, 59–61.
———. "Piłsudski i Lenin o ruchach rewolucyjnych i narodowych." *N* (London) 3 (1951): 60–117; 4 (1952): 128–65.
———. "Polska wobec Europy południowo-wschodniej na przełomie 1918/1919." *N* (London) 10 (1976): 52–90.
———. "Tajny układ między Austro-Węgrami a Ukrainą z 8 lutego 1918 r." *N* (London) 12 (1979): 60–6.
Biernacki, Mieczysław. "Bitwa pod Równem, 2. VII. – 9. VII. 1920." *B* (Warsaw), no. 2, 123–41; no. 3, 291–313.
———. "Bitwa z Budiennym nad Uszą, 19–21 czerwca 1920 r." *B* (Warsaw), no. 1, 74–106; no. 2, 190–210.

———. *Działania Armji Konnej Budiennego w Kampanji Polsko-Rosyjskiej 1920 r., 26. V. – 20. VI. 1920*. Warsaw: Wojskowy Instytut Naukowo-Wydawniczy, 1924.
Bierzanek, Remigiusz. *Państwo polskie w politycznych koncepcjach mocarstw zachodnich, 1917–1919*. Warsaw: Polski Instytut Spraw Międzynarodowych, 1964.
Bihl, Wolfdieter. "Beiträge zur Ukraine-Politik Österreich-Ungarns 1918." *JGO* 14, no. 1 (March 1966), 51–62.
———. "Einige Aspekte der Österreichisch-ungarischen Ruthenenpolitik, 1914–1918." *JGO* 14, no. 4 (December 1966), 539–50.
———. "Die Tätigkeit des ukrainischen Revolutionärs Mykola Zaliznjak in Österreich-Ungarn." *JGO* 13, no. 2 (June 1965), 226–30.
Bilas, Dmytro. "Iak pol'skyi marshal Pilsuds'kyi pomahav nam buduvaty Ukraïnu." *Nasha derzhava* (Toronto), 1954, nos. 10–11 (48–9).
Bocheński, Adolf M. *Między Niemcami a Rosją*. Warsaw: "Polityka," 1937.
———. "Jeszcze o Traktacie Ryskim." *BPU*, 1933, no. 4, 12–15.
Bocheński, Aleksander, Stanisław Łoś, and Włodzimierz Bączkowski. *Problem polsko-ukraiński w Ziemi Czerwieńskiej*. Warsaw: "Polityka," 1938.
Bohusz-Szyszko, Zygmunt. *Działania wojenne nad Dolną Wisłą w 1920 r*. Warsaw: Wojskowe Biuro Historyczne, 1931.
Boi. "Ukraïns'ki sichovi stril'tsi (U.S.S.) i Sichovi stril'tsi (S.S.)." *IKAChK na 1924 rik*, 68–78.
Bój pod Zasławem, 23 września 1920. Warsaw: Wojskowy Instytut Naukowo-Wydawniczy, 1925.
Bołtuć, Mikołaj. "Budienny pod Zamościem." *B* (Warsaw), 1926, no. 3, 203–29. A Polish perspective on the defense of Zamość by UNR and Polish troops against Budennyi's cavalry army in August 1920.
Boncza, St. J. *Joseph Pilsudski: Founder of Polish National Independence and Chief of the Polish State*. London: S. Low, 1921.
Bondorowski, M. "Mniejszości narodowe na Ukrainie." *SN*, 1928, no. 1, 107–12.
Borkiewicz, Adam. "Koncentracja nad Wieprzem." *B* (Warsaw), 1925, no. 2, 169–209.
Borshchak, Il'ko (Borschak, Elie). "Evropa i vidrodzhennia Ukraïny, 1914–1923." *LChK*, 1936, no. 10, 5–8; no. 11, 8–12; no. 12, 7–12.
———. "La paix ukrainienne de Brest-Litovsk." *Le Monde Slave* 2 (1929), no. 4, 33–62; 3, no. 7, 63–84; 3, no. 8, 199–225.
———. "Pol's'kyi nastup na Ukraïnu 1920 r. u mizhnarodnii politytsi." *ChSh*, 1925, no. 9, 76–92; 1927, no. 7–8, 109–43.
Bortnowski, Władysław. "Osłona na Bugu." *N* (London) 3 (1951): 138–49.
Borzecki. "Walki w Galicji." *B* (Warsaw), 1920, no. 4, 257–73; no. 5, 326–32.
Bradley, John F. N. *Allied Intervention in Russia*. New York: Basic Books, 1968.
———. "The Allies and Russia in the Light of French Archives, 7 November 1917–15 March 1918." *SS* 16, no. 2 (1964), 166–85.
———. *La Légion tchecoslovaque en Russie, 1914–1920*. Paris: Delmas, 1965.
Brazhnev, E. "Partizanshchina." *Novyi mir*, 1925, no. 7, 61–84.
Bril, I. "Politicheskaia podgotovka letnei operatsii 16-i armii v 1920 g." *VR*, 1926, no. 11, 86–105.

Brinkley, George A. *The Volunteer Army and the Allied Intervention in South Russia, 1917–1921: A Study in the Politics and Diplomacy of the Russian Civil War.* Notre Dame: University of Notre Dame Press, 1966.
Brown, Philip M. "The New Balkans of Central Europe." *North American Review* 211 (1920): 182–93.
Bryk, Oleksander. *Ternystyi shliakh Ukraïns'koho Uriadu (1918–1921): U 50-littia vidnovlennia Ukraïns'koï Derzhavy.* Winnipeg: the author, 1960.
Brzozowski, Władysław. "Początki P. O. W., VIII. 1–22. X. 1914 r." *N* (Warsaw) 16 (1937): 473–90.
Buchanan, George W. "Great Britain and Russia." *LA* 10 May 1919, 582–92.
Budecki, Zdzisław. *Stosunki polsko-litewskie po Wojnie Światowej, 1918–1928.* Warsaw: Koło Naukowe Szkoły Nauk Politycznych, 1928.
Buiskii, Anatolii A. *Krasnaia Armiia na vnutrennem fronte: Bor'ba s belogvardeiskimi vostaniiami, povstanchestvom i banditizmom.* 3d ed. Moscow: Gos. izd-vo, 1929.
Bukowiecki, Stanisław. "Role czynników wewnętrznych w utworzeniu nowej państwowości Polski." *N* (Warsaw), 2, no. 2 (1930), 1–24.
Bulavenko. "Borot'ba na Kubani v druhii polovyni 1918 r." *RN*, 1934, no. 1–2 (72–3), 14–24.
———. "Kuban' i 'moskovs'kyi shliakh'." *RN*, 1934, no. 7–8 (78–9), 187–97.
———. "Kuban' u pershii polovyni 1919 r." *RN*, 1934, no. 5–6 (76–7), 133–42.
———. "Vyzvolennia Kubani z pid bol'shevyts'koï vlady v 1918 r." *RN*, 1933, no. 11–12 (70–1), 265–75.
Burnatovych, Oleksa. *Ukraïns'ka ideol'ogiia revoliutsiinoï doby.* Lviv: Ukraïns'kyi prapor, 1922.
Butler, Ralph. "Józef Piłsudski: Aristocrat-Revolutionary." *Atlantic Monthly*, August 1923, 269–77.
———. *The New Eastern Europe.* London: Longmans and Green, 1919.
Bykovsky, Lev. *Solomon I. Goldelman: A Portrait of a Politician and Educator, 1885–1974; A Chapter in Ukrainian-Jewish Relations.* New York: Ukrainian Historical Association, 1980.
Camon, Hubert. *Zwycięski manewr marszałka Piłsudskiego przeciw bolszewikom, sierpień 1920: Studjum strategiczne.* Translated by Józef Andrzej Telsar. Warsaw: Wojskowy Instytut Naukowo-Wydawniczy, 1930.
Carley, Michael J. *Revolution and Intervention: The French Government and the Russian Civil War, 1917–1919.* Montreal: McGill-Queen's University Press, 1983.
Cartwright, W. P. *The Big Three of Poland's Drama: President Ignatius Moscicki, Marshal Smigly-Rydz and Colonel Joseph Beck.* London: Pilot Press, n.d.
Cepnik, Henryk. *Józef Piłsudski, twórca niepodległego państwa polskiego: Zarys życia i działalności popularnie określony.* Warsaw: Instytut Państwowo-Twórczej, 1933.
Chaikovs'kyi, Bohdan. "Pid moskovs'kym panuvanniam." *VSVU*, no. 21–2 (1915), 10–12.
Chalyi, S. "Aneksiia Skhidn'oï Halychyny i Radians'ka Ukraïna." *NH*, 1923, no. 1, 85–92.
Chaplenko, V. "Moï pryhody z V. Vynnychenkom." *VU*, no. 63 (1970), 33–40.
Charaszkiewicz, Edmund. "Przebudowa Wschodu Europy: Fragmenty faktów z lat 1917–21." *N* (London) 9 (1974): 229–85.

———. "Przebudowa Wschodu Europy: Materiały do polityki wschodniej Józefa Piłsudskiego w latach 1893–1921." *N* (London) 5 (1955): 125–67.
Chebotariv, Mykola. "Lytsar bez rekliamy." *Nedilia* (Augsburg), 1951, no. 13, 3–8.
Cherenovich, S. "Takticheskie uroki otkhoda 3-i Pol'skoi armii v iiune 1920 g." *VR*, 1932, no. 1, 47–60.
Chernets'kyi, A. "Rolia mista, industriï ta robitnytstva v ukraïns'kii vyzvol'nii borot'bi." *UV* (Neu-Ulm), no. 101 (1950).
Chesna, Iona D. "Trahichna smert' Symona Petliury." *Tr* (New York), no. 39 (1966), 6–8.
Chesterton, G. K. "The True Case against Bolshevism." *LA*, 13 September 1919, 647–9.
Chetyrkin, A. "Krest'ianstvo iuga Rossii pod vlastiu Denikina: Agrarnaia politika denikinshchiny." *IM*, 1941, no. 5 (93), 61–73.
Chocianowicz, Wacław. "Historia Dywizji Litewsko-Białoruskiej w świetle listów Józefa Piłsudskiego." *N* (London) 7 (1962): 200–18.
———. "Szkic dziejów Litewsko-Białoruskiej Dywizji." *ZH* 28 (1974): 124–52.
Chojnowski, Andrzej. *Koncepcje polityki narodowościowej rządów polskich w latach 1921-1939*. Wrocław: Zakład Narodowy im. Ossolińskich, 1970.
———. "Kwestia mniejszości narodowych a bezpieczeństwo państwa w myśli politycznej Narodowej Demokracji i Sanacji." In *Na warsztatach historyków polskiej myśli politycznej*, 217–22. Edited by Jan St. Miś. Wrocław: Zakład Narodowy im Ossolińskich.
Chołodecki, Józef Białyna. *Zakładnicy miasta Lwowa w niewoli rosyjskiej, 1915–1918*. Lviv: Wschód, 1930.
Chornohor, Bohdan. "Dukh stepiv—chy otamanshchyna." *LChK*, 1937, no. 1, 16–18.
Choulgine, Alexandre [Shul'hyn, Oleksander]. *L'Ukraine et le cauchemar rouge: Les massacres en Ukraine*. Paris: J. Tallandier, 1927.
Chubaty, Nicholas. "The Modern Ukrainian Nationalist Movement." *JCEA* 4 (1944): 281–305.
———. "Ukraine—between Poland and Russia." *RP* 8 (1946): 331–53.
———. "The Ukrainian and Polish-Russian Border Dispute." *UQ* 1 (1940): 52–71.
Chulyi, Petro. "Moskali na Ukraïni: Paralieli." *LNV*, 1922, no. 8, 172–8.
"Chuzhynets'ki predstavnyky v Ukraïns'kii derzhavi." *"Ukraïns'kyi invalid": Kaliendar na 1936*, 89–90.
Ciałowicz, Jan. *"Manewr na Mozyr i Kalinkowicze, 4. III.–12. III. 1920. r."* Warsaw: Wojskowy Instytut Naukowo-Wydawniczy, 1925.
———. "O genezie Legionów: Z powodu książki Andrzeja Garlickiego." *NDP* 10 (1966): 187–206.
Ciechanowski, Jan. "Woodrow Wilson in the Spotlight of Versailles." *PoR* 1, no. 2–3 (1956), 12–21.
Ciechowski, St. "Na paryz'kim bruku." *BPU*, 1937, no. 30 (221), 337–8.
Cienciała, Anna M. "Polityka brytyjska wobec odrodzenia Polski, 1914–1918." *ZH* 16 (1969): 67–94.
———, and Titus Komarnicki. *From Versailles to Locarno: Keys to Polish Foreign Policy, 1919–25*. Lawrence: University Press of Kansas, 1984.

Ciołkosz, Adam. *Ludzie P.P.S.* London: Centralny Komitet Polskiej Partii Socjalistycznej, 1967.
Cochenhausen, Friedel von. "Die antibolschewistische Bewegung in Südrussland." *Die Woche* (Berlin), 4 October 1919, 1095–8.
Cohen, I. "My Mission to Poland, 1918–19." *Jewish Social Studies* 3, no. 2 (1951), 149–72.
Crisp, Olga. "Some Problems of French Investment in Russian Joint-Stock Companies, 1894–1914." *SEER* 35 (1956–7): 223–40.
Czarski, Andrzej. *Od Borysowa do Rygi: Uwagi krytyczne o dyplomacji, wojnie i pokoju 1920 r.* Warsaw, 1930.
Czerniawski, Emil J. *Dmowski wobec Piłsudskiego.* Sydney: Nuof, 1969.
Czerniewski, W. "The Future of Ukraina." *LA*, 2 November 1918, 733–45.
"Czy ukraińskość zagraża polskości?" *BPU*, 1936, no. 6 (145), 45–7.
Czyżewski, Ludwig. "Bój spotkaniowy 7 Dywizji Piechoty z grupą uderzeniową Woroszyłowa." *B* (Warsaw), 18, no. 2–3 (1936), 331–48.
D'Abernon, Edgar V. *The Eighteenth Decisive Battle of the World: Warsaw, 1920.* London: Hodder and Stoughton, 1931.
Dąbrowski, Jerzy. *Bój odwrotowy nad Niemnem i Rosią 1-ej Dywizji Litewsko-Białoruskiej, 21–25 lipca 1920 roku.* Warsaw: Wojskowe Biuro Historyczne, 1933.
Dąbrowski, Marjan. *Kampania na Wołyniu, 2. IX. 1915 r.–8. X. 1916 r.* Warsaw: Wydawnictwo Księgarni Wojskowej, 1919.
———, ed. *Dziesięciolecie Polski odrodzonej: Księga pamiątkowa, 1918–1928.* Cracow and Warsaw: "Ilustrowany Kuryer Codzienny," "Światowid," and "Na Szerokim Świecie," 1928.
Dąbrowski, Stanisław. "The Peace Treaty of Riga." *PoR* 5, no. 1 (1960), 3–34.
Danilewiczowa, Maria. "Dyplomaci angielscy o Marszałku Piłsudskim." *ZH* 23 (1973): 208–11.
Daniłowski, G. "Józef Piłsudski." In *Szlakiem legjonów*, 20. Chicago: Komitet Obrony Narodowej w Ameryce, 1914.
Danko, M. "Idea Petlury a społeczeństwo ukraińskie." *BPU*, 1936, no. 5 (144), 37–8.
———. "Konflikt mizh velykoderzhavamy i sprava vyzvolennia Ukraïny." *Tr* (Paris), 1939, no. 26 (676), 2–6.
Danylevs'kyi, K. *Petliura v sertsiakh i pisniakh svoioho narodu.* Pittsburgh, 1951.
Danylovych, Kost'. *Kil'ka zustrichiv z Holovnym otamanom na Velykii Ukraïni 1919 roku.* Chicago: the author, 1954.
Dashkevych, Roman. *Artyleriia Sichovykh stril'tsiv u borot'bi za Zoloti kyïvs'ki vorota.* New York: Chervona Kalyna, 1965.
Daszyński, Ignacy. *Wielki człowiek w Polsce: Szkic psychologiczno-polityczny.* Warsaw: Wydawnictwo Warszawskiego Oddziału Towarzystwa Uniwersytetu Robotniczego w Warszawie, 1925.
Dats'kiv, T. "Masakra halychan v Odesi v r. 1920." *URob*, 14 September 1951.
Davies, Norman. "Lloyd George and Poland, 1919–20." *JCH*, 6, no. 3 (1971), 132–54.
———. "Sir Horace Rumbold w Warszawie. 1919–1920," *DN* 3, no. 3 (1971), 39–54.
———. *White Eagle, Red Star: The Polish-Soviet War, 1919–20.* London: Macdonald, 1972.

Davis, Richard S. "With the Polish Army." *The Outlook* (New York) 126 (1920): 21–4.
Dębicka, Elżbieta. "Polskie organizacje w Tarnopolu w 1918–19 r." *N* (Warsaw) 18 (1938): 108–34.
Debo, Richard K. *Survival and Consolidation: The Foreign Policy of Soviet Russia, 1918–1921.* Montreal and Kingston: McGill-Queen's University Press, 1992.
Degot, V. "Men'shevizm i belogvardeishchina vo vremia grazhdanskoi voiny v Odesse." *Katorga i ssylka* (Moscow), 1931, no. 7 (80), 26–39.
Demkowski, Piotr. *Bój pod Wołkowyskiem, 23–24 września 1920 r.* Warsaw: Wojskowy Instytut Naukowo-Wydawniczy, 1924.
Derosh, Alen [Desroches, Alain]. "Ukraïns'ka problema i S. Petliura." *Tr* (New York), no. 39 (1966), 8–10.
Deruga, Aleksy. "Inicjatywa Lenina w sprawie uregulowania stosunków z Polską na przełomie lat 1918–1919." *DN* 2, no. 2 (1970), 89–103.
———. "O federalizmie i polityce wschodniej obozu belwederskiego." *PH*, 55, no. 2 (1964), 317–30.
———. "Początek rokowań o sojusz między Piłsudskim a Petlurą, styczeń–lipiec 1919." *ZDSPR* 6 (1970): 45–67.
———. *Polityka wschodnia Polski wobec ziem Litwy, Białorusi i Ukrainy (1918–1919).* Warsaw: Książka i Wiedza, 1969.
———. "Przed i po Wyprawie Wileńskiej 1919 r." *ZDSPR* 10 (1973): 51–72.
"Desiata richnytsia isnuvannia Armii U.N.R." *T*, no. 4 (1927), 88–96.
Desroches, Alain. *The Ukrainian Problem and Symon Petlura (The Fire and the Ashes).* Chicago: Ukrainian Research and Information Institute, 1970.
Dillon, Emile J. *The Peace Conference.* London: Hutchinson, 1919.
———. *The Inside Story of the Peace Conference.* New York: Harper and Brothers, 1920.
"Dlaczego Niemcy tak długo Podlasia nie opuszczali." *RW*, 20 April 1919.
Dmowski, Roman. *Niemcy, Rosja i kwestja polska.* Częstochowa: A. Gmachowski, 1938.
———. *Polityka polska i odbudowanie państwa.* 3d ed. 2 vols. Hannover: Księgarnia Perzyński, Niklewicz, 1947.
———. *Problems of Central and Eastern Europe.* London, 1917.
———. *Świat powojenny i Polska.* Warsaw: M. Niklewicz, J. Załuska, 1931.
Dmytryshyn, Basil. *Moscow and the Ukraine, 1918–1953: A Study of Russian Bolshevik Nationality Policy.* New York: Bookman Associates, 1956.
Dnisttrans'kyi, Stanyslav. *L'Ukraine et la Conférence de la Paix.* N.p. [Paris?], 1919.
"Do istoriï italiis'ko-ukraïns'kykh vidnosyn v 1919 r." *P*, 1941, no. 11, 658–89.
"Do istoriï Ukraïns'koho polku im. Bohdana Khmel'nyts'koho." *VSVU*, no. 153 (1917), 362–4.
"Do przywódców narodu ukraińskiego." *RW*, 1919, no. 21 (52).
"Do 40-kh rokovyn vidrodzhennia Ukraïns'koho viis'ka." *BUNDS*, no. 28 (1958), 25–7.
Dobrotvors'kyi, Osyp. "Lystopad 1921 roku na Velykii Ukraïni: Korotkyi narys povstancho-partyzans'koho rukhu pid komanduvanniam generala Iurka Tiutiunnyka." *IKAChK na 1923 rik*, 142–50.

Dobrowolska, Barbara. "Stosunek mocarstw sprzymierzonych do sprawy zachodnich granic Polski w pierwszej fazie Konferencji Pokojowej w Paryżu w 1919 r." *NDP* 1 (1958): 35–76.
Dobrowolski, A. "Centralna Rada na Ukrainie." *PD*, 1920, no. 6, 271–80.
Domarats'kyi. Oborona Zamostia. Aleksandrów Kujawski, 1921. Ms.
Dontsov, Dmytro. "Mazepyns'kyi myr, 1918–1928." *IKAChK na 1928 rik*, 37–43.
———. "Memento: Do paryz'koho protsesu." *LNV*, 1927, no. 11, 261–6.
———. "Symon Petliura." *LNV*, 1926, no. 7–8, 321–8.
Doroshenko, Dmytro. *History of Ukraine, 1917–1923*. Vol. 2. Translated by D. M. Elcheshen. Winnipeg: Hetman Movement Leadership, 1973.
———. *Istoriia Ukraïny 1917–1923. rr.* 2 vols. Uzhhorod, 1930, 1932. Reprint, New York: Bulava, 1954.
Doroshenko, Volodymyr. "Literaturna diial'nist' Symona Petliury." *UPS*, 1973, no. 5, 6–7.
Dotsenko, Oleksander. "Geneza Zymovoho pokhodu, 6, XII. 1919–6 V. 1920." *IKAChK na 1934 rik*, 44–51.
———. "Reid otamana Sahaidachnoho, Kholodnyi Iar–Kherson: Z tsykliu Chotyry povstans'ki reidy i ïkh likvidatsiia." *LChK*, 1932, no. 11, 4–5.
Douglas, James. "W zaraniu dyplomacji polskiej: Misja Ligi Narodowej i P. P. S. w Japonji, 1904–1905." *N* (Warsaw) 5 (1932): 177–99, 363–78.
"Dovkruhy smerty Torresa." *UPS*, 1966, no. 3, 11–12.
Drazhevs'ka, L. "Rozmova pro Petliuru." *KAV na 1954 rik*, 42–4.
Droga życia Józefa Piłsudskiego. Prepared by Wanda Piłsudska et al. London: Fundusz im. Aleksandry Piłsudskiej, 1977.
Drozdowski, Marian Marek. *Ignacy Jan Paderewski: A Political Biography*. Warsaw: Interpress, 1981.
"Druhyi Vseukraïns'kyi viis'kovyi z'ïzd u Kyïvi." *VSVU*, no. 161 (1917), 488–91; no. 163, 522–3.
Dryhynycz, Jarosław. "Symon Petlura." *Ws*, 1936, no. 1–2, 44–51.
Dublański, Anatol. "Wyprawa Karola XII na Ukrainę a wyprawa kijowska 1920 r." *BPU*, 1937, no. 23, 254–6.
Duda, M. "Vidhuky revoliutsiï na Slobozhanshchyni v 1917, r." *IKAChK na 1937 rik*, 151–5.
Dudko, Fedir. "Z bol'shevyts'koho Kyieva do Kyieva ukraïns'koho." *IKAChK na 1938 rik*, 54–65.
Dugdale, Blanche E. C. "The Case of East Galicia." *NE*, 11 March 1920, 202–6.
Dumin, O. *Ukraïns'ko-pol's'ka viina, 1918–1919*. Prague, 1929.
Dunin-Borkowski, P. "Wytyczne programu zbliżenia polsko-ukraińskiego." *Droga* (Warsaw), 1931.
Dushnyck, Walter. "The Kerensky Provisional Government and the Ukrainian Central Rada." *UQ*, 1967, no. 2, 109–29.
———. "Russia and the Ukrainian National Revolution." *UQ*, 1946, no. 2, 363–75.
———. "The Russian Provisional Government and the Ukrainian Central Rada." *UQ*, 1946, no. 3, 66–79.

Dyboski, Roman. "Two Neighbors of Russia and Their Policies: Poland." *NCA*, June 1924, 804–14.
Dzierżykraj-Stokalski, Tadeusz. "Powody naszej klęski w pierwszej połowie Wojny Polsko-Bolszewickiej." *KL*, 25 August 1932.
Dziewanowski, M. K. *Joseph Piłsudski: A European Federalist, 1918–1922*. Stanford: Hoover Institution Press, 1969.
———. "Joseph Piłsudski, 1867–1967." *EEQ* 2, no. 4 (1969), 359–83.
E., Al. "Niebezpieczeństwo obecnej polityki Piłsudskiego." *RW*, 13 July 1919.
———. "Pokój a sprawa Ukrainy." *RW*, 12 November 1920.
Egorov, A. I. *L'vov-Varshava, 1920 god: Vzaimodeistvie frontov*. Moscow: Voennoe izdatel'stvo, 1929.
A polemical account of the Bolshevik campaign in Poland in 1920 by the commander of the Bolshevik Southwestern Front.
Eideman, R., and Nikolai E. Kakurin. *Hromadians'ka viina na Ukraïni*. Kharkiv: Derzhavne vydavnytstvo Ukraïny, 1928.
A brief survey of the Bolshevik struggle for power in Ukraine. The authors stress the campaign against the partisan groups and the strategic and political causes of the Polish-Ukrainian offensive in 1920 and Budennyi's counteroffensive.
Elcock, H. J. "Britain and the Russo-Polish Frontier, 1919–1921." *The Historical Journal* 12, no. 1 (1969), 137–54.
Epstein, Klaus. "The Development of German-Austrian War Aims in the Spring of 1917." *JCEA* 17, no. 1 (1957), 24–47.
Eudin, Xenia H. "The German Occupation of the Ukraine in 1918: A Documentary Account." *RR* 1 (1941): 90–105.
———. "Soviet National Minority Policies, 1918–1921." *SEER* 21, no. 2 (1943), 31–55.
Farman, Jr., Elbert E. "The Polish-Bolshevik Cavalry Campaigns of 1920." *Cavalry Journal* (London), July 1921, 223–39.
Fedenko, Panas. "The Period of the Directory." In *Ukraine: A Concise Encyclopaedia*, vol. 1, 754–70. Edited by Volodymyr Kubijovyč. Toronto: University of Toronto Press, 1963.
———. "1917 rik v istoriï Ukraïny." *KAD rik 1937*, 52–62.
Fedorenko, Ievhen V. "Symon Petliura—velykyi derzhavnyi muzh." *Sv*, 25 May 1979.
Fedyshyn, Oleh S. *Germany's Drive to the East and the Ukrainian Revolution, 1917–1918*. New Brunswick: Rutgers University Press, 1971.
Felinski, M. *The Ukrainians in Poland*. London: the author, 1931.
Fiddick, Thomas C. *Russia's Retreat from Poland, 1920: From Permanent Revolution to Peaceful Coexistence*. London: Macmillan, 1990.
Filipowicz, Tytus. "Józef Piłsudski w Japonii w 1904 roku." *Świat* (Warsaw), 1934, no. 11.
Finot, Jean. "France, Poland and the Reds." *AR* 62 (1920): 543.
Fischer, Louis. *The Soviets in World Affairs: A History of the Relations between the Soviet Union and the Rest of the World, 1917–1929*. 2 vols. Princeton: Princeton University Press, 1951.
Footman, David. *The Russian Revolution*. New York: G. P. Putnam and Sons, 1964.

Frants, G. "Evakuatsiia germanskimi voiskami Ukrainy, zima 1918–1919 g." *IS*, 1922, no. 2, 262–9.
An account of German-Ukrainian negotiations concerning the German evacuation from Ukraine in the fall of 1918, including Hryhor'ïv's ultimatum to the German garrison in Mykolaiv.
Friedman, Philip. "The First Millenium of Jewish Settlement in the Ukraine and in the Adjacent Areas." *Annals of the Ukrainian Academy of Arts and Sciences in the U.S.* 7, no. 1–2 (1959), 1483–1516.
Friedman, Saul S. *Pogromchik: The Assassination of Simon Petlura*. New York: Hart, 1976.
Fuller, J. F. C. *Decisive Battles: Their Influence upon History and Civilization*. New York: Charles Scribner and Sons, 1940.
G. "Z lwowskiego frontu." *RW*, 13 November 1919.
Gai, G. *Na Varshavu: Deistviia 3-go konnogo korpusa na Zapadnom fronte*. Moscow: Gos. izd-vo, 1928.
Gałęzowska, Irena. "Józef Piłsudski wobec swej misji i jej wykonania." *N* (London) 8 (1972): 5–12.
———. "Myśl Józefa Piłsudskiego w świetle filozofii współczesnej." *N* (London) 7 (1962): 127–45.
"Galicia—the Latest Victim." *LA*, 21 February 1920, 513–14.
"Galicja." *RW*, 25 February 1918.
"Galicya tylko przy Polsce rozwijać się może." *GW*, 25 December 1921.
Garczyński, Leon S. *Problem polsko-ukraiński*. Toronto: Związkowiec, 1941.
Garlicki, Andrzej. *Geneza legionów: Zarys dziejów Komisji Tymczasowej, skonfederowanych stronnictw niepodległościowych*. Warsaw: Książka i Wiedza, 1964.
———. *U źródeł obozu belwederskiego*. Warsaw: Państwowe Wydawnictwo Naukowe, 1978.
Gąsiorowski, Wacław. *Historja Armji Polskiej we Francji*. 2 vols. Warsaw: Dom Książki Polskiej, 1931, 1939.
Gąsiorowski, Zygmunt J. "Joseph Piłsudski in the Light of British Reports." *SEER* 50 (1972): 558–69.
———. "Stresemann and Poland before Locarno." *JCEA* 18, no. 1 (1958), 23–47.
Gasser, Roger. "Weygand en Pologne." *Le Monde*, 24 June 1966.
"General-chetar Arnol'd Vol'f." *Sv*, 29 December 1924.
"General Petlura was Fatally Shot in Paris by Russian Student Seeking Revenge." *NYT*, 26 May 1926.
"General Wrangel, the Russian Anti-Bolshevist Leader." *AR* 62 (1920): 433.
"German Policy in Poland." *NE*, 18 October 1917, 1–12.
Gerson, Louis L. *Woodrow Wilson and the Rebirth of Poland, 1914–1920*. New Haven: Yale University Press, 1953.
Gervais, Céline, ed. *La Guerre polono-soviétique de 1919–20: Colloque organizé par le Laboratoire de slavistique, Paris, 4 mai 1973*. Paris: Institut d'études slaves, 1975.
Gets, M. "Ukraïns'ka Derzhava 1918 r. iak pidmet mizhnarodn'oho prava." In *Za velych natsiï: U dvadtsiati rokovyny vidnovlennia Ukraïns'koï Het'mans'koï Derzhavy*, 104–15. Edited by Mykola Pasika, Mykhailo Karpyshyn, and Teofil'

Kostruba. Lviv, 1938. Reprint, New York: Bulava, 1955.
Gibbons, Herbert A. "The Ukraine and the Balance of Power." *CM*, July–October 1921, 463–71.
Giertych, Jędrzej. "Dyskusja o Traktacie Ryskim." *ML*, 8 January 1933, 18–21.
———. *Józef Piłsudski, 1914–1919*. 2 vols. London: the author, 1979, 1982.
———. *O program polityki kresowej*. Warsaw: the author, 1932.
———. *O przeszłość ziem wschodnich Rzeczypospolitej: Bilans dwudziestolecia, skutki ostatniej wojny, stan obecny, propozycje i wnioski*. London: the author, 1946.
———. *Pół wieku polskiej polityki: Uwagi o polityce Dmowskiego i polityce polskiej lat 1919–1939 i 1939–1947*. London: the author, 1947.
Giza, Stanisław. "Obrona Lwowa w listopadzie 1918 roku w świetle literatury ukraińskiej." *N* (Warsaw) 13, no. 3 (1936), 312–22.
Glovins'kyi, Ie. "27 travnia 1926: Pid bezposerednim vrazhinniam." *StV*, 1926, no. 7–8, 32–3.
Głuziński, Tadeusz. *Sprawa ukraińska*. Warsaw, 1936.
Goldelman, Solomon I. *Jewish National Autonomy in Ukraine, 1917–1920*. Chicago: Ukrainian Research and Information Institute, 1968.
Golubev, A. V. "Desant Vrangelia na Kubani, Avgust–sentiabr 1920 g." *VR*, 1928, no. 8, 53–75.
Gonta, Dmytro. "Na pantsyrnyku 'Khortytsia'." *IKAChK na 1932 rik*, 71–86.
———. "Otamanshchyna." *Kyïv* (Philadelphia), 1957, no. 1, 16–19; no. 2, 107–15; no. 3, 159–62; no. 4, 197–200; no. 5, 262–7.
Górka, Olgierd. "Dziejowa rzeczywistość a racja stanu Polski na południowym wschodzie." *Polityka Narodowa* (Warsaw), 1933, no. 1–2, 6–33.
Gostyńska, Weronika. "Rola Juliana Marchlewskiego w tajnych rokowaniach polsko-radzieckich, czerwiec-lipiec 1919 r." *ZPW*, 1966, no. 2, 23–40.
———. *Stosunki polsko-radzieckie, 1918–1919*. Warsaw: Książka i Wiedza, 1972.
———. "Stosunki polsko-radzieckie a państwa bałtyckie, wrzesień-grudzień 1919 r." *ZDSPR* 14 (1976): 25–55.
———. "Tajne rokowania polsko-radzieckie w Mikłaszewiczach, sierpień-grudzień 1919 r." *ZPW*, 1967, no. 10, 53–78.
Gostyński, Władysław. "'Cud Wisły' w świetle zasad strategji." *RW*, 14 August 1921.
Gots'kyi. V. "Pliany Pilsuds'koho perebudovy Skhodu Evropy." *VK*, 1980, no. 2 (106), 47–59.
Grabski, Stanisław. "Jeszcze o rokowaniach ryskich." *MN*, 1933, no. 8, 82–6.
———. *Na nowej drodze dziejowej*. Warsaw: Państwowy Instytut Wydawniczy, 1946.
———. *The Polish-Soviet Frontier*. London: Keliher, Hudson and Kearns, 1943.
———. "Prawda o Traktacie Ryskim." *ABC* (Warsaw), 6 November 1932.
———. *Uwagi o bieżącej historycznej chwili Polski*. Warsaw: Księgarnia Perzyński, Niklewicz, 1922.
———. *Z codziennych walk i rozważań*. Poznań: Wielkopolska Księgarnia Nakładowa Karola Rzepeckiego, 1923.
———. *Z zagadnień polityki narodowo-państwowej*. Warsaw: Księgarnia i Skład Nut Perzyński, Niklewicz, 1925.

Grappin, Henri. *Polonais et Ruthènes: La question de Galicie.* Paris: Imprimerie de Vaugirard, 1919.
Grebing, Helga. "Österreich-Ungarn und die ukrainische Aktion 1914–18." *JGO* 7, no. 3 (1959), 270–96.
Grigorov, A. "Berezinskaia operatsiia." *VR,* 1920, no. 1.
Grinberg, Maria. "Z zagadnień Wojny Polsko-Radzieckiej." In *Ruch robotniczy i ludowy w Polsce (1914–1923),* 475–523. Edited by A. Kozłowski. Warsaw: Książka i Wiedza, 1960.
Grocholski, Kazimierz, and Michał Mińkowski, eds. *Dzieje Pułku Ułanów Podolskich, 1809–1947.* London: Koło 12 Pułku Ułanów Podolskich, 1982.
Grosfeld, Leon. "Piłsudski i Sawinkow." In *Studia historyczne: Księga Jubileuszowa z okazji 70 rocznicy urodzin prof. dra. Stanisława Arnolda,* 108–31. Warsaw: Książka i Wiedza, 1965.
———. *Polityka państw centralnych wobec sprawy polskiej w latach Pierwszej Wojny Światowej.* Warsaw: Państwowe Wydawnictwo Naukowe, 1962.
———. *Polskie reakcyjne formacje wojskowe w Rosji, 1917–1919.* Warsaw: Państwowe Wydawnictwo Naukowe, 1956.
———. "Wpływ Rewolucji Lutowej na Królewstwo w świetle świadectw austriackich." *KH,* 1956, no. 4, 381–94.
———, and Henryk Zieliński, eds. *Historia Polski,* vol. 4, pt. 1, *1918–1926.* Warsaw: Państwowe Wydawnictwo Naukowe, 1969.
1974. Grunberg, Karol. *Polskie koncepcje federalistyczne, 1864–1918.* Warsaw: Książka i Wiedza, 1971.
Grużewski, T. "Traktat Brzeski i jego następstwa." *NiP* 30 May 1918, 148–51.
Gukovskii, A. I. *Frantsuzskaia interventsiia na iuge Rossii, 1918–1919 g.* Moscow: Gos. izd-vo, 1928.
———. "Inostrannaia interventsiia na Ukraine v 1917–1919 godakh." *IM,* 1939, no. 1 (71), 76–100.
H., V. "Velykyi syn ukraïns'koho narodu." *UPS,* 1973, no. 5, 4–6.
Haivas, Ia. "Symon Petliura v mynulomu i v suchasnosti." *Sv,* 2–3 November 1979.
Halaichuk, Bohdan. "Chy Spolucheni Shtaty vyznaly Ukraïnu?" *O* (Buenos Aires), 1954, no. 5 (58), 1–2.
———. "Khto uvil'nyv 1918 r. Krym vid bol'shevykiv." *LChK,* 1938, no. 9, 11–13.
———. "Organizatsiia ukraïns'koï dyplomatychnoï sluzhby." *IKAChK na 1938 rik,* 35–8.
Halecki, Oskar. "Dwie Ukrainy." *Świat* (Warsaw), 29 May 1920.
———. "Kijów a Polska." *Tygodnik Ilustrowany* (Warsaw), 15 May 1920.
———. *Polish-Russian Relations—Past and Present.* Notre Dame: The University Press, 1943.
———. "The Problem of Federalism in the History of East Central Europe." *PoR,* 5, no. 3 (1960), 5–19.
Haller, Stanisław. "Nasz stosunek do Denikina." *KW,* 13 June 1937.
Halyniak, B. "Ukraïns'ka Narodnia Respublika: V rokovyny Tret'oho universalu." *O* (Buenos Aires), December 1949, 2–3.

———. "Ukraïns'ka 'zrada': Ukraïna mizh Antantoiu i Tsentral'nymy Derzhavamy." *O* (Buenos Aires), February 1951, 1–2.
Hamrets'kyi, Iu. M. "Pro chysel'nyi sklad bil'shovykiv na Ukraïni v 1917 r." *UIZh*, 1962, no. 5, 15–23.
Hankevych, Lev. "Zaprysiazhennia pershoho uriadu ZUNR u L'vovi: U 43-ti rokovyny Lystopadovoho zryvu." *VK*, 1961, no. 4, 9–16.
Hausner, Artur. "Józef Piłsudski o budowie Wojska Polskiego i Radzie Stanu." *N* (Warsaw) 19, no. 1 (1939), 83–96.
Helczyński, Bronisław. "Józef Piłsudski jako Naczelnik Państwa, listopad 1918–grudzień 1922." *N* (London) 9 (1974): 286–307.
Hempel, Stanisław. "O przyjazd do kraju gen. Hallera." *N* (London) 5 (1955): 202–5.
"Heneral-khorunzhyi Vsevolod Petriv: V 15-tu richnytsiu smerty." *BSBUVK*, no. 16–17 (1963), 29–30.
Herrnstadt, Rudolf. "Piłsudski in Japan." *LA*, February 1935, 499–501.
Het'man, Mykhailo. "Sichovi stril'tsi: Spivtvortsi 'Tsudu nad Vislov'." *UK*, 1976, no. 5 (39), 28.
Hladkyi, Hryts'. "Sichovi stril'tsi." *IKAChK na 1923 rik*, 40–50.
Hleb-Koszańska, Helena. "Józef Piłsudski na Syberji w świetle współczesnych jego listów (1887–1889)." *N* (Warsaw) 14 (1936): 198–208.
Hnatiuk, Nazar. "'Heroï' z-pid Krutiv." *LNV*, 1928, no. 9, 17–19.
Hołówko, Tadeusz. "Czy statut Wschodniej Galicji jest do przyjęcia?" *RW*, 20 December 1919.
———. "Dość już dmowszczyzny." *R*, 18 December 1919.
———. "Skutki pokoju w Rydze." *Przymierze* (Warsaw), no. 28 (November 1920).
———. "Stosunek Państwa Polskiego do jego sąsiadów." *Przedświt* (Warsaw), 1919, no. 1–2.
———. "Wieści z Ukrainy." *RW*, 6 February 1921.
Holzer, Jerzy. *Polska Partia Socjalistyczna w latach 1917–1919*. Warsaw: Państwowe Wydawnictwo Naukowe, 1962.
Homzyn, B. "Symon Petliura v perspektyvi istoriï." *A*, 16 January 1951.
Horak, Stephan M. *The First Treaty of World War I: Ukraine's Treaty with the Central Powers of February 9, 1918*. Boulder: East European Monographs, 1988.
———. *Poland and Her National Minorities, 1919–1939: A Case Study*. New York: Vantage Press, 1961.
Horbach, N. "Symon Petliura: V 35-tu richnytsiu smerty Holovnoho otamana." *UPS*, 1961, no. 5, 1961, 5–6.
Hordiienko, Havrylo. "'Pomylka' Symona Petliury." *VK*, 1981, no. 3, 22–4.
Horoszkiewicz, R. W. "Szlachta zaściankowa na Ziemiach Wschodnich." *Rocznik Ziem Wschodnich i Kalendarz na Rok 1937* (Warsaw), 171–6.
Horst, Leonhard. "At the Riga Peace Conference." *LA*, 20 November 1920, 458–60.
Hostowiec, P. "Wyprawa kijowska." *K*, 1955, no. 12, 3–10.
Hrushevs'kyi, Mykhailo S. *The Historical Evolution of the Ukrainian Problem*. 2d ed. Cleveland: John T. Zubal, 1981.
———. "V ohni i buri." *Literaturnyi i hromads'ko-politychnyi kaliendar-al'manakh*

Dnipro na rik 1937, 78–80.
———. *Vil'na Ukraïna*. New York: Ukraïns'ka drukars'ka i vydavnycha spilka, 1918.
Hryhoriïv, Nykyfor. "Do spravy pro rozstril polk. Bolbachana." *TU*, 1932, no. 9, 12–13; no. 10, 15–16.
———. "Kruty." *Ukraïns'ke hromads'ke slovo* (New York), 1954, no. 2.
———. "Pidstavy ukraïns'koï natsional'no-derzhavnoï polityky." *NU*, 1923, no. 4, 70–8; no. 5, 47–56.
———. *Pidstavy ukraïns'koï nezalezhnoï polityky*. Detroit: Kosmos, 1939.
———. *Poliaky na Ukraïni: Pol's'ko-ukraïns'ki vidnosyny v istorychnii perspektyvi*. Scranton: Ukrainian Workingmen's Association, 1936.
———. *Ukraïns'ka borot'ba za derzhavu v rokakh 1917–1920: Chomu ukraïntsi ne vderzhaly svoieï derzhavy*. Scranton: Ukrainian Workingmen's Association, 1934.
Hryhorovych, M. "Ukraïns'kyi viis'kovyi rukh na Prydniprianshchyni 1917 r." *IKAChK na 1937 rik*, 17–20.
Hrynevych, Iaroslav. *V im'ia pravdy: Analiza bezparalel'noï trahediï Ukraïns'koï Halyts'koï Armiï*. New York: Moloda hromada, 1972.
Hryshko, Vasyl'. "Real'no-istorychnyi i suchasno-aktual'nyi Petliura." *NDni*, 1980, no. 4, 27–30.
Hryshyn, Artamon. "Lystopad ... na dumku prykhodyt' Shcherbak." *BSBUVK*, 1964, no. 3, 7–9.
Hrytsak, Evhen. "Z istoriï knyzhkovoho rukhu na Velykii Ukraïni, 1917–1922." *LNV*, 1923, no. 9, 55–64.
Hrytsai, Ostap. "Shliakhamy slavy: U chetverti rokovyny zdobuttia Kyïva 31. serpnia 1919–31. serpnia 1923." *US*, no. 39–40 (1923), 1–7.
———. "Ukraïns'ka Halyts'ka Armiia v 'Chotyrokutnyku smerty' na Skhidnii Ukraïni." *US*, no. 45–6 (1923), 1–7.
Huddleston, Sisley. "Piłsudski and the New Poland." *The Fortnightly Review* (London) 107 (1920): 261–70.
Humphrey, Grace. *Piłsudski: Builder of Poland*. New York: Scott and More, 1936.
Hunczak, Taras. "A Reappraisal of Symon Petliura and Ukrainian-Jewish Relations, 1917–1921." *Jewish Social Studies*, 1969, no. 3, 163–83.
———, ed. *The Ukraine, 1917–1921: A Study in Revolution*. Cambridge: Harvard Ukrainian Research Institute, 1977.
Hupert, Witold. *Walki o Lwów: Od 1 listopada 1918 do maja 1919 roku*. Warsaw: Księgarnia Wojskowa, 1933.
———. *Zajęcie Małopolski Wschodniej i Wołynia w roku 1919*. Lviv: B. Połoniecki, 1928.
"Iak Piłsuds'kyi zaiouvav ukraïns'ki zemli." *NH*, 1923, no. 2, 86–8.
Iakovlev, Iakov A. "Nasha politika na Ukraine i ukrainskii seredniak." *Ezhenedel'nik pravdy* (Moscow), 1919, no. 12, 13–19.
Iakovliv, Andrii. "Do pytannia pro legal'nist' uriadu UNR." *Tr* (Paris), 1928, no. 43, 5–15.
———. "Istorychni tradytsiï ukraïns'koï derzhavnosty." *Tr* (Paris), 1937, no. 5, 3–13.
———. *Osnovy konstytutsiï U.N.R.* Paris: Mech, 1935.

———. *Paryz'ka trahediia 25 travnia 1926 roku: Do protsesu Shvartsbarda*. Prague: Mizhorhanizatsiinyi komitet dlia vshanuvannia pam'iati Symona Petliury v Prazi, 1930.
Iaroslavyn, Sydir. *Vyzvol'na borot'ba na zakhidn'o-ukraïns'kykh zemliakh u 1918–1923 rokakh*. Philadelphia: Hurtok prykhyl'nykiv, 1956.
Iavorivs'kyi, Evhen. "Chortkivs'ka ofenzyva i vidvorot za Zbruch v osvitlenni Nachal'noï komandy." *LChK*, 1935, no. 12, 4–8.
Iavors'kyi, Oleksa. *V richnytsiu smerty sv. pam. Symona Petliury*. Winnipeg: "Ukraïns'kyi holos," 1972.
Ieroshevych, Petro. "Z borot'by ukraïns'koho narodu za svoiu nezalezhnist'." *ZD* 8 (1938) 9–65; 9 (1938): 18–59.
Ihnatov, N. "Chervonoarmiis'kyi zahin u borot'bi za khlib." *LR*, 1933, no. 1–2, 175–87.
Iłłakowiczówna, Kazimiera. *Ścieżka obok drogi*. Warsaw: Rój, 1939.
Ilovaiskii, Vladimir. *God puti: Zhizn' Dobrovol'cheskoi armii*. Rostov-na-Donu: Obnovlenie, 1919.
Iosypyshyn, Iaroslava. "Symon Petliura, 1879–1979." *Ukraïns'ka biblioteka im. S. Petliury: Informatisiinyi biuleten'* (Paris), no. 42 (1980), 10–11.
"Isaak Mazapa—publitsyst." *NSl*, no. 3 (1973): 128–81.
"Istnienie Rzeczypospolitej bez Wsch. Małopolski nie do pomyślenia." *GW*, 25 December 1921.
"Istorychnyi akt 22. sichnia 1919 r." *NIKTP na rik 1939*, 87–103.
Ivankiv, O. "V 10-tu richnytsiu smerty S. Petliury." *H*, no. 17–18 (1936), 24–6.
Ivanov, A. V. "Tsentral'naia Rada i Kievskii sovet v 1917–1918 g.g." *LR*, 1922, no. 1, 2–15.
Ivanov, L. "Revoliutsiia 1905 goda na Ukraine." *VI*, 1945, no. 5–6, 23–43.
Ivanys, Vasyl'. "Petliura na Kubani." *Sv*, 23 May 1951.
———. "Symon Petliura iak hromadianyn, polityk i derzhavnyi muzh: U 38-mi rokovyny smerty." *NL*, no. 12 (1964), 51–63.
———. *Symon Petliura—prezydent Ukraïny, 1879–1926*. Toronto: Ukrainian War Veterans' League of Canada, 1952.
A valuable biography of Petliura.
Iwanowski, Jerzy. "Gdyby Denikin zwyciężył ... czerwony totalizm zostałby zastąpiony białym." *Dziennik Żołnierza* (London), 19 August 1947.
Iwański, Gereon. "Z dziejów Komunistycznej Partii Galicji Wschodniej." *ZPW*, 1967, no. 4, 25–52.
"Iz istorii frantsuzkoi interventsii v Odesse." *KA* 45 (1931): 53–80.
Iżykowski, Zygmunt. "Polityka imperializmu niemieckiego wobec ziem ukraińskich w 1918 r." *Uniwersytet im. Adama Mickiewicza w Poznaniu: Historia*, 1968, no. 8, 189–205.
Jabłoński, Henryk. "Międzynarodowe warunki odbudowy niepodległości Polski w 1918 r." In *Ruch robotniczy i ludowy w Polsce (1914–1923)*, 1–62. Edited by A. Kozłowski. Warsaw: Książka i Wiedza, 1960.
———. "Ministerium Spraw Polskich Ukraińskiej Republiki Ludowej, 1917–1918." *N* (Warsaw) 20, no. 1 (1939): 65–88.

———. "Piłsudski a konserwatyści krakowscy (kilka faktów z lat 1926–1927)." In *Studia historyczne: Księga Jubileuszowa z okazji 70 rocznicy urodzin prof. dra. Stanisława Arnolda*, 150–65. Warsaw: Książka i Wiedza, 1965.
———. *Polska autonomia narodowa na Ukrainie, 1917–1918*. Warsaw: Towarzystwo Miłośników Historii, 1948. Reprinted in his *Z rozważań o II Rzeczypospolitej*, 244–359. Wrocław, Warsaw, Cracow, Gdańsk, and Łódź: Polska Akademia Nauk, 1987.
———. "Powstanie Drugiej Rzeczypospolitej Polskiej w 1918 r. na tle dziejów Europy." *KH*, 1958, no. 4, 1035–54.
———. "Rewolucja Październikowa a odbudowa państwa polskiego w 1918 r." *ZPW*, 1958, no. 1, 8–39.
———. "Z dziejów genezy sojuszu Piłsudski-Petlura: Początki konfliktu zbrojnego XI. 1918–III. 1919 r." *WAP*, 1961, no. 5, 40–58. Reprinted in his *Z rozważań o II Rzeczypospolitej*, 360–81. Wrocław, Warsaw, Cracow, Gdańsk, and Łódź: Polska Akademia Nauk, 1987.
———. "Ze studiów nad początkami Narodowej Demokracji." *PH*, 1953, no. 4, 481–536.
Jabłoński, Tadeusz. *Zarys historii P. P. S.* 2d. ed. Warsaw: Spółdzielnia Wydawnicza "Wiedza," 1947.
"Jak tworzył się 'rząd' ukraiński we Lwowie w r. 1918?" *KL*, 4 November 1931.
"Jak zamordowano Petlurę?" *IKC*, 30 May 1926.
Jaworznicki, Bolesław. "Wyprawa kijowska Piłsudskiego." *SM*, 1955, no. 5, 43–55.
Jędruszczak, Tadeusz. "Stanowisko Polski i mocarstw Ententy w sprawie polskiej granicy wschodniej, 1918–1921." *SM*, 1959, no. 6, 58–77.
Jędrzejewicz, Janusz. *Józef Piłsudski*. Warsaw: Ogniwo, 1920.
———. "Piłsudski—prekursor przyszłości." *N* (London) 2 (1950): 3–17.
Jędrzejewicz, Wacław. "Front litewsko-białoruski podczas wojny 1920 r." *N* (London) 8 (1972): 26–87.
———. *Kronika życia Józefa Piłsudskiego, 1867–1935*. 2 vols. London: Polska Fundacja Kulturalna, 1977–8.
———. *Piłsudski: A Life for Poland*. New York: Hippocrene Books, 1982.
———. "Rokowania borysowskie w 1920 roku." *N* (London) 3 (1951): 47–59.
———. "Sprawa 'Wieczoru': Józef Piłsudski a Wojna Japońsko-Rosyjska 1904–1905." *ZH* 27 (1974): 3–103.
———. "Sprawa Wilna w lipcu 1920 roku." *ZH* 17 (1970): 127–63.
Jeleński, K. A. "Wywiad z gen. Weygand." *K*, 1953, no. 6, 83–8.
Johnston, G. R. "The Battle of Warsaw, August 1920." *Army Quarterly* (London), 1923, no. 2, 235–46.
Jones, H. A. *Over the Balkans and South Russia, 1917–1919*. Greenhill: Aeolus, 1987.
Józef Piłsudski, 1867–1935. Cracow: Spółka Wydawnicza Kurjera, 1935.
Józef Piłsudski i jego legjony w muzyce i pieśni. Edited by Mateusz Gliński et al. Warsaw: "Muzyka," 1935.
Juryłko, Stefan. "Niemcy na Ukrainie." *PEW* 1939, no. 4, 225–30.
Juzwenko, Adolf. "Polityka mocarstw zachodnich wobec Rosji w roku 1919 przed załamaniem się ofensywy Kolczaka." *SDZSRR* 9 (1973): 123–41.

———. "Stosunek 'Białej' Rosji do odrodzającego się państwa polskiego i jego granic." *KH*, 1973, no. 3, 621–39.
K. "Armeis'ka hrupa gen. Kravsa v nastupi na Kyïv." *US*, no. 8 (1921), 308.
K., K. "Ulychni boï v Kyievi." *US*, no. 8 (1921), 9–14; no. 10 (1921), 5–6.
K., L. "Ekspozytura Ministerstwa Spraw Wojskowych do spraw ukraińskich w roku 1920." *N* (London) 7 (1962): 236–45.
K., M. "Ukraïns'ka natsional'na terytoriia i kil'kist' ukraïntsiv v Pol'shchi." *NIKTP na rik 1926*, 57–60.
———. "Zhydy v Ukraïns'kii Narodnii Respublitsi." *My i svit* (Toronto), no. 49 (1958), 6–10.
Kakurin, Nikolai E. *Kak srazhalas' revoliutsiia*. 2 vols. Edited by N. N. Popov. Moscow: Gos. izd-vo, 1925–6.
A survey of the Red Army campaigns from 1918 to 1920.
———. *Russko-pol'skaia kampaniia 1918–1920: Politiko-strategicheskii ocherk*. Moscow: Vysshii voennyi redaktsionnyi sovet, 1922.
A brief survey of the Polish-Soviet War, with emphasis on the Polish-Ukrainian spring offensive in 1920 and Budennyi's counteroffensive.
———. *Strategicheskii ocherk grazhdanskoi voiny*. Moscow: Gosudarstvennoe voennoe izdatel'stvo, 1926.
———. *Voina s belopoliakami 1920 g.* Moscow: Gosudarstvennoe voennoe izdatel'stvo, 1925.
———. *Volkovyskoe srazhenie v rangakh Nemanskoi operatsii*. Moscow: Gos. izd-vo, 1927.
———. *Vstrechnoe srazhenie 1-oi Konnoi i 2-oi Pol'skoi armii na podstupakh k L'vovu*. Moscow: Voenizdat, 1925.
———, and K. Berends. *Kievskaia operatsiia poliakov 1920 goda*. Moscow: Gos. izd-vo, 1928.
Kaleniczenko, Pawło M. "Działalność internacjonalistów polskich na Ukrainie w 1919 r." *ZDSPR* 3 (1968): 118–36.
Kamenets'kyi, Ihor. *Nimets'ka polityka suproty Ukraïny v 1918 rotsi ta ïï istorychna geneza*. Munich: "Ukraïns'kyi istoryk," 1969.
Kamenev, S. S. "Bor'ba s beloi Polshei." *VV*, 1922, no. 12, 7–15.
A critical study of the Polish-Soviet War.
Kamieńskaja, Nina W. "Białoruś w okresie Wojny Polsko-Radzieckiej." *ZDSPR* 3 (1968): 79–96.
Kampanja roku 1920 w świetle prawdy. Lviv: Księgarnia Polska, 1924.
Kantorovich, Vl. "Frantsuzy v Odesse." *Byloe* (Petrograd), no. 19 (1922), 198–210.
Kapustians'kyi, Mykola. "Holovnyi otaman Symon Petliura: Promova." *Ukraïns'ke slovo* (Paris), 27 May 1956.
———. "Otamany–heneral-khorunzhi Vasyl' i Iurko Tiutiunnyky." *RD* (Toronto), 1958, no. 1 (22), 1–6.
A valuable description of Gens. Vasyl' and Iurii Tiutiunnyk, set against the background of the UNR defensive campaign against the Bolsheviks and Polish policy vis-à-vis the campaign.

———. *Pokhid ukraïns'kykh armii na Kyïv-Odesu v 1919 rotsi: Korotkyi voienno-istorychnyi ohliad*. 2d ed. 2 vols. Munich: Vydavnytstvo Khvyl'ovoho. 1946.
———. "Symon Petliura." *RN*, 1930, no. 5–6, 103–6.
———. *Ukraïns'ka zbroina syla i ukraïns'ka natsional'na revoliutsiia*. Saskatoon: "Novyi shliakh," 1936.
Karpeniuk, Mariian. "Velykden' pid L'vovom 1919 r.: Narys z krivavykh boïv." *NIKTP na rik 1925*, 56–63.
Karpenko, H. "Selians'kyi rukh na Kyïvshchyni za chasiv avstro-hermans'koï okupatsiï ta het'manshchyny." *LR*, 1931, no. 1–2, 67–91.
Kashuba, I. "Symon Petliura—velykyi ukraïns'kyi patriot i revoliutsioner." *HU*, 9 July 1986.
Kasprzycki, Tadeusz. *Józef Piłsudski and His Ideas on International Peace*. New York: Piłsudski Centennial Memorial Committee, 1968.
Katelbach, Tadeusz. "Piłsudski i Sosnkowski." *ZH* 34 (1975): 35–42.
———. "Rola Piłsudskiego w sprawie polsko-litewskiej." *N* (London) 1 (1948): 101–16.
Kawalec, Tadeusz. *Historja IV-ej Dywizji Strzelców Generała Żeligowskiego w zarysie*. Vilnius: Harcerska Spółka Wydawnicza, 1921.
Kawalkowski, Aleksander. *Z dziejów odbudowy państwa: Szkice*. Warsaw: Instytut Naukowo-Wydawniczy, 1933.
Kazanivs'kyi, P. "Sv. pam'iati heroiam—kozakam zhynuvshym pid Bazarom: Iz dopovidi." *UK*, 1974, no. 4, 30–3.
Kedryn, Ivan. "Chetvertyi universal i Beresteis'kyi myr." *AUNS na iuvileinyi rik 1968*, 85–97.
———. "Brześć-Ryga-Paryż." *BPU*, 1926, no. 12 (151), 112–15.
———. "Chomu S. V. Petliura?" *Sv*, 3 April 1951.
———. "Istota Traktatu Ryskiego." *BPU*, 1933, no. 3, 10–14.
———. "Pol's'kyi general pro l'vivs'ki liegendy." *LChK*, 1933, no. 1, 20–1.
———. "Rik 1918 v istoriï ukraïns'koï politychnoï dumky." *Kalendar "Svobody" na rik 1958*, 79–86.
———. "Shliakh dumky i chynu: Z nahody 50-kh rokovyn stvorennia legionu USS." *VK*, 1964, no. 3 (15), 4–8.
———. "Symon Petliura." *IKAChK na 1927 rik*, 143–51.
Kędzierski, Jerzy. "Józef Piłsudski a pokolenie współczesne." *N* (London) 1 (1948): 18–40.
Kellogg, Vernon. "Paderewski, Piłsudski, and Poland." *The World's Work* (New York), no. 38 (1919): 109–12.
Kenez, Peter. "A. I. Denikin." *RR*, 1973, no. 2, 139–52.
Kennan, George. "The Situation in Southeastern Russia." *The Outlook* (New York), September–December 1920, 136–7.
Kerensky, Alexander. "Bolshevism Condemned." *LA*, 26 November 1921, 541–3.
———. *Russia and History's Turning Point*. New York: Duell, Sloan, and Pearce, 1965.
Khronoviat, Mykhailo. "Orhanizatsiia Ukraïns'kykh sichovykh stri'tsiv u Peremyshli." *VK*, 1972, no. 1 (57), 33–40.

Khrystiuk, Pavlo. "Provyna pered ukraïns'koiu revoliutsieiu." *Boritesia—Poborete!* (Vienna), 1920, no. 5, 36–66.

"Kiedy głos zabiera p. Dienikin." *BPU*. 1937, no. 15, 161–2.

Kihichak, Andrii. "Zustrich USS-iv pid provodom Vasylia Vyshyvanoho z zaporozhtsiamy pid provodom Bolbachana." *VK*, 1972, no. 5–6 (61–2), 33–5.

Kirkien, Leszek. *Russia, Poland and the Curzon Line*. Duns: Caldra House, 1945.

Kish, Guido. "Woodrow Wilson and the Independence of Small Nations in Central Europe." *The Journal of Modern History* (Chicago) 19 (1947): 235–8.

Klings, Sigismund St. *Piłsudski*. Paris: Editions Kra, 1929.

Kliuev, Leonid L. *Boiova put' Pershoï kinnoï armiï*. Kharkiv: "Na varti." 1931.

———. *Bor'ba za Tsaritsyn, 1918–1919 gg*. Moscow: Gos. izd-vo, 1928.

———. *Pervaia Konnaia Krasnaia armiia na pol'skom fronte v 1920 godu*. Moscow: Gosudarstvennoe voennoe izdatel'stvo, 1932.

Klymchuk, Vasyl'. "Pokhid na Kyïv: Na pidstavi spohadiv uchasnykiv ta ochevydtsiv." *Ukraïns'kyi invalid: Zahal'nyi kaliendar dlia ukraïns'koho narodu na rik 1939*, 89–92.

Kn., H. "Jeszcze w sprawie ukraińskiej." *RW*, 20 July 1919.

Knysh, Zynovii. *Varshavs'kyi dohovir v svitli natsionalistychnoï krytyky*. Winnipeg: the author, 1950.

———. "Viis'kova diial'nist' Mykoly Mikhnovs'koho." In his *Take pero pyshe: Vybrani statti*, 127–43. Toronto: Sribna surma, 1965.

———. "Vynnychenko chy Petliura?." *RD*, 1953, no. 2 (10), 1–7; no. 3 (11), 4–10.

Koć, Adam. "Powrót Józefa Piłsudskiego z Magdeburga." *N* (Warsaw) 15 (1937): 234–5.

———. "Przyjazd Józefa Piłsudskiego do Warszawy 10 listopada 1918 roku." *N* (London) 7 (1962): 224–36.

Koch, Hans. *Dohovir z Denikinom vid 1 do 17 lystopada 1919 r.* Lviv: Chervona kalyna, 1930.

A justification of the UHA agreement with Denikin in November of 1919.

Komarnicki, Tytus. *Piłsudski a polityka wielkich mocarstw zachodnich*. London: Instytut Józefa Piłsudskiego, 1952.

———. *Rebirth of the Polish Republic: A Study in the Diplomatic History of Europe, 1914–1920*. Melbourne: Heinemann, 1957.

———. "Odbudowa państwowości polskiej na Ziemiach Wschodnich." *Rocznik Prawniczy Wileński* (Vilnius) 3 (1929): 2–46.

Konovalov, S., ed. *Russo-Polish Relations: An Historical Survey*. Princeton: Princeton University Press, 1945.

Kopylins'kyi, M. "Sotsiial-demokraty i viis'kova sprava 1917 roku." *UK*, 1982, no. 1, 38–49.

Korbel, Josef. *Poland between East and West: Soviet and German Diplomacy toward Poland, 1919–1933*. Princeton: Princeton University Press, 1963.

Korbut, Sydir. *Symon Petliura*. Lviv: Ukraïns'ke vydavnytstvo, 1941.

Korduba, F. "Heneral-polkovnyk Mykola Kapustians'kyi." *VK*, 1969, no. 3–4 (40–1), 16–20.

Korduba, M. "Etnografichna terytoriia Ukraïny." *VSVU*, no. 181 (1917), 802–8; no. 182, 819–24; no. 183, 836–9.

Kormanowa, Żanna, and Walentyna Najdus, eds. *Historia Polski,* vol. 3, pt. 3, *1914–1918.* Warsaw: Państwowe Wydawnictwo Naukowe, 1974.

Koroliv-Staryi, Vasyl'. *Simon Petlura, héros national ukrainien.* Prague: Čas, 1919.

——. "Tsentral'na Rada ta ïï rolia v vidnovlenni ukraïns'koï derzhavnosty." *Tr* (Paris), 1927, no. 16 (74), 7–23.

Korotkov, I. S. *Razgrom Vrangelia.* Moscow: Voennoe izdatel'stvo, 1951.

A study, based largely on archival material, of the Bolshevik campaigns against Wrangel during the second half of 1920.

Korybut-Woroniecki, H. J. "Stowarzyszenie 'La Pologne et la guerre' w Szwajcarii." *N* (Warsaw) 15 (1937): 198–226, 389–99.

Kosogov, I. "Konnaia armiia na vrangelevskom fronte." *VR*, 1935, no. 11, 13–20.

Kostruba, Teofil'. "Istorychne znachennia Ukraïns'koï Derzhavy 1918 r." In *Za velych natsiï: U dvadtsiati rokovyny vidnovlennia Ukraïns'koï Het'mans'koï Derzhavy,* 91–6. Edited by Mykola Pasika, Mykhailo Karpyshyn, and Teofil' Kostruba. Lviv, 1938. Reprint, New York: Bulava, 1955.

Kostyshyn, S. "Chykalenko pro Vynnychenka." *URob*, 19 January 1951.

Kosyk, Volodymyr. *La politique de la France à l'égard de l'Ukraine, mars 1917–février 1918.* Paris: Université de Paris-I, Institut d'histoire des relations internationales contemporaines, 1981.

——, ed. *Symon Petliura: Zbirnyk studiino-naukovoï konferentsiï v Paryzhi, traven' 1976: Statti, zamitky, materiialy.* Munich: Ukraïns'kyi vil'nyi universytet, 1980.

Kotowicz, Fr. "O stosunkach do Ukrainy." *GW*, 15 March 1920.

Koval', Bohdan. "Provid v profili." In *Ideï i liudy vyzvol'nykh zmahan' 1917–1923,* 167–96. Edited by Bohdan Koval'. New York: Bulava, 1968.

——. "U denikins'kii tiurmi." *Sv*, 25 November 1924.

Koval's'kyi, M. "Symon Petliura." *M*, 1966, no. 1 (36).

Kowalski, Włodzimierz T. "At Brest and at Versailles." *Polish Perspectives* 21, no. 11 (1978), 16–28.

——. *Rok 1918.* Warsaw: Krajowa Agencja Wydawnicza, 1978.

——, and Andrzej Skrzypa. *Stosunki polsko-radzieckie, 1917–1945.* Warsaw: Krajowa Agencja Wydawnicza, 1980.

Kozak, Ivan. "Ukraïns'ka Halyts'ka Armiia." *VK*, 1969, no. 1, 3–8.

Kozicki, Stanisław. *Bój pod Lidą.* Warsaw: Wojskowe Biuro Historyczne, 1930.

——. *Sprawa granic Polski na konferencji pokojowej w Paryżu.* Warsaw: Księgarnia Perzyński, Niklewicz, 1921.

A concise description of the question of Poland's boundary at the Paris Peace Conference, by a supporter of Dmowski and opponent of Piłsudski.

Kozłowski, Leon. *Rewolucja rosyjska i niepodległość Polski: Geneza aktu 30 marca.* Warsaw: "Zjednoczenie," 1922.

Kozłowski, Maciej. *Między Sanem a Zbruczem: Walki o Lwów i Galicję Wschodnią, 1918–1919.* Cracow: ZNAK, 1990

Krasnov, P. N. "Na vnutrennom fronte." *ARR* 1 (1921): 97–190.

Krat, Mykhailo. "Bazar: U 50-ti rokovyny rozstrilu 359." *Sv*, 20 November 1971.

———. "Pol's'ki ofitsery pro diï Armiï UNR v 1920 r." *VK*, 1962, no. 1 (5), 13–16.

Kretschmer, Hauptmann. "Durchbruch der russischen Reiter-Armee durch die polnische Front im Frühjar 1920." *WW*, 1931, no. 3, 147–64.

Kronik, Aleksander L. "Zachodnia Dywizja Strzelców, 1918–1919." *ZDSPR* 3 (1968): 51–64.

Krushyns'kyi, Fedir. "Petliura i Piłsuds'kyi." *MU*, 1936, no. 4–5, 5–8.

Krypiakevych, Ivan, et al. *Istoriia ukraïns'koho viis'ka*. Winnipeg: Kliub pryiateliv ukraïns'koï knyzhky, 1953.

Krysiński, A. "Liczba i rozmieszczenie Ukrainców w Polsce." *SN*, 1928, no. 6, 651–70.

Kryvolap, Iurii. "Symon Petliura." *UPS*, 1972, no. 5, 8–9.

Krzewski, Stanisław. *Zasady federacji w polskiej polityce kresowej*. Cracow, 1920.

Krzyżanowski, Adam. *Rządy marszałka Piłsudskiego*. Cracow: the author, 1928.

———. "Z historji stosunków polsko-rosyjskich nazajutrz po Wojnie Światowej." *PW*, 1936, no. 58, 72–5.

Kubiak, Stanisław. *Niemcy a Wielkopolska, 1918–1919*. Poznań: Instytut Zachodni, 1969.

Kubijovyč, Volodymyr. *Western Ukraine within Poland, 1920–1939: Ethnic Relationships*. Chicago: Ukrainian Research Information Institute, 1963.

Kuchabs'kyi, Vasyl'. "Zovnishn'o-politychne polozhennia ob'iednanykh ukraïns'kykh armii u 'Chotyrokutnyku smerty' v lypni–serpni 1919." *LChK*, 1931, no. 10, 13–17; no. 11, 7–10.

Kucher, Mykhailo. "Manifest otamana Hryhor'ïva." *Tr* (New York), no. 27 (1964), 10–14.

———. "Symon Petliura." *Tr* (New York), no. 80 (1976), 2–7.

Kukiel, Marian. *Bitwa pod Wołoczyskami, 11–24 lipca, 1920*. Warsaw: Wojskowy Instytut Naukowo-Wydawniczy, 1923.

———. "Dramat generała Weygand." *B* (London), April–June 1949, 3–11.

———. "Miejsce kampanji 1920 r. w historji wojen." *B* (Warsaw) 16, no. 2 (November 1924), 125–36.

———. "Na ukraińskich szlakach." *OB*, May 1977, 8–9.

———. *The Polish-Soviet Campaign of 1920*. Edinburgh: Oliver and Boyd, n.d. [1940s].

———. "Z doświadczeń kampanji r. 1920 na Ukrainie i w Małopolsce." *B* (Warsaw) 3, no. 10 (1920), 721–8; no. 11, 814–19.

Kukułka, Józef. "Niektóre aspekty międzynarodowe polityki Piłsudskiego wobec ziem litewsko-białoruskich w pierwszej połowie 1919 roku." *SNDP* 2 (1962): 35–61.

———. "Sprawa Galicji Wschodniej w stosunkach polsko-francuskich przed podpisaniem Traktatu Wersalskiego." *SNDP* 5 (1963): 163–85.

Kulichenko, M. I. *Bor'ba Kommunisticheskoi partii za reshenie natsional'nogo voprosa v 1918–1920 godakh*. Kharkiv: Izdatel'sto Kharkovskogo gosudarstvennogo universiteta, 1963.
A biased analysis of the role of the Bolsheviks and their subversive activities in Ukraine and Belarus in the years 1918–20.

Kulyk, I. "Ekonomichni chynnyky frantsuz'koï interventsiï." *ChSh*, 1923, no. 3, 122–8.
Kumaniecki, Jerzy. "Uznanie wschodniej granicy Polski przez Radę Ambasadorów." *KH* 76 (1969): 73–92.
Kupchanko, K. "Armiina grupa gen. Kravsa v nastupi na Kyïv v serpni 1919 roku." *IKAChK na 1923 rik*, 108–17.
Kurcjusz, T. "Pierwsze spotkanie 13-ej Dywizji Piechoty z Budiennym." *B* (Warsaw), 1921, no. 1, 475–87; no. 2, 577–89; no. 3, 696–704; no. 4, 781–92.
    An account, based on official reports and personal observations, by a Polish officer of the campaign of the Polish Thirteenth Infantry Division against Budennyi's Cavalry Army in the Koziatyn region from May to June 1920, and of the Polish troops' relations with the Ukrainian partisans and civilian population.
Kurinnyi, Petro. "Bol'shevyts'ka agresiia proty Ukraïny, 1917–1921." *Ukraïns'kyi zbirnyk* (Munich) 1 (December 1954): 11–22.
Kurmanovych, Viktor. "Do spravy vidvorotu U.H.A. za Zbruch." *RN*, 1934, no. 3–4, 82–6.
Kuryłło, Stefan. "Niemcy na Ukrainie." *PEW* 1, no. 4 (1939), 224–34.
Kushnir, Mykhailo. "Bii pid Krutamy." *UK*, 1982, no. 1, 21–7.
Kusielewicz, Eugene. "New Light on the Curzon Line." *PoR*, 1956, no. 2–3, 82–8.
———. "Paderewski and Wilson's Speech to the Senate, January 22, 1917." *Polish American Studies* 13, no. 3–4 (1956), 65–71.
———. "Wilson and the Polish Cause at Paris." *PoR*, 1956, no. 1, 64–79.
Kutiakov, I. "'Kievskie Kanny' 1920 g." *VR*, 1932, no. 10, 42–61; no. 11–12, 94–112; 1933, no. 3–4, 59–70.
Kutrzeba, Stanisław. *Kongres, traktat i Polska*. Warsaw: Gebethner i Wolff, 1919.
———. *Królewstwo i Galicya: Uwagi z czasu wojny*. Warsaw: Towarzystwo Wydawnicze, 1917.
Kutrzeba, Tadeusz. *Bitwa nad Niemnem, wrzesień–październik 1920*. Warsaw: Wojskowy Instytut Naukowo-Wydawniczy, 1926.
———. "Odpowiedź Generałowi Denikinowi." *Gazeta Polska* (Warsaw), December 1938.
———. *Wyprawa Kijowska 1920 roku*. Warsaw: Gebethner i Wolff, 1937.
    An account by a Polish general and historian of the 1920 Polish-Ukrainian alliance and joint campaign against the Bolsheviks.
Kutschabsky, W. *Die Westukraine im Kampfe mit Polen und dem Bolschevismus in den Jahren 1918–1923*. Berlin: Junker und Dünnhaupt, 1934.
Kuzelia, Zenon. *Rik 1918 na Ukraïni*. Salzwedel: Soiuz vyzvolennia Ukraïny, 1918.
Kuz'min, N. F. *Krushenie poslednego pokhoda Antanty*. Moscow: Gos. izd-vo politicheskoi literatury, 1958.
———. *Krushenie tretego pokhoda Antanty*. Moscow: Gos. izd-vo politicheskoi literatury, 1961.
"Kwestja Armji Polskiej po stronie rosyjskiej." *Demokrata Polski* (Warsaw), 30 April 1917, 3–7.
L., Iurii. "Slidamy Symona Petliury: Pro mistsia v Paryzhu, de proviv vin ostanni dni svoho zhyttia." *Ukraïns'kyi samostiinyk* (Munich), 24 May 1953.
Landau, Rom. *Piłsudski, Hero of Poland*. London: Jarrolds, 1930.

Lashchenko, Rostyslav. "Iak obyraly Dyrektoriiu U.N.R." *KAD na rik 1923*, 7–14.
Lasocki, Zygmunt. "Wyzwolenie Małopolski: Polska Komisja Likwidacyjna i Komisja Rządząca." In *Dziesięciolecie Polski odrodzonej: Księga pamiątkowa, 1918–1928*, 115–21. Edited by Marjan Dąbrowski: Cracow: "Ilustrowany Kuryer Codzienny," 1928.
Latawski, Paul, ed. *The Reconstruction of Poland, 1914–23*. London: Macmillan, 1992.
Lawton, Lancelot. *The Russian Revolution (1917–1926)*. London: Macmillan, 1927.
―――. *The Ukrainian Question and Its Importance to Great Britain*. London: Anglo-Ukrainian Committee, 1935.
Lazarevs'kyi, Borys. "Oblychchia Symona Petliury." *Tr* (Paris) 1938, no. 22, 27–30.
Lazarevs'kyi, Hlib. "Het'manshchyna." *ZD* 2 (1930): 197–216; 3 (1931): 234–68.
Łączyk, Marian. *Komitet Narodowy Polski a Entanta i Stany Zjednoczone, 1917–1919*. Warsaw: Państwowe Wydawnictwo Naukowe, 1966.
Lebedovych, Ivan, ed. *Polevi dukhovnyky Ukraïns'koï Halyts'koï Armiï: U 45-richchia uchasty u vyzvol'nykh zmahanniakh; materiialy do istoriï*. Winnipeg: Ivan Lebedovych, 1963.
Lednicki, Aleksander. *Nasza polityka wschodnia*. Warsaw: "Zjednoczenie." 1922.
A collection of articles by a prominent Polish lawyer and politician about Poland's Eastern policy.
Lehovich, Dymitry V. "Denikin's Offensive." *RR*, 1973, no. 2, 173–86.
Leinwand, Artur. *Polska Partia Socjalistyczna wobec Wojny Polsko-Radzieckiej 1919–1920*. Warsaw: Państwowe Wydawnictwo Naukowe, 1964.
Leonhardt, Horst. "General Budyonny." *LA*, 4 September 1920, 565–8.
Lepecki, Mieczysław. *Sybir bez pzekleństw: Podróż do miejsc zesłania Marszałka Piłsudskiego*. Warsaw: "Rój," 1936.
Levyts'kyi, Kost'. "Pershyi Derzhavnyi Sekretariiat u L'vovi." *US*, no. 33 (1923), 15–19.
Lewandowski, Józef. *Federalizm: Litwa i Białoruś w polityce obozu belwederskiego, XI. 1918–IV. 1920*. Warsaw: Państwowe Wydawnictwo Naukowe, 1962.
An analysis of Piłsudski's federalist policy vis-à-vis Lithuania and Belarus from November 1918 to April 1920.
―――. *Imperializm słabości: Kształtowanie się koncepcji polityki wschodniej piłsudczyków, 1921–1926*. Warsaw: Państwowe Wydawnictwo Naukowe, 1967.
―――. "O wojnie 1920 roku ... inaczej." *ZH* 20 (1971): 200–4.
―――. "Prometeizm—koncepcja polityki wschodniej Piłsudczyzny." *Biuletyn Wojskowej Akademii Politycznej: Seria Historyczna*. Warsaw, 1958, no. 2, 100–37; 1959, no. 1, 31–52.
―――. "U źródeł wyprawy kijowskiej." *WAP* 7 (1962): 90–111.
Lewandowski, Krzysztof. "Sprawa ukraińska a Państwa Centralne w latach 1914–1916." *SDZSRR* 8 (1972): 25–37.
―――. *Sprawa ukraińska w polityce zagranicznej Czechosłowacji w latach 1918–1932*. Wrocław: Zakład Narodowy im. Ossolińskich, 1974.
Lewiński, Zbigniew. "Zagon na Koziatyn." *B* (Warsaw), April 1921, 306–16.
Libicki, Konrad. "Szkic ustroju politycznego i społecznego Rosji Denikinowskiej." *PD*, 1919, no. 15, 750–5.

Ligocki, Edward. *O Józefie Hallerze: Życie i czyny na tle współczesności dziejowej.* Warsaw: Komitet Obywatelski Obrony Państwa, 1923. A glorification of Haller's military activities in the Austrian army during World War I and as commander in chief of the Polish Army in France, based on Haller's own account and other secondary sources.

Linster, B. "Iz istorii revoliutsionnogo dvizheniia v Elizavetgrade." *LR*, 1928, no. 5, 100–15.

Lipiński, Wacław. *Bajończycy i Armja Polska we Francji.* Warsaw: Wojskowe Biuro Historyczne, 1929.

———. "Powrót Józefa Piłsudskiego z Magdeburga i przewrót listopadowy w r. 1918 według relacyj Adama Koca, ks. Zdzisława Lubomirskiego i kardynała Aleksandra Kakowskiego." *N* (Warsaw), 15, no. 2 (1937), 233–42.

———. "Sprawy wojskowych formacyj polskich na Wschodzie według relacji ks. Kazimierza Lutosławskiego." *N* (Warsaw) 16 (1937), 633–45.

———. *Wielki Marszałek, 1867–1935.* Warsaw: Gebethner i Wolff, 1937.

———. *Wojna Polska: Rok 1919–1920.* Warsaw: Gebethner i Wolff, 1936.

———. "Z historji Armji Polskiej we Francji." *N* (Warsaw) 6, no. 3 (1932), 467–75.

———. "Związek Walki Czynnej i Związek Strzelecki w świetle korespondencji władz austriackich." In his *Z dziejów dawnych i najnowszych: Szkice i studja historyczne*, 187–201. Warsaw: Wojskowy Instytut Naukowo-Wydawniczy, 1934.

———. "Zwolnienie Józefa Piłsudskiego z Magdeburga w świetle relacji niemieckiej." In his *Z dziejów dawnych i najnowszych: Szkice i studja historyczne*, 423–39. Warsaw: Wojskowy Instytut Naukowo-Wydawniczy, 1934.

Litwiński, Stanisław. "Z dziejów antynarodowej polityki reakcji polskiej." *SM*, 1951, no. 1–2, 110–22.

Livyts'kyi, Andrii. "Śmierć Marszałka Piłsudskiego a Ukraińcy." *BPU*, 1935, no. 22 (109), 252–3.

Livyts'kyi, Mykola. "Slovo pro Petliuru." *Kalendar-KUNS na 1967 rik*, 81–7.

———. "Symon Petliura: Borets' za suverennu derzhavnist'." *Sv*, 1976, nos. 229–34.

Lloyd George, David. *The Truth about the Peace Treaties.* London: V. Gollancz, 1938.

Łobodowski, Józef. "Koncepcje wschodnie Piłsudskiego." *W*, 7 June 1964.

Łoś, Stanisław. *O konstruktywną politykę na Rusi Czerwonej.* Warsaw: F. Hoesick, 1932.

Łossowski, Piotr. *Między wojną a pokojem: Niemieckie zamysły wojenne na wschodzie w obliczu Traktatu Wersalskiego, marzec-czerwiec 1919 roku.* Warsaw: Książka i Wiedza, 1976.

———. "Próba przewrotu polskiego w Kownie w sierpniu 1919 r." *NDP* 8 (1964): 51–74.

———. *Stosunki polsko-litewskie w latach 1918–1920.* Warsaw: Książka i Wiedza, 1966.

Lotots'kyi, Oleksander. *Derzhavnyi provid Symona Petliury.* Paris, 1930.

———. "Istorychni osnovy nashoï derzhavnoï nezalezhnosty." *Tr* (Paris), 1926, no. 17, 3–7.

———. *Symon Petliura.* Warsaw: Komitet dlia vshanuvannia X. richnytsi smerty Symona Petliury, 1936.

———. "Symon Petliura—derzhavnyi symvol natsiï." *UV* (Detroit), 30 May 1979.

———. *Symon Petliura iak polityk i derzhavnyi muzh.* Paris: Soborna Ukraïna, 1951.

———. "Symon Petliura pro kul'turnu pratsiu emigratsiï." *Tr* (Paris), 1931, no. 20–1, 8–23.

———. "Ukraïnska myśl polityczna." *Ws* 4, no. 1–2 (1932–3), 7–19.

Łowczowski, Gustaw. "Bitwa pod Kostiuchnowką." *B* (London), 1956, no. 3, 3–24.

Lozyns'kyi, Mykhailo. *Halychyna v rr. 1918–1920.* Vienna: Institut sociologique ukrainien, 1922. Reprint, New York: Chervona Kalyna, 1970.

An authoritative political history of Eastern Galicia in 1918–20 by the former ZUNR undersecretary of foreign affairs and member of the ZUNR delegation to the Paris Peace Conference. Many documents are cited.

———. *Notes sur les relations ukraino-polonaises en Galicie pendant les 25 dernières années, 1895–1919.* Paris: Bureau ukrainien, 1919.

———. "Polozhennia Skhidn'oï Halychyny zi stanovyshcha mizhnarodn'oho prava." *Kaliendar tovarystva Prosvity na rik 1923,* 183–96.

———. "Pol's'kyi naïzd na Halychynu i rolia Aliiantiv." *KUNS na rik 1920,* 47–50.

———. "V desiatyrichchia halyts'koï revoliutsiï: Fakty i sproba otsinky." *ChSh,* 1928, no. 11, 180–91.

Lucas, Richard C. "The Seizure of Vilna, October 1920." *The Historian* 23, no. 2 (1961), 234–46.

Łukasiewicz, Juljusz. "Uwagi o polityce ukraińskiej Marszałka Piłsudskiego." *WP,* 14 December 1941.

A survey of Piłsudski's Ukrainian policy, set against the background of his Soviet Russian policy in 1919–1920, by the head of the Department of East European Affairs in the Polish Ministry of Foreign Affairs.

Lundgreen-Nielsen, Kay. *The Polish Problem at the Paris Peace Conference: A Study of the Policies of the Great Powers and the Poles, 1918–1919.* Odense: Odense University Press, 1979.

"The Lurid Trial of Petlura's slayer." *LD,* 19 November 1927, 36, 41–2.

Lutosławski, Wincenty. *Bolshevism and Poland.* Paris: M. Flińkowski, 1919.

———. *Lithuania and White Ruthenia.* Paris: Levé, 1919.

L'vov, N. "Beloe dvizhenie: K 20-tiletiiu ego zarozhdeniia." *F,* no. 37 (1937), 5–11.

L-yi, I. "Nad trunoiu Symona Petliury: Ohliad varshavs'koï presy." *Tr* (Paris), 1926, no. 44, 29–31.

Lypa, Iurii. "Petliura." *KAD na rik 1938,* 9–13.

Lystopadovyi reid. Toronto: Ukraïns'kyi voienno-istorychnyi instytut, 1957.

M. "Ukraïns'ka sotsiial-demokratiia i sprava stvorennia ukraïns'koï armiï v 1917 r." *RN,* 1933, no. 11–12 (70–1), 260–5.

M., M. "Dopovid' pro Petliuru i pohromy 1919–1920 rr." *Sv,* 26 April 1973.

Macfarlane, L. J. "Hands Off Russia: British Labour and the Russo-Polish War, 1920." *Past and Present* (London), no. 38 (1967), 126–52.

Machalski, Tadeusz. *Generał Tadeusz Kutrzeba.* London: Veritas Foundation Press, 1983.

———. *Ostatnia epopeja: Działania kawalerii w 1920 roku.* London: B. Świderski, 1969.

Machray, Robert. *The Poland of Piłsudski: Incorporating 'Poland, 1914–1931,' Much Condensed, and Carrying on the History of Poland till Mid-July 1936*. London: Allen and Unwin, 1936.

Mackiewicz, Stanisław. *Historja Polski od 11 listopada 1918 r. do 17 wrzesnia 1939 r.* London: M. I. Kolin, 1941.

———. *Klucz do Piłsudskiego*. London: the author, 1943.

Magalias, S. "Heneral-khorunzhyi Volodymyr Sikevych: V desiati rokovyny smerty." *BUNDS*, 1962, no. 12, 25–7.

Majstrenko, Iwan. *Borot'bism: A Chapter in the History of Ukrainian Communism*. New York: Research Program on the U.S.S.R., 1954.

Makarenko, Hr. "Polkovnyk P. Bolbachan: Ostannii akt zhyttia." *LChK*, 1930, no. 7–8, 10–11.

Makeev, P. V. *Na Denikina: Rol' latyshskikh streltsov v razgrome denikinskikh polchishch*. Riga: Latviiskoe gos. izd-vo, 1960.

Makovskii, V. "Operatsii na Visle v pol'skom osvetlenii." *VR*, 1931, no. 7, 127–34.

Maksakova, L. V. *Agitpoezd "Oktiabr'skaia revoliutsiia," 1919–1920*. Moscow: Izdatel'stvo Akademii nauk SSSR, 1956.

Malaniuk, Evhen. "Natsional'na proskomiddia." *StV*, 1926, no. 7–8, 1–28.

———. "Slovo v desiatylittia 25. V. 1926–25. V. 1936." *KAD na rik 1937*, 63–74.

Malinowski, Władysław. *Józef Piłsudski, 1867–1914*. London: Komitet Wydawniczy, 1964(?).

Maliszewski, Edward. *Polacy i polskość na Litwie i Rusi*. Warsaw: W. Lazarski, 1916.

Mal't, M. "Denikinshchina i krest'ianstvo." *PR*, 1924, no. 1, 140–57.

Mamatey, Victor S. *The United States and East Central Europe, 1914–1918: A Study in Wilsonian Diplomacy and Propaganda*. Princeton: Princeton University Press, 1957.

Mandzenko, K. "Petliura, petliurivtsi, petliurivstvo: Do storichchia vid dnia narodzhennia Holovnoho otamana Symona Petliury, 1879–1979." *AUNS na rik 1979*, 7–36.

Manuil'skii, Dmitrii. "O rizhskikh peregovorakh." *KI*, 1920, no. 15, 3077–82.

Marak, Volodymyr. "Korotka istoriia 9 harmatn'oho polku UHA." *LChK*, 1932, no. 1, 17–21.

Marchand, René. "French Policy in Russia." *LA*, 3 July 1920, 17–23.

Marchlewski, Julian (Markhlevskii, I.). "Mir s Polshei." *KI*, 1920, no. 14, 2751–4.

———. *Voina i mir mezhdu burzhuaznoi Polshei i proletarskoi Rossiei*. Moscow: Gos. izd-vo, 1921.

Marcinkowski, Karol. *Boje w Zbarażu 25 i 26 lipca 1920 oraz rzeź w Bystryku 1 czerwca 1920*. Philadelphia: Doraźny Zespół w Filadelfii. 1983.

Margolin, Arnold D. *The Jews of Eastern Europe*. New York: Seltzer, 1926.

———. "Moï zustrichi z Petliuroiu: Do 30-littia smerty Symona Petliury." *NDni*, no. 64 (1955), 8–9.

Maritchak, Oleksander. "Mizhnarodnie polozhennie halyts'koï spravy: Politychnyi ohliad za ostanni roky." *US*, no. 24 (1923), 15–19.

Martenko, Ihor R. "Denikin and Ukraine." *Ukraïns'ka trybuna* (Munich), 24 August 1947.

Martynets', Volodymyr. "S. V. Petliura i ukraïns'ke natsional'ne vidrodzhennia." *StV*, 1926, no. 7–8, 15–21.

———. *Zhydivs'ka problema na Ukraïni*. London, 1938.

Maruszewski, Artur. "Propaganda bolszewicka podczas kampanji polsko-sowieckiej 1920 roku." *B* (Warsaw) 39 (1932): 174–83.

Masliuk, Hr. "Dlia nas—Petliura." *Tr* (New York), 1961, no. 3, 7–10.

Matkowski, Karol, and Stanisław Biegański. "Sprawa polska na konferencji międzynarodowej w Spa." *B* (Warsaw) 39 (1932): 1–50.

Max of Baden. "The Eclipse of the Fourteen Points." *LA*, 23 August 1919, 449–53.

Mazepa, Isaak. *Bol'shevyzm i okupatsiia Ukraïny: Sotsiial'no-ekonomichni prychyny nedozrilosty syl ukraïns'koï revoliutsiï*. Lviv: "Znattia to syla." 1922.

———. *Ohneva proba: Ukraïns'ka polityka i strategiia v dobi Zymovoho pokhodu 1919–1920*. Prague: "Proboiem," 1941.

———. "Shcho oslabliuvalo nashu borot'bu v rokakh 1917–1920?" *Kaliendar dlia ukraïns'kykh pratsiuiuchykh liudei "Pryiatel' narodu" na rik 1937*, 62–5.

———. *Ukraïna v ohni i buri revoliutsiï, 1917–1921*. 3 vols. Munich: Prometei, 1950–1.

One of the best works on the Ukrainian revolution. Written by a former UNR prime minister, it is especially valuable because of its wealth of information on all political parties.

———. "Ukrainia under Bolshevist Rule." *SEER* 12 (1934): 323–46.

———. "Winnica." *K*, 1952, no. 9, 104–9.

———. "Zymovyi pokhid i partyzans'kyi rukh na Ukraïni v 1919 r." *KAD na rik 1936*, 89–96.

An account of the UNR Army's Winter Campaign of 1919–20 and partisan activities, including those led by Makhno and Hryhor'ïv, against the Bolsheviks and Whites.

Mękarski, Stefan. "Z problemów polsko-ukraińskich." *OB* (Brussels), 13 September 1958.

Melikov, Vladimir A. *Marna—1914 goda, Visla—1920 goda, Smirna—1922 goda*. Moscow: Gos. izd-vo, 1928.

———. "Srazhenie na Visle v svete opyta maisko-avgustovskoi kampanii 1920 g.: Politiko-strategicheskii etiud." *VR*, 1930, no. 10, 9–44.

Mel'nyk, Mykola. *Ukraïns'ka derzhava 1917–1920 rokiv u svitli mizhnarodn'oho prava*. London: Vyzvol'nyi shliakh, 1971.

Menchukov, E. A. *Istoricheskii ocherk boev v usloviiakh okruzhenii*. Moscow: Gos. izd-vo, 1930.

A valuable, well-documented work on twenty selected military operations involving encirclement, mostly during the First World War and Russian Civil War: it includes accounts of the fighting against Makhno.

Merkun, Osyp. "Nashi poloneni v Italiï." *Volia* (Vienna), 1920, no. 8, 368–72.

Merlot, A. *L'armée Polonaise: Constitution en France et organisation, juin 1917–avril 1919*. Paris: Levé, 1919.

Mezheninov, S. A. *Nachalo bor'by s poliakami na Ukraine v 1920 g. (XII armiia)*. Moscow: Gos. izd-vo, 1926.

Michelotti, Gigi. "Why Poland Fails." *LA*, 11 September 1920, 630–4.

Międziński, B. "Piłsudski i Sosnkowski." *K*, 1968, no. 1, 158–84.
———. "Polityka wschodnia Piłsudskiego." *ZH* 31 (1975): 3–45.
———. "Wojna i pokój." *K*, 1966, no. 5, 107–20; no. 6, 93–104; no. 9, 85–97; no. 11, 108–22; no. 12, 124–36.
On the Polish-Soviet War of 1920, the Peace Treaty of Riga, and their results.
Migdal, Stefan. *Piłsudczyzna w latach Pierwszej Wojny Światowej: Zarys działalności i ideologii*. Katowice: Śląsk, 1961.
Mikulicz, Sergiusz. *Prometeizm w polityce II Rzeczypospolitej*. Warsaw: Książka i Wiedza, 1971.
Mikulin, V. "L'vov-Varshava." *VR*, 1929, no. 10, 141–51.
Milis, "Legjony i Piłsudski." *NiP*, 1918, no. 22, 41–6; no. 23, 63–9.
Mitkiewicz, Leon. "Marszałek Piłsudski o swoich generałach." *W*, 1 September 1966.
———. *W Wojsku Polskim, 1917–1921*. London: Veritas Foundation Press, 1976.
Młynarski, Feliks J. *Do broni! Prawda o Naczelnym Komitecie Narodowym i Polskich Legjonach*. New York: Polish Book Importing Co., 1915.
Modelski, Izydor R. *Józef Haller w walce o Polskę niepodległą i zjednoczoną*. Toruń: Drukarnia Robotnicza, 1936.
Molenda, Jan. *Piłsudczycy a Narodowi Demokraci, 1908–1918*. Warsaw: Książka i Wiedza, 1980.
Mongirdowa, Marja. "Jeńcy Polacy w obozach państw centralnych na tle koncepcji tworzenia armji w latach 1916–1918." *N* (Warsaw) 10 (1934), no. 1 (24), 97–120; no. 2 (25), 263–92; no. 3 (26), 431–47.
Montanus, B. *Polish-Soviet Relations in the Light of International Law*. New York: University Publications, 1944.
Morei de Moran, I. L. "Partyzans'kyi otriad 30 kvitnia." In *Ukraïns'ka strilets'ka hromada v Kanadi, 1928–1938*, 117–20. Saskatoon: Ukraïns'ka strilets'ka hromada v Kanadi, 1938.
Morkotun, P. "Nachal'nyi otaman i vozhd' Ukraïns'koï Natsional'noï Armiï, 1879–1926." *Kalendar "Ukraïns'koho khliboroba" na rik 1935* (Curitiba), 31–3.
Moskalenko, Andrew. "The Hetmanate in 1918 and Bolshevik Aggression in Ukraine." *UR* (London) 11, no. 2, 81–4.
Moszczeński, Józef. "Francuska Misja Wojskowa w Polsce w czasie Bitwy Warszawskiej w 1920 roku." *N* (London) 1 (1948): 83–8.
———. "Młodzież postępowo-niepodległościowa na terenie Kijowa i Moskwy." *N* (London) 6 (1958): 94–101.
———. "Natarcie i odwrót XV Armji sowieckiej, maj–czerwiec 1920 r." *B* (Warsaw) 12 (1924), no. 1–2, 88–114; no. 3, 204–25.
———. "Przegląd najnowszej literatury sowieckiej tyczącej się Wojny Polsko-Rosyjskiej 1918–20 r." *B* (Warsaw) 12 (1924), no. 3, 311–15.
———. "Przygotowanie i plan drugiej ofensywy Tuchaczewskiego." *B* (Warsaw) 17, no. 2 (1925), 269–93; 18, no. 1 (1925), 44–59.
———. "Rosyjski plan bitwy nad Wisłą w 1920 r." *B* (Warsaw) 19 (1925), no. 2, 135–68.
Motyl, Alexander J. *The Turn to the Right: The Ideological Origins and Development of Ukrainian Nationalism, 1919–1929*. Boulder: East European Monographs, 1980.

Mouttjoy, Desmond. "Ukraine Politics, 1917–1920." *NE*, 24 June 1920, 249–56.
Movchin, N. *Polsledovatel'nye operatsii po opytu Marny i Visly*. Moscow: Gos. izd-vo, 1928.
M-t., P. "Ukraïns'ka viis'kova deliegatsiia u Vrangelia, 10. IX. 1920." *LChK*, 1933, no. 7–8, 5–7.
Murdered by Moscow: Petlura, Konovalets, Bandera; Three Leaders of the Ukrainian National Liberation Movement Assassinated at the Orders of Stalin and Khruschov. London: Ukrainian Publishers, 1962.
Murray, Kenneth, M. *Wings over Poland: The Story of the 7th (Kosciuszko) Squadron of the Polish Air Service, 1919, 1920, 1921.* New York: D. Appleton, 1932.
Musiałek, Józef M. *Rok 1914: Przyczynek do dziejów brygady Józefa Piłsudskiego.* Cracow: the author, 1914.
Mykhailiuk, Bohdan [Knysh, Zynovii]. *Varshavs'kyi dohovir v svitli natsionalistychnoï krytyky*. Winnipeg: the author, 1950.
Mykhailivs'kyi, M. "Dva svity—dvi kul'tury: Het'man Pavlo Skoropads'kyi i Volodymyr Vynnychenko pro Symona Petliuru." *URob*, 28 September 1951.
———. "Pavlo Skoropad'skyi." In *Ideï i liudy vyzvol'nykh zmahan' 1917–1923*, 231–7. Edited by Bohdan Koval'. New York: Bulava, 1968.
"Myśli ś. p. Symona Petlury." *BPU*, 1936, no. 20, 198.
Mytrovych, K. "100-littia vid narodzhennia Symona Petliury i zavdannia ukraïns'koï emigratsiï." *Ukraïns'ka biblioteka im. S. Petliury: Informatsiinyi biuleten'* (Paris), no. 42 (1980), 2–4.
N. "Z naszych frontów." *RW*, 1919, nos. 36, 40–3.
N., A. "Wschodnia Małopolska integralną częścią Rzeczypospolitej." *GW*, 25 December 1921.
"Na Kyïv! Narys pokhodu zluchenykh ukraïns'kykh armii na Kyïv u serpni 1919 roku." *NIKTP na rik 1939*, 99–103.
"Na moskala! Wymarsz strzelców z Krakowa." In *Szlakiem Legjonów*, 21–2. Chicago: Komitet Obrony Narodowej w Ameryce, 1914.
"Na Ukrainie." *NiP*, 13 April 1918, 61–4.
"Nachal'nyi otaman Semen Vasyl'ovych Petliura." *KUNS na rik 1920*, 78–81.
"Nachalo Vrangelevshchiny." *KA* 21 (1927): 174–81.
Nahaievs'kyi, I. *Istoriia ukraïns'koï derzhavy dvadsiatoho stolittia.* Rome: Universitatis Catholicae Ucrainorum S. Clementis Papae, 1989.
Nahornyi, I. "Do desiatyrichchia zvil'nennia Donbasu vid denikinshchyny." *LR*, 1930, no. 1 (40), 194–7.
Najdus, Walentyna. "Polacy we władzach Republiki Litewsko-Białoruskiej, 1919 r." *KH*, 1967, no. 3, 611–24.
———. *Szkice z historii Galicji*. Vol. 1. Warsaw: Książka i Wiedza, 1958.
———. "Uchodźcy Polscy w Rosji w latach 1917–1919." *KH*, 1957, no. 1, 24–40.
Nakashidze, Iurii. "Pol'shcha i prometeïvs'kyi rukh." *Tr* (New York), no. 27 (1964), 16–19; no. 28, 13–14.
Nałęcz, Tomasz. "Józef Piłsudski w Tymczasowej Radzie Stanu." In *Historia XIX i XX wieku: Studia i szkice; prace ofiarowane Henrykowi Jabłońskiemu w*

siedemdziesiątą rocznicę urodzin, 112–25. Edited by Andrzej Garlicki et al. Wrocław: Zakład Narodowy im. Ossolińskich, 1979.

———. *Polska Organizacja Wojskowa, 1914–1918*. Wrocław: Ossolineum, 1984.

Narski, Zygmunt. "Z rozmyślań nad Ukrainą." *RW*, 28 September 1919.

Nash, Hr. "Petliurivshchyna." *NU*, 1925, no. 1, 3–26.

Naumenko, Iurii. "Kwestia ukraińska i Ukraincy na tle Wyprawy Kijowskiej: Na marginesie książki gen. T. Kutrzeby." *BPU*, 1937, no. 27 (218), 301–3; no. 28 (219), 311–13.

———. "Rola armji ukraińskiej w kampanji polsko-rosyjskiej 1920 r." *BPU*, 1935, no. 20 (107), 230–1.

Naumovych, Sofiia. "Za shcho vbyly Symona Peliuru?" *A*, 11 June 1981.

Nazaruk, Osyp. *Do istoriï revoliutsiinoho chasu na Ukraïni: Ukraïns'ki politychni partiï, ïkh soiuzy i teoriï*. Winnipeg, 1924.

———. *Halychyna i Velyka Ukraïna: Traktat prysviachenyi ukraïns'kym zhinkam i viis'kovym*. Lviv: Nova zoria, 1936.

———. *Nad Zolotoiu Lypoiu: V taborakh Ukraïns'kykh sichovykh stril'tsiv*. Vienna: Ukraïns'ka boieva uprava, 1917.

"Neprymyrenist' moskovs'koho natsionalizmu z ukraïnstvom." *VSVU*, no. 135 (1917), 65–7.

Nevezhin, K. *Russko-pol'skaia voina*. Moscow, 1923.

"Nezborymi dukhom: U treti rokovyny perekhodu ostankiv UHA cherez Karpaty 31. serpnia 1920–31. serpnia 1923." *US*, 1923, no. 19–20 (41–2), 1–6.

"Niepodległa Ukraina." *RW*, 16 February 1919.

"Niezwykła wyprawa Piłsudskiego." In *Szlakiem Legjonów*, 22–3. Chicago: Komitet Obrony Narodowej w Ameryce, 1914.

Nikulin, Lev. V. "Pochód za Wisłę." *ZH* 4 (1963): 145–66.

———. *Tukhachevskii: Biograficheskii ocherk*. Moscow: Voennoe izdatel'stvo, 1963.

Nimchuk, Ivan. *Ukraïns'ka viis'kova organizatsiia u Vidni v dniakh perevorotu: Prychynok do istoriï budovy ukraïns'koï derzhavy v Halychyni*. Vienna: Ukraïns'kyi prapor. 1922.

Nishchenko, Kornel'. "Symon Petliura." *Tr* (New York), no. 46 (1967), 3–10.

Nizhegorodtsev, A. *Pochemu Dobrovol'cheskaia armiia voiuet protiv kommunistov, Lenina i Trotskago*. Kharkiv, 1919.

N-ko, O. "Symon Vasyl'ovych Petliura." *NP*, 1954, no. 6, 2–3.

Nötzel, Karl. *Die Unabhängigkeit der Ukraine also einzige Rettung vor der russischen Gefahr, zugleich eine Würdigung der Kulturaufgabe Österreichs*. Munich: Hans Sach Verlag, 1915.

Norris, David. "Caspian Naval Expedition, 1918–1919." *Journal of the Central Asian Society* 10, no. 1 (1923), 216–40.

"Nota Ukraińskiego Sowieckiego Rządu." *PD*, 1919, no. 11, 481–4.

Novosivs'kyi, I. M. "Vidrodzhennia ukraïns'koï derzhavnosty 1917–1918 rr. ta uchast' Bukovyny v ïï vidbudovi." *Kyïv: Kalendar-al'manakh "Novoho shliakhu," 1978* (Toronto), 99–107.

Nowak, Antoni. "Józef Piłsudski w oblężonym mieście." *N* (London), 11 (1978): 161–6.

Nowak-Kielbikowa, Maria. "Polityka Wielkiej Brytanii wobec Europy Środkowo-Wschodniej w latach 1918–1921." *SDZSRR* 6 (1970): 89–126.

———. *Polska-Wielka Brytania w latach 1918–1923: Kształtowanie się stosunków politycznych.* Warsaw: Państwowe Wydawnictwo Naukowe, 1975.

Nozdrunov. "Pochemu ne udalos' okruzhit' Pol'skuiu armiiu 4–7 iiulia 1920 g. na Zapadnom fronte." *VR*, 1930, no. 7, 78–100.

O granice wschodnie Państwa Polskiego: Sprawozdania z wiecu zwołanego w Warszawie dnia 22. IX. 1918 roku przez grupę Polaków pochodzących z polskich Ziem Wschodnich. Warsaw: Drukarnia Polska, 1918.

O., A. "Kolonizacja i rozwój gospodarczy naszego Wschodu." *WsP*, 1921, no. 6–7, 271–2.

———. "Ukraina i sprawa ukraińska." *WsP*, 1921, no. 4–5, 179–81.

Obukh, Klym. "L. Vasilevs'kyi pro I. Pilsuds'koho." *Sv*, 10 August 1935.

Ochmański, Jerzy. *Historia Litwy.* Wrocław: Zakład Narodowy im. Ossolińskich, 1982.

———. "Kulisy wyprawy wilenskiej Piłsudskiego 1919 r." *ZDSPR* 3 (1968): 65–78.

Ochota, Jan. "Unieważnienie aktów rozbiorowych przez Rosję." *Sprawy Obce* (Warsaw), 1930, no. 1, 283–314.

Odarchenko, Petro. "S. V. Petliura iak literaturnyi i teatral'nyi krytyk." *Slovo: Zbirnyk* (New York) 3 (1968): 345–53.

Ohiienko, Ivan. *Riatuvannia Ukraïny: Na tiazhkii sluzhbi svoiemu narodovi.* 2d rev. ed. Winnipeg: Society of Volyn, 1968.

Ohliadivs'kyi. "Den' 1. lystopada." *US*, no. 19 (1922), 1–10.

Okulicz, Kazimierz. "Ostatni akt dramatu Józefa Piłsudskiego, 1920–1922." *ZH* 9 (1966): 7–45.

An informative account of Piłsudski's Lithuanian policy by the head of the government of "Central Lithuania."

Oleksiienko, Petro. "Heneral-khorunzhyi Borys Palii-Neïlo." *BSBUVK*, no. 14 (1963), 20–2.

———. *Trydtsiati rokovyny Lystopadovoho zryvu, 1918–1948.* Regensburg: Chervona kalyna, 1948.

Olesiiuk, T. "Pivnichni kordony Ukraïns'koï Narodn'oï Respubliky." *T*, no. 14 (1930), 65–95; no. 15 (1931), 48–68.

———. "S. V. Petliura ta ukraïns'ke studenstvo." *StV*, 1926, no. 7–8, 9–15.

Ol'khivs'kyi, Borys. "Symon Petliura." *TM*, 1937, no. 4, 22–7.

Olszański, Prochor N. (Ol'shanskii, Prokhor N). "Od preliminariów pokojowych do traktatu pokojowego." *ZDSPR* 3 (1968): 97–117.

———. *Rizhskii mir: Iz istorii bor'by Sovetskogo pravitel'stva za ustanovlenie mirnykh otnoshenii s Pol'shei, konets 1918–mart 1921 g.* Moscow: Nauka, 1969.

Olszański, Tadeusz Andrzej. *Historia Ukrainy XX w.* Warsaw: Volumen, 1990(?).

Omelianovych-Pavlenko, Mykhailo. "Derzhavna inspektura." *KAD na rik 1933*, 33–44.

Oplustill, Zdzisław. *Polskie formacje wschodnie, 1918–1919.* Warsaw: Perzyński, Niklewicz, 1922.

Ordon, W. "Polska ofenzywa na Ukrainie." *RW*, 1920, nos. 19–20.

"Organizatsiia ukraïns'koho viis'ka." *VSVU*, no. 150 (1917), 307–9.

Orzel, Laurence J. "A 'Hotly Disputed' Issue: Eastern Galicia at the Paris Peace Conference, 1919." *PoR*, 1980, no. 1, 1980, 49–68.
Ostrovershenko, Ivan. "Bii pid Motovylivkoiu v 1918 rotsi." *BSBUVK*, 1964, no. 3, 3–6.
Otreshko-Ars'kyi, Mykola. "Voienni shkoly Armiï UNR." *Tr* (New York), no. 71 (1973), 9–18.
Overkovych, M. "Zymovyi anabazis." *H*, no. 13 (1934), 12–14.
Ozerians'kyi, V. "Symon Petliura i my." *Tr* (Paris), 1937, no. 21–2, 23–5.
P. "Sytuacja strategiczna na Ukrainie." *RW*, 1920, no. 2.
P., M. "Głos żołnierza w sprawie Litwy i Ukrainy." *RW*, 1919, nos. 24–5.
———. "Polska a Ukraina." *RW*, 1919, no. 21.
P., V. "Dilo Mykoly Mikhnovs'koho." *URob*, 2 January 1951.
Padalka, Mykola. *Vystup polubotkivtsiv 4–6 lypnia 1917 roku v m. Kyïvi na foni politychnoï sytuatsiï toho chasu*. Lviv: the author, 1921.
Paderewski, Ignacy. *Archiwum polityczne Ignacego Paderewskiego*. 4 vols. Wrocław: Zakład Narodowy im. Ossolińskich, 1973–4.
Page, Stanley W. "Lenin and Self-Determination." *SEER* 28 (1950): 342–55.
———. "Lenin, the National Question and the Baltic States, 1917–1919." *The American Slavic and East European Review*, no. 7 (1948), 15–31.
Pajączkowski, Franciszek. "Życie kulturalne Lwowa w czasie walk polsko-ukraińskich 1. XI. 1919 – 1. VI. 1919." *N* (Warsaw) 18, no. 1 (1938), 1–28.
Pajewski, Janusz. "Polityka mocarstw centralnych wobec Polski podczas Pierwszej Wojny Światowej." *Rocznik Historyczny* (Poznań) 28 (1962): 9–56.
———. *Wokół sprawy polskiej: Paryż-Lozanna-Londyn, 1914–1918*. Poznań: Wydawnictwo Poznańskie, 1970.
Palamar, Hryts'. "Skhidnia Halychyna—zhertva frantsuz'koho imperiializmu." *NU*, 1923, no. 11, 17–34.
Palij, Michael. *The Anarchism of Nestor Makhno, 1918–1921: An Aspect of the Ukrainian Revolution*. Seattle and London: University of Washington Press, 1976.
"Pam'iati henerala Mykoly Iunakova." *Tr* (New York), 1961, no. 5 (11), 9–11.
"Pam'iati henshtabu hen.-khor. Ievhena Meshkovs'koho." *Tr* (New York), 1960, no. 4, 8–10.
"Pam'iati nezabutn'oho." *T*, no. 5 (1927), 15–19.
Panchenko, Ivan. "Pershyi Ukraïns'kyi korpus." *UK*, 1972, no. 2, 8–17.
Paneyko, Basil (Paneiko, Vasyl'). "Conditions of Ukrainian Independence." *The Slavonic Review*, December 1923, 336–45.
———. "Germany, Poland and the Ukraine." *NCA*, January 1939, 34–43.
Pannenkowa, Irena. *Punkty Wilsona a Galicja Wschodnia*. Warsaw: Książnica Polskiego Towarzystwa Nauczycieli Szkół Wyższych, 1919.
Pap, Michael S. *Ukraine's Struggle for Sovereignty, 1917–1918*. New York: Shevchenko Scientific Society, 1961.
Papierzyńska-Turek, Mirosława. *Sprawa ukraińska w Drugiej Rzeczypospolitej, 1922–1926*. Cracow: Wydawnictwo Literackie, 1979.
Paprocki, Stanisław J. *Kwestia ukraińska*. London: Reduta, 1949.

———. "Polska i Ukraina." *Za Wolność i Niepodległość* (London), no. 20 (1948), 398–402.

Pasichnyk, Dmytro. "Kruty-Paryzh." *StV*, 1926, no. 7–8, 28–30.

Patterson, Eric J. *Piłsudski, Marshal of Poland*. London: Arrowsmith, 1935.

Pauka, I. "Eshche o kontrudare Iugo-zapadnogo fronta v mae-iiune 1920 g." *VR*, 1935, no. 5–6, 15–25.

———. *Razgrom belopoliakov pod Kievom v 1920 g.* Moscow: Gosudarstvennoe voennoe izdatel'stvo, 1938.

Pavlovych, Mykhailo. *Ukraïna iak ob'iekt mizhnarodn'oï kontr-revoliutsiï*. Winnipeg: Ukraïns'ki robitnychi visty, 1922.

———. "Ukraine." *SoR*, 4 December 1920, 545–8.

"Perebih protsesu." *T*, no. 5 (1927), 83–9.

Perkowicz, Edward. "Bitwa pod Warszawą w sierpniu 1920 i jej kryzys." *B* (Warsaw) 19, no. 2 (1925), 242–87.

"Persha richnytsia z dnia smerty holovy Dyrektoriï, Holovnoho otamana viis'k U.N.R. sv. pam'iati S. V. Petliury." *T*, no. 4 (1927), 97–100.

Petliura, Semen. *Do Holovnoho rumuns'koho komanduvannia*. 26 June 1919.

———. "Pam'iati polehlykh za derzhavnist'." *Tr* (Paris), 22 January 1926.

———. "Poslednii ukrainskii shestidesiatnik: K polugodovshchine smerti K. P. Mikhal'chuka." *Golos minuvshago* (Moscow) 2, no. 10 (1914), 236–43.

"Petlura and the Ukraine." *NYT*, 1 June 1926.

"Petlura and the Vatican." *SoR*, 28 August 1920, 214–15.

"Petlura and Washington." *NYT*, 4 June 1926.

Petriv, Vsevolod. "Do istoriï formuvannia viis'ka na Ukraïni pidchas revoliutsiï." *LNV*, 1930, no. 11, 981–7.

———. "Vidrodzhennia nezalezhnoï zbroinoï syly ukraïns'koho narodu." *H*, no. 20–1 (1936), 9–13.

Piatkowski, Henryk. "Krytyczny rozbiór Bitwy Warszawskiej 1920 roku." *B* (London), 1957, no. 1, 3–36.

———. "Marszałek Piłsudski jako wódz wojska w polu." *B* (London), 1953, no. 1, 3–14.

Pidhainy, Oleh S. *The Ukrainian-Polish Problem in the Dissolution of the Russian Empire, 1914–1917*. Toronto: New Review Books, 1962.

Piłsudski, Józef. "Karta z historji." *BPU*, 9 June 1935, 261.

Piotrkiewicz, Teofil. *Kwestia ukraińska w Polsce w koncepcjach piłsudczyzny, 1926–1930*. Warsaw: Wydawnictwo Uniwersytetu Warszawskiego, 1981.

Piotrowski, Marian. "O przyszłą równowagę." *Jutro Polskie* (London), 24 December 1950.

Piskorf, Tadeusz. *Działania Dywizji Kawalerji na Ukrainie od 20. IV. do 20. VI. 1920 roku*. Warsaw: Wojskowy Instytut Naukowo-Wydawniczy, 1926.

An account by a Polish officer, based on archival material, personal experiences, and secondary sources, of the Polish Cavalry Division in Right-Bank Ukraine from 20 April to 20 June 1920.

———. "Myśl manewru z nad Wieprza." *N* (London) 3 (1951): 129–37.

———. *Wyprawa Wileńska*. Warsaw: Księgarnia Wojskowa, 1919.

"Pislia protsesu." *T*, no. 5 (1927) 10–14.
Piszczkowski, Tadeusz. *Anglia a Polska, 1914–1939, w świetle dokumentów brytyjskich*. London: Oficyna Poetów i Malarzy, 1975.
———. *Odbudowanie Polski, 1914–1921: Historia i polityka*. London: Orbis, 1969.
Pliska, Stanley R. "The 'Polish-American Army,' 1917–1921." *PoR*, 1965, no. 3, 46–59.
Plomieńczyk, Adam. "Polskie warunki pokoju." *RW*, 5 September 1920.
———. "W przededniu wznowienia sprawy Galicji Wschodniej." *RW*, 12 December 1920.
Plutyński, Antoni. *Romana Dmowskiego świat powojenny i Polska*. Warsaw: Wydawnictwo "Przeglądu Politycznego," 1932.
"Po zwycięstwie nad Wisłą w 1920 roku." *N* (London) 2 (1950): 213–17.
Pobóg-Malinowski, Władysław. *Józef Piłsudski*. 2 vols. Warsaw: Gebethner i Wolff, 1935.
———. "Laboratorja organizacji bojowej P.P.S." *N* (Warsaw) 10 (1934): 464–9.
———. *Najnowsza historia polityczna Polski*. Vol 2. *1914–1939*. 3d rev. ed. London: the author, 1985.
———. "Tokijski epizod." *OB* (Brussels), no. 500 (1952).
Podil's'kyi, M. "Pol'shcha i ukraïntsi." *Khliborobs'kyi shliakh* (Lviv), 1933, no. 12, 35–40.
Podlaski, Kazimierz [Skaradziński, Bohdan]. *Białorusini—Litwini—Ukraińcy: Nasi wrogowie—czy bracia?* Warsaw: Przedświt, 1984. Ukrainian translation: *Bilorusy—lytovtsi—ukraïntsi: Nashi vorohy—chy braty?* Introduction by Iaroslav Pelens'kyi. Munich: Vidnova, 1986.
Podleski, Franciszek. *Układy pokojowe w Brześciu Litewskim, 1918*. Żelibory, 1933.
———. *Zagadnienie "ukraińskie" na tle stosunków austrjackich*. Lviv: Księgarnia Polska Bernarda Polonieckiego, 192?
Poker, Jim. *Błękitni rycerze*. Warsaw: Rój, 1931.
Pokrovskii, Georgii. *Denikinshchina: God politiki i ekonomiki na Kubani, 1918–1919 g*. Berlin: Z. I. Grzhebin, 1923.
"Poland and the Soviet Republics of Russia and Ukraine: Peace Treaty Signed at Riga, March 18, 1921." *Société des nations: Recueil des traités* 6 (1921): 51–169.
"Poland at Peace with Russia." *CH* 13 (1921): 452–4.
"Poland's Campaign against Russia." *CH* 13 (1921): 83–6.
"Poles and Ukrainians." *KUNS na rik 1932*, 153–7.
Polianskii, N. "Stavropol'skaia operatsiia 11-i Krasnoi armii v 1920 g." *VR*, 1935, no. 5–6, 31–49.
Polish Americans and the Curzon Line: President Roosevelt's Statement at Yalta. Edited by D. S. Wandycz. New York: Józef Piłsudski Institute of America, 1954.
"Politychni i militarni tsili pokhodu na Kyïv." *Tr* (Paris), 1937, no. 21–2, 31–5.
"Polkovnyk Oleksander Petliura." *Dorohovkaz*, 1965, no. 5–6 (24–5), 7–8.
Polons'ka-Vasylenko, N. "Ostanni roky zhyttia i smerty Mykhaila Hrushevs'koho." *Kalendar "Ukraïns'kykh vistei,"* 1964 (Edmonton), 36–48.
"Pol'sha i iuzhno-russkaia kontrrevoliutsiia." *KA* 47–8 (1931): 91–111.

Polska Armja Błękitna. Poznań: Drukarnia Św. Wojciecha, 1929.
Poltava, L. "Povstantsi na pivdni Ukraïny v 1920–21 rokakh." *VK*, 1967, no. 3, 32–5.
———. "Ukraïns'ki povstans'ki zahony v 1919–1920 rokakh." *VK*, 1967, no. 5–6, 26–33.
Pomarański, Stefan. *Józef Piłsudski: Życie i czyny*. Warsaw: Okręg Stołeczny Związku Peowiaków, 1934.
———. "Na marginesie niemieckich planów organizacji wojska polskiego w czasie Wojny Światowej." *N* (Warsaw) 2, no. 2 (1930), 229–34.
Ponomarenko, P. M. "O politike partii v ukrainskoi derevne v 1919–1920 gg." *VI*, 1956, no. 8, 105–7.
Popov, N. A. "Uchastie kitaiskikh internatsional'nykh chastei v zashchite Sovetskoi Respubliki v period grazhdanskoi voiny, 1918–1920 gody." *VI*, 1957, no. 10, 109–23.
Popov, P. "Petliurovskoe podpol'e na Pravoberezhnoi Ukraine: Puteshestvie v UNR." *LR*, 1926, no. 3, 31–42.
Porokhivs'kyi, Hnat. "Ukraïns'ka armiia ta ïï vozhd'." *Sh*, no. 3–4 (1953), 22–3.
———. "Ukraïns'ka viis'kova emigratsiia v Rumunii." *T*, no. 11 (1929), 76–86; no. 12 (1930), 75–82; no. 13 (1931), 57–68; no. 16 (1932), 74–90; no. 17 (1932), 70–8.
"Povstancheskoe dvizhenie na Ukraine." *Revoliutsionnaia Rossiia* (Berlin), no. 11 (1921), 22–5.
"POW w Stanisławowie od 1 listopada 1918 do 30 maja 1919." *RW*, 28 September 1919.
Poznański, Marceli. "Koncepcja ukraińska a odwrót z Kijowa." *RW*, 11 June 1920.
P-pa, N. "Protybol'shevyts'ki povstannia v Ukraïni 1921 r." *VK*, 1969, no. 6 (43), 57–67.
Pragier, Adam. "Piłsudski w Japonii." *WP*, 1942, no. 122.
———. "Polityka ukraińska Piłsudskiego." *WP*, 1941, no. 42.
"Pratsia het'mana Pavla Skoropads'koho z pershykh dniv vyzvol'nykh zmahan'." *Na vidsich* (Berlin), no. 8–9 (1940), 6–16.
Premysler, I. "Razgrom banditizma na Ukraine, 1921 g." *Voenno-istoricheskii zhurnal* (Moscow), 1940, no. 9, 34–44.
Preobrazhenskii, E. "Evgeniia Bogdanovna Bosh." *PR*, 1925, no. 2 (37), 5–16.
"Prezydent A. Livyts'kyi pro ukraïns'ku polityku 1917 roku." *KAD na rik 1937*, 75–85.
Primakov, V. "Srazhenie pod Orlom, oktiabr' 1919–noiabr' 1919 goda." *Bor'ba klassov* (Moscow), 1931, no. 2, 50–60.
A survey of Denikin's campaign against the Bolsheviks in Orel and Kursk gubernias in the second half of 1919; it includes an account of the Latvian and Estonian troops fighting Denikin and of Makhno's operations in his rear.
"Pro kyïvs'ku operatsiiu." *Tr* (Paris), 1937, no. 32–3 (582–3), 15–19.
Procyk, Anna. "The Treatment of the Ukrainian Question at the Yassy Conference of November 1918." In *Zbirnyk na poshanu prof. dr. Oleksandra Ohloblyna*, 400–10. Edited by Vasyl' Omel'chenko. New York: Ukrainian Academy of Arts and Sciences in the U.S., 1977.
Prokhoda, Vasyl'. "Boï sirozhupannykiv na pol's'komu fronti." *VK*, 1969, no. 6 (43), 41–8.

———. "Optymizm S. Petliury." *Tr* (Paris), 1935, no. 21–2 (475–6), 3–8.
———. *Ukraïns'ka armiia ta Holovnyi otaman S. Petliura*. Prague: Mizhorhanizatsiinyi komitet dlia vshanuvannia pam'iati Symona Petliury v Prazi, 1930.
———. "Zmarnovana natsional'na syla." *UK*, 1971, no. 1, 25–8.
Protopopov, L. "Otkhod III. pol'skoi armii ot g. Kieva v iiune 1920 g." *VR*, 1929, no. 7, 109–19; no. 8, 27–37.
"Protses." *Tr* (Paris), 1927, no. 1, 1–4; no. 2, 1–4; no. 3, 1–4; no. 4, 1–4; no. 5, 1–4; no. 6, 1–4; no. 7, 1–4; no. 8, 1–4.
"Provokatsiinyi krivavyi napad na eshelony Polku im. Bohdana Khmel'nyts'koho u Kyïvi." *VSVU*, no. 167 (1917): 580–2.
Pruszyński, Mieczysław. *Dramat Piłsudskiego: Wojna 1920*. Warsaw: Polska Oficyna Wydawnicza „BGW", 1994.
Prykhod'ko, Viktor. "Volodymyr Vynnychenko." *Sv*, 1951, nos. 87, 89, and 90–1.
Przybylski, Adam. "Działania 1. Dywizji Piechoty Legjonów na Ukrainie 1920 r." *B* (Warsaw) 13 (1924), no. 3, 236–52; 14 (1924), no. 1, 53–69; no. 2, 161–76.
———. *Działania wstępne w Wojnie Polsko-Rosyjskiej, 1918–1920*. Warsaw: Wojskowy Instytut Naukowo–Wydawniczy, 1928.
———. *Wojna Polska, 1918–1921*. Warsaw: Wojskowy Instytut Naukowo-Wydawniczy, 1930.
Purtal, Antoni. "Drukarnia konspiracyjna w Łodzi w okresie okupacji niemieckiej, VI. 1916–VII. 1918." *N* (Warsaw) 10 (1934): 404–30.
Putna, Vitovt K. *K Visle i obratno*. Moscow: Voennyi vestnik, 1927.
Puzyts'kyi A. "Boï syrykh za Korosten': rik 1919." *ZD* 2 (1930): 73–96.
——— "Borot'ba za dostupy do Kyïva." *ZD* 5 (1935): 9–61; 6 (1936): 13–64; 7 (1937): 9–56.
P-yi, A. "'Chetvertyi universal'." *Vyz*, 1923, no. 1, 46–51.
R. "Britain and Poland." *The Fortnightly Review* (London) 108 (1920): 430–9.
R., J. "Z dziejów prometeizmu polskiego." *Ws*, 1937, no. 1–2, 1–19.
R., S. *Ekonomichni osnovy halyts'koï derzhavnosty*. Lviv: Ukraïns'kyi prapor, 1921.
———. *Nafta Skhidn'oï Halychyny*. Vienna: Ukraïns'kyi prapor, 1922.
Radek, Karl. *Voina polskikh belogvardeitsev protiv Sovetskoi Rossii: Doklad na sobranii agitatorov moskovskikh organizatsii K.P. 8. V. 1920 g*. Moscow: Gos. izd-vo, 1920.
———. "The War with Poland." *LA*, 1920, nos. 3975–6, 635–40, 699–703.
Radziejowski, Janusz. "Ruch narodowy i rewolucyjny na Ukrainie w okresie działalności Centralnej Rady, marzec 1917–kwiecień 1918 r." *SDZSRR* 9 (1973): 53–84.
Radziwiłł, Stanisław A. *Les ukrainiens pendant la guerre*. Paris: E. de Boccard, 1937.
Rakhmannyi, Roman. *Aktual'nist' samostiinyts'kykh idei Symona Petliury*. London: Ukrainian Publishers, 1983.
Rakovskii, Grigorii. *Konets belykh ot Dnepra do Bosfora: Vyrozhdenie, agoniia i likvidatsiia*. Prague: Volia Rossii, 1921.
A sequel to the author's *V stane belykh* (Istanbul, 1920) dealing with the final phase of the Russian Civil War in 1920.

Rakovskii, Kh. G. *Bor'ba za osvobozhdenie derevni*. Kharkiv: Politotdel Ukrsovtrudarmii, 1920. An authoritative and unique account of the Bolshevik regime's struggle against the Ukrainian partisan uprisings and peasant revolts during the Bolshevik invasion of 1919, based on the records of the Red Army, Cheka, and Commissariat of Internal Affairs.

Rawita-Gawroński, Fr. "Ruś i my." *KW*, 2 March 1920.

Rdułtowski, K. "Józef Piłsudski w Mińsku." *ZH* 22 (1972): 124–6.

Reddaway, William F. *Marshal Piłsudski*. London: Routledge, 1939.

Rekis, O. "Z bil'shovyts'koho pidpillia v Odesi, 1918–1919 rr." *LR*, 1931, no. 1–2 (46–7), 169–86.

Reshetar Jr., John S. *The Ukrainian Revolution, 1917–1920: A Study in Nationalism*. Princeton: Princeton University Press, 1952.

Ripets'kyi, Stepan. *Ukrainian-Polish Diplomatic Struggle, 1918–1923*. Chicago: Ukrainian Research and Information Institute, 1963.

———. *Ukraïns'ke sichove striletstvo: Vyzvol'na ideia i zbroinyi chyn*. New York: Chervona kalyna, 1956.

———. "Vidrodzhennia ukraïns'koho viis'ka i ioho rolia v ukraïns'kii revoliutsiï." *VU*, no. 54 (1967), 3–15.

Riubi. "Operatsii konnitsy Budennogo vo vremia pol'skogo otstupleniia s Ukrainy, mai–iiun' 1920 g." *VR*, 1926, no. 12, 10–31.

"Rocznica śmierci Symona Petlury." *BPU*, 1936, no. 22 (161), 226–7.

Rohatyns'kyi, I. "Chortkivs'ka ofenzyva." *IKAChK na 1931 rik*, 58–64.

———. "Pam'iati ot. Kyryla Karasia, komendanta X. harmatn'oho polku U.H.A." *IKAChK na 1932 rik*, 97–112.

Romanów-Głowacki, Wiktor. "Jeszcze o Zamościu w 1920 roku." *DP*, 22 August 1964.

———. "Symon Petlura." *DP*, 21 April 1962.

Romer, Eugeniusz. *W obronie Galicyi Wschodniej*. Lviv: Książnica Polska, Towarzystwo Nauczycieli Szkoł Wyższych, 1919.

"Rosiia i avstriis'ka Ukraïna." *VSVU*, no. 21–2 (1915), 1–4.

Roszkowski, Stanisław. "Tworzenie Armji Polskiej w Austro-Węgrzech." *N* (Warsaw) 6 (1932), no. 2, 256–90; no. 3, 398–434.

Rothschild, Joseph. *Piłsudski's Coup d'Etat*. New York: Columbia University Press, 1966.

Roure, Rémy (Pierre Fervacque, pseud.) *Le chef de l'Armée Rouge, Mikail Toukatchevski*. Paris: Bibliothèque-Charpentier, 1928.

Royek, M. A. "Polish-Ukrainian Conflict over Lvov and East Galicia, 1918–1920." MA thesis, Columbia University, 1960.

Rozhin, Ivan. "Symon Petliura—Holovnyi otaman." *Tr* (New York), 1961, no. 3 (9), 406.

Rozwadowski, Jan M. *My a Ruś i Litwa*. Cracow: Księgarnia J. Czerneckiego, 1917.

Różycki, Tadeusz. "Możliwość interwencji Konnej Armji Budiennego w Bitwie Warszawskiej." *B* (Warsaw) 19, no. 2 (1925), 288–93.

R-t. "Shche dekil'ka faktiv pro V. Vynnychenka." *RD*, 1952, no. 2–3 (6–7), 16–19.
Rubach, M. "K istorii grazhdanskoi bor'by na Ukraine: K vosprosu ob organizatsii Vremennogo Raboche-Krest'ianskogo Pravitel'stva Ukrainy." *LR*, 1924, no. 4, 151–65.
A useful account of political conditions in Ukraine at the end of 1918 and the organization of the Soviet Provisional Workers' and Peasants' Government there. A number of documents are included.
Rudnev, V. *Krakh belopol'skoi okkupatsii na Ukraine v 1920 g.* Kharkiv, 1941.
Rudnicki, Szymon. "Lwowska grupa Ligi Narodowej w świetle własnych protokołów z lat 1918–1919." *PH*, 1977, no. 3, 711–32.
Rudychiv, Ivan. "Symon Petliura uchnem Poltavs'koï dukhovnoï shkoly i seminariï." *UPS*, 1954, no. 5, 10–12.
"Russia's reign of terror ... Sentiment in Ukraine." *CH*, October 1918, 74–81.
Rutkowski, Stanisław. "Geneza i przebieg odsieczy Lwowa w listopadzie 1918 r." *B* (Warsaw) 23 (1926), no. 1, 33–48; no. 2, 137–54.
——. "Pierwsze walki z Armją Konną pod Koziatynem, 28, V. 1920 – 6. VI. 1920." *B* (Warsaw) 31 (1928), no. 1–2, 1–24; no. 3, 231–52.
Rybalka, I. K. *Rozhrom burzhuazno-natsionalistychnoï Dyrektoriï na Ukraïni.* Kharkiv: Vydavnytstvo Kharkivs'koho derzhavnoho universytetu, 1962.
Rzymowski, Wincenty. *J. Piłsudski: Życie i czyny.* Zamość: Z. Pomarański, 1920.
S., B. "Perebih protsesu." *T*, no. 5 (1927), 83–9.
"S. Petliura pro ukraïnizatsiiu armiï." *VSVU*, no. 46 (1917), 727–8.
Sahaidachnyi, Petro. *V ioho tini: Symon Petliura v istoriï ukraïns'koho narodu.* New York: Ukraïns'ke vydavnytstvo, 1951.
Salitan, I. "Operativnaia deiatel'nost' armeiskoi konnitsy po opytu voiny s Pol'shei 1920 g." *VR*, 1928, no. 12, 67–86.
Sal's'kyi, V. "Holovni pidstavy tvorennia Armiï U.N.R. v mynulomu i maibutn'omu." *T*, no. 4 (1927), 3–8.
——. "Holovnyi otaman Symon Petliura i Armiia U.N.R." *T*, no. 3 (1924), 5–13.
——. "Symon Petliura iak istorychna postat'." *UIn*, no. 19–23 (1929), 4–7.
Samchuk, Hryhir. "Chomu tragediia Bazaru?" *Tr* (Paris), 1938, no. 1–2, 29–32.
Samovydets', P. *Zymovyi pokhid: Trydtsiati rokovyny, 1919–1949; politychnyi ohliad.* n. p., 1949.
Savchenko, Volodymyr. "Do 35-tylittia smerty S. Petliury." *Tr* (New York), 1961, no. 5 (11), 12–16.
——. "Narys borot'by Viis'ka U.N.R. na Livoberezhzhi naprykintsi 1918 ta pochatku 1919 rr." *ZD* 5 (1936): 158–85; 6 (1936): 119–54.
——. "Vtracheni mozhlyvosti dlia peremohy v lystopadi 1920 r." *T*, no. 2 (1924), 99–151.
Savoika, Liubomyr. "Iak povstala armiia Halliera." *Visti* (Munich), no. 122 (1966), 64–6.
Schaetzel, Tadeusz. "Racja stanu Polski na Wschodzie." *N* (London) 8 (1972): 225–49.
Senn, Alfred E. *The Emergence of Modern Lithuania.* New York: Columbia University Press, 1959.

———. *The Great Powers, Lithuania and the Vilna Question, 1920–1928*. Leiden: E. J. Brill, 1966.

Sergeev, I. N. *Od Dźwiny ku Wiśle*. Translated, with an introduction, by Józef Moszyński. Warsaw: Wojskowy Instytut Naukowo-Wydawniczy, 1925.

Sew-Sey. "Cele gospodarcze polityki polskiej na wschodzie." *RW*, 1920, nos. 19–20.

Shandruk, Pavlo (Szandruk, Paweł). *Arms of Valor*. New York: Robert Speller and Sons, 1959.

———. "Geneza umowy polsko-ukraińskiej z 21. IV. 1920 r." *Ws*, 1935, no. 2, 36–55.

———. "Organizacja wojska ukraińskiego na Podolu z początkiem r. 1920 i wyprawa na Mohylów, 26–28 kwietnia 1920 r." *B* (Warsaw), 29, no. 2 (1928), 202–18.

———. "Symon Petliura iak organizator ukraïns'koho viis'ka." *T*, no. 5 (1930), 2–4.

———. "Ukraïns'ka armiia v borot'bi z Moskovshchynoiu, 18 zhovtnia–21 lystopada 1920 r." *ZD* 4 (1934): 201–36.

An officer's detailed account of the UNR Army's defensive campaign against the Bolshevik occupational forces in Right-Bank Ukraine in late 1920.

Shankovs'kyi, Lev. "Na perelomi 1918 i 1919 rokiv: Pochatok druhoï viiny Moskvy proty Ukraïny i prychyny nevdach Ukraïns'koï armiï." *AKP, na rik 1969*, 65–84.

———. *Ukraïns'ka Halyts'ka Armiia: Voienno-istorychna studiia*. Winnipeg: Dmytro Mykytiuk, 1974.

———. "Ukraïns'ka natsional'no-vyzvol'na revoliutsiia." *AKP, na rik 1969*, 124–56.

———. "Za Ukraïnu—proty Moskvy: Ukraïns'kyi narodnii povstans'kyi rukh proty Moskvy pid chas vyzvol'noï viiny 1917–1920 rr. i pislia zakinchennia viiny v 1921–1924 rr." *AKP, na rik 1971*, 111–26.

Shaposhnikov, B. *Na Visle: K istorii kampanii 1920 goda*. Moscow: Gosudarstvennoe voennoe izdatel'stvo, 1924.

Shapoval, Mykyta. "Do prohramy ukraïns'koho vyzvolennia." *NU*, 1923, no. 9, 3–18; no. 10, 21–35.

———. *Liakhomaniia: Nasha doba; sotsiial'no-politychynyi narys*. Prague: Vil'na spilka, 1931.

———. "Pro smert' S. Petliury." *Kaliendar Ukraïns'koho robitnychoho soiuzu na rik 1929* (Scranton), 69–85.

Sharp, Samuel L. *Poland: White Eagle on a Red Field*. Cambridge: Harvard University Press, 1953.

Shchurovs'kyi, Volodymyr. "Ukraïns'ki sichovi stril'tsi na Zaporizhu." *IKAChK na 1929 rik*, 40–4.

Shekeryk-Donykiv, Petro. "Pro sproby Sichovoï organizatsiï na Velykii Ukraïni." *Zaporozhets': Kaliendar dlia narodu na rik 1921* (Vienna), 123–32.

Shelukhyn, Serhii. "Myrovi perehovory mizh Ukraïns'koiu Derzhavoiu i RSFSR v 1918 rotsi." *VU*, no. 47 (1965), 23–30.

———. *Ukraine, Poland and Russia and the Right of the Free Disposition of the Peoples*. Washington: Friends of Ukraine, 1919.

———. *Varshavs'kyi dohovir*. Toronto: Ukraïns'kyi robitnyk, 1947.

Shelygin, Ia. "Partizanskaia bor'ba s getmanshchinoi i avstro-germanskoi okkupatsiei."

LR, 1928, no. 6 (33), 61–101.
Shemet, Serhii. "Polkovnyk Petro Bolbachan: Zamitky do istoriï Zaporozh'skoho korpusu 1917–1919 rr." *KhU* 4 (1922–3): 200–36.
Shevchenko, Volodymyr. "Kruty." *UIn*, no. 31 (1931), 4–7.
Shevchuk, Semen. *Pora skazaty pravdu pro nashi vyzvol'ni zmahannia, dobytysia voli dlia Halyts'koï zemli, 1918–1939*. Toronto: the author, 1965.
Shilovskii, E. A. *Na Berezine: Deistviia XVI armii na r. Berezine v marte–iiule 1920 goda*. Moscow: Gos. izd-vo, 1928.
Shkrumeliak, Iura. *Krivavyi shliakh: Vyïmky z dniv nedoli Ukraïns'koï Halyts'koï Armiï*. Philadelphia: Ameryka, 1922.
———. *Poïzd mertsiv: Kartyna zhertv i trudiv*. New York: Hoverlia, 1962.
Shlikhter, A. "Bor'ba za khleb na Ukraine v 1919 godu." *LR*, 1928, no. 2 (29), 96–135.
Shmerling, Vl. "Grigorii Kotovskii." *VV*, 1940, no. 8, 9–13.
Shotwell, James Thomson, and Max M. Laserson. *Poland and Russia, 1919–1945*. New York: King's Crown Press, 1945.
Shteifon, M. B. *Krizis dobrovol'chestva*. Belgrade: Russkaia tipografiia, 1928.
Shtif, N. I. *Pogromy na Ukraine: Period Dobrovol'cheskoi armii*. Berlin: Vostok, 1922.
Shul'hyn, Oleksander (Shulgin, Alexander). *Derzhavnist' chy haidamachchyna: Zbirnyk stattei ta dokumentiv*. Paris: Mech, 1931.
———. "Elementy ukraïns'koï derzhavnosty v 1917 r." *Tr* (Paris), 1926, no. 31, 6–9; no. 32, 12–16.
———. "Ukraine and Its Political Aspirations." *The Slavonic Review* 13 (1934–5): 350–62.
Shumyts'kyi, Mykola. "Symon Petliura—tvorets' ukraïns'koho viis'ka." In *Symon Petliura: Zbirnyk studiino-naukovoï konferentsiï v Paryzhi*, 19–26. Edited by Volodymyr Kosyk. Munich: Ukraïns'kyi vil'nyi universytet, 1980.
Shvarts, N. "Nekotorye uroki varshavskoi operatsii 1920 goda." *VR*, 1931, no. 4, 34–60.
Sichovi stril'tsi: Viis'ko sobornoï Ukraïny. Prague: Proboiem, 1942.
Siedlecki, K. "Brześć Litewski: Rokowania pokojowe i traktaty." *B* (Warsaw) 15 (1924), no. 2, 113–36; no. 3, 239–58; 16 (1924), no. 1, 16–29.
Sieradzki, Józef. *Białowieża i Miklaszewicze: Mity i prawdy; Do genezy wojny pomiędzy Polską a RSFRR w 1920 r*. Warsaw: Wydawnictwo Ministerstwa Obrony Narodowej, 1959.
Sierociński, Józef. *Armia Polska we Francji: Dzieje wojsk generała Hallera na obczyźnie*. Warsaw: the author, 1929.
Sieroszewski, Wacław, ed. *Idea i czyn Józefa Piłsudskiego*. Warsaw: Biblioteka Dzieł Naukowych, 1934.
Sikorski, Władysław. *La campagne polono-russe de 1920*. Paris: Payot, 1928.
———. *Nad Wisłą i Wkrą: Studjum z Polsko-Rosyjskiej Wojny 1920 roku*. Lviv: Zakład Narodowy im. Ossolińskich, 1928.
A comprehensive work on the Polish-Soviet War of 1920 focusing on the left

section of the Polish front, where the author was a commander.

Simański, P. "Oblicze moralno-polityczne Czerwonego Wojska." *B* (Warsaw) 39, no. 3 (1932), 509–45.

Simonds, Frank H. "The Armistice of Riga." *AR*, November 1920, 486–96.

———. "The Saving of Poland." *AR*, October 1920, 371–9.

Simonov, B. *Razgrom denikinshchyny: Pochemu my pobedili v oktiabre 1919 g.* Moscow: Gos. izd-vo, 1928.

Singalewicz, Wladimir, and Richard Kimens. *Les ukrainiens et la Guerre Universelle.* Paris: n.p., 1919.

"Situation in the Baltic States: Zeligowski's Seizure of Vilna." *CH* 13 (1921): 454–6.

Skaba, A. D. et al, eds. *Ukraïns'ka RSR v period hromadians'koï viiny, 1917–1920.* 3 vols. Kyiv: Vydavnytstvo politichnoï literatury Ukraïny, 1967–70.

Składkowski, Wiesław. *Opinia publiczna we Francji wobec sprawy polskiej w latach 1914–1918.* Wrocław: Zakład Narodowy im. Ossolińskich, 1976.

Skliarenko, Ie. M. *Borot'ba trudiashchykh Ukraïny proty nimets'ko-avstriis'kykh okupantiv i het'manshchyny v 1918 rotsi.* Kyïv: Vydavnytstvo Akademii nauk ursr, 1960.

Skoropys-Ioltukhovs'kyi, Olaksander. *Znachinnie samostiinoï Ukraïny dlia evropeis'koï rivnovahy.* Vienna: Soiuz vyzvolennia Ukraïny, 1916.

Skrzypek, A. "Układ polsko-bałtycki z 17 marca 1922 r." *ZDSPR* 8 (1972): 37–57.

Skrzypek, Józef. "Lwów w listopadzie 1918 r. w oświetleniu uczestników walk." *N* (Warsaw) 14, no. 2 (1936), 304–18.

———. *Ukraińcy w Austrii podczas Wielkiej Wojny i geneza zamachu na Lwów.* Warsaw, 1939.

———. "Zagadnienie ukraińskie w pracach Leona Wasilewskiego." *N* (Warsaw), 16 (1937): 11–16, 101–63, 193–201.

———. *Zamach stanu płk. Januszajtisa i ks. Sapiehy 4–5 stycznia, 1919 r.* Warsaw: Spółdzielnia Wydawnicza, 1948.

Skrzypek, Stanisław. *The Problem of Eastern Galicia.* London: Polish Association for the South-Eastern Provinces, 1948.

———. *Sprawa ukraińska.* London: Stronnictwo Narodowe, 1953.

———. *Ukraiński program państwowy na tle rzeczywistości.* London: Związek Ziem Południowo-Wschodnich Rzeczypospolitej Polskiej, 1948.

Skwarczyński, Adam. "Polska a Ukraina." *RW*, 25 May 1919.

———. "Ukraina i państwa Ententy." *RW*, 9 May 1920.

Sladek, Ždenek, and Jaroslav Valenta. "Sprawy ukraińskie w czechosłowackiej polityce wschodniej w latach 1918–1922." *ZDSPR* 3 (1968): 137–69.

Slavins'kyi, Maksym. "Symon Petliura, 1926–1936." *Tr* (New York), no. 75 (1974), 13–15.

———. "Symon Petliura, 1879–1926." *Iliustrovanyi kaliendar "Ukraïns'koho holosu" na 1935 rik* (Winnipeg), 99–107.

Śliwiński, Artur. "Marszałek Piłsudski o sobie." *N* (Warsaw) 16 (1937): 367–73.

Slyvka, Iu. Iu. *Zakhidna Ukraïna v reaktsiinii politytsi pol's'koï ta ukraïns'koï burzhuaziï (1920–1939).* Kyiv: Naukova dumka, 1985.

Smogorzewski, Kazimierz Maciej. *About the Curzon Line and the Other Lines.* London: Free Europe, 1944.

———. *La guerre polono-soviétique, d'apres les livres des chefs polonais.* Paris: Gebethner et Wolff, 1928.

———. *Lwow and Wilno.* London: Free Europe, 1944.

———. *La Pologne restaurée.* Paris: Gebethner et Wolff, 1927.

Sokolnicki, Michał. "Józef Piłsudski a zagadnienie Rosji." *N* (London) 2 (1950): 51–70.

———. "Kryzys legionowy 1916 roku." *N* (London) 7 (1962): 146–55.

———. "Na przełomie polityki legionowej." *N* (London) 5 (1955): 5–28.

———. *Polska między niemcami a Rosją.* London: Instytut Józefa Piłsudskiego, 1952.

Solonar. "Vidrodzhennia Ukraïns'koï armiï." *H*, no. 9 (1931), 20–4.

Solovei, Dmytro. "Vynyshchennia ukraïnstva—osnovna meta Rosiï u viini 1914 roku." *NL*, 1963, no. 4, 55–82.

Solovii, Volodymyr. "Ukraïns'ki vyzvol'ni zmahannia na tli mizhnarodn'oï politychnoï sytuatsiï." *Tr* (Paris), 1940, no. 11–12, 7–11; no. 13–14, 3–7; no. 15–16.

Solukha, Petro. *Den' 25-ho travnia 1926 roku.* Toronto, 1976.

Sopotnicki, Józef. *Kampanja polsko-ukraińska: Doświadczenia operacyjne i bojowe.* Lviv: Odrodzenie, 1921.

Sosnkowski, Kazimierz. *Legionary Piłsudskiego.* Toronto: Związek Narodowy Polski w Kanadzie, 1964.

———. *O Józefie Piłsudskim.* London: Komitet Uczczenia Pamięci w 25-lecie Jego Zgonu, 1961.

Spanchak, Mykola. "Starshyny UHA u Moskvi i Kozhukhovi." *VK*, 1969, no. 6, 56–60.

"Sprava rozstrilu bohdanivtsiv na zasidanni Maloï Rady i protesty proty rozstrilu." *VSVU*, no. 173 (1917), 675–7.

Srokowski, Konstanty. *Sprawa narodowościowa na Kresach Wschodnich.* Cracow: Gebethner i Wolff, 1924.

Stachiewicz, Julian. *Działania zaczepne 3. Armii na Ukrainie.* Warsaw: Wojskowy Instytut Naukowo-Wydawniczy, 1925.

———. "Manewr na Żytomierz w kwietniu 1920 r." *B* (Warsaw) 13 (1924): 125–38.

———. "Niemieckie plany organizacji wojska polskiego w czasie Wojny Światowej." *N* (Warsaw) 1, no. 1 (1929), 12–29.

Stachiw, Matthew, and Jaroslaw Sztendera. *Western Ukraine at the Turning Point of Europe's History, 1918–1923.* Shevchenko Scientific Society, 1969.

Stakhiv, Matvii. "Perekhid cherez Zbruch i nevykorystani mozhlyvosti." *VU*, no. 22 (1959), 22–7.

———. *Ukraïna v dobi Dyrektoriï UNR.* 7 vols. Scranton: Ukrainian Workingmen's Association, 1962–6.

Stalin, Joseph. *Marxism and the National and Colonial Questions: A Collection of Articles and Speeches.* London: Martin Lawrence, 1935.

Stanymyr, Osyp. "Z italiis'koho frontu na ukraïns'kyi v lystopadi 1918 r." *VK*, 1966, no. 2, 26–33.

Starzewski, Jan. *Józef Piłsudski: Zarys psychologiczny.* Warsaw: F. Hoesick, 1930.
Steblik, Władysław. "Epizod z walk 12 Pułku Piechoty w Wojnie 1920 roku." *B* (Warsaw), 1926, no. 2, 167–78.
Stebnitsky, R. *L'Ukraine et les ukrainiens.* Berne: R. Suter, 1918.
Stechyshyn, M. "Ubyvstvo vozhdia: Kyïvs'ki vrazhinnia." *UIn*, no. 28–30 (1930), 7–14.
Stefaniv, Zenon. *Ukraïns'ki zbroini syly 1917–21 rr.* 2d ed. Munich: Soiuz ukraïns'kykh veteraniv, 1947.
Steffen, Gustaf F. *Russia, Poland and the Ukraine.* 2d ed. Translated by Jacob Wittmer Hartmann. Cleveland: John T. Zubal, 1981.
Stempowski, Stanisław. "Z historii stosunków polsko-ukraińskich." *K*, 1952, no. 9 (59), 104–9.
Stepanenko, Mykola. "Symon Petliura i Mykhailo Hrushevs'kyi pro novitniu rosiis'ku koloniial'nu imperiiu." *A*, 1980, nos. 86 and 88.
Stoiko, Volodymyr. "Z'ïzd narodiv u Kyievi 1917 roku." *UIs*, 1977, no. 3–4 (55–6), 14–25.
Stokalski, Wiktor D. *Dzieje jednej partyzantki z lat 1917–1920.* Lviv: the author, 1927.
Stolarzewicz, Ludwik. *Pierwszy żołnierz odrodzonej Polski.* Łódź: Księgarnia Ludwika Fiszera, 1928.
Stovba, Oleksander. "Ukraïns'ka students'ka hromada v Moskvi 1860-kh rokiv." In *Zbirnyk na poshanu prof. d-ra Oleksandra Ohloblyna*, 411–53. Edited by Vasyl' Omel'chenko. New York: Ukrainian Academy of Arts and Sciences in the U.S., 1977.
Strowski, Fortunat. "Paradoksy Marszałka Józefa Piłsudskiego." *PW*, no. 182 (1937), 3–17.
Strumiński, J. "Wrażenia z Galicji Wschodniej." *RW*, 6 July 1919.
Stsibors'kyi, M. "Dohovir han'by." *SD*, 1933, no. 4, 118–22.
A critique of the agreement between the UNR Directory under Petliura and the Polish government under Piłsudski.
Stukov, N. I. "Iugo-Zapadnyi front v iiule 1920 g." *VR*, 1929, no. 10, 129–41.
Sukiennicki, Wiktor. "Amerykański memoriał Paderewskiego." *ZH*, no. 26 (1973), 166–85.
———. "Moskwa a Ukraina po klęsce Niemiec w 1918 r." *ZH*, no. 5 (1964), 133–43.
———. "Stalin and Byelorussia's 'Independence'." *PoR*, 1965, no. 4, 84–107.
Sullivant, Robert S. *Soviet Politics and the Ukraine, 1917–1957.* New York: Columbia University Press, 1962.
Suprunenko, N. I. "Bor'ba ukrainskikh partizan protiv denikinshchiny." *Istoricheskii zhurnal*, 1942, no. 5, 27–37.
———. "Ustanovlenie Sovetskoi vlasti na Ukraine." *VI*, 1957, no. 10, 49–70.
Suslov, P. V. *Politicheskoe obespechenie sovetsko-pol'skoi kampanii 1920 goda.* Moscow: Gos. izd-vo, 1930.
Swianiewicz, Stanisław. "Niezrealizowane plany Piłsudskiego." *K*, 1960, no. 5 (151), 3–9.

Święcicki, Tadeusz. "Wobec decyzji wersalskiej w sprawie Galicji: Polska i Ukraina." *RW*, 1 December 1919.
Sydorenko-Saporai, Serhii. "Sotsiialistychna spadshchyna natsionalistam voiakam: Vstup do strategichno-politychnoho narysu Zymovoho pokhodu." *Nemezida* (Warsaw), no. 1 (1936), 5–19.
Symmons-Symonolewicz, Konstantin, "Polish Political Thought and the Problem of the Eastern Borderlands of Poland, 1918–1939." *PoR*, 1959, no. 1–2, 65–81.
"Symon Petliura." *UR* (London), June 1956, 27–34.
Symon Petliura: Do 20–richchia smerty. Heidenau: Soiuz veteraniv, 1946.
Symon Petliura—derzhavnyi muzh. Edited by Nataliia Livyts'ka-Kholodna, Zakhar Ivasyshyn, and Artem Zubenko. New York: Ukraïns'kyi natsional'no-derzhavnyi soiuz v SShA, 1957.
"Symon Petliura proty zhydivs'kykh pohromiv." *VK*, 1966, no. 2 (23), 57–9.
Symon Petliura: Symvol nashoï derzhavnosty. Buenos Aires: Rada, 1959.
Symon Petliura: Zbirnyk studiino-naukovoï konferentsiï v Paryzhi, traven' 1976; statti, zamitky, materiialy. Edited by Volodymyr Kosyk. Munich: Ukraïns'kyi vil'nyi universytet, 1980.
Symon Petliura: Zum 100. Geburtstag. Munich, 1979.
Symonenko, R. H. *Proval polityky mizhnarodnoho imperializmu na Ukraini: Druha polovyna 1919–berezen' 1921 r.* Kyïv: Naukova dumka, 1965.
Tardie, André. "The Allies and Bolsheviks." *LA*, 25 September 1920, 750–61.
Tarnavs'kyi, Ostap. "Politychnyi dorohovkaz Symona Petliury." *VU*, no. 9 (1956), 10–19.
Temnyts'kyi, Volodymyr. *Ukraïns'ki sichovi stril'tsi*. Vienna: Soiuz vyzvolennia Ukraïny, 1915.
Temperley, H. W. V., ed. *A History of the Peace Conference of Paris*. Vol. 6. London: Henry Frowde and Hodder and Stoughton, 1924.
Terlets'kyi, Omelian. "Iak poloneni ukraïntsi u vetsliars'komu tabori pryvytaly revoliutsiiu v 1917 rotsi." *LChK*, 1932, no. 11, 6–8; no. 12, 4–5.
———. "Velyka podiia: Beresteis'kyi myr, 9. II. 1918." *NIKTP na 1938 rik*, 105–8.
Teslar, Tadeusz. *Polityka Rosji Sowieckiej podczas wojny z Polską: Trzy momenty*. Warsaw: Gebethner i Wolff, 1937.
———. *Propaganda bolszewicka podczas Wojny Polsko-Rosyjskiej 1920 roku*. Warsaw: Wojskowy Instytut Naukowo-Oświatowy, 1938.
Tillman, Seth P. *Anglo-American Relations at the Paris Peace Conference of 1919*. Princeton: Princeton University Press, 1961.
Tiulenev, Ivan V. *Pervaia konnaia v boiakh za sotsialisticheskuiu rodinu: Ocherk boevykh deistvii*. Moscow: Gosudarstvennoe voennoe izdatel'stvo, 1938.
Tiutiunnyk, Iurii. *Z poliakamy proty Ukraïny*. Kharkiv, 1924.
———. *Zymovyi pokhid 1919–20 rr.* Kolomyia, 1923. Reprint, New York: Vydavnytstvo Chartoryis'kykh, 1966.
"To defend Schwartzbard." *NYT*, 18 June 1926.
Todorskii, A. I. *Marshal Tukhachevskii*. Moscow: Izdatel'stvo politicheskoi literatury, 1963.

Tokarzhevs'kyi-Karashevych, Ian. *Simon Petlura, 22 (10) mai 1870–25 (12) mai 1926.* Paris: France-Orient, 1927.

———. "Symon Petliura v Paryzhi, 1924–1926." *Tr* (Paris), 1931, no. 20–1, 33–42.

Tomashivs'kyi, Stepan. *Pid kolesamy istoriï.* New York: Bulava, 1962.

Tomkiewicz, Władysław. "Ukraina między Wschodem i Zachodem." *SN* 12, no. 1–2 (1938), 1–41.

———. "Zasięg kolonizacji polskiej na ziemiach ruskich." *Przegląd Powszechny*, 1933, 32–57.

Toporowicz, Wiesława. "Rosyjskie koła rządowe wobec kwestii polskiej w latach 1914–1917." *DN*, 1972, no. 4, 21–52.

Torzecki, Ryszard. *Kwestia ukraińska w Polsce w latach 1923–1929.* Cracow: Wydawnictwo Literackie, 1989.

Toynbee, Arnold J. *Survey of International Affairs, 1920–1923.* London: Oxford University Press, 1925.

Tragediia dvokh narodiv: Materiialy do sporu mizh Ukraïns'koiu ta Rosiis'koiu sotsiial-demokratychnymy partiiamy z pryvodu ubyvstva S. Petliury. Prague, 1928.

Trembits'kyi, V. "Osnovy sanitarno-medychnoï sluzhby v UNR, lystopad 1917–berezen' 1918." *VK*, 1972, no. 1 (57), 29–33.

———. "Sanitarna bl'okada Ukraïny 1919 roku." *VK*, 1973, no. 5–6, 59–66.

———. "Vseukraïns'ke tovarystvo Chervonoho khresta, 1918–1923." *VK*, 1972, no. 4 (60), 17–21.

———. "Zakhody ukraïns'kykh uriadiv u spravi zvil'nennia voiakiv ukraïntsiv z italiis'koho polonu." *VK*, 1973, no. 1 (63), 55–63.

Triandafilov, V. "Zaimodeistvie mezhdu Zapadnym i Iugo-zapadnym frontami vo vremia letnego nastupleniia Krasnoi Armii na Vislu v 1920 g." *VR*, 1925, no. 3, 21–51.

Trotskii, Lev. *Sovetskaia Rossiia i burzhuaznaia Pol'sha: Rech na mitinge v Gomele 10 maia 1920 goda.* Moscow: Literaturno-izdatel'skii otdel Politicheskogo upravleniia Revvoensoveta respubliki, 1920.

Trzciński, Witold. "Uznanie niepodległości Polski przez Rosję." *N* (Warsaw), 8, no. 2 (1933), 301–4.

Tsapko, Ivan. "Boievi aktsiï ukraïns'koï kinnoty u veresni 1920 roku." *VK*, 1964, no. 4 (16), 6–8.

———. "Rolia Vil'noho kozatstva u vyzvol'nii borot'bi." *VK*, 1967, no. 5–6 (30–1), 19–25.

Tukhachevskii, M. N. *Pokhod za Vislu.* Moscow: Gos. izd-vo, 1923.

A survey of the Soviet campaign in Poland in 1920, based largely on the author's memories and official documents. Originally lectures delivered to the advanced class at the Moscow Military Academy, 7–10 February 1923.

Turians'kyi, Osyp. "Prezydent Zakhidn'o-Ukraïns'koï Narodn'oï Respublikly pro nashu spravu." *US*, no. 19 (1922), 14–20.

———. "Reaktsiinyi plian Antanty v Rosiï i samostiinist' Pol'shchi." *Vo*, 1919, no. 4, 150–6.

Turkalo, Kost'. "Holovnyi otaman Symon Petliura." *AUNS na rik 1968*, 99–103.

Tymtsiurak, Volodymyr. "Prychynky do zhyttiepysu polkovnyka Dmytra Vitovs'koho." *VK*, 1972, no. 5–6 (61–2), 21–32.
"U 35-ti rokovyny slavnoho Zymovoho pokhodu, 6, XII. 1919–6. V. 1920." *BUNDS*, no. 15 (1955), 4–6.
Udovychenko, Oleksander. *Ukraïna u viini za derzhavnist': Istoriia orhanizatsiï i boiovykh dii Ukraïns'kykh Zbroinykh Syl, 1917–1921*. Winnipeg: D. Mykytiuk, 1954. A valuable survey of the organization and activities of the Ukrainian armed forces.
Ukrainian National Committee of the United States. *Ukraine on the Road to Freedom: Selection of Articles, Reprints and Communications Concerning the Ukrainian People in Europe*. New York: Ukrainian National Association, 1919.
Ukraïns'ka deliegatsiia Skhidn'oï Halychyny v Ryzi. Vienna: Uriad presy i propagandy ZUNR, 1920.
"Ukraïns'ka manifestatsiia u Kyïvi." *VSVU*, no. 149 (1917), 291–2.
"Ukraïns'ka Tsentral'na Rada." *KUNS*, 1919, 46–63.
"Ukraïns'ka zbroina syla tomu dvadsiat' rokiv." *NIKTP na rik 1939*, 91–8.
"Ukrainskaia operatsiia belopoliakov: Berezinskoe srazhenie; kontrmanevr Krasnykh armii na Ukraïne." In *Grazhdanskaia voina, 1918–1921*, vol. 3, 327–64. Edited by A. S. Bubnov, S. S. Kameneva, and R. P. Eideman. Moscow: "Voennyi vestnik," 1930.
"Ukraïns'ki poloneni v Italii." *Vo*, 1919, no. 4, 161–6.
"Ukraïns'kyi viis'kovyi z'ïzd u Kyïvi." *VSVU*, no. 156 (1917), 402–4.
"Ukraïntsi do Vil'sona." *VSVU*, no. 138 (1917), 113–14.
"Ukraïntsi-katolyky na Pravoberezhnii Ukraïni." *VSVU*, no. 168 (1917), 600.
Ullman, Richard H. *Anglo-Soviet Relations, 1917–1921: Intervention and the War*. Princeton: Princeton University Press, 1961.
Uzdowski, Marjan. "Na marginesie chwili: W sprawie Ukrainy." *RW*, 19 June 1921.
———. "O warunkach porozumienia się z nową Rosją." *RW*, 2 May 1920.
———. "Sprawa niepodległości Ukrainy a Polska." *RW*, 1 May 1920, 7–10.
V., O. "Dmovs'kyi i ukraïns'ke pytannia." *LNV*, 1930, no. 10, 914–24.
———. "Varshavs'ka kryza." *LNV*, 1922, no. 5, 150–7.
V., P. "Symon Petliura i zhydivs'ke pytannia v Rosiï." *Sv*, 9 June 1951.
"V 4-litni rokovyny smerty polk. Dmytra Vitovs'koho, pershoho ministra viiny ZUNR." *US*, no. 37 (1923), 1–3.
Val', E. G. F. *Kak Pilsudskii pogubil Denikina*. Tallinn: the author, 1938.
Valiis'kyi, Arkadii. "Chuzhynets'ki avtory pro roliu Armii U.N.R. v bytvi pid Varshavoiu." *Holos kombatanta* (New York), 1959, no. 2 (8), 6–8.
———. "Povstanchyi rukh v Ukraïni i otamaniia." *Sv*, 21 March 1957.
Vasyliuk, Pavlo. "Katerynoslavs'ki podiï." *NSl*, no. 3 (1973), 77–88.
Vasyl'kivs'kyi, L. "Prychynky do istoriï ukraïns'koï dyplomatiï v 1917–21 rokakh." *S*, 1970, no. 6, 109–23; no. 7–8, 140–52.
Vel'tman, Mikhail L. *Ukraina kak ob"ekt mezhdunarodnoi kontr-revoliutsii*. Moscow: Gos. izd-vo, 1920.
———. *Voina s pol'skimi panami: Pol'sko-shliakhetskaia avantiura*. Kharkiv: Izdatel'stvo PUR RVS Iugo-zapadnogo fronta, 1920.

Veryha, Vasyl'. *Halyts'ka Sotsiialistychna Soviets'ka Respublika (1920 r.) (Persha bol'shevyts'ka okupatsiia Halychyny).* New York: Shevchenko Scientific Society, 1986.

"Vesna dlia narodiv Rosiï i voskresenie ukraïns'koho zhyttia." *Kaliendar "Kanadyis'koho rusyna" na rik 1918* (Winnipeg), 225–36.

Vesnians'kyi, Z. "U piatdesiatu richnytsiu Bazaru." *Tr* (New York), no. 65 (1971), 4–6.

———. "U 50-littia Zymovoho pokhodu." *Tr* (New York), no. 56 (1969), 11–16.

———. "U 45-ti rokovyny smerty S. Petliury." *Tr* (New York), no. 64 (1971), 5–9.

Vityk, Semen. "Halychyna i Velyka Ukraïna." *NH*, 1923, no. 2, 1–23.

———. "Skhidnia Halychyna i skhidni kordony Pol'shchi." *ChSh*, 1923, no. 3, 116–21.

Voinarovych, Bohdan. *Symon Petliura.* Lviv: the author, 1925.

———. *Symon Petliura: Z nahody deviatoï richnytsi trahichnoï ioho smerty.* Lviv: the author, 1935.

Voloshyn, Rostyslav. "Polityka bol'shevykiv na Ukraïni za Tsentral'noï Rady." *V*, 1937, no. 3, 192–201.

Volyn' S. Petliuri, 1926–1936. Rivne: Volyns'ke ob'iednannia, 1936.

Vovk-Siromanets'. *Symon Petliura: Ioho zhyttia i pratsia.* Kyiv: Vidrodzhennia, 1918.

"Vrangelevshchina: Iz materialov Parizhskogo posol'stva Vremennogo pravitel'stva." *KA* 39 (1930): 3–46; 40 (1930): 3–40.

"Vseukraïns'kyi natsional'nyi z'ïzd u Kyievi." *VSVU*, no. 151 (1917), 327–32; no. 152, 344–5.

"Vseukraïns'kyi selians'kyi z'ïzd u Kyïvi." *VSVU*, no. 159 (1917), 455–61.

"Vseukraïns'kyi viis'kovyi z'ïzd." *VSVU*, no. 160 (1917), 474–9.

Vynnychenko, Volodymyr. "Iedynyi revoliutsiino-demokratychnyi natsional'nyi front." *NU*, 1923, no. 1–2, 56–71.

———. "Ievreis'ke pytannie na Ukraïni." *NU*, 1923, no. 7–8, 20–31.

Vyslots'kyi, Ivan. *Het'man Pavlo Skoropads'kyi v osvitlenni ochevydtsiv.* Toronto: Ukraïns'kyi robitnyk, 1940.

Vytanovych, Illia. "Agrarna polityka ukraïns'kykh uriadiv rokiv revolutsiï i vyzvol'nykh zmahan', 1917–20." *UIs*, 1967, no. 3–4, 5–60.

Wachowiak, Andrzej. "Zagadnienie niepodległości wśród przedwojennej zarobkowej emigracji polskiej we Francji." *N* (Warsaw) 10 (1934): 206–18.

Walewski, Witold. "Cukrownictwo na Ukrainie." *PK* 2 (1963): 167–94.

Walichnowski, Tadeusz, ed. *U źródeł niepodległości Polski.* Warsaw: Państwowe Wydawnictwo Naukowe, 1980.

Waligóra, Bolesław. *Bój na przedmieściu Warszawy w sierpniu 1920 r.* Warsaw: Wojskowe Biuro Historyczne, 1934.

———. *Walka o Wilno: Okupacja Litwy i Białorusi w 1918–1919 r. przez Rosję Sowiecką.* Vilnius: Wydawnictwo Zarządu Miejskiego, 1938.

Wandycz, Damian S., ed. *Polish Americans and the Curzon Line: President Roosevelt's Statement at Yalta.* New York: Józef Piłsudski Institute of America, 1954.

Wandycz, Piotr S. *France and Her Eastern Allies, 1919–1925: French-Czechoslovak-Polish Relations from the Paris Peace Conference to Locarno*. Minneapolis: University of Minnesota Press, 1962.
———. "French Diplomats in Poland, 1919–1926." *JCEA*, 1964, no. 4, 440–50.
———. "General Weygand and the Battle of Warsaw of 1920." *JCEA*, 1960, no. 4, 357–89.
———. "Henrys i Niessel: Dwaj pierwsi szefowie Francuskiej Misji Wojskowej w Polsce, 1919–1921." *B* (London) 44, no. 1–2 (1962), 3–19.
———. "Nieznany listy Petlury do Piłsudskiego." *ZH*, no. 8 (1965), 181–6.
———. "The Polish Precursors of Federalism." *Journal of Central East Europe*, January 1953, 346–55.
———. *Soviet-Polish Relations, 1917–1921*. Cambridge, Mass.: Harvard University Press, 1969.
———. "Z zagadnień współpracy polsko-ukraińskiej w latach 1919–20." *ZH*, no. 12 (1967), 3–24.
Wąpiński, Roman. "Endecka koncepcja polityki wschodniej w latach II Rzeczypospolitej." *SDZSRR* 5 (1969): 55–100.
———. "Endcja wobec kwestii ukraińskiej i białoruskiej." *Słowianie w dziejach Europy: Studia historyczne ku uczczeniu 75 rocznicy urodzin i 50-lecia pracy naukowej Profesora Henryka Łowmiańskiego*, 301–8. Edited by Jerzy Ochmański. Poznań: Wydawnictwo Uniwersytetu im. A. Mickiewicza, 1974.
———. *Narodowa Demokracja, 1893–1939: Ze studiów nad dziejami myśli nacjonalistycznej*. Wrocław: Zakład Narodowy im. Ossolińskich, 1980.
Wasilewski, Leon. *Kresy Wschodnie: Litwa i Białoruś, Podlasie i Chełmszczyzna, Galicya Wschodnia, Ukraina*. Warsaw: Towarzystwo Wydawnicze w Warszawie, 1917.
———. *Sprawa kresów i mniejszości narodowych w Polsce*. Warsaw: Wydawnictwo Warszawskiego Oddziału Towarzystwa Uniwersytetu Robotniczego, 1925.
———. "Sprawa podziału Galicji na tle stosunków austrjacko-ukraińskich." *PW*, 1925, no. 41, 459–64.
———. *Stosunki polsko-litewskie w dobie popowstaniowej*. Jerusalem: Wydział Kultury i Prasy DTWA Jednostek Wojska na Śr. Wschodzie, 1946.
———. *Ukraina i sprawa ukraińska*. Cracow: Książka, 1912.
———. "Wschodnia granica Polski." *B* (Warsaw) 17, no. 2 (1925), 125–35.
———. "Z burzliwej doby Ukrainy." *PW*, 1925, no. 33, 33–44.
Wasiutyński, Wojciech. *Zagadnienie Ziem Wschodnich*. Warsaw: the author, 1936.
Watt, Richard M. *Bitter Glory: Poland and Its Fate, 1918 to 1939*. New York: Simon and Schuster, 1979.
Wawrzkowicz, Eugeniusz. *Walczący Lwów w listopadzie 1918*. Lviv: Książnica-Atlas, 1939.
Weber, Leopold. "Przebicie się 51 Pułku Piechoty strzelców kresowych przez grupę Jakira w dniu 20 sierpnia 1920 roku." *B* (Warsaw) 15, no. 3 (1924), 259–66.
Weinstein, H. R. "Land Hunger and Nationalism in the Ukraine, 1905–1917." *The Journal of Economic History* 2 (1942): 24–35.

Wereszycki, Henryk. "Jeden z projektów niemieckiego rozwiązania sprawy polskiej w czasie Wielkiej Wojny: Memoriał o wytycznych przy zawieraniu pokoju z Rosją z r. 1915." *N* (Warsaw) 16 (1937): 458–62.

Wereszycki, Tadeusz. "Pierwszy etap obrony Lwowa." *N* (Warsaw) 1, no. 2 (1930), 370–7.

Weryha-Darowski, Aleksander. *Kresy Ruskie Rzeczypospolitej: Województwa Kijowskie, Wołyńskie, Bracławskie i Podolskie*. Warsaw: Koło Polaków Ziem Ruskich, 1919.

Weygand, Maximilien. *Bitwa o Warszawę: Odczyt wygłoszony w Brukseli*. Warsaw: Mazowiecka Spółka Wydawnicza, 1930.

———. "The Repulse of the Bolshevik Invasion of Poland." *The American Army and Navy Journal*, 1922, no. 47, 1141–2; no. 48, 1166, 1174–5.

Wheeler-Bennett, John W. *Brest-Litovsk: The Forgotten Peace, March 1918*. New York: W. W. Norton, 1938.

"Widmo Kijowa." *BPU*, 1935, no. 25, 283–4.

"Wiec Ligi Ziem Wschodnich." *R*, 22 January 1919.

Wielhorski, Władysław. *The Importance of the Polish Eastern Provinces for the Polish Republic*. Glasgow: Książnica Polska, 1943.

———. *Ziemie ukrainne Rzeczypospolitej: Zarys dziejów*. London: Koło Kijowian, 1959.

Wielopolska, M. J. *Pliszka w jaskini lwa: Rozważania nad książką panny Iłłakowiczówny "Ścieżka obok drogi."* Warsaw: Józef Zielony, 1939.

Wierny, Adam. *Na szlakach dziejowych Romana Dmowskiego*. Piotrków: the author, 1939.

Wierzejski, Witold K. "Fragmenty z dziejów młodzieży akademickiej w Kijowie, 1864–1920." *N* (Warsaw) 19, no. 3 (1939), 418–70.

Wilczyński, Jan. "Polskie Kolegium Uniwersyteckie w Kijowie, 1917–1919." *PK* 2 (1963): 195–216.

Wilder, Jan A. "Wpływ rosyjskiej Rewolucji Październikowej na stanowisko Zachodnich Aliantów wobec sprawy polskiej." *KH*, 1957, no. 6, 3–23.

Wilson and Poland: Four Essays Commemorating the Woodrow Wilson Centennial, 1856–1956. New York: Polish Institute of Arts and Sciences in America, 1956.

"Wojna z Rosją czy wojna z Ukrainą." *RW*, 20 April 1919.

"Wojska sprzymierzeńcze na Ukrainie." *PD*, 1919, no. 12, 515–18.

Wojstomski, Stefan W. *Russia and the Principle of Self-Determination, 1917–1918*. London, 1955.

———. *Traktat Brzeski a Polska: Sprawa polska w pertraktacjach pokojowych w Brześciu Litewskim pomiędzy Czwór-przymierzem a Rosją Sowiecką i Ukrainą*. London: Polska Fundacja Kulturalna, 1969.

———. "Weygand-Rozwadowski-1920." *ZH* 15 (1969): 221–4.

Wollenberg, Erich. *The Red Army: A Study of the Growth of Soviet Imperialism*. London: Secker and Warburg, 1940.

Woropay, Valentyna. "The Struggle for Ukrainian Independence in 1917–1918." *UR* (London) 1967, no. 3, 20–36; no. 4, 33–43; 1968, no. 1, 62–72; no. 2, 67–73; 1969, no. 1, 67–87; no. 2, 65–75; no. 3, 73–86; 1970, no. 2, 76–93.

Wraga, Ryszard. "Piłsudski a Rosja." *K*, 1947, no. 2–3, 43–54.
———. *Polska a kapitalistyczna interwencja w ZSSR*. Rome, 1945.
Wroniak, Zdzisław. "Geneza rządów Paderewskiego." *Historia* (Poznań), 1959, no. 4, 129–84.
———. *Sprawa polskiej granicy zachodniej w latach 1918–1919*. Poznań: Wydawnictwo Poznańskie, 1963.
Wroński, Stanisław. "Współdziałanie rządu polskiego z emigracyjnymi organizacjami antyradzieckimi w latach 1918–1938." *ZDSPR* 3 (1968): 262–90.
Wrzosek, Mieczysław. "Idea wojska polskiego w Rosji po obaleniu caratu i walka o jej realizację." *NDP* 12 (1967): 67–85.
———. *Polskie korpusy wojskowe w Rosji w latach 1917–1918*. Warsaw: Książka i Wiedza, 1969.
"Wschodnia granica Polski na zasadzie Pokoju Ryskiego." *Komunistyczna Trybuna* (Warsaw), 21 November 1920.
Z., F. "Po zgonie Wodza." *BPU*, 19 May 1935, 225–6.
"Z działalności P.O.W. na kresach wschodnich: Na podstawie raportów." *RW*, 1919, nos. 25–6.
"Z lystopadovykh dniv." *KUI na rik 1938*, 33–6.
"Z powodu przybycia generała Hallera." *RW*, 1919, no. 17.
"Z promov i pysan' Symona Petliury." *Sv*, 2 June 1951.
"Z sudovoï spravy: Na dopyti." *Tr* (Paris), 1926, no. 46, 20–3.
Zahorska, Anna. "Z dziejów P.P.S. w Moskwie." *N* (Warsaw) 40 (1934): 470–4.
Zaitsev, Pavlo. "Ol'ha Petliura." *M*, 1960, no. 1 (32).
Zając, Józef. "Bitwa 5-ej Armji nad Wkra." *B* (Warsaw) 19, no. 2 (1925), 210–41.
———. *Dwie wojny: Mój udział w wojnie o niepodległość i w obronie powietrznej Polski*. London: Veritas Foundation Press, 1964.
Zaks, Zofia. "Galicja Wschodnia w polityce Zachodnio-Ukraińskiej Republiki Ludowej i Ukraińskiej Republiki Ludowej w drugiej połowie 1919 r." In *Naród i państwo: Prace ofiarowane Henrykowi Jabłońskiemu w 60 rocznicę urodzin*, 387–405. Warsaw: Państwowe Wydawnictwo Naukowe, 1969.
———. "Galicja Wschodnia w polskiej polityce zagranicznej, 1921–1923." *ZDSPR* 8 (1971): 3–36.
———. "Problem Galicji Wschodniej w czasie Wojny Polsko-Radzieckiej." *SDZSRR* 8 (1972): 79–109.
———. "Sprawa Galicji Wschodniej w Lidze Narodów, 1920–1922." *NDP* 12 (1967): 127–53.
Zalewski, Antoni. "W sprawie polityki narodowościowej na Wołyniu." *WsP*, 1921, no. 6–7, 261–70.
Zalizniak, Mykola. "Ukraïns'ka armiia i general graf St. Sheptyts'kyi." *Nedilia* (Lviv), 1928, no. 15.
Zambrowski, Roman. "Uwagi o Wojnie Polsko-Radzieckiej 1920 roku." *ZH* 38 (7976): 3–30.
Zaremba, Zygmunt (Czarski, A., pseud.) *Od Borysowa do Rygi: Uwagi krytyczne o dyplomacji, wojnie i pokoju w r. 1920*. Warsaw, 1930.

———. "Ukraina Sowiecka i Ukraina niepodległa." *R*, 10 September 1920.
Zaslavskii, David Z. *Poliaki v Kieve v 1920 godu*. Petrograd: "Byloe," 1922.
Zatorski, Aleksander. "Emigracja polska w Rosji wobec władzy Rad, 1917–1918." *ZDSPR* 2 (1966): 176–223.
Za-vych, Iv. "Chuzhozemni viis'kovi formuvannia v ukraïns'kii derzhavi." *IKAChK na 1939 rik*, 88–101.
Zawadzki, Bolesław. "Nasz system obrony w kampanji 1920 r.: Geneza i zasady." *B* (Warsaw) 7, no. 2 (1922), 120–34.
———. *System obrony w 1920 roku*. Warsaw: Wojskowy Instytut Narodowo-Wydawniczy, 1926.
Zawiszanka, Zofja. "Do historji Drużyn Strzeleckich." *N* (Warsaw) 2, no. 2 (1933), 267–84.
Zbierański, Czesław. *Granice Polski a imperjalizm Rosji: Ogólny zarys stosunków polsko-sowieckich i roszczeń terytorjalnych Z.S.R.R*. Toronto: Polish Alliance Press, 1944.
Zbirnyk pamiati Symona Petliury, 1897–1926. Prague: Mizhorhanizatsiinyi komitet dlia vshanuvannia pamiati Symona Petliury v Prazi, 1930.
Zbyszewski, W. A. "Denikin: Zdolny generał, ograniczony polityk." *DP*, 12 August 1947.
———. "Generał Haller." *K*, 1960, no. 10 (156), 106–11.
———. "Nieznane 'Testimonium' o Piłsudskiem." *ZH* 4 (1963): 45–51.
Zdziechowski, Marian. "Pierwiastek zachowawczy w idei ukraińskiej." *PW*, 1937, no. 179, 85–102; no. 180, 53–64.
———. "Z historji stosunków polsko-rosyjskich nazajutrz po Wojnie Światowej." *PW*, 1936, no. 58.
Żegota-Januszajtis, Marjan. "Strategiczne granice Polski na Wschodzie." *B* (Warsaw) 2, no. 3 (1919), 174–80.
Zelenskii, P. *Pervaia Konnaia v boiakh 1920 goda*. Moscow: "Voiennyi vestnik." 1928.
Zgorniak, Marian. "Austro-węgierskie władze polityczne i wojskowe wobec polskich organizacij paramilitarnych w Galicji przed wybuchem I Wojny Światowej." In *Polska-Niemcy-Europa: Studia z dziejów myśli politycznej i stosunków międzynarodowych*, 261–72. Edited by Antoni Czubiński. Poznań: UAM, 1977.
Zhuk, Andrii. "Do istoriï ukraïns'koï politychnoï dumky pered svitovoiu viinoiu." *Vyz*, 1923, no. 2, 30–43.
———. "Symon Petliura: Z nahody 10-oï richnytsi smerty, 1879–1926." *LChK*, 1936, no. 5, 2–5.
———. "Ukraïns'ka hromada v Peterburzi i iï rolia v buduvanni ukraïns'koï derzhavy." *VSh*, 1964, no. 2, 149–56; no. 4, 369–402.
Zhurba, Halyna. "Mikhnovs'kyi na I-mu viis'kovomu z'ïzdi." *KAD na rik 1937*, 120–1.
Zhyvotko, Arkadii. *Iak Sovitska Moskva zvoiuvala Ukraïnu*. Introduction by N. Hryhoriïv. Lviv: Soimovyi kliub U.S.R.P., 1933.
Zieleniewski, Leon. "Zasada samookreślenia narodów." *SN* 3, no. 1 (1929), 5–15.
"Z'ïzd ponevolenykh narodiv u Kyievi." *S*, 1972, no. 9 (141), 54–8.

Zinkevych, Osyp. "Heneral P. Samutyn—voiak, strateh, doslidnyk." *Sv*, 30 July 1983.
Zlenko, Petro. *Symon Petliura: Materiialy dlia bibliografichnoho pokazhchyka*. Paris, 1939.
Zlepko, Dmytro. "Ukraïns'ko-pol's'ki vzaiemyny periodu 1919–1923 rr." *Vidnova* (Munich), no. 3 (1985), 93–105.
Żochowski, Stanisław. *Brytyjska polityka wobec Polski, 1916–1948*. Brisbane and London: Maria i Stanisław Żochowski, 1979.
Zotov, S. "Proryv pol'skogo fronta." *VR*, 1935, no. 5–6, 36–45.
Zozulia, Iakiv. "Pro sanitarno-medychnu sluzhbu v UNR." *VK*, 1972, no. 1 (60), 57–64.
———. *Velyka ukraïns'ka revoliutsiia: Materiialy do istoriï vidnovlennia ukraïns'koï derzhavnosty; kalendar istorychnykh podii za liut. 1917 r.-ber. 1918 r.* New York, 1967.
Zubenko, A. "V 40-vi rokovyny Zymovoho pokhodu." *Tr* (New York), 1960, nos. 1–6.
Zuev, Fedor G. *Mezhdunarodnii imperializm—organizator napadeniia panskoi Pol'shi na Sovetskuiu Rossiiu, 1919–1920*. Moscow: Gos. izd-vo politicheskoi literatury, 1954.
Żułowski, Mieczysław. *Wojna z Rosją o niepodległość, 1918–20*. Warsaw: Wydawnictwo Polskie, 1978.
"Zustrich armii Denikina i Petliury." *Vo* 4, no. 1 (1919), 44–5.
Zygmuntowicz, Zygmunt. "Wyzwolenie Małopolski: Obrona Lwowa." In *Dziesięciolecie Polski odrodzonej: Księga pamiątkowa, 1918–1928*, 122–30. Edited by Marjan Dąbrowski. Cracow: "Ilustrowany Kuryer Codzienny," 1928.

Index

Accame, Capt., 50
Aleksandrów Kujawski, 178
Alekseev, Mikhail, 44
Alekseev, S. A., 214n. 25
Alexander II, 246n. 5
Alexander III, 24
Allied Powers. *See* Entente
All-Russian Union of Zemstvos and Cities, 17
All-Ukrainian Council of Military Deputies, 3, 18
All-Ukrainian military congresses, 196; First, 3, 17; Second, 3, 18; Third, 4, 19
All-Ukrainian National Congress, 2
All-Ukrainian peasants' congresses, 196; First, 3; Second, 9
All-Ukrainian Union of Zemstvos, 21
All-Ukrainian Workers' Congress, 196; First, 3; Second, 9
Alsberg, Henry G., 225n. 28, 226n. 20, 242n. 32, 242n. 36
Anderson, Edgar, 229n. 3
Andriievs'kyi, D., 212n. 15
Andriievs'kyi, Panas, 10
Andriievs'kyi, Viktor, 209n. 12
Antonchuk, Dmytro, 68, 227n. 2, 227n. 3
Antoniny, 96
Antonov, Vladimir, 5
Archangel, 189
Archinard, Louis, 37
Armistice Convention of 1918, 81
Arski, Stefan, 217n. 23, 229n. 3
Askenazy, Szymon, 225n. 3
Austria, 1, 5, 21, 27, 30, 31, 41, 49, 51, 55, 67, 68, 70, 144, 148, 160, 170
Austrian army, 2, 6, 7, 9, 10, 20, 31, 41, 94, 106, 133, 196, 197;

Supreme Command, 31, 32; Second Polish Brigade, 41
Auta River, 115, 125

Babruisk, 84, 124
Bachyns'kyi, Ievhen, 245n. 1
Bączkowski, Włodzimierz, 246n. 1
Baidok, Ivan, 236n. 27
Bakunin, Mikhail, 24
Balkan Wars, 28, 30
Balta: county, 94; town, 189
Baltic Sea, 49, 69, 81, 82
Baltic states, 64, 84, 85. *See also under specific states*
Bar, 109, 136
Baran, S., 221n. 1, 222n. 9
Baranavichy, 154
Barlicki, Norbert, 137, 154, 155
Bartoszewicz, Jachim, 232n. 2
Barysau, 84, 89, 90, 124
Bataglia, Roman, 219n. 9
Bayonne, 36
Bazar, 123, 183, 200
Bazyl's'kyi, Havrylo, 171
Belarus, 35, 59, 60, 61, 63, 65, 66, 78, 79, 81, 83, 84, 85, 86, 89, 90, 133, 134, 138, 141, 143, 144, 145, 148, 151, 152, 153, 154, 155, 160, 165, 170, 198; Belarusian Socialist Soviet Republic, 81, 140–1, 144, 148, 151, 152, 155, 165–6, 169; Socialist Soviet Republic of Lithuania and Belarus, 81
Belgium, 118
Belovezha, 134, 148
Bemko, Volodymyr, 234n. 2, 235n. 21, 236n. 31
Berdychiv, 100, 107, 116, 117
Bereza Kartuzka, 82
Berezhanskii, Nik., 223n. 17, 239n.

8, 239n. 10, 240n. 17, 240n. 3,
241n. 11, 241n. 20, 241n. 26,
241n. 29, 242n. 38, 242n. 7,
243n. 11
Berlin, 33, 62, 120, 186, 189
Berthélemy, Joseph, 52
Berthelot, Henri, 46
Beseler, Hans Hartwig von, 33
Bessarabia, 8, 10, 46, 102
Bezpal'ko, Iosyf, 98
Bezruchko, Marko, 106, 107, 108, 117, 123, 171, 175, 210n. 12, 214n. 25, 236n. 31
Biała Podlaska, 131
Białystok, 125, 128, 129, 131
Biarezina River, 84, 115, 124, 125
Bidnov, Vasyl', 211n. 4, 211n. 7
Biegański, Stanisław, 217n. 28, 219n. 9, 221n. 20
Bierzanek, Remigiusz, 221n. 20
Bila Tserkva, 10, 104, 112, 116
Bilska Volia, 122
Birzulia, 110
Bisanz, Alfred, 109
Biuletyn Polsko-Ukraiński (Warsaw), 186
Black Sea, 45, 49, 69, 82
Boerner, Ignacy, 87
Boh River, 100, 101
Bolesław the Brave (King of Poland), 105
Boltuc, Mikołaj, 238n. 60, 240n. 11
Bordeaux, 37
Borius, Albert, 45
Borodianka, 117, 122
Borot'ba publishing house (St. Petersburg), 14
Boryslav, 52
Bosh, Evgeniia, 5
Bosnia and Herzegovina, 30
Botha, Louis, 52
Boulogne-sur-Mer, 37
Bowman, Isaiah, 50
Brazil, 40, 41

Bredov, Nikolai, 107
Breiter, Ernest, 141, 142
Brest-Litovsk, 5, 20, 75, 82, 106, 124, 125, 131, 134, 140, 148, 183, 197
Brody, 121, 126, 154
Browder, Robert Paul, 213n. 18
Brusilov, Aleksei, 2, 31, 114
Brussels, 65
Buchach, 122, 136
Bucharest, 46, 186
Budapest, 184, 189
Budennyi, Semen, 104, 115, 116, 117, 121, 123, 127, 132, 200
Budny, Michał, 220n. 16, 222n. 9
Buell, Raymond Leslie, 217n. 25, 217n. 28
Buh River, 82, 87, 125, 129, 132, 134
Bukovyna, 5, 10, 41, 46, 47, 95, 197
Bulgaria, 21
Bunyan, James, 208n. 4, 209n. 6
Butler, Ralph, 215n. 1, 215n. 6, 215n. 13
Butler, Rohan, 217n. 28, 223n. 21, 229n. 1
Bykovsky, Lev, 248n. 26
Bytyns'kyi, M., 238n. 60, 245n. 4

Cachoeira, 40
Cambon, Jules-Martin, 50
Cambridge Springs, Penn., 40
Camp Borden, Ont., 40
Campinchi, César, 190, 192, 194
Canada, 40, 185
Capua Vettere, 41
Carpathian Mountains, 122, 175
Carr, Edward Hallet, 231n. 20, 240n. 15
Carton de Wiart, Adrian, 50, 54
Casa Giare, 41
Caucasia, Northern, 115
Central Jewish Commission in France, 189

Central National Committee, 24
Central Powers, 1, 5, 6, 8, 9, 20, 31, 32, 33, 34, 36, 38, 40, 41, 45, 51, 81, 93, 196, 197
Central Rada, 1–2, 3, 4, 5, 6, 7, 8, 9, 10, 18, 19, 21, 22, 94, 188, 196, 197; First Universal, 3, 18; Second Universal, 3; Third Universal, 4, 6, 188; Fourth Universal, 5, 6; General Secretariat, 3, 4, 5, 18; Jewish Social Democratic Bund, 188. *See also* UNR government
Chamberlin, William Henry, 221n. 20, 230n. 9, 237n. 46, 239n. 7, 239n. 10, 240n. 15
Charaszkiewicz, Edmund, 226n. 20
Cheka, 109, 110, 128
Chekhovych, Kostiantyn, 68
Cherkasy, 104
Chernihiv gubernia, 93
Chernivtsi, 46, 47
Chernov, Victor M., 208n. 5, 216n. 22
Chernyshevskii, Nikolai, 24
Chicherin, Georgii, 88, 89, 90, 138, 140, 163
Chief National Committee (Cracow), 31
Chorna Khmara (partisan leader), 180
Chornobyl, 104
Chornyi Ostriv, 68
Chornyi, Serhii, 178, 180, 245n. 4
Chortkiv, 54, 121, 136
Chudek, Józef, 217n. 23
Chudniv, 109, 121
Churchill, Winston, 102, 234n. 6
Chykalenko, Ievhen, 208n. 3, 214n. 21
Chyzhevs'kyi, M., 245n. 4
City of Marseille (ship), 42
Clemenceau, Georges, 83
Committee of Assistance to Pogrom Victims of the Russian Red Cross, 188
Committee of Friendship of Caucasia, Turkestan, and Ukraine, 186
Committee of Polish Volunteers for Service in the French Army, 36
Conference of Ambassadors: of 1920, 34; of 1923, 56, 65, 80, 169
Congress of Nations Formerly Ruled by Tsarist Russia (1917), 186
Côtes-du-Nord, 37
Cracow, 27, 29, 30, 31
Crimea, 8, 44, 134, 145, 200
Curitiba, 40
Curzon Line, 82, 134, 144
Curzon, Lord George, 82, 89
Czechoslovakia, 34, 106, 122, 175, 189

D'Abernon, Lord Edgar Vincent, 120, 133, 234n. 13, 238n. 55, 238n. 57, 239n. 6, 239n. 9, 240n. 14
Dąbie, 173
Dąbrowski, Stanisław, 241n. 31, 242n. 34, 242n. 35, 242n. 36, 242n. 5
Dąbski, Jan, 137, 139, 140, 143, 145, 147, 150–4, 160, 161–5, 169, 241n. 9, 241n. 10, 241n. 20, 241n. 25, 241n. 26, 241n. 27, 241n. 30, 242n. 35, 242n. 36, 242n. 2, 242n. 4, 242n. 5, 242n. 6, 242n. 7, 242n. 8, 243n. 11, 243n. 13, 243n. 14, 243n. 15
Daniłowski, G., 216n. 14, 217n. 22
Danzig (Gdansk), 43, 119, 120, 125
Dashkevych, R., 223n. 11
Daszyński, Ignacy, 34, 120
Dats'kiv, T., 236n. 27
Daugavpils, 83, 84, 87, 88
Davies, Norman, 234n. 2, 235n. 14, 237n. 44, 237n. 51, 238n. 57, 240n. 17

Davnyi, R., 236n. 31
Dęblin, 125, 126, 130
Degras, Jane, 231n. 15, 239n. 4
Del'vig, Serhii, 68
Demchuk, O., 238n. 58
Denikin, Anton, 44, 56, 57, 78, 79, 80, 81, 84–8, 90, 115, 116, 188–9, 210n. 13, 220n. 17, 220n. 19, 221n. 20, 222n. 3, 225n. 26, 230n. 9, 231n. 14, 231n. 18
Denikin's Army. *See* Russian Volunteer Army
Derazhnia, 180
Deruga, Aleksy, 221n. 20, 222n. 4, 222n. 9, 227n. 1, 228n. 17, 230n. 9, 231n. 20
Desna River, 117
Desroches, Alain, 210n. 1, 244n. 9, 245n. 1, 246n. 2, 248n. 12, 248n. 14, 248n. 16, 248n. 18, 248n. 26
Diakiv, Iaromyr, 224n. 24
Didkovs'kyi, Maksym, 75
Dienstl-Dąbrowa, 41
Dłuski, Kazimierz, 43, 60, 63, 225n. 2, 226n. 6, 226n. 15, 226n. 20
Dmowski, Roman, 28, 37, 42, 59, 60, 61, 62, 77, 78, 139, 152, 153, 198, 201, 225n. 1
Dnieper River, 76, 77, 103, 104, 117, 140, 145, 168, 180, 200
Dniester River, 47, 70, 84, 100, 101, 104, 109, 117, 120, 121, 122, 123, 126, 127, 135, 136, 138, 148, 154, 172, 200
Dobkowski, Elia, 189–91, 248n. 11, 248n. 15, 248n. 26
Dobrians'kyi, Agaton, 213n. 21
Dobroliubov, Nikolai, 24
Dobrotvors'kyi, Osyp, 244n. 4
Dol'nyts'kyi, Myron, 224n. 23
Dolud, Andrii, 108
Domarats'kyi, 238n. 60
Dombrovs'kyi, I., 244n. 2, 244n. 4
Don region, 5, 99

Don River, 46, 81
Dontsov, Dmytro, 209n. 11
Doroshenko, Dmytro, 209n. 10, 209n. 11, 209n. 12, 210n. 13, 212n. 15, 214n. 25, 232n. 5
Doroshenko, Volodymyr, 211n. 7
Dostoevskii, Fedor, 24
Dotsenko, Oleksander, 224n. 24, 224n. 25, 224n. 26, 225n. 31, 227n. 1, 227n. 2, 227n. 5, 228n. 11, 233n. 18, 233n. 19, 236n. 26
Douglas, James, 216n. 18
Drabatyi, I., 210n. 13, 214n. 25
Drazhevs'ka, L., 210n. 1, 212n. 15, 235n. 21
Drohobych, 52
Drozdowski, Marian Marek, 218n. 5, 218n. 6
Drużyny Strzeleckie (Riflemen's Units), 30, 31
Dryhynycz, Jarosław, 245n. 1
Dubno: county, 71; town, 32, 121
Dukhonin, Nikolai, 18
Dulles, Allen W., 246n. 2
Dulove, 41
Dumin, Osyp (pseud. Krezub, A.), 210n. 12, 214n. 25, 235n. 25, 238n. 58, 243n. 1
Dvina River, 84, 115, 124, 154, 158, 168
Dvinsk, 32
Dziabenko, Ia., 208n. 3, 213n. 16
Działdowo, 127
Dzierżykraj-Stokalski, Wiktor, 232n. 6, 233n. 12, 233n. 15
Dzierżyński, Feliks, 128
Dziewanowski, M. K., 227n. 20, 229n. 5, 229n. 7, 230n. 9, 233n. 22, 237n. 40

Ecochard, Joseph, 42
Egorov, Aleksandr, 116, 121, 126, 127, 130
Eichhorn, Hermann von, 6, 7, 42

Emelchyn region, 181
Engels, Friedrich, 24
Entente, 8, 9, 10, 11, 20, 21, 22, 33, 35, 36, 37, 38, 40, 43, 44, 45, 46, 49, 50, 51, 53, 55, 56, 57, 58, 59, 65, 66, 67, 69, 78, 79, 80, 81, 82, 83, 85, 86, 87, 88, 89, 90, 106, 108, 111, 118, 119, 125, 129, 134, 142, 143, 144, 162, 169, 177, 184, 196, 198, 199. *See also* Principal Allied and Associated Powers
Erfurt, 44
Erickson, John, 235n. 14, 237n. 51, 238n. 1, 240n. 11
Erzberger, Matthias, 44
Estonia, 63, 64, 70, 81, 89

Fastiv, 48, 116
Fastiv Agreement, 48
Fedenko, Panas, 211n. 8, 212n. 12, 214n. 25, 228n. 11, 245n. 1
Fervacque, Pierre, 116, 237n. 48
Finland, 63, 64, 70, 118; Finnish army, 185
Fischer, Fritz, 209n. 9
Fischer, Louis, 228n. 10, 231n. 22, 239n. 10, 241n. 22
Fisher, H. H., 208n. 4, 209n. 6, 217n. 28, 227n. 20
Florinsky, Michael T., 212n. 9
Flory, Judge, 190
Foch, Ferdinand, 43, 44, 83, 120
Foch Line, 83
Footman, David, 243n. 12
France, 36, 37, 38, 39, 40, 41, 42, 43, 44, 45, 49, 50, 53, 56, 60, 83, 105, 116, 169, 185, 190–4
Franco-Polish Military Mission, 37, 38, 39, 40, 41
Franko, Ivan, 14
French army, 10, 37, 42, 45, 46, 185, 189, 193; High Command, 37; 156th Division, 45; Foreign Legion, 189; ———, First Regiment, 36; ———, 363d Infantry Regiment, 189
Freydenberg, Henri, 192–3
Frinovskii (Soviet officer), 183
Frolov, Mykhailo, 107
Fuller, J. F. C., 239n. 1, 239n. 3, 240n. 11, 240n. 12, 240n. 13, 240n. 15, 240n. 16
Fürstenberg-Hanecki, Jakub, 161
Fylonovych, V., 209n. 7, 211n. 2, 212n. 12, 213n. 21, 214n. 22, 214n. 25, 245n. 1

Galan, Volodymyr, 224n. 23
Galichina, Bukovina, Ugorskaia Rus' (Petliura, ed.), 16
Galicia, 14, 30, 42, 44, 46, 47, 48, 49, 50, 52, 55, 68, 69, 82, 83, 98, 111, 126, 135, 142–3, 199; Eastern, 5, 10, 36, 41, 49, 51, 52, 54, 55, 56, 59, 61, 68, 69, 70, 76, 78, 79, 82, 119, 138, 141–5, 148, 150, 151, 153, 173, 197; Western, 82
Garlicki, Andrzej, 215n. 2, 215n. 6
Gąsiorowska-Grabowska, Natalia, 222n. 11, 226n. 20, 227n. 2, 230n. 9, 236n. 31, 240n. 16, 240n. 2, 243n. 9
Gąsiorowski, Wacław, 215n. 6, 218n. 1, 218n. 3, 218n. 5
Gazeta Warszawska (Warsaw), 77
Geneva, 185
German army, 2, 6, 7, 9, 10, 20, 34, 36, 37, 41, 46, 81, 93, 94, 133, 196, 197; Oberkommando-Ostfront, 81; Heeresgruppe Kiew, 6; German Soldiers' Council, 34
Germany, 1, 5, 9, 20, 29, 33, 34, 37, 40, 43, 44, 51, 52, 58, 59, 60, 64, 67, 79, 81, 83, 88, 116, 118, 154, 160, 162, 170, 198, 201
Gerus, Oleh W., 210n. 13

Ghai (Gai), Ghaia, 124, 127, 237n. 45
Gibbons, Herbert Adams, 222n. 8
Gillie, D. R., 215n. 3, 219n. 8
Głąbiński, Stanisław, 217n. 26, 219n. 9, 229n. 20
Goldelman, Solomon I., 188, 248n. 8
Gol'denveizer, A. A., 210n. 13, 214n. 25
Golikov, Aleksandr, 116
Góra Kalwaria, 126
Górecki, Roman, 219n. 9
Gorlice, 31
Gostyńska, Weronika, 231n. 18
Gouston, Sophie, 230n. 13
GPU (secret police), 189
Grabski, Stanisław, 60, 61, 77, 137, 138, 139, 152–4, 169, 226n. 7, 226n. 8, 242n. 33, 242n. 35, 243n. 16
Grabski, Władysław, 118, 119, 134
Grajewo, 131, 144
Gratz, Gustav, 209n. 9
Great Britain, 37, 49, 50, 56, 62, 69, 116, 153, 169
Greek army, 47
Grishin-Almazov, Aleksei, 46
Groener, Wilhelm, 6
Group of Polish Socialists Abroad, 26
Grunberg, Karol, 226n. 20
Gvazava, Georgi, 186

Habsburg monarchy, 48, 197
Halahan, Mykola, 208n. 3, 237n. 41
Haller, Józef, 41, 42, 44, 45, 46, 53, 95, 125, 219n. 9, 220n. 16, 231n. 14, 233n. 12
Haller's army. *See* Polish army in France. *See under* Polish army
Haller, Stanisław, 123, 125, 135, 231n. 20
Halych, 122, 126
Hankevych, Lev, 211n. 6, 211n. 7
Hankevych, Mykola, 14

Hankey, Sir Maurice, 120
Harbin, 186
Harkavyi, Illia, 183
Havryliuk, Il'ko, 214n. 21, 246n. 1
Havryliv, H., 236n. 27
Helsinki, 186
Helsinki Conference of 1920, 64
Henning, Eugeniusz Michaelis de, 95
Herchanivs'kyi, Dmytro, 236n. 31
Hetman government, 8, 9
Hirniak, Nykyfor, 236n. 27
Hladkyi, Hryts', 236n. 31
Hlyns'kyi, Pavlo, 2
Hnatiuk, Volodymyr, 14
Holland, 37
Holovins'kyi, Iuliian, 109, 110
Hołówko, Tadeusz, 230n. 11, 233n. 9, 233n. 10, 233n. 14, 233n. 15
Holub, Andrii, 224n. 24
Holyns'kyi, Petro, 236n. 27
Horbachevs'kyi, Antin, 70
Horbuliv, 117
Horodenka, 136
Horst, Leonhard, 240n. 1
Horyn River, 59, 120, 121
Howard, Sir Esme W., 50, 54, 222n. 9, 223n. 14
Hrodna, 83, 125, 131, 134, 135
Hrubeshiv, 122, 123, 135
Hrushevs'kyi, Mykhailo, 2, 10, 17
Hrybovytsia, 148
Hryhor'iïv, Nykyfor, 46, 95, 220–1n. 19
Hulyi-Hulenko, Andrii, 108, 179
Humphrey, Grace, 215n. 1, 215n. 2, 215n. 6, 215n. 12, 216n. 13, 216n. 15, 216n. 17, 216n. 19, 216n. 21, 216n. 22, 217n. 23, 217n. 26, 238n. 54, 240n. 15
Hunczak, Taras, 248n. 12, 248n. 26
Hungary, 46, 184, 189; Hungarian army, 133; Hungarian government, 184

Husiatyn, 121, 179
Hymans, Paul, 65

Iakir, Iona, 116, 183
Iakovlev, Capt., 172, 173
Iakovliv, Andrii, 209n. 7, 248n. 12, 248n. 26
Ialtushkiv, 136
Iampil, 104, 121
Ianchenko, Mykola, 178
Ianovs'kyi, Viktor, 244n. 10, 244n. 3, 245n. 4
Ianushkevich, Nikolai N., 93
Iaruha, 41, 136
Iaryshiv, 172
Iaselda River, 145
Iezupil, 136
Imperial Bank of Russia, 89, 155, 159, 162
International Federation of League of Nations Societies, 185
International League of Invalids, 185
International League of Women for Peace and Freedom, 185
Ioffe, Adol'f, 137–41, 143–5, 147, 150–1, 153–5, 160, 161–5, 169
Ipa River, 124
Irkutsk, 24
Istanbul, 186
Italy, 37, 41, 43, 49, 50, 56, 77, 106, 169
Iudenich, Nikolai, 84
Iushkevych, O., 107
Ivanets', Ivan, 236n. 31
Ivanov (Soviet officer), 183
Ivanys, Vasyl', 209n. 11, 210n. 1, 211n. 5, 211n. 6, 213n. 16, 245n. 1, 248n. 9, 248n. 26
Ivasyshyn, Zakhar, 246n. 2
Iwanowski, Jerzy, 85, 230n. 9, 231n. 14
Iwaszkiewicz, Wacław, 84, 100
Iziaslav, 180
Izvol'skii, Aleksandr, 36

Jabłoński, Henryk, 228n. 16, 232n. 2
Jabotinsky, Vladimir, 191
Japan, 27, 28, 50, 56, 169
Jassy, 46
Jaworski, Feliks, 96
Jędrzejewicz, Janusz, 219n. 9, 230n. 11
Jędrzejewicz, Wacław, 75, 215n. 1, 215n. 2, 215n. 5, 215n. 6, 215n. 8, 215n. 11, 216n. 13, 216n. 14, 216n. 15, 216n. 17, 216n. 18, 216n. 19, 216n. 20, 216n. 22, 217n. 23, 217n. 26, 218n. 29, 232n. 26, 234n. 14, 235n. 17, 237n. 51, 238n. 57, 239n. 11, 240n. 16
Josefov, 122
Józewski, Henryk, 76
Jundziłł, Zygmunt, 227n. 20
Jusserand, Jules, 120
Juzwenko, Adolf, 229n. 3

Kakowski, Aleksander (Archbishop of Warsaw), 33
Kakurin, Nikolai E., 86, 231n. 16, 234n. 10, 239n. 1, 240n. 11
Kaledin, Aleksei, 5
Kalinowski, Józef, 232n. 28
Kalisz, 173, 175, 186
Kamianets-Litovsk, 148
Kamianets-Podilskyi: city, 8, 57, 74, 97–8, 107, 139, 142; county, 59, 96, 98
Kamieniecki, Witold, 137, 153
Kamins'kyi, Col., 68
Kaniv, 42, 44, 104
Kapkan, Iurii, 2
Kapustians'kyi, M., 223n. 16, 245n. 4
Karnachev (commissioner), 94
Karnicki, Aleksander, 85, 86
Katelbach, Tadeusz, 227n. 20
Katerynodar, 13, 14
Kaunas, 62, 63, 64, 65, 81, 82, 83

Kauzik, Stanisław, 161, 164
Kawalec, Tadeusz, 220n. 17, 221n. 20
Kawalkowski, Aleksander, 229n. 2
Kedrovs'kyi, Volodymyr, 208n. 3, 213n. 17, 213n. 21, 245n. 1
Kedryn, Iwan, 241n. 9, 245n. 1
Kerensky, Aleksandr, 3, 4, 18, 19, 212n. 9, 213n. 18, 213n. 19
Kernan, Francis J., 50
Kessler, Count Harry, 33
Keyes, Gen., 80
Kharkiv: city, 12, 23; gubernia, 13
Kharkiv University, 23
Kherson, 46
Kholm (Chełm): city, 122, 127, 131, 135; region, 5, 8, 41, 56, 79
Khrystiuk, Pavlo, 208n. 2, 208n. 4, 209n. 9, 209n. 11, 209n. 12, 214n. 21, 214n. 25, 221n. 3
Khust, 41
Khvostov, A. A., 93
Kielce, 31
Kiernik, Władysław, 137, 154, 155
Kiev. See Kyiv
Kievskaia starina (Kyiv), 15
Kin, D. See Plotkin, David
Kirensk, 24
Kirov, Sergei, 137
Kish, Col., 54
Klodnyts'kyi, Vasyl', 236n. 31
Kmeta, Arkhyp, 213n. 21
Knittel, R., 108
Knoll, Roman, 50, 51, 68
Kobeliaky county, 12
Kolchak, Aleksander, 84, 85
Kołłątaj, Hugo, 60
Kollard, Iurii, 211n. 2
Kolno, 131
Komarnicki, Titus, 219n. 9, 227n. 20, 228n. 17, 232n. 24, 232n. 26, 237n. 52, 242n. 36
Kon, Feliks, 128
Konovalets', Evhen, 106, 111

Konovalov, S., 232n. 24, 232n. 26
Kopaihorod, 173
Korbel, Josef, 226n. 20, 231n. 24, 232n. 26, 240n. 15
Korbut, Sydir, 246n. 2
Korets, 180, 181
Kork, Avgust, 115
Kornilov, Lavr, 44
Koroliv-Staryi, V., 210n. 1, 211n. 2, 211n. 6, 212n. 15, 214n. 24
Korosten, 21, 117, 122, 180, 181, 183
Korsh, Fedor, 16
Korwin-Sokołowski, Adam Ludwik, 234n. 8, 235n. 24
Koshyts', Oleksander, 185
Kossak, Sophia, 233n. 15, 233n. 16
Kossakowski, Michał Stanisław, 87
Kossowski, Michał Stanisław, 90
Kostiukivka, 31
Kostopil region, 179
Kosyk, Volodymyr, 245n. 1
Kotovs'kyi, Hryhorii, 104, 172, 176, 180, 182, 183
Kotsiubyns'kyi, Iurii, 161, 169
Kovalevs'kyi, Mykola, 209n. 11, 221n. 1
Kovel, 44, 135, 179
Kowalski, Włodzimierz T., 219n. 9, 222n. 9
Kozelets, 117
Koziatyn, 100, 101, 116, 117
Kozlovs'kyi, H., 212n. 12
Koz'ma, I. K., 245n. 4
Kozova, 68
Krajowski, Franciszek, 107, 108, 135
Kraków. See Cracow
Krasin, Leonid, 163, 164
Krasnystaw, 122, 123
Kraus, Antin, 122
Kremianets, 13, 71
Kremianets Hills, 70
Krezub, A. See Dumin, Osyp

Krivoshein, Aleksandr V., 93
Kryzhopil, 104
Krzyżanowski, Adam, 231n. 20
Kuban, 8, 13, 44, 95, 99, 134
Kubijovyč, Volodymyr, 221n. 1, 223n. 17, 228n. 11
Kuchabs'kyi, Vasyl', 236n. 31
Kucharzewski, Jan, 33
Kukiel, Marian, 217n. 28, 219n. 8, 223n. 11, 227n. 20, 230n. 9, 231n. 20, 234n. 2, 238n. 56, 239n. 11, 240n. 15
Kukułka, Józef, 219n. 11, 221n. 20, 230n. 9
Kuliński, Mieczysław, 137, 152
Kun, Béla, 184
Kurakh, Mykhailo, 235n. 21, 236n. 31
Kurcjusz, T., 237n. 35, 237n. 49, 237n. 51
Kurdynovs'kyi, Borys, 67
Kurovs'kyi (partisan leader), 112, 116
Kushch, Viktor, 186, 243n. 1
Kutrzeba, Tadeusz, 87, 103, 105, 117, 123, 222n. 3, 227n. 4, 228n. 9, 228n. 11, 228n. 18, 231n. 18, 231n. 20, 232n. 26, 233n. 2, 234n. 11, 234n. 12, 234n. 14, 235n. 15, 235n. 18, 235n. 24, 237n. 41, 237n. 50, 237n. 51, 238n. 60, 238n. 61, 240n. 16
Kutyłowski, Bohdan, 78, 85
Kuzelia, Zenon, 223n. 17
Kviring, Emmanuel, 161, 165
Kwiatka, Józef, 28
Kyiv: city, 2, 3, 4, 5, 8, 9, 10, 11, 12, 13, 14, 15, 18, 19, 20, 21, 22, 27, 42, 48, 56, 57, 62, 77, 99, 100, 101, 102, 103, 104, 105, 107, 110, 112, 114, 116, 117, 122, 140, 177, 180, 181, 186, 187, 188, 192, 199; gubernia, 15, 92, 93; region, 56

Kyiv Gubernial Zemstvo, 21
Ładoś, Aleksander, 137, 139, 150, 153, 161, 241n. 8, 241n. 25, 242n. 34, 242n. 35, 242n. 1, 242n. 5, 242n. 7, 243n. 13, 243n. 15
La Mandria di Chivasso, 41
Łańcut, 106
Landau, Rom, 216n. 17, 216n. 18, 216n. 19, 216n. 20, 217n. 23, 217n. 26
Lansing, Robert, 222n. 7
La Revue de Prométhée (Paris), 186
Lasocki, Zygmunt, 82
Latvia, 63, 64, 70, 81, 87, 88, 118, 137, 139, 154, 157; Latvian army, 88; Latvian government, 139, 169
Lausanne, 37
Laval, 37
Lavrov, Petr, 24
Lawton, Lancelot, 243n. 12
Lazurenko, Stepan, 208n. 3, 209n. 7, 214n. 25
League of Nations, 65, 185, 186
Lechowicz, Edward, 161
Lector, 238n. 59
Le Havre, 42
Leinwand, Artur, 225n. 4, 230n. 9, 238n. 57
Leipzig, 44
Lemakhiv, 100
Lemberg. *See* Lviv.
Lemko region, 82
Lenin, Vladimir Illich, 4, 62, 87, 88, 90, 114, 137, 144, 145, 155, 170, 241n. 21, 241n. 23
Leonivka, 180, 181, 182
Le petit parisien (Paris), 90
Leslay, 37
Levyns'kyi, Volodymyr, 14, 211n. 6, 211n. 7
Levyts'kyi, Dmytro, 48
Levyts'kyi, Kost', 141, 142, 151

Levyts'kyi, Osyp, 223n. 16, 224n.
24, 224n. 26, 225n. 30
Lewandowski, Józef, 227n. 2, 227n.
3, 227n. 5, 228n. 6, 228n. 7,
228n. 8, 228n. 11, 228n. 14,
229n. 19, 231n. 20, 232n. 29,
232n. 2
Lewiński, Zbigniew, 234n. 2, 234n.
12
Liatychiv: county, 94; town, 136,
180
Liberec, 122
Lida, 135, 154
Liepāja, 157, 160
Ligocki, Edward, 218n. 3, 218n. 5,
218n. 6, 219n. 8, 219n. 9, 220n.
16, 222n. 11
Lille, 37
Lipiński, Wacław, 215n. 1, 215n. 8,
216n. 13, 217n. 26, 217n. 27,
218n. 1, 218n. 2, 218n. 3, 218n.
4, 218n. 5, 218n. 6, 219n. 7,
219n. 8, 219n. 9, 220n. 16, 220n.
17, 221n. 20
Listowski, Antoni, 84, 100, 107, 115
Literaturno-naukovyi vistnyk (Lviv,
later Kyiv), 14, 15
Lithuania, 23, 24, 27, 35, 59, 60, 61,
63, 64, 65, 66, 70, 78, 79, 81, 83,
84, 86, 118, 119, 134, 138, 141,
148, 152, 153, 154, 155, 165,
198; Government of Central
Lithuania, 65; Grand Duchy of,
62, 64, 83; Lithuanian army, 125;
Lithuanian Socialist Soviet
Republic, 81, 148; Socialist
Soviet Republic of Lithuania and
Belarus, 81
Litvinov (Soviet officer), 183
Lityn: county, 94, 96, 109; town,
136, 173
Liubar, 180
Liuboml, 148
Livshits (Soviet officer), 183

Livyts'ka-Kholodna, Nataliia, 209n.
7, 210n. 1, 246n. 2
Livyts'kyi, Andrii, 70, 98, 138, 184,
199
Lloyd George, David, 42, 44, 53, 55,
56, 220n. 15, 223n. 13, 223n. 18,
224n. 22
Łódź, 26, 28, 44
Lokański, Henryk, 218n. 6
Łomża, 131
London, 26, 27, 29, 37, 69, 118, 119
Longhena, Romei, 50
Lord, Robert Howard, 50
Lorenz, J., 137, 150
Lotots'kyi, Oleksander, 16, 211n. 2,
212n. 10, 212n. 13, 216n. 14
Lozyns'kyi, Mykhailo, 222n. 9,
223n. 11, 223n. 16, 223n. 19,
225n. 30
Lubartów, 130
Lublin, 27, 34, 126, 130, 131
Lubomirski, Prince Zdzisław, 33
Łukasiewicz, Juljusz, 229n. 3
Luninets, 154
Lutosławski, Wincenty, 222n. 6
Lutsk, 87, 106, 111, 135
Lviv, 13, 14, 15, 27, 43, 46, 48, 50,
52, 68, 121, 122, 126, 127, 130,
132, 138, 142, 179, 197
Lviv University, 13
Lyon, 37
Lypa, Iurii, 209n. 7, 213n. 21
Lypnyts'kyi, Iuliian, 68
Lypovets, 104
Lysenko, Mykola, 13
Lytvynivka, 102

Machalski, Tadeusz, 234n. 14, 237n.
51
Machray, Robert, 215n. 1, 216n. 13,
216n. 14, 216n. 15, 216n. 17,
217n. 23, 217n. 25, 217n. 26,
217n. 28, 220n. 16, 232n. 24,
232n. 26, 238n. 57

Mackiewicz, Stanisław, 215n. 1, 215n. 5
Mackinder, Mr., 80
Mahileu, 18
Mai-Maevskii, Vladimir, 85
Mainz, 44
Majewski, Lieut., 182
Majstrenko, Iwan, 209n. 11
Makarenko, Andrii, 10
Makarenko, Oleksander, 2
Makarenko, Pavlo, 2
Makarushka, Liubomyr, 224n. 23
Makhno, Nestor, 84, 111, 176, 220–1n. 19
Mala Divytsia, 15
Maladzechna, 83, 84, 115, 124
Malam, Ia. D., 13
Mali Minky, 182
Malyn, 117, 122, 180
Manchuria, 28
Mans, 37
Manuïl's'kyi, Dmytro, 126, 137, 143, 144, 160, 170, 239n. 2, 243n. 18
Marchlewski, Julian, 87, 128, 132, 237n. 46, 239n. 10, 240n. 12, 242n. 34
Margolin, Arnold D., 188, 210n. 13, 214n. 25, 222n. 11, 225n. 31, 246n. 5, 248n. 10, 248n. 12, 248n. 26
Margulies, Vladimir, 221n. 20
Martos, B., 208n. 3, 208n. 4
Martynets', Hnat, 224n. 23
Marushchenko-Bohdanivs'kyi, A., 209n. 7, 243n. 2, 244n. 10, 245n. 4
Marx, Karl, 24
Maslivets', Hr., 244n. 4
Matkowski, Karol, 217n. 28
Matsiievych, Kost', 67, 214n. 25
Matuszewski, Ignacy, 68, 161, 162
Mayenne, 37
Mazepa, Isaak, 98, 107, 209n. 11, 210n. 1, 212n. 8, 214n. 25, 221n. 3, 224n. 24, 225n. 31, 228n. 11, 228n. 14, 230n. 9, 231n. 20, 233n. 19, 233n. 21, 234n. 4, 235n. 21, 235n. 22, 235n. 24, 235n. 26, 237n. 37, 237n. 41, 238n. 58
Mazurkiewicz, Bronisław, 26
Meierovics, Zigfrids, 139
Meijer, Jan M., 234n. 5
Melikov, V. A., 234n. 10, 239n. 1, 240n. 11
Merlot, A., 218n. 2, 218n. 4
Mezheninov, Sergei, 100
Miaskivka, 104, 121
Michelotti, Gigi, 222n. 9
Mieczkowski, Adam, 137
Międziński, Bogusław, 232n. 1
Mikhailovskii, Nikolai, 24
Mikhnovs'kyi, Mykola, 2
Mikulicz, Sergiusz, 246n. 1
Militant Organization (Organizacja Bojowa), 29, 30
Miller, David Hunter, 219n. 12, 220n. 16, 222n. 10, 223n. 12, 229n. 4
Minkiewicz, Antoni, 98
Minsk: city, 17, 59, 61, 62, 63, 81, 84, 115, 125, 128, 129, 132, 134, 135, 137, 139, 144, 153, 154, 155, 169; gubernia, 59, 71
Mława, 127, 131
Modelski, Izydor, 219n. 9, 220n. 16, 220n. 17, 223n. 11
Modlin, 125, 126, 129, 130, 131
Mohyla, Stepan. *See* Petliura, Symon
Mohyliv-Podilskyi, 41, 107, 136, 172
Mokra, 94
Molenda, Jan, 216n. 22
Montagna, Giulio-Cesare, 50
Moraczewski, Jędrzej, 34, 35
Mordalevych (partisan leader), 176
Moscow: city, 14, 15, 16, 20, 21, 42, 62, 70, 84, 85, 86, 87, 89, 90,

102, 109, 128, 129, 140, 144, 151, 154, 162, 163, 167, 189, 191, 192, 201; gubernia, 145
Moshchanytsia, 180
Mozyr, 124
Mshanets'kyi, Petro, 70
Mstyslav (Patriarch of the Ukrainian Autocephalous Orthodox Church), 12, 210n. 1, 211n. 2
Mumm, Philip, 21
Muravev, Mikhail, 5, 20
Murmansk, 42, 44
Murtazin, M., 104
Mykhailiv, Leonid, 70
Mykhailova, Liubov, 211n. 2, 244n. 4, 245n. 1
Mykhalevych, Afanasii, 24
Mykolaiv, 46, 106
Mykytka, Osyp, 109
Myshuha, Luka, 141, 223n. 16, 224n. 24, 225n. 26
Myśl Polska (Warsaw), 186

Napoleon I (Emperor of France), 77
Narew River, 125, 127
Narodna Wola (Narodnaia Volia), 23
Naruszewicz (Polish officer), 96
Nasielsk, 131
National Cossack Council, 177, 178
Naumenko, Iurii, 235n. 25, 238n. 58, 243n. 1
Nazaruk, Osyp, 141, 143, 210n. 12, 210n. 13, 214n. 25, 223n. 16, 241n. 15, 241n. 16, 241n. 28, 241n. 31
Nel'hovs'kyi, Gen., 181
Neman River, 99, 123, 124, 133, 134, 135, 148, 200
Netreba, 179
New York, 40
Nezvyska, 68
Niagara Fort, N.Y., 40
Niagara-on-the-Lake, Ont., 40
Niasvizh region, 158

Nice, 37
Nicholas, Grand Duke, 32
Nieniewski, A., 51
Niessel, Henri Albert, 50
Nimylovych, Osyp, 236n. 27
Nitti, Francesco, 49, 56, 221n. 2, 224n. 22
Nizhyn region, 104
Noulens, Joseph, 50
Nova Chortoryia, 111
Novakivs'kyi, Mykhailo, 70
Nova Ushytsia, 136
Novo-Aleksandriia. *See* Puławy.
Novohrad-Volynskyi, 180
Novokostiantyniv, 142
Novorossiisk, 45
Nyzhniv, 68, 136

Obolenskii, Leonid, 137, 161
Ocetkiewicz, Capt., 98
Ochmański, Jerzy, 229n. 3
Odessa: city, 11, 45, 46, 47, 56, 57, 58, 101, 107, 110, 191; region, 10, 46, 110
Ogiński Canal, 145
Ohiienko, Ivan, 98, 233n. 19, 233n. 20
Okulicz, Kazimierz, 226n. 20
Olesiiuk, T., 212n. 15
Olesko, 181
Olszański, Prochor N., 239n. 5, 242n. 5, 243n. 15
Omelianovych-Pavlenko, Ivan, 108, 171
Omelianovych-Pavlenko, Mykhailo, 58, 100, 102, 108, 110, 111, 123, 126, 136, 138, 142, 225n. 27, 227n. 3
Onats'kyi, Ievhen, 248n. 12
Onyshchuk, Denys, 236n. 27
Oplustill, Zdzisław, 219n. 9, 220n. 18, 221n. 20
Ordon, W., 234n. 2, 236n. 32
Oriental Institute, 186

Oriental Youth Circle, 186
Orłowski, Xawery, 233n. 19
Orsha, 90
Orzel, Laurence J., 222n. 9, 224n. 23
Ostapowicz, Gustaw, 46
Oster, 117
Ostrih: county, 180; town, 94
Ostrów Mazowiecki, 127
Ostrowski, Józef, 33
Otchiai, K. M., 50
Otmarshtain, Iurii, 178, 181
Otynia, 47
Ovruch, 120

Padalka, Mykola, 213n. 21
Padalka, Vasyl', 245n. 4
Paderewski, Ignacy, 34, 35, 37, 39, 43, 44, 46, 50, 54, 55, 62, 67, 68, 82, 229n. 5
Palii-Sydorians'kyi, Mykhailo, 178, 180, 245n. 4
Paliïv, Dmytro, 225n. 30, 225n. 31
Palij, Michael, 209n. 11, 221n. 20
Paneiko, Vasyl', 14
Paris, 26, 33, 34, 35, 36, 37, 38, 39, 42, 45, 51, 52, 53, 55, 65, 69, 78, 82, 169, 185–6, 189–91, 193, 201
Paris Peace Conference, 34, 35, 46, 52, 53, 67, 69, 82, 83, 143; Botha Commission (Inter-Allied Commission), 52, 53; Commission on Polish Affairs, 43, 50, 52; Council of Four, 55; Inter-Allied Commission in Poland, 46, 54; Polish Ukrainian Armistice Committee, 54; Secretariat-General, 46; Supreme Council, 42, 43, 50, 52, 53, 55, 56, 82, 83, 118–9, 143
Paszkiewicz, G., 230n. 9
Patek, Stanisław, 55, 88, 89, 90
Patterson, Eric J., 215n. 2, 216n. 13, 216n. 14, 216n. 17, 216n. 22, 217n. 23, 217n. 26
Pauka, I., 183
Pavlenko, Viktor, 19
Pavlenky, 12
Pavliuk, Klym, 68
Peace Treaty of Andrusovo, 60
Peace Treaty of Riga, 56, 60, 61, 140, 161–70, 175, 201, 202
Peace Treaty of Versailles, 34, 49, 50, 80, 83, 118
Peace Treaty of Warsaw, 66, 67–79, 100, 105, 109, 112, 137, 138, 140, 153, 169, 199, 201, 202
Pekarchuk, Kharytyna, 244n. 10
Peremykin, I., 171, 173
Petliura, Fedir, 12
Petliura, Ivan, 12
Petliura, Larysa, 15, 185
Petliura, Mariianna, 12
Petliura, Maryna, 12
Petliura, Oleksander, 12, 190, 210n. 1
Petliura, Ol'ha (mother, née Marchenko), 12
Petliura, Ol'ha (wife, née Bil's'ka), 15, 185, 190
Petliura, Symon (pseud. Mohyla, Stepan; Tagon, Sviatoslav), 228n. 15, 235n. 21; as head of state, 66, 67–70, 75–7, 99, 138–40, 142, 153, 198, 199; as commander in chief of the UNR Army, 11, 22, 56, 57, 58, 70, 102, 105, 110–1, 113, 220n. 19, 246–7n. 6; assassination of, 187–95, 201; early years, 12–7; early revolutionary activity, 17–8, 19–22; in exile, 177, 184–7, 194, 201; in the UNR Directory, 10, 11, 22, 57, 198; in the Central Rada, 18, 19; policy toward Jews, 188, 191–4, 246–7n. 6; relations with Poland, 97, 101, 106, 138, 140, 199, 201

Petliura, Teodosiia, 12
Petliura, Vasyl' (father), 12
Petrenko, 244n. 4
Petriv, Vsevolod, 209n. 7
Petrograd. *See* St. Petersburg
Petrushevych, Evhen, 57, 68, 141, 142
Peyere, Magistrate, 188, 191
Piast Party, 119–20
Piątkowski, Henryk, 239n. 1
Pidhaitsi, 136
Pigido, F., 248n. 26
Piłsudska, Alexandra, 216n. 18, 216n. 19, 216n. 20, 216n. 22, 217n. 23, 217n. 26, 226n. 13, 226n. 17
Piłsudski, Bronisław (brother), 24
Piłsudski, Józef, 215n. 3, 215n. 5, 215n. 6, 215n. 7, 215n. 8, 215n. 9, 215n. 11, 215n. 13, 216n. 13, 216n. 15, 216n. 16, 216n. 17, 216n. 18, 216n. 19, 216n. 20, 216–7n. 22, 217n. 23, 217n. 26, 219n. 8, 220n. 16, 226n. 14, 226n. 19, 227n. 2, 229n. 5, 229n. 6, 234n. 3, 235n. 16, 238n. 1, 240n. 16; as leader of Polish army and state, 34–5, 44, 46, 52, 53, 54, 59, 64, 78–9, 80, 82, 90–1, 108; as leader of the PPS, 29, 59, 152, 198; early revolutionary activity, 26–33, 40, 51, 93; early years, 23–6; policy regarding Lithuania and Belarus, 81–3; policy toward the East, 59, 60, 61–6, 67, 77, 78, 139, 152, 153, 160, 198, 201, 226n. 16; relations with UNR, 68–9, 76, 91, 97, 101, 104–5, 113, 138, 140, 175, 179, 199, 201, 226n. 16; retirement from political life, 175, 184, 201; return to power in 1926, 175, 187, 201; war with Soviet Russia, 80–3, 84–90, 99–100, 114, 116–20, 125, 129–31, 134–5, 200
Pinsk, 32, 59
Pisarev, Dmitrii, 24
Pishcha, 148
Piszczkowski, Tadeusz, 223n. 11, 237n. 39
Pliska, Stanley, 217n. 26, 218n. 5, 218n. 6, 219n. 9, 220n. 16
Płock, 131
Płomieńczyk, Adam, 241n. 6
Plotkin, David (pseud. Kin, D.), 208n. 5
Pobóg-Malinowski, W., 215n. 1, 216n. 17, 216n. 18, 229n. 3, 231n. 14, 241n. 25
Poděbrady, 175
Podillia, 46, 94, 97, 98, 100, 102, 107; gubernia, 59, 92, 93, 94, 189
Podlachia, 79
Poincaré, Raymond, 37, 40
Poker, Jim, 218n. 3, 220n. 16
Polatsk, 84, 124
Poliakov, I. A., 208n. 5
Polish army, 45, 47, 55–6, 68, 72–4, 80, 81, 87, 88, 96, 97, 98, 100–5, 106, 108, 110–22, 124–7, 129–32, 134–6, 144, 145, 148, 155, 158, 179, 185, 200, 201; Supreme Command, 72–5, 104, 105, 120, 134, 155, 161; First Army, 115, 124, 126, 130–1, 134; Second Army, 100, 107, 115, 121, 126, 134–5; Third Army, 100–1, 103, 107, 109, 115, 116, 117, 120, 122, 126, 130–1, 135; Fourth Army, 115, 124, 126, 130–1, 134–5; Fifth Army, 125, 126, 130–1, 134; Sixth Army, 100–1, 103, 109, 112, 115, 116, 120, 121, 122, 126, 135; Haller's army, 53, 54, 83, 84; Polish Second Corps, 41, 94; Polish Third Corps, 94, 95, 96; Second Division, 124; Seventh Division,

97; Tenth Division, 131; Twelfth Division, 112; Eighteenth Division, 107; Polish Fourth Division, 53 (*see also under* Russian Volunteer Army); First Legionary Infantry Division, 129; Second Legionary Infantry Division, 123; Third Legionary Infantry Division, 129; Eighth Infantry Division, 121; Thirteenth Infantry Division, 116; Lithuanian-Belarusian Division, 65; First Legionary Infantry Brigade, 103; Second Brigade, 95; First Light Cavalry Regiment, 103; S. Haller's Polish Army Group, 123, 135; Polesie Group, 115, 120, 124; Romer's Cavalry Group, 115, 120; Irregular Light-Cavalry Squadron, 96. *See also* Polish army in France; Polish Legion
Polish army in France, 37, 38–9, 40, 41, 42, 43, 44; Polish First Division, 42, 44; ———, First Regiment of Polish Riflemen, 42
Polish Central Committee of Safety, 39; National Division, 39
Polish Committee General (Switzerland), 39
Polish Communist party, 127
Polish government, 73–5, 88, 102, 113, 118, 128, 137–9, 153, 163, 167, 169, 184, 198, 201; Ministry of Foreign Affairs, 50–1; ———, Foreign Affairs Committee, 70, 77; Ministry of Military Affairs, 74, 106; State Defence Council, 118, 119, 128
Polish Insurrection of 1863–4, 31
Polish Legion, 31, 33, 36, 40; First Brigade, 31, 32
Polish-Lithuanian Commonwealth, 63, 64

Polish Military Board, 42, 44
Polish Military Mission in Ukraine, 46
Polish Military Organization (POW), 31, 33
Polish National Committee (Lausanne), 37
Polish National Committee (Paris), 35, 38, 39, 41, 42, 78; Polish Interparty Council, 42; ———, Executive Committee, 42
Polish National Committee (Rome), 41
Polish National Council (Brazil), 40; Central Committee, 40
Polish National Democratic party, 28, 29, 32, 35, 37, 59, 60, 62, 77, 78, 105, 152, 178, 198, 199
Polish Provisional Council of State, 32, 33; Military Commission, 33
Polish Regency Council, 33, 34
Polish Sejm, 35, 55, 65, 105, 118, 137–9, 152, 160, 161
Polish Socialist Party (PPS), 26, 27, 28, 29, 30, 59, 120, 152, 198; Central Committee, 26, 27; "Lithuanian Section," 26; PPS-Left Wing, 29; PPS-Revolutionary Faction, 29
Polish State Bank, 162
Polissia, 84, 124, 125, 165, 181; Southern, 122; Western, 56
Polonne, 94
Poltava: city, 8, 12, 13; gubernia, 12, 13, 15, 19, 93
Poltava, Leonid, 210–1n. 1, 244n. 10, 245n. 4
Poltava Theological Seminary, 12
Poniatenko, Prokip, 70
Porsh, Mykola, 211n. 5, 211n. 6, 211n. 7, 212n. 8
Potigny-Ussy, 37
Potocki, Count Józef, 96
Povolozky, J., 210n. 13

Poznań: city, 34, 43, 52; region, 130
Poznański, Karol, 242n. 35, 242n. 5, 243n. 10, 243n. 11
Prague, 175, 186
Pratsia (Lviv), 13
Pravda (Moscow), 114
Primakov, Vitalii, 172, 183
Principal Allied and Associated Powers, 50, 55, 56, 80. *See also* Entente
Próchniak, Edward, 128
Prokhoda, Vasyl', 210n. 12, 210n. 13, 212n. 12, 213n. 16, 213n. 21, 214n. 25, 227n. 5
Prokopovych, V'iacheslav, 67, 184, 185, 246n. 1
Promethean League, 186–7
Prométhée (Paris), 186
Proskuriv: city, 96, 142, 180; county, 59
Provisional Commission of Confederated Independence Parties, 30
Provisional Revolutionary Committee of Poland, 128
Prussia, 52; East, 52, 81, 126, 131, 132; West, 43
Pruszyński, Mieczysław, 218n. 1, 231n. 14
Pryluky, 15
Prypiat River, 71, 100, 104, 116, 117, 120, 124, 129, 135, 200
Przedświt (London), 26
Przybylski, Adam, 218n. 28, 229n. 9, 231n. 20, 234n. 2, 234n. 14, 237n. 51, 238n. 57, 238n. 1, 240n. 11, 240n. 16, 240n. 17
Ptsich River, 84
Ptych River, 124
Puchalski, Stanisław, 31
Puławy, 12, 130
Putnyk-Hrebeniuk, Demian, 2
Pylypchuk, Pylyp, 68, 69, 184

Quintin, 37

Rada (Kyiv), 14
Radcliffe, Sir Percy, 120
Radomyshl, 100, 117, 122
Radziwiłł, Leon, 41
Radzymin, 130, 131
Rafes, Moisei, 188, 222n. 3
Rakovskii, Khristian, 140, 142, 163
Rarancha, 41
Raszewski, Kazimierz, 121
Ratne, 135
Rawita-Gawroński, Franciszek, 232n. 2
Red Army, 11, 56, 57, 66, 81, 82, 83, 84, 86–8, 90, 99, 100, 102–5, 107, 109–18, 121–2, 124–36, 145, 148, 151, 158, 171–2, 176, 180–3, 188–9, 192, 197, 198, 199, 200, 201; Supreme Command, 130–2, 134, 200; Third Army, 124–5, 127, 130–1, 134–5; Fourth Army, 124–5, 127, 131–2, 134; Sixth Army, 176; Twelfth Army, 100–4, 109, 116, 117, 120, 124, 126–7, 130, 135; Fourteenth Army, 100–4, 121, 124, 126–7, 130, 135–6; Fifteenth Army, 115, 124–5, 127, 130–1, 134–5; Sixteenth Army, 115, 124–5, 127, 130–1, 134–5; Army of the Southwestern Front, 127; Budennyi's First (Red) Cavalry Army, 115–7, 120–2, 124, 126–7, 135; Russian Second Guard Corps, 4; Third Cavalry Corps, 124–5, 127, 131–2; Sixth Division, 180; Seventh Division, 176; Twenty-fifth Division, 104; Fifty-First Division, 180; Eighth Cavalry Division (Red Cossack Cavalry Corps), 172, 183; Kotovs'kyi's Cavalry Division, 104, 172, 180–2; Forty-First

Infantry Division, 172; Bashkir Cavalry Brigade, 104, 172; Golikov's Strike Group, 116; Mozyr Group, 124, 126–7, 130–1; Northern Group, 115
Reddaway, W. F., 238n. 57
Rembolovych, Ivan, 245n. 4
Reshetar, John S., Jr., 209n. 11, 211n. 1, 221n. 20, 222n. 3, 222n. 9, 224n. 24, 228n. 11, 228n. 14
Revolutionary Ukrainian party (RUP), 13, 14
Revyuk, Emil, 223n. 17
Reynaudel, Pierre, 190, 194
Riflemen's Union (Union of Active Struggle), 30, 31
Riga, 32, 137, 138, 139, 140, 141, 142, 143, 152, 153, 155, 161, 163, 201
Riga Peace Conference of 1920, 143; General Commission, 147, 150; Polish Railway Subcommission, 163
Rio de Janeiro, 40
Rivne: city, 106, 111, 121, 135, 154, 179; county, 71, 179
Robotnik (Vilnius), 26, 27
Rohatyns'kyi, I., 224n. 23
Rohoznyi, Hryts', 244n. 1, 244n. 4
Romania, 46, 47, 57, 77, 109, 148, 172, 179, 189
Romanów-Głowacki, 238n. 60
Rome, 37, 41
Romer, Jan, 100, 101, 115
Romer, Michał, 64
Roos, Hans, 220n. 16, 222n. 11
Ros River, 112, 116
Roska River, 112, 116
Rosolivtsi, 96
Rossiia insurance society, 15
Rozdilna, 180
Rozwadowski, Jan, 226n. 20
Rozwadowski, Tadeusz, 68, 120, 125

Różycki, Tadeusz, 238n. 60
Rudnia, 148
Rudnytsia, 102
Rudychiv, Ivan, 210n. 1, 211n. 2
Rumbold, Sir Horace George, 80, 84, 89
Rummel, Col. von, 96
Russian army (Imperial), 2, 3, 6, 17, 18, 20, 28, 31, 32, 37, 68, 93, 94, 105, 133, 171, 196; Supreme Command, 18, 19; Fifth Army, 96; Ninth Army, 41, 94; First Ukrainian Regiment, 2; Second Military School, 19
Russian army (Soviet). *See* Red Army
Russian Communist party: Central Committee, 102, 114; Ninth All-Russian Conference, 127
Russian government (Imperial): Council of Ministers, 93; Ministry of War, 17
Russian government (Soviet), 88, 138, 141, 144, 151, 153, 160, 169; Council of People's Commissars, 86, 155; Supreme Central (All-Russian) Executive Committee, 147, 151; War Council, 90
Russian Imperial State Bank. *See* Imperial Bank of Russia
Russian Military Mission, 189
Russian Political Conference of 1919 (Paris), 82
Russian Political Liberation Committee, 172
Russian Provisional Government, 2, 3, 4, 7, 18, 19, 33, 36, 37, 85, 114; Russian Constituent Assembly, 85
Russian Revolution of 1905, 1, 13, 14, 29
Russian Revolution of 1917, 1, 16, 17, 36, 59, 61, 78, 92, 196, 201;

March (February) Revolution, 1, 17, 36; November (October) Revolution, 4
Russian State Duma: First, 14; Second, 15
Russian Volunteer Army, 8, 10, 44, 45, 46, 47, 56, 57, 58, 66, 69, 78, 79, 80, 84–6, 95, 97, 99, 105, 107, 116, 133, 134, 188, 192, 197, 198, 199; High Command, 45; Third Corps, 46; Polish Fourth Division, 44, 45, 46, 47, 95 (*see also under* Polish army)
Russo-Japanese War, 27, 28, 29
Rybak, Col., 100
Rybnytsia, 102
Rydz-Śmigły, Edward, 88, 100, 107, 116, 121, 122, 134
Rzhepets'kyi, Borys, 70, 226n. 16

Sabaliunas, Leonas, 215n. 2
Sadovs'kyi, V., 211n. 6, 211n. 7, 212n. 8, 212n. 10
Sahaidachnyi, Petro, 228n. 15
Saint Petersburg, 4, 14, 15, 19, 24, 26, 50, 89, 162
Sakhalin Island, 24
Salikovs'kyi, Oleksander, 15, 212n. 15
Salonika, 45
Sals'skyi, Volodymyr, 108, 234n. 2, 235n. 24, 243n. 1
Samchuk, Hryhir, 245n. 4
Samhorodok, 116
Samutyn, Petro, 234n. 14, 235n. 22
Santa Maria (Italy), 41
Sapieha, Prince Eustachy, 118, 120, 138, 139, 152, 163
Saratov (ship), 45
Sarny, 121, 154
Savchenko, V. P., 239n. 1, 240n. 11, 240n. 16, 240n. 17, 243n. 1
Savinkov, Boris, 172
Savoika, Liubomyr, 222n. 11

Schulder, Richard, 209n. 9
Schwartzbard, Samuel, 187–91, 193–5, 201
Selianyn (Lviv), 13
Senn, Alfred E., 226n. 18
Serbia, 30
Seret River, 121
Sergeev, Evgenii, 115
Shamanek, Alfred, 58
Shandruk, Pavlo, 221n. 20, 224n. 23, 224n. 26, 225n. 27, 225n. 31, 227n. 1, 233n. 22, 234n. 2, 235n. 24, 235n. 26, 237n. 51, 240n. 17, 243n. 1, 244n. 4, 244n. 7, 244n. 4, 245n. 1, 248n. 26
Shankovs'kyi, Lev, 234n. 2, 235n. 26, 237n. 37
Shaparovych, Edmund, 108
Shapiro, Leonard, 242n. 38, 243n. 9, 244n. 5
Shapoval, Mykola, 190, 192
Shapoval, Mykyta, 210n. 13, 214n. 25
Shapoval, Oleksander, 107
Sharhorod, 172, 173
Shchara River, 134, 135, 145
Shcherbak (UPA soldier), 183
Shcherbyna, Fedir, 13, 211n. 3, 211n. 4, 211n. 5
Shelukhyn, S., 228n. 12, 228n. 14
Shemet, Serhii, 208n. 3, 209n. 12
Shemiakin (Ioffe's secretary), 165
Sheparovych, Iuliian, 109
Shepetivka, 56
Shevchenko, Taras, 15
Shmerling, 244n. 10
Shpak (partisan leader), 180
Shpilins'kyi, O., 245n. 4
Shul'hyn, Oleksander, 176, 186, 214n. 25
Shustykevych, A., 235n. 21, 236n. 27, 236n. 30
Shvets', Fedir, 10
Siberia, 24, 90, 93

Sich Riflemen, 10, 19, 111; Second Division (later Third Iron Riflemen Division), 100, 107, 108, 113, 171, 173; Third Division, 100; Sixth Division, 100, 103, 106, 108, 111, 117, 120, 122, 123, 126, 171; Fourth Brigade, 107; Ninth Brigade, 173. *See also* UNR Army
Siedlce, 131
Sienkiewicz, Henryk, 39
Sieradzki, Józef, 231n. 20
Sierociński, Józef, 218n. 1, 218n. 3, 218n. 5, 218n. 6, 219n. 7, 219n. 8, 219n. 9, 220n. 16, 221n. 20
Sieroszewski, Wacław, 215n. 1, 215n. 2, 215n. 6, 215n. 8, 215n. 9, 215n. 10, 215n. 13, 216n. 17, 216n. 19, 216n. 22, 217n. 23
Sikevych, Volodymyr, 211n. 8
Sikorski, Stanisław, 174
Sikorski, Władysław, 115, 124–5, 131, 135
Silesia: Teschen, 34; Upper, 34, 162
Sillé-le-Guillaume, Sarthe, 37, 42
Sinkler, Volodymyr, 75
Siropolko, St., 212n. 15, 214n. 25
Skarzyński, Wincenty, 218n. 3, 218n. 5, 218n. 6, 219n. 9
Skierski, Leonard, 131, 134
Skirmut, Konstanty, 41
Składkowski, Sławoj Felicjan, 217n. 26
Skoropads'kyi, Pavlo, 5, 7, 8, 9, 10, 21, 188, 192, 197, 208n. 3, 214n. 25
Skrypnyk, Ivan, 12
Skrypnyk, Stepan. *See* Mstyslav
Skrzyński, Aleksander, 86, 224n. 23, 231n. 17, 231n. 20
Skrzyński, Władysław, 69
Skrzypek, Józef, 218n. 29, 226n. 6, 229n. 3
Skulski, Leopold, 117
Skvortsov-Stepanov, Ivan, 239n. 7

Skvyra, 104
Skwarczyński, Adam, 234n. 2
Skwarczyński, Stanisław, 216n. 18, 216n. 19, 217n. 22, 217n. 23
Slavins'kyi, Maksym, 210n. 1, 211n. 5, 212n. 11, 212n. 12, 212n. 14
Sławek, Walery, 75
Sliusarchuk, Kostiantyn, 68
Slovo (Kyiv), 15
Sluch River, 59, 61, 84, 120
Slutsk, 84
Smal'-Stots'kyi, Roman, 186, 211n. 7, 212n. 12, 246n. 1
Smogorzewski, Kazimierz Maciej, 227n. 20
Smolensk, 90, 124, 189, 201
Smovs'kyi, K., 209n. 7, 214n. 21, 214n. 23
Social Democratic party of the Kingdom of Poland and Lithuania, 29, 32
Society of Ukrainian Progressives (TUP), 1, 15
Sokal, 135
Sokhots'kyi, Izydor, 236n. 27
Sokół gymnastic society, 30
Sokolnicki, Michał, 61, 215n. 13, 217n. 22, 217n. 23, 217n. 26, 226n. 11, 227n. 20
Sokołów Podlaski, 127
Sokyrnytsia, 41
Sologub, Nikolai, 115
Solovets Islands, 110
Sopotnicki, Józef, 223n. 15
Sosnkowski, Kazimierz, 30, 33, 115, 120
Sosnowiec, 28
South Africa, 52
Spa, 44, 118, 119, 134
Spa Conference of 1920, 120, 134
Spencer, Herbert, 24
Stachiewicz, Julian, 47, 215n. 13
Stachiw, Matthew. *See* Stakhiv, Matvii

Stajner, Karlo, 236n. 28
Stakhiv, Matvii, 221n. 20, 223n. 17, 227n. 2
Stalin, Joseph, 126
Stanimir, Osyp, 109, 235n. 26
Stankiewicz, Jan, 41, 44, 94
Stanyslaviv, 54
Stara Syniava, 96
Starokostiantyniv: county, 96; town, 106
Staroviit, Mykola, 244n. 4
Steblivka, 41
Steczkowski, Jan, 163, 164
Stefaniv, Zenon, 210n. 12, 224n. 23
Stempowski, Stanisław, 76, 95, 232n. 6, 233n. 7, 233n. 9, 233n. 13, 233n. 17
Stettin (Szczecin), 141
Stokhid River, 31
Stovba, Oleksander, 210n. 1, 212n. 10
Strasburger, Henryk, 161
Strypa River, 121
Strzałkowo, 173
Strzelec Society, 30
Styr River, 31, 70, 121, 135, 145
Sudetenland, 122
Sujkowski, Andrzej, 216n. 18
Sujkowski, Antoni, 64
Sukhanov, N. N., 208n. 3
Sułkiewicz, Aleksander, 26
Sushko, Roman, 19, 178
Suslov, P. V., 231n. 19, 237n. 45
Suwałki Armistice, 65
Svislach River, 148
Świderski, B., 223n. 11
Switzerland, 39, 185
Symmons-Symonolewicz, Konstantin, 226n. 20
Szczepiórno, 173, 175
Szeptycki, Stanisław, 51, 82, 83, 115, 124–5
Szpotański, Stanisław, 216n. 14
Sztendera, Jaroslaw, 221n. 20

Szumlakowski, Marian, 67, 68
Szwarce, Bronisław, 24

Tabor (Kalisz, later Warsaw), 186
Tabouis, Georges, 192
Tagon, Sviatoslav. *See* Petliura, Symon
Tahanrih, 85
Tarnavs'kyi, Myron, 57, 58
Tarnów, 31, 184
Tatars'kyi, V., 244n. 4
Tehran, 186
Temperley, H. W. V., 218n. 28, 221n. 3, 224n. 23, 226n. 20, 229n. 9
Ternopil, 32, 68, 135
Teschen, 119
Teteriv River, 100, 117, 180, 182
Titus Flavius Vespasianus, 191
Tiutiunnyk, Iurii, 57, 58, 108, 111, 178, 179, 181–2, 225n. 29, 225n. 30, 236n. 33, 244n. 8
Tokarzewski, Marjan, 232n. 2
Tokarzhevs'kyi-Karashevych, Ian, 246n. 4, 248n. 26
Tokhary, Prince Jean de, 191
Tokyo, 27, 28
Tolstoi, Lev, 24
Torrès, Henri, 190–5
Torreta, Pietro Thomasi, 50
Trampczyński, Wojciech, 105
Transcarpathia, 41, 197
Treaty of Saint-Germain, 55
Trotsky, Leon, 88, 102, 132, 176, 234n. 7
Trypillia, 104
Tryzub (Paris), 185
Tsehel's'kyi, L'onhyn, 48, 210n. 13, 221n. 1, 221n. 3
Tsirits, Gustav, 109
Tsyhanivka, 96
Tuchola, 111
Tukhachevskii, Mikhail, 115, 116, 122, 124–9, 130–5, 200

Tuliup, Volodymyr, 68
Tunka, 24
Turgenev, Ivan, 24
Turkey, 186; Turkish army, 185
Tyraspil, 109, 180
Tyrrell, William George, 50

Uborevich, E., 100
Ubort River, 84, 120
Udovychenko, Oleksander, 107, 108, 110, 171, 209n. 7, 213n. 21, 224n. 26, 234n. 2, 235n. 14, 235n. 24, 235n. 26, 237n. 34, 238n. 58, 240n. 17, 243n. 1, 244n. 4, 244n. 10, 245n. 4
Ukraïna (Kyiv), 15
Ukrainian army. *See* UNR Army; Ukrainian Galician Army; Ukrainian Partisan Army
Ukrainian Autocephalous Orthodox Church, 12
Ukrainian Club (St. Petersburg), 14
Ukrainian Congress of Toilers, 48
Ukrainian Free University, 175
Ukrainian Galician Army (UHA), 44, 46, 47, 48, 50, 51, 53, 54, 55, 56, 57, 58, 68, 82, 83, 84, 102, 103, 106–13; Red UHA, 102, 109; —, First Brigade, 103, 109–11; —, Second Brigade, 103, 109–11; —, Third Brigade, 103, 109–11; UHA Military Committee, 110; UHA Revolutionary Committee, 109
Ukrainian Higher Pedagogical Institute, 175
Ukrainian Husbandry Academy, 175
Ukrainian Military Club, 2, 3
Ukrainian Military General Committee, 3, 4, 18, 19
Ukrainian Military Organizational Committee, 2
Ukrainian National State Union, 9
Ukrainian National Union (UNS), 9, 10, 22
Ukrainian National University, 8
Ukrainian Orthodox Church in the USA, 12
Ukrainian Partisan Army (UPA), 178–82; Bessarabian Strike Group, 179; Podillian Group, 178–82; Volynian (Northern) Group, 178–82; Main Partisan Staff and Civil Administration, 178
Ukrainian party of Socialist Revolutionaries (SR), 20
Ukrainian People's Republic (UNR), 4, 5, 9, 10, 22, 48, 53, 56, 63, 66, 67, 68, 69, 70, 71, 74, 75, 76, 83, 84, 87, 97, 98, 99, 101, 111–2, 123, 139, 140, 142, 153, 169, 171, 172, 174, 176, 184, 185, 188, 192, 196, 200. *See also* UNR Army; UNR government
Ukrainian Republican Choir, 185
Ukrainian Social Democratic party, 11, 198
Ukrainian Social Democratic Workers' party (USDRP, SD), 14, 15, 20
Ukrainian Socialist-Federalist party, 8
Ukrainian Socialist Revolutionary party, 11, 198
Ukrainian Socialist Soviet Republic, 56, 139, 140–1, 143, 144, 148, 151–3, 155, 163, 165–9, 180, 201
Ukrainian state university (Kamianets-Podilskyi), 8
Ukrainian Station (Kalisz internment camp), 175; Ukrainian Central Committee, 175
Ukrainskaia zhizn' (Moscow), 15, 16
Ukrainskii vopros (Petliura, ed.), 16
Ulman, W., 127
Ulrych, Juliusz, 175
Uman, 116

Union of Active Struggle. *See* Riflemen's Union
Union of Landowners in Ukraine, 7, 21
Union of Railroad Workers in Ukraine, 10
United States of America (USA), 28, 37, 38, 39, 40, 50, 62, 89, 169, 185; US Army, 40; US Congress, 39
University of Toronto, 39
UNR. *See* Ukrainian People's Republic
UNR Army, 5, 8, 11, 44, 45, 51, 54, 56, 57, 72, 75, 84, 95, 97, 99–114, 117, 120–3, 124, 126–7, 129, 132, 135–6, 139, 145, 162, 171–3, 176, 179, 184, 187, 192–3, 198, 199, 200, 201; Supreme Command, 72–4, 171; Third Russian Cavalry Army, 171; First Ukrainian Corps, 5; Ukrainian Graycoats Corps, 68; First Machine-Gun Division, 171; First Zaporozhian Division, 108, 171; Second Volynian Division, 108, 171; Fourth Kyiv Division, 108, 171, 178; Fifth Kherson Division, 100, 108, 122, 171; UNR Sixth Division, 120, 178; Separate Cavalry Division, 108, 171; Cossack Cavalry Brigade, 172; Separate Infantry Brigade, 107; Don Cossacks cavalry regiment, 107; Kuban Cossacks cavalry company, 107; Fastiv Army Group, 116; Black Haidamakas, 19; Red Haidamakas (Kish Slobids'koï Ukrainy), 19, 21; Sich Riflemen (*see separate entry*). *See also* Ukrainian Galician Army; Ukrainian Partisan Army
UNR Directory, 10, 11, 22, 45, 46, 48, 49, 54, 56, 58, 66, 67, 68, 70, 76, 142, 188, 193, 197, 198. *See also* UNR government
UNR government, 3, 7, 57, 70, 73–5, 76, 85, 88, 97, 98, 99, 101, 102, 105, 106, 113, 137–8, 169, 175, 184, 188, 196, 197, 198, 199, 201; Ministry of Agriculture, 7; Ministry of Foreign Affairs, 68; Ministry of Military Affairs, 75, 106; UNR Constituent Assembly, 4, 7, 48, 71; UNR government-in-exile, 175–7, 178, 185–7. *See also* Central Rada; UNR Directory
Unszlicht, Józef, 128
Ural Mountains, 90, 104
Uzh River, 120, 182

Val', E. G., 231n. 20, 232n. 4, 233n. 1
Vapniarka, 57, 136
Vashchenko, Petro, 245n. 4
Vasylkiv, 10
Vasyl'ko, Baron Mykola, 185
Vaukavysk, 134, 135, 144
Vernadsky, George, 208n. 3, 217n. 26
Vetlugin, A., 212n. 12
Viazlov, Andrii, 94
Vienna, 29, 30, 141, 184, 189
Vignon, M., 120
Vil'na Ukraina (St. Petersburg), 14
Vilnius: city, 23, 24, 25, 26, 27, 29, 62, 63, 64, 65, 81, 82, 83, 125; gubernia, 23, 59, 165; region, 64, 65, 82, 154
Vinnykivtsi, 94
Vinnytsia, 11, 95, 104, 106, 109
Vistnyk, 18
Vistula River. *See* Wisła River
Vitebsk, 124
Volochyska, 173
Volodava, 135
Volodin, Mikhail, 189–91
Volodymyr-Volynskyi, 68, 148

Volunter Army. *See* Russian Volunteer Army
Volynia, 13, 61, 83, 84, 87, 94, 100, 121, 135, 181; gubernia, 59, 92, 93; Northern, 69; Western, 10, 56, 70, 76
Voskanov, Gaspar, 100
Vyborg, 14
Vynnychenko, Volodymyr, 10, 11, 17, 18, 19, 22, 191, 198, 209n. 8, 209n. 12, 221n. 1, 248n. 7
Vyshhorodok, 70
Vyshyvanyi, Vasyl', 219n. 9
Vytvyts'kyi, Stepan, 70, 221n. 1, 222n. 9

Wadowice, 173
Walewski, Witold, 232n. 6
Walka (Cracow), 27
Wandycz, Piotr, 227n. 20, 227n. 2, 228n. 8, 229n. 9, 231n. 20, 235n. 24, 237n. 41, 238n. 57, 238n. 1, 239n. 11, 241n. 31, 242n. 35, 242n. 5, 243n. 15
Wapiński, Roman, 216n. 18
Warsaw, 24, 26, 28, 33, 34, 35, 44, 55, 67, 68, 70, 71, 75, 77, 78, 82, 85, 89, 105, 120, 122, 124, 125, 126, 127, 128, 129, 130, 131, 132, 133, 137, 151, 152, 153, 161, 162, 168, 174, 179, 184, 186, 199, 200, 201
Warsaw Citadel, 26
Washington, D.C., 39, 120
Wasilewski, Leon, 61, 62, 65, 137, 140, 152, 153, 154, 161, 165, 215n. 2, 216n. 22, 217n. 23, 217–8n. 28, 226n. 10, 226n. 12, 241n. 13
Waszkiewicz, Ludwik, 137
Watt, Richard M., 218n. 28, 218n. 29, 239n. 10, 240n. 17
Węgrów, 127
Weryha-Darowski, Aleksander, 232n. 2
Western Ukrainian People's Republic (ZUNR), 43, 48, 49, 50, 52, 53, 54, 57, 67, 68, 70, 78, 118, 141–3, 197; ZUNR government, 49, 51, 52, 53, 54, 55, 58, 68, 141, 143; ZUNR National Rada, 48, 141–3, 197. *See also* Ukrainian Galician Army
Weygand, Maximilien, 116, 120, 129, 130, 218n. 6, 237n. 47, 238n. 57, 239n. 1, 239n. 11, 240n. 15, 240n. 16
Wheeler-Bennett, John W., 209n. 9
White Sea, 110
Wichliński, Michał, 137
Wielowiejski, Józef, 219n. 9, 219n. 11
Wieprz River, 126, 130, 131
Wierny, Adam, 239n. 10
Willm, Albert, 190, 192, 193, 194
Wilson, Woodrow, 39, 43, 44, 50, 51, 53, 82
Wisła (Vistula) River, 23, 43, 85, 99, 123, 125, 126, 129, 130, 131, 132, 134, 168
Wisłocki, Włodzimierz, 233n. 19
Witos, Wincenty, 119, 242n. 36
Witte, Count Sergei, 14
Wkra River, 127, 131
Włodawa, 127
Wojciechowski, Stanisław, 26
Wollenberg, Erich, 243n. 1
Woodward, E. L., 217n. 28, 223n. 21, 229n. 1
Wrangel, Peter, 81, 85, 134, 144, 145, 154, 162, 171, 200, 230n. 13
Wschód (Warsaw), 186
Wyhowska de Andreis, Wanda, 232n. 3, 233n. 8
Wyszków, 128

Yugoslavia, 77

Zagłoba-Mazurkiewicz, 68
Zahrods'kyi, Oleksander, 108
Zaitsev, Pavlo, 212n. 10
Zając, Józef, 220n. 17
Zaleski, August, 68
Zalishchyky, 122
Zaliztsi, 68
Zamość, 44, 122, 123, 132, 200
Zamoyski, August, 69
Zamoyski, Maurycy, 69
Zapysky Naukovoho tovarystva im. Shevchenka (Lviv), 14
Zaryts'kyi, Vas., 245n. 4
Zaslav county, 96
Zastavtsi, 68
Zatons'kyi, Volodymyr, 183
Zawadzki, Bolesław, 230n. 9
Zawiszanka, Zofja, 217n. 23
Zbruch River, 54, 55, 56, 70, 78, 84, 121, 136, 142, 154, 173, 179
Zbyszewski, W. A., 231n. 18
Zdolbuniv, 70
Żeligowski, Lucjan, 44, 45, 47, 65, 95, 130, 131, 135, 221n. 20, 239n. 1, 240n. 11

Zelins'kyi, Viktor, 106
Zhmerynka, 100, 136, 173
Zhuk, Andrii, 210n. 1, 211n. 2, 211n. 7, 212n. 12
Zhytomyr, 5, 20, 116, 117, 122, 139, 180
Zieliński, Henryk, 229n. 3
Zieliński, Tadeusz, 31
Zieliński, Zygmunt, 44, 122, 131
Zmiienko, Vsevolod, 117, 235n. 22, 238n. 60
Zolota Lypa River, 68
Zorenko, Dmytro, 245n. 4
Zozulia, Iakiv M., 208n. 3, 208n. 4, 213n. 21, 214n. 25
Zubenko, Artem, 246n. 2
Zulavas, 23
ZUNR. *See* Western Ukrainian People's Republic
Zürich, 185
Zviahel, 120
Zygadłowicz, Gen., 124

* In the index and throughout this volume, personal names are transliterated according to the standard Library of Congress system, while geographic names follow the modified Library of Congress system.